CRIMINAL JUSTICE 90/91

Fourteenth Edition

Editor

John J. Sullivan
Mercy College, Dobbs Ferry, New York

John J. Sullivan, professor and former chairman of the Department of Law, Criminal Justice, and Safety Administration at Mercy College, received his B.S. in 1949 from Manhattan College and his J.D. in 1956 from St. John's Law School. He was formerly captain and director of the Legal Division of the New York City Police Department.

Editor

Joseph L. Victor
Mercy College, Dobbs Ferry, New York

Joseph L. Victor is professor and chairman of the Department of Law, Criminal Justice, and Safety Administration at Mercy College, and coordinator of Criminal Justice Graduate Study at the Westchester Campus of Long Island University. Professor Victor has extensive field experience in criminal justice agencies, counseling, and administering human service programs. He earned his B.A. and M.A. at Seton Hall University, and his Doctorate of Education at Fairleigh Dickinson University.

Annual Editions

A Library of Information from the Public Press

Cover illustration by Mike Eagle

The Dushkin Publishing Group, Inc.
Sluice Dock, Guilford, Connecticut 06437

The Annual Editions Series

Annual Editions is a series of over fifty volumes designed to provide the reader with convenient, low-cost access to a wide range of current, carefully selected articles from some of the most important magazines, newspapers, and journals published today. Annual Editions are updated on an annual basis through a continuous monitoring of over 200 periodical sources. All Annual Editions have a number of features designed to make them particularly useful, including topic guides, annotated tables of contents, unit overviews, and indexes. For the teacher using Annual Editions in the classroom, an Instructor's Resource Guide with test questions is available for each volume.

VOLUMES AVAILABLE

Africa
Aging
American Government
American History, Pre-Civil War
American History, Post-Civil War
Anthropology
Biology
Business and Management
Business Ethics
Canadian Politics
China
Comparative Politics
Computers in Education
Computers in Business
Computers in Society
Criminal Justice
Drugs, Society, and Behavior
Early Childhood Education
Economics
Educating Exceptional Children
Education
Educational Psychology
Environment
Geography
Global Issues
Health
Human Development
Human Resources
Human Sexuality
Latin America
Macroeconomics
Marketing
Marriage and Family
Middle East and the Islamic World
Money and Banking
Nutrition
Personal Growth and Behavior
Psychology
Public Administration
Social Problems
Sociology
Soviet Union and Eastern Europe
State and Local Government
Third World
Urban Society
Violence and Terrorism
Western Civilization, Pre-Reformation
Western Civilization, Post-Reformation
Western Europe
World History, Pre-Modern
World History, Modern
World Politics

Library of Congress Cataloging in Publication Data
Main entry under title: Annual editions: Criminal justice. 1990/91.
1. Criminal Justice, Administration of—United States—Addresses, essays, lectures.
I. Sullivan, John J., *comp.* II. Victor, Joseph L., *comp.* III. Title: Criminal justice.
HV 8138.A67 364.973.05 LC 77-640116
ISBN: 0-87967-837-2

Fourteenth Edition

Manufactured by The Banta Company, Harrisonburg, Virginia 22801

Editors/ Advisory Board

Members of the Advisory Board are instrumental in the final selection of articles for each edition of Annual Editions. Their review of articles for content, level, currency, and appropriateness provides critical direction to the editor and staff. We think you'll find their careful consideration well reflected in this volume.

EDITOR

ADVISORY BOARD

STAFF

To the Reader

In publishing ANNUAL EDITIONS we recognize the enormous role played by the magazines, newspapers, and journals of the *public press* in providing current, first-rate educational information in a broad spectrum of interest areas. Within the articles, the best scientists, practitioners, researchers, and commentators draw issues into new perspective as accepted theories and viewpoints are called into account by new events, recent discoveries change old facts, and fresh debate breaks out over important controversies.

Many of the articles resulting from this enormous editorial effort are appropriate for students, researchers, and professionals seeking accurate, current material to help bridge the gap between principles and theories and the real world. These articles, however, become more useful for study when those of lasting value are carefully *collected, organized, indexed,* and *reproduced* in a *low-cost format*, which provides easy and permanent access when the material is needed. That is the role played by *Annual Editions*. Under the direction of each volume's *Editor*, who is an expert in the subject area, and with the guidance of an *Advisory Board*, we seek each year to provide in each *ANNUAL EDITION* a current, well-balanced, carefully selected collection of the best of the public press for your study and enjoyment. We think you'll find this volume useful, and we hope you'll take a moment to let us know what you think.

During the 1970s, criminal justice emerged as an appealing, vital, and unique academic discipline. It emphasizes the professional development of students who plan careers in the field, and attracts those who want to know more about a complex social problem and how this country deals with it. Criminal justice incorporates a vast range of knowledge from a number of specialties, including law, history, and the behavioral and social sciences. Each specialty contributes to our fuller understanding of criminal behavior and of society's attitudes toward deviance.

In view of the fact that the criminal justice system is in a constant state of flux, and because the study of criminal justice covers such a broad spectrum, today's students must be aware of a variety of subjects and topics. Standard textbooks and traditional anthologies cannot keep pace with the changes as quickly as they occur. In fact, many such sources are already out of date the day they are published. *Annual Editions: Criminal Justice 90/91* strives to maintain currency in matters of concern by providing up-to-date commentaries, articles, reports, and statistics from the most recent literature in the criminal justice field.

This volume contains units concerning crime and justice in America, victimology, the police, the judicial system, juvenile justice, and punishment and corrections. The articles in these units were selected because they are informative as well as provocative. The selections are timely and useful in their treatment of ethics, punishment, juveniles, courts, and other related topics.

Included in this volume are a number of features designed to make it useful for students, researchers, and professionals in the criminal justice field. These include a topic guide, for locating articles on specific subjects; the table of contents abstracts, which summarize each article and feature key concepts in italics; and a comprehensive bibliography, glossary, and index. In addition, each unit is preceded by an overview which provides a background for informed reading of the articles, emphasizes critical issues, and presents challenge questions.

We would like to know what you think of the selections contained in this edition. Please fill out the article rating form on the last page and let us know your opinions. We change or retain many of the articles based on the comments we receive from you, the user. Help us to improve this anthology—annually.

John J. Sullivan

Joseph L. Victor

Editors

Contents

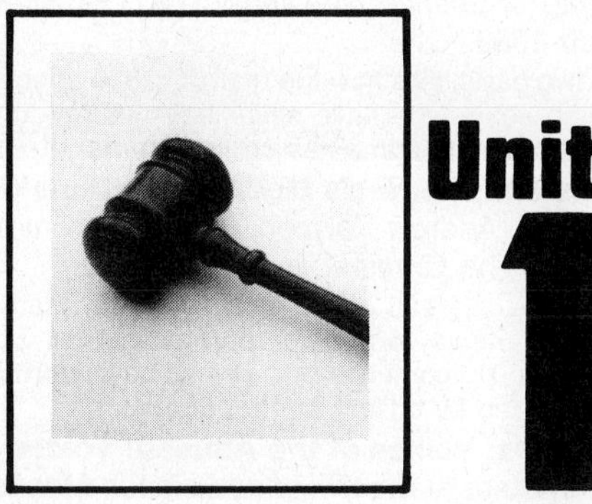

Unit 1

Crime and Justice in America

Eight selections focus on the overall structure of the criminal justice system in the United States. The current scope of crime in America is reviewed; topics such as criminal behavior, drugs, organized crime, and white collar crime are discussed.

The concepts in bold italics are developed in the article. For further expansion please refer to the Topic Guide, the Index, and the Glossary.

Unit 2

Victimology

Six articles discuss the impact of crime on the victim. Topics include the rights of crime victims, the consequences of family violence, and the ethics of the news media's treatment of crime victims.

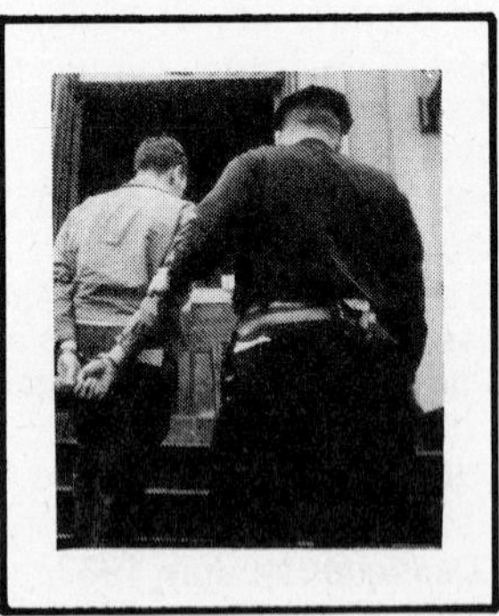

Unit 3

Police

Nine selections examine the role of the police officer. Some of the topics discussed include police response to crime, utilization of policewomen, and managing police corruption.

The Judicial System

Ten selections discuss the process by which the accused are moved through the judicial system. Prosecutors, courts, the jury process, and judicial ethics are reviewed.

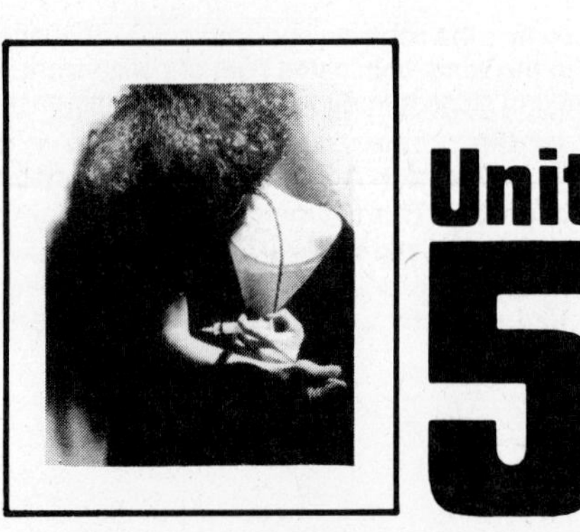

Unit 5

Juvenile Justice

Six selections review the juvenile justice system. The topics include effective ways to respond to violent juvenile crime, juvenile detention, female delinquency, and the impact of teenage addiction.

Unit 6

Punishment and Corrections

Nine selections focus on the current state of America's penal system, and the effects of sentencing, probation, overcrowding, and capital punishment on criminals.

The concepts in bold italics are developed in the article. For further expansion please refer to the Topic Guide, the Index, and the Glossary.

Charts and Graphs

Topic Guide

This topic guide suggests how the selections in this book relate to topics of traditional concern to criminal justice students and professionals. It can be very useful in locating articles which relate to each other for reading and research. The guide is arranged alphabetically according to topic. Articles may, of course, treat topics that do not appear in the topic guide. In turn, entries in the topic guide do not necessarily constitute a comprehensive listing of all the contents of each selection.

TOPIC AREA	TREATED AS AN ISSUE IN:
AIDS	45. AIDS in Prison
Attorneys	25. The Duty of the Defense Counsel 26. The Prosecutor as a "Minister of Justice" 30. Convicting the Innocent
Battered Families	11. Battered Families
Children	*See* Juveniles
Civilian Review	23. Civilian Review Boards
Constitutional Rights	33. Liberals and Crime
Corrections	40. Sentencing and Corrections 41. State Prisons: Crucibles for Justice 42. Prison Crowding in the United States 43. You're Under Arrest—AT HOME 44. Whipping 45. AIDS in Prison 46. Alternatives to Incarceration
Corruption	20. Confronting Police Corruption
Courts	24. The Judicial Process 25. The Duty of the Defense Counsel 26. The Prosecutor as a "Minister of Justice" 27. White Justice, Black Defendants 28. A Prosecutor's View of Plea Bargaining 29. Genetics Meets Forensics 31. After 200 Years
Crime	1. An Overview of the Criminal Justice System 2. What Is Crime? 3. Are Criminals Made or Born? 7. Guardian Angels
Crime Victims	*See* Victimology
Criminal Behavior	3. Are Criminals Made or Born?
Criminal Justice	1. An Overview of the Criminal Justice System 2. What Is Crime? 7. Guardian Angels 25. The Duty of the Defense Counsel 26. The Prosecutor as a "Minister of Justice" 32. A Criminal Lack of Common Sense
Death Penalty	48. 'This Man Has Expired'
Defense Counsel	25. The Duty of the Defense Counsel
Delinquency	*See* Juveniles
Discrimination	18. Women On the Move? 22. Living as a "Black in Blue" 27. White Justice, Black Defendants
DNA	29. Genetics Meets Forensics
Drugs	4. A Law Enforcement Response 39. Teenage Addiction
Education	17. The State of Police Education
Ethics	20. Confronting Police Corruption 25. The Duty of the Defense Counsel 26. The Prosecutor as a "Minister of Justice"
Family Violence	11. Battered Families
Fear of Crime	7. Guardian Angels 9. The Fear of Crime
Guardian Angels	7. Guardian Angels
Gun Control	5. Guns
House Arrest	43. You're Under Arrest—AT HOME
Jails	38. The Hard Facts About Children in Jails
Judges	24. The Judicial Process 28. A Prosecutor's View of Plea Bargaining 32. A Criminal Lack of Common Sense
Jury	31. After 200 Years
Juveniles	34. Handling of Juvenile Crime 35. Do Status Offenders Get Worse? 36. Our Violent Kids 37. Girls' Crime and Woman's Place 38. The Hard Facts About Children in Jails 39. Teenage Addiction
Law Enforcement	*See* Police
Mafia	*See* Organized Crime

TOPIC AREA	TREATED AS AN ISSUE IN:	TOPIC AREA	TREATED AS AN ISSUE IN:
Mediation	14. Victim-Offender Mediation	**Prosecution**	24. The Judicial Process 26. The Prosecutor as a "Minister of Justice" 28. A Prosecutor's View of Plea Bargaining
Minorities	22. Living as a "Black in Blue" 27. White Justice, Black Defendants	**Punishment**	*See* Corrections
Narcotics	*See* Drugs	**Racism**	22. Living as a "Black in Blue" 27. White Justice, Black Defendants
Organized Crime	6. Hitting Kingpins in Their Assets 8. As Racketeering Law Expands	**Restitution**	46. Alternatives to Incarceration
Parole	46. Alternatives to Incarceration	**RICO**	8. As Racketeering Law Expands
Plea Bargaining	28. A Prosecutor's View of Plea Bargaining	**Sentencing**	28. A Prosecutor's View of Plea Bargaining 40. Sentencing and Corrections
Police	15. Police Response to Crime 16. The Police in the United States 17. The State of Police Education 18. Women On the Move? 19. Making Neighborhoods Safe 20. Confronting Police Corruption 22. Living as a "Black in Blue" 23. Civilian Review Boards	**Victimology**	9. The Fear of Crime 10. Crime Victims and the News 11. Battered Families 12. Victims of Crime 13. Death of a Bard 14. Victim-Offender Mediation
Press	10. Crime Victims and the News	**Whipping**	44. Whipping
Prisons	41. State Prisons: Crucibles for Justice 42. Prison Crowding in the United States 45. AIDS in Prison 47. Models and Opportunities	**Women**	11. Battered Families 18. Women On the Move? 37. Girls' Crime and Woman's Place
Private Security	15. Police Response to Crime 21. From Private Security to Loss Control		
Probation	43. You're Under Arrest—AT HOME 46. Alternatives to Incarceration		

Crime and Justice in America

Crime continues to be a major problem in the United States. Court dockets are full, our prisons are overcrowded, the probation and parole caseloads are overwhelming, and our police are being urged to do more. The bulging prison population places a heavy strain on the economy of the community.

Crime is a complex problem that defies simple explanations or solutions. While the more familiar crimes of murder, rape, and assault are still with us, drugs are an ever-increasing scourge, and international crime is an issue to be dealt with.

The articles presented in this section are intended to serve as a foundation for the materials that are presented in subsequent sections. "An Overview of the Criminal Justice System" charts the sequence of events in the administration of justice. The response to crime is a very complex process that involves citizens as well as many agencies, levels, and branches of government. "What Is Crime?" offers definitions and characteristics of the most common serious crimes. It also considers such topics as the differences between felonies and misdemeanors, organized crime, and white-collar crime.

Why do people commit crimes? In spite of the best efforts of experts, human behavior is still not fully understood. There is much diversity of opinion regarding the causes of criminal behavior, a topic addressed in "Are Criminals Made or Born?" The authors of this article stimulate thought and discussion on this complex issue by presenting evidence that suggests that both biological and sociological factors affect the degree of criminal behavior.

One of the most controversial topics in recent years is the legalization of illicit drugs. Efforts on the part of the federal and local governments have been costly both in terms of money and judicial resources; success has been minimal and the flow of illegal drugs has continued unabated. This subject is examined in "A Law Enforcement Response to Legalizing Illicit Drugs," and the authors conclude that drug use in any degree of legality is a significant threat to our common welfare.

In the United States, guns have long been viewed by many people as a constitutional right. These people have lobbied so successfully that laws governing gun ownership are virtually nonexistent. Recent events have once again brought up the subject of gun control. This ongoing debate is examined in the article "Guns," where various opinions about what should be done are considered.

Organized crime has been a part of our lives for many decades, and how to eradicate or control it has been a constant job of all our enforcement agencies. In recent years drug sales have injected enormous quantities of cash into crime organizations. Recently the feds have started to go after drug lords' bank accounts and other properties. As the article "Hitting Kingpins in Their Assets" points out, this new tactic does indeed work, but has stirred up defense lawyers who question the legality of these seizures.

Crime in recent years, especially in the cities, has grown worse. The concept of a vigilante-type enforcement has gained notoriety, and in many communities, acceptance. One of the most famous groups that represents this form of citizen crime prevention is the Guardian Angels. The article "Guardian Angels: A Unique Approach to Crime Prevention" examines their activities and assesses their impact on crime and citizens' fear of crime.

Looking Ahead: Challenge Questions

What is crime?

What is the sequence of events in the criminal justice system?

Should drugs be legalized?

Are the Guardian Angels a positive factor in the criminal justice system?

Unit 1

1,24,30

An Overview of the Criminal Justice System

The response to crime is a complex process that involves citizens as well as many agencies, levels, and branches of government

The private sector initiates the response to crime

This first response may come from any part of the private sector: individuals, families, neighborhood associations, business, industry, agriculture, educational institutions, the news media, or any other private service to the public.

It involves crime prevention as well as participation in the criminal justice process once a crime has been committed. Private crime prevention is more than providing private security or burglar alarms or participating in neighborhood watch. It also includes a commitment to stop criminal behavior by not engaging in it or condoning it when it is committed by others.

Citizens take part directly in the criminal justice process by reporting crime to the police, by being a reliable participant (for example, witness, juror) in a criminal proceeding, and by accepting the disposition of the system as just or reasonable. As voters and taxpayers, citizens also participate in criminal justice through the policymaking process that affects how the criminal justice process operates, the resources available to it, and its goals and objectives. At every stage of the process, from the original formulation of objectives to the decision about where to locate jails and prisons and to the reintegration of inmates into society, the private sector has a role to play. Without such involvement, the criminal justice process cannot serve the citizens it is intended to protect.

What is the sequence of events in the criminal justice system?

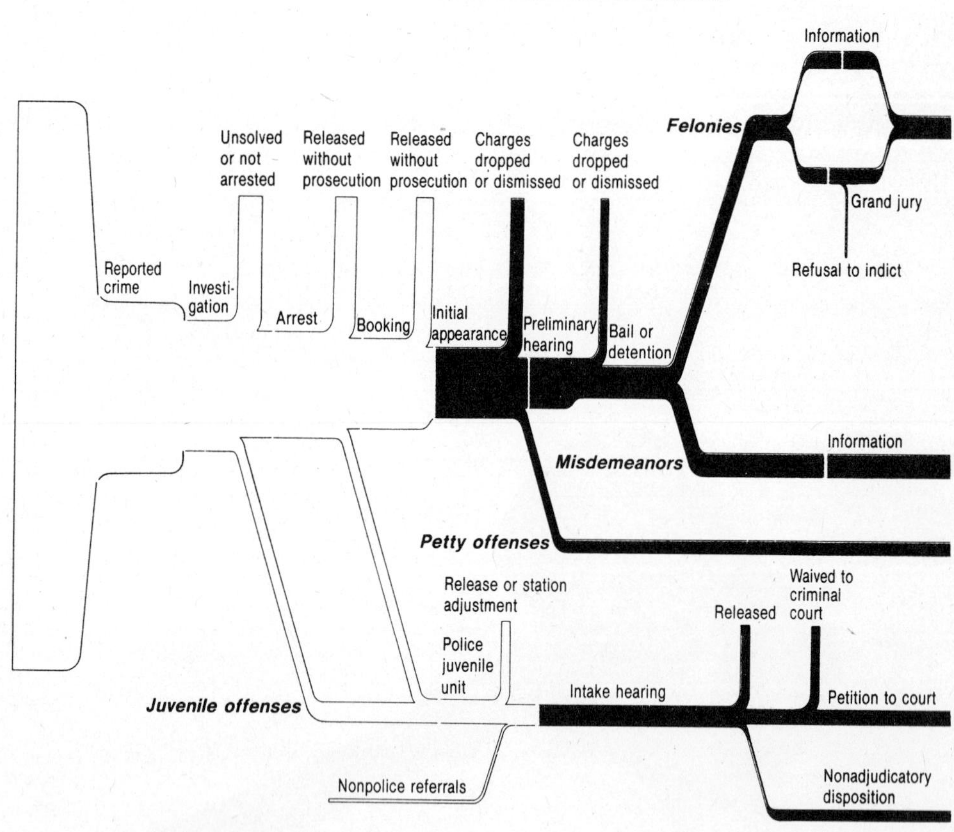

Note: This chart gives a simplified view of caseflow through the criminal justice system. Procedures vary among jurisdictions. The weights of the lines are not intended to show the actual size of caseloads.

The government responds to crime through the criminal justice system

We apprehend, try, and punish offenders by means of a loose confederation of agencies at all levels of government. Our American system of justice has evolved from the English common law into a complex series of procedures and decisions. There is no single criminal justice system in this country. We have many systems that are similar, but individually unique.

Criminal cases may be handled differently in different jurisdictions, but court decisions based on the due process guarantees of the U.S. Constitution require that specific steps be taken in the administration of criminal justice.

The description of the criminal and juvenile justice systems that follows portrays the most common sequence of events

From *Report to the Nation on Crime and Justice*, Bureau of Justice Statistics, U.S. Department of Justice, March 1988, pp. 56-60.

in the response to serious criminal behavior.

Entry into the system

The justice system does not respond to most crime because so much crime is not discovered or reported to the police. Law enforcement agencies learn about crime from the reports of citizens, from discovery by a police officer in the field, or from investigative and intelligence work.

Once a law enforcement agency has established that a crime has been committed, a suspect must be identified and apprehended for the case to proceed through the system. Sometimes, a suspect is apprehended at the scene; however, identification of a suspect sometimes requires an extensive investigation. Often, no one is identified or apprehended.

Prosecution and pretrial services

After an arrest, law enforcement agencies present information about the case and about the accused to the prosecutor, who will decide if formal charges will be filed with the court. If no charges are filed, the accused must be released. The prosecutor can also drop charges after making efforts to prosecute *(nolle prosequi)*.

A suspect charged with a crime must be taken before a judge or magistrate without unnecessary delay. At the initial appearance, the judge or magistrate informs the accused of the charges and decides whether there is probable cause to detain the accused person. Often, the defense counsel is also assigned at the initial appearance. If the offense is not very serious, the determination of guilt and assessment of a penalty may also occur at this stage.

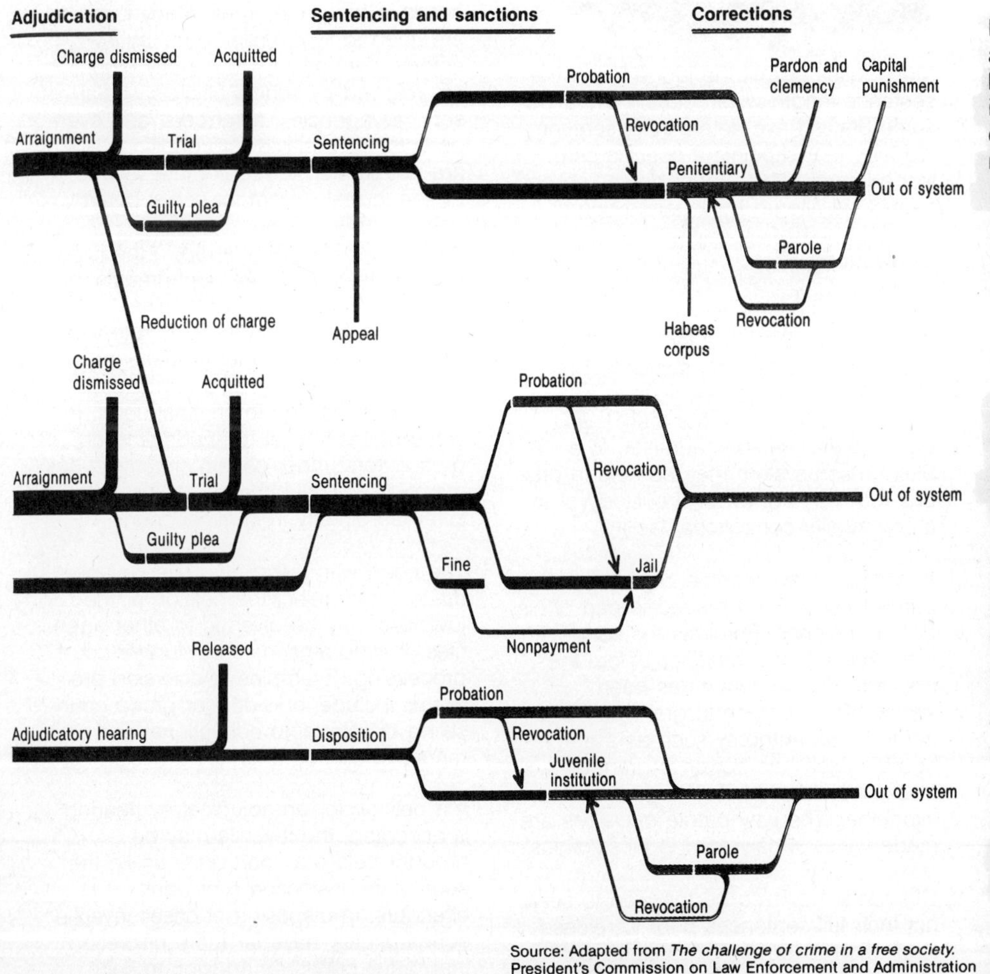

Source: Adapted from *The challenge of crime in a free society.* President's Commission on Law Enforcement and Administration of Justice, 1967.

In some jurisdictions, a pretrial-release decision is made at the initial appearance, but this decision may occur at other hearings or may be changed at another time during the process. Pretrial release and bail were traditionally intended to ensure appearance at trial. However, many jurisdictions permit pretrial detention of defendants accused of serious offenses and deemed to be dangerous to prevent them from committing crimes in the pretrial period. The court may decide to release the accused on his/her own recognizance, into the custody of a third party, on the promise of satisfying certain conditions, or after the posting of a financial bond.

In many jurisdictions, the initial appearance may be followed by a preliminary hearing. The main function of this hearing is to discover if there is probable cause to believe that the accused committed a known crime within the jurisdiction of the court. If the judge does not find probable cause, the case is dismissed; however, if the judge or magistrate finds probable cause for such a belief, or the accused waives his or her right to a preliminary hearing, the case may be bound over to a grand jury.

A *grand jury* hears evidence against the accused presented by the prosecutor and decides if there is sufficient evidence to cause the accused to be brought to trial. If the grand jury finds sufficient evidence, it submits to the court an indictment (a written statement of the essential facts of the offense charged against the accused). Where the grand jury system is used, the grand jury may also investigate criminal activity generally and issue indictments called grand jury originals that initiate criminal cases.

Misdemeanor cases and some felony cases proceed by the issuance of an *information* (a formal, written accusation submitted to the court by a prosecutor). *In some jurisdictions*, indictments *may be* required in felony cases. However, the accused may choose to waive a grand jury indictment and, instead, accept service of an information for the crime.

Adjudication

Once an indictment or information has been filed with the trial court, the accused is scheduled for arraignment. At the arraignment, the accused is informed of the charges, advised of the rights of criminal defendants, and asked to enter a plea to the charges. Sometimes, a plea of guilty is the result of negotiations between the prosecutor and the defendant, with the defendant entering a guilty plea in expectation of reduced charges or a lenient sentence.

If the accused pleads guilty or pleads *nolo contendere* (accepts penalty without admitting guilt), the judge may accept or reject the plea. If the plea is accepted, no trial is held and the offender is sentenced at this proceeding or at a later date. The plea may be rejected if, for example, the judge believes that the accused may have been coerced. If this occurs, the case may proceed to trial.

If the accused pleads not guilty or not guilty by reason of insanity, a date is set for the trial. A person accused of a serious crime is guaranteed a trial by jury. However, the accused may ask for a bench trial where the judge, rather than a jury, serves as the finder of fact. In both instances the prosecution and defense present evidence by questioning witnesses while the judge decides on issues of law. The trial results in acquittal or conviction on the original charges or on lesser included offenses.

After the trial a defendant may request appellate review of the conviction or sentence. In many criminal cases, appeals of a conviction are a matter of right; all States with the death penalty provide for automatic appeal of cases involving a death sentence. However, under some circumstances and in some jurisdictions, appeals may be subject to the discretion of the appellate court and may be granted only on acceptance of a defendant's petition for a *writ of certiorari*. Prisoners may also appeal their sentences through civil rights petitions and writs of habeas corpus where they claim unlawful detention.

Sentencing and sanctions

After a guilty verdict or guilty plea, sentence is imposed. In most cases the judge decides on the sentence, but in some States, the sentence is decided by the jury, particularly for capital offenses such as murder.

In arriving at an appropriate sentence, a sentencing hearing may be held at which evidence of aggravating or mitigating circumstances will be considered. In assessing the circumstances surrounding a convicted person's criminal behavior, courts often rely on presentence investigations by probation agencies or other designated authorities. Courts may also consider victim impact statements.

The sentencing choices that may be available to judges and juries include one or more of the following:

- the death penalty
- incarceration in a prison, jail, or other confinement facility
- probation—allowing the convicted person to remain at liberty but subject to certain conditions and restrictions
- fines—primarily applied as penalties in minor offenses
- restitution—which requires the offender to provide financial compensation to the victim.

In many States, State law mandates that persons convicted of certain types of offenses serve a prison term.

Most States permit the judge to set the sentence length within certain limits, but some States have determinate sentencing laws that stipulate a specific sentence length, which must be served and cannot be altered by a parole board.

Corrections

Offenders sentenced to incarceration usually serve time in a local jail or a State prison. Offenders sentenced to less than 1 year generally go to jail; those sentenced to more than 1 year go to prison. Persons admitted to a State prison system may be held in prisons with varying levels of custody or in a community correctional facility.

A prisoner may become eligible for parole after serving a specific part of his or her sentence. Parole is the conditional release of a prisoner before the prisoner's full sentence has been served. The decision to grant parole is made by an authority such as a parole board, which has power to grant or revoke parole or to discharge a parolee altogether. The way parole decisions are made varies widely among jurisdictions.

Offenders may also be required to serve out their full sentences prior to release (expiration of term). Those sentenced under determinate sentencing laws can be released only after they have served their full sentence (mandatory release) less any "goodtime" received while in prison. Inmates get such credits against their sentences automatically or by earning it through participation in programs.

If an offender has an outstanding charge or sentence in another State, a detainer is used to ensure that when released from prison he or she will be transferred to the other State.

If released by a parole board decision or by mandatory release, the releasee will be under the supervision of a parole officer in the community for the balance of his or her unexpired sentence. This supervision is governed by specific conditions of release, and the releasee may be returned to prison for violations of such conditions.

The juvenile justice system

The processing of juvenile offenders is not entirely dissimilar to adult criminal processing, but there are crucial differences in the procedures. Many juveniles are referred to juvenile courts by law enforcement officers, but many others are referred by school officials, social services agencies, neighbors, and even parents, for behavior or conditions that are determined to require intervention by the formal system for social control.

When juveniles are referred to the juvenile courts, their *intake* departments, or prosecuting attorneys, determine whether sufficient grounds exist to warrant filing a petition that requests an *adjudicatory hearing* or a request to transfer jurisdiction to criminal court. In some States and at the Federal level prosecutors under certain circumstances may file criminal charges against juveniles directly in criminal courts.

The court with jurisdiction over juvenile matters may reject the petition or the juveniles may be diverted to other agencies or programs in lieu of further court processing. Examples of diversion programs include individual or group counseling or referral to educational and recreational programs.

If a petition for an adjudicatory hearing is accepted, the juvenile may be brought before a court quite unlike the court with jurisdiction over adult offenders. In disposing of cases juvenile courts usually have far more discretion than adult courts. In addition to such options as probation, commitment to correctional institutions, restitution, or fines, State laws grant juvenile courts the power to order removal of children from their homes to foster homes or treatment facilities. Juvenile courts also may order participation in special programs aimed at shoplifting prevention, drug counseling, or driver education. They also may order referral to criminal court for trial as adults.

Despite the considerable discretion associated with juvenile court proceedings, juveniles are afforded many of the due-process safeguards associated with adult criminal trials. Sixteen States permit the use of juries in juvenile courts; however, in light of the U.S. Supreme Court's holding that juries are not essential to juvenile hearings, most States do not make provisions for juries in juvenile courts.

The response to crime is founded in the intergovernmental structure of the United States

Under our form of government, each State and the Federal Government has its own criminal justice system. All systems must respect the rights of individuals set forth in court interpretation of the U.S. Constitution and defined in case law.

State constitutions and laws define the criminal justice system within each State and delegate the authority and responsibility for criminal justice to various jurisdictions, officials, and institutions. State laws also define criminal behavior and groups of children or acts under jurisdiction of the juvenile courts.

Municipalities and counties further define their criminal justice systems through local ordinances that proscribe additional illegal behavior and establish the local agencies responsible for criminal justice processing that were not established by the State.

Congress also has established a criminal justice system at the Federal level to respond to Federal crimes such as bank robbery, kidnaping, and transporting stolen goods across State lines.

The response to crime is mainly a State and local function

Very few crimes are under exclusive Federal jurisdiction. The responsibility to respond to most crime rests with the State and local governments. Police protection is primarily a function of cities and towns. Corrections is primarily a function of State governments. More than three-fifths of all justice personnel are employed at the local level.

	Percent of criminal justice employment by level of government		
	Local	State	Federal
Police	77%	15%	8%
Judicial (courts only)	60	32	8
Prosecution and legal services	58	26	17
Public defense	47	50	3
Corrections	35	61	4
Total	62%	31%	8%

Source: *Justice expenditure and employment, 1985,* BJS Bulletin, March 1987.

Discretion is exercised throughout the criminal justice system

Discretion is "an authority conferred by law to act in certain conditions or situations in accordance with an official's or an official agency's own considered judgment and conscience."[1] Discretion is exercised throughout the government. It is a part of decisionmaking in all government systems from mental health to education, as well as criminal justice.

Concerning crime and justice, legislative bodies have recognized that they cannot anticipate the range of circumstances surrounding each crime, anticipate local mores, and enact laws that clearly encompass all conduct that is criminal and all that is not.[2] Therefore, persons charged with the day-to-day response to crime are expected to exercise their own judgment within *limits* set by law. Basically, they must decide—

- whether to take action
- where the situation fits in the scheme of law, rules, and precedent
- which official response is appropriate.

To ensure that discretion is exercised responsibly, government authority is often delegated to professionals. Professionalism requires a minimum level of training and orientation, which guides officials in making decisions. The professionalism of policing discussed later in this chapter is due largely to the desire to ensure the proper exercise of police discretion.

The limits of discretion vary from State to State and locality to locality. For example, some State judges have wide discretion in the type of sentence they may impose. In recent years other States have sought to limit the judges' discretion in sentencing by passing mandatory sentencing laws that require prison sentences for certain offenses.

Who exercises discretion?

These criminal justice officials...	...must often decide whether or not or how to—
Police	Enforce specific laws Investigate specific crimes Search people, vicinities, buildings Arrest or detain people
Prosecutors	File charges or petitions for adjudication Seek indictments Drop cases Reduce charges
Judges or magistrates	Set bail or conditions for release Accept pleas Determine delinquency Dismiss charges Impose sentence Revoke probation
Correctional officials	Assign to type of correctional facility Award privileges Punish for disciplinary infractions
Paroling authority	Determine date and conditions of parole Revoke parole

More than one agency has jurisdiction over some criminal events

The response to most criminal actions is usually begun by local police who react to violation of State law. If a suspect is apprehended, he or she is prosecuted locally and may be confined in a local jail or State prison. In such cases, only one agency has jurisdiction at each stage in the process.

However, some criminal events because of their characteristics and location may come under the jurisdiction of more than one agency. For example, such overlapping occurs within States when local police, county sheriffs, and State police are all empowered to enforce State laws on State highways.

Congress has provided for Federal jurisdiction over crimes that—
- materially affect interstate commerce
- occur on Federal land
- involve large and probably interstate criminal organizations or conspiracies
- are offenses of national importance, such as the assassination of the President.[3]

Bank robbery and many drug offenses are examples of crimes for which the States and the Federal Government both have jurisdiction. In cases of dual jurisdiction, an investigation and a prosecution may be undertaken by all authorized agencies, but only one level of government usually pursues a case. For example, a study of FBI bank robbery investigations during 1978 and 1979 found that of those cases cleared—
- 36% were solved by the FBI alone
- 25% were solved by a joint effort of the FBI and State and local police
- 40% were solved by the State and local police acting alone.

In response to dual jurisdiction and to promote more effective coordination, Law Enforcement Coordinating Committees have been established throughout the country and include all relevant Federal and local agencies.

Within States the response to crime also varies from one locality to another

The response differs because of statutory and structural differences and differences in how discretion is exercised. Local criminal justice policies and programs change in response to local attitudes and needs. For example, the prosecutor in one locality may concentrate on particular types of offenses that plague the local community while the prosecutor in another locality may concentrate on career criminals.

The response to crime also varies on a case-by-case basis

No two cases are exactly alike. At each stage of the criminal justice process officials must make decisions that take into account the varying factors of each case. Two similar cases may have very different results because of various factors, including differences in witness cooperation and physical evidence, the availability of resources to investigate and prosecute the case, the quality of the lawyers involved, and the age and prior criminal history of the suspects.

Differences in local laws, agencies, resources, standards, and procedures result in varying responses in each jurisdiction

The outcomes of arrests for serious cases vary among the States as shown by Offender-based Transaction Statistics from nine States:

	% of arrests for serious crimes that result in . . .		
	Prosecution	Conviction	Incarceration
Virginia	100%	61%	55%
Nebraska	99	68	39
New York	97	67	31
Utah	97	79	9
Virgin Islands	95	55	35
Minnesota	89	69	48
Pennsylvania	85	56	24
California	78	61	45
Ohio	77	50	21

Source: Disaggregated data used in *Tracking offenders: White-collar crime*, BJS Special Report, November 1986.

Some of this variation can be explained by differences among States. For example, the degree of discretion in deciding whether to prosecute differs from State to State; some States do not allow any police or prosecutor discretion; others allow police discretion but not prosecutor discretion and vice versa.

What is crime?

Crimes are defined by law

In this report we define crime as all behaviors and acts for which a society provides formally sanctioned punishment. In the United States what is criminal is specified in the written law, primarily State statutes. What is included in the definition of crime varies among Federal, State, and local jurisdictions.

Criminologists devote a great deal of attention to defining crime in both general and specific terms. This definitional process is the first step toward the goal of obtaining accurate crime statistics.

To provide additional perspectives on crime it is sometimes viewed in ways other than in the standard legal definitions. Such alternatives define crime in terms of the type of victim (child abuse), the type of offender (white-collar crime), the object of the crime (property crime), or the method of criminal activity (organized crime). Such definitions usually cover one or more of the standard legal definitions. For example, organized crime may include fraud, extortion, assault, or homicide.

What is considered criminal by society changes over time

Some types of events such as murder, robbery, and burglary have been defined as crimes for centuries. Such crimes are part of the common law definition of crime. Other types of conduct traditionally have not been viewed as crimes. As social values and mores change, society has codified some conduct as criminal while decriminalizing other conduct. The recent movement toward increased "criminalization" of drunk driving is an example of such change.

New technology also results in new types of conduct not anticipated by the law. Changes in the law may be needed to define and sanction these types of conduct. For example, the introduction of computers has added to the criminal codes in many States so that acts such as the destruction of programs or data could be defined as crimes.

What are the characteristics of some serious crimes?

Crime	Definition	Facts
Homicide	Causing the death of another person without legal justification or excuse, including UCR crimes of murder and nonnegligent manslaughter and negligent manslaughter.	• Murder and nonnegligent manslaughter occur less often than other violent UCR Index crimes. • 58% of the known murderers were relatives or acquaintances of the victim. • 20% of all murders in 1985 occurred or were suspected to have occurred as the result of some felonious activity.
Rape	Unlawful sexual intercourse with a female, by force or without legal or factual consent.	• Most rapes involve a lone offender and a lone victim. • About 32% of the rapes recorded by NCS in 1985 were committed in or near the victim's home. • 73% of the rapes occurred at night, between 6 p.m. and 6 a.m. • 58% of the victims of rape in 1985 were under 25 years old.
Robbery	The unlawful taking or attempted taking of property that is in the immediate possession of another, by force or threat of force.	• Robbery is the violent crime that most often involves more than one offender (in almost half of all cases in 1985). • About half of all robberies reported by NCS in 1985 involved the use of a weapon.
Assault	Unlawful intentional inflicting, or attempted inflicting, of injury upon the person of another. Aggravated assault is the unlawful intentional inflicting of serious bodily injury or unlawful threat or attempt to inflict bodily injury or death by means of a deadly or dangerous weapon with or without actual infliction of injury. Simple assault is the unlawful intentional inflicting of less than serious bodily injury without a deadly or dangerous weapon or an attempt or threat to inflict bodily injury without a deadly or dangerous weapon.	• Simple assault occurs more frequently than aggravated assault. • Most assaults involve one victim and one offender.

(continued on next page)

What are some other common crimes in the United States?

Drug abuse violations—Offenses relating to growing, manufacturing, making, possessing, using, selling, or distributing narcotic and dangerous nonnarcotic drugs. A distinction is made between possession and sale/manufacturing.

Sex offenses—In current statistical usage, the name of a broad category of varying content, usually consisting of all offenses having a sexual element except for forcible rape and commercial sex offenses, which are defined separately.

Fraud offenses—The crime type comprising offenses sharing the elements of practice of deceit or intentional misrepresentation of fact, with the intent of unlawfully depriving a person of his or her property or legal rights.

Drunkenness—Public intoxication, except "driving under the influence."

Disturbing the peace—Unlawful interruption of the peace, quiet, or order of a community, including offenses called "disorderly conduct," "vagrancy," "loitering," "unlawful assembly," and "riot."

Driving under the influence—Driving or operating any vehicle or common carrier while drunk or under the influence of liquor or drugs.

From *Report to the Nation on Crime and Justice*, Bureau of Justice Statistics, U.S. Department of Justice, March 1988, pp. 2-3, 8-9.

Liquor law offenses—State or local liquor law violations, except drunkenness and driving under the influence. Federal violations are excluded.

Gambling—Unlawful staking or wagering of money or other thing of value on a game of chance or on an uncertain event.

Kidnaping—Transportation or confinement of a person without authority of law and without his or her consent, or without the consent of his or her guardian, if a minor.

Vandalism—Destroying or damaging, or attempting to destroy or damage, the property of another without his or her consent, or public property, except by burning, which is arson.

Public order offenses—Violations of the peace or order of the community or threats to the public health through unacceptable public conduct, interference with governmental authority, or violation of civil rights or liberties. Weapons offenses, bribery, escape, and tax law violations, for example, are included in this category.

How do violent crimes differ from property crimes?

The outcome of a criminal event determines if it is a property crime or a violent crime. Violent crime refers to events such as homicide, rape, and assault that may result in injury to a person. Robbery is also considered a violent crime because it involves the use or threat of force against a person.

Property crimes are unlawful acts with the intent of gaining property but which do not involve the use or threat of force against an individual. Larceny and motor vehicle theft are examples of property crimes.

In the National Crime Survey a distinction is also made between crimes against persons (violent crimes and personal larceny) and crimes against households (property crimes, including household larceny).

What are the characteristics of some serious crimes?

Crime	Definition	Facts
Burglary	Unlawful entry of any fixed structure, vehicle, or vessel used for regular residence, industry, or business, with or without force, with the intent to commit a felony or larceny.	• Residential property was targeted in 2 out of every 3 reported burglaries; nonresidential property accounted for the remaining third. • In 1985, 42% of all residential burglaries occurred without forced entry. • About 37% of the no-force burglaries were known to have occurred during the day between 6 a.m. and 6 p.m.
Larceny-theft	Unlawful taking or attempted taking of property other than a motor vehicle from the possession of another, by stealth, without force and without deceit, with intent to permanently deprive the owner of the property.	• Less than 5% of all personal larcenies involve contact between the victim and offender. • Pocket picking and purse snatching most frequently occur inside nonresidential buildings or on street locations. • Unlike most other crimes, pocket picking and purse snatching affect the elderly about as much as other age groups.
Motor vehicle theft	Unlawful taking or attempted taking of a self-propelled road vehicle owned by another, with the intent of depriving him or her of it, permanently or temporarily.	• Motor vehicle theft is relatively well reported to the police. In 1985 89% of all completed thefts were reported. • The stolen property is more likely to be recovered in this crime than in other property crimes.
Arson	The intentional damaging or destruction or attempted damaging or destruction by means of fire or explosion of property without the consent of the owner, or of one's own property or that of another by fire or explosives with or without the intent to defraud.	• Single-family residences were the most frequent targets of arson. • 16% of all structures where arson occurred were not in use.

Sources: BJS *Dictionary of criminal justice data terminology*, 2nd edition, 1981. BJS *Criminal victimization in the U.S., 1985*. FBI *Crime in the United States 1985*.

How do felonies differ from misdemeanors?

Criminal offenses are also classified according to how they are handled by the criminal justice system. Most jurisdictions recognize two classes of offenses: felonies and misdemeanors.

Felonies are not distinguished from misdemeanors in the same way in all jurisdictions, but most States define felonies as offenses punishable by a year or more in a State prison. The most serious crimes are never "misdemeanors" and the most minor offenses are never "felonies."

What is organized crime?

Although organized crime has been considered a problem throughout the century, no universally accepted definition of the term has been established. The President's Commission on Organized Crime, for example, defines the criminal group involved in organized crime as "a continuing, structured collectivity of persons who utilize criminality, violence, and a willingness to corrupt in order to gain and maintain power and profit."

Some characteristics of organized crime are generally cited:
- **Organizational continuity:** Organized crime groups ensure that they can survive the death or imprisonment of their leaders and can vary the nature of their activities to take advantage of changing criminal opportunities.
- **Hierarchical structure:** All organized crime groups are headed by a single leader and structured into a series of subordinate ranks, although they may vary in the rigidity of their hierarchy. Nationwide organizations may be composed of multiple separate chapters or "families," each unit generally headed by its own leader who is supported by the group's hierarchy of command. Intergroup disputes, joint ventures, and new membership are generally reviewed by a board composed of the leaders of the most powerful individual chapters. For example, La Cosa Nostra currently is estimated to include 24 individual "families" all under the general authority of a "National Commission" comprised of an estimated nine bosses.
- **Restricted membership:** Members must be formally accepted by the group after a demonstration of loyalty and a willingness to commit criminal acts. Membership may be limited by race or common background and generally

Organized crime includes many traditional crimes as well as offenses such as racketeering

involves a lifetime commitment to the group, which can be enforced through violent group actions.

- **Criminality/violence/power:** Power and control are key organized crime goals and may be obtained through criminal activity of one type or in multiple activities. Criminal activity may be designed directly to generate "income" or to support the group's power through bribery, violence, and intimidation. Violence is used to maintain group loyalty and to intimidate outsiders and is a threat underlying all group activity. Specific violent criminal acts include, for example, murder, kidnaping, arson, robbery, and bombings.
- **Legitimate business involvement:** Legitimate businesses are used to "launder" illegal funds or stolen merchandise. For example, illegal profits from drug sales can be claimed as legitimate profits of a noncriminal business whose accounting records have been appropriately adjusted. Legitimate business involvement also elevates the social status of organized crime figures.
- **Use of specialists:** Outside specialists, such as pilots, chemists, and arsonists, provide services under contract to organized crime groups on an intermittent or regular basis.

Organized crime groups often are protected by corrupt officials in the government and private sector

Such officials include inspectors who overlook violations, accountants who conceal assets, financial officers who fail to report major cash transactions, law enforcement officers who provide enforcement activity information to drug traffickers, and attorneys who have government witnesses intimidated to change their testimony. The public also supports organized crime by sometimes knowingly or unknowingly purchasing illegal goods and "hot" merchandise.

Organized crime groups are involved in many different activities

In addition to its well known involvement in illegal drugs, organized crime is also involved in prostitution, gambling, and loan sharking operations and has been shown to have infiltrated legitimate industries such as construction, waste removal, wholesale and retail distribution of goods, hotel and restaurant operations, liquor sales, motor vehicle repairs, real estate, and banking.

How much does organized crime cost?

A recent survey for the President's Commission on Organized Crime estimates that 1986 net income from organized crime activity ranged between $26.8 billion (a low estimate) and $67.7 billion (the high estimate).

The indirect costs of organized crime affect all consumers through increased consumer prices. Kickbacks, protection payments, increased labor and material costs, and lack of competition in industries controlled by organized crime all increase consumer costs. Unpaid taxes on illegal activities result in higher tax burdens for legal wage earners.

Racketeer Influenced and Corrupt Organization (RICO) statutes are key tools in the fight against organized crime

The Federal RICO statute was enacted in 1970 and was amended most recently in 1986. Unlike other existing statutes that address individual criminal acts such as murder or robbery, the RICO statute was specifically designed to target the overall and continuing operations of organized crime organizations. Specifically, the act prohibits the use of racketeering activities or profits to acquire, conduct, or maintain the business of an existing organization or "enterprise." Racketeering activities are defined to include any act or threat involving murder, kidnaping, gambling, arson, robbery, bribery, extortion, dealing in narcotic or dangerous drugs, fraud, and other crimes. The act also provides for forfeiture of illegally obtained gains and interests in enterprises.

Twenty-three States had enacted RICO statutes by 1986. Most of them are very similar to the Federal statute.

The government also has other tools to fight organized crime, including witness protection programs, electronic surveillance procedures, and immunity statutes.

There is much debate about how to define "white-collar" crime

Reiss and Biderman define it as violations of law "that involve the use of a violator's position of significant power, influence or trust . . . for the purpose of illegal gain, or to commit an illegal act for personal or organizational gain." Another researcher, Sutherland, defines white-collar crime as "a crime committed by a person of respectability and high social status in the course of his occupation." Edelhertz defines it as "an illegal act or series of illegal acts committed by nonphysical means and by concealment or guile to obtain money or property, to avoid the payment or loss of money or property, or to obtain business or personal advantage."

Although specific definitions vary, the term is generally construed to include business-related crimes, abuse of political office, some (but not all) aspects of organized crime, and the newly emerging areas of high-technology crime. White-collar crimes often involve deception of a gullible victim and generally occur where an individual's job, power, or personal influence provide the access and opportunity to abuse lawful procedures for unlawful gain.

Specific white-collar crimes include embezzlement, bribery, fraud (including procurement fraud, stock fraud, fraud in government programs, and investment and other "schemes"), theft of services, theft of trade secrets, tax evasion, and obstruction of justice.

Unlike violent crimes, white-collar crimes do not necessarily cause injury to identifiable persons

White-collar crime instead can cause loss to society in general as in cases of tax evasion, for example. For this reason, white-collar crimes, unlike violent crimes, may not always be detected and are more difficult to investigate.

Little data are available on the extent of white-collar crime

Measuring white-collar crime presents special problems:

- **No uniform definitions** exist that define either the overall scope of white-collar crime or individual criminal acts.
- **Wide variations** in commercial recordkeeping procedures make it difficult to collect and classify data on the loss.
- **Uncertainty over the legal status** of financial and technical transactions complicates the classification of data.

White-collar crime refers to a group of nonviolent crimes that generally involve deception or abuse of power

• **Computer technology** can conceal losses resulting from computer crimes.
• **Crimes may not be reported** to protect consumer confidence.

Almost three-fourths of the white-collar crimes prosecuted at the State level resulted in convictions

A study of 8 States and the Virgin Islands found that 12% of the white-collar crime cases that originated with an arrest and for which dispositions were reported in 1983 were not prosecuted. The study defined white-collar crimes as forgery/counterfeiting, fraud, and embezzlement.

Prosecution rates for white-collar crimes were similar to those for violent crimes (murder, rape, robbery, kidnaping, and assault), property crimes (stolen vehicles, burglary, and arson), and public order crimes (drug and weapons offenses and commercial vice). Because the study focused on white-collar crime cases that were reported through the criminal justice system, the sample does not take into account the large number of white-collar crimes that were not discovered, not reported to authorities, or did not result in an arrest.

The study also found the conviction rate for cases prosecuted to be about 74%, slightly higher than for violent crimes (66%) and public order crimes (67%) and about the same as for property crimes (76%).

About 60% of the persons convicted for white-collar crime vs. about 67% of those convicted for violent crimes were sentenced to prison. Eighteen percent of white-collar offenders sentenced to prison were sentenced to more than 1 year (about the same as persons convicted of public order offense) vs. 39% of violent offenders.

ARE CRIMINALS MADE OR BORN?

Evidence indicates that both biological and sociological factors play roles.

Richard J. Herrnstein and James Q. Wilson

Richard J. Herrnstein is a professor of psychology and James Q. Wilson a professor of government at Harvard.

A revolution in our understanding of crime is quietly overthrowing some established doctrines. Until recently, criminologists looked for the causes of crime almost entirely in the offenders' social circumstances. There seemed to be no shortage of circumstances to blame: weakened, chaotic or broken families, ineffective schools, antisocial gangs, racism, poverty, unemployment. Criminologists took seriously, more so than many other students of social behavior, the famous dictum of the French sociologist Emile Durkheim: Social facts must have social explanations. The sociological theory of crime had the unquestioned support of prominent editorialists, commentators, politicians and most thoughtful people.

Today, many learned journals and scholarly works draw a different picture. Sociological factors have not been abandoned, but increasingly it is becoming clear to many scholars that crime is the outcome of an interaction between social factors and certain biological factors, particularly for the offenders who, by repeated crimes, have made public places dangerous. The idea is still controversial, but increasingly, to the old question "Are criminals born or made?" the answer seems to be: both. The causes of crime lie in a combination of predisposing biological traits channeled by social circumstance into criminal behavior. The traits alone do not inevitably lead to crime; the circumstances do not make criminals of everyone; but together they create a population responsible for a large fraction of America's problem of crime in the streets.

Evidence that criminal behavior has deeper roots than social circumstances has always been right at hand, but social science has, until recent years, overlooked its implications. As far as the records show, crime everywhere and throughout history is disproportionately a young man's pursuit. Whether men are 20 or more times as likely to be arrested as women, as is the case in Malawi or Brunei, or only four to six times as likely, as in the United States or France, the sex difference in crime statistics is universal. Similarly, 18-year-olds may sometimes be four times as likely to be criminal as 40-year-olds, while at other times only twice as likely. In the United States, more than half of all arrests for serious property crimes are of 20-year-olds or younger. Nowhere have older persons been as criminal as younger ones.

It is easy to imagine purely social explanations for the effects of age and sex on crime. Boys in many societies are trained by their parents and the society itself to play more roughly and aggressively than girls. Boys are expected to fight back, not to cry,

Intelligence and temperament have heritable bases and influence behavior.

and to play to win. Likewise, boys in many cultures are denied adult responsibilities, kept in a state of prolonged dependence and confined too long in schools that many of them find unrewarding. For a long time, these factors were thought to be the whole story.

Ultimately, however, the very universality of the age and sex differences in crime have alerted some social scientists to the implausibility of a theory that does not look beyond the accidents of particular societies. If cultures as different as Japan's and Sweden's, England's and Mexico's, have sex and age differences in crime, then perhaps we should have suspected from the start that there was something more fundamental going on than parents happening to decide to raise their boys and girls differently. What is it about boys, girls and their parents, in societies of all sorts, that leads them to emphasize, rather than overcome, sex differences? Moreover, even if we believed that every society has arbitrarily decided to inculcate aggressiveness in males, there would still be the greater criminality among *young* males to explain. After all, in some cultures, young boys are not denied adult responsibilities but are kept out of school, put to work tilling the land and made to accept obligations to the society.

But it is no longer necessary to approach questions about the sources of criminal behavior merely with argument and supposition. There is evidence. Much crime, it is agreed, has an aggressive component, and Eleanor Emmons Maccoby, a professor of psychology at Stanford University, and Carol Nagy Jacklin, a psychologist now at the University of Southern California, after reviewing the evidence on sex differences in aggression, concluded that it has a foundation that is at least in part biological. Only that conclusion can be drawn, they said, from data that show that the average man is more aggressive than the average woman in all known societies, that the sex difference is present in infancy well before evidence of sex-role socialization by adults, that similar sex differences turn up in many of our biological relatives—monkeys and apes. Human aggression has been directly tied to sex hormones, particularly male sex hormones, in experiments on athletes engaging in competitive sports and on prisoners known for violent or domineering behavior. No single line of evidence is decisive and each can be challenged, but all together they convinced Drs. Maccoby and Jacklin, as well as most specialists on the biology of sex differences, that the sexual conventions that assign males the aggressive roles have biological roots.

That is also the conclusion of most researchers about the developmental forces that make adolescence and young adulthood a time of risk for criminal and other nonconventional behavior. This is when powerful new drives awaken, leading to frustrations that foster behavior unchecked by the internalized prohibitions of adulthood. The result is usually just youthful rowdiness, but, in a minority of cases, it passes over the line into crime.

The most compelling evidence of biological factors for criminality comes from two studies—one of twins, the other of adopted boys. Since the 1920's it has been understood that twins may develop from a single fertilized egg, resulting in identical genetic endowments—identical twins—or from a pair of separately fertilized eggs that have about half their genes in common—fraternal twins. A standard procedure for estimating how important genes are to a trait is to compare the similarity between identical twins with that between fraternal twins. When identical twins are clearly more similar in a trait than fraternal twins, the trait probably has high heritability.

There have been about a dozen studies of criminality using twins. More than 1,500 pairs of twins have been studied in the United States, the Scandinavian countries, Japan, West Germany, Britain and elsewhere, and the result is qualitatively the same everywhere. Identical twins are more likely to have similar criminal records than fraternal twins. For example, the late Karl O. Christiansen, a Danish criminologist, using the Danish Twin Register, searched police, court and prison records for entries regarding twins born in a certain region of Denmark between 1881 and 1910. When an identical twin had a criminal record, Christiansen found, his or her co-twin was more than twice as likely to have one also than when a fraternal twin had a criminal record.

In the United States, a similar result has recently been reported by David Rowe, a psychologist at the University of Oklahoma, using questionnaires instead of official records to measure criminality. Twins in high school in almost all the school districts of Ohio received questionnaires by mail, with a promise of confidentiality as well as a small payment if the questionnaires were filled out and returned. The twins were asked about their activities, including their delinquent behavior, about their friends and about their co-twins. The identical twins were more similar in delinquency than the fraternal twins. In addition, the twins who shared more activities with each other were no more likely to be similar in delinquency than those who shared fewer activities.

No single method of inquiry should be regarded as conclusive. But essentially the same results are found in studies of adopted children. The idea behind such studies is to find a sample of children adopted early in life, cases in which the criminal histories of both adopting and biological parents are known. Then, as the children grow up, researchers can discover how predictive of their criminality are the family histories of their adopting and biological parents. Recent studies show that the biological family history contributes substantially to the adoptees' likelihood of breaking the law.

For example, Sarnoff Mednick, a psychologist at the University of Southern California, and his associates in the United States and Denmark have followed a sample of several thousand boys adopted in Denmark between 1927 and 1947. Boys with criminal biological parents and noncriminal adopting parents were more likely to have criminal records than those with noncriminal biological parents and criminal adopting parents. The more criminal convictions a boy's natural parents had, the greater the risk of criminality for boys being raised by adopting parents who had no records. The risk was unrelated to whether the boy or his adopting parents knew about the natural parents' criminal records, whether the natural parents committed their crimes before or after the boy was given up for adoption, or whether the boy was adopted immediately after birth or a year or two later. The results of this study have been confirmed in Swedish and American samples of adopted children.

Because of studies like these, many sociologists and criminologists now accept the existence of genetic factors contributing to criminality. When there is disagreement, it is about how large the genetic contribution to crime is and about how the criminality of biological parents is transmitted to their children.

Both the twin and adoption studies show that genetic contributions are not alone responsible for crime — there is, for example, some increase in criminality among boys if their adopted fathers are criminal even when their biological parents are not, and not every co-twin of a criminal identical twin becomes criminal himself. Although it appears, on average, to be substantial, the

precise size of the genetic contribution to crime is probably unknowable, particularly since the measures of criminality itself are now so crude.

We have a bit more to go on with respect to the link that transmits a predisposition toward crime from parents to children. No one believes there are "crime genes," but there are two major attributes that have, to some degree, a heritable base and that appear to influence criminal behavior. These are intelligence and temperament. Hundreds of studies have found that the more genes people share, the more likely they are to resemble each other intellectually and temperamentally.

Starting with studies in the 1930's, the average offender in broad samples has consistently scored 91 to 93 on I.Q. tests for which the general population's average is 100. The typical offender does worse on the verbal items of intelligence tests than on the nonverbal items but is usually below average on both.

Criminologists have long known about the correlation between criminal behavior and I.Q., but many of them have discounted it for various reasons. Some have suggested that the correlation can be explained away by the association between low socioeconomic status and crime, on the one hand, and that between low I.Q. and low socioeconomic status, on the other. These criminologists say it is low socioeconomic status, rather than low I.Q., that fosters crime. Others have questioned whether I.Q. tests really measure intelligence for the populations that are at greater risk for breaking the law. The low scores of offenders, the argument goes, betray a culturally deprived background or alienation from our society's values rather than low intelligence. Finally, it is often noted that the offenders in some studies have been caught for their crimes. Perhaps the ones who got away have higher I.Q.s.

But these objections have proved to be less telling than they once seemed to be. There are, for example, many poor law-abiding people living in deprived environments, and one of their more salient characteristics is that they have higher I.Q. scores than those in the same environment who break the law.

Then, too, it is a common misconception that I.Q. tests are invalid for people from disadvantaged backgrounds. If what is implied by this criticism is that scores predict academic potential or job performance differently for different groups, then the criticism is wrong. A comprehensive recent survey sponsored by the National Academy of Sciences concluded that "tests predict about as well for one group as for another." And that some highly intelligent criminals may well be good at eluding capture is fully consistent with the belief that offenders, in general, have lower scores than nonoffenders.

If I.Q. and criminality are linked, what may explain the link? There are several possibilities. One is that low scores on I.Q. tests signify greater difficulty in grasping the likely consequences of action or in learning the meaning and significance of moral codes. Another is that low scores, especially on the verbal component of the tests, mean trouble in school, which leads to frustration, thence to resentment, anger and delinquency. Still another is that persons who are not as skillful as others in expressing themselves verbally may find it more rewarding to express themselves in ways in which they will do better, such as physical threat or force.

For some repeat offenders, the predisposition to criminality may be more a matter of temperament than intelligence. Impulsiveness, insensitivity to social mores, a lack of deep and enduring emotional attachments to others and an appetite for danger are among the temperamental characteristics of high-rate offenders. Temperament is, to a degree, heritable, though not as much so as intelligence. All parents know that their children, shortly after birth, begin to exhibit certain characteristic ways of behaving — they are placid or fussy, shy or bold. Some of the traits endure, among them aggressiveness and hyperactivity, although they change in form as the child develops. As the child grows up, these traits, among others, may gradually unfold into a disposition toward unconventional, defiant or antisocial behavior.

Lee Robins, a sociologist at Washington University School of Medicine in St. Louis, reconstructed 30 years of the lives of more than 500 children who were patients in the 1920's at a child guidance clinic in St. Louis. She was interested in the early precursors of chronic sociopathy, a condition of antisocial personality that often includes criminal behavior as one of its symptoms. Adult sociopaths in her sample who did not suffer from psychosis, mental retardation or addiction, were, without exception, antisocial before they were 18. More than half of the male sociopaths had serious symptoms before they were 11. The main childhood precursors were truancy, poor school performance, theft, running away, recklessness, slovenliness, impulsiveness and guiltlessness. The more symptoms in childhood, the greater the risk of sociopathy in adulthood.

Other studies confirm and extend Dr. Robins's conclusions. For example, two psychologists, John J. Conger of the University of Colorado and Wilbur Miller of Drake University in Des Moines, searching back over the histories of a sample of delinquent boys in Denver, found that "by the end of the third grade, future delinquents were already seen by their teachers as more poorly adapted than their classmates. They appeared to have less regard for the rights and feelings of their peers; less awareness of the need to accept responsibility for their obligations, both as individuals and as members of a group, and poorer attitudes toward authority."

Traits that foreshadow serious, recurrent criminal behavior have been traced all the way back to behavior patterns such as hyperactivity and unusual fussiness, and neurological signs such as atypical brain waves or reflexes. In at least a minority of cases, these are detectable in the first few years of life. Some of the characteristics are sex-linked. There is evidence that newborn females are more likely than newborn males to smile, to cling to their mothers, to be receptive to touching and talking, to be sensitive to certain stimuli, such as being touched by a cloth, and to have less upper-body strength. Mothers certainly treat girls and boys differently, but the differences are not simply a matter of the mother's choice — female babies are more responsive than male babies to precisely the kind of treatment that is regarded as "feminine." When adults are asked to play with infants, they play with them in ways they think are appropriate to the infants' sexes. But there is also some evidence that when the sex of the infant is concealed, the behavior of the adults is influenced by the conduct of the child.

Premature infants or those born with low birth weights have a special problem. These children are vulnerable to any adverse circumstances in their environment — including child abuse — that may foster crime. Although nurturing parents can compensate for adversity, cold or inconsistent parents may exacerbate it. Prematurity and low birth weight may result from poor prenatal care, a bad diet or excessive use of alcohol or drugs. Whether the bad care is due to poverty, ignorance or anything else, here we see criminality arising from biological, though not necessarily genetic, factors. It is now known that these babies are more likely than normal

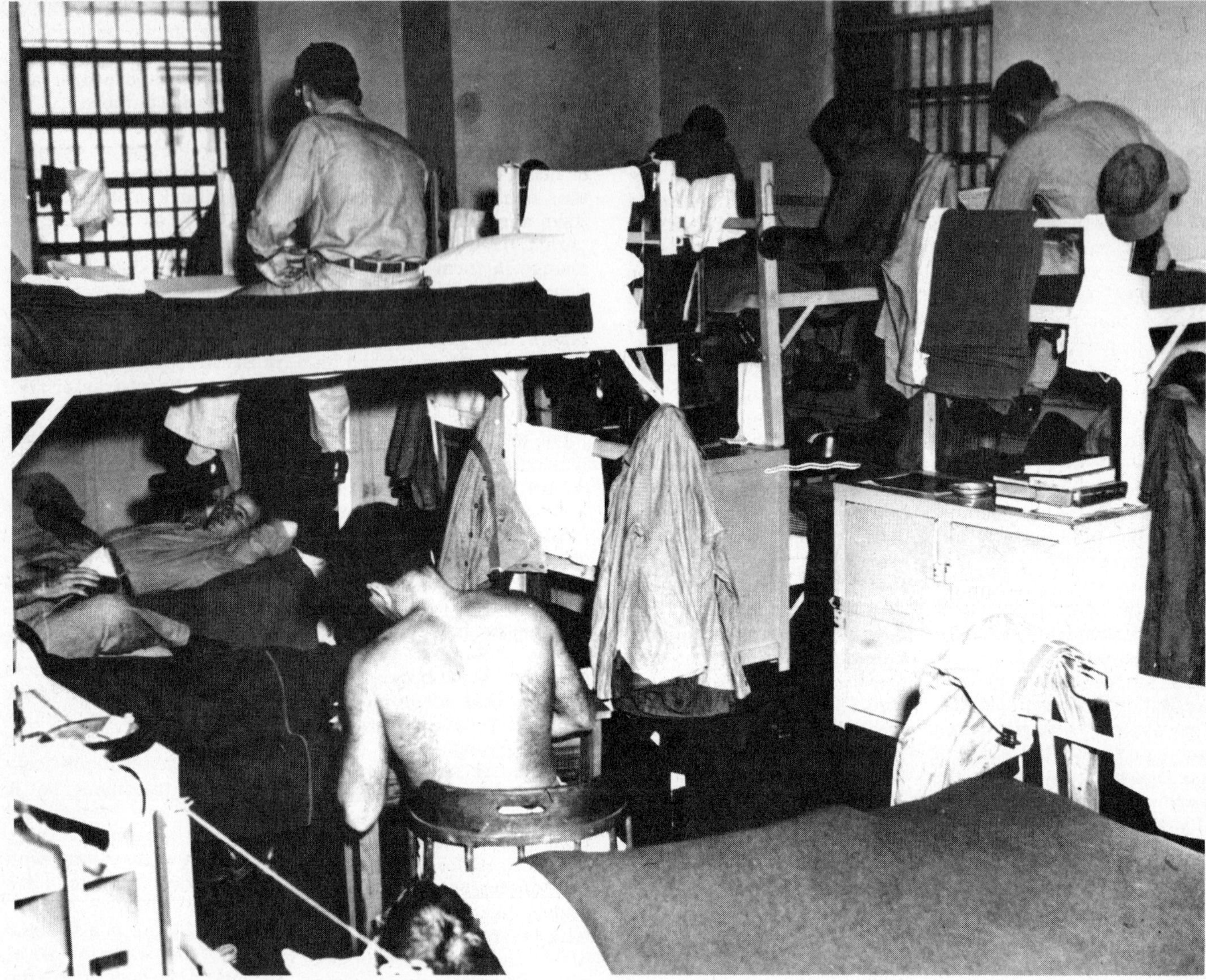

A majority of criminals are young and male; this is a worldwide phenomenon. Also, there is a correlation between criminal behavior and IQ. These facts indicate that both biological and sociological factors play a role in the development of a criminal.

babies to be the victims of child abuse.

We do not mean to blame child abuse on the victim by saying that premature and low-birth-weight infants are more difficult to care for and thus place a great strain on the parents. But unless parents are emotionally prepared for the task of caring for such children, they may vent their frustration at the infant's unresponsiveness by hitting or neglecting it. Whatever it is in parent and child that leads to prematurity or low birth weight is compounded by the subsequent interaction between them. Similarly, children with low I.Q.s may have difficulty in understanding rules, but if their parents also have poor verbal skills, they may have difficulty in communicating rules, and so each party to the conflict exacerbates the defects of the other.

THE STATEMENT that biology plays a role in explaining human behavior, especially criminal behavior, sometimes elicits a powerful political or ideological reaction. Fearful that what is being proposed is a crude biological determinism, some critics deny the evidence while others wish the evidence to be confined to scientific journals. Scientists who have merely proposed studying the possible effects of chromosomal abnormalities on behavior have been ruthlessly attacked by other scientists, as have those who have made public the voluminous data showing the heritability of intelligence and temperament.

Some people worry that any claim that biological factors influence criminality is tantamount to saying that the higher crime rate of black compared to white Americans has a genetic basis. But no responsible work in the field leads to any such conclusion. The data show that of all the reasons people vary in their crime rates, race is far less important than age, sex, intelligence and the other individual factors that vary within races. Any study of the causes of crime must therefore first consider the individual factors. Differences among races may have many explanations, most of them having nothing to do with biology.

The intense reaction to the study of biological factors in crime, we believe, is utterly misguided. In fact, these discoveries, far from implying that "criminals are born" and should be locked up forever, suggest new and imaginative ways of reducing criminality by benign treatment. The opportunity we have is precisely analogous to that which we had when the biological bases of other disorders were established. Mental as well as physical illness — alcoholism, learning disabilities of various sorts, and perhaps even susceptibilities to drug addiction — now seem to have genetic components. In each case, new understanding energized the search for treatment and gave it new direction. Now we know that many forms of depression can be successfully treated with drugs; in time we may learn the same of Alzheimer's disease. Alcoholics are helped when they understand that some persons, because of their predisposition toward addiction to alcohol, should probably never consume it at all. A chemical treatment of the predisposition is a realistic possibility. Certain types of slow learners can already be helped by special programs. In time, others will be also.

Crime, admittedly, may be a more difficult program. So many different acts are criminal that it is only with considerable poetic license that we can speak of "criminality" at all. The bank teller who embezzles $500 to pay off a gambling debt is not engaging in the same behavior as a person who takes $500 from a liquor store at the point of a gun or one who causes $500 worth of damage by drunkenly driving his car into a parked vehicle. Moreover, crime, unlike alcoholism or dyslexia, exposes a person to the formal condemnation of society and the possibility of imprisonment. We naturally and rightly worry about treating all "criminals" alike, or stigmatizing persons whom we think might become criminal by placing them in special programs designed to prevent criminality.

But these problems are not insurmountable barriers to better ways of thinking about crime prevention. Though criminals are of all sorts, we know that a very small fraction of all young males commit so large a fraction of serious street crime that we can properly blame these chronic offenders for most such crime. We also know that chronic offenders typically begin their misconduct at an early age. Early family and preschool programs may be far better repositories for the crime-prevention dollar than rehabilitation programs aimed — usually futilely — at the 19- or 20-year-old veteran offender. Prevention programs risk stigmatizing children, but this may be less of a risk than is neglect. If stigma were a problem to be avoided at all costs, we would have to dismantle most special-needs education programs.

Having said all this, we must acknowledge that there is at present little hard evidence that we know how to inhibit the development of delinquent tendencies in children. There are some leads, such as family training programs of the sort pioneered at the Oregon Social Learning Center, where parents are taught how to use small rewards and penalties to alter the behavior of misbehaving children. There is also evidence from David Weikart and Lawrence Schweinhart of the High/Scope Educational Research Foundation at Ypsilanti, Mich., that preschool education programs akin to Project Head Start may reduce later deliquency. There is nothing yet to build a national policy on, but there are ideas worth exploring by carefully repeating and refining these pioneering experimental efforts.

Above all, there is a case for redirecting research into the causes of crime in ways that take into account the interaction of biological and social factors. Some scholars, such as the criminologist Marvin E. Wolfgang and his colleagues at the University of Pennsylvania, are already exploring these issues by analyzing social and biological information from large groups as they age from infancy to adulthood and linking the data to criminal behavior. But much more needs to be done.

It took years of patiently following the life histories of many men and women to establish the linkages between smoking or diet and disease; it will also take years to unravel the complex and subtle ways in which intelligence, temperament, hormonal levels and other traits combine with family circumstances and later experiences in school and elsewhere to produce human character.

A Law Enforcement Response to Legalizing Illicit Drugs

Edward J. Tully and Margo Bennett

Edward J. Tully, Chief, Education/Communication Arts, and Margo Bennett, Special Agent Supervisor, FBI Academy, Quantico, Virginia

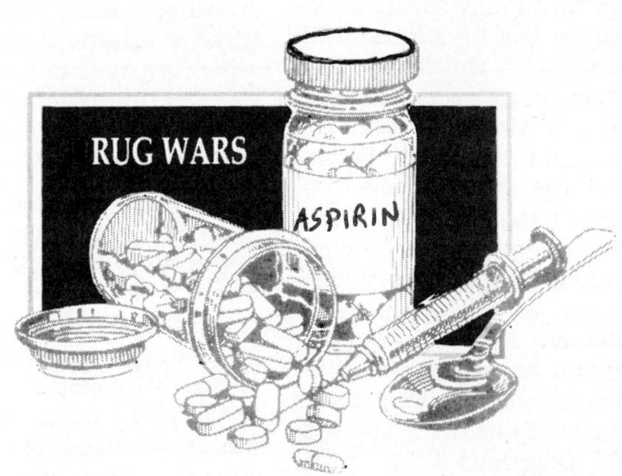

"Those who cannot remember the past are condemned to repeat it."

— George Santayana
Life of Reason, Volume 1

When the question of legalizing illicit drugs was raised at the October 1988 meeting of the Major City Chiefs (an organization consisting of 48 chief executive officers of the largest law enforcement organizations in the United States and Canada), the chiefs responded with disappointment, having believed that the merits of this issue had long since been settled. Their next step was to encourage the preparation of an appropriate response, reflecting the general thinking of the law enforcement community.

The objective of the following article is to present the reasonable legalization arguments and provide the persuasive rebuttals known to law enforcement officials. Our purpose is not to chill debate, or to demean those who are, in good faith, calling for some aspect of legalization. Neither should this be viewed as an attempt to glorify, justify or rationalize law enforcement's efforts to control drug problems during the past 20 years or so. We have made many mistakes in the past and will probably make more in the future. When these errors occur, we encourage the community to call them to our attention so that we can make appropriate corrections and adjustments.

Both sides of the legalization argument agree that North America has a serious drug abuse problem that involves both legal and illegal substances. The stated goals of both sides are to protect individual rights, reduce general and violent crime, promote the mental and physical health of the people and ensure a better quality of life for all citizens. Thus, the discussion should center on the path we take to ensure that our mutual objectives are met. The law enforcement community argues that legalization advocates propose dangerous experiments in social policy. In our view, the legalization of illicit drugs promises no significant benefit to anyone in our society. Therefore, we view the experiments as risks that we should not entertain.

Following are basic arguments presented by proponents of legalization.

The Protection of Individual Rights

The central, underlying theme of many arguments to legalize illicit drugs is that individuals in a free society have a right to make their own choices, even if their exercise of liberty leads to their own destruction. This argument was offered by Dr. Ethan Nadelman in the Summer 1988 issue of *Public Interest.* "Legalization is . . . a recognition of the right to make . . . choices free of the fear of criminal sanction." Once again, as often in the past, the debate over legalization centers around the delicate balance between the liberty and rights of individuals and the well-being of the community. Americans have frequently held that as long as an individual's behavior does not adversely affect others, then he ought to be free to do as he chooses. This position safeguards free speech, freedom of religion, freedom of association and the freedom to live a reasonable lifestyle. The conflict comes when an individual's action threatens the community. If the community decides that the potential threat to the citizenry legitimately overrides the freedom exercised by the individual, it handles the problem through laws or cultural norms, or both.

In order for the "individual rights" argument to succeed, the proponents of legalization must successfully argue that the abuse of currently illicit drugs does not pose a significant threat. In practice, proponents offer the rationale that drugs are not harmful; that many individuals who use them are perfectly competent; that users and addicts are not primarily to blame for their actions while under the influence; that actions

Reprinted from *The Police Chief* magazine, Vol. LVI, No. 8, August 1989, pp. 57-59, 61-64. Copyright held by The International Association of Chiefs of Police, Inc., P. O. Box 6010, 13 Firstfield Road, Gaithersburg, MD 20878, USA.

of the community to protect itself are more of a threat to the public good than the actions of drug abusers; and, finally, that there would be fewer social problems if current criminal sanctions were lifted and education and treatment were emphasized instead.

No one denies the importance of drug prevention, education and treatment. But the real issues are (1) whether society and government have the authority to protect the public from the harmful acts of drug abusers and other persons who would do it harm either intentionally or otherwise; (2) whether society should protect an individual from himself; and (3) what measure—or combination of measures—is acceptable in terms of diminished individual rights, to promote the common welfare?

In response to the first issue, all sides agree, in general terms, that certain aspects of drug abuse (violence to others, for example) pose a significant threat to our society and that, in these cases, society does have a fundamental right to take measures to protect itself from danger.

Second, American and Canadian societies have a long history of taking appropriate measures to protect people from their own unwise actions. They have established mandatory social security regulations, seat belt laws and child labor laws, among others.

Finally, America's traditions of government and social policy are based on the recognition that individuals are responsible for the consequences of their actions. Some legalization advocates have sought to shift responsibility from the individual, blaming society for drug use. Thus, a person who freely chooses to become drug dependent is excused of any blame for act or consequences. Usually the first to be blamed are the poor parents, who must obviously have erred in parenting. Next in line are the schools, churches and the individual's peers. Finally, the laws are blamed. If this argument is accepted, it follows that the drug-induced actions should be legalized on the logical assumption that the attendant problems will fade.

Proponents of "individual rights" have used this argument in the past with respect to sexual conduct, speech and a host of other issues, successfully at times and unsuccessfully at others. In the case of drug abuse, however, it is difficult to accept the argument that individuals must not be held accountable for their lifestyles. A large number of our citizens have freely chosen to ignore the law and to engage in activities that are a threat not only to themselves, but also to the community.

In this situation, the law was not wrong, unjust or an unacceptable infringement on individual rights. The responsibility of government is to do what it can do to ensure that its citizens are able to enjoy and exercise their very considerable freedoms. Government "of the people, by the people and for the people" requires a population physically and mentally able to make prudent decisions.

Punitive Measures Lead to Violence, Corruption and Crime

According to legalization advocates, the law enforcement approach and the use of punitive and repressive measures have led to violence, corruption of public officials and a significant increase in general crime.

It is true that levels of violence, general crime and, to a lesser extent, corruption of public officials have increased over the past 20 years. These trends can be tied directly or indirectly to legal or illegal drug abuse. However, to suggest that the increase in crime levels is caused by the illegality of some substances, or marketing practices, stretches logic to the breaking point. It requires acceptance of the implausible claim that individuals who choose to use or distribute drugs, and subsequently become involved in additional unlawful activities, somehow bear no responsibility. The government is blamed because it has made the ingested substance illegal, difficult to obtain or expensive.

This argument is naive. One reason people use mind-altering drugs is because they want to feel good. Individuals who continue drug use do so because they want to, or until they reach a point where they lose individual control over their lives. Up to this point, use of drugs is strictly voluntary. Thus, the inexorable drift to addiction on the part of some drug users is the result of a multitude of individual choices made over time.

The violence and criminal behaviors exhibited by people under the influence of drugs are not motivated by legal sanctions. The law, per se, does not cause their behavior. Individuals choose their behavior. If that behavior violates a law, harms another person or corrupts a public official, it is not reasonable to blame the law. We have not yet blamed the law in the case of the bank robber, wife beater or shoplifter. In reality, most individuals involved in criminal activity are either oblivious to or contemptuous of the law. Social rules are for other people, not for them. In our experience, there are few drug addicts, drug dealers or drug-induced criminals who would argue that the law, or law enforcement, caused his behavior. More to the point of the argument is that few drug traffickers would "go straight" if narcotics were legalized.

One final note on the corruption of public officials: It is true that present illegal drug activities have provided the wealth needed to corrupt police officers, judges or others involved in the criminal justice system. But this should not be viewed as part of the drug problem. It is the result of having public servants who are susceptible to corruption and hence not fit for public service. Whether the motivation is drugs, money or power, the problem of corruption is, in reality, a problem of character. In the final analysis, the problem of public corruption can be solved if we first select men and women of good character to be public servants.

The proponents of "individual rights" have made the individual's freedom of choice the centerpiece of their argument for the legalization of drugs. While the law enforcement community acknowledges the importance of individual rights and liberty, it considers the probable common good to be endangered by the legalization of drugs. We hold that it is destructive of the common good to legitimize patterns of behavior with drugs by which individuals become a threat to others and an enormous community liability. Thus, we reject the argument that current drug laws have made the drug problem worse. What has made the problem worse are individuals who have made some very poor choices.

Supply Reduction Policies Have Failed

Proponents of legalization insist that despite law enforcement's best efforts, the supply and substance purity of drugs have increased while price has decreased. Thus, they argue, law enforcement has failed. This is far from true, and it misleads reflections about wise social policy. Of all illicit drugs, only cocaine has increased in availability and purity at decreased prices. Marijuana, heroin and hashish have remained relatively stable and high priced, which is the objective of supply reduction. The principal reason cocaine has become more widely available is that the cocaine cartels have a huge supply of the easily stored drug, which they have been dumping on the North American market in order to increase demand. Despite recent events in Afghanistan, Iran and Lebanon that have wiped out previously supportive law enforcement activities in those nations, our interdiction efforts have kept the supplies of other drugs fairly stable.

On the other hand, to claim that law enforcement has been completely successful with its reduction efforts is not justified. The law enforcement community now recognizes that it will not be able to eliminate the flow of illicit drugs into North America. The demand for drugs is too high and the ease of smuggling drugs over the borders is too well known for our efforts to be totally successful. However, capitulation in this area means a significant increase in drugs or—in the case of several countries that have *de facto* capitulation—the possible loss of the entire country. The recognition of this fact has led law enforcement to open a second front by devoting more resources to demand reduction programs. The Drug Enforcement Administration, and the Los Angeles police and sheriff's departments have been leaders in the development of demand reduction programs. As these programs have spread throughout the United States, they have been acclaimed by educators and parents as very effective. These modest programs will not, in and of themselves, solve the drug problem, but they do vividly point out that drug demand reduction efforts need to be greatly expanded, with more institutions directly involved in addressing the problem.

To claim that law enforcement supply reduction efforts have "failed" is also to deny the fact that arrests, seizures and forfeitures have significantly increased each year. The legalization argument does not address the issue of what the magnitude of the supply problem would be if *no* effort had been made. Considering the complex problems involved in supply reduction efforts, law enforcement would argue that our efforts have neither failed nor succeeded as well as we had hoped. Each year as we learn more about the problem, we make adjustments in our tactics and strategies. Each year, it becomes more difficult to smuggle all types of contraband into North America. Each year, it becomes more difficult to grow and conceal marijuana and tougher to transport the product from point to point. As we continue to improve our reduction efforts, seizures will continue to show modest increases. We would argue that we should stay the course on the supply reduction issue and not give in to a problem just because we have had only partial success.

Drug Prohibition Laws Cause Crime

Advocates of legalization argue that if we repealed laws presently making the production, distribution, purchase and consumption of drugs illegal, we would reduce the number of crimes. This is not only misleading but untrue. The issue is whether, as advocates claim, repeal would take the profit out of drug dealing and thus result in less drug-marketing violence. We believe the answer is no. Unless the legalization proponents intend to sell any drug, to any person, at any time, in any amount desired, then a black market for drugs—and the attendant problems of crime and violence—will continue to exist. If drugs are freely available in the legal market and present addiction rates are maintained, it is reasonable to expect that the number of persons and the amount of drugs dispensed in the illegal market will increase. Thus, any short-term reduction of crime, however unlikely, would be rapidly negated. In the long term, the problems would probably be worse.

The argument that legalization would reduce the costs of drugs rests on the assumption that government can manufacture and distribute drugs more efficiently than the present illegal system, thus making drugs cheaper. Cheap drugs should, the argument states, reduce the necessity to commit crimes to finance drug purchases. Both of these assumptions are questionable. First, it is doubtful the government could compete against the present illegal system of distribution, particularly if the illegal system chose to compete with the government. The current cost of the production of a kilogram of cocaine is approximately $300. This amount of cocaine presently sells on the streets of Canada or the United States for anywhere from $15,000 to $30,000. Today, the price of cocaine is set by the cocaine cartel and not subject to usual market forces. Firmly in control of supplies, enjoying a huge profit margin and not burdened by the bureaucracy that would be required by government market participation, the cartels would make competitive pricing by government difficult and might well require government subsidies—themselves a drain on economic resources—if implemented.

Furthermore, drug users not only have to buy drugs but also have the usual expenses of food and housing. Most heavy users are not able, or willing, to hold full-time employment after they pass a certain stage of addiction, yet they still need money. Since most addicts have found crime to be the easiest way to fund their lifestyles, it is reasonable to conclude that they will continue their predatory habits.

Finally, if the number of abusers increased as a result of legalization, then the amount of crime committed would also increase. Any reduction of violent crime achieved by the availability of inexpensive narcotics through government distribution would be negated by an increase in the number of drug users. The number of crimes such as assault, child abuse and violence committed routinely by drug users would tend to increase as the drugs became more readily available. This is a lesson we have learned from our experience with alcohol abuse. It need not be repeated.

High Cost of Law Enforcement

Proponents of legalization estimate the cost of law enforcement in regard to the drug problem at about $10 billion annually, and suggest that this money could be better spent on drug rehabilitation programs. While $10 billion is a lot of money, it is only a tiny fraction of the funds spent annually to promote the public good. It is not even a great deal of money in comparison to private expenditures for personal comfort. In July 1988, as reported by CBS News, Americans spent $4.3 billion on electricity to run air conditioners. Put another way, the $10 billion amounts to $40 per year per person. When viewed in this context, the amount we spend on drug enforcement is modest. One other mitigating factor is the dollar value of seizures of assets from drug organizations. In 1987, for example, DEA seizures amounted to more than their annual budget allocation.

The law enforcement community would certainly endorse building more drug treatment centers and is already working to build community support for such projects. Considering the gravity of the drug problem, the law enforcement community believes that an informed public would support allocation of funds to build adequate drug treatment centers without sacrificing our enforcement efforts. Since this is presently occurring throughout the United States and Canada, it would tend to support our contention that the public is quite willing to help with drug treatment, without yielding on the illegality of drug use or the cost of law enforcement. Protection of the public by law enforcement is not in competition with drug education and treatment; these purposes are not a zero-sum game.

Legalization Will Not Result in High Drug Use

Most proponents of legalization suggest that it would not lead to a dramatic rise in drug abuse. But even Nadelman suggested this might be risky when he stated, "It is thus impossible to predict whether legalization would lead to greater levels of drug abuse, and exact costs comparable to most of alcohol and tobacco abuse."

Faced with the evidence of what has happened in terms of alcohol and tobacco abuse after sanctions were lifted on those substances, it is difficult to understand why it is impossible to predict the consequences of legalization of illicit drugs. Other historical examples show what happens when dangerous substances are not controlled. China's experience with opium from 1830 to 1930 is revealing. The Moslem Empire of the 11th century, the Inca Indians, Japan and Egypt all experienced significant drug dependency problems in their histories. The recent British attempt to control heroin abuse through the medical process has been a significant failure. We should also remember that morphine and cocaine were readily available in the form of patent medicines after the Civil War. The result was that America experienced a drug abuse problem similar in scope to what we see today. In general terms, most societies throughout history have had problems with drugs or drug abuse. Those societies that solved the problem did so in the same fashion we are trying today.

Relevant information can also be drawn from levels of abuse of currently legal drugs such as valium. Our experience with methaqualone (Quaaludes), oxycondone (Percodan) and hydromorphone (Dilaudid) gives sufficient evidence that the control of legal drugs is difficult, expensive and not always successful. In each case, the drug has been widely abused, despite the prescription process. These substances have found their way into the black market, having been illegally diverted or manufactured. All these facts indicate that if presently illicit drugs were legalized, whether they were distributed by the private or the public sector under specific controls, people disposed to drug use would in fact use them. Generalized use could rise, and illegal means of meeting demand would continue.

Consideration must be given to the claim that illicit drugs are not, and would not, become as popular as tobacco and alcohol. This is a hazardous assumption. The most dangerous drugs might not become widely popular, but use of debilitating narcotics that adversely affect behavior could. The drug traffickers have shown themselves to be extremely shrewd at marketing strategies, and they will continue to promote demand. Much more important than legalization is the mobilizing of community pressure against illegal narcotics, as has been done with tobacco and alcohol.

Law enforcement officials do not predict that legalization would cause "doomsday." We argue that legalization promises no improvement and unnecessarily risks an increasing of drug abuse.

Illicit Drugs Are Not as Dangerous as Believed

Legalization arguments depend on two additional assumptions: first, that illicit drugs are not as dangerous as is commonly believed and, second, that since some illicit drugs are highly dangerous, they are not likely to be popular. With respect to the first assumption, it is enough to say the medical community disagrees, as does every police officer who comes into contact with people debilitated by drugs from marijuana to "crack." The claim that illicit drugs are not dangerous falls of its own weight in the face of experience. The medical research community admits that current progress of research is insufficient to say *exactly how dangerous* illicit drugs are to physical and mental health. Funding for additional medical research should be a high priority so that the full measure of risk can be grasped. For the present, we have enough information from emergency room and morgue records, accident statistics and overall costs of lost productivity from drug abuse to know that the dangers are real. As drug epidemics ebb and flow, and new substances are introduced into the marketplace, we tend to neglect such evidence. It was just a few years ago that cocaine was thought by many to be safe and nonaddicting. The early studies of marijuana indicated some potential long-term health hazards, but most studies were done with samples containing half the THC now present in the sinsemilla and hydroponic varieties of marijuana. Current research tends to support the hypothesis that marijuana is a significant health hazard with a debilitating effect on motor skills. These are important skills used in driving, flying or handling a locomotive. Results of impairment have become all too familiar.

The claim that illicit drugs are not as dangerous as believed is wrong, and those who make it diminish the realism of the debate about legalization.

Conclusion

In our view, the proponents of legalization have not made a case for the freedom of individuals to choose to use illicit drugs regardless of the consequences. We believe the threat of intemperate drug use, whether legal or illegal, is a significant threat to our common welfare. The problem incurred by removing current sanctions would only make the threat more pronounced. We should protect ourselves by legislation where sanctions meet the combined test of common sense and the constitutions of the United States and Canada.

It is interesting to note that those making an argument for the legalization of illicit drugs have not recently made similar arguments on behalf of the common drunk. The drunk has become the "leper" in our society as a result of his behavior while intoxicated. The alcoholic is no longer considered in some quarters to be without responsibility for his conduct, but rather to be in violation of standards of common decency. Being drunk is not given any weight, in any quarter, as an excuse for violent or abusive behavior, and the drunk driver is being punished more severely than ever before in our history. Where are the defenders of the drunk? Where are the defenders of the smoker these days? Simply put, staunch defenders of the drunk and the smoker are gone because many have recognized that tolerance adversely affects the individual and the society. Laws have been strengthened and the sanctions of custom are being used to discourage consumption.

While some commentators would suggest the problem of drug abuse is made worse by repressive measures of the criminal justice system, it is more reasonable to assume that the underlying cause of our problems lies within ourselves. Whether the causes reflect an absence of high personal standards, greed, inability to cope with rapid change or involuntary confinement to poverty, we must come to grips with the fact that a large number of people in our culture turn to drugs for relief. Law enforcement cannot address these basic problems alone. Considering the nature and the complexities of the underlying problems, it is obvious to us that the institutions of the family, education, religion, business, industry, media and government all have crucial stakes in the solution of the problem. Drug abuse is no longer the other fellow's problem!

Even though the problems of drug abuse are severe in both the United States and Canada, we should pause and consider the success we have had in reducing the number of people who are smoking cigarettes, and the steps that the Mothers Against Drunk Drivers

destruction of the common good

only cocaine dropped in price

(MADD), Students Against Drunk Driving (SADD) and Alcoholics Anonymous (AA) have taken to bring alcohol abuse problems under control. Some recent surveys indicate that our teenagers' drug use may have peaked and perhaps dropped a bit in recent years as a result of an effective demand reduction program. This is evidence that we have made some significant progress in curbing the problem.

We need not haggle over how much each of us should do to bring the problem under control. We should not vilify those who suggest a different approach, or pass additional legislation in a hysterical atmosphere. This is a time to determine our best means and remedies for facing the problems and to move forthrightly to the task of reducing the problem to tolerable levels. For the short term, the law enforcement community hopes to continue to maintain reasonable and prudent pressure on supply interdiction and vigorous enforcement of existing laws, while at the same time continuing the development of demand reduction programs. This will buy time so that additional solutions can be developed and more players brought into the contest. In this regard, we in the law enforcement community stand ready to share our knowledge, resources and dedication to solving the problem with any institution, public or private, at any time.

We are sensitive to the fact that mistakes have been made in the attempt to control drug abuse. However, rather than dwell on finding a scapegoat, we really should be working together, as men and women of good faith, in an attempt to safeguard present and future generations. Controlling the problems of narcotics will take a long time, and it is not going to be as simple—or ostensibly as easy—as the mere legalization of drugs.

Editor's note: The Major City Chiefs of Police unanimously endorsed this article at their October 6, 1988, meeting in Portland, Oregon.

GUNS

Guns have long stirred America's primal passions. But escalating violence by armed drug dealers and a schoolyard massacre in Stockton, Calif., in January have pushed the debate to a new apogee. State legislatures are considering new controls on guns, and the gun lobby is furiously resisting. Lost in the fight is a sense of the many other shades of opinion about what to do.

For all their differences on the gun issue, most Americans have one thing in common. They respond to the mystique about shooting. Gun-control advocates worry about the fearsome force loosed in shooting, while gun enthusiasts emphasize the satisfaction of being the master of such force. Those polarized sensibilities are now in full-scale war again as Americans debate what to do about guns.

For the first time since the assassinations of the late 1960s, the country is seriously considering significant new limitations on firearms. But this time, instead of assailants named Sirhan or Ray, the main catalysts for the debate are the nameless drug lords whose feral deeds fill the news every day. They possess and actively traffic in arsenals of weapons so threatening that they have police outgunned, and many Americans want those guns taken away. Another catalyst was not a drug dealer, but a deranged welder named Patrick Edward Purdy. Last January, he killed five schoolchildren and wounded 30 other adults and children in Stockton, Calif. His gun of choice was a Chinese-made semiautomatic version of the AK-47.

The reaction has been astounding. More than a dozen localities, from Los Angeles to Cleveland to Stockton, itself, have adopted assault-weapon bans. On the state level, an assault-rifle prohibition moved swiftly through the California legislature but is now on hold while details are ironed out. Several other state legislatures also are considering bills. Twenty-two states have already enacted waiting-period legislation, including conservative Virginia, which voted earlier this year to institute a limited background check on all gun buyers. At the federal level, bills to limit assault rifles have been introduced, while the Justice Department is studying expansion of the existing computer system to review the backgrounds of all gun purchasers.

However, the forces opposed to gun control, led by the 2.8-million-member National Rifle Association, have rallied to thwart or slow down many antigun initiatives. Their most dramatic turnaround could soon be in evidence when President Bush, an NRA life member who received wide support from gun owners in last year's election, unveils a new anticrime initiative, perhaps as early as this week. A month ago, Bush switched his long-standing opposition to limiting semiautomatic weapons and endorsed a temporary ban on the importation of assault weapons. Now, ac-

From *U.S. News & World Report,* May 8, 1989, pp. 20-22, 24-25.

cording to White House sources, the President plans to address the public's clamor for action by introducing a plan to de-emphasize gun control in favor of stern anticrime measures; the plan will largely embrace the NRA's notion that criminals are the issue, not guns. The Bush plan will seek an end to federal plea bargains with drug dealers who use guns; a beefing up of prosecutorial forces; more mandatory sentences; a widening of death-penalty statutes and ways to "make prisons less pleasant," perhaps by creating tent prisons with bare amenities. It is not yet clear what Bush will do about assault rifles, but any backing away from a permanent ban will be viewed as a victory for the NRA.

Still, the NRA has been uncharacteristically on the defensive in recent years and especially now on the assault-rifle issue. It held its 118th annual convention last week in St. Louis in a combative mood and reaffirmed its position that anticrime measures are the way to conquer urban violence, not antigun measures. The NRA board decided to add a plank to its platform that would back bond issues to build more prisons. NRA Executive Vice President J. Warren Cassidy regards the latest opposition as a media-inspired assault to deny basic rights. "[Gun opponents] make pretenses and sounds as if 'We only want the killer rifles, the cop-killer bullets, the plastic guns,' " he mimics his adversaries. "The campaign is to disarm the law-abiding American public."

For many Americans who oppose all guns and those who are more ambivalent, the attractiveness of guns is lost amid growing concerns about their tragic misuse. Antigun advocates seize on that concern, using words and conjuring up mystiques of their own that only help Cassidy make his case. "To many gun opponents, weapons equal evil," says Leonard Supenski, a Baltimore, Md., policeman and gun-control advocate who enjoys firearms. Between those extremes of emotion lies a much more complex reality.

Name: *James Coombe*
Age: *30*
Occupation: *Lawyer*

Coombe takes no chances with his guns, which include several assault rifles. A Cincinnati native and Yale graduate, he is so worried that gun opponents might try to take his weapons that he has hidden them in a bank vault. Coombe liked shooting as a child because it helped him compete with his athletic brothers and father, despite his allergies. He views guns as a foil against government authority. "If the government doesn't trust me to keep an AR-15, why should I trust the government?" Coombe thinks gun controls are a slippery slope. "If you can ban an Uzi, you can ban a double-barreled skeet gun." He applies libertarian views to other controversies. He once volunteered to stand guard at a firebombed abortion clinic.

Name: *Dan Harbin*
Age: *30*
Occupation: *Gun-store owner*

Harbin's love of hunting led him to build a private mountain retreat, paint a deer on the door of his camouflaged truck and open a gun shop in New Middletown, Ohio, so he could spend more time with other hunters. In 20 years, he has killed 39 deer, and last year he went hunting 41 times. When he opened his shop a month ago, his first dozen customers wanted semi-automatic guns. Harbin is trying to pass on his interest to his 2-year-old twin sons. Following a cue he picked up playing with his father, one of the twins mimics Dirty Harry, saying "Go ahead, make my day," whenever he points his toy guns at Harbin. "I guess it's cute in a way," says Harbin. "But, you know, I'm going to train him right."

The vast number of guns at large in America suggests that there is no single solution to the nation's "gun problem." A Harris Survey released last month showed that nearly every other household in the country has a gun. Purdy's was apparently a popular choice. The federal Bureau of Alcohol, Tobacco and Firearms estimates Americans own 2 million to 3 million semiautomatic assault weapons. In the last 18 months alone, BATF has received applications to import nearly a million assault weapons. Accurate statistics about the absolute number of guns are as hard to come by as agreement about what to do with them; but recent estimates show that 70 million Americans own approximately 140 million rifles and 60 million handguns. In other words, the nation's private arsenal is big enough to supply one gun to nearly every man, woman and child in the country.

Americans own guns for manifold reasons. Hunters like Tom Hudson, an electrical engineer in Phoenix, Ariz., view their guns as a way

Name: *Gus Koutroulakis*
Age: *59*
Occupation: *Restaurant owner*

Above the lunchtime din at Pete's Famous Hot Dogs, a popular Birmingham, Ala., eatery, Koutroulakis talks about being robbed nine years ago. "It was 10 minutes after 10 on December 22." Koutroulakis was not carrying his .32-caliber pistol that night. While he was outside, a robber entered his restaurant, held a gun to a woman's head and shot a man in the neck. Koutroulakis does not worry that having a gun could do more harm than good. For him, the safer route is to be armed. "That gun is the equalizer," he says. "You got a lot of nuts out here, man. You don't know what's going to happen." He supports the NRA wholeheartedly, although, like the vast majority of gun owners, he is not a member. "No one ever asked me to join," he explains. He wants to have the maximum firepower to halt the next robber, which means he wants to buy an M-1 rifle. "I know you can stop somebody with that."

to escape the "stoplight-and-concrete jungle." Target shooters emphasize the calmness, the discipline, the self-control involved in shooting. Devotees of much reviled assault rifles are drawn to the technology and the brute impact of these weapons. Collectors see beauty and craftsmanship. Their fascination represents nothing more menacing, they profess, than an antique-car buff's or a computer jock's mild obsessions. The millions of Americans who keep guns for self-protection are buying talismans they hope will ward off a seeming epidemic of evil spirits. "I don't want to be a hero, but I want to be a victim even less," says Derek Singh, a Brooklyn businessman who believes he saved his life six years ago when he scared off attackers with the .38-caliber handgun he carries. Some gun owners see their weapons as foils against government tyranny. "I never gave any consideration to owning an AK-47, but I do now because of what those nuts in Washington are doing," says George Grahovac of Springfield, Ohio. Grahovac cannot help remembering his adolescence in Yugoslavia, when, he says, Nazis massacred his relatives after confiscating all private weapons. For men in particular, guns evoke a near mystical return to their youths, swathed in memories of standing alongside their fathers in dawn-lighted blinds. Or they recall traipses down dirt roads in long-lost haunts with a bunch of pals, carting a Daisy BB rifle or that first .22 on an idyllic *Boy's Life* summer afternoon.

"Hitting America in the teeth"

The abundance of guns is nothing new. A 1624 survey at Jamestown, Va., counted a firearm for each colonist. Many a critic of gun ownership has pondered why the United States, almost alone among industrial nations, has persisted in maintaining a gun culture. The late sociologist Herman Kahn provided a partial answer in 1973 while criticizing a plan to ban schoolchildren from shooting on rifle ranges. "You were hitting America in the teeth," he said. "You think it's making a minor change, just taking the gun away. It's right at the center of the culture."

That culture arose from a mingling of the practical and the philosophical reasons why Americans have been drawn to guns. The practical reasons are simple: Pioneers needed to eat and to protect themselves from the wild. The philosophical reason relates to the political tyranny that immigrants, particularly those from Europe, had suffered when governments limited access to weapons. Those fears bred a long-lived political creed, bordering today on theology among some followers, in favor of popular access to arms as a counter to tyranny.

The U.S. Constitution's Second Amendment reads, "A well regulated Militia, being necessary to the security of a free State, the right of the people to keep and bear Arms, shall not be infringed." The NRA says that means government has no power to control weapons, while gun opponents argue it relates only to the right of states to maintain militias. A complete reading of court interpretations raises questions about both approaches. Even the Supreme Court has not touched the question in 50 years, and neither gun-control advocates nor their opponents can take much comfort from the 1939 ruling. In that decision, the Court upheld a control on sawed-off shotguns because they were not ordinary military equipment explicitly protected by the Second Amendment. That kind of reasoning, in the current debate, might make skeet guns more controllable than AK-47s.

Whatever the Constitution's framers really meant, America's peculiar frontier experience fueled its attachment to guns. There, in log cabins and isolated farmhouses, the separate practical and philosophical reasons for America's gun devotion merged. "The ultimate fear," wrote historians Lee Kennett and James LaVerne Anderson in *The Gun in America,* was "not that government will tyrannize, but that it will fail to protect." The absence, not the excess, of government control became the most compelling practical reason to own guns.

The nation has never completely lost its frontier *Zeitgeist*. "Every Walter Mitty has had his moment when he is Gary Cooper,

Names: *James and Sarah Brady*
Ages: *48, 47*
Occupations: *Vice chairman, National Organization on Disability; Chairwoman, Handgun Control, Inc.*

A handgun changed the Bradys' lives forever. As White House press secretary, James Brady was with Ronald Reagan in 1981 when John Hinckley shot the President, striking Brady in the forehead. A brain injury left him disabled. In 1985, amid an NRA drive to weaken the 1968 Gun Control Act, Sarah Brady, daughter of an FBI agent, supported gun control. Ever since, she has advocated seven-day waiting periods for all handgun purchases—a measure now known as the Brady Bill. NRA opposition has blocked the proposal, but the Bradys still hope the reform will come.

stalking the streets in 'High Noon' with his gun at the ready," wrote the late historian Richard Hofstadter in a 1970 antigun essay. Beyond the romance, the Wild West's most lasting legacy is the suspicion that when it comes to protection, one can count on no one else. James Jones said it well in his novel, *The Pistol:* "The world was rocketing to hell in a bucket, but if he could only hold on to his pistol, remain in possession of the promise of salvation its beautiful blued-steel bullet-charged weight offered him, he would be saved."

Some police experts believe the greatest growth in gun ownership in recent years has been among people who want guns for self-protection. That fact underscores that they are increasingly an urban phenomenon, even though the greatest attraction for sporting purposes continues in the South and the West, where rural roots remain strongest. Indeed, according to data cited as credible by both sides, fewer than half the handguns in circulation are primarily used for recreation. And women are increasingly buying guns for protection. Between 1983 and 1986, there was a 53 percent increase in female gun owners, according to a Gallup poll for Smith & Wesson.

Not until the turn of this century, as the frontier receded, did reformers take organized steps to control guns. The earliest legislation regulating concealed weapons emerged in, of all places, the South. The white majority, despite its own devotion to guns, was scared enough by rising ownership of guns among freed slaves to impose stiff license fees, a regulation analogous to poll taxes. The South was not alone in its fears. "As cities filled with unassimilated masses of immigrants from Southern and Eastern Europe," wrote Kennett and Anderson, "the swarthy, hirsute and wild-eyed anarchist became the new shibboleth."

A political upheaval

That scare has political resonance today, especially as the country is inundated with reports of runaway drug trafficking. The result, says political analyst Kevin Phillips, is a "coalescing into a high-powered new 'crime'-issues complex rapidly gaining importance." According to Phillips, the public's fear of drugs could turn gun control into a potent crime issue among voters, minimizing the electoral benefits conservatives have always reaped from opposing any gun controls. Liberal gun opponents are still vulnerable, says Phillips, because their usual opposition to the death penalty is also wrapped into the public's outrage about rising crime. But he foresees that the drug menace could reshuffle political alignments as some moderates and conservatives turn to supporting gun control. This could have an impact on key

ASSAULT-RIFLE DEBATE

The hottest gun issue now is how to control semiautomatic assault rifles without limiting hunters' favorite weapons.

Automatic assault rifle. *This AK-47 fires 30 rounds with a trigger squeeze. Only the military, police and licensed citizens can use it. Semiautomatic AK-47s look the same.*

Semiautomatic hunting rifle. *This rifle fires one shot per trigger pull, the same mechanical function used in semiautomatic assault rifles. Gun advocates argue a ban on semiautomatics would affect their rifles.*

USN&WR—Basic data: National Rifle Association, 1989

Names: *Il Ling and Ilson New*
Ages: *28, 53*
Occupations: *Marketing executive, lawyer*

Guns provide rites of passage for daughters as well as sons. Il Ling New recalls her father teaching her to shoot near their California home with no ammunition in her rifle. "I was terribly embarrassed. I always thought everyone was laughing," says Il Ling, who became the first female captain of Yale's skeet team. Ilson learned about hunting when he was sent to live with a family in Nebraska as a child. "It was Americana," says Korean-born Ilson. "I would be embarrassed to be in a field with an AK-47," says Ilson. "But as a minority, I'm concerned about restrictions based upon appearance."

gubernatorial races in the next two years in places like Virginia and New York, where some candidates have already adjusted their positions to address these concerns.

The result may well be a patchwork quilt of laws with only marginal effect in keeping weapons out of criminal hands. The key problem is the difficulty in drafting laws that will separate assault weapons used in crime from semiautomatics frequently used for target practice and sometimes for hunting. Pro-gun forces insist that gun critics base their objections on the menacing appearance of firearms. "They're really talking about banning something because it's ugly," says Neal Knox, a former NRA executive. Even defining the much maligned Saturday night special has been elusive for the Maryland panel that is supposed to implement a ban on such weapons that voters passed last year. Despite the optimism surrounding waiting-period legislation, no one can warrant that background checks will slow the acquisition of guns by criminals, who tend to get their weapons illegally anyway.

Still, the recent debate has made a difference, and a clearer middle course in handling the gun issue is emerging. Its basic tenets include the creation of a strong registration system for most weapons, the institution of a waiting period before the purchase of many firearms and substantially expanded gun-education programs. Even the NRA has modified its opposition to waiting periods. It now goes along with checks to determine if a purchaser has a criminal record, so long as the check is conducted instantly. That shift is attributable to the changing feelings of gun owners. The recent Harris Survey revealed that over half the country's gun owners favor a ban on assault rifles, although NRA members are split on this question. Many argue that there is no easy way to make a legal distinction between a semiautomatic assault rifle and common hunting rifles because they operate on the same mechanical principle: One squeeze of the trigger yields one shot. Nevertheless, some gun enthusiasts like Judith Bishop, a suburban-Chicago riflery teacher, are showing impatience with those who embrace assault guns. "There is no use for that weapon in hunting or international competition," she says.

The predominant hope among many NRA members is that the organization will emphasize education about guns. That, along with organizing target competition, was its main purpose before it felt compelled to fight gun controllers after the assassinations of Martin Luther King, Jr., and Robert Kennedy in 1968. The need for greater understanding about guns, about who uses them and why and about how to use them safely is a central problem in the current debate. "I wish the NRA were able to expose more non-gun owners to what guns are all about," says NRA member Il Ling New, an Orange County, Calif., gun owner. Whether

Names: *Judith Bishop, Michael Youtsey*
Ages: *48, 17*
Occupations: *Riflery teacher, student*

A mother of two, Bishop is active in the Evanston (Ill.) Junior League and is a substitute teacher. She also teaches riflery. She thinks shooting has an undeserved bad reputation. "Kids suffer tremendous damage in contact sports, but no one is on a rampage to restrict those activities." Michael Youtsey, a high-school senior and one of Bishop's students, has won scores of shooting competitions. Since last year, when a deranged woman shot seven people in nearby Winnetka, killing one of them and then herself, antigun forces have been building in the area. While Bishop, an NRA member, worries about intolerance among nongun owners, she favors extensive background checks and mandatory training for gun buyers. "There has to be some limit on the Second Amendment," she says.

conducted by the NRA or some other body, a form of mandatory safety training geared to the lethal power of particular weapons could help reduce the prospects for tragedy.

Calm compromises will be hard to achieve as long as outspoken advocates on either side persist in fanning the flames. Gun-control groups suspect that if they do not push the issues hard and, sometimes, emotionally, while fears run high, they will never win crucial support. Gun organizations know that they keep moderates on their side by playing to apprehensions. "The key to the gun organizations is to keep gun owners convinced that they are a hated minority," says Don Kates, a gun-law expert in San Francisco. While returning fire for fire may do wonders for their membership lists, the opposing groups are not helping to build a more suitable role for guns in this society. "For the last 20 years, people representing the two extreme poles have been screaming at each other past the general public," says Supenski. "Lost in the middle is that great body of common sense and logic necessary to solve this dilemma." Until each side, and the people in the middle, set aside the myths they bring to the gun issue and get down to business, the noise will be all that builds.

by Donald Baer with Ted Gest and Lynn Anderson Carle

Hitting kingpins in their assets

The feds have started to go after drug lords' bank accounts and other properties. The new tactic works, but defense lawyers are screaming

In Naples, Fla., a hearse and five mountain lions were seized. In Muskogee, Okla., 517 cattle were auctioned. In Sausalito, Calif., a seized recording studio got the street nickname "Club Fed" when the U.S. Marshals Service took it over. And in Pewaukee, Wis., U.S. Marshal Robert Keating found himself making sales calls to assure customers that a foundry snatched by the government would remain a reliable supplier.

In growing numbers, authorities around the nation are hitting drug lords where it hurts most—in their assets. While most of the public ferment in the drug war has been focused on President Reagan's recent signing of omnibus drug legislation and attendant saber rattling about death penalties and user sanctions, a little-heralded policy is making much greater impact. The auction block may hold more promise than the electric chair in turning the war around as law-enforcement officials seize prize status symbols such as boats, cars and even farther-out baubles bought with the profits of drug traffickers.

Robin Hood to the rescue. The incentive for police is cold cash. Some of the proceeds from the asset seizures are plowed right back into community law enforcement under a Robin Hood arrangement that allows the federal government to share the wealth with local crime fighters. Gross seizures by the federal government mushroomed from about $100 million in fiscal year 1981 to more than $1 billion in fiscal year 1987, thanks largely to the work of Justice Department agencies and the Customs Service.

While there is no magic solution in the struggle against drugs, some criminologists argue that asset seizure is a more effective deterrent than prison. Drug kingpins see jail time as little more than the cost of doing business, analysts say, and there are always lieutenants ready to take over. By contrast, removing assets strikes at the underpinning of major organizations by "taking away what they need to keep operating—their financial base," asserts Gwen Holden of the National Criminal Justice Association. By having a large chunk of those forfeited assets devoted to local-level narcotics enforcement, "the crooks are funding their own demise," says Howard Safir of the U.S. Marshals Service.

This "equitable sharing" of the proceeds of seized assets with state and local cops began in August, 1985, after it was authorized by Congress in the Comprehensive Crime Control Act of 1984. Before that, federal authorities kept all the assets themselves and there was little reason for local police to cooperate in federal drug probes. The 1984 law allowed the Attorney General to share property forfeited to the federal government with state and local law enforcement in proportion to the locals' participation in the case and thereby encouraged a lot more local interest in helping feds make big busts.

State and local law-enforcement agencies have gotten $182 million in cash and property from the federal government since the change in the law. They have used it to purchase vehicles, firearms and surveillance equipment, as well as to support overtime pay for narcotics officers, funding for informants and new investigative units to go after major traffickers. Los Angeles police alone have netted more than $18 million in shared proceeds and see about $25 million more in the pipeline. "We wouldn't have a war on drugs in Los Angeles if it weren't for equitable sharing," says Deputy Chief Glenn Levant. "This program is the greatest thing that ever happened to local law enforcement." Other facets of federal law enforcement are being rewarded, too. Some $95 million in seized assets was earmarked for federal prison construction.

Not everyone is thrilled with the more aggressive asset-seizure policy. Defense lawyers, for instance, have been horrified to see their fees threatened by the crackdown. The law can be used to keep ill-gotten drug profits from being used to pay attorneys, either by freezing accused drug lords' assets in pretrial proceedings so that attorneys cannot be paid or by seizing fees allegedly paid from drug proceeds at a later time. In one prominent example, the Washington, D.C., law firm of Caplin & Drysdale took what it thought was a criminal income-tax case for a client who was later charged with drug trafficking. The government seized the assets of the defendant, who then had no way to pay the firm's $170,513 bill.

Defense lawyers say the prospect of seized fees violates the Sixth Amendment right to counsel of choice, interferes with the attorney-client relationship and precludes an effective defense since these cases require specialized expertise. Justice Department officials counter that neither the Sixth Amendment nor any other law guarantees the right to high-priced counsel paid with illegally obtained assets. After a round of conflicting federal circuit-court decisions on the issue, the Supreme Court decided recently to review it.

BUSTED BOOTY

In their crackdown on drug kingpins, federal authorities have taken possession of a wide range of properties and other assets purchased with the proceeds of drug sales. The seized goods, worth $1.1 billion, range from fancy cars and exclusive real estate to aircraft such as the 1950s-vintage C-97 Air Force transport, above, that was bought as surplus. Here is a partial list of the current inventory at the U.S. Customs Service and the U.S. Marshals Service:

	Value
■ Cash	$442.9 mil.
■ 1,829 parcels of real estate	$283.8 mil.
■ 6,086 miscellaneous items, including jewelry	$184.7 mil.
■ 8,849 vehicles	$61.2 mil.
■ 1,015 financial instruments	$36.6 mil.
■ 499 boats	$32.4 mil.
■ 245 aircraft	$26.8 mil.
■ 54 businesses	$11.9 mil.
■ Laboratory equipment and chemicals	$7.6 mil.
■ Foodstuffs	$3.8 mil.
■ 265 pieces of electronic equipment	$2.1 mil.
■ 68 art objects, antiques	$1.3 mil.
■ 47 animals	$1.2 mil.
■ 148 weapons	$1.1 mil.

Note: Customs handles assets seized by its agents, the Coast Guard and the Secret Service; the Marshals Service handles assets seized by Justice Department agencies.

Civil vs. criminal procedure. Civil libertarians, lawyers and some judges also have more-basic misgivings about asset seizure. Especially troublesome is the widespread use of civil, rather than criminal, procedure to go after specific properties used in or acquired through drug trafficking. The result is cases with names like *United States v. A Single Family Residence,* where the property itself, not a criminal defendant, is the object of the government's case. In civil complaints, the government need only show probable cause that a crime was committed in order to seize property. And the burden of proof for upholding the charge is that there be a preponderance of evidence, not the tougher criminal standard that the evidence prove guilt beyond a reasonable doubt. Attorney David Smith, who previously worked in the Justice Department's asset-forfeiture effort, argues that these kinds of civil proceedings could replace "the whole criminal-justice system with a very peculiar, constitutionally anomalous system of civil sanctions."

Others felt the asset-seizure strategy was abused last year when vehicles and boats were seized even though only minuscule amounts of drugs were found on them. It was part of the Reagan administration's "zero tolerance" policy aimed at making casual drug users feel the pinch. Congressional critics said innocent boat owners such as commercial fishermen were being deprived of their livelihoods because, unknown to them, someone had been caught smoking a joint on board their vessels. As a result, Congress included provisions in the recent drug bill to provide relief. Boats and cars will be returned if owners can prove they were unaware of the violation, and the Justice Department must decide more quickly whether to pursue forfeiture in such cases.

Given the promise and rewards of asset seizure, it is hard to believe the government has not been pursuing that policy aggressively for a long time. The biggest problem lay with bureaucratic hindrances. In 1981, for instance, the General Accounting Office, a watchdog arm of Congress, criticized the Justice Department for not using asset seizure enough. The GAO said the department had not given prosecutors or investigators the guidance or the incentive to pursue seizure; it also noted that existing forfeiture statutes were ambiguous or incomplete.

Most of those problems were addressed in the 1984 law. Nevertheless, the policy has had rocky moments. The government must often operate seized businesses pending their forfeiture and resale, a situation that can present daunting management challenges. For example, when the Marshals Service seized the Plant Recording Studio in Sausalito, Calif., a popular venue for rock-and-rollers, "at first, there was some question in the minds of the clientele," says supervisory Deputy U.S. Marshal Alan Jeannerett. Customers "were concerned that trench-coated G-men would be hanging around all the time." Instead, the Marshals Service hired the previous manager to run the place and tried to stay out of her hair. In Chicago, Deputy Marshal Edward Scheu was obliged to appear at a neighborhood meeting to answer complaints of loitering and noise near a reggae bar—the Wild Hare and Singing Armadillo Frog Sanctuary—in federal custody. Scheu and a Chicago Police Department representative promised to keep a closer watch on the bar's patrons.

A floating junkyard. Other administrative problems arose as the program's inventory value grew to $1.1 billion. In 1985, it was discovered that the Customs Service had been using the Miami River to store 145 boats, some of which had been deteriorating for years while losing resale value and transforming the river "from a scenic waterway to a floating junkyard," according to Senator Lawton Chiles (D-Fla.). By January, 1987, understaffing at the DEA had produced a backlog of 9,500 seizure cases. Now, most cases are being addressed promptly because property and cash management have been centralized and private contractors are being hired to help warehouse and sell new acquisitions.

As the kinks gradually get worked out, asset seizures will surely grow more important. The DEA is adding more teams of special agents to concentrate on such cases, and the latest drug bill authorizes the hiring of scores more federal prosecutors who will focus their efforts on asset confiscation. States and localities are following the lead of Arizona and Florida, which have already developed a sophisticated seizure capability. European nations are considering new asset-seizure laws as well. No one says it is a panacea. But in this war, the first place to determine whether the good guys really have a chance of winning is the bottom line.

GUARDIAN ANGELS: A UNIQUE APPROACH TO CRIME PREVENTION

Susan Pennell, Christine Curtis, Joel Henderson, and Jeff Tayman

Susan Pennell: Director of the Criminal Justice Research Unit of the San Diego Association of Governments. Christine Curtis: Assistant Director of the Criminal Justice Research Unit of the San Diego Association of Governments. Joel Henderson: Professor in the School of Public Administration and Urban Studies at San Diego State University. Jeff Tayman: Statistician/Demographer with the San Diego Association of Governments.

This project was supported by Grant Number 83-IF-CX-0037, awarded to the San Diego Association of Governments by the National Institute of Justice, Department of Justice, under the Omnibus Crime Control and Safe Streets Act of 1968, as amended. Points of view or opinions stated in this document are those of the authors and do not necessarily represent the official position or policies of the U.S. Department of Justice.

The Guardian Angels represent a form of citizen crime prevention that has fostered interest and concern regarding the group's impact, motives, leadership, and organizational structure. Led by their founder, Curtis Sliwa, these volunteers patrol the streets and subways in over 50 cities. The purpose of this exploratory study was to document the activities of the Angels, assess their impact on crime and citizen fear of crime, and describe features of the group that differentiate it from other citizen patrols. Recent research suggests that citizen patrols may reduce crime and make citizens feel safe by imposing social order. Study findings suggest that Angels may not reduce the violent offenses they seek to prevent, although they may have limited impact on property crimes. Segments of the population feel safe when Angels patrol, which may be associated with the Angels performing an order-maintenance role. Sliwa's efforts to mobilize minority youth to be positive role models is a unique feature of the Angels. Ultimately, the effectiveness of the Angels may depend on the extent to which Sliwa can seek rapprochement with law enforcement and community leaders.

As this special issue demonstrates, citizens become involved in crime prevention efforts in a variety of ways, but few strategies or groups have generated the interest, media attention, and controversy sparked by the Guardian Angels. Led by their self-proclaimed leader and founder, Curtis Sliwa, this nationwide organization consists of unarmed, red-bereted, peace-seeking, racially mixed youth who "dare to care" by patrolling the streets as a visual deterrent to crime. Sliwa advocates putting the "crudballs and slimebuckets" out of business through a reawakening of traditional values that involve people reaching out to one another and caring about their community.

Although the philosophy is admirable, the means to operationalize the approach have been viewed with skepticism and suspicion. Since the inception of the Guardian Angels in 1977, the motives and methods of Curtis Sliwa have been sources of concern for government officials and law enforcement administrators alike. The approach of the Guardian Angels differs from traditional community crime prevention efforts in its leadership, membership, longevity, and methods for reducing crime. A brief review of the literature highlights these differences.

TRADITIONAL COMMUNITY CRIME PREVENTION

Participation in crime prevention activities can be on an individual basis, characterized by Lavrakas as self-imposed behavioral restrictions to avoid victimization; or participation can involve collective behavior, not necessarily as a result of fear of crime, but as a result of participation in neighborhood groups (Lavrakas, 1981). Typical forms of collective participation behavior are neighborhood watch, citizen patrol, senior escort, and attendance at community meetings.

Similar to other volunteer organizations, citizen patrols have problems with recruitment, training, and commitment. The problems have given rise to programs that are short-lived, of poor quality, and understaffed. Factors that make the difference in the quality or success of the programs include existence of charismatic leadership, urgency or saliency of the immediate problem, and the characteristics of the population attempting the program (Yin et al., 1977). The focus of citizen patrols is, for the most part, local citizens in cooperation with law enforcement.

The literature cites two approaches to account for community responses to crime: the victimization approach and the social order approach (Lewis and Salem, 1981). With respect to the victimization perspective, individuals who are victimized by an event declared by statute to be illegal may tend toward isolation or avoidance responses. Collective responses seek to increase awareness of risk and educate the community

Reprinted from *Crime & Delinquency*, Vol. 35, No. 3, July 1989, pp. 378-400.

about ways to reduce opportunities for victimization (Lewis and Salem, 1981).

The social order approach describes fear of crime as indicative of the community's lack of social control. Prevention programs are designed to increase the social control capacity of a community as well as enhance social integration. The significance of informal social control and its association to fear of crime has been recognized as a critical factor in the crime prevention literature (Wilson and Kelling, 1982; Greenberg, Rohe, and Williams, 1985).

RESEARCH FOCUS

The research literature suggests that the Guardian Angels represent a unique citizen patrol because they are nationally controlled, largely made up of young minorities, do not rely on government funding, maintain independence from local police, and are willing to intervene in crimes. This research, sponsored by the National Institute of Justice, sought to assess the extent to which the Guardian Angels achieve their objectives: to prevent crime and increase citizens' feelings of safety.

METHOD

The objectives of the study were to do the following:

- Document the organization and activities of the Guardian Angels.
- Evaluate the effectiveness of the Angels in preventing or deterring crime in the areas patrolled.
- Assess the effectiveness of the Guardian Angels in increasing citizens' feelings of safety and reducing fear of crime, and examine citizen perceptions of the Angels.
- Assess the perceptions of law enforcement personnel and local government officials regarding the Guardian Angels.
- Compare the Guardian Angels with other citizen volunteer crime prevention groups with respect to leadership, organizational structure, and membership.

Documentation of Angel Organization and Activities

At the beginning of the research (October 1983), Curtis Sliwa reported 48 chapters of the Guardian Angels in the United States and Canada. Discussions with Leaders and features of cities determined the final selection of 21 cities for study. Factors included accessibility to the Angel leader, location, city population, crime rate, Angels' perception of police attitude toward Angels, longevity of chapter, and number of Angel members and activities (e.g., street patrol, transit patrol). The chapters studied reflect a representative cross-section of all Angel chapters.

Eight cities were considered primary sites. These cities are urban areas and include representation from both Eastern and Western regions: Boston, Chicago, Cleveland, Dallas, New York, Sacramento, San Diego, and San Francisco. In these cities, two site visits were conducted by the research team at six-month intervals. During the initial visit, interviews were conducted with Angel leaders and members and police administrators. Guardian Angel training procedures were observed and the researchers joined regularly scheduled Angel patrols for nonparticipant observation. Angels were asked to maintain information about patrol activity on patrol logs. On the return visit, data were collected from logs and membership applications; follow-up interviews were carried out with the Angel leader and police administrator, and surveys were conducted of police line officers and citizens.

In the remaining thirteen cities, considered secondary sites, telephone interviews were conducted with chapter leaders. In one of these chapters, Angel members completed mail surveys. In another chapter, personal interviews were conducted with members in a city that was not a primary site. A list of cities involved in each research phase is provided in Table 1.

In total, 25 Guardian Angel leaders, representing 21 cities, responded to a personal or telephone interview about their chapter. Overall, 12 of the respondents were in the 8 primary sites visited by the researchers. (Borough leaders in New York were interviewed individually.) The questions addressed the nature and scope of patrol activities, recruitment and training, internal management of chapters, and relationship with police.

A total of 117 Angel members participated in personal or mail interviews (106 in primary sites). The Angels represented 10 cities (8 primary sites plus 2 chapters for which comparable information was received). The personal interviews were conducted prior to patrols and those members who patrolled on a particular day were included. It is possible that the sample reflects Angels who were more active (e.g., more likely to patrol). This is an advantage in that these members were more aware of Angel activities; however, this may affect the representativeness of their estimates of level of participation (i.e., number of patrols per week). Angel members were asked about their motivation for joining the Angels, their experiences on patrol, level of participation, and sociodemographic characteristics.

Patrol logs maintained by Angels were the primary source of information on Angel activities. Each chapter leader was asked to include specific data as part of the patrol logs for a six-month period (April 1, 1984 to September 30, 1984). In particular, data requested included number of members on patrol, date, time, prepatrol activity (e.g., weapons checks, calisthenics), nature of contacts with citizens and police, and disci-

TABLE 1: Cities Contacted, by Type of Respondent: Guardian Angel Study

City	*Police Administrators*	*Police Community Relations Officers*	*Patrol Officers*	*Angel Chapter Leaders*	*Angel Members*	*City Government Officials*	*Citizens*
Boston, MA	X[a]	X	X	X	X	X	X
Buffalo, NY	X						
Camden, NJ	X						
Chicago, IL	X[a]		X	X	X	X	X
Cleveland, OH	X[a]			X	X	X	X
Dallas, TX	X	X	X	X	X	X	
Detroit, MI	X						
Fresno, CA	X	X		X	X		
Hammond, IN	X						
Harrisburg, PA	X	X		X			
Houston, TX	X	X		X			
Indianapolis, IN		X					
Kalamazoo, MI	X			X			
Las Vegas, NV	X			X			
Miami, FL	X	X		X			
Montreal, Canada	X						
New Haven, CT	X						
New York, NY	X[a]	X	X	X	X	X	X
Oakland, CA	X	X					
Ontario, Canada	X	X					
Philadelphia, PA				X			
Pittsburgh, PA				X			
Portland, ME	X			X			
Portland, OR		X		X			
Sacramento, CA	X	X	X	X	X	X	
San Diego, CA	X	X	X	X	X	X	X
San Francisco, CA	X	X	X	X	X	X	
Santa Ana, CA	X	X		X	X		
St. Louis, MO	X	X					
Seattle, WA		X					
Stockton, CA	X			X			
Toronto, Canada	X						
Syracuse, NY	X	X		X			
Toledo, OH	X	X					
Vancouver, Canada	X						

NOTE: Cities in bold type were primary sites.
a. Includes transit police administrators.

pline problems. A total of 672 patrol logs were reviewed for the study period.

Effect of Angels in Preventing Crime

One of the primary objectives of the Guardian Angels is to reduce or deter violent crime in the areas patrolled. The target offenses, according to the national leader, include assault, battery, rape, robbery, and other crimes that involve force or personal injury. While property crimes (e.g., theft, burglary) are not considered target offenses, Angels will intervene to assist victims and apprehend offenders. For this reason, both violent and property crimes were included in the assessment of Guardian Angel effectiveness.

The study site for this phase of the analysis was San Diego, California, where the Angels patrol in the downtown redevelopment area. The quasi-experimental design used to assess changes in crime is a modification of the multiple time-series design, which compares reported crimes in an experimental area, where the Angels patrol, to a non-equivalent control area.

The Guardian Angels began patrolling in San Diego in July 1982. The study period was from January 1, 1982, through December 1984. Reported crimes occurring between 7:00 p.m. and 11:00 p.m. were compared because this is when Angel patrols occur. In this study, the pretest period does not provide an equivalent number of observations as in the post-test period (6 months compared to 30 months after Angel patrols began) because comparable data prior to January 1982 were not available. The fact that the pretest period is limited to six months affects the statistical analyses that could be performed. The number of crimes was analyzed monthly and for six-month intervals to establish trends during the study period.

Effect of Angels on Citizen Feelings of Safety and Perception Toward Angels

To obtain detailed information on citizens' attitudes toward the Guardian Angels, personal interviews were conducted with 110 merchants and 130 residents in downtown areas of San Diego where the Guardian Angels patrol. The purpose of conducting citizen interviews was to gather *subjective* information on the effect of Guardian Angels on fear of crime and crime incidence. The 1980 Census data show that most downtown residents are male (81%), single (45%), and likely to rent (99%); a significant proportion are not high school graduates (46%), and the median annual income is $5,187. The population characteristics presented unique problems for sampling and conducting interviews, which could affect the representativeness of the sample. In addition, the fact that the interviews were conducted in an urban redevelopment area in one city affects the extent to which the findings can be generalized.

To obtain a comprehensive picture of citizen reaction to the Guardian Angels, a survey of transit riders was also conducted. Researchers surveyed transit riders in four Eastern cities while they were on the subway train or at the bus stop (in Cleveland). The sample was based on availability and willingness to participate. The forms were returned before the rider got off the train (or on the bus in Cleveland). A total of 286 surveys were completed.

Perceptions of Local Law Enforcement and Government Representatives

To address the nature of police and Angel interaction and obtain opinions of law enforcement toward the Guardian Angels, personal interviews were undertaken with city and transit police administrators at the eight primary sites. Additionally, to provide a broader cross-section of responses, surveys were mailed to police administrators in the remaining 40 cities known to have an active Guardian Angels chapter. A total of 33 agencies participated in both interviews and surveys. In total, 35 police and transit administrators and 34 community relations or liaison officers responded.

The position of local governments toward the Guardian Angels was assessed through interviews with mayors and city administrative personnel in the primary sites. No information from local city governments was obtained from secondary sites.

Preliminary data collected during the first site visit to eight cities suggested that opinions of line officers and police administrators regarding the Guardian Angels may vary and that attitudes of officers may differ according to experiences in different cities. Therefore, a brief questionnaire was developed for city police and transit officers and administered during the second site visit. The surveys were conducted at six of the primary sites. In some of the Eastern cities, transit police officers were surveyed. Only precincts or divisions in which the Angels patrol were included in the study. A total of 444 line officer surveys were completed.

Comparison with Other Citizen Crime Prevention Efforts

An empirical examination of fifteen citizen crime prevention groups was conducted through personal interviews with their leaders (presidents, chairpersons). In the groups with a citizen patrol component, active members were surveyed using self-administered questionnaires. These groups were compared to the Angels on several variables, including purpose, activities, organizational structure, internal management, financial support, interaction with police, and characteristics of the membership. Groups were selected based on discussions with law enforcement personnel, listings of groups provided by large citizen organizations, and focus of groups (e.g., neighborhood watch, citizen patrol).

RESEARCH FINDINGS

Guardian Angel Organization and Activities

To place the research results in perspective, it may be helpful to describe the Guardian Angels' organization and primary activities. The organization is controlled nationally by the founder, Curtis Sliwa. Angel chapters are initiated either by citizen request or by Sliwa when he perceives a community in need of Angel support. Following an announcement of an Angel chapter and accompanied by extensive media coverage, Sliwa selects a local chapter leader and begins a recruitment effort. Interviews with members revealed that they joined the Angels to prevent or deter crime (64%) and to help others (49%).

According to the organization's National Rules and Regulations, a three-month training program must be completed to graduate and earn a red beret and T-shirt. At the time of the study, all original members of the eight primary sites had received training in martial arts, physical and mental conditioning, citizen arrest procedures, cardio-pulmonary resuscitation (CPR), and first aid.

A significant turnover rate coupled with the need to maintain patrol activities led most chapters to resort to less rigorous "on-the-job" training. This practice may be associated with perceptions of law enforcement toward the Angels, presented later in this article.

Angels on patrol are not to be under the influence of drugs or alcohol and are not allowed to carry weapons. Each member is searched prior to patrol. Street patrols occurred in all primary sites; however, patrol of the subways was more prevalent in the Eastern cities. Areas patrolled include inner-city areas as well as parks, commercial districts, and residential developments.

National guidelines suggest that Angel chapters should patrol three times a week with at least eight members per patrol. Review of patrol logs indicated that the majority of primary sites patrolled less than three times a week and had difficulty maintaining the required number for patrol.

Interviews and patrols with Angel members and review of patrol logs provided information about the types of activities that constituted typical patrols. These included providing directions, calling police, assisting drunks, escorting senior citizens, and helping people on buses and across the street. Based on patrol log data, 17% of the patrols involved incidents in which citizens were assisted, which may be an underestimate based on observations of patrols and interviews with Angels and law enforcement personnel. Of the 672 patrols studied during a six-month period, only two citizen arrests were recorded. Also only ten crime-related incidents resulted in the Angels contacting police. Although the validity of the logs may be questionable, supplementary information supports the presumption that the most common patrol activity was assisting citizens.

Guardian Angels' Impact on Crime

It was hypothesized that the presence of the Guardian Angels would prevent or deter violent crime. Findings indicated that this was not the case in San Diego. Reported major violent offenses declined by 22% in the experimental area where Angels patrolled compared to a 42% drop in the control area. This suggests that factors other than Angel patrols may explain the crime reduction. This finding was supported by using *monthly* Angel activity data and reported violent offenses. Results showed that the number of patrols and violent crime incidents were not associated ($r = -.10$, n.s.).

The Angels may have had an impact on property offenses but this assumption is not conclusive. The experimental area where Angels patrolled showed a 25% reduction in property crimes compared to the six-month period before Angels patrolled. The decline in the control area was 15%. Findings demonstrated a significant association between Angel patrols and theft-related crimes ($r = -.55$, $p = .003$). When Angel patrols increased in frequency, the number of reported crimes was lower. However, the San Diego Police Department initiated a foot patrol in the experimental area during the post-test period. The effects of this strategy and the potential for displacement of property crimes to other areas could not be measured. It may be that Angels are most effective in times of high visibility such as during extensive media coverage and when patrols are very frequent (six days a week). This hypothesis requires further testing.

Impact of Guardian Angels on Citizens' Feelings of Safety

Citizen perceptions. The household and merchant interviews conducted in areas patrolled by the Guardian Angels in San Diego provide the following information on interactions with the Guardian Angels from the citizens' perspective:

- In total 90% of the 240 respondents had heard of the Guardian Angels.
- A smaller percentage (42%) were aware that the Angels patrolled in their neighborhood.
- Most of the respondents who knew of the Angel patrols had actually observed them.
- Over one-third had seen the Angels once a week or more and 27% had talked to Angel members.
- Five of those interviewed had been assisted by the Angels and 36% had seen the Angels help someone else.
- In total, 11% of the respondents had seen the Angels act in a way they thought was inappropriate (e.g., overreact, patrol where they were not wanted, act in a rowdy manner).

In four Eastern cities, the majority of the transit riders surveyed knew of the Angels (97%), and 83% had seen the Angels patrolling. In total, 11% had received assistance from the Angels and over one-third had observed the Angels help another person.

A basic tenet of the Guardian Angel approach is that their presence in selected areas increases citizens' feelings of safety or, conversely, reduces fear of crime. Citizens were asked to rate how effective the Angels are in increasing citizens' feelings of safety and if they felt more safe when they knew Angels were patrolling in their areas. Citizens rated Angel effectiveness with a mean score of 3.5 based on a scale of 1 to 5 (with 1 being not at all effective and 5 very effective). Over half (60%) of the citizens who were aware that Angels patrolled in their neighborhood observed that they felt more safe as a result of the presence of Angels.

Law Enforcement and Local Government Reaction to Guardian Angels

It was presumed that the activities and impact of the Guardian Angels would be influenced by the perceptions and reactions of law enforcement. Based on interviews with police administrators and surveys of patrol personnel in the primary cities, the responses of these groups were less favorable than citizens' responses toward the Angels. Although police agreed that the Angel presence may increase citizens' feelings of safety, they questioned their impact on crime reduction. Respondents were reluctant to describe their official position toward the Angels as supportive, and expressed concerns about the physical safety of both citizens and Angels if Angels intervene in incidents.

The following findings summarize the responses of law enforcement personnel and city government representatives.

- Upon request by the Angels, most police administrators (77% of 35) and city government staff members surveyed (6 of 8) have held meetings with Angels. Meetings generally focused on Angels' requests for support or recognition of their activities. In some agencies, Angels were provided with identification cards and police conducted record checks on potential Angel recruits.
- Although nearly half of the police administrators (46%) agreed that the Angels have assisted patrol officers, 37% observed that their agencies have received complaints from citizens about the Angels. Concerns from citizens included: Angels soliciting contributions, patrolling in areas in which their presence was not wanted, and acting in an aggressive manner.
- Almost half of the police administrators (49%) observed that no conflicts have arisen between police and Angels for two reasons: Angel visibility has been minimal *or* Angels have adhered to the ground rules established by police.
- About half of the administrators (51%) agreed that there is a benefit to the Angels' patrols and 46% indicated that Angel activities in their cities should continue. Proportionately, line patrol officers were less likely to hold these views.
- The majority of city government respondents indicated that Angel patrols are beneficial and should continue. However, only two of eight city representatives characterized their city's position toward the Angels as supportive. Most took a neutral position.
- Similarly, the majority of police administrators adopted a neutral stance toward the Angels (57%). In total, 23% described their view as supportive while 17% reported an unsupportive position.
- Supportive opinions were reflected in statements such as "any type of citizen help is welcome" and the "Angels provide a positive means for youth to become involved in their community." Less positive views were associated with the belief that patrolling the streets is the responsibility of the police. Some respondents spoke unfavorably about the Angels' demeanor and style of dress (e.g., appearance similar to gang members).
- In total, 11 of the 35 police and transit administrators have developed either formal or informal agreements with the Angels. In four of the cities studied (Boston, Cleveland, Portland, and Syracuse), the Angels are provided with free subway or bus passes and identification cards. In exchange, the Angels are asked to notify the transit personnel of trains or routes they intend to patrol. Informal agreements with city police agencies are characterized by police departments assigning a liaison person to meet with the Angels and in some cases providing identification cards, training facilities, and information relative to citizen's arrest procedures. Some departments have issued in-house bulletins to police personnel describing the department position toward the Angels and the administrative expectations with respect to officer interaction with the Angels.

Police in six cities completed a questionnaire during line up or roll call. The majority of the officers surveyed were familiar with the Angels. Almost half (49%) had talked with Angels; however, only 6% stated that they had received assistance. Of the officers who were knowledgeable of Angel activities (152), the majority agreed that Angels had

- helped citizens (61%)
- made citizen's arrests (66%)
- detained a suspect (61%)
- identified a suspect (51%)
- acted inappropriately (70%)

The fact that Curtis Sliwa has publicly stated that his group's autonomy and independence could be adversely affected by close ties to police has not endeared the Angels to the law enforcement community. Despite research findings that suggest citizen crime prevention groups are more effective when a strong liaison is developed with local law enforcement (Garofalo and McLeod, 1988), the Sliwa approach minimizes this interaction.

Citizens Views Compared to Police and City Officials

A series of opinion statements about the Guardian Angels (Ostrowe and DiBiase, 1983) were presented to all groups (Table 2). Results indicate that Eastern transit riders and San Diego citizens were more likely than others to feel that ore Angels should be patrolling, that Guardian Angels should expand to other cities, and that local governments should support the Angels. In contrast, line police officers revealed the least favorable opinions regarding these statements. Police administrators and city officials generally scored in the midrange, reflecting a no opinion response. Groups tended to agree that crime fighting should be done only by professional police. Similar responses by citizens on the issue of crime fighting may be related to reluctance on the part of citizens to grant "crime-fighting" status to a civilian group. Citizens may also perceive the Angels in a helping or good Samaritan role.

TABLE 2: Opinions Toward Guardian Angels Survey Results, 1984

	Mean Scores				
	Police & Transit Administrators n = 13	Patrol Officers n = 429	City Officials n = 9	Eastern Transit Riders n = 274	San Diego Citizens n = 210
I wish there were more Guardian Angels patrolling the streets.	3.2	2.3	2.8	4.1	3.7
Crime fighting should be done only by professional police.	3.2	1.9	3.4	3.4	3.2
The mayor and city officials should support the Guardian Angels.	3.2	2.4	2.8	4.1	3.6
I would like to see the Guardian Angels expand to other American cities which have a crime problem.	3.0	2.5	3.2	4.0	3.7
In general, I oppose the actions of the Guardian Angels.	3.8	2.7	3.7	3.9	3.9

NOTE: 1 = Least favorable toward Angels—5 = Most favorable toward Angels

It is of interest to note that a random telephone survey of 239 Chicago citizens conducted in 1982 also revealed favorable attitudes toward Angels. The majority of those surveyed believed that the Angels were helpful in preventing crime, thought the city administration should give official recognition to the group, and observed that they would feel safer on the subway if the Angels were present (Lavrakas, 1985).

San Diego citizens and transit riders perceived the Angels as more effective in reducing fear than the other groups surveyed based on mean scores (3.5). Police administrators perceived the Angels as minimally effective in increasing citizens' feelings of safety (2.0). Line officers and community relations officers indicated only slightly higher scores (2.2 and 2.3). Angel members rated themselves the highest with a mean score of 4.2.

Citizens interviewed in San Diego, transit riders surveyed in the East, and Angel members rated the Guardian Angels higher than police respondents or city officials on Angel effectiveness in reducing crime. Respondents in the primary sites were asked to rate the effectiveness of the Guardian Angels in reducing crime on a scale from 1 to 5, with 5 being very effective and 1 being not at all effective. Mean scores on this question were as follows:

- police administrators 2.1
- police line officers 1.9
- San Diego citizens 3.5
- transit riders 3.5
- city officials 2.5
- Angel members 4.0

Police respondents offered comments on the "crime-fighting" abilities of the Guardian Angels. Several indicated that the low visibility of the Angels minimizes their impact on crime, although they may increase citizens' perceptions of safety. Less favorable remarks characterized the Angels as vigilantes who lack motivation and leadership. Some law enforcement personnel suggested that Angels could be more effective by joining other crime prevention groups, projecting a better image, increasing their visibility, and coordinating their efforts with the police.

Organizational Structure-Comparative Analysis of Citizen Volunteer Crime Prevention Groups

The Guardian Angels were compared to fifteen other citizen crime prevention groups to examine differences and similarities with respect to organizational structure and membership characteristics. The comparative analysis addressed the following organizational features:

- perceived purpose and activities
- recruitment procedures and training
- factors related to membership

Purpose and Activities

Organizations with patrol components as part of their program are located in Lower Merion Township, Pennsylvania; Long Island, New York; Florence, New Jersey; and Stockton, California. Although program activities vary, these groups have similar purposes that include: increasing citizen awareness of crime by community education, promoting active participation in crime prevention efforts, and enhancing neighborhood security. The patrols in the East operate with assistance and direction from the local police departments. No weapons or force are employed on patrols and volunteers are expected to report suspicious activity to the police. Members are strongly discouraged from intervening in possible crime-related incidents. In Florence and Stockton, members engage in both walking and mobile patrols, usually consisting of two people. The other groups engage only in mobile patrols. The Stockton group functions to "observe and report," yet the leader indicated that this group will physically intervene in incidents if necessary.

While the citizen groups restrict their activities to local communities, the Guardian Angels is a national organization. Over a third of the Angel chapters in this study were initiated by Curtis Sliwa with the remaining chapters started by Angel members in other cities or on the basis of a community request. The major purposes of the Guardian Angels are to be a visual deterrent to crime, to increase citizens' feelings of safety, and to provide positive role models for young people. In contrast to most citizen patrols examined, the Angels *will* intervene if they encounter a crime in progress, although physical intervention is viewed as a last resort to be used only to protect others from harm.

In addition to foot patrols, many Angel chapters also become involved in community-related activities based on requests from citizens, which provide the opportunity to increase their visibility with the public and a means to maintain the interest of the members. The supplementary activities are more typical of Eastern chapters, perhaps because these groups have been in existence longer than Western chapters. Some Angel groups have developed Junior Angel programs for youth from ages 11 to 15. Although these younger members are not permitted to patrol, they are encouraged to understand the value of community involvement by assisting senior citizens with various jobs such as raking leaves and shoveling snow. According to the Guardian Angels, the purpose of the junior program is "to help younger people feel better about themselves and bridge the gap between younger and older people." Other activities in which Angel chapters become involved include: assisting senior citizens with groceries, providing escort services to and from events to ensure personal safety, collecting and distributing food and toys for local civic organizations, participating in community festivals and blood drives, searching for missing and runaway youth, and giving community presentations about self-protection and ways to avoid victimization.

Most of the San Diego organizations do not require any specific training of volunteers. The four groups with patrol components do require training, although only one specifies a certain number of hours. With the exception of the Stockton group, other citizen groups are assisted by law enforcement in training of members. Instructions relate to accurate completion of patrol logs and procedures for observing and reporting suspicious activity.

Relationship with Police

Thirteen of the fifteen citizen groups have informal agreements with local police agencies. Law enforcement may provide support with respect to crime statistics, training, and designating a liaison position to interact with the groups. The groups with citizen patrols are expected to notify police of areas patrolled. Patrols are likely to be directed by police when members do not patrol in their own neighborhoods.

Recruitment Issues

Community presentations and media coverage were the primary means of recruiting volunteers for citizen groups. The organizations with multiple purposes generally have more difficulty recruiting and retaining members than groups with a neighborhood orientation.

Seven of the fifteen citizen leaders indicated that screening of volunteers is not applicable to their groups. The remaining group screen volunteers with some receiving assistance from police to determine potential criminal backgrounds. Eleven leaders observed that a known specific criminal background would exclude an individual from membership or result in termination. Disobeying the guidelines for citizen patrols would also lead to termination. More than half (8) of the groups have no specific requirements for joining beyond a willingness to become involved. Some of the citizen groups solicit dues, and two groups have minimum age requirements for members who participate in patrols. The most desirable characteristic for volunteers, according to the majority of leaders of citizen groups, was a caring and concerned attitude.

Features Unique to the Angels

A comparative analysis of the Angels with other citizen crime prevention groups (mobile patrols and neighborhood watch groups) revealed features of the Angel organization that both contribute to and detract from its stability and effectiveness, as well as affect its attractiveness to potential recruits. Members of the Angels are recruited primarily from young minorities who come predominantly from inner-city areas. They are drawn by Sliwa's charisma, which combines macho street language with the notion that it is "cool to be an Angel" and help others in the community. Sliwa's national leadership is pervasive, a factor that, like the composition of the membership, differentiates the Angels from typical groups organized to prevent crime. While other groups reflect "the eyes and ears" of local police, the Angels are willing to intervene physically in street situations.

DISCUSSION OF FINDINGS

In varying degrees, the Guardian Angels' organization has some features that contribute to stability and maintenance of citizen crime prevention groups (Marx and Archer, 1973). These include:

- Approval of the community they presume to represent.
- strong charismatic leader.
- positive ideology that affirms what the group supports as well as what it opposes.

Other factors related to group maintenance, according to Marx and Archer (1973) are financial support and legitimacy from local government. Neither of these conditions are applicable to the Guardian Angels. With regard to finances, Sliwa acknowledges, Sliwa acknowledges that contributions from private citizens and organizations are helpful, but he is reluctant to accept funds from any government entity and does not actively encourage fund-raising by local chapters. His justification for this position is associated with his feelings about the concept of the Guardian Angels and his desire to remain independent and autonomous. He observes that the motivation for helping and protecting people could be diluted with a focus on fund-raising. He feels that commitment to the Angel concept might be negatively redirected if the organization became financially comfortable.

Sliwa also believes that positive relationships with police and city officials are not necessary for Angels to fulfill their mission. While he recognizes that formal agreements may urge local officials to communicate with Angels and such communication can reduce potential conflicts, he is unwilling to encourage close ties with public entities. It should be noted that some individual chapters have developed positive associations with police agencies. Sliwa accepts these interactions and in most situations respects the chapter leaders' efforts to sustain such communication. This is in line with another feature of stability: varying regulation by police (Marx and Archer, 1973). The authors of "The Urban Vigilante" conclude their study by observing that the groups most likely to survive are those that accommodate to the official power structure. However, they add an interesting paradox by stating that the "accommodations that help a group stay in business can estrange it from its presumed constituents. It is difficult to enjoy official toleration without being exploited or subverted by authorities" (Marx and Archer, 1973). Sliwa appears to recognize this potential.

Our study of the Guardian Angels reflects some of the reasons discussed by Marx and Archer to explain why local officials are reluctant to support groups that attempt to deter disorders or prevent crime:

- groups are not held accountable
- power of groups is not legally subscribed
- screening of members is inadequate

In *Reactions to Crime,* McPherson and Silloway (1981) elaborate on the inherent tension between police and private citizen groups that take the initiative to prevent crime. These authors state that most crime reduction programs that are government funded define crime in the legalistic sense and have strong ties to the police, who are most comfortable when they direct the prevention activities. When citizens take the lead and exclude law enforcement, or activities do not correspond with police opinions, officers feel threatened (McPherson and Silloway, 1981). This rationale may underlie the reluctance of police administrators to support the Guardian Angels openly and explain the negative and often hostile remarks by line officers. Our research suggests that law enforcement and local government officials may be unclear about the Angel organization and mission, and are uneasy about features relative to membership.

The National Rules and Regulations of the Guardian Angels state that the first fifty volunteers cannot have arrest records that include felonies. Thereafter, only individuals with arrests for serious crimes are excluded. However, in most cases, the screening process is inadequate because it relies on the volunteer to provide this information.

The results from this study do not support the label of vigilantism often attached to the Guardian Angels by the popular press and representatives of law enforcement. However, the reluctance of police administrators to support the Angels officially may stem from a police perception that places the Angels within the context of vigilantism. In their study of 28 vigilante groups prevalent in the 1960s, Marx and Archer found that supplemental or adversarial relationships with police did not determine positive or negative feelings of police toward such groups. The authors suggest that police often oppose supplemental groups (organized to provide assistance to police) because of the professionals' dislike of sharing authority and prestige with an amateur, even nominally. Probably more relevant to the Angels, the authors also state that the police fear the groups will make tactical mistakes and abuse their power (Marx and Archer, 1973). The potential for abuse by Angels was mentioned by many police personnel in the present study.

Although our evidence is limited, few specific instances were noted in which Angels intervened inappropriately; however, most line officers felt that this had occurred. Inconsistent or inadequate training of members may be associated with such actions and can also affect the physical safety of the Angel members or result in false arrests. Police administrators expressed concern about liability of police agencies if Angels were endorsed by law enforcement.

Features of the Guardian Angel organization suggest the potential for generating an informal social control mechanism. Conditions such as a cohesive, small group, frequent contacts, and similarity in beliefs and social characteristics foster informal social control, which may be linked to crime prevention and fear of crime (Greenberg, Rohe, and Williams, 1985; Wilson and Kelling, 1982; Lavrakas, 1982). Findings from studies on police foot patrol have shown that more police officers walking the beat may not reduce crime but may increase citizens' feelings of safety due to the presence of informal social controls (Trojanowicz and Banas, 1985; McGovern, 1983).

Citizen perceptions toward the Angels may be related to perceived assurance that the Angels will seek and maintain a sense of order. In areas where there is an imbalance of "respectable" versus "unrespectable" people, the citizenry desires a social control mechanism (Wilson and Kelling, 1982). The Angels may contribute to this sense of control and be perceived as a potential for intervention.

The most significant feature of the Guardian Angels may be that they represent a group of young people who are generally recognized as contributing to the crime problem. Several Angels admitted to previous affiliation with gangs. The gang, for many inner-city youth, provides a vehicle for the symbolic evidences of manhood such as physical prowess, status, and power. As Yablonsky (1966) has noted, the gang structure provides the potential to develop the characteristics of loyalty, leadership, and individual competence.

Curtis Sliwa exhibits charismatic qualities that motivate minority youth to be positive role models by becoming involved in volunteer crime prevention efforts. Sliwa recognizes the underlying motivations associated with volunteerism such as a desire to be liked, a desire to perform, a need for a position of authority, and an opportunity to meet an unfulfilled need in their lives (see Routh, 1972). Sliwa also realizes the value of recognition, feedback, reinforcement, and mobility within an organization (see Naylor, 1967).

The frustrations experienced by inner-city youth as well as the basic problems faced by adolescents may be associated with the motivations of young people who join the Guardian Angels. The Guardian Angels provide an opportunity for youth to meet their own needs in a constructive manner and also allow a positive contribution to the community.

Consideration of youth as a resource rather than a collection of problems to be solved by adults is the central theme expressed in the book, *The Value of Youth*. The contributing authors observe that there are few opportunities for youth in American culture to gain a sense of usefulness and meaningful participation. Young people need to feel competent and useful. Like all individuals, youth need confirmation that their efforts are appreciated. If they are not provided with opportunities to fulfill these needs in an acceptable way, they will seek their own means, which may be unacceptable as well as destructive.

Programs such as the Guardian Angels have the potential for providing youth with a stake in the larger community in a way that brings about the meaningful development of their own abilities. The positive outcomes of such an approach are described by Arthur Pearl (1978): "a means to develop initiative and self-determination with opportunities to gain a sense of satisfaction by participating in the decision-making process."

The results of this study contribute to the current knowledge regarding citizen patrols. Such patrols represent a unique form of crime control and have increased in this country, yet research has been limited regarding their effectiveness, their potential for involvement of youth, and their relationship to law enforcement. It is suggested that more extensive research be conducted based on the exploratory findings presented in this study of the Guardian Angels.

REFERENCES

Garofalo, James and Maureen McLeod, 1988. *Improving the Use and Effectiveness of Neighborhood Watch Programs* Washington, D.C; National Institute of Justice.

Greenberg, Stephanie W., William M. Rohe, and Jay R. Williams, 1985, *Informal Citizen Action and Crime Prevention at the Neighborhood Level*, Washington, D.C.; National Institute of Justice.

Lavrakas, Paul J., 1981, *Factors Related to Citizen Involvement in Personal, Household, and Neighborhood Anti-Crime Measures: An Executive Summary*, Washington, D.C; National Institute of Justice.

______ 1982. *Citizen Self-Help and Neighborhood Crime Prevention*, Evanston, IL; Northwestern University, Center for Urban Affairs and Policy Research.

______ 1985, *Chicagoans' Attitudes Toward the Guardian Angels*. Evanston, IL; Northwestern University, Medill School of Journalism and Center for Urban Affairs and Policy Research.

Lewis, Dan A. and Greta Salem. 1981. "Community Prevention: An Analysis of a Developing Strategy." *Crime and Delinquency* 27:405–421.

McGovern, Rebecca, ed. 1983. "The Fortress Mentality: A Look at the Public Fear of Crime." In *The Criminal Justice Newsletter* 14(10).

McPherson, Marlys and Glenn Silloway, 1981. "Planning to Prevent Crime." In *Reactions to Crime*, edited by Dan Lewis. Beverly Hills, CA: Sage.

Marx, Gary T. and Dane Archer, 1973. "The Urban Vigilante," *Psychology Today*, pp. 45–50.

Naylor, Harriet, 1967. *Volunteers Today: Finding, Training and Working with Them*. New York: Association Press.

Ostrowe, Brian B. and Rosanne DiBiase, 1983. "Citizen Involvement as a Crime Deterrent: A Study of Public Attitudes Toward an Unsanctioned Civilian Patrol Group." *Journal of Police Science and Administration*, 11:185–193.

Pearl, Arthur, 1978. "Youth in Lower Class Settings," In *The Value of Youth*, edited by Arthur Pearl, Douglas Grant, and Ernst Wenk, Davis, CA: Responsible Action.

Routh, Thomas A., 1972. *The Volunteer and Community Agencies*, Springfield, IL; Charles C. Thomas.

Trojanowicz, Robert C. and Dennis W. Banas, 1985. *The Impact of Foot Patrol on Black and White Perceptions of Policing*, Michigan State University, National Neighborhood Foot Patrol Center.

Wilson, James O. and George L. Kelling, 1982. "Broken Windows," *Atlantic Monthly* (March).

Yablonsky, Lewis, 1966. *The Violent Gang*, New York: Penguin.

Yin, Robert, Mary E. Vogel, Jan M. Chaiken, and Deborah Roth, 1977. *Citizen Patrol Projects*, Washington, D.C.; Government Printing Office.

The Nation

As Racketeering Law Expands, So Does Pressure to Rein It In

Laura Mansnerus

The Federal racketeering law, passed in 1970 as a weapon against mobsters, has in recent years been used to sue Fortune 500 companies, hundreds of accountants and stockbrokers, the Long Island Lighting Company, Claus von Bulow and an occasional spouse in a divorce case. This month an appeals court upheld the use of the law, known as RICO, in a civil suit against protesters who disrupted an abortion clinic in Philadelphia.

The decision illustrated the reach of the Racketeer Influenced and Corrupt Organizations Act, which was originally intended to bring broader powers to bear against criminals who had proved difficult to prosecute. It has since become extraordinarily popular among plaintiffs' lawyers—and especially unpopular with business.

The law permits criminal prosecution of those in an "enterprise" that has engaged in "a pattern of racketeering activities," which range from wire fraud to murder for hire. Congress sought to encourage private parties to do the same in civil suits. But no law could constitutionally single out a class of defendants; instead, the law has to be directed against specific types of acts. And those acts, plaintiffs' lawyers note, are committed by all kinds of defendants, the great majority of whom are not mobsters.

By now, complaints about RICO are well established. Criminal defense lawyers and civil libertarians detest the criminal provision that allows prosecutors to seize a defendant's assets before trial. They say overzealous prosecutors use that leverage—as United States Attorney Rudolph W. Giuliani did last year against the investment banking house of Drexel Burnham Lambert—to coerce settlements before any misconduct has been formally charged, let alone proved in court.

The civil provisions have outraged the businesses, securities dealers and accountants who have become the most frequent targets. They contend that RICO complaints are used to harass legitimate businesses and are clogging the Federal courts with litigation brought by plaintiffs who belong in state courts, but want the triple damages that this Federal law provides. These defendants say the Congress that enacted RICO could not have had them in mind.

Today, the civil provision faces the greatest pressure for change. Hearings on restrictive amendments are expected in Congress this spring.

RICO does have its defenders. G. Robert Blakey, one of the law's drafters, said the objections amount to "a large hue and cry from people who don't like to be held responsible for what they do."

Michael Waldman, legislative director of the Public Citizen's Congress Watch, a Washington group affiliated with Ralph Nader, said: "Most people who support reform take the position that it should be used against mobsters but not against criminals who wear pin-striped suits instead of fedoras. But white-collar crime, like organized crime, leaches hundreds of billions out of the economy each year."

Civil RICO, with the inducement of triple damages in attorney's fees for successful plaintiffs, was meant to create "private attorneys general" to enforce what prosecutors, with limited funds and staffs, could not. But for the first decade or so of its existence, the law did not accomplish that at all. Few cases were brought, and the lower Federal courts tended to require that the misconduct alleged bear some resemblance to organized criminality.

Visions and Realities

The number of civil RICO suits nevertheless increased in the early 1980's, and many more followed a 1985 Supreme Court decision rejecting the proposition that the law applied only to "racketeering injuries." The decision, Sedima v. Imrex Company, acknowledged that RICO was being applied in unexpected contexts, but said, "This defect—if defect it is—is inherent in the statute as written, and its correction must lie with Congress."

In the recent abortion clinic case, the United States Court of Appeals for the Third Circuit relied heavily on the Sedima decision. Many other courts have responded similarly. The trend is reflected in the number of civil RICO suits filed in the Federal courts. There were 19 in 1981, 117 in 1984 and 1,095 in the year that ended June 30, 1987. In the year ending last June 30, 959 civil RICO suits were filed, according to the Administrative Office of the U.S. Courts.

What still seems most troublesome to opponents of the law is RICO's divergence from Congress's 1970 vision. Judge Jack B. Weinstein of Federal District Court in Brooklyn said as much last month when he set aside a RICO award against the Long Island Lighting Company and ruled that the suit by Suffolk County, which maintained that the company systematically lied in applications for rate increases, properly belonged with state regulators. "The 'major purpose' of the RICO statute was to help block the criminal predations of organized crime upon legitimate businesses," he wrote. "Care must be taken to insure that the RICO statute is not extended beyond the reach envisaged by Congress."

Mr. Blakey, now a law professor at the University of Notre Dame, has no such reservations. The law "was not meant to be limited in scope," he said, and it "covers nothing that is not criminal." He said the abortion clinic case was well within RICO's purpose. "From the point of view of the abortion clinic, would it have made any difference whether the person who put the arm on them was named Corleone or O'Neal?" he said.

The courts still have issues to resolve, but the fight has shifted largely to Congress. There, the third proposal in three Congresses focuses on damages. The bill, which is designed to deter civil RICO suits by eliminating triple damages in most instances, is supported by insurance companies, securities dealers, accountants and the A.B.A., but strenuously opposed by groups including Mr. Waldman's organization, plaintiffs' lawyers and state attorneys general. By most accounts the debate is more heated than before. But for now, Mr. Waldman said, "the politics of it is unclear."

Victimology

The crime victim, traditionally the forgotten person in the criminal justice system, is now the center of attention for those who want to change the system. Indeed, historians might call the 1980s the decade in which a move was finally made toward acknowledging victims of crime as central characters in the criminal event, worthy of compassion and concern.

From 1981 to 1989 Presidents Reagan and Bush have proclaimed a National Victims of Crime Week annually with a view to focusing attention on the problems and concerns of crime victims. In December 1982 the President's Task Force on Victims of Crime published a 144-page report on the treatment of crime victims throughout the country. This publication contained 68 recommendations for addressing the problems of victims. While studying the experiences of crime victims, the task force recognized that family violence is often more complex in its causes and solutions than crime committed by unknown perpetrators.

Victims of crime have also been the subject of legislation during the 1980s. For example, the 1982 Omnibus Victim and Witness Protection Act requires the use of victim impact statements at sentencing in federal criminal cases, and provides for greater protection of federal victims and witnesses from intimidation. The Comprehensive Crime Control Act and the Victims of Crime Act of 1984 authorize federal funding for state victim compensation and victim assistance programs.

Comprehensive legislation which protects the interests of the victim has been enacted in more than 35 states. State victim compensation programs have continued to expand—43 states and the District of Columbia now have these programs—as have victim assistance services in the community.

Thus, recent developments have been supportive of the crime victim. The articles in this unit provide sharper focus on some key issues. From the lead essay, "The Fear of Crime," we learn that the fear of being victimized is pervasive among people, including some who have never been victims of crime. This article addresses the effects of crime on its victims.

Andrew Karmen contends that victims have rights which ought to be respected by both editors and reporters, in his article, "Crime Victims and the News Media." Battered families are the focus of "Battered Families: Voices of the Abused; Voices of the Abusers."

The following article, "Victims of Crime," gives the reader a sense that the pain and suffering victims undergo come not only at the hands of the assailant, but from the way the criminal justice system leaves no place for them or their survivors.

Thomas Moore, in his engaging essay "Death of a Bard," relates recollections of and describes in detail the murder of his childhood friend who fell victim to a random murder. The unit closes with a report on victim-offender mediation as a dispositional alternative.

Looking Ahead: Challenge Questions

How does crime affect the victim's psyche?

Are you familiar with victim service programs in your area?

What comes to mind when you think of family violence? Are there any known effective intervention strategies?

Unit 2

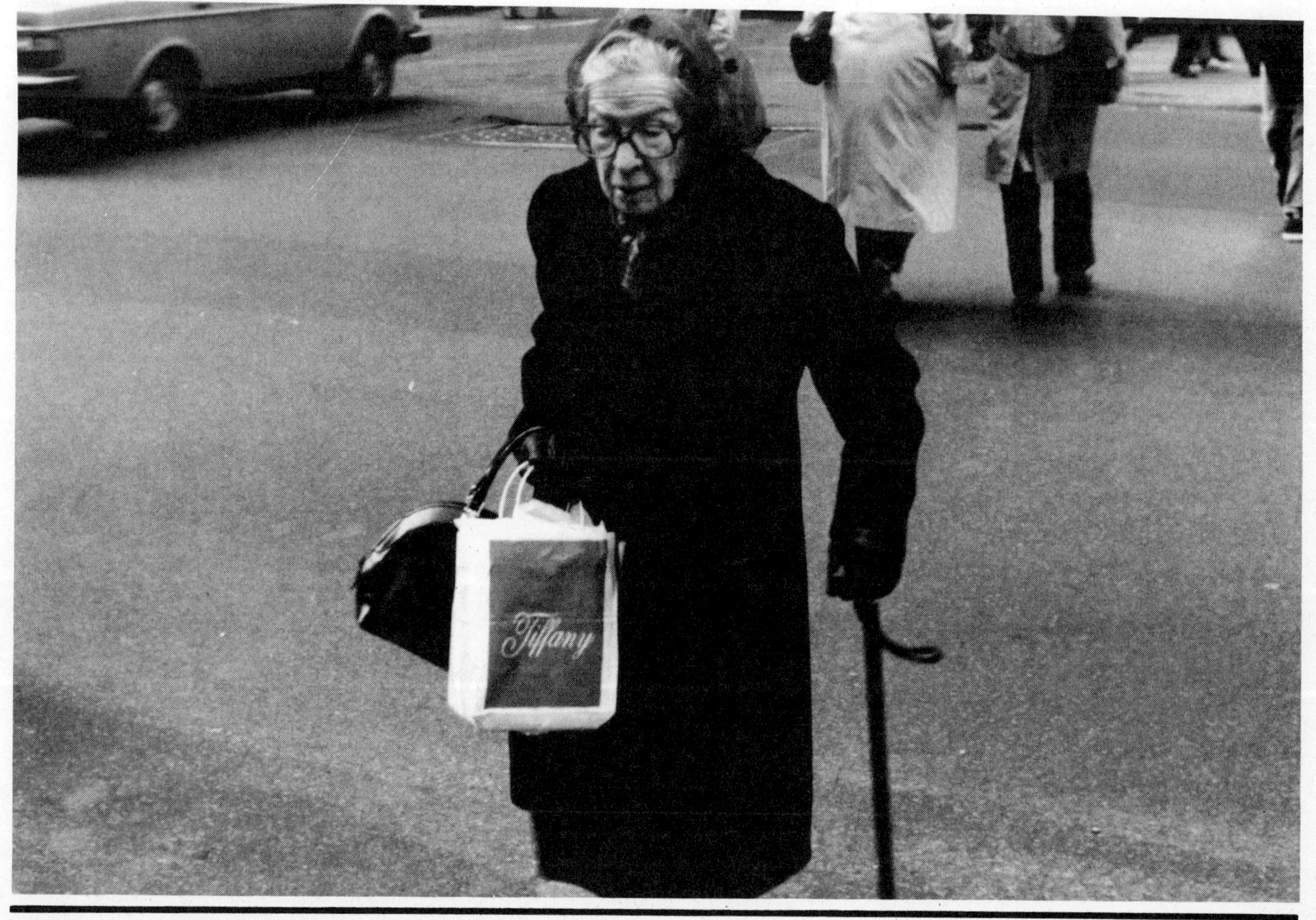

The Fear of Crime

The fear of crime affects many people, including some who have never been victims of crime

How do crime rates compare with the rates of other life events?

Events	Rate per 1,000 adults per year*
Accidental injury, all circumstances	242
Accidental injury at home	79
Personal theft	72
Accidental injury at work	58
Violent victimization	31
Assault (aggravated and simple)	24
Injury in motor vehicle accident	17
Death, all causes	11
Victimization with injury	10
Serious (aggravated) assault	9
Robbery	6
Heart disease death	4
Cancer death	2
Rape (women only)	2
Accidental death, all circumstances	.5
Pneumonia/influenza death	.3
Motor vehicle accident death	.2
Suicide	.2
Injury from fire	.1
Homicide/legal intervention death	.1
Death from fire	.03

These rates approximate your chances of becoming a victim of these events. More precise estimates can be derived by taking account of such factors as your age, sex, race, place of residence, and lifestyle. Findings are based on 1982-84 data, but there is little variation in rates from year to year.

*These rates exclude children from the calculations (those under age 12-17, depending on the series). Fire injury/death data are based on the total population, because no age-specific data are available in this series.

Sources: *Current estimates from the National Health Interview Survey: United States, 1982,* National Center for Health Statistics. "Advance report of final mortality statistics, 1983," *Monthly Vital Statistics Report,* National Center for Health Statistics. *Estimates of the population of the United States, by age, sex, and race: 1980 to 1984,* U.S. Bureau of the Census. *The 1984 Fire Almanac,* National Fire Protection Association. *Criminal victimization 1984,* BJS Bulletin, October 1985.

The chance of being a violent crime victim, with or without injury, is greater than that of being hurt in a traffic accident

The rates of some violent crimes are higher than those of some other serious life events. For example, the risk of being the victim of a violent crime is higher than the risk of death from cancer or injury or death from a fire. Still, a person is much more likely to die from natural causes than as a result of a criminal victimization.

About a third of the people in the United States feel very safe in their neighborhoods

The fear of crime cannot be measured precisely because the kinds of fears people express vary depending on the specific questions asked. Nevertheless, asking them about the likelihood of crime in their homes and neighborhoods yields a good assessment of how safe they feel in their own immediate environment.

In the Victimization Risk Survey, a 1984 supplement to the National Crime Survey, most people said that they felt at least fairly safe in their homes and neighborhoods. Yet, the people who said that they felt "fairly safe" may have been signaling some concern about crime. Based on a "very safe" response, a little more than 4 in 10 people felt entirely safe in their homes and about 1 in 3 felt totally safe in their neighborhoods—

- homeowners felt safer than renters
- people living in nonmetropolitan areas felt safer than those living in cities
- families with incomes of $50,000 or more were most likely to report their neighborhoods were very safe from crime.

The Victimization Risk Survey found that—

- 9 in 10 persons felt very or fairly safe in their places of work
- few persons—about 1 in 10—felt in danger of being a victim of a crime by a fellow employee, but persons working in places that employ more than 50 people were more likely to express fear of possible victimization.

The groups at the highest risk of becoming victims are not the ones who express the greatest fear of crime

Females and the elderly generally express a greater fear of crime than do people in groups who face a much greater risk. The Reactions to Crime project found that such impressions are related to the content of information about crime. Such information tends to emphasize stories about elderly and female victims. These stories may influence women and the elderly in judging the seriousness of their own condition. Perhaps groups such as females and the elderly reduce their risk of victimization by constricting their activities to reduce their exposure to danger. This behavior would account, at least in part, for their high levels of fear and their low levels of victimization.

Relatives, friends, and neighbors who hear about a crime become as fearful as the victim

When one household in a neighborhood is affected by a crime, the entire neighborhood may feel more vulnerable. This suggests that people who have not been victimized personally may be strongly affected when they hear about how others have been victimized. The Reactions to Crime project found that

From *Report to the Nation on Crime and Justice,* Bureau of Justice Statistics, U.S. Department of Justice, March 1988, pp. 24-25.

How does crime affect its victims?

indirect reaction to crime is often very strong.

$13 billion was lost from personal and household crimes in 1985

The direct cash and property losses from personal robberies, personal and household larcenies, household burglaries, and privately owned motor vehicle theft in 1985 was slightly more than $13 billion. This NCS finding probably underestimates the amount covered by insurance because the claims of many respondents had not been settled at the time of the NCS interview.

UCR data show that in 1985 losses from reported robberies, burglaries, and larceny/theft surpassed $5.9 billion. Among the many economic consequences of crime are lost productivity from victims' absence from work, medical care, and the cost of security measures taken to deter crime.

Other costs of crime include the economic costs of the underground economy, lowered property values, and pain and suffering of victims, their families, friends, and neighbors. A fuller discussion of the cost of crime is in Chapter V.

The economic impact of crime differs for different groups

The cost of crime is borne by all segments of society, but to different degrees. A study on the economic cost of crime using NCS data for 1981 shows that the dollar loss from crimes involving money, property loss, or destruction of property rises with income.

- Median losses were higher for households with incomes of $15,000 or more than for households with incomes of less than $7,500 from burglary ($200 vs. $100) and from motor vehicle theft ($2,000 vs. $700).

- Median losses from personal crimes were higher for blacks ($58) than for whites ($43).
- Median losses from household crimes were higher for blacks ($90) than for whites ($60).
- More than 93% of the total loss from crime was in crimes without victim-offender contact (such as burglary, theft without contact, and motor vehicle theft).

Many victims or members of their families lose time from work

Along with injuries suffered, victims or other members of their household may have lost time from work because of a violent crime. Lost worktime was reported in 15% of rapes and 7% of assaults (11% of aggravated assaults, 6% of simple assaults).

Violent crimes killed 19,000 and injured 1.7 million in 1985

NCS data for 1985 show that of all rape, robbery, and assault victims—
- 30% were injured
- 15% required some kind of medical attention
- 8% required hospital care.

The likelihood of injury was—
- greater for females than males even when rape was excluded from the analysis
- about the same for whites and blacks
- greater for persons from lower than from higher income households.

Who is injured seriously enough to require medical attention?

An analysis of NCS data for 1973-82 found that—
- Female victims are more likely than male victims to be injured, but they have about the same likelihood of requiring medical attention (13% of female vs. 12% of male victims).
- Blacks are more likely than whites to require medical attention when injured in violent crimes; 16% of black violent crime victims and 16% of the victims of all other racial groups required medical attention, while 11% of white victims required such care.

How seriously a victim is injured varies by type of crime

	Percent of all violent victimizations requiring:			
	Medical attention	Treatment in hospital emergency room	Overnight hospital stay	Median stay for those hospitalized overnight
Rape	24%	14%	3%	4 days
Robbery	15	7	2	5
Assault	11	5	1	5
Aggravated	18	9	3	5
Simple	7	3	—	2

—less than .5%

Source: BJS National Crime Survey, 1973-82.

CRIME VICTIMS AND THE NEWS MEDIA: QUESTIONS OF FAIRNESS AND ETHICS

Dr. Andrew Karmen

Associate Professor, Sociology Department, John Jay College of Criminal Justice, New York City.

THE NATURE OF THE PROBLEM:

- *A T.V. network special about murders anchored by a talk show host grabbed the audience's attention with the following opening film clips: a gruesome scene of a man found dead behind the wheel of his car; a grisly picture of a corpse lying in a pool of blood on the ground; dead bodies under sheets wheeled off to the morgue on stretchers; interviews with grieving relatives who break into tears as they call out for vengeance; excerpts from a slain policeman's funeral; a close-up of a son who has just been told his mother was killed; and uncut footage caught by a surveillance camera in a convenience store of an innocent bystander being shot in the head by a robber (Rivera, 1988).*
- *A young woman was found murdered in a New York City housing project. The "eyewitness" news crew started filming as police officers carried the victim's body into an ambulance. That night, on the six o'clock news, a teenager was shown pounding on the ambulance door, moaning "That's my sister in there!" (Greenfield, 1987).*
- *The remains of young women murdered by a serial killer were unearthed in Green River, Oregon. The cameras were rolling at the crime scene as a medical examiner picked up one of the victims' skulls and held it aloft. That scene of sand sifting out of the brain cavity was aired on all three of Seattle's T.V. stations. The families of the victims watching the news that evening were shocked and dismayed to see what their daughters had been reduced to (Barker, 1987).*
- *Beneath the tabloid's front page headline was a picture of the victim's smiling face. Next to it appeared a photo of her father, caught off-guard by an enterprising journalist as he opened his front door. The caption read: "The tortured face of ______ ______ displays the anguish of a father over the brutal murder of his 14-year-old daughter, ______ ______, who was found raped and bludgeoned to death in Queens yesterday"* (N.Y. Post, 1988:1).

At its best, crime reporting in newspapers and magazines, and on television and radio, provides the public with a valuable service. The accounts can convey in rich detail just how it feels to be victimized. By remaining faithful to the facts, journalists can enable audiences to transcend their own limited experiences and to see emergencies, tragedies, triumphs, and adventures from other people's points of view. Skillfully prepared accounts can effectively get across the drama, raw emotions, dilemmas, and accommodations that arise from lawless deeds. Nonvictims can better understand and empathize with the feelings and actions of crime victims when they are presented with sufficient background information, well-founded interpretations, and keen insights.

Unfortunately, the news media's depictions of the depredations of offenders and the plight of their victims furnish endless opportunities for commercial exploitation. A desire for financial gain is the root cause of any tendency to depart from accurate portrayals. Media outlets are profit-oriented businesses. Shocking news attracts viewers, listeners, and readers. Screaming headlines, gripping accounts, colorful descriptions, catchy phrases, memorable quotes, and other forms of media hype are useful packaging devices to build the huge audiences that permit media corporations to charge sponsors high rates for advertisements. Consid-

Reprinted from *Ethics and Fairness in Criminal Justice*, published by The Criminal Justice Institute, C. W. Post Campus, Long Island University, pp. 18-32, by permission of the author.

erations of personal advancement, like "scooping" the competition or revealing the "inside story" might motivate reporters and editors to hurriedly broadcast or publish an unbalanced or incomplete account of events. Organizational imperatives, like space limitations and time deadlines, might impose further distortions of the full truth surrounding criminal incidents.

Many victims harbor grievances against the news media for what they consider to be "sensationalism," "scandal-mongering," "pandering," and "yellow journalism" in the coverage of their cases. One way to approach the problem of reporting which smacks of "insensitivity" or "bad taste" is to acknowledge that victims have rights which ought to be respected and protected. It is difficult to assert that people who have been murdered still have rights. But it is easy to comprehend that the survivors of murder victims have rights, as do victims of less terrible offense, vis-à-vis the news media and their audiences.

For example, overzealous members of the press can be criticized for maintaining a death watch vigil in front of a kidnap victim's home; and they can be chastised for shouting questions and shoving a microphone towards a dazed, hysterical, or grief-stricken individual. By turning a personal tragedy into a media circus and then a public spectacle, news reporters invade the victim's personal space and symbolically disparage the seriousness of the incident for the injured party (Briggs-Bunting, 1982). Journalists and editors have obligations towards the subjects of their stories as well as to those who consume their products. It is not necessary to deliver up victims to the cameras, and voyeuristically parade their misfortunes before curious audiences merely to satiate some gluttonous appetite for the prurient (Kempton, 1987).

Questions of professional ethics and standards for fair treatment raised by these examples of excesses are now being addressed. Editors, journalists and activists within the victims' rights movement are grappling with these issues at conferences, at legislative sessions, in courtrooms, and during confrontations and demonstrations. The specific indictment of news media coverage by advocates of victims' rights reads as follows:

Media portrayals of the victims' plight are condemned as offensive, abusive, unfair and unethical if . . .

1. Names and exact addresses are needlessly made public, and repeated over and over again in subsequent accounts.
2. The victim's family finds out about the crime from media coverage rather than from personal notification by the victim or the police.
3. Victims are hounded at home or at work by packs of reporters and camera crews seeking interviews and impromptu press conferences.
4. Reporters use deceit or intense pressure to convince victims to consent to interviews or photographs.
5. Reporters insensitively intrude at intensely private moments of shock and grief, such as when first discovering facts about the crime, or during funerals.
6. Camera crews shoot pictures in poor taste, such as blood stains at the scene of the crime, dead bodies, or hysterical relatives.
7. Reporters conduct interviews with children who were victimized or who were relatives or eyewitnesses.
8. Editors impose headlines and captions which demean the victim and reduce him or her to less than a person, merely a category, like "blonde" or "preppie" or "model."
9. Reporters reveal to the public comments that were uttered in private, in confidence, or "off the record."
10. Reporters recklessly spread half-truths, inaccuracies, and unchecked or misinterpreted details (Thomason, 1987; Greenfield, 1987; Seymour, 1987).

SOME DILEMMAS:

The question boils down to this: What rights do victims (and their survivors, in cases of murder) have which ought to be respected when editors and journalists report about their cases? Also, should these matters be appropriate subjects for additional government regulations, or are they best formulated as a matter of ethics and fairness?

A consensus exists that the public should be kept informed about instances of criminal behavior, and that the reporting of these acts should be free of censorship. But the growing commitment to the well-being of crime victims and their families intrudes upon this complex equation. The issue goes beyond simply striking a balance between the needs of people who potentially might be victimized (the general public) and the needs of persons who just have joined the ranks of crime victims. The issue may not be "What do newspapers, radio stations, and T.V. networks have a right to do, legally" but rather "What ought the news media do, ethically?" Put another way, the crucial question is not "Can these details be made public?" but rather, "Why should these facts about the victim's private life and personal relationships be made public?" (Grotta, 1987; Greenfield, 1987; Thomason, 1987).

Since criminal acts are not just harmful to particular individuals but threaten society at large, the public has a right and a need to know about the emergence of dangerous conditions and troublesome developments like outbreaks of theft and violence. It is the media's role, or perhaps even "duty" to probe into, disclose fully, and disseminate widely all important and relevant details surrounding significant criminal acts. Arising from the protection of "free speech," the news media has a constitutional right to report public events without the impediments of government censorship. But the dilemma is sharpest when the public's right to know and the media's right to report clash with the privacy rights of persons who through some misfortune are targeted by criminals and find themselves in the unwanted glare of lights, microphones, and cameras.

POSSIBLE SOLUTIONS:

Several remedies are being proposed to curb the abusive treatment of victims by the news media. The first rests upon new legislation. The second relies upon self-policing by journalists of a professional code of ethics. The third counts on educating victims to know and exercise their rights.

Government regulations that restrain media coverage have been enacted in several parts of the country. For example, in Oregon and Minnesota, any local police chief is authorized to censor news stories by withholding the identity of the victim if that is what the victim requests and if release would pose some danger to him or her (CVD, 1984). However, critics argue that such practices only create opportunities for local police and elected officials to impose a "none-of-your-business" policy on reporters that will result in rumor, panic, or cover-ups of incompetence (Detroit Free Press Editors, 1987). Some states have laws to keep the identities of rape victims confidential. For example, New York's civil rights law assures that the name of any sex-offense victim under the age of 18 shall remain confidential. However, in 1975, the Supreme Court struck down a Georgia law (in *Cox Broadcasting v. Cohn*) which prohibited the publication of rape victims' names once they were revealed in open court. The court held that states cannot impose restrictions on the dissemination of truthful information contained in official court records open to public inspection (CVD, 1984). If the battle over withholding names has been lost, the chance to keep at least the victim's address from the public remains open. The President's Task Force on Victims of Crime (1982) recommended that legislation should be proposed and enacted to ensure that addresses of victims and witnesses are not made public (or available to the defense attorney and defendant) unless there is a clear need recognized by the judge.

Another approach, which serves as an alternative to the legislative strategy, is to develop and adopt a professional code of ethics for journalists who cover crime news. The kinds of provisions that this code of ethics would contain have been sketched out by editors, reporters and victim advocates at conferences. Reporters who abide by the restrictions in the code of ethics would "read victims their rights" at the outset of any interviews, in the same way that police officers are required to read suspects their Miranda rights. The professional ethics would assure victims that they have a right to . . .

1. Refuse a request for a statement or an interview.
2. Distinguish between comments that are "on the record" and "off the record."
3. Request a chance to review any direct quotations attributed to them which might be inaccurate or misleading due to editing.
4. Demand a retraction to correct any errors of fact in a story.
5. Decline to have any pictures taken.
6. File a formal complaint against a journalist whose behavior was abusive or whose actions were unethical (SVB, 1986; Barker, 1985).

Some victim advocates are understandably skeptical of the willingness and ability of the media to police itself through the use of a code of ethics. Furthermore, some media insiders will concede that "the media's collective ethics are no stronger than those of its least scrupulous member" (Alter and Clift, 1987). (This refers to the tendency of different outlets to pick up and repeat information that might have been obtained through unethical means.) Therefore, the third alternative to curb exploitive handling of the victim's plight is to educate victims about their rights so they can effectively exercise them and protect their own interests. Such a strategy of education preparation and empowerment faces a major obstacle: victims must know about their rights before they encounter media representatives. Since victims are selected by offenders from the general public, this means that everyone needs to know in advance what their rights are should they become victimized and thereby thrust into the public spotlight.

Clearly, victim advocates and organizations have a formidable task in front of them. They need assistance from other people who adopt the two alternative approaches. Reporters must be trained about their professional responsibilities and ethical obligations in journalism schools as well as on the job. New laws are needed to protect victims from commercial exploitation, and civil lawsuits must be launched to provide an avenue of redress for those individuals who wind up victimized twice, once by the criminal and then by the news media. In the foreseeable future, a heated debate will continue over questions of ethics and fairness concerning the coverage of the victims' plight, and over the most effective ways of curbing abuse by commercial news media outlets.

BIBLIOGRAPHY

Alter, Johnathan, and Clift, Elinor. 1987. "Test Cases For A New Political Generation." *Newsweek*, Vol. 110, No. 20 (November 16): 48–49.

Barker, Linda. 1985. "The Media Victims Of Crime." NOVA (National Organization For Victim Assistance) Newsletter, Vol. 9, No. 4, (April): 4–5.

______ 1987. "Quotes From The Symposium." P. 23 in Thomas Thomason and Anatha Babbili (Eds.) Crime Victims And The

News Media. Fort Worth, Texas: Texas Christian University Dept. of Journalism.

Briggs-Bunting, Jane. 1982. "Behind The Headlines: News Media Victims." Pp. 80–97 in Jacqueline Scherer and Gary Shepard (Eds.) *Victimization Of The Weak: Contemporary Social Reactions.* Springfield, Illinois: Charles C. Thomas.

Crime Victims Digest (CVD). 1984. "Publishing The Names Of Victims And Witnesses: What Can Police And Prosecutors Do To Stop It?" Vol. 1, No. 5. (February): 1–6.

Detroit Free Press Editors. 1987. "Police: A Policy Of Withholding Information Would Be A Poor Way To Fight Crime." Sept. 22: 15.

Greenfield, Jeff. 1987. "TV: The Media Determines Impact of Crime Stories." Pp. 19–23 in Thomas Thomason and Anantha Babbili (Eds.) *Crime Victims And The News Media.* Fort Worth, Texas: Texas Christian University Dept. of Journalism.

Grotta, Gerald. 1987. "Pilot Study Probes Attitudes In Media Coverage." Pp. 26–30 in Thomas Thomason and Anantha Babbili (Eds.) *Crime Victim And The News Media.* Fort Worth, Texas: Texas Christian University Dept. of Journalism.

Kempton, Murray. 1987. "Delivering the Victim to the Cameras." *Long Island Newsday,* November 29:8.

President's Task Force On Victims of Crime. 1982. Final Report. Washington, D.C.: U.S. Government Printing Office.

Rivera, Geraldo. 1988. "Murder." ABC Network, April 13, 1988.

Seymour, Ann. 1987. "Victim Advocate Suggests Code For Journalists." Pp. 31–33 in Thomas Thomason and Anantha Babbili (Eds.) *Crime Victims And The News Media.* Fort Worth, Texas: Texas Christian University Dept. of Journalism.

Sunny Von Bulow National Victim Advocacy Center (SVB). 1986. *Victims' Rights and the Media.* Fort Worth, Texas: SVB Center.

Thomason, Thomas. 1987. "The Issue Is Ethics." Pp. 2–3 in Thomas Thomason and Anantha Babbili (Eds.) *Crime Victims And The News Media.* Fort Worth, Texas: Texas Christian University Dept. of Journalism.

BATTERED FAMILIES

VOICES OF THE ABUSED

Mistreated wives tell their stories of physical threat

By Ellen Steese
Staff writer of The Christian Science Monitor

Boston

At the request of the women interviewed for this story, their names have been changed, and some details have been altered to protect anonymity.

Battered wives in shelters are invisible refugees in our midst, fleeing a war declared on them alone.

Many are in hiding, innocent prisoners on the lam. You meet them in basements with no name on the door, in quiet, incurious, residential neighborhoods. The sorts of places where a succession of exhausted-looking wives and their children can come and go unremarked.

Routine information is oddly absent. It's an act of supreme trust to give someone your full name—and unthinkable to tell anyone where you live.

But if you listen carefully enough and stay long enough, you find in these shelters the story of women emerging from the shadow of secret violence into a world that, if not free of fears, is at least a safe haven from physical abuse.

Cathy is short, cute, a little plump, and she has a sensible, understanding, reassuring air, like a nurse, which she is. Life is peaceful now. She is about to receive an advanced nursing degree. She is safe and divorced, with full custody of her seven-year-old daughter. This is the calm after a storm.

Her relationship with her ex-husband started out like a fairy tale, with no dark shadows. "I thought I was so ugly, and how could I get a man as tall and dark and handsome as George?" Cathy says. They had a very romantic courtship, with flowers and dinners out: "He treated me like a queen."

Then, a month before the wedding, he pushed her. "I thought it was because of the tension of the marriage," she continues. He said it would never happen again.

He always said it would never happen again. Her life became a round of slaps and punches—always below the neck, so the bruises would be out of sight. Sometimes once a week. Sometimes every day. Sometimes there'd be a respite of two weeks.

Her job as a nurse supported the family (he had 18 jobs in seven years, she says), but that was no guarantee of independence: "He told me when to go to sleep and when not to go to sleep. . . ."

Cathy was always tiptoeing around, not knowing what was going to set him off. Her home was like a concentration camp for one. One terrifying day she was forced to sit in a chair, without doing anything, for 12 hours, while he got drunk and said things like "I'm going to break your . . . head and then tear you to pieces."

"I used to wait for the beating. It seemed like an *eternity,*" Cathy comments. She thought things would be better after Janey was born, but then she says, "I was torn between being a mother and surviving."

One evening, because Janey was crying, her husband knocked Cathy down and held a butcher knife at her throat. Missing a tooth and with a concussion, she ran into the January night in her nightgown and slippers, the several miles to her father's house.

In situations like this a person has to make instant, terrifying decisions. Asked if she felt comfortable leaving Janey behind, Cathy says her husband had never injured her. She feels now that leaving the baby saved her own life. To get her child back, however, she had to return to the marriage.

Her father-in-law had been a batterer, too. So when Cathy asked her mother-in-law for help, she said, "You'll just have to get used to it."

Cathy evokes these dark memories as we sit in a plain but warm and comfortable room. It has the feeling of a refuge.

In the other room, her daughter, Janey, and a friend are industriously playing house. There is a vigorous debate about whether some imaginary pork chops had, or had not, already been cooked. But in between the girls' housewifely comments you hear prattling references to foster parents, jail, police.

"He stay in jail so long," one little voice says.

Why did Cathy stay? Because afterward there would be a 'honeymoon" period, she says.

"They're so sorry for what they've done. They're going to kill themselves if you leave. You want so much to believe it's not going to happen again."

Another problem: Her husband threatened to kill members of her family if she left: "I always thought I was protecting them by staying." And he threatened her with loss of custody of her daughter. Cathy says it was a happy moment when the judge at her divorce trial said, " 'Nobody has the right to hurt anybody, and yes, that baby is yours.' "

The neighbors would hear her screams and call the police, and then she would be blamed for the disturbance and beaten again.

"People think we like it, and that's why we put up with it. We're afraid he'll come after the person [who intervenes]," she says. "You show me the person who likes to get beaten. I think that's a myth that needs to be stopped."

Cathy also says that other women should be alert, rather than thinking nothing like this could ever happen to them. She emphasizes that she had come from a loving family, and that she had been confident as a teen-ager.

Once, at 16, she saw a friend being

Reprinted by permission from *The Christian Science Monitor,* July 14, 1988, pp. 25-26, and July 15, 1988, pp. 23-24.

What statistics and shelters say about battered women

Advocates commonly quote a Bureau of Justice Statistics figure that a woman is beaten in the United States every 15 seconds. That is based on figures for the number of reported beatings that took place between 1978 and 1982.

The National Coalition Against Domestic Violence (NCADV) estimates that somewhere between 2 and 6 million women are battered each year.

(To put this in perspective, according to the Bureau of the Census in Washington, there are 97.3 million women 15 and older in the US, of which 58 million are married and living with spouse, married but spouse absent, or a partner in an unmarried couple with no other adult in the household.)

Getting out of the marriage or relationship does not guarantee protection. According to Bureau of Justice Statistics figures, in three-fourths of spouse-on-spouse assaults, the victim was divorced or separated at the time of the incident.

Battering tends to escalate over time, and homicide is sometimes the culmination. In 1986, 40 percent of all female homicide victims were killed by relatives or boyfriends.

Many statistics are based on a fairly small sample, but these still provide some interesting clues to the whole picture of domestic violence.

Women who murdered their husbands were often battered women. Accordingly to a study in Cook County (Chicago),Ill., 40 percent of the women who committed homicides were battered women who killed their batterer.

A five-year study at Yale-New Haven Hospital concluded that 40 percent of all injury-related visits to the hospital by women were the result of battering. The study also disclosed that battering was a major precipitating factor in cases of female alcoholism and drug abuse, child abuse, attempted suicide, and situational disorders.

The children are victims, too. Not only is child abuse more likely in homes where the wife is battered, but also, children are very often witnesses to the battering. The NCADV estimates that, of these children, 60 percent of the boys will grow up to be batterers, and 50 percent of the girls will grow up to be battered women. The NCADV also estimates that in one-quarter of violent families, the wife is attacked while pregnant.

One study showed that three-fourths of all battered women reported that their abuser was not violent in public, and that they were not believed when they reported instances of brutality.

Advocates insist that emotional abuse is as devastating as physical abuse. Among the behaviors considered abusive are ridiculing a woman's beliefs or women as a group, criticizing and shouting, attempting to control, and refusal to work or to share money.

Other characteristics of a batterer include extreme suspiciousness and possessiveness, poor self-image, strongly traditional ideas about men's and women's roles, and a tendency to isolate a woman from her family or friends.

It is commonly thought that battering is largely a problem in poorer neighborhoods, but advocates insist that the problem extends across the social spectrum.

"Any woman, rich or poor, black, white, or Latina [or otherwise], could be a battered woman," says Alba Baerga, who is on the staff of Casa Myrna Vazquez shelter in Boston. Upper-class or upper-middle-class women are less likely to *report* abuse, however.

All over the US, there are shelters offering help to women who are battered. The National Coalition Against Domestic Violence, in Washington, D.C., has a toll-free hotline, 800-333-SAFE. Women who call there can get information on shelters and programs near them.

Shelters also share information. A shelter in one state, for instance, will refer a woman fleeing for her life to a shelter in other state. Some shelters in Boston offer transitional housing. And there is a long-established network in Massachusetts of "safe homes"—homes in the community that take in battered women. This is not common in most parts of the country, according to the NCADV.

Not all women who come to a shelter leave the batterer. "Some have been in shelters before," Ms. Baerga says.

"Some come for half an hour and decide to give another chance to the relationship. Some come determined to be independent, to find an apartment. Our main goal is to provide a safe place where they can make their own decision."

Katrina Pope, on the staff of Elizabeth Stone House, concurs. "We aren't here to say you can't go back. We're here to provide as many resources as possible, and to say there are possibilities in your life, there are options. No one deserves to be beaten."

One of the main obstacles to putting a stop to battering is that women want to deny that there is a problem.

"Some of them are strong enough to say 'Yes, I am a battered woman.' Some of them are very open about it," says Baerga. "Others are there for two months—and don't even remember they were in the shelter. It can take your whole life and you still never admit you were [battered].

"The way we measure success here: Only one phone call might be a success. It might take the woman her whole life to make that phone call." —E. S.

slapped, and she thought at the time she would never allow anyone to treat her that way. She continues, "And look what happened to me. . . ."

The keynote of domestic violence is confusion. What is unclear is what love is, how it is properly expressed, how you recognize it, or its absence.

"You're practically *mesmerized,*" Cathy says.

But physical violence is not the only battering that women fear. "Emotional abuse is just as damaging," says Katrina Pope, from the staff of Elizabeth Stone House, in Boston. This is supported even by women with stories of attempted strangulation and broken bones.

Viola is a small, confident woman who tells her story in a pizza parlor. For her, it was a relationship that degenerated slowly, taking with it her self-respect. She stopped bathing and combing her hair—but saw to it that the children were fed and the rent paid.

Her family stopped coming; "He created an atmosphere where my family wouldn't come to visit. . . . I was so depressed." A friend pointed out the change in her: "And this is when I began to see some light."

Like many of the women, Viola says drugs were a large part of the problem, causing a complete personality change.

On one occasion, after she had taunted him, her husband started to strangle her and knocked her to the floor. She told him "You can't deal with the truth—knocking someone down to shut them up."

Unlike many women, who stay to ever-intensifying physical abuse, that was the end for Viola. "Some people stay in a cage forever. They believe they're powerless," she continues.

The question you ask after meeting Sarah is, Where did she learn about love? Abused as a child, she lived for 10 years with a man who among other injuries, fractured her skull nine times.

"I was used to it because that's how it was when I grew up. I would get beaten for leaving toys on the floor or for not doing the dishes right," she says.

Mostly Sarah's injuries came from interposing her 5-foot-2 self between her 6-foot-4 husband and one of the children.

"When you're looking at a two-year-old getting a beating for leaving a toy on the floor, you have to put a stop to it," Sarah comments, firmly.

"The abuse started even before we got married. I was cooking supper one day, and he didn't like what I was cooking. He threw me up against the wall and broke a kneecap." Asked if she had been concerned about marrying a man who had broken her kneecap, she paused. "I had *doubts,*" she said hesitantly.

But it was his hitting the children that finally made Sarah leave. One boy lost several teeth. She says, "If you raise your hand, he will duck automatically. He was afraid of moving out of the shelter. He felt 'safe'—that's the word he used to use. 'I feel safe here.' "

His teachers have commented on the seven-year-old's improvement in the nine weeks since they left home.

Now it's a triumph that her children will go off into the living room to play by themselves. "All the people around them are showing them love. I think that's what's bringing them out of it."

Sarah is not optimistic or ecstatic, however, about being free for the first time in 10 years. Asked why not, she said simply, "He hasn't found me yet."

The question you want to ask, over and over, is, Why don't you leave? One of many reasons is that it's hard to leave someone who won't be left.

Stephanie met Danny when she was 16 and moved in with him. She realized this was a major mistake when he held her over the porch edge of the third-story apartment and threatened to throw her over if she ever left him.

The offhand way she tells her terrible story shows you the happy-looking young woman still ought to have been going to school and giggling with her friends. Now in her early 20s, Stephanie has spent the last seven years fighting off a nightmare of rape and harassment, by herself.

"After a while, you get used to it. It's like a way of life." Danny said he didn't mean it, so Stephanie took him back, and then he left her when she was three months pregnant. But he didn't leave for good. After the birth he came back with a knife and gun, threatening to kill the little girl.

According to Stephanie, he told the Department of Social Services that she was abusing the child, and she was put on probation for three months. "He said, 'Now you have to be nice to me and do what I say.' That's when the rapes started."

According to her, Danny would throw rocks in the window and come sit in her apartment with a gun. He called her 100 times a day. He would threaten to get visitation rights and cut the daughter to pieces. He would have her electricity and phone shut off. And when she was out, he would try to drag her into his car.

As a result Stephanie stayed in her apartment most of the time.

"I used to call the police, and they wouldn't come. I'd say, 'he's outside!' and they'd say, 'Call us when he comes to the door. This isn't "Hawaii 5-0." ' I stopped calling the police."

Meeting an advocate from a shelter—she didn't even know of their existence—made the difference for Stephanie. Now she has an apartment, a job, and a car. "I started dating late last year," she says.

Stephanie is gradually relaxing her precautions. She doesn't, for instance, keep a butcher knife under the bed anymore. She no longer pursues her ritual of checking the closets and windows to make sure Danny isn't lurking somewhere. But freedom won and freedom felt are two different matters. Now she says, she just checks under the bed.

VOICES OF THE ABUSERS

Husbands who have mistreated wives discuss need for help

Ellen Steese
Staff writer of The Christian Science Monitor

Cambridge, Mass.

At the request of the men interviewed for this story, their names have been changed. The counselors' names are their own.

We think of the family as a bulwark against the world. But there is a down side to this: It sometimes makes people feel that whatever happens within the family, short of murder, is private—a personal, not a legal, matter.

In this context, while smacking your next-door neighbor would be reasonable cause for assault charges, doing the same to your wife can seem like a family argument that just got a little out of control.

"Many men we see—it just never occurred to them that what they do is against the law," comments David Adams of Emerge, an 11-year-old counseling service for men who batter, in Cambridge, Mass. So, he says, you often get very respectable people—"doctors, lawyers, ministers"—battering their wives.

"So often, men have the attitude that what they do in private should not count . . . that they should only be judged according to their public behavior."

A common image of a batterer is a man who cannot control his temper, who lashes out in frustration. But Mr. Adams says that at Emerge, battering is thought of as a deliberate strategy, a way of maintaining control.

Some batterers are so violent that this behavior spills over into all areas of their lives. But for many, home is the one place they can express violence without being punished for it.

Thus, batterers "are able to have the

last word in arguments," he remarks.

"They are able to secure compliance on the part of the woman. They are able to not deal with her grievances. The woman is perpetually on the defensive. She's always dealing with *his* grievances."

Adams points out that "every husband gets angry at times, but if once a month or twice a year you get violent, your anger has more weight."

Don Conway-Long, of Raven, a men's counseling service in St. Louis, uses words such as "choose" and "choice" a lot to discuss the actions of batterers.

He says that there are men who have witnessed battering as children—a very common prelude to becoming batterers themselves—who *choose* not to. He points out that there are men who had terrible experiences in Vietnam, who again *choose* not to become batterers.

Many men choose violence against women as a way of releasing anger, he comments.

"We live in a culture that permits us to make that choice and supports that choice . . . that provides ways for men to show they have dominance over women."

There are groups all over the country that offer counseling. Unfortunately, batterers seldom perceive themselves to be in need of these services.

Mr. Conway-Long estimates that they reach "about 1 percent" of all the men who need help.

Many men come to Emerge because they are required to by the courts, "rather than genuinely seeing that they have a problem. Internal motivation often doesn't develop until later," says Mr. Adams.

"The men we see are very susceptible to which way the law leans. If the law is taking a laissez-faire approach, it's much easier for the men to minimize or deny their violence.

"If the law is imposing clear sanctions, then battering men take it more seriously. They see it not just as a domestic affair, but as a crime against the state."

The main way Emerge works with batterers is through group counseling. Two Emerge therapists are present at each session, but almost more important are the support and perspective the men give each other.

A visit to a group session at Emerge changes your image of a batterer. "People think a batterer should have a tattoo on his ear," as Conway-Long puts it. "Usually we meet Dr. Jekyll—we never get to meet Mr. Hyde." In fact, all the clients are so handsome, likable, well dressed, and articulate, you become positive that you have stumbled into the wrong pale, perhaps the Divorced Dads Workshop.

But faces tighten and smiles disappear when you mention the grimly clinical words "domestic violence."

You have to really respect people for having a problem and trying to deal with it. And deal with it head-on they did. The men were pretty hard on each other. The attitude seemed to be, "We're here to do a job, so let's get down to it."

This particular group hadn't had an incident of violence for some months, but Emerge sessions try to cope with all aspects of abusive and controlling behavior.

For instance, one man, Steve, had left his wife of many years, taken up with a girlfriend, broken off with her, and now is in couples therapy with his wife, although he doesn't want to resume the marriage. "Of course, the couples sessions are not to put our marriage back together. It's more of an autopsy," as he puts it.

The other men spend about 20 minutes telling him that this behavior is abusive. John points out, "You don't take a car to the repair shop that you're going to junk next week. You're really hurting her—giving her some false hopes." Jim describes Steve's behavior as "wishy-washy" about six times.

"I appreciate your help, guys," says Steve finally.

The topics discussed, like dealing with a partner's anger, reflect the sort of thing any couple learns to deal with. The subject of women getting angry is particularly touchy, since the men are trying to learn to control this reaction in themselves.

Adams points out that in many relationships "there's not a whole lot of room for the woman's anger. For men, there is a great tendency to translate everything into anger. You're good at expressing anger. We'd like you to be good at responding to your partner's anger."

The trap here, he says, is getting into a pattern where "you are willing to give up abuse as long as she follows the rules. If she gets angry, that gives us the 'right' to be abusive."

Jim points out that in business, men handle other people's anger very differently. For instance, in his job, if someone points out that he has made a mistake: "I'd say, 'Wait a minute. I'm sorry. It's my fault. And I understand why you're angry.' "

He says that when he went home—"of course, now I don't have a home to go to"—he would start giving explanations and justifications.

"If you say, 'You're right. I can see why you're angry,' it defuses the whole thing. What used to be an hour argument is now four minutes. It takes the strain off . . ."

Most men who are batterers rather naturally do not want to talk about it. But some are so eager to escape from this cycle that they are willing. Some even speak up in public.

Paul, who has been going to Emerge since September, says it helps him to stand up and say, "I used to be a batterer."

He is poised, clean cut, and athletic looking, with a wide, friendly smile. In yellow tie, gray pants, and leather pilot jacket slung over a shoulder, he looks like a cover for Gentlemen's Quarterly. You believe him when he says that if you told his co-workers that he used to beat up his girlfriend, they'd say, "Oh, no—Paul's a nice guy!"

"My father was an alcoholic. I grew up watching my father come home drunk and start arguing with my mother—sometimes money, sometimes bills," he says. "He'd smack her. My brother and I, we started to protect her. I see myself as my father. I thought it was a normal kind of thing, a way of controlling women."

His face wrinkles in pain as he talks about his relationship with his girlfriend, Laura, a relationship marked by jealousy and suspicion and arguments that sometimes ended with grabbing and hitting.

"I'd feel sorry about all the thoughts that were in my head after the anger was released. I could never control it *during* the anger."

Paul would deliberately take a drink before provoking a fight, so that he could use the drink as an excuse afterward.

"I did a lot of ignoring—that's a kind of control, too. I was jealous—not trusting and not being trustworthy. I wasn't understanding anything she said or anything she talked about. I would take it in the wrong context and start an argument about that.

"I was always being negative, never positive. I did things like date other girls. I was very dishonest.

"I always felt that Laura was very

A battered wife tells her story

Not all women are completely passive in the face of violence.

Karen (not her real name) was a battered wife. She grew up in New York housing projects with her mother and three sisters.

"New York is a very fast paced life. You have to know how to protect yourself," she says.

Her husband was violent, and she defended herself: "I had weapons all over my house. If this were my kitchen I'd have a weapon under the stove and in the fridge. In the living room I'd have a weapon behind the chair and under the cushions."

Most of their fights took place at 3, 4, or 5 a.m.

"Before I left, I apologized to all the neighbors. I had holes in the wall from his punching the wall, throwing me against the wall and stuff. Particularly the way they build houses nowadays—the walls are *paper*-thin!

"I'm not a fighter. Being with him, I changed. I became a violent person. . . . I picked up a pipe. I picked up some scissors. I was going to stab him.

"To know I was capable of hurting someone—that really scared me. I said, 'It's time for me to leave.' One of us was going to die, and he's not worth going to jail for."

Her advice to other women in her situation:

"Get out before it's too late. He'll kill you and get five to 10 years, and be out two years on good behavior. You're six feet under, and *he'll* get the children.:"

Karen got up the courage to leave and to go to Boston—with $30, her small daughter, and possessions in plastic bags.

"Material things you can always buy. The emotion and respect is free, and that's what you need," she comments with conviction.

Karen is grateful to her husband for the times he was good to her, and says that she stayed with him for four years because she thought she was in love with him.

"I realize now, being here, that I wasn't. I'm a very loving person. I love a lot of people.

"But as far as a relationship, and somebody loving me back, I guess I don't know what love is." **—E. S.**

attractive. I always felt unattractive. I thought, "I'm not cute enough for her. She'll find a nicer-looking guy with a better car.' But she wasn't looking for that. She was looking for a little compassion and honesty. I didn't give her any of that."

Laura's sister was a counselor, and she told Paul about Emerge. Initially he was skeptical: "I didn't think I was getting anything. Look at these guys telling me about their problems."

Paul's worst problem had been spying on Laura when she was with other people. He made a promise to the group that he wouldn't do this anymore—a promise he wasn't always able to keep. On one 30-degree winter day, he stood freezing outside a bar where Laura was talking with her friends. "You want to do good, but you have *so much* hate and anger inside you."

The men in the group recommended another line of behavior.

"They're not only scolding me. They're comforting me, too. They want to stick by me and help me," says Paul. "Discussing my last violent act, I shed a tear, not feeling sorry for myself. It was a tear of 'look at what I am doing to this woman.' "

Ability to take criticism in the group is a key success in the program, Paul feels. He says that when a man in the "hot seat" (being critiqued by the group) "becomes totally negative and aggressive, I know he's not going to stay in the program. You can see it in a person when they change."

Batterers tend to have very traditional ideas about the relationship between men and women. Paul characterizes his old attitude: The man should be "like a god. I should be *first,*" he says. "Now I look on a woman more as an equal."

At Emerge, men learn to treat women in a different way. "Walking down the street and whistling at a woman—I would never do that now. I *have* done it," Paul says. "Picking up a woman in a bar—I wouldn't do that.

"Everyone in the group has a full deep respect for women while they're sitting in that room. I think it's great that Emerge has that effect on men." Asked what about when they're not in the room, he says, "If they're lying to the group, they're only lying to themselves."

"I feel I've really progressed a lot. I'm going to stick it out at Emerge. I know it will take longer . . . I feel now as if I'm achieving something in life. I felt no good, really rotten sometimes. I was scared to face the truth. Facing the truth is the biggest obstacle to any problem."

Paul asks to have his advice to other batterers put in bold letters: "It's going to be hard [maintaining the relationship], because the woman is always going to have that question at the back of her mind: Is he going to be violent like he was before?"

Paul says he's lucky because he's only 26 and has time to resolve his problem. He wants to be married and have a family, and be "compassionate, caring, loving."

He'd like to get back together with Laura. "I want her to learn that there is good in me. The only way I can ever get married or have a relationship is by showing that the violence is gone."

Local women's shelters often have information on counseling for men. Raven, a service in St. Louis, has a national directory: Write PO Box 24159, St. Louis MO, 63130, or call (314) 725-6137. Emerge has its office at 280 Green St., Cambridge, MA 02139; telephone, (617) 547-9870.

VICTIMS OF CRIME

The nation's crime siege has continued through the 1980s despite predictions it would ease. In a typical year:

- *There are 8.1 million serious crimes like murder, assault and burglary*
- *Only 724,000 adults are arrested*
- *Only 193,000 of them are convicted*
- *Only 149,000 of them go to prison*
- *And 36,000 serve less than a year*
- *Fewer than half the crimes committed are reported to authorities*

A violent crime is committed every 5 seconds, leaving an anguished victim and a scarred community. Sometimes the wounds reopen with a vengeance, especially when the public believes a heinous act has been grievously mishandled. Much of California rose in revolt in 1987 when a convict named Larry Singleton was released on parole eight years into a 14-year sentence for raping 15-year-old Mary Bell Vincent, chopping off her arms with an ax and leaving her to die in a ditch. Singleton was forced out of six California communities by outraged citizens. A similar outcry greeted revelations that John Mack, top aide to then-House Speaker Jim Wright, attempted to murder a woman named Pamela Small 16 years ago and served only two years in jail because Wright helped him get a job. Mack resigned amid a storm of criticism once Small spoke publicly about her ordeal.

For every such notorious case there are many millions of less noticed, but no less traumatizing crimes. And for most of the victims, suffering comes not only at the hands of the assailant but from the way the criminal-justice system leaves no place for victims or their survivors. Last week, in Worcester, Mass., the beleaguered justice system delivered the second knockout blow to May Foy, the widow of a cabdriver slain last year. Two men agreed to admit killing Thomas Foy in return for parole eligibility within 15 years. But the widow pleaded that the deal was unfair and called for a jury trial to ensure "justice done in the American way." Unexpectedly last month, a judge accepted her argument, rejected the plea bargain and ordered a trial. But last week, prosecutors went before another judge and had the first ruling overturned, sealing the plea bargain and outraging the family.

There is another victim when a violent crime occurs. It is the community. After any serious crime, neighborhoods change as fear grows and morale drops. If enough crimes are committed, signs of massive decay set in, most alarmingly in the growing number of instances when police are unable to address the kind of routine street crimes that befall many. In big cities, they must ignore burglaries, purse snatchings and radio pilfering from cars just to keep pace with the attacks that draw blood.

Abused by the system

Most harrowing of all is the way the bloodletting has become pervasive and unpredictable. Victimization is a chronic state. The U.S. Bureau of Justice Statistics estimates that 83 percent of children now 12 years old will become victims of actual or attempted violence if crime continues at current rates. The innocent (called "mushrooms" by gangs) increasingly are being hurt. The number of bystanders gunned down in New York City, Boston, Los Angeles and Washington, D.C., tripled in three years. Last week, 33-year-old Rhonda Anthony was killed

From *U.S. News & World Report*, July 31, 1989, pp. 16-19. Copyright, 1989, U.S. News & World Report.

in a crossfire while sitting on her front porch in a residential Washington, D.C., neighborhood overrun with drug dealers.

After they are assaulted, victims must continue their struggle in a legal environment that pays more attention to their adversaries than to them. The system's lack of concern for victims derives from traditions of English law that insist justice is best served when the legal clash is between the defendant and the state rather than the defendant and the victim. In the United States, that means the rights enshrined in the law are those accorded criminal suspects. The Supreme Court in the past three decades has vastly extended defendants' rights by limiting police powers to question suspects without defense attorneys present and to seize evidence without warrants.

Even the more conservative Rehnquist Court has bitterly disappointed victims when they argued their interests were on the line. Two years ago, Justices rejected the use in death-penalty cases of "victim-impact statements" that tell juries about the victim's background and how a murder affected the family. Last month, the Court voted 5 to 4 to void a death sentence against a South Carolina killer. The Justices ruled a victim's personal attributes such as importance to a family and a community are not pertinent to the "moral culpability" of the defendant.

Slow and uncertain punishment

More infuriating for victims are the faults in the system itself. Punishment of society's wrongdoers is neither sure nor swift. Nationwide, the police are able to solve only 1 in 5 major crimes. When a cop does manage to collar a suspect, it may take more than a year in crowded urban court systems to dispose of the case. A new study reports the *average* disposition time in crime-ridden Newark, N.J., as 308 days. In the meantime, about 1 in 6 defendants who are free on bail is arrested for new crimes. Resources are so scarce throughout the system that up to 9 cases in 10, depending on the city, end in plea bargains that reduce the charges against criminals. Such procedures are necessary because courts and prosecutors are far too strapped for funds to provide a jury trial for every defendant. But that is no comfort to those who have been violated. A spate of tough sentencing laws has extended terms for many crimes, and prison rolls have more than doubled since 1980 to 630,000. Yet penal institutions are so overcrowded that only 1 case in 6 leads to a prison term, and space limits dictate that the average time in custody remains short, as inmates are freed early to make room for newcomers. Most "life" terms end before 10 years are spent behind bars. In Los Angeles County, where the jail population of 22,000 could fill a city, inmates serve one day for every 30 days stated in the sentence.

Many victims blame the gravest violations on juvenile courts. Created decades ago to provide special treatment for youths under 17, who presumably were not hardened criminals, the system has been intensely criticized for not responding to the increasingly vicious behavior of young criminals. A recent Justice Department report estimated that nearly half of juveniles picked up for violent offenses are put on probation or released outright. Even if a young criminal is imprisoned, the term generally cannot extend beyond age 17. Drug peddlers often use young teens to do their dirty work because they know they will not do serious jail time.

The result of these systemic failures is a sense of bitterness and frustration that can be felt across the nation:

- Jacob McGrogan, 48, a Pittsburgh bartender, was walking home in his working-class neighborhood last year when two young men offered him a ride. They promptly robbed him of $70, in the process beating him brutally with a baseball bat, blinding him permanently and wrecking his hearing. McGrogan was furious to learn that, at the time of the attack, one of the accused, Brian Wolfe, was at large after being released pending trial for an earlier assault. "If the system had worked right, he wouldn't have been out on the street and I wouldn't be blind," says McGrogan, who soon will enter a home for the disabled.
- In Queens, N.Y., John and Maureen Woods faced an ordeal after a teenager fatally stabbed their 16-year-old son David in the heart as the honor student tried to settle a quarrel. The couple complains that, without telling them, a prosecutor allowed the jury to choose between murder and manslaughter charges. The sentence could have run to 25 years, but the judge imposed a 4-to-12-year term that could lead to the killer's parole in four years. "He had more sympathy for the murderer than for us," says John Woods. His wife adds: "We have been victimized twice—by the killer and the system."
- Tamra Wimler's suffering began when Jerry Gallo, a former boyfriend, kidnapped her and forced her into an abandoned warehouse, where he raped her repeatedly and threatened to kill her. Wimler soon became prime witness in the case of *People v. Gallo.* First, the 27-year-old bank aide says, she was followed by "goons" everywhere she went. Then the defense accused her of stealing from Gallo's bank account. One day, she was "scared to death" when she learned that he might win release on bail and come after her. A judge delayed the case again and again when the defense pleaded for more time. "You can't recuperate," she says of the woes that did not end even after Gallo received a 35-year prison term, which he is appealing. "It's not like what happens on TV."

Not surprisingly, as such frustrations mounted, victims began to organize in their own defense. Fully 7,000 groups have sprung up to ease the inner pain and some of the financial difficulties of victims. And an increasingly potent movement has arisen to address what many see as imbalances in the way the law treats victims. In the past decade, reports the Washington-based National Organization for Victim Assistance, states have passed 1,500 laws aimed at giving victims broad new rights to participate in the cases against their assailants. Many states have toughened penalties for those who threaten victims, and have barred criminals from profiting when their stories are told in books and movies. Many changes were designed to help victims cope with the aftermath of attacks on them by providing counseling and some measure of financial relief for the losses they suffered.

Second-generation reforms

For all its success, the victims'-rights movement continues to face the indifference of many authorities to its demands. "Many officials believe that it is just too time-consuming and cumbersome to involve victims in such decisions as pretrial release and sentencing," says Jane Burnley, chief of the U.S. Office for Victims of Crime. One result is that most victims are unaware of their rights to participate. In 1982, Californians voted a constitutional amendment giving victims the right to address judges at their assailants' sentencing. Mostly because of ignorance, 97 percent failed to appear. Those who did speak in court had little effect on the sentencing outcome.

Undaunted, victim supporters are seeking a second generation of protections. They succeeded last year in Florida and Michigan, which enacted constitutional amendments that guarantee victims the right to take part in each stage of the justice process, from being notified of arraignments to being able to speak at parole hearings. "Our primary goal is not harsh punishments or money but to be involved," says Roberta Roper, who led a campaign to change Maryland laws after her daughter was murdered in 1982. At another level, many victims would like a chance to confront their assailants. Some states are experimenting with mediation sessions where victims and offenders talk out their differences, prodding assailants to acknowledge the damage they have wrought and in some cases easing the emotional trauma of the victim.

Restitution pays

Some promising reforms involve new sentencing schemes. "We need to create interim punishments that make convicts accountable without overstraining the corrections system," says James Stewart, chief of the Justice Department's research arm. One answer is restitution. More judges are ordering defendants to repay victims for losses, although the procedure still is underutilized. California plans to open "restitution centers," where selected inmates would live and hold down jobs in the community, paying one third of earnings to their victims and splitting the rest with the state. Victim advocates lobbied for the program, but it has been delayed by objections to convicts' living in residential neighborhoods.

States and localities also have fallen short with their own programs to provide for the financial losses suffered by crime victims. Their reimbursements do not come close to covering the more than $15 billion lost to crime annually. Payments to victims average less than $1,900. And limitations in some states make it impossible for any but the poor to qualify.

Victim advocates are laying more ambitious plans to overhaul the system. California prosecutors, police chiefs and Republican leaders are pushing for voter approval of a plan that would speed preliminary hearings, streamline jury selection and curb stalling tactics of defense lawyers. Reformers are less sanguine about retooling the juvenile system. Victims back transferring particularly violent cases to adult court, but the evidence is mixed on whether the tactic results in harsher penalties for chronic offenders.

If history is any guide, the needs of victims will be addressed only by fits and starts. Many hope the Supreme Court will get another conservative member and change in favor of victims. And taxpayers furious about rampaging drug use may even be willing to pay for the kind of prosecutorial and prison resources to keep the worst offenders behind bars longer and perhaps even provide more compensation for victims. But even if the scales begin to tip more toward them, victims will never get enough from the government to assuage the awful, unique violation each has endured. Some wounds never heal.

---

by Ted Gest with Pamela Ellis-Simons in Los Angeles, Scott Minerbrook in New York, Anne Moncreiff Arrarte in Miami and bureau reports

DEATH OF A BARD

A search for the meaning of a childhood friend's murder

THOMAS MOORE

Let me not die ingloriously and without struggle, but let me first do some great things that shall be told among men thereafter.
—Hector, in Homer's Iliad

No one could die like Frank. His favorite game when we were kids, playing in sand dunes behind his family's summer home in northern Michigan, was war. Frank, his younger brother Bill and I would spend long afternoons digging trenches in the sand, making forts and playing out epic battles with stick guns, painstakingly whittled and sandpapered to look like old flintlocks. A virtuoso of sound effects, he would animate the battle of the moment with a soundtrack of exploding howitzers and hacking machine guns, popping rifles and bullets ricocheting off rocks, pinging, ptooing and finally finding their mark, thudding into a body.

When he went down, which was often, the fall generally started in midair, as he was leaping over a sumac bush in a last-ditch surprise attack. His face would grimace with the imagined pain from the first bullet to his leg. Heroically, he'd squeeze off a couple more shots, nailing the last Nazis in the bunker. He'd take a few more bullets, to the chest, the arm, the neck, and, dropping his spent gun, flinging his arms and legs out and emitting a fatal "aahyeeeeh," he would crumple onto the sand. Only after some terminal flourishes sure to elicit laughter from his rapt audience of two would he expire.

His real death this year was violent but had none of the glory he had imagined. It snuck up on him in the middle of the night, when no one was watching. Frank Fuller Fowle III, 42, was murdered last January 19, stabbed in the heart in a motel parking lot in Georgia by a 23-year-old cocaine user who had asked him for a quarter. Frank was driving home to St. Louis at the time, and pulled off the interstate around midnight to get some sleep. There were two motels at the exit ramp; he picked the one where the man who would kill him waited.

He parked his car, a Mercedes 300E, outside Room 112 at the Days Inn on the edge of Forsyth, a small town 65 miles southeast of Atlanta, and took in some of his things. He dictated a few thoughts into his recorder, part of a daily chronicle of his travels and observations he kept for offspring and posterity. Frank took a sweeping view of his life. He was a bard, a latter-day Homer who traveled to schools around the country enacting scenes from Greek classics and, as he put it, "telling of the deeds of heroes." Still pumped up from a performance he had given that evening, he went back out to his car to get some books to read when a man approached him.

He fought his assailant

According to investigating officers, who obtained a confession from the alleged assailant after his capture the next morning, Frank retrieved a change purse from his car to get a quarter. The man, a construction worker from Forsyth named Darrell Bowden, apparently wasn't satisfied with small change from the owner of a Mercedes and attacked him with a knife. Frank did what some victims are advised not to do: He fought back. He grappled with the man against the car, and then down on the ground amid the spilled change. The assailant cut and stabbed him several times in the back, puncturing a lung. A witness behind a curtained window heard Frank cry out, ". . . But I'll give you what you want!"

Frank managed to break away and, bleeding profusely, adrenaline coursing through his body, he ran toward the motel office. If his assailant was looking for a chance to escape from an incident that had escalated beyond his control, this was it. For whatever reasons, he did not take that choice. Instead, according to authorities, he ran after Frank and stabbed him fatally in the chest. Frank fell to the pavement, rolled onto his back and died. The assailant took his wallet with $200 in it and ran off into the night.

Thus abruptly ended the life of one of my best childhood friends. He was an innocent victim of a random crime and, as his father put it, extraordinary bad luck. "There is no meaning in the act itself of Frank's death," the rabbi asserted sensibly at the funeral, trying to head off a troubled disposition of the grief-stricken to seek just such a meaning. I couldn't accept that at the time, and I don't accept it now. If nothing else, Frank's death marked the end of my own childhood.

In the months that followed, as I sorted out facts, speculations and jumbled feelings about Frank's death by talking with his family and other friends, I tried to make sense out of his senseless murder, to seek a connection between his existence and his death. Others shared this urge, wondering whether Frank had been predestined to be killed this way, whether he had asked for it, or whether God had just taken the way He gives, for reasons unrevealed to ordinary mortals. Shock, anger and grief overwhelmed all else at the funeral, but underneath, this disturbing insistence on meaning had already been born, resisting the seeming randomness of his death and leading each of us "survivors" to question what our own lives were really about.

He looked for adventure and romance

That his death stirred such questions would have made Frank smile, because that is what he tried to do in his life. He championed free will and the heroic ideal and would have argued that, as a philosophical matter, there is no such thing as an innocent victim, that we are not simple pawns of external circumstances, that we all shape in some way our own fate.

Frank was most certainly an innocent. He grew up in Winnetka, a wealthy Chicago suburb, the son of a corporate attorney and a corporate attorney's daughter. Suburban affluence tends to breed innocence in children, but Frank was innocent by nature. As a boy he was a charmer who regaled the family at dinner with mimicry of movie actors and teased his brother, sisters and mother to distraction. Much like Herman Melville's Billy Budd, a favorite character of his, he was a handsome, carefree sailor bobbing about on sunny seas, looking for adventure and romance and generally oblivious to the possibility of squalls or dangers beneath the surface.

As he grew up, his winning, childlike innocence seemed increasingly eccentric to people. In an odd, preposterous way, Frank never let go of the dreams, ideals and glory days of his youth, investing them with prodigious enthusiasm and transforming them into a lonesome crusade that eventually steered him off the interstate to that desolate parking lot.

Like other American boys, he wanted to be a hero, a doer of great deeds. Unlike most of us, however, the increasing gap between his dreams and troublesome realities hardened his conviction that he was destined for some great role, to lead a life that was noble. A landscape of malls and money, of career moves and family obligations proved dishearteningly ill-suited for noble deeds and heroic action. It did not beckon like the storied whaling towns of New England or the frontiers of the Wild West he read about as a child. And his romanticism set him up for disappointment. He journeyed up to Alaska one summer with another buddy, Giff, to seek his fortune on the fishing boats. He came back in debt and disillusioned with the less-than-noble natures of the commercial fishermen he worked with.

After college, the Vietnam War offered a promising opportunity for heroic experience, by either resisting it or fighting in it. But, a campus carouser and basically apolitical, he was oddly disconnected from the great events of the moment and did not have strong feelings about the war. He fell in love instead, got married and then joined the Navy, following in his father's footsteps. To Frank, The Navy was The Sea, the province of Joseph Conrad's sea sagas and Melville's Moby Dick. Few of his shipmates shared his romantic views, however, much less respected the hearty gusto with which he threw himself into his duties as an officer and a disciplinarian. Frank came to be regarded as something of an oddball, rushing up to the bow of the ship in storms to feel the sea heave and the salt water burn his face, imagining what Captain Ahab felt tied to the Great White Whale. Officers didn't do that.

When he was blamed for running a ship aground in San Diego, an accident for which a board of inquiry later exonerated him, he abandoned the Navy. He and his wife had a son but then divorced. He hawked encyclopedias, Fuller brushes and Charmin toilet paper; played guitar, sang songs and did comic routines in saloons, and completed law school. But law practice turned out to be tedious and did not hold him long.

He roamed from one great adventure to another

In the end, he simply conjured up a career to meet his grandiose expectations. He became a traveling bard, roaming at will from one great adventure of literature to another, dramatizing for students scenes from Homer's *Iliad,* Plato's *Republic,* Pericles' "Funeral Oration," Coleridge's "The Rime of the Ancient Mariner" and the Declaration of Independence. He also conducted discussions on how the heroic ideals embodied in these works related to people's lives today. "What nobler deed can I perform than to inspire others to noble deeds," he noted in his journal.

It was an improbable vocation, inspired by a set of the "Great Books of the Western World" that he bought for $125 at a flea market and read cover to cover, a Socratic law-school professor of jurisprudence and a Richard Burton recording of the "Ancient Mariner." He was so moved by the recording that he memorized the poem and persuaded a college group to let him perform it for a $15 fee. Soon he mastered Book 22 of the *Iliad,* the tale of Hector's death at the hands of fleet-footed Achilles, Frank's all-time hero, and took his show on the road to schools in St. Louis and Chicago.

His act took off fast after the *Wall Street Journal* featured him on the front page in 1981 under a skeptical headline, "Evangelical Lawyer Spans U.S. to Preach a Gospel of Homer; Frank Fowle, Alias The Bard, Is a One-Man 'Iliad' Show; Just Greek to Some Pupils." The more preposterous his career seemed to others, the more Frank fastened on it as his unique calling in life. "A true bard is an inspired performer" is how he described what he did for prospective schools. "He unites the soul of the poet with the soul of the audience. And since a bard tells of the deeds of heroes, the audience is united with greatness." At times, he believed that God spoke through him, that he was carrying out God's will. "I have strange power of speech," he wrote, invoking Coleridge's Mariner.

He was also seized by doubt, worried by practical considerations and fearful of distracting temptations. Each spring, he anguished over bookings. He imagined that various setbacks would make him lose heart. Before his second marriage, he worried that no one would marry him because of the constant travel and lack of financial stability. Once he found a woman who loved and accepted him, he worried that he couldn't be the husband and father he wanted to be for the same reasons.

Irene, his second wife, is Jewish, and after they married Frank converted to Judaism. He was an Episcopalian, and this leap of faith didn't set right with either family at first, particularly Irene's. Her father never accepted him. He thought Frank "a showman," she says. Others agreed. "My friends think I'm a little crazy," he wrote in his journal. But he had come to believe in what he was doing as an end in itself. "Dad was happiest performing," says Frank IV, 19.

Last year, Frank did 115 shows, bringing his total to nearly 1,000. He was on the road over 100 days. A lawyer who had given up work to rear their children, Irene did not like Frank's being away from home so much, and she worried about all the driving. Money was no longer a problem. She came from a wealthy family, and Frank's income was nearing six figures. He barely broke even when he first started barding in 1978, logging thousands of miles in a Honda Civic that he turned into his office, and a way of life. When one school couldn't pay him, he accepted two basketballs. But last year, he charged up to $1,500 a show.

He bought a Mercedes and later traded it in for a bigger

model, which he christened "Fleet Achilles." Frank was a bard, but deep down, maybe out on the interstate somewhere, pushing the Mercedes up over 100 on a moonlit night, it is easy to imagine that the spirit of the great runner Achilles stirred inside him. "Frank was out there, teasing the gods," says his sister Margaret, 45.

When someone close to you is murdered, you exhibit an obsessive curiosity about the details of the crime. Bill paced out his brother's final steps in the motel parking lot; it was something he had to do. Others speculated about whether Frank might have done anything to tilt the event. Should he have fought back or could he have talked the guy out of it? Or if he talked to him, did he prolong the exchange unnecessarily? One unavoidable speculation was that he sized up this midnight approach as a moment for the heroism he glorified.

He could not believe anyone would kill him

Frank had but a few seconds to influence what was happening to him. Whether he saw an opportunity to be the hero he told tales of or was simply trying to give the assailant what he wanted, the sad irony may be that his nature could not anticipate, would not allow, the idea that anyone would want to kill him for real. Or the truth may be that the very inspiration that made him seem innocent and out of place, an enthusiastic prophet of ancient virtues in a time of amorality and despair, led him to recognize evil and refuse to compromise with it.

If Frank's attempt to defend himself signifies his character and spirit, it does not change the fact that he was the victim of an assault, and does not suggest he shares blame for what happened. His assailant, awaiting trial for murder and a possible death sentence, will argue to the contrary. Bowden pleaded not guilty and declined to be interviewed for this article. He also escaped from jail on July 14 and was caught two hours later. His defense attorney, Harold Martin, claims that mutual combat occurred, making a case for voluntary manslaughter, not murder.

Assailants often justify their crimes by saying they were provoked, and defense attorneys try to discredit victims or raise doubt to lessen a charge or soften a sentence. The prosecutor in Forsyth, Dist. Atty. Tommy Floyd, says such a claim is unlikely to stand up: "In Georgia, you can't claim self-defense if you start a sequence of events with an armed robbery that leads to murder."

Frank dedicated his performances to the idea of justice and labored hard to define the concept. "What is the mark, the sign, the indication of injustice?" he wrote in a law quarterly essay entitled "Just Decisions." "The answer is pain, suffering, hurt, injury. . . . Many people would like to say healing or repairing the injury is the sign of justice. But wouldn't the parties have preferred it if no injury had occurred in the first place? Therefore, justice is a state or condition of no injury. A good word that describes an injury-free condition is healthy. Thus, I say that justice is health."

By his definition, no justice can atone for his murder. There can be no repair of the injury, no health. His family suffers enduring hurt. "I'm very proud of Frank," says Frank's father, 81. "And it makes me really good and sad that he's not around here any more." His oldest sister, Lisa, 47, plans to attend every day of the trial. "I can't get past the murder," she says. "Frank didn't die; he was killed. I want to be there to see justice done, or if it is not done, to know why." Another sister, Susan, Margaret's twin, wrote to public officials in Georgia and Congress, pleading that society redress the injustices that lead people to cocaine and murder. "Frank F. Fowle had a tremendous gift to give the world," she wrote. "Now we must live out the extent of our lives without him; we will never stop grieving, for we loved him dearly, our beloved dreamer who taught us to live our dreams."

BE SMART AND FOLLOW YOUR INSTINCTS

IF CRIME STRIKES YOU

A nervous-looking man with one hand in his pocket surprises you from behind as you head for your car and demands your wallet. What should you do? No handbook covers every situation, but the best course is to "follow your instincts, judging the robber and the environment," says Anne Seymour of the Texas-based National Victim Center. If the assailant is armed and you clearly are outmatched, resisting may be deadly. If you believe someone is within shouting distance, "scream your head off," Seymour says. Study the attacker's appearance so that you can testify about it later.

Every guideline for victims has exceptions. It often makes sense, for example, to offer your money to a robber in the hope you will not be injured. But if the assailant is bent on inflicting pain, "trying to reason with such a person may only egg him on," says Dean Kilpatrick of the Crime Victim Research and Treatment Center at the Medical University of South Carolina. "If you are convinced someone intends to kill you, you might as well scream and resist." The scary thing is that a victim has only a few seconds to size up the situation and decide on the best course of action to follow.

After the crime, victims should immediately report the incident to the police and seek medical attention, if necessary. Do not ignore psychological consequences. Kilpatrick reports that up to 1 in 3 crime victims suffers from posttraumatic-stress disorder, regardless of whether there was physical injury. The problem can usually be treated in up to a dozen sessions with mental-health professionals or social workers.

If you suffered losses that are not covered by insurance, you may be eligible for compensation in the 45 states that provide recompense for victims. Immediate aid may be available, but only if you can prove you are in dire straits. Otherwise, it may be anywhere from several months to a year or more before you receive payment, and it probably will fall short of your losses.

Because victim services vary widely among states, ask your police department or local prosecutor's office for information on whom you may consult for help and on your rights in dealing with the criminal-justice system, rights that are spelled out in 1,500 laws passed by state legislatures in recent years. Many law-enforcement organizations have special units that are assigned to help crime victims, but you may be forced to seek private help if public agencies in your area are not attuned to victims' needs. Two national groups monitor 7,000 public and private organizations that help crime victims of all kinds, including several hundred groups that offer support to relatives of murder victims. For a referral, write or call the National Organization for Victim Assistance, 717 D Street, N.W., Washington, D.C. 20004, (202) 393-6682, or the National Victim Center, P.O. Box 17209, Fort Worth, Tex. 76102, (817) 877-3355.

Frank's wife Irene, a 35-year-old mother of two young children, is a widow before her time. Her life, one day full of the happy wonder and domestic pulls of early motherhood, is now filled with sadness and anger. "I live in torture," she says. Her youngest child, Sam, 2, cannot comprehend what has happened. Sunny-natured and irrepressible like Frank, he often stares out the front door, looking for his father's car to drive up. Rachel, 3, understands her father won't be coming home any more but feels he can still see and hear her, that he is a star looking down from heaven. When she brings a painting home from preschool, she likes to take it outside in the early evening before she goes to bed and hold it up for her father to see, who sparkles down his approval. "I wish I could touch Daddy," she tells her mom.

"There's this feeling of unfinished business"

At his funeral, on a Sunday a few days after his murder, I watched Frank's coffin being lowered into the ground, stunned that the life of a man with such vigor could be stopped so suddenly, so prematurely and for so little cause. He was a man hitting his stride, and I had not had time to appreciate it. "There's Frank's death, but there's also the death of the relationship," says Lisa. "None of us got a chance to close. There's this feeling of unfinished business."

I remembered the last time I saw him, up in Michigan, leading my oldest boy and Bill's two young sons up to the sand dunes to learn the ritual of our summer afternoons of childhood. I followed and he drew me into the game. We chose up sides, planted flags to be defended and scrambled into the underbrush to hide. The kids giggled and ran about madly. And before long Frank did one of his dramatic deaths. That's the image that came to me at his graveside, Frank leaping headlong over the sumac, his teeth flashing white against the blue sky, the falling hero.

The Monday after the funeral, I went back to work as usual. Life went on callously as if nothing had happened, a lake swallowing a skipping stone that hit the water wrong. The emotional wounds had already started a mysterious and unstoppable healing, concentric ripples fading out into calm.

I pass, like night, from land to land / I have strange power of speech / That moment that his face I see, / I know the man that must hear me; / To him my tale I teach.

—*"The Rime of the Ancient Mariner"*

Victim-Offender Mediation: A Survey of Program Characteristics and Perceptions of Effectiveness

Stella P. Hughes and Anne L. Schneider

Stella P. Hughes: Associate Professor of Sociology in the Liberal Arts Department at South Dakota School of Mines and Technology. Anne L. Schneider: Professor and Head in the Department of Political Science at Oklahoma State University.

Funding for this research was supplied in part by a grant from the Office of Juvenile Justice and Delinquency Prevention, U.S. Department of Justice, #84-JS-AX-K045. The authors would like to thank Dr. Richard A. Dodder of Oklahoma State University for his helpful suggestions in preparing the final draft of this manuscript.

Victim-offender mediation as a dispositional alternative is a fairly recent addition to the juvenile justice system. The number of mediation programs has been increasing during the past decade, but little is evident about the design and implementation of these programs. This article reports findings from a survey of 240 juvenile justice organizations in the United States. Program designs, goals, and perceptions of effectiveness are discussed.

Criminal and juvenile justice systems in the United States have operated under the principle that crimes are committed against the state and that society, rather than the individual who actually suffered the loss or consequence, is the "victim" of delinquent acts. The offender may expunge the crime by "paying a debt to society," but this approach often leaves the one who has been wronged feeling resentful and deprived of any voice in the justice system (e.g., Schafer, 1976).

There have been efforts in recent years to supply some services to victims, and a major change in juvenile justice has been an emphasis on restitution as a part of treatment or sanction for offenders (Galaway and Hudson, 1981; McDonald, 1976; Schneider et al., 1981). Reports generally have been favorable, and in-depth studies of four juvenile programs found recidivism rates to be lower in those components using restitution as opposed to detention, counseling, or probation (Schneider, 1986).

A number of organizations, particularly those dealing with juveniles, have begun using mediation between victim and offender as a means of reconciliation and of determining amount and type of restitution. When designing new programs such as these, the usual strategy is to copy models that have been used by others (Brewer and deLeon, 1983; Schneider and Ingram, 1988). Little is known, however, about the actual use of mediation in juvenile courts, and information is lacking on the prevalence of such programs, how they are organized, and whether they are considered effective. Quite often, then, important policy decisions have been made about how programs should be designed or implemented without any real knowledge of available alternatives.

In order to assist program personnel in policy design and to attempt to fill some of the gaps in understanding how mediation is used in the juvenile court system, a nationwide survey was undertaken to locate and examine mediation programs. This article presents findings from the survey. The purposes of the article are (1) to describe what is happening with mediation across the country in terms of program characteristics; (2) to examine perceptions of the effectiveness of mediation and compare perceived effectiveness of this dispositional alternative with that of restitution, probation, and incarceration; (3) to report reasons for not using mediation; and (4) to describe program differences between larger and smaller counties, older and newer programs, and programs handling larger or smaller numbers of cases.

The first mediation organization to receive widespread recognition was the Victim Offender Reconciliation Program (VORP) instigated in Canada during the mid-1970s (Umbreit, 1985). The purpose of the original VORP project was to provide an alternative method of dealing with crime, to allow victim and offender an opportunity to reconcile and mutually agree on restitution, to use a third party to mediate and facilitate reconciliation, and to deal with crime as a conflict to be resolved (McKnight, 1981).

A few surveys have identified some organizations that provide mediation. Umbreit (1986) located 32 such programs; the Prisoners and Community Together (PACT) Institute of Justice in Valparaiso, Indiana, published a directory of 47 mediation programs in 17 states (Gehm, 1986); and a restitution directory cited 67 jurisdictions with mediation components (Warner and Burke, 1987).

Some comprehensive studies of individual programs have also added to the available information. In a survey of 14 project leaders across the United States and Canada, Wright (1985) explored perceptions of difficulties associated with mediation and identified two primary areas of concern: a need to set priorities among goals and lack of research or monitoring to determine program success. Coates and Gehm (1985) conducted an in-depth examination of juvenile and adult VORP programs in six Indiana and Ohio counties and found that both offenders and victims expressed a fairly high level of satisfaction with the process, although offenders appeared more satisfied than victims. The authors concluded that the concept has considerable potential as an alternative sanction.

Dittenhoffer and Erickson (1983), in assessing two Canadian VORPs, found that judges and prosecutors were not particularly interested in either alternatives to incarceration or reconciliation of victim and offender, thus diluting some of the project objectives, and they concluded that VORP was only partially obtaining its goals.

SAMPLING PROCEDURE

Since victim-offender mediation is almost always utilized in conjunction with restitution or community service programs, the *Juvenile Restitution Program Profiles and Directory* (Warner and Burke, 1987) was used as a primary sampling source. This directory was compiled from a survey of all U.S. cities of over 100,000 population and a sample of cities under 100,000. Questionnaires were mailed to all programs listed in the restitution directory as having a victim-offender mediation component and to all mediation programs in the VORP directory (Gehm, 1986). From the above sources, 171 programs reportedly using mediation were identified and included in the sample along with a random selection of a similar number of programs from the restitution directory that did not indicate a mediation component. Responses were received from representatives of 240 organizations (a return rate of over 70%), with 79 indicating a victim-offender component.

The project was designed to capture the diversity of program representation across the country rather than variation in opinions about a given organization; therefore, only one questionnaire was sent to each jurisdiction with the request that it be completed by the person most knowledgeable about the mediation or restitution program. Responses came from all but three states in the continental United States (New Mexico, North Dakota, and West Virginia), and those with mediation programs represented 31 states. Returned questionnaires were almost evenly distributed between those thought to use mediation and the comparison group; however, a number of respondents in the "mediation" group indicated that they had no such program. A possible reason for this is that an earlier, positive answer to the original restitution survey was reconsidered when confronted with definitive program statements.

Questionnaires were completed by individuals representing a variety of organizations and occupations. Some respondents were directly involved with mediation programs; others worked with larger organizations such as the court, probation and parole, or restitution. Those in administrative positions (program directors, coordinators, supervisors, and so on) made up about 61% of the total; the remainder were parole officers, social workers, caseworkers, court intake personnel, counselors, and court judges.

Mediation programs were found in counties with populations ranging from as small as 3,000 to over two million. Around 25% were in counties of under 50,000 inhabitants, and another 25% in areas of over 400,000. The median size of the counties in which programs were located was approximately 140,000. The oldest program began in 1965 and five programs were less than six months old. Almost 18% were started between 1965 and 1979, approximately 44% between 1980 and 1984, and around 39% between 1985 and 1987. Most mediation programs were rather small with 25% handling fewer than ten mediation cases during 1986 and over half reporting fewer than 50 cases. However, some rather large programs were found, as 21% reported handling over 200 cases. Most of the programs surveyed were part of the juvenile justice system; therefore, unless otherwise noted, responses reflect data pertaining to juveniles only.

A 1987 survey of randomly selected counties in the United States revealed that approximately 20% of cities with populations of 10,000 to 100,000 and 45% of cities with over 100,000 inhabitants had formal restitution programs (Schneider and Warner, 1987). Based on responses to the current survey, it is estimated that approximately 5.2% of restitution programs in cities of 10,000 to 100,000 population and 11.7% of those in cities of over 100,000 contain a mediation component.

CHARACTERISTICS OF PROGRAMS

Seven major organizational dimensions or program characteristics were examined: (1) program purposes and goals, (2) target population, (3) program organization/administration, (4) characteristics of mediators and mediation, (5) characteristics of the final contract, (6) support for the mediation program, and (7) role of evaluation.

Purposes and Goals

All respondents were asked to rate the importance of seven possible goals of mediation and mark them on a ten-point scale ranging from "Not at all important" to "Very important" with the midpoint of "5" being the neutral position. Holding the offender accountable was considered to be the most important mediation goal (an average score of 9.5). One respondent commented, "being accountable in and of itself is a value whether or not the person later commits another criminal act." The next most important goals were providing restitution (8.8), making the victim whole (8.2), reconciling victim and offender (7.9), rehabilitating the offender (7.5), and providing an alternative to institutionalization (6.3). These scores were all above the neutral position and thus represented goals that were considered important. Punishing the offender, with a score of 3.8, was rated as relatively unimportant.

Target Population

Although in some mediation programs there were no restrictions on the types of cases considered appropriate, in most (80%) some kinds of offenders or offenses were excluded. Violent offenses or offenders were mentioned most often; but in some programs sex offenders, chronic offenders, those with drug, alcohol, or mental health problems, and the retarded were excluded. Others excluded offenders considered to be sociopathic, cases of child abuse, offenders showing no remorse or denying involvement, and overly angry victims. A few respondents reported mediating only minor misdemeanors or property offenses while others set a monetary limit on the amount of damage or loss. One respondent said the agency took "whomever the court orders into the program."

Program Organization/Administration

Some programs were stand-alone mediation units; however, most were components of larger organizations. Administratively, programs were primarily governed by private, nonprofit organizations (43%), but some were under the direction of probation departments (21%), state or county agencies (17%), the court (7%), or other miscellaneous groups. In total, 27 respondents reported programs that were modeled directly after the VORP

TABLE 1: Sources of Program Funding

Funding Source	*Total Amount*	*Average N = 30*	*% of Total*
Gov't Grants	1,044,549	30,722	84
Religious Org.	85,314	7,110	7
Community	60,302	7,538	5
Foundations	54,663	9,110	4
Total	1,244,828	20,747	100

TABLE 2: Program Organization

	Average Score N = 79		*Average Score N = 79*
Frequency of Referrals to Program		Frequency of Occurrence	
Probation	5.6	More than one session held	1.6
Court	5.6	Parties do not agree on contract	1.8
Police	2.1	Judge overrules contract	0.6
Schools	0.8	Contract too easy	1.4
Frequency of Inclusion in Contract		Contract too difficult	1.7
		Victim lies about offense	2.0
Monetary restitution	6.9	Victim overly concerned with punishment	2.4
Work for community	4.5		
Both monetary & community	4.2	Parents attend mediation session	6.9
Behavioral requirements	3.8		
Work for victim	2.3	Attorney attends mediation session	1.2
No activities	1.0		
		Level of Satisfaction	
		Victim with agreement	8.2
		Offender with agreement	7.7
		Victim with outcome	7.6

The following scales were used to answer frequency and satisfaction questions.

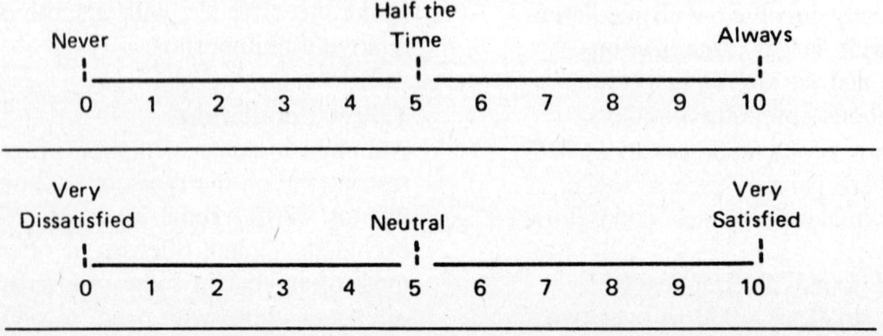

concept and others showed elements of VORP influence. Most programs (77%) were governed by written policies or procedures.

Information was elicited concerning source and amount of financial support for mediation programs during the previous year. Less than half of respondents (38%) supplied a monetary amount, but those that did accounted for well over $1,000,000 in funding (see Table 1). Financial support ranged from private donations to federal grants, but government funding (local, state, and federal) appeared to be the major source of income for most programs. Also mentioned were religious organizations, local businesses or community groups, and foundations or trust funds. Many programs were funded by more than one agency or group.

Respondents were asked how often clients were referred to their program by the court, the police, intake officials, or school systems. As Table 2 indicates, referrals tended to come either from the court or from probation/intake officials, with police and school referrals being relatively infrequent. Also mentioned by some respondents were attorneys, clergy, the victim, and individuals in the community.

Characteristics of Mediators and Mediation

Program staff alone were used as mediators in 55% of programs. In another 37% a combination of staff and volunteers were used, and in the remaining 8%, only volunteers served as mediators. A wide variation in the number of mediators was also reported. Respondents from 13 programs (17%) indicated having only one mediator and 25 (32%) claimed fewer than three. At the other extreme, in six programs (8%) 50 or more mediators were used, and one respondent reported over 100. The median number was 5.

Mediator training was conducted by program staff in the majority of programs (59%), but outside professionals were used in some (19%), and volunteers who had been mediators (3%) or probation department staff (3%) were used in others. A number of respondents reported a combination of training sources (13%), and a few reported that their programs required no mediator training at all (4%). One of these said that mediation was done by "trial and error," and another that training was "on the job." At the other extreme, two respondents reported offering 80 hours of training. The median amount of training time was 20 hours with 9 hours of follow-up or in-service training.

In only a few programs (15%) were mediators required to be certified, but a number of other qualifications were mentioned. Some respondents cited educational or professional requirements (a college degree or being a probation officer); others mentioned a certain score on a written exam or experience in working with youth, and a number listed such attributes as good listening skills, commitment to the mediation philosophy, and patience.

Mediation sessions varied in length from ten minutes to two hours, although most lasted about an hour. In most cases there was only one mediation session per case, but four respondents indicated that in at least half the cases, more than one session was held.

Characteristics of the Final Contract

Respondents were asked to estimate how often a number of components or requirements were included in their mediation contract (see Table 2). Most often cited was a contract that included monetary restitution to the victim. Less frequently mentioned were community service, a combination of monetary restitution and community service, and behavioral requirements of the offender (e.g., school attendance, counseling, or achieving minimum school grades). Working for the victim was not a common practice, perhaps, as one respondent indicated, because of concerns for liability.

Contracts requiring no activities on the part of the offender were mentioned by only 37% of respondents, but in two programs this approach was used more than half the time. Other respondents added that they occasionally required return or replacement of lost property, participation in workshops, charitable contributions, or an apology.

The parties involved usually agreed on the final contract and the judge rarely overruled the decision (Table 2). One respondent, however indicated that the judge overruled about half the time and three reported that the contract was "court ordered," or "the court officer makes this decision," an apparent contradiction of some of the basic concepts of victim-offender mediation. Most respondents felt that the contract was neither too easy nor too difficult for the offender, nor did they believe that the victim often lied about the offense or was overly concerned with punishment. Parents frequently attended mediation sessions, but attorneys rarely did so. Both victim and offender were generally seen as satisfied with the agreement, although the offender appeared somewhat less satisfied. The victim reportedly was usually satisfied with the outcome of the contract.

In almost all programs (91%) the contract was monitored to make sure that the offender completed all requirements. As a general rule, this was done either by program staff (35%) or probation department staff (33%). In some cases monitoring was done by a combination of personnel (25%), and in a few programs (6%) the mediator did all of the contract monitoring.

Support for the Mediation Program

Information was elicited concerning the amount of support received from organizational sources in the juvenile justice system, from various local and community groups, and from families of offenders. Also included were questions concerning the importance of this support (questionnaire items were derived from Severy et al., 1982).

Support of juvenile court judges was considered to be the most important (see Table 3), followed by support of parents or other family members, state juvenile service providers, city/county commissioners, public defenders, alternative juvenile program providers, law enforcement officials, prosecutors, local service organizations, and state legislators.

The amount of support received from each of the above generally followed the same pattern, although *importance* of support from juvenile court judges, family, and commissioners was rated somewhat higher than *actual* support. Alternative service providers and service

TABLE 3: Mean Scores on Importance of Program Support, Actual Support

Support Area	*Importance of Support N = 79*	*Actual Support N = 79*
Juvenile court judges	9.4	8.6
Parents or other family	8.4	7.8
State juvenile service providers	7.4	7.5
City/county commissioners	7.3	6.9
Public defenders	7.2	7.2
Alternative juvenile program providers	7.1	7.6
Law enforcement officials	6.9	6.8
State attorneys	6.7	6.8
Local service organizations	6.3	6.8
State legislators	6.0	6.2

The following scales were used to answer support questions.

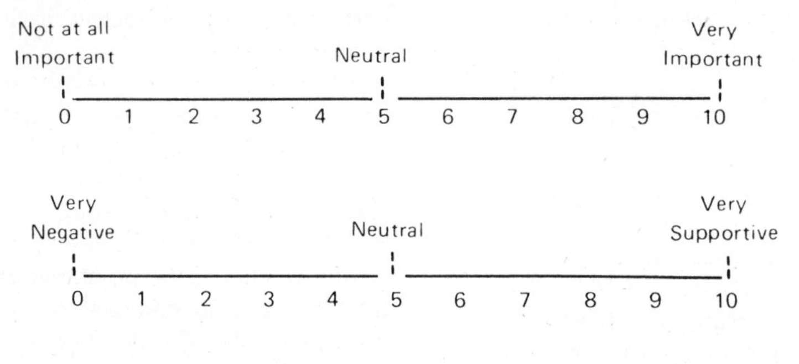

organizations, on the other hand, were rated somewhat lower in importance than in actual support. Overall, juvenile court judges were seen as providing the most support.

Most program personnel (64%) received no assistance from community groups in the form of volunteer mediators, funding, staff, or training. Those that did receive such assistance most often were provided funding (in 18 programs) or volunteer mediators (in 16 programs). Three respondents reported that the community supplied mediation training, and another three used staff from community organizations. Some also received such assistance as office space in local churches, clerical help from senior citizens, publicity, and so on.

Role of Evaluation

Respondents were asked if an evaluation of program effectiveness had been conducted during the past five years. Less than half (41%) indicated that an evaluation had been done. Among those responding affirmatively, evaluations were most often done every year (61%); the remainder were conducted on an irregular basis. Many programs, however, were fairly new, and several respondents commented that their program had not been in existence long enough to warrant assessment. Evaluations were usually conducted by internal staff (57%), although some were done by outside evaluators (30%), and a few by a combination of both (13%). Outside evaluators tended to be personnel from universities, private institutions, VORP/PACT agencies, or private consultants. Respondents appeared generally satisfied with the evaluations and gave them a mean score of 7.2 on the 10-point satisfaction scale.

MEDIATION EFFECTIVENESS

Respondents representing mediation programs were asked for perceptions of the effectiveness of the program in their jurisdiction, and information was elicited from all respondents concerning the effectiveness of mediation in general. In addition, the effectiveness of mediation was compared with that of the dispositional alternatives of probation, incarceration, and restitution.

Perceptions of Program Effectiveness

Mediation in general received an average score of 8.4 on the 10-point effectiveness scale whereas individual programs scored 7.9. There was also a high level of satisfaction with individual program components. Respondents believed that in their program victim interests had been served (a score of 8.5), that offender interests had been served (8.4), and that mediators had done a good job (8.5). One respondent, however, commented, "potential is great but funding is needed."

Comparisons of Dispositional Alternatives

In comparing the four dispositional alternatives, respondents were uniformly positive about the effectiveness of mediation and indicated more confidence in both mediation and restitution than in the more traditional

TABLE 4: **Average Scores for Effectiveness of Dispositional Alternatives**

	Mediation *N = 240*	*Restitution* *N = 240*	*Probation* *N = 240*	*Incarceration* *N = 240*
Reduces Recidivism				
Total	7.2	6.9	5.2	3.8
Administrators	7.5	6.9	4.9	3.5
Staff	6.5	7.0	5.9	4.3
Rehabilitates Offender				
Total	7.2	7.3	5.6	2.9
Administrators	7.4	7.4	5.1	2.4
Staff	6.8	7.0	6.7	4.0
Victims Are Satisfied				
Total	8.6	8.8	5.1	6.4
Administrators	8.8	8.7	4.6	5.9
Staff	8.1	9.0	6.1	7.6
Offenders Held Accountable				
Total	8.4	8.7	5.7	5.5
Administrators	8.6	8.7	5.1	5.2
Staff	7.9	8.5	7.1	6.3
Fair to Offender				
Total	8.5	8.8	6.4	4.5
Administrators	8.9	9.0	5.9	4.1
Staff	7.8	8.0	7.4	5.2
Fair to Victim				
Total	8.6	9.1	5.2	4.5
Administrators	8.8	9.3	4.9	4.2
Staff	8.0	8.6	5.9	5.0

The following scale was used to answer agreement questions.

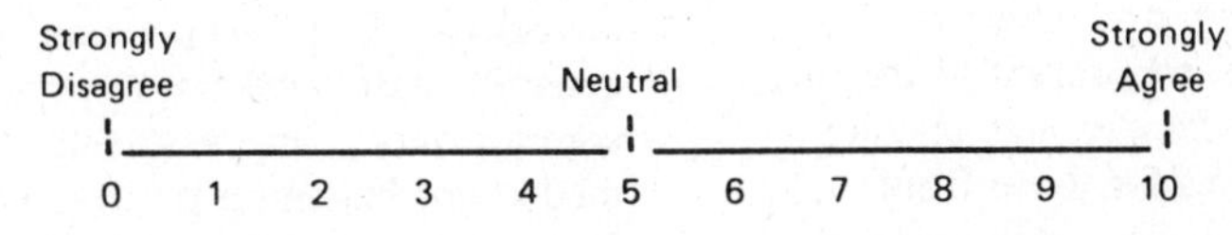

dispositions of incarceration and probation (see Table 4). Although this would be expected since program personnel may be biased toward their own programs, it also indicates that mediation and restitution are viewed as viable alternatives by those who know the most about them. As a whole, probation was seen as being more effective than incarceration.

A number of occupational differences were also apparent. Those holding administrative positions gave somewhat higher scores to the effectiveness of mediation, and to a lesser extent to restitution, than did staff members. Staff members, on the other hand, tended to view the effectiveness of the other dispositional alternatives (incarceration and probation) more favorably than did administrators. It is possible that the administrative group exhibited more enthusiasm because their jobs are more visionary in nature, while those working more closely with victims and offenders are faced with a less-than-ideal reality.

RESTITUTION WITHOUT MEDIATION

Respondents representing jurisdictions without mediation were asked some questions concerning the reasons why such a program had not been implemented. The primary reason was lack of resources (staff and funding), although some indicated that the concept had not been discussed or knowledge about such programs was lacking. Rejected as reasons were lack of need, opposition to such a program, and the philosophical issues of mediation not protecting the interests of victims and offender and the inability of victim and offender to reach a good understanding. The idea that the victim should not be required to confront the offender, however, received minimal support.

The question might be asked as to whether respondents without mediation components might have had different perceptions of the effectiveness of this alternative when compared with representatives of restitution programs that utilized mediation. The current research data tend to support this contention, as respondents from programs without mediation indicated significantly lower mean scores on all of the questions relating to mediation effectiveness than did those from programs utilizing mediation. Perhaps this is because individuals become more favorable toward mediation as a result of gaining experience in working with the concept; or perhaps it is because those who are more favorably disposed toward mediation are more likely to develop such programs. In either case, there is no evidence that people who do not work with mediation programs have an overblown view of their possible effectiveness; on the contrary, they may underestimate it.

PROGRAM DIFFERENCES

In spite of differences in program age, in number of cases mediated, or in size of county population, the programs surveyed were found to be quite similar in structure, and very few significant differences were noted among programs from various sized counties, in older or younger programs, or programs of different sizes. In general, larger counties had larger programs, that is, they mediated more cases; both older programs and those that had been in operation longer tended to be larger; and there appeared to be a slight trend for the development of new programs in the smaller counties. More differences were apparent between older and newer programs, particularly those developed before 1980, than with either county size or size of program.

For the most part, the same goals were stressed, regardless of population size or program size and age. Exceptions were that in the newer programs, those started from 1980 on, respondents gave more importance to the goals of reconciling the victim and offender and making the victim whole; and there was a trend for those from the smaller counties to give more emphasis to the goals of rehabilitating the offender and providing restitution.

There was a trend for newer programs to be administered more often by private/nonprofit organizations and less often by the court, and newer programs reportedly had a greater inclination to use written policies and procedures and to employ training manuals for conducting mediation training. In the largest programs, it was more likely that an evaluation of program effectiveness had been conducted and that mediation was used as an alternative to probation. Referrals cam primarily from the same sources; however, larger programs, older programs, and programs from larger counties tended to receive more referrals from police and from the schools.

Mediation contracts that called for the offender to work for the victim were used less often as programs became larger, and this was also true with the use of monetary restitution. Respondents from the largest programs were somewhat more inclined to report the use of behavioral requirements on the part of the offender, and those from both smaller and newer programs were more apt to indicate the use of contracts having no requirements or activities at all.

Respondents from the largest counties reported receiving less support from juvenile court judges and from state juvenile service providers than did those from smaller counties. On the other hand, those with programs in the larger counties considered the support of juvenile court judges to be less important than did individuals in smaller areas. Respondents from programs mediating larger numbers of cases also indicated that they received more support from state legislators. Individuals from older programs considered the support of alternative juvenile program providers to be more important than did those from newer programs, but those from older programs also rated state juvenile service providers as somewhat less important.

SUMMARY AND CONCLUSIONS

As a whole, mediation programs appeared to be fairly widespread and functioning well. In administration, they were most often governed by private/nonprofit organizations and received referrals primarily from the court or probation/intake officials. The majority of mediators were paid program staff, and mediator training was almost always utilized. The final contract usually involved monetary restitution to the victim, and in most cases, this was monitored. Mediation programs generally were supported by the community and those working with juveniles, and financial support came largely from local, state, and federal grants or allocations. Program evaluation was not commonly used.

The concept and philosophy of victim-offender mediation was viewed favorably by both those with programs and those without, and program respondents considered their components to be highly successful. In general, staff workers were less optimistic than program administrators in assessing the effectiveness of mediation, but more positive concerning the effects of incarceration and probation.

These data give a more comprehensive picture of victim-offender mediation than has been available in the past, but information is still far from complete. A more in-depth study of selected organizations that differ in such things as administration, source of funding, target population, or mediator training could be of interest and add to the knowledge that is being accumulated about effective mediation. Additional data could be gathered on such items as characteristics of both offenders and victims referred, the proportion of victims participating, reasons for nonparticipation on the part of both victims and offenders, and a more comprehensive assessment of the kinds of crimes and offenders accepted.

REFERENCES

Brewer, Garry D. and Peter deLeon. 1983. *The Foundations of Policy Analysis.* Homewood, IL: Dorsey.

Coates, Robert B. and John Gehm. 1985. *Victim Meets Offender: An Evaluation of Victim-Offender Reconciliation Programs.* Valparaiso, IN: PACT Institute of Justice, PACT Inc.

Dittenhoffer, Tony and Richard V. Erickson. 1983. "The Victim/Offender Reconciliation Program: A Message to Correctional Reformers," *University of Toronto Law Journal* 33:315–347.

Galaway, Bert and Joe Hudson, eds. 1981. *Perspectives on Crime Victims.* St. Louis: C. V. Mosby.

Gehm, John, ed. 1986. *National VORP Directory: A Directory of Programs Offering Victim-Offender Reconciliation and Mediation Services,* 2nd ed. Valparaiso, IN: National Victim-Offender Reconciliation Resource Center, PACT Institute of Justice, PACT, Inc.

McDonald, William F. 1976. "Criminal Justice and the Victim: An Introduction." Pp. 17–55 in *Criminal Justice and the Victim,* edited by W. F. McDonald. Beverly Hills, CA: Sage.

McKnight, Dorothy. 1981. "The Victim-Offender Reconciliation Project." Pp. 292–299 in *Perspectives on Crime Victims,* edited by B. Galaway and J. Hudson. St. Louis: C. V. Mosby.

Schafer, Sheldon. 1976. "The Victim and Correctional Theory: Integrating Victim Reparation with Offender Rehabilitation." Pp. 227–236 in *Criminal Justice and the Victim,* edited by W. F. McDonald. Beverly Hills, CA: Sage.

Schneider, Anne L. 1986. "Restitution and Recidivism Rates of Juvenile Offenders: Results from Four Experimental Studies." *Criminology* 24:533–552.

______ and Helen Ingram. 1988. "Systematically 'Pinching' Ideas: An Analytical Approach to Policy Design." *Journal of Public Policy.*

Schneider, Anne Larason and Jean Shumway Warner. 1987. "The Role of Restitution in Juvenile Justice Systems." *Yale Law and Policy Review* 2:382–401.

Schneider, Peter R., Anne L. Schneider, Paul D. Reiter, and Colleen M. Cleary. 1981. "Restitution Requirements for Juvenile Offenders: A Survey of the Practices in American Juvenile Courts." Hearing before the Subcommittee on Human Resources of the Committee on Education and Labor, House of Representatives, Ninety-Seventh Congress, Washington, D. C.

Severy, Lawrence J., Pauline Houlden, Gregory H. Wilmoth, and Starr Silver. 1982. "Community Receptivity to Juvenile Justice Program Planning." *Evaluation Review* 6:25–46.

Umbreit, Mark. 1985. *Victim Offender Mediation: Conflict Resolution and Restitution.* Valparaiso, IN: PACT Institute of Justice, PACT, Inc.

______ 1986. "Victim Offender Mediation and Judicial Leadership." *Judicature* 69:202–204.

Warner, Jean S. and Vincent Burke, eds. 1987. *Juvenile Restitution Program Profiles and Directory (Pre-Publication Edition).* Stillwater, OK: Office of Juvenile Justice and Delinquency Prevention, U.S. Department of Justice. Policy Sciences Group, Oklahoma State University.

Wright, Martin. 1985. "The Impact of Victim/Offender Mediation on the Victim." *Victimology: An International Journal* 10:631–644.

Police

Police officers are the guardians of our freedoms under the Constitution and the law, and as such they have an awesome task. They are asked to prevent crime, to protect citizens, to arrest wrongdoers, to preserve the peace, to aid the sick, to control juveniles, to control traffic, and to provide emergency services on a moment's notice. They are also asked to be ready to lay down their lives, if necessary. In recent years the job of the police officer has become even more complex and dangerous; illegal drug use and trafficking is at epidemic levels, racial tensions are explosive, and violent crime continues to increase at alarming rates.

"Police Response to Crime" details some of the duties of the police and presents statistics on how well they are fulfilling their duties. It also looks at the roles of other public agencies, as well as private security, in crime and protection.

The United States police system is not all that complex, but it is vast and involves more than 20,000 separate and distinct law enforcement agencies that employ more than half a million people. The diverse role of policing is illustrated in "The Police in the United States."

As a reflection of today's need for a sophisticated police system, education has become of increasing importance. Police departments are demanding college-educated officers in their recruiting drives. The article "The State of Police Education: Critical Findings" assesses the increasing role education plays in the career of an officer.

Traditionally policing was a male-dominated career. The 1972 amendments to the Civil Rights Act caused significant progress in eliminating discrimination in the hiring and promotion of women. There is still much to be done to reach total equality, and the article "Women On the Move? A Report on the Status of Women in Policing" examines the current state of women's role in police work.

The concept of "community-based policing" is discussed in "Making Neighborhoods Safe." "Confronting Police Corruption: Organizational Initiatives for Internal Control" details the specifics for implementing anti-corruption programs within police agencies, while "Civilian Review Boards: A Means to Police Accountability" discusses the pros and cons of outside review of the police.

Racial tension within the police ranks is the focus of "Police Officers Tell of Strains of Living as a 'Black in Blue.' " In an effort to reduce the stress that discrimination can cause, most police departments are now stressing sensitivity to racial issues in their training programs.

Private security has become a major form of "policing" in the United States. "From Private Security to Loss Control: What Does the Future Hold?" discusses several areas of concern that the industry must deal with in the next decade.

Looking Ahead: Challenge Questions

Is a college education a valid requirement for being a police officer?

Have women reached their full potential as police officers?

Should the police be involved in community problems not directly concerned with crime?

Unit 3

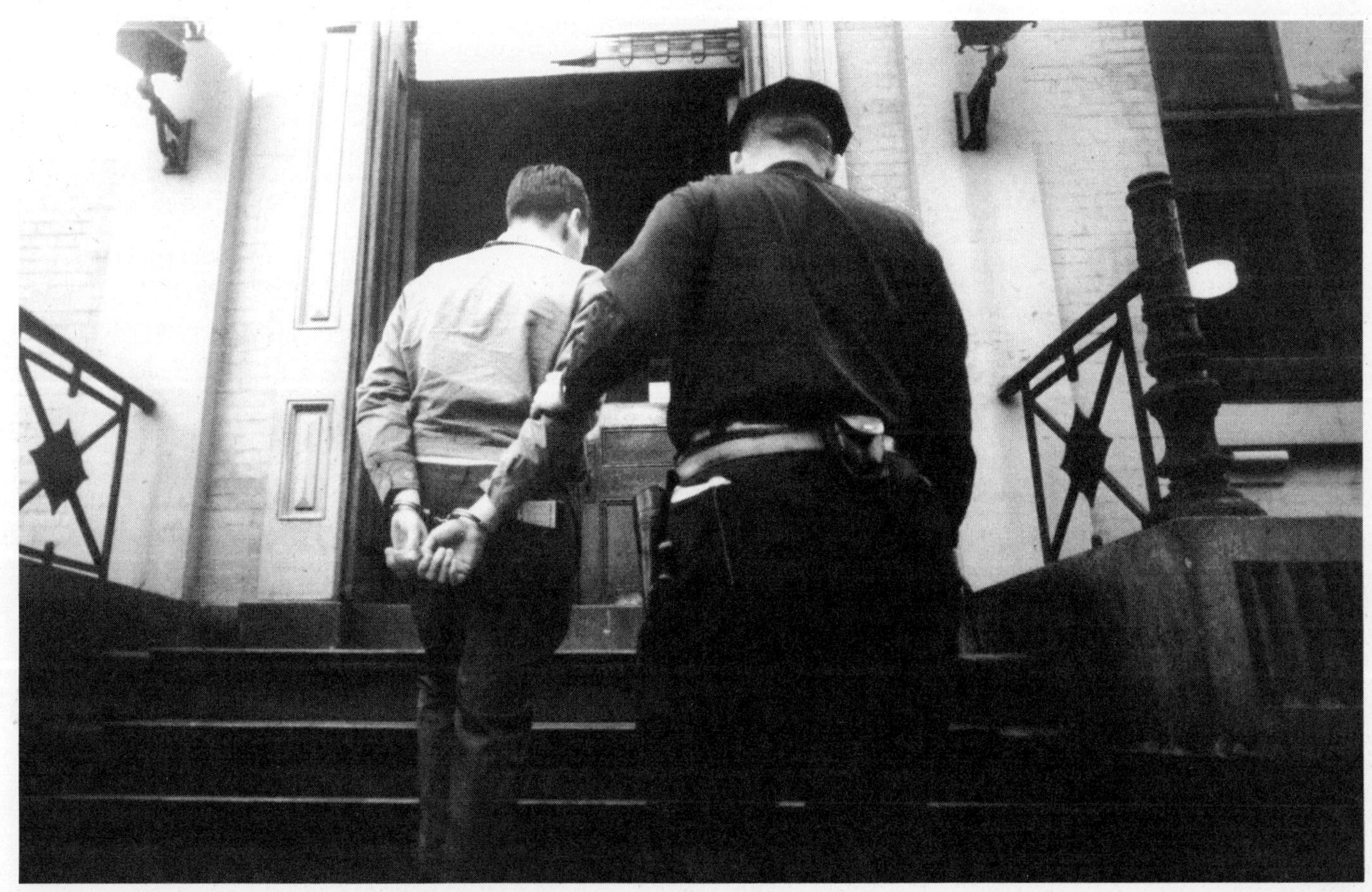

Police Response to Crime

The system responds directly to a fraction of crime

Most crime is not reported to police

As noted in chapter II, only about a third of all crimes are reported to police. The crimes most likely to be reported are those most serious in terms of injury and economic loss.

The criminal justice system responds to crimes brought to its attention by reports from citizens or through direct observation by law enforcement officers. Crimes are reported most often by the victim or a member of the victimized household. Police discover 3% of reported personal crimes and 2% of reported household crimes.

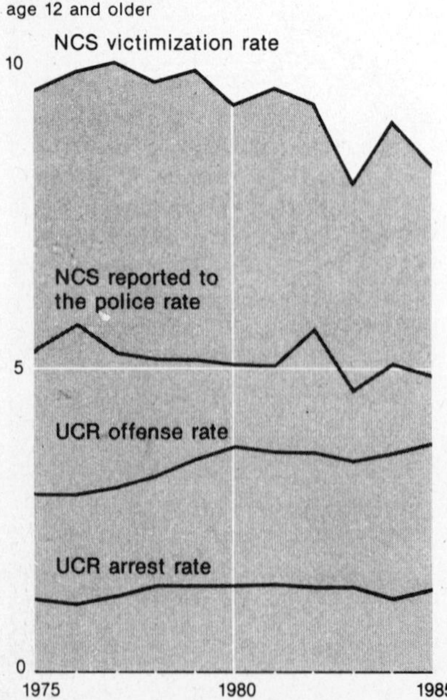

Most reported crimes are not solved by arrest. For that reason the proportion of crimes handled directly by the criminal justice system through the processing of suspects is relatively small. Indirectly, the criminal justice system may be dealing with more crime than appears from arrest data because the offenders who are processed may have committed much more crime than that for which they are arrested (see chapter III).

Fallout for the crime of aggravated assault is shown in this chart:

The first contact with the criminal justice system for most citizens is the police dispatcher

In many cities citizens can report crimes through a universal number, such as 911. In other cities the citizen must call the police directly. The dispatcher will ask for facts about the crime, such as what happened, where, when, whether or not it involved injury or loss. This information helps the police to select the most appropriate response.

Law enforcement is one of several police roles

The roles of police officers are—
- **Law enforcement**—applying legal sanctions (usually arrest) to behavior that violates a legal standard.
- **Order maintenance**—taking steps to control events and circumstances that disturb or threaten to disturb the peace. For example, a police officer may be called on to mediate a family dispute, to disperse an unruly crowd, or to quiet an overly boisterous party.
- **Information gathering**—asking routine questions at a crime scene, inspecting victimized premises, and filling out forms needed to register criminal complaints.
- **Service-related duties**—a broad range of activities, such as assisting injured persons, animal control, or fire calls.

Wilson's analysis of citizen complaints radioed to police on patrol showed that—
- 10% required enforcement of the law
- more than 30% of the calls were appeals to maintain order
- 22% were for information gathering
- 38% were service-related duties.

Most crime is not susceptible to a rapid police response

A study by the Police Executive Research Forum suggests that police response time is important in securing arrests only when they are called while the crime is in progress or within a few seconds after the crime was committed. Otherwise, the offender has plenty of time to escape.

In a study of response time in Kansas City, only about 6% of the callers reported crimes in progress. Where discovery crimes are involved (those noticed after the crime has been completed), few arrests may result even if citizen reporting immediately follows discovery; by this time the offender may be safely away. If a suspect is arrested, the length of delay between the offense and arrest may crucially affect the government's ability to prosecute the suspect successfully because of the availability of evidence and witnesses.

From *Report to the Nation on Crime and Justice,* Bureau of Justice Statistics, U.S. Department of Justice, March 1988, pp. 62-63, 66.

A variety of public agencies provide protection from crime

Today, police officers do not always respond to calls for service

Based on research and the desire for improved efficiency, many police departments now use a number of response alternatives to calls for service. The type of alternative depends on a number of factors such as whether the incident is in progress, has just occurred, or occurred some time ago and whether anyone is or could be injured. Police officers may be sent, but the call for service may also be responded to by—

- **Telephone report units** who take the crime report over the telephone. In some departments, more than a third of the calls are initially handled in this way.
- **Delayed response** if officers are not needed at once and can respond when they are available. Most departments state a maximum delay time, such as 30 to 45 minutes, after which the closest unit is assigned to respond.
- **Civilian personnel** trained to take reports; they may be evidence technicians, community service specialists, animal control officers, or parking enforcement officers.
- **Referral to other noncriminal justice agencies** such as the fire department, housing department, or social service agencies.
- **A request for a walk-in report** where the citizen comes to the police department and fills out a report.

Law enforcement evolved throughout U.S. history

In colonial times law was enforced by constables and a night watch made up of citizens who took turns watching for fires and unruly persons. By the beginning of the 19th century, most citizens who could afford it paid for someone else to take their watch.

The first publicly supported, centralized, consolidated police organization in the United States was established in New York in 1844. It was modeled after the London Metropolitan Police created in 1829 by Sir Robert Peel. Other major American cities adopted the same system soon after. Today, more than 90% of all municipalities with a population of 2,500 or more have their own police forces.

Rural policing in the United States developed from the functions of sheriffs

The office of sheriff, a direct import from 17th century England, was used primarily in the rural colonies of the South. As elected county officials, sheriffs had detention and political functions along with law enforcement responsibilities.

Originally responsible for large, sparsely populated areas, many sheriffs were faced with big city law enforcement problems because of urban growth after World War II. In some counties the sheriff's office has retained its detention functions, but law enforcement functions are handled by county police departments. In other counties the sheriff's office resembles many big city police departments. There are more than 3,000 sheriff's departments in the United States today.

Traditionally, the police function has been dominated by local governments

- In 1986 there were 11,743 municipal, 79 county, and 1,819 township general-purpose police agencies in the United States. Together, they employ 533,247 full-time equivalent employees.
- Other State and local law enforcement groups include State agencies such as the 51 State police and highway patrols and some 965 special police agencies including park rangers, harbor police, transit police, and campus security forces. Along with their independent responsibilities, these agencies often support local law enforcement on technical matters such as forensics and identification.
- The Federal Government employs 8% of all law enforcement personnel. Among the more than 50 Federal law enforcement agencies are the Federal Bureau of Investigation (FBI), the Drug Enforcement Administration (DEA), the Bureau of Alcohol, Tobacco, and Firearms (BATF), the Secret Service, and the Postal Inspection Service.

Urbanization and social change have had great impact on policing

- The dramatic shift in population to urban areas since World War II has had great impact on the demand for police service. The percentage of police officers employed in urban areas rose from 68% in 1977 to 82% in 1982.
- During the recent period of increasing concern about employment discrimination against women and minorities, mostly white, male police departments have added women and minorities to their ranks. The proportion of sworn officers who were women went from 2% in 1971 to almost 7% in 1985. The proportion of police officers and detectives who were black went from 9% in 1983 to 12% in 1985.

Professionalism and advanced technology have also transformed policing in the past half century

- In 1982, 79% of police officers in a sample survey conducted by the FBI reported that they had done some college work. 23% of the respondents had received baccalaureate degrees.[1] Basic and in-service training is now regarded as indispensable. More than 670 training academies now exist in the United States.[2]
- In 1964 only one major police department was using automated data processing.[3] More recent surveys suggest that virtually all jurisdictions of 50,000 or more population were using computers by 1981.[4]
- In 1922 less than 1,000 patrol cars were in use in the entire country.[5] At that time, only one city had radio-equipped cars. Today, the patrol car has almost replaced the "beat cop" and police communications enable the patrol officer to have access to citizen calls for service as well as data banks on a variety of critical information, including outstanding warrants and stolen property.

Private security continues to grow

After public police agencies were formed in the mid-1800s, organized pri-

Increased civilian employment has also changed police agencies

The increase results from the—
- desire to free up sworn officers for patrol duties
- need for technical expertise, such as data processing.

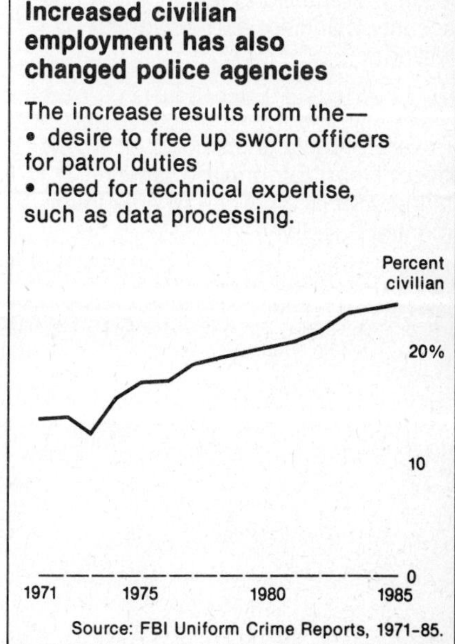

Source: FBI Uniform Crime Reports, 1971-85.

Private security plays an important role in crime control

vate law enforcement developed in response to—
• the lack of public police protection in the expanding West
• problems with interstate jurisdiction
• development of the railroad
• increased industrialization.

The first private security officer, Allan Pinkerton, had a tremendous impact on private security through his work with the railroads and through his establishment of the first private security firm. Owing to the lack of a Federal law enforcement agency, Pinkerton's security agency was hired by the Federal Government in 1861. More recently there has been increased need for private security, particularly to protect defense secrets and defense supplies provided by the private sector. More recent growth in private security is in response to growth of crime and security needs in businesses.

The private security industry protects private concerns against losses from accidents, natural disasters, or crime

This for-profit industry provides—
• personnel, such as guards, investigators, couriers, bodyguards
• equipment, including safes, locks, lighting, fencing, alarm systems, closed circuit television, smoke detectors, fire extinguishers, and automatic sprinkler systems
• services, including alarm monitoring; employee background checks and drug testing; evacuation planning; computer security planning; and polygraph testing.

Private security is provided either by direct hiring (proprietary security) or by hiring specific services or equipment (contract security).

1.1 million people are estimated to be employed in private security

Proprietary security	**448,979**
Guards	346,326
Store detectives	20,106
Investigators	10,000
Other workers	12,215
Manager and staff	60,332
Contract security	**640,640**
Guards and investigators	541,600
Central alarm station	24,000
Local alarm	25,740
Armored car/courier	26,300
Security equipment	15,000
Specialized services	5,000
Security consultants	3,000
Total	1,100,000

Source: Cunningham and Taylor, *Private security and police in America: The Hallcrest report* (Portland, Oreg.: Chaneller Press, 1985).

The authority of private security personnel varies among States and localities

Many States give private security personnel authority to make felony arrests when there is "reasonable cause" to believe a crime has been committed. Unlike sworn police officers, private personnel are not obligated to tell arrestees of their rights. Private security usually cannot detain suspects or conduct searches without the suspect's consent. In some States laws give private security authority to act as "special police" within a specific jurisdiction such as a plant, a store, or university campus.

Many private security firms are licensed or regulated

In some jurisdictions both State and local requirements must be met to obtain a license to provide private security.

At the State level—
• 35 States license guard and patrol firms.
• 22 States and the District of Columbia require the registration of guards.
• 37 States license private investigators.
• Alarm companies must obtain a license in 25 States and are regulated in 10 States.
• 8 States license armored car companies and 6 States license couriers.
• In fewer than 12 States, the same agency or board regulates alarm companies and armored car firms, as well as guard, patrol, and investigative firms.
• 3 States have independent regulatory boards; 6 States have such boards in State agencies.
• Private security is regulated by the department of public safety or State police in 15 States, the department of commerce or occupational licensing agency in 7 States, and the department of state in 5 States.

Public police are often employed by private security firms

Some police officers "moonlight" as private security officers in their off-duty hours. According to the Hallcrest survey, 81% of the surveyed police departments permit moonlighting, but most estimated that 20% or less of their officers are working as private security personnel. Acting like a contract security firm, some police departments provide personnel to private concerns and use the revenue for the department.

Private security has continued to outnumber public police since the 1950s

Public police protection grew most rapidly in the late 1960s and early 1970s in response to increasing urbanization and crime rates. Public police protection has stabilized in the 1980s, but private security has continued to grow. Further growth of the private security industry is expected, particularly in relation to products using high technology, such as electronic access control and data encryption units for computer security systems.

The Police in The United States

Beverly Sweatman and Adron Cross

Beverly R. Sweatman is public affairs assistant to the chief of INTERPOL and Adron Cross is assistant chief , Interpol /State Liasion Program. Both Sweatman and Cross work at the Interpol National Central Bureau in Washington, D.C.

The United States police system is neither as complicated nor as confusing as it might appear on the surface. It is, however, vast and complex, and involves more than 20,000 separate and distinct law enforcement agencies that employ more than half a million people. The differences between these law enforcement agencies are generated primarily by the jurisdictional authority or boundaries under which they operate and the specific laws they are empowered to enforce.

The U.S. does not have a national police force. Instead, the United States is served by a multi-layered network of police jurisdictions that include town, city, county, and state police, as well as federal law enforcement agencies.

One reason for this diverse structure lies at the foundation of the Nation's governmental system. The U.S. Constitution provides for a federal system of government, which is a two-level structure consisting of distinct and separate state governments functioning under a central national government.

Federal jurisdictions encompass crimes of interstate and international proportions, such as the illegal transporting of persons or property across state borders and crimes that endanger national security or affect the integrity of the U.S. monetary system or national borders.

At the state level, law enforcement becomes a bit more complex since each state has the right to govern itself within the parameters of the Constitution and must enforce its own law enforcement agency, which in most cases is a state police force. The states themselves are further divided into counties, metropolitan areas, cities and towns, and each of these divisions enacts its own local ordinances. Enforcing these ordinances and maintaining local law and order are thousands of county sheriffs, city and county police, and town marshals. These men and women are the first in line of law enforcement in all U.S. communities, and citizens look primarily to them for protection from criminal activity.

HISTORICAL BACKGROUND

To fully understand the police system in the United States, it is helpful to look back in colonial days in America. Many natural differences existed between the early colonies, such as size, location, population, commerce, and industry. Because of the independent nature of these colonies and the vast territory that separated them, each one developed its own system of order and authority to meet its particular needs. There was no central authority with power over all the colonies to enact or enforce laws and regulations.

The methods used to provide protection for citizens and maintain order against criminal activities varied between the colonies. For example, early in the seventieth17th century Boston established a system of nightwatchmen to supplement their military guard. New Amsterdam (later New York) and Philadelphia soon adopted a similar system. Throughout the colonies, an assortment of law enfor-

From *C.J. International,* January/February 1989, pp. 11-18. Originally appeared in *International Criminal Police Review,* official publication of Interpol. Reprinted by permission.

cement officials such as constables, marshals, and sheriffs gradually developed. [1]

When the original thirteen colonies joined together to form the United States of America, they established the aforementioned federal system of government whereby power was distributed between a central national government and separate state governments. The individual states were not willing to turn over complete authority to the federal government, and they stringently guarded their rights to govern themselves within the parameters of the Constitution and to enact and enforce their own laws. Consequently, the federal government was granted jurisdiction only as set forth by the Constitution, as interpreted by the courts, and all other jurisdictions remained with the states. This action worked against the establishment of a national police force.

Development of police entities that met the specific needs of the towns and cities continued. In 1838 Boston supplemented its nightwatch with a day police force. Other cities followed, and in 1844 the New York legislature passed a law authorizing creation of "the first unified day and night police" force. Philadelphia soon followed suit and by the late nineteenth century most major American cities had municipal police forces. These forces were commanded by a chief or commissioner who was either elected or appointed. Appointments sometimes required the consent of a city council.

Thus, the mid-nineteenth century saw the emergence of the main structural elements of American policing. These

Police check on a highway in the United States.

included municipal (city or town) police, supplemented by county sheriffs in rural areas. The gradual addition of two other elements, state police and federal agencies, complete the present-day system. [3]

The Texas Rangers, created in 1835 to supplement Texas military forces, were the forerunners of today's state police forces. Other states followed after the turn of the century. Some state police agencies are restricted to enforcing traffic laws and protecting life and property on the highways. Others, however, have general policing authority in criminal matters throughout the state. [4]

In keeping with its constitutional authority to regulate international and interstate commerce and to protect U.S. property both at home and abroad, Congress enacted federal laws against a wide range of criminal activity, and the federal government slowly expanded its police capacity.

The Revenue Cutter Service was established in 1789 to help prevent smuggling, and thirteen U.S. marshals were appointed by the president, concurrent with enactment of

Alabama State Police patrol car and helicopter

the Judiciary Act, which created the original court system for the United States. In 1836 agents responsible for investigating infringements involving postal matters were added to the staff of the Postmaster General, and in 1865, the U.S. Secret Service was formed to investigate counterfeiting that was rampant during the Civil War. Later in the century, inspectors with law enforcement powers joined the Immigration and Naturalization Service. Among the more important law enforcement responsibilities later recognized by Congress were internal revenue investigations and narcotics control. Investigators hired by the Department of Justice in late 1800 became the Bureau of Investigation in 1908, and later, in 1930, became the present day Federal Bureau of Investigation.

For some crimes, such as espionage, federal law stands alone. For others, such as arson, bank robbery, counterfeiting, or possession of illegal drugs, federal as well as state and local authorities have concurrent jurisdiction. [5]

None of the federal law enforcement agencies of today has unlimited jurisdiction over all federal laws. Each agency was created to "enforce specific laws and cope with particular situations." [6] In addition, "Federal police agencies have no particular rank order or hierarchy of command or responsibility, and each reports to the specific department or bureau to which it is responsible." [7]

Federal authority is divided primarily between two major departments of the executive branch of government - the Department of the Treasury and the Department of Justice. Other Federal organizations, such as the various inspector general offices that investigate crime within the government itself, and the U.S. Coast Guard, an agency within the Department of Transportation, which is responsible for enforcing maritime laws, all have important roles in law enforcement. The Postal Inspection Service is the law enforcement arm of the postal service and handles all postal crimes such as mail fraud and assaults upon postal employees while exercising their duties. In 1986, the State Department's Bureau of Diplomatic Security was granted law enforcement authority to investigate matters involving passport and visa fraud and special internal matters within that agency.

In addition to the civilian law enforcement authority listed above, federal statutes also grant law enforcement authority to military operations and security and crimes committed against U.S. military personnel or property or by U.S. military personnel. The three separate military investigative agencies are the Naval Investigative Service, the Air Force Office of Special Investigation, and the Army

ATF officers at the scene of a bombing

Criminal Investigation Command. Military agencies are forbidden to enforce civilian laws.

STATE LAW ENFORCEMENT (Police Agencies)

It is not possible within the scope of this article to present a description of the police structure in each of the 50 states and the District of Columbia (Washington, D.C.). Instead, we will provide an overview of the police structure of one representative state. This overview, with minor variations, is reflective of many of the police departments throughout the United States.

POLICE JURISDICTIONS IN THE STATE OF ILLINOIS

Within the state of Illinois, there are 793 town and city (municipal) police departments, employing more than 25,000 full- and part-time sworn police officers who investigate all types of crimes and enforce local ordinances of the towns and cities as well as state laws, with implicit authority to arrest for violations of federal laws. Approximately 12,000 of these sworn officers are employed by the Chicago Police Department.

The state has 102 county sheriff departments, which employ more than 3,300 sworn officers. These officers, also investigate all types of crime and have the same arrest authority as the municipal officers.

The Illinois State Police Department, which has police powers throughout the state, employs 2,168 full-time sworn officers. There are other state agencies, such as the Secretary of State, which is responsible for driver licensing and vehicle registrations and employs 170 sworn officers who are responsible for fishing, hunting, forestry, and boating laws. These agencies, too, enforce state laws with implicit authority to arrest for violations of federal laws.

The total of 31,475 sworn officers described above does not include the officers of railroads, airports, hospitals, park districts, forest preserves, colleges, and universities that maintain law enforcement agencies of their own.

Although each of the aforementioned officers has taken an oath to enforce local ordinances as well as county, state, and federal laws, their powers of arrest are restricted to the jurisdictional boundaries of the police departments that employ them.

Illinois also has more than 700 licensed private security and detective agencies that provide guard, patrol and investigative services to businesses, corporations, and private individuals (celebrities). These private agencies must confine their services to the properties of their employers.

JURISDICTIONAL BOUNDARIES

A police officer's powers of arrest are restricted to the geographical boundaries of his employer, whether it is a town, city, state or other police department, such as airport, university, etc.

The cities of Normal, Illinois, and Bloomington, Illinois, as well as Illinois State University and Bloomington Municipal Airport, have distinct corporate and municipal boundaries. Police officers employed by these entities, therefore, are restricted to investigating crimes and enforcing laws within their respective boundaries.

The above-mentioned entities are located in the county of McLean. McLean county has a county sheriffs department to investigate crimes and enforce all laws in the unincorporated areas outside the jurisdiction of the cities of Normal and Bloomington, Illinois State University and the Bloomington Airport Authority. However, the sheriff's officers have full arrest powers anywhere within McLean County, including the cities of Normal and Bloomington, the university and the airport.

Arrest of a fugtitive by two U.S. Marshals

The Illinois State Police have full arrest powers within the 102 counties that comprise the state of Illinois, including all municipal communities.

An Illinois State Supreme Court ruling has stipulated that a local police officer has no authority to make an arrest outside his jurisdiction without the aid of an arrest warrant that is valid anywhere in the state of Illinois. The various law enforcement agencies, by utilizing mutual assistance agreements, multi-jurisdictional aid compacts, and state laws, effectively assist each other in arresting criminals who have travelled from one jurisdiction to another.

Federal law enforcement agencies such as the FBI, the DEA, the U.S. Secret Service, the U.S. Customs Service, the U.S. Marshals Service, etc., have the authority to initiate arrests in any state or U.S. territory for offenses that are a violation of federal law, specifically, offenses such as bank robbery, flight to avoid prosecution, kidnapping, counterfeiting, and treason, to name a few. This is especially true when the criminal travels across a state boundary into another state jurisdiction. For example, in the case of a bank robbery, local police would respond to the initial alert and notify the FBI, subsequently releasing control of the investigation to them. Mutual assistance agreements between federal and state agencies, however, enable both agencies to join resources and collectively pursue the investigation of the bank robbery. This type of cooperation diminishes jurisdictional problems between town, city, county, state and federal police agencies.

Cooperation is further enhanced through the task force concept, a system whereby the various municipal, state and federal agencies combine information and investigative resources to address a specific criminal problem in a specific area.

FUNCTIONS OF A POLICE DEPARTMENT

Municipal police departments range in size from one- or two-man offices, such as Smithsburg, Maryland, and Ridgeway, South Carolina, to elaborate and extensive facilities, such as the cities of New York, Chicago, and Los Angeles, which, together, employ more than 46,000 police officers, according to figures reported in the 1986 *Uniform Crime Report* published by the FBI.

The departments are operationally structured to meet the needs of the town or city in which they are located. For example, larger departments generally assign squads to address specific types of crimes, while the smaller departments, which experience lower crime rates, handle whatever type of crime or investigation arises. Assistance is always available should a situation extend beyond the capability of the police entity involved.

FEDERAL LAW ENFORCEMENT AGENCIES

Division of law enforcement authority at the federal level is not only between major departments but within them as well. As indicated earlier, each federal law enforcement agency reports to the head of the specific department to which it is responsible. The heads of these departments comprise a segment of the president's cabinet.

The Department of the Treasury, for example, has four distinct law enforcement agencies: the Bureau of Alcohol, Tobacco, and Firearms, the U.S. Customs Service, the U.S. Secret Service, and the Internal Revenue Service. Each has specific duties and jurisdictions related to the mission of the U.S. Treasury.

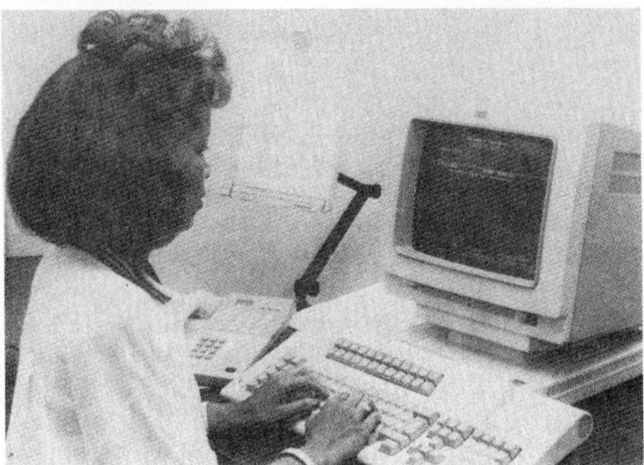

Computerized file of missing persons in the state of Alabama

For instance, the Bureau of Alcohol, Tobacco, and Firearms, also known as ATF, enforces federal laws pertaining to the manufacture, sale, and possession of firearms and explosives and uses these laws to investigate the use of firearms or explosives to commit violent crimes. Since federal laws require that manufacturers and dealers keep records on all sales of firearms and explosives, ATF is the nation's leading agency for tracing such weapons for domestic and international law enforcement agencies.

ATF also investigates major arson cases, particularly interstate arson-for-profit schemes, and initiates joint federal, state, and local anti-arson task forces. At the same time, ATF collects federal taxes on alcohol and tobacco products, suppresses illegal traffic in these commodities, and regulates alcohol industry trade practices.

Like ATF, the U.S. Customs Service is an agency with many responsibilities. Foremost among these is the collection of import duties and taxes at more than 300 ports of entry, from both individuals and commercial carriers. At the same time, the Customs Service detects and intercepts illegal drugs, counterfeit consumer goods, and other contraband entering the United States and prevents strategic high technology from being smuggled out of the country. Recent seizures of boats, planes and other vehicles used to transport illegal drugs into the United States have received widespread media attention and are an integral part of the federal government's efforts to stem the drug trade in America.

The U.S. Secret Service is best known for its role of protecting the president and vice president and their families, as well as other elected officials and foreign heads of state visiting the United States. But, as an agency of the Treasury Department, the Secret Service also investigates crimes related to the U.S. monetary system, such as counterfeiting of currency, coins, stamps, and bonds, forgery of government checks, and credit card fraud. And, together with the FBI, the Secret Service works to stem the growing tide of computer fraud in the United States.

The Internal Revenue Service is the nation's primary revenue-collecting agency, responsible for enforcing the revenue laws and tax statutes. However, because of drug smuggling, organized crime, and other criminal operations that involve large sums of undeclared income, the Internal Revenue Service is often included in investigations in these areas.

Two officers guard a suspect

Within the Department of Justice, law enforcement also falls primarily within four agencies: the FBI, the Drug Enforcement Administration, the U.S. Marshals Service, and the Immigration and Naturalization Service. And occupying a unique category all its own is IP-Washington, the U.S. National Central Bureau for Interpol.

The FBI focuses on organized crime activities, among them racketeering, corruption, bank robbery, pornography, and prostitution. The FBI also investigates "white collar" crimes - crimes that rely on deceit and concealment rather than force or violence. As the primary agency responsible for investigating terrorist activity in the United States, the FBI also trains special antiterrorist teams to prevent and respond to terrorist attacks and tracks foreign intelligence agents and their activities within the United States. In addition, the FBI operates an extensive forensic science laboratory and a computerized fingerprint identification service that performs identifications for federal, state and local law enforcement agencies, and maintains the National Crime Information Center (NCIC), which provides investigators with data on everything from known criminals and stolen property to missing persons and unsolved violent crimes.

The Drug Enforcement Administration, or DEA, spearheads the United States' intensifying war on illegal drugs. As part of its activities, the DEA conducts surveillance operations and infiltrates drug rings. The agency also tracks illicit drug traffic, registers manufacturers and distributors of pharmaceutic drugs, tracks the movement of chemicals used to manufacture illegal drugs, and leads the nation's domestic marijuana eradication program.

The U.S. Marshals Service was created in 1789 with the appointment of thirteen federal marshals by President George Washington. Today, in addition to ensuring the security of court facilities, U.S. marshals apprehend most federal fugitives and execute federal arrest warrants. In addition, they operate the Witness Security Program, ensuring the safety of endangered witnesses. The Marshals Service has its own Air Wing to transport federal prisoners to court appearances and then to prison. At the same time, the Marshals Service is responsible for handling the seizure and disposal of property resulting from criminal activity.

The Immigration and Naturalization Service (INS) controls the entry of aliens along thousands of miles of land and sea borders, and investigates smuggling rings that bring thousands of illegal immigrants into the country each year. The INS also facilitates certification of naturalized citizens and entry of qualified aliens into the country.

IP-Washington, known in the United States as the USNCB, is also an agency within the Department of Justice. It fulfills a unique position in the U.S. police structure by coordinating investigative request for international assistance from both domestic and foreign police. Through the USNCB, state, and local police departments, as well as federal law enforcement agencies, are able to pursue international investigative leads. Conversely, foreign police seeking criminal investigative assistance anywhere in the United States can do so by contacting the USNCB through their own Interpol National Central Bureau. To meet the demands of both the domestic and foreign police communities, the USNCB makes wide use of computerization and the latest modern communications technology, effectively tying together the more than 20,000 state, local, and federal agencies and their foreign counterparts.

COOPERATION AND TRAINING

The success of American law enforcement efforts can be attributed to numerous formal and informal programs of cooperation and training. Chief among the formal cooperative programs are the special task forces mentioned earlier, such as the Organized Crime/Drug Enforcement Task Forces operating throughout the United States. These task forces bring together the expertise of state and local law enforcement authorities and federal agencies in a concentrated effort against organized crime, illicit drug operations, and other areas of mutual interest and concern. Most often, U.S. attorneys are included as important members of the task forces.

Numerous training programs offered by both federal and state agencies keep police officers current with the latest

A Massachusetts State Police officer

investigative techniques and equipment. For example, the Federal Law Enforcement Training Center (FLETC) at Glynco, Georgia, is an interagency training facility serving sixty federal law enforcement organizations. The major training effort at the center is in the area of basic programs to teach common areas of law enforcement skills to police and investigative personnel. The center also conducts advanced programs and provides the facilities and support services for other agencies to conduct advanced training for their own law enforcement personnel. In addition, the center offers selective, highly specialized training programs to state and local officers.

The FBI National Academy at Quantico, Virginia, is open to senior law enforcement officers from federal, local, and state agencies as well as foreign police departments. The academy offers a wide array of course curricula covering police management, police science, firearms, forensic science, crisis management, legal problems of police administrators, fitness for police officers, and applied criminal psychology. Also, specialized courses are provided concerning death investigations, crime scenes, identification, photography, and fingerprint science. The FBI Academy also offers college credit to police officers through its affiliation with the University of Virginia.

The U.S. Secret Service offers courses to state and local police officers in the examination of questioned (forged) documents. In addition, they train firearms instructors at the James J. Rowley Training Center in Beltsville, and offer briefings in protective techniques to state and local police who are engaged in the protection of their local dignitaries. These briefings better enable the state and local police to work with the Secret Service when that agency's protectees visit their areas.

On the state level, a police agency may have its own training facility for the training of officers. In addition, municipalities with a population of 100,000 or more also offer a basic training program for new officers, and this can result in a particular state having several police academies.

To ensure uniformity in the degree and quality of training given to police at the academies, most of the 50 states have local training boards that are responsible for the establishment of training standards. Course curricula to be presented to the officers must be approved by the training board prior to being offered. The basic curriculum generally consists of courses in criminal law, humanities, first aid, weapons, self defense, and investigative procedures, to name but a few. The length of the training programs varies within each state, from a minimum of 10 weeks to a maximum of 18 weeks.

Periodic inservice and specialized training is provided to all law enforcement officers by the training academies within the states. A minimum of forty hours per year has been set as a standard requirement.

Other police training institutions within the United States include the Northwestern Traffic Institute, Southern Police Traffic Institute, the Institute of Police Technology and Management, and the San Luis Obispo Training Facility, all of which provide specialized training for supervisors and managers of police agencies.

In addition to programs within agencies, professional associations, such as the International Association of Chiefs of Police and the National Sheriff's Association, offer law enforcement executives a forum for sharing ideas and provide the spark for many successful law enforcement programs.

States also form associations among themselves, such as the Association for State Criminal Investigative Agencies, which meets twice annually to share common problems and solutions and to work toward the betterment of state investigative agencies. This association's membership numbers approximately 24 states whose state police agencies have been given general policing authority throughout the state and carry out criminal investigative functions.

The states also sponsor training sessions for law enforcement personnel throughout their state that address specific types of criminal activity. For example, the Colorado Springs Police Department, in conjunction with the District Attorney's office in that district, recently hosted a seminar to address the problems of fugitives and missing persons and the law enforcement response to these problems. This seminar, with more than 200 attendees, was open to police at all levels -- municipal, county, state, and federal. In addition, the South Carolina Law Enforcement Officers Association meets annually for a retraining conference at which seminars covering various topics are held.

The Kansas Sheriffs Association, the Kansas Peace Officers Association and the Kansas Association of Chiefs of Police, recently held their second annual Joint Law Enforcement Conference for the purpose of strengthening ties between that state's various police agencies and offering workable solutions to problems of mutual interest.

A Michigan State Police Officer

Similar conferences include, to name but a few: the Western States Crime Conference, sponsored by the Arizona Department of Public Safety; the New England State Police Administrator's Conference, which is a meeting of commissioners and other representatives of six New England States, including Connecticut, Maine, Massachusetts, New Hampshire, Rhode Island, and Vermont; and the California Attorney General's Annual Criminal Intelligence Training Conference, hosted by the California Department of Justice.

These meetings, seminars, and conferences provide excellent opportunities for sharing ideas and new programs, and enhance the effectiveness of police throughout the country.

Other formal efforts include periodic crime reports that give law enforcement personnel reliable information on criminal activities and trends. For example, the Bureau of Justice Statistics (BJS) within the Department of Justice collects, analyzes, publishes, and disseminates statistical information on crime, victims of crime, criminal offenders, and the operations of justice systems at all levels of government. BJS also provides financial and technical support to state statistical agencies and analyzes national information policy on such issues as the privacy, confidentiality, and security of data and the interstate exchange of criminal records.

The National Institute of Justice (NIJ) is the primary federal sponsor of research on crime and justice. Its goal is to answer real world questions about crime control and ensure that this new knowledge is disseminated to those who can use it. NIJ publishes *Issues and Practices* reports and research summaries to highlight findings for busy criminal justice policy makers. NIJ's National Criminal Justice Reference Service (NCJRS) gives the criminal justice community access to a data base of over 83,000 reference materials.

The Bureau of Justice Assistance (BJA) administers the Department of Justice's state and local justice assistance program to improve criminal justice operations. BJA sets priorities for and awards discretionary grants, makes block awards to the states and territories, and administers the Public Safety Officers' Benefits Program.

These and innumerable other programs provide the U.S. law enforcement community with the means to obtain their mutual objectives of enforcing laws and protecting citizens.

The activties enumerated in this article by no means include every function and activity associated with law enforcement operations in the United States. They do, however, present a brief overview of the variety and types of interaction practiced by the members of the law enforcement community, whether they represent a federal, state, or local agency.

Despite its vastness and complexity, the American police system works. It successfully serves more than 235 million people in a country that covers more than 3.5 million square miles, a monumental task by any standard.

REFERENCES

The writers gratefully acknowledge the cooperation of all those who provided them with access to the reference sources listed below and, in particular, that of the Bureau of Alcohol, Tobacco, and Firearms in granting permission to use excerpts from their video *Teamwork and the Law,* and that of Dr. David Lester of Stockton State College in Pomona, New Jersey, who provided the excerpts from **Introduction to Criminal Justice.**

Encyclopedia of Crime and Justice, McMillan & Free Press, New York, 1984 (References Nos. 1, 3 and 5).

Joseph J. Senna, L.J. Siegel, **Introduction to Criminal Justice,** West Publishing Co., St. Paul, Minn., 1981 (References Nos. 2, 4, 6 and 7).

Illinois Criminal Justice Information Authority Illinois Revised Statutes.

Illinois Department of Transportation.

Inbau, **Criminal Law for Police.**

O. Wilson, **Police Administration.**

Annual Report of the Attorney General of the U.S., 1986.

U.S. Government Manual, 1988.

THE STATE OF POLICE EDUCATION: CRITICAL FINDINGS

David L. Carter, Ph.D. and Allen Sapp, Ph.D.

David L. Carter, Ph.D. - School of Criminal Justice Michigan State University; Allen Sapp, Ph.D. - Department of Criminal Justice Central Missouri State University

INTRODUCTION

The purpose of this study was to determine the status of education in policing today. Both the President's Commission on Law Enforcement and Administration of Justice (1967) and the National Advisory Commission on Criminal Justice Standards and Goals (1973) recommended that police officers have baccalaureate degrees. In fact, the National Advisory Commission stated:

> Every police agency, not later than 1982, require as a condition of initial employment the completion of at least 4 years of education (120 semester units or baccalaureate degree) at an accredited college or university (Police, p. 369).

Police officials do not know how far they have come in achieving this goal. The lack of evidence showing continuing interest in this on a national level caused some police leaders to express concern that the apparent trend of the 1970's, to increase the educational level of law enforcement, might be reversed. The Forum's belief in the importance of education for the continuing improvement of the police was the primary impetus for conducting this study.

This project, like all Forum projects was conducted from a policy perspective. The information from the study is intended to provide police executives with a basis for comparing their own department with others and to assist in the preparation of educational policies. It is also hoped that the information will be useful to academic policy makers to shape curricula and programming in degree programs for law enforcement.

This report is a summary of the study's results. An in-depth technical report is available from the Forum. The summary has been developed to provide timely feedback to police agencies that took the time to share this important information. It has also been designed to highlight the more significant findings of the research.

RESULTS

- Police Departments are increasingly employing college educated officers.
- These results portray the picture that despite the few agencies which formally require a college education for promotion, the preference for college clearly exists, at least as an informal criterion.
- Educational requirements, by themselves, do not seem to discriminate against minority applicants.

RESEARCH METHODS

The project's objective was to determine the status of the higher education in policing today. To address this question three approaches were used. First, a comprehensive search and analysis of the literature was conducted. Second, a survey of all state and local police agencies serving populations of 50,000 or more and/or agencies with more than 100 sworn officers was carried out. (A total response rate of 76% of the 699 agencies in the survey population was achieved.) Finally, site visits were made at seven geographically distributed police departments of varying sizes which responded to the survey. The site visits were designed to closely examine the policies, practices, and effects higher education

"The State of Police Education: Critical Findings," by David L. Carter and Allen Sapp, *Police Executive Research Forum*, 1988, pp. 3-8. Reprinted by permission.

has on police operations and management. They also provided invaluable insight into understanding the results of the survey and the literature.

SURVEY FINDINGS

Educational Policies for Sworn Officers

- 62% of the responding agencies have at least one formal policy in support of officer pursuit of higher education; most agencies have more than one such policy. These policies serve as a measure of demonstrated support for higher education.
- 58% of agencies with educational support policies require that the coursework be job-related.
- "Job related" may include various subject areas:
  - 49% indicated a preference for criminal justice majors.
  - 46% indicated no preference for the major.
  - Related majors, indicated from comments and site visits, include business administration, sociology, psychology, and social sciences. Some also indicated a preference for "general liberal arts" degrees.
  - Those indicating a preference for criminal justice graduates did so because of the enhanced knowledge of the entire criminal justice system and issues in policing.
  - Supporters of the liberal arts degrees argue that such college preparation gives the individual a wider range of tolerance and decision-making resources.
- Only 25% of the agencies with educational policies required that the coursework be part of a degree program.
  - This is somewhat surprising; without requiring coursework to follow a degree plan would mean personnel could take a variety of unrelated courses.
  - Those in support of a college degree as a symbol of a "professional" would find this approach wasteful of resources and lacking direction for professional achievement.
  - Conversely, one may also argue it takes a variety of skills to be an effective police officer.
- 61% of the responding agencies had a collective bargaining agreement.
  - 54% of these had educational incentive provisions as part of the contract.
  - Based on comments and information from the site visits, it is reasonable to assume that the incentive provisions were, for the most part, proposed by the POA's, not management. POA's appear to give initial support for educational requirements for employment under the belief this may lead to increased salaries.

Educational Policies for Police Civilian Employees

- 51% of responding agencies provided some form of educational support for civilians.
- It appears most of these policies are local government programs rather than exclusively police department policies.
- The most common civilian educational policy is tuition assistance for job-related courses.

Requirements for Entry into Police Service

- 14% of the police departments had a formal college requirement for employment; a somewhat lower level than anticipated.
- Municipal agencies are more likely to have a college requirement than consolidated, sheriff's, or state agencies.
- The most common higher education requirement was a 2 year, 60 credit hour, Associate's degree.
- The basis for the number of college credits required for employment seems to be an intuitive decision based loosely on the recommendations of the President's Commission and National Advisory Commission, the ability to recruit persons with college credits, and the effects of the college requirement on potential minority applicants.
- The practice of police employment indicates the majority of police departments have an *informal* policy to at least give preference to those with college.
- Reasons agencies do not establish a formal educational requirement for employment include:
  - A presumed discriminatory effect of the higher education requirement;
  - The fear of a discrimination lawsuit for an educational requirement;
  - Establishing the educational requirement requires validation and agencies are unsure how to validate higher education as a Bona Fide Occupational Qualification (BFOQ);
  - Agencies fear that some good police candidates may be lost as a result of the requirement;
  - Agencies and parent jurisdictions fear that POA's may seek increases in salaries and benefits if a higher education requirement is established;
  - With higher education there must be more aggressive, hence more expensive, recruitment efforts;
  - Agencies fear they may be unable to fill academy classes;
  - Administrators *feel* that higher education is a necessity—or at least a benefit—yet they are not totally convinced;
  - Interference by POA's and/or city personnel departments make the establishment of an educational requirement more difficult.

3. POLICE

Promotional Policies

- 75% indicated no policy or practice requiring college education for promotion.
- 8% had written policy requiring some college hours for promotion, however, the number of required credits varies.
- 3% reported *informal* policies requiring college hours for promotion. Survey comments indicated that even more than the 3% may have the informal requirement, however, they did not report it.
- 4% provided early promotional eligibility for persons with college hours.
- 82%—while not *requiring* college credits for promotion—recognize college education as an important element in promotion decisions.

Recruiting

- 54% directed recruiting equally at college students and the general public.
- 7% primarily directed recruiting efforts toward college students.
- Survey comments indicated that many agencies directed recruiting efforts toward minorities and women regardless of education.
- 27% had either a full or part-time education liaison officer.
- The most prevalent student-oriented program was a Scout Explorer Post associated with the police department (59%). Site visit information indicated that the Explorer Posts were educational, but relatively few Explorers pursued a law enforcement career with the agency.
- Other significant student-oriented programs were internships (55%) and ride-along programs (43%).
- A wide range of innovative student-oriented programs exist indicating many departments have policies and practices to establish liaisons with college educated groups.

Important Factors Relating to Colleges

- The most important factors in officer selection of a college to attend are location (82%); cost (72%); and degree offerings (72%).
- 70% of police chief executives indicated that they have been consulted by area colleges/universities at least a few times on curricular and/or research matters.

Advantages and Disadvantages of College Education for Police

- Overall, the results suggest that police executives find more advantages to college educated officers than disadvantages.
- Among the more salient indicators reported by the respondents were that college educated officers:
  - Communicate better with the public;
  - Write better reports;
  - Perform more effectively;
  - Receive fewer citizen complaints;
  - Show more initiative in performing police tasks;
  - Are more professional;
  - Use discretion wisely;
  - Are more likely to be promoted;
  - Are better decision makers;
  - Show more sensitivity to racial and ethnic groups; and
  - Have fewer disciplinary problems.

The Profile of the Police

- Police staffing distributions nationwide:
  - 75% of all sworn personnel were line/patrol officers;
  - 12% are first line supervisors;
  - 13% are management and command officers;
  - Ratio of first line supervisors to patrol officers is 1:6.4;
  - Ratio of management/command officers to patrol officers is 1:5.6;
  - Ratio of management/command personnel to first line supervisors is 1:.87;
- Minority representation in law enforcement agencies is:
  - 12% Black;
  - 6% Hispanic;
  - 1% Other;
  - These proportions reflect favorably with the general population distributions (12% Black; 7% Hispanic; 3% Other).
- 12% of all sworn officers are female.

Education, Race, Sex:

- The average educational level for police in 1967 was 12.4 years; barely more than a high school diploma.
- Current average educational level is well into the sophomore year of college—given the time involved for social change to occur and the large number of police officers involved, this increase is qualitatively significant.
- The variance among the educational levels of the racial/ethnic groups is small.
- The consistency of no college and some undergraduate work between blacks, whites, and hispanics is particularly striking. The data indicate that minority group members with higher education *can and are* being effectively employed by law enforcement agencies.
- While the raw numbers of minorities are obviously lower than whites, the *proportion* of minorities (as noted above) is roughly close to the national level.
- It is further significant to note that the proportion of law enforcement personnel holding graduate degrees is highest by Blacks followed respectively by Other, Hispanics, and Whites.

Educational Levels of Officers by Race/Ethnicity:

	Average Level of Education	No College	Some Undergraduate Work	Graduate Degree
Blacks	14 years	28%	63%	9%
Hispanics	13 years	27%	68%	5%
Whites	14 years	34%	62%	4%
Other Race/Ethnicity	14 years	19%	73%	8%

- Not only has law enforcement made significant strides in the employment of minorities, the numbers with a college education is a finding of particular importance.
  - + This suggests that higher education does not have an inherent discriminatory effect on minorities for police employment;
  - + That college educated minority group members can be effectively recruited for law enforcement;
  - + That there may not be a need to establish differential educational criteria for minority group members to meet affirmative action goals.

Educational Levels of Officers by Sex

	Average Level of Education	No College	Some Undergraduate College	Graduate Degree
Male	14 years	35%	62%	3%
Female	15 years	24%	46%	30%

IMPLEMENTING EDUCATIONAL REQUIREMENTS

All cities visited had policies and practices in support of higher education. The sites visited were: San Diego, San Jose, and Sacramento, California; Tulsa, Oklahoma; New York City; Kansas City, Missouri; and Largo, Florida. These visits revealed a number of implementation issues:

- Educational requirements for entry and promotion can be effectively implemented.
- Educational requirements are most successful when supported by a plan for implementation and programming.
- Agencies with higher education requirements for employment tend to have non-traditional recruitment programs.
- Innovative policy alternatives to facilitate the attendance of college were noted in most agencies.
- Organizational commitment to the educational program was fundamental to the program's success.
- On-going dialogue with police officer associations prior to implementation of any educational criteria facilitates program development.
- Educational requirements are best implemented as a matter of policy—not informal mechanisms.
- On-going communications between the police department and local colleges and universities (most notably through criminal justice programs) enhances the ability to implement higher educational policies (a factor which was strongly evident to all cities visited).

- In those agencies with a higher educational standard, educational support policies were evident (e.g., policies may include incentive pay, tuition assistance, permit on-duty class attendance, permit officers to exchange days-off and/or shift assignments to facilitate class attendance).

WOMEN ON THE MOVE? A Report on the Status of Women in Policing

Susan E. Martin

This report has been made possible through funding from the Ford Foundation. Its author, Dr. Susan Martin, is a project director and member of the Police Foundation research team. The Police Foundation is a public nonprofit organization devoted to improvement and innovation in policing.

Abstract

In the years following the passage of the 1972 Amendments to the Civil Rights Act, policing made significant progress in eliminating discrimination in the hiring and promotion of women. The proportion of women in both officer and supervisory ranks has increased substantially. That progress notwithstanding, there is still much to be done to correct the overall underrepresentation of women in policing.

From the entry of the first sworn female into policing in 1910 until 1972, women officers were selected according to separate criteria from men, employed as "policewomen," and limited to working with "women, children and typewriters" (Milton, 1972). The passage of the 1972 Amendments to the Civil Rights Act of 1964, however, extended the act's coverage to state and local government employees and thus guaranteed under law equal opportunity in policing. Since that date, many departments, often under the threat of a court order, have eliminated discriminatory personnel policies.

How far had these changes gone through the mid-1980s? Although most experts assumed some significant progress had been made, it was apparent that there was more to be done. Just how much, however, was unclear. The research evidence was limited.[1] The Police Foundation had completed its last research on this matter in 1978. And so, in an effort to quantify change and provide data that would guide future policies, the Police Foundation initiated in 1987 a study that included a mail survey of personnel practices in municipal and state police agencies. This report summarizes the survey findings from municipal agencies and points to some of their policy implications.

Figure 1

MEAN PERCENTAGE OF FEMALE POLICE IN 1978 AND 1986 BY CITY SIZE

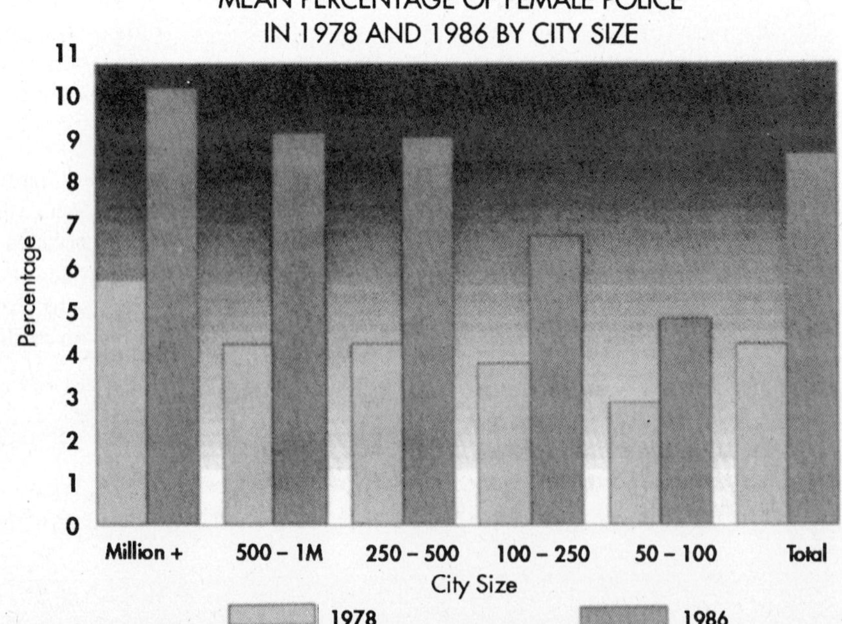

Reprinted by permission from *Police Foundation Reports*, May 1989, pp. 1-8, published by the Police Foundation.

Figure 2

PERCENTAGE OF FEMALE POLICE
IN 1978 AND 1986 BY RANK

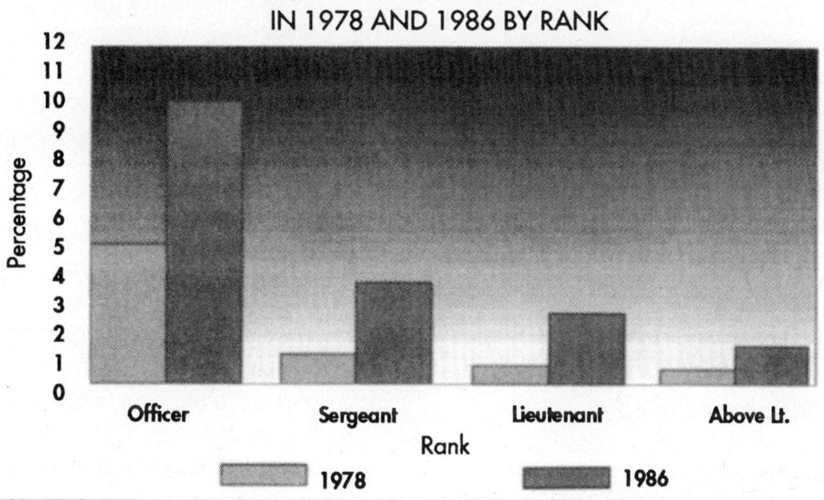

THE SURVEY

The national mail survey of police personnel practices sought information on: (1) departmental policies and practices regarding recruitment, selection, and promotion; (2) the number and percentage of male and female officers by ethnic group, rank, and assignment; (3) male and female officer turnover rates; and (4) the existence and nature of other personnel policies related to women, including those on affirmative action, sexual harassment, and pregnancy and maternity leave.

Questionnaires were sent to all 446 municipal police departments serving populations of 50,000 and all state police agencies. This was the same sample used by the Police Foundation in its 1978 survey of women in policing.[2] Seventy-two percent of the municipal departments returned usable surveys.[3]

THE RESULTS

Representation of Women in Policing

The proportion of women among sworn police personnel has grown steadily since 1972. In that year, a survey of cities serving populations of 250,000 or more revealed that women comprised only 2 percent of uniformed law enforcement personnel (ICMA, 1972). In 1978, women made up 4.2 percent of sworn personnel in municipal departments serving

Table 1

WOMEN'S PROMOTIONS IN MUNICIPAL DEPARTMENTS BY CITY SIZE

	SERGEANT		LIEUTENANT	
CITY SIZE	MEAN % ELIGIBLE (N=192)	MEAN % PROMOTED (N=192)	MEAN % ELIGIBLE (N=157)	MEAN % PROMOTED (N=157)
> 500,000	9.5	15.8	2.9	3.4
250,000-500,000	6.1	8.0	3.1	7.7
100,000-250,000	6.6	7.1	3.0	3.2
50,000-100,000	4.5	6.2	1.8	0.9
TOTAL	6.8	8.8	2.7	3.5

Both the proportion of women eligible for promotion and the rate at which women were promoted were directly related to size of the city served; the larger the city, the higher the percentage. The biggest gains for women came in departments serving populations of over half a million, where women made up 9.5 percent of those eligible for promotion and 15.8 percent of those achieving the rank of sergeant in 1986.

populations over 50,000 (see Figure 1). By the end of 1986, the proportion of women had risen to 8.8 percent of all sworn officers in these agencies.

Figure 1 indicates that women's representation in policing in both 1978 and 1986 was directly related to city size. Although there has been growth in the proportion of women officers in cities of all sizes, the increase has been greater in departments in the largest cities. For example, in cities over a million, women made up 5.8 percent of the officers in 1978 and 10.4 percent in 1986; in cities of 50,000 to 100,000, they made up only 2.6 percent of the total in 1978 and 4.9 percent in 1986. In both years minority women made up a disproportionately large share of all women in policing — 38 percent in 1978 and 40 percent in 1986. In contrast, minority men constituted 10 and 21 percent of all the male officers, respectively, in 1978 and 1986. Minority female representation was closely related to city size; white female representation was not.

Regional differences in the proportion of women in policing were small but related to variations in minority representation. Women constituted 7.6 percent of all officers in the west, where the proportion of minority women is the smallest, and 9.4 percent in the south, where the proportion of minority women is largest.

How one views the representation of women in policing depends on the standard one uses to measure it. Since women make up 44.7 percent of the labor force, it can be argued that they are underrepresented in policing. In addition, in contrast to traditionally "male" professions such as law and medicine, policing appears to be lagging. According to U.S. Department of Labor data, in May 1987, women made up 21 percent of the nation's lawyers and judges; 15 percent of the health diagnosing occupations.

In comparison with other skilled "blue collar" craft occupations, however, women in policing have done well; females made up only 4 percent of mechanics and repairers and 2 percent of workers in construction trades in May 1987 (U.S. Dept. of Labor cited by Powell, 1988:76-78).

Women in Supervisory Positions

Although the proportion of women in supervisory ranks grew between 1978 and 1986, the increase was smaller than that in the rank of officer. In 1978, women made up one percent of municipal police supervisors, only 20 percent of whom were minority women. In 1986, women made up 3.3 percent of all supervisors, with 30 percent of these being minorities. While minority women continued to be under-represented in supervisory ranks, they did make gains on white female counterparts.

The size of the jurisdiction studied in

1978 made little difference because women's representation was so uniformly small. In 1986, however, a higher proportion of women supervisors were found in agencies serving populations over 250,000 (4.0 percent) than those in the smaller cities (2.1 percent).

Most of the increase in female supervisors occurred at the rank of sergeant (Figure 2). In general, the higher the rank, the smaller the percentage of women in it. For example, the proportion of women among all officers, detectives and corporals increased from 5 percent in 1978 to 10 percent in 1986. The proportion of women sergeants among all sergeants increased from 1.0 to 3.7 percent; the proportion of women lieutenants from .7 to 2.5 percent; and the proportion of those in the higher ranking command staff from .5 to 1.4 percent. These differences are attributable in part to the fact that women have not been policing in significant numbers long enough to have shown up in the highest ranks. Nonetheless, their virtual exclusion from upper level management in police departments is similar to their near absence in corporate board rooms and law partnerships.[4]

Data on the proportion of male and female officers eligible for promotion, promoted, or likely to be promoted in 1986, however, are somewhat more encouraging. As shown in Table 1, although 6.8 percent of all persons eligible for promotion to the rank of sergeant were female, 8.8 percent of those actually promoted were women; similarly, at the rank of lieutenant, women made up 2.7 percent of those eligible, but 3.5 percent of those actually promoted or likely to become lieutenants in 1986. Furthermore, across the various city size categories, with only one exception (agencies in cities with populations under 100,000), women were promoted in greater numbers than would be expected based on their representation in the eligible pools for sergeant and lieutenant.

Both the proportion of women eligible for promotion and the rate at which women were promoted were directly related to size of the city served; the larger the city, the higher the percentage. The biggest gains for women came in departments serving populations of over half a million, where women made up 9.5 percent of those eligible for promotion and 15.8 percent of those achieving the rank of sergeant in 1986.

The low proportion of women in police supervisory positions can be explained by several factors. First, a smaller proportion of women are eligible for promotion due to service requirements. Among the 226 municipal agencies providing promotion data, 41 (18 percent) indicated that no women were eligible for promotion to sergeant in 1986; men were eligible for promotion in every case. Second, promotional systems that give substantial weight to seniority beyond minimal eligibility requirements limit women's promotional opportunities and actual promotion rates. While this lack of seniority still handicaps women, it is expected that in another decade the discriminatory effects of seniority will largely disappear (one possible exception being imbalances caused by higher turnover rates for women officers).

A third factor that seems to limit promotional opportunities for women is the supervisor's evaluation—considered for final placement on promotional lists in more than half the responding departments. Although job performance is a relevant consideration in a promotion system, effective measures of police performance have not been developed, most rating systems tend to be subjective, and as such may result in subtle downgrading of women who do not fit supervisors' conscious or unconscious definition of the ideal officer.

In agencies placing greater weight on objective measures, opportunities for moving into middle management increase. In fact, the percentage of eligible women promoted to sergeant was significantly higher in agencies using an assessment center as part of the promotional process (12.2 percent) than those that did not (4.9 percent).

Sex Differences in Officer Selection and Training

It has long been known that application and selection rates are influenced by eligibility criteria and mechanisms used to recruit, screen, and select candidate officers. For many years minimum height and weight standards greatly limited the pool of female

Figure 3

IMPACT OF AFFIRMATIVE ACTION ON PROPORTION OF FEMALES AMONG APPLICANTS AND PERSONS SELECTED BY DEPARTMENTS

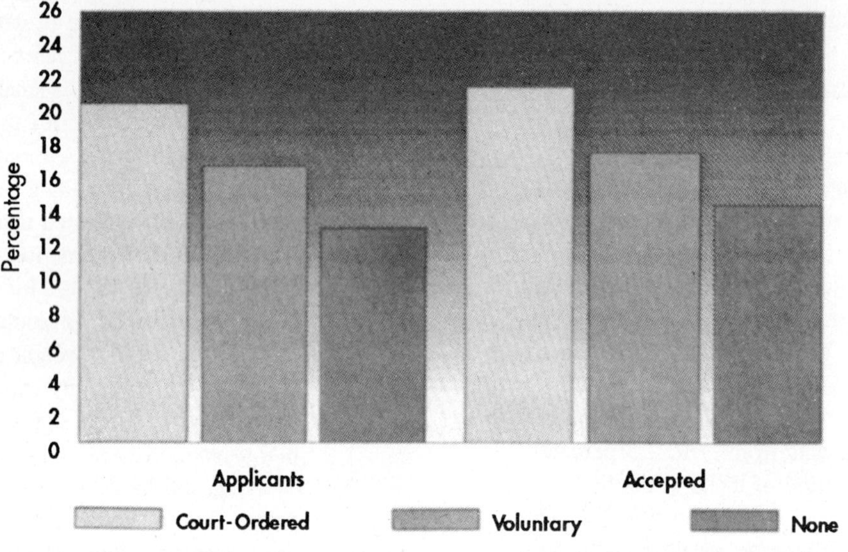

applications (Milton, 1972; Sulton and Townsey, 1981).

In the past 15 years, however, these criteria have changed dramatically, thereby enlarging the pool of eligible women. By 1986, fewer than 4 percent of municipal departments still had minimum height (mean = 5' 4") and weight (mean = 135.3) standards. Instead, the use of physical fitness tests and standards making weight proportional to height are becoming the norm (Fyfe, 1986:5). Furthermore, women applicants in the past have often been found "unsatisfactory" as a result of oral interviews in which neither questions nor responses were standardized (Gray, 1975). In 1986, the Police Foundation found that 76 percent of the responding agencies

Figure 4

1986 PERCENTAGE OF MALE AND FEMALE TURNOVER BY TYPE OF SEPARATION

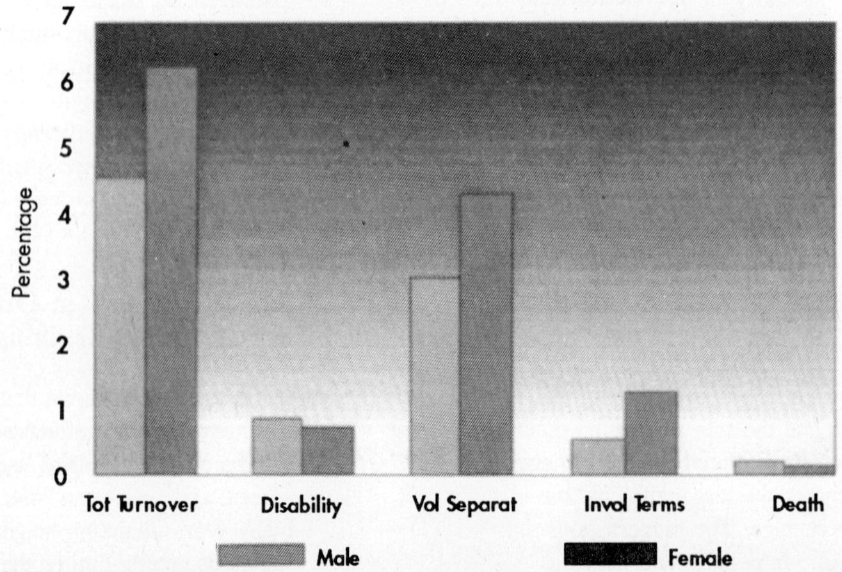

reported that they used standardized questions and 60 percent reported having predetermined acceptable answers.

Data on those who applied and were accepted for police jobs, and on those who entered and completed the training academy in municipal agencies, suggest that there is no systematic sex discrimination in the applicant selection process.

While 20 percent of the applicants were female, women comprised 20.6 percent of all those accepted by departments; 19.9 percent entering an academy; and 19.2 percent of those completing academy training. These data show that there are no significant sex differences in rates of offers of employment, or entry into and completing of the academy.[5]

A variety of actors were found to be related to the proportion of women among a department's applicants, accepted candidates, academy entrants, and new trainees. City size, for example, was directly related to each stage of selection. The proportion of women applicants in departments in cities over a million (29 percent) is more than twice the proportion in agencies in cities of 50,000 to 100,000 (13 percent). While the proportions of women accepted, entering the academy, and completing it also decreased substantially with city size, variation among departments in each size category was so great that the finding did not achieve statistical significance.

A breakdown by region suggests that there was a higher proportion of female applicants in the south and a smaller proportion in the northeast than in the north central and western states, but there were no significant regional differences in acceptance, academy entrance, or academy completion rates.

Among the selection criteria, the absence of a pre-training physical agility test was significantly associated with female application rates (19 percent versus 15 percent) and with female acceptance rates (22 percent versus 15 percent of those accepted).

A department's selection criteria and the presence and nature of its affirmative action policy also appear to have an impact on both the size of the female applicant pool and the number of female applicants accepted. Figure 3 shows that in agencies with court-ordered affirmative action plans, 21 percent of the applicants were female, in contrast to 17 percent in agencies with voluntary affirmative action plans, and 13 percent in those with no plan. Women also made up a significantly larger proportion of the applicants accepted in agencies with court-ordered affirmative action plans (21 percent), as compared to agencies with voluntary plans (18 percent) or no plans (14 percent).

Sex Differences in Turnover

Just as rates of entry into policing affect representation of women as a whole, so do turnover and separation rates. Figure 4 shows non-retirement turnover for males and females during 1986 and the four primary types of turnover, i.e., disability, voluntary separations, involuntary terminations, and death (but NOT normal retirement). During 1986, 6.3 percent of women officers and 4.6 percent of male officers separated from their departments. Although there were no sex differences in the rates of turnover due to disability or death, women had higher rates than men of both voluntary (4.3 percent versus 3.0 percent) and involuntary (1.2 versus .6 percent respectively) separations.

City size had virtually no relationship to turnover rates; women's turnover, however, was much lower in departments serving cities with populations over a million (4.2 percent) than in those serving smaller jurisdictions (7.8 percent). The factor most strongly associated with the female turnover rate was male turnover rate; where women tend to leave, men also are more likely to leave. Both male and female turnover was higher in the west than other regions.

A variety of factors related to women employees' slightly higher turnover rates may explain these findings (Kanter, 1977; O'Farrell and Harlan, 1982; Jurik, 1985). The association between male and female turnover rates suggests that departmental policies (such as willingness to eliminate trainees from the academy or during their probationary period) and local labor market conditions affect male and female officers in similar ways.

Some of the factors that probably do

contribute to higher turnover rates for women include:

- a work environment that is hostile or unpleasant for women but not for men (Martin, 1980; Hunt, 1984);
- difficulties in meshing policing with family life (particularly for a single parent on rotating shifts);
- inadequate light duty and pregnancy leave policies that make having a family and continuing to work difficult or impossible;
- an unrealistically positive picture of the work acquired from television or from recruiters seeking to meet goals; and
- the problems, e.g. performance pressures, faced by "tokens" (Kanter, 1977).

Because of the nature of police patrol, most police agencies permit or require pregnant officers to leave patrol assignments. Yet only 74 percent of the agencies reassign a pregnant officer to a light duty assignment until delivery; 14 percent force the woman to go on leave when she can no longer continue in her "normal" assignment. Twelve percent of the agencies had not yet had to deal with a pregnancy. It is likely that many of the women forced to leave policing for six to eight months in order to have a child resign temporarily or permanently from their departments.

Impact of Affirmative Action

Affirmative action policies have a major impact not only on the rates at which females apply and enter policing, but, over the long term, on women's overall representation in policing. In 1986, 15 percent of the municipal agencies responding to our survey had court-ordered affirmative action hiring policies; 42 percent had voluntary affirmative action plans in effect; and 43 percent had none.

In those agencies under court order to increase the representation of women and minorities, women made up 10.1 percent of the sworn personnel in 1986; in those with voluntary affirmative action plans, women made up 8.3 percent of the personnel, and in those without affirmative action plans women constituted only 6.1 percent of the personnel.

Affirmative action also is related to the proportion of women in supervisory positions; in departments with court-ordered affirmative action, women made up 3.5 percent of the supervisors; in those with voluntary affirmative action 2.4 percent; and in those without affirmative action 2.2 percent of the supervisory personnel.

Because the representation of women and presence of affirmative action policies were also related to other factors, the Police Foundation study used multivariate analysis to control for the effects of size, region, minority representation, and the proportion of women officers in 1978 to determine whether affirmative action policies have an independent effect. After including these variables in several regression models, we found that both court-ordered and voluntary affirmative action remained significantly associated with the proportion of women in a department in 1986 and that the presence of an affirmative action policy also was significantly associated with an increase in the representation of female officers over the 8-year period.

Because several factors also were found to be related to application and acceptance rates, researchers conducted a similar multivariate analysis to isolate the effects of affirmative action. For each test, two regression models, identical except that the second one omitted the affirmative action variables, were developed and compared (Namboodiri, Carter, and Blalock, 1975).[6]

Although we found that both court-ordered and voluntary affirmative action remained significantly associated with female application rates, after controlling for the other variables neither was found to be significantly related to the proportion of female applicants accepted for employment. This suggests that affirmative action policies make a favorable impact on recruitment, primarily in widening the applicant pool; but once that is enlarged, women are usually selected in proportion to their presence in that pool. If current selection procedures continue, women will eventually make up as much as 20 percent of police personnel. If the proportion of women is to increase beyond that, however, recruiting efforts to encourage more female applicants to enter the applicant pool may be required.

CONCLUSION AND POLICY IMPLICATIONS

The survey findings suggest that there has been some positive change in the status of women in policing in the past decade. The proportion of female officers has increased in police departments in each population category and geographic region. By the end of 1986, women made up nearly 9 percent of officers in municipal departments in cities over 50,000. This has occurred despite federal efforts to weaken affirmative action programs, which are found in more than half the agencies responding to the survey and are associated with the increased female representation.

The *pace* of change is, nonetheless, relatively slow; women still constitute less than 9 percent of all police personnel and 3.3 percent at the supervisory level. They thus continue to face the problems experienced by "tokens," e.g. performance pressures, heightened boundaries against "outsiders," and entrapment in stereotyped roles (Kanter, 1977).

Recruitment, selection, retention, and promotion rates paint an equivocal picture regarding women's status in police work. About 20 percent of both the current applicants and recruits are female, which suggests that once women apply, there does not seem to be systematic discrimination against them. There is wide variation among departments, however, in both application and acceptance rates. This points to the fact that some agencies attract women and others do not, leaving considerable room for more effective recruitment efforts. Such efforts are particularly important because women have higher turnover rates than men, and thus more women are needed to enter policing even to maintain current sex ratios.

Although women are being promoted at a rate slightly higher than might be expected based on their proportion among those eligible, current trends would indicate that women are not likely to assume departmental leadership and policymaking positions for many years in more than a handful of agencies.

What policies do these findings suggest for the next decade?

- Since affirmative action policies have substantially changed the composition of the larger departments, it is important to see that such policies are adopted where they are absent and continued where they exist.
- Voluntary affirmative action hiring policies should focus on enlargement of the pool of recruits. This will permit selection of more and more well qualified women, while avoiding imposition of court-ordered changes in hiring procedures that cause a backlash of resentment.
- To increase the rate of female promotion, departments need to alter promotion standards to eliminate criteria irrelevant to identifying supervisory ability or potential. They need to adopt policies and procedures which clearly state that promotions are based on merit.
- Increasing the number of women in recruitment and training assignments as well as in high visibility supervisory posts will create more role models for both potential recruits and women already on the job.
- Active, vigorous enforcement of existing sexual harassment policies might reduce turnover rates.
- The adoption of a pregnancy policy permitting pregnant women to remain on the job in a non-contact assignment and allowing new mothers to take leave beyond the brief period needed for physical recovery, would also have a salutary effect.

Footnotes

1. Several early studies indicated that women can perform effectively as patrol officers (Bloch and Anderson, 1974; Sherman, 1975; Sichel et al., 1978) and identified the problems and coping strategies of the first generation of women assigned to patrol work (Martin, 1980). More recent surveys of personnel practices (Fyfe, 1987; Sulton and Townsey, 1981) have found continuing changes in police agency selection criteria but lack information on changes in selection and promotion practices and turnover rates. For a critique of these early evaluations, see Morash and Greene (1986); for a discussion of the shortcomings of statistical information, see Walker (1985).

2. We subsequently discovered that the 1986 sample included all departments in Sulton and Townsey's 1978 survey, as well as 50 departments that they did not include. Forty-one of these departments were in the 50,000 to 100,000 size category in 1986 but previously had fewer than 50,000 inhabitants. The other nine were larger departments, six of which appear to have been used for a pretest.

3. Sulton and Townsey obtained usable surveys from 74 percent of the municipal agencies.

4. In 1985 only 2 percent of the top corporate executives of Fortune 500 companies were women (Powell 1988:75) and 6 percent of law firm partners were women according to a study conducted by the ABA's Commission on Women in the Profession.

5. Because in many jurisdictions, county or municipal personnel boards administer the initial entry test and "certify" qualified applicants from a list ranked by written exam score, only 60 percent of the departments were able to provide data on the number of applicants; in contrast, 72 percent provided data on academy entrance and completion. Several departments that did not provide the latter information indicated that no officers had been hired or completed training in 1986.

6. Both models included as independent variables agency size, region, percent black, percent Hispanic, percent female, whether the agency had increased its authorized sworn personnel since 1982, whether women had been assigned to patrol prior to 1974, the total percentage of applicants accepted, whether the agency uses a pre-training agility test, and whether there is either female or minority representation on the oral panel.

References

Bloch, P. and D. Anderson
1974 *Policewomen on Patrol: Final Report.* Washington: Urban Institute.

Fyfe, J.
1986 *Police Personnel Practices, 1986.* (Baseline Data Report Volume 18, Number 6). Washington, D.C.: International City Management Association.

Gray, T.C.
1975 "Selecting for a Police Subculture," pp. 46-56 in Skolnick, J.H. and T.C. Gray (eds.) *"Policing in America."* Boston: Little Brown.

Hunt, J.
1984 "The Logic of Sexism Among Police." Unpublished paper presented at the American Society of Criminology an nual meeting in Cinncinati, Ohio.

International City Management Association
1972 "Personnel Practices in Municipal Police Departments" Urban Data Service 5.

Jurik, N.
1985 "An Officer and a Lady: Organizational Barriers to Women Working as Correctional Officers in Men's Prisons." *Social Problems* 32:375 388.

Kanter, R.M.
1977 *Men and Women of the Corporation.* New York: Basic Books.

Martin, S.E.
1980 *"Breaking and Entering": Policewomen on Patrol.* Berkeley: University of California Press.

Milton, C.
1972 *Women in Policing.* Washington: Police Foundation.

Morash, M. and J. Greene
1986 "Evaluating Women on Patrol: A Critique of Contemporary Wisdom." *Evaluation Review* 10:230-255.

Namboodiri, H.K., L.F. Carter, and H.M. Blalock
1975 *Applied Multivariate Analysis and Experimental Designs.* New York: McGraw Hill.

O'Farrell, B. and S. L. Harlan
1982 "Craftworkers and Clerks: The Effects of Male Coworker Hostility on Women's Satisfaction with Non-Traditional Jobs." *Social Problems* 29:252-265.

Powell, G.N.
1988 *Women and Men in Management.* Sage: Beverly Hills, CA.

Sherman, L.J.
1975 "Evaluation of policewomen on patrol in a suburban police department." *Journal of Police Science and Administration* 3:434-438.

Sichel, J.L., L.N. Friedman, J.C. Quint, and M.E. Smith
1978 *Women on Patrol: A Pilot Study of Police Performance in New York City.* Washington, DC: National Institute of Law Enforcement and Criminal Justice.

Sulton, C. and R. Townsey
1981 *A Progress Report on Women in Policing.* Washington: Police Foundation.

Walker, S.
1985 "Racial minority and female employ ment in policing: the implications of 'glacial' change." *Crime and Delinquency* 31:555-572.

Sometimes "fixing broken windows" does more to reduce crime than conventional "incident-oriented" policing

MAKING NEIGHBORHOODS SAFE

JAMES Q. WILSON AND GEORGE L. KELLING

James Q. Wilson and George L. Kelling write widely about crime. Wilson is the Collins Professor of Management at UCLA and the chairman of the board of directors of the Police Foundation, a private research group in Washington, D.C. George L. Kelling is a professor at the College of Criminal Justice at Northeastern University, in Boston, and a fellow in the Program in Criminal Justice at the John F. Kennedy School of Government, at Harvard.

NEW BRIARFIELD APARTMENTS IS AN OLD, RUNdown collection of wooden buildings constructed in 1942 as temporary housing for shipyard workers in Newport News, Virginia. By the mid-1980s it was widely regarded as the worst housing project in the city. Many of its vacant units provided hiding places for drug users. It had the highest burglary rate in Newport News; nearly a quarter of its apartments were broken into at least once a year.

For decades the police had wearily answered calls for assistance and had investigated crimes in New Briarfield. Not much came of this police attentiveness—the buildings went on deteriorating, the burglaries went on occurring, the residents went on living in terror. Then, in 1984, Detective Tony Duke, assigned to a newly created police task force, decided to interview the residents of New Briarfield about their problems. Not surprisingly, he found that they were worried about the burglaries—but they were just as concerned about the physical deterioration of the project. Rather than investigating only the burglaries, Duke spent some of his time investigating the *buildings*. Soon he learned that many city agencies—the fire department, the public-works department, the housing department—regarded New Briarfield as a major headache. He also discovered that its owners were in default on a federal loan and that foreclosure was imminent.

The report he wrote to Darrel Stephens, then the police chief, led Stephens to recommend to the city manager that New Briarfield be demolished and its tenants relocated. The city manager agreed. Meanwhile, Barry Haddix, the patrol officer assigned to the area, began working with members of other city agencies to fix up the project, pending its eventual replacement. Trash was carted away, abandoned cars were removed, potholes were filled in, the streets were swept. According to a study recently done by John E. Eck and William Spelman, of the Police Executive Research Forum (PERF), the burglary rate dropped by 35 percent after Duke and Haddix began their work.

Stephens, now the executive director of PERF, tells the story of the New Briarfield project as an example of "problem-oriented policing," a concept developed by Professor Herman Goldstein, of the University of Wisconsin Law School, and sometimes also called community-oriented policing. The conventional police strategy is "incident-oriented"—a citizen calls to report an incident, such as a burglary, and the police respond by recording information relevant to the crime and then trying to solve it. Obviously, when a crime occurs, the victim is entitled to a rapid, effective police response. But if responding to incidents is all that the police do, the community problems that cause or explain many of these incidents will never be addressed, and so the incidents will continue and their number will perhaps increase.

This will happen for two reasons. One is that a lot of serious crime is adventitious, not the result of inexorable social forces or personal failings. A rash of burglaries may occur because drug users have found a back alley or an abandoned building in which to hang out. In their spare time, and in order to get money to buy drugs, they steal from their neighbors. If the back alleys are cleaned up and the abandoned buildings torn down, the drug users will go away. They may even use fewer drugs, because they will have difficulty finding convenient dealers and soft burglary targets. By the same token, a neglected neighborhood may become the turf of a youth gang, whose members commit more crimes together in a group than they would if they were acting alone. If the gang is broken up, former members will still commit some crimes but probably not as many as before.

Most crime in most neighborhoods is local: the offenders live near their victims. Because of this, one should not assume that changing the environmental conditions conducive to crime in one area will displace the crime to other areas. For example, when the New York City police commissioner, Ben Ward, ordered Operation Pressure Point, a crackdown on drug dealing on the Lower East Side, dealing and the criminality associated with it were reduced in that neighborhood and apparently did not immediately reappear in other, contiguous neighborhoods. Suburban customers of the local drug dealers were frightened away by the sight of dozens of police officers on the streets where these customers had once shopped openly for drugs. They could not—at least not right away—find another neighborhood in which to buy drugs as easily as they once had on the Lower East Side. At the same time, the local population included some people who were willing to aid and abet the drug dealers. When the police presence made drug dealing unattractive, the dealers could not—again, at least not for the time being—find another neighborhood that provided an equivalent social infrastructure.

The second reason that incident-oriented police work fails to discourage neighborhood crime is that law-abiding citizens who are afraid to go out onto streets filled with graffiti, winos, and loitering youths yield control of these streets to people who are not frightened by these signs of urban decay. Those not frightened turn out to be the same people who created the problem in the first place. Law-abiding citizens, already fearful, see things occurring that make them even more fearful. A vicious cycle begins of fear-induced behavior increasing the sources of that fear.

A Los Angeles police sergeant put it this way: "When people in this district see that a gang has spray-painted its initials on all the stop signs, they decide that the gang, not the people or the police, controls the streets. When they discover that the Department of Transportation needs three months to replace the stop signs, they decide that the city isn't as powerful as the gang. These people want us to help them take back the streets." Painting gang symbols on a stop sign or a storefront is not, by itself, a serious crime. As an incident, it is trivial. But as the symptom of a problem, it is very serious.

IN AN EARLIER ARTICLE IN *THE ATLANTIC* (MARCH, 1982) we called this the problem of "broken windows": If the first broken window in a building is not repaired, then people who like breaking windows will assume that no one cares about the building and more windows will be broken. Soon the building will have no windows. Likewise, when disorderly behavior—say, rude remarks by loitering youths—is left unchallenged, the signal given is that no one cares. The disorder escalates, possibly to serious crime.

The sort of police work practiced in Newport News is an effort to fix the broken windows. Similar projects are under way in cities all over America. This pattern constitutes the beginnings of the most significant redefinition of police work in the past half century. For example:

• When a gunfight occurred at Garden Village, a low-income housing project near Baltimore, the Baltimore County police responded by investigating both the shooting and the housing project. Chief Cornelius Behan directed the officers in his Community Oriented Police Enforcement (COPE) unit to find out what could be done to alleviate the fears of the project residents and the gang tensions that led to the shooting. COPE officers worked with members of other agencies to upgrade street lighting in the area, trim shrubbery, install door locks, repair the roads and alleys, and get money to build a playground. With police guidance, the tenants organized. At the same time, high-visibility patrols were started and gang members were questioned. When both a suspect in the shooting and a particularly troublesome parole violator were arrested, gang tensions eased. Crime rates dropped. In bringing about this change, the police dealt with eleven different public agencies.

• When local merchants in a New York City neighborhood complained to the police about homeless persons who created a mess on the streets and whose presence frightened away customers, the officer who responded did not roust the vagrants but instead suggested that the merchants hire them to clean the streets in front of their stores every morning. The merchants agreed, and now the streets are clean all day and the customers find the stores more attractive.

• When people in a Los Angeles neighborhood complained to the police about graffiti on walls and gang symbols on stop signs, officers assigned to the Community Mobilization Project in the Wilshire station did more than just try to catch the gang youths who were wielding the spray cans; they also organized citizens' groups and

Boy Scouts to paint over the graffiti as fast as they were put up.

• When residents of a Houston neighborhood became fearful about crime in their area, the police not only redoubled their efforts to solve the burglaries and thefts but also assigned some officers to talk with the citizens in their homes. During a nine-month period the officers visited more than a third of all the dwelling units in the area, introduced themselves, asked about any neighborhood problems, and left their business cards. When Antony Pate and Mary Ann Wycoff, researchers at the Police Foundation, evaluated the project, they found that the people in this area, unlike others living in a similar area where no citizen-contact project occurred, felt that social disorder had decreased and that the neighborhood had become a better place to live. Moreover, and quite unexpectedly, the amount of property crime was noticeably reduced.

These are all examples of community-oriented policing, whose current popularity among police chiefs is as great as the ambiguity of the idea. In a sense, the police have always been community-oriented. Every police officer knows that most crimes don't get solved if victims and witnesses do not cooperate. One way to encourage that cooperation is to cultivate the good will of both victims and witnesses. Similarly, police-citizen tensions, over racial incidents or allegations of brutality or hostility, can often be allayed, and sometimes prevented, if police officers stay in close touch with community groups. Accordingly, most departments have at least one community-relations officer, who arranges meetings between officers and citizens' groups in church basements and other neutral locales.

But these commonplace features of police work are add-ons, and rarely alter the traditional work of most patrol officers and detectives: responding to radio calls about specific incidents. The focus on incidents works against a focus on problems. If Detective Tony Duke had focused only on incidents in New Briarfield, he would still be investigating burglaries in that housing project; meanwhile, the community-relations officer would be telling outraged residents that the police were doing all they could and urging people to call in any useful leads. If a tenant at one of those meetings had complained about stopped-up drains, rotting floorboards, and abandoned refrigerators, the community-relations officer would have patiently explained that these were not "police matters."

And of course, they are not. They are the responsibility of the landlord, the tenants themselves, and city agencies other than the police. But landlords are sometimes indifferent, tenants rarely have the resources to make needed repairs, and other city agencies do not have a twenty-four-hour emergency service. Like it or not, the police are about the only city agency that makes house calls around the clock. And like it or not, the public defines broadly what it thinks of as public order, and holds the police responsible for maintaining order.

Community-oriented policing means changing the daily work of the police to include investigating problems as well as incidents. It means defining as a problem whatever a significant body of public opinion regards as a threat to community order. It means working with the good guys, and not just against the bad guys.

The link between incidents and problems can sometimes be measured. The police know from experience what research by Glenn Pierce, in Boston, and Lawrence Sherman, in Minneapolis, has established: fewer than 10 percent of the addresses from which the police receive calls account for more than 60 percent of those calls. Many of the calls involve domestic disputes. If each call is treated as a separate incident with neither a history nor a future, then each dispute will be handled by police officers anxious to pacify the complainants and get back on patrol as quickly as possible. All too often, however, the disputants move beyond shouting insults or throwing crockery at each other. A knife or a gun may be produced, and somebody may die.

A very large proportion of all killings occur in these domestic settings. A study of domestic homicides in Kansas City showed that in eight out of ten cases the police had been called to the incident address at least once before; in half the cases they had been called *five times* or more. The police are familiar with this pattern, and they have learned how best to respond to it. An experiment in Minneapolis, conducted by the Police Foundation, showed that men who were arrested after assaulting their spouses were much less likely to commit new assaults than those who were merely pacified or asked to leave the house for a few hours. Research is now under way in other cities to test this finding. Arrest may prove always to be the best disposition, or we may learn that some kind of intervention by a social agency also helps. What is indisputable is that a domestic fight—like many other events to which the police respond—is less an "incident" than a problem likely to have serious, long-term consequences.

Another such problem, familiar to New Yorkers, is graffiti on subway cars. What to some aesthetes is folk art is to most people a sign that an important public place is no longer under public control. If graffiti painters can attack cars with impunity, then muggers may feel they can attack the people in those cars with equal impunity. When we first wrote in these pages about the problem of broken windows, we dwelt on the graffiti problem as an example of a minor crime creating a major crisis.

The police seemed powerless to do much about it. They could arrest youths with cans of spray paint, but for every one arrested ten more went undetected, and of those arrested, few were punished. The New York Transit Authority, led by its chairman, Robert Kiley, and its president, David Gunn, decided that graffiti-free cars were a major management goal. New, easier-to-clean cars were bought. More important, key people in the Authority were held accountable for cleaning the cars and keeping them clean. Whereas in the early 1980s two out of every three cars were covered with graffiti, today fewer than one in six is. The Transit Police have played their part by arresting those who paint the cars, but they have been more successful at keeping cars from being defaced in the first place than they were at chasing people who were spraying already defaced ones.

WHILE THE PHRASE "COMMUNITY-ORIENTED POLICING" comes easily to the lips of police administrators, redefining the police mission is more difficult. To help the police become accustomed to fixing broken windows as well as arresting window-breakers requires doing things that are very hard for many administrators to do.

Authority over at least some patrol officers must be decentralized, so that they have a good deal of freedom to manage their time (including their paid overtime). This implies freeing them at least partly from the tyranny of the radio call. It means giving them a broad range of responsibilities: to find and understand the problems that create disorder and crime, and to deal with other public and private agencies that can help cope with these problems. It means assigning them to a neighborhood and leaving them there for an extended period of time. It means backing them up with department support and resources.

The reason these are not easy things for police chiefs to do is not simply that chiefs are slaves to tradition, though some impatient advocates of community-oriented policing like to say so. Consider for a moment how all these changes might sound to an experienced and intelligent police executive who must defend his department against media criticisms of officer misconduct, political pressure to cut budgets, and interest-group demands for more police protection everywhere. With decentralized authority, no one will know precisely how patrol officers spend their time. Moreover, decentralized authority means that patrol officers will spend time on things like schmoozing with citizens, instead of on quantifiable tasks like issuing tickets, making arrests, and clearing cases.

Making the community-oriented officers generalists means letting them deal with other city agencies, a responsibility for which few officers are well trained and which cuts across sensitive questions of turf and public expectations.

If officers are left in a neighborhood, some of them may start taking money from the dope dealers and after-hours joints. To prevent that, officers are frequently moved around. Moreover, the best people are usually kept in the detective squad that handles the really big cases. Few police executives want their best people settling into a neighborhood, walking around the bus stops and shopping malls.

The enthusiasts for community-oriented policing have answers for all these concerns, but sometimes in their zeal they forget that they are contending with more than mere bureaucratic foot-dragging—that the problems are real and require thoughtful solutions. Many police executives get in trouble not because the crime rate goes up but because cops are accused of graft, brutality, laziness, incivility, or indifference.

In short, police management is driven more by the constraints on the job than by the goals of the job. You cannot cope with those constraints without understanding them. This may be why some of the biggest changes toward community-oriented policing have occurred in cities where a new chief has come in from the outside with a mandate to shake up a moribund department. Lee Brown brought a community orientation to the Houston Police Department under precisely those circumstances—the reputation of the department was so bad that almost any change would have been regarded as an improvement.

What can we say to the worried police chief who is already running a pretty good department? Start with corruption: For decades police executives and reformers have believed that in order to prevent corruption, you have to centralize control over personnel and discourage intimacy between police officers and citizens. Maybe. But the price one pays for this is very high. For example, many neighborhoods are being destroyed by drug dealers, who hang out on every street corner. The best way to sweep them off the streets is to have patrol officers arrest them for selling drugs and intimidate their customers by parking police cars right next to suspected drug outlets. But some police chiefs forbid their patrol officers to work drug cases, for fear they will be corrupted. When the citizens in these cities see police cars drive past scenes of open drug dealing, they assume the police have been paid off. Efforts to prevent corruption have produced the appearance of corruption.

Police Commissioner Ben Ward, in New York, decided that the price of this kind of anti-corruption strategy was too high. His Operation Pressure Point put scores of police officers on the streets to break up the drug-dealing bazaar. Police corruption is no laughing matter, especially in New York, but some chiefs now believe that it will have to be fought in ways that do not require police officers to avoid contact with people.

Consider the problem of getting police resources and managing political pressures: resources can be justified with statistics, but statistics often become ends in themselves. One police captain we interviewed said that his department was preoccupied with "stacking widgets and counting beans." He asked his superior for permission to take officers out of radio cars and have them work on community problems. The superior agreed but warned that he would be watching to see what happened to "the stats." In the short run the stats—for example, calls answered, average response time—were likely to get worse, but if community problems were solved, they would get better as citizens had fewer incidents to report. The captain worried, however, that he would not be given enough time to achieve this and that the bean counters would cut off his program.

A better way to justify getting resources from the city is to stimulate popular demand for resources devoted to problem-solving. Properly handled, community-oriented policing does generate support for the department. When Newark police officers, under orders from Hubert Williams, then the police director, began stopping city buses and boarding them to enforce city ordinances against smoking, drinking, gambling, and playing loud music, the bus patrons often applauded. When Los Angeles police officers supervised the hauling away of abandoned cars, onlookers applauded. Later, when some of the officers had their time available for problem-solving work cut back, several hundred citizens attended a meeting to complain.

In Flint, Michigan, patrol officers were taken out of their cars and assigned to foot beats. Robert Trojanowicz, a professor at Michigan State University, analyzed the results and found big increases in citizen satisfaction and officer morale, and even a significant drop in crime (an earlier foot-patrol project in Newark had produced equivalent reductions in fear but no reductions in crime). Citizen support was not confined to statements made to pollsters, however. Voters in referenda twice approved tax increases to maintain the foot-patrol system, the second time by a two-to-one margin. New Briarfield tenants unquestionably found satisfaction in the role the police played in getting temporary improvements made on their housing project and getting a commitment for its ultimate replacement. Indeed, when a department experiments with a community-oriented project in one precinct, people in other precincts usually want one too.

POLITICIANS, LIKE POLICE CHIEFS, HEAR THESE VIEWS and respond. But they hear other views as well. One widespread political mandate is to keep the tax rate down. Many police departments are already stretched thin by sharp reductions in spending that occurred in the lean years of the 1970s. Putting *one* additional patrol car on the streets around the clock can cost a quarter of a million dollars or more a year.

Change may seem easier when resources are abundant. Ben Ward could start Operation Pressure Point because he had at his disposal a large number of new officers who could be thrown into a crackdown on street-level drug dealing. Things look a bit different in Los Angeles, where no big increases in personnel are on the horizon. As a result, only eight officers are assigned to the problem-solving Community Mobilization Project in the Wilshire district—an economically and ethnically diverse area of nearly 300,000 residents.

But change does not necessarily require more resources, and the availability of new resources is no guarantee that change will be attempted. One temptation is to try to sell the public on the need for more policemen and decide later how to use them. Usually when that script is followed, either the public turns down the spending increase or the extra personnel are dumped into what one LAPD captain calls the "black hole" of existing commitments, leaving no trace and producing no effects.

What may have an effect is how the police are deployed and managed. An experiment jointly conducted by the Washington, D.C., Police Department and the Police Foundation showed that if a few experienced officers concentrate on known repeat offenders, the number of serious offenders taken off the streets grows substantially. The Flint and Newark experiences suggest that foot patrols in certain kinds of communities (but not all) can reduce fear. In Houston problem-oriented tactics seem clearly to have heightened a sense of citizen security.

The problem of interagency cooperation may, in the long run, be the most difficult of all. The police can bring problems to the attention of other city agencies, but the system is not always organized to respond. In his book *Neighborhood Services*, John Mudd calls it the "rat problem": "If a rat is found in an apartment, it is a housing inspection responsibility; if it runs into a restaurant, the health department has jurisdiction; if it goes outside and dies in an alley, public works takes over." A police officer who takes public complaints about rats seriously will go crazy trying to figure out what agency in the city has responsibility for rat control and then inducing it to kill the rats.

Matters are almost as bad if the public is complaining about abandoned houses or school-age children who are not in school. The housing department may prefer to concentrate on enforcing the housing code rather than go through the costly and time-consuming process of getting an abandoned house torn down. The school department may have expelled the truant children for making life miserable for the teachers and the other students; the last thing it wants is for the police to tell the school to take the kids back.

All city and county agencies have their own priorities and face their own pressures. Forcing them to cooperate by knocking heads together at the top rarely works; what department heads promise the mayor they will do may bear little relationship to what their rank-and-file employees actually do. From his experiences in New York City government Mudd discovered that if you want agencies to cooperate in solving neighborhood problems, you have to get the neighborhood-level supervisors from each agency together in a "district cabinet" that meets regularly and addresses common concerns. This is not an easy task (for one thing, police district lines often do not match the district boundaries of the school, housing, traffic, and public-works departments), but where it has been tried it has made solving the "rat problem" a lot easier. For example, Mudd reports, such interagency issues as park safety and refuse-laden vacant lots got handled more effectively when the field supervisors met to talk about them than when memos went up the chain of command of one agency and then down the chain of command of another.

COMMUNITY ORGANIZATIONS ALONG THE LINES OF Neighborhood Watch programs may help reduce crime, but we cannot be certain. In particular, we do not know what kinds of communities are most likely to benefit from such programs. A Police Foundation study in Minneapolis found that getting effective community organizations started in the most troubled neighborhoods was very difficult. The costs and benefits of having patrol officers and sergeants influence the delivery of services from other city agencies has never been fully assessed. No way of wresting control of a neighborhood from a street gang has yet been proved effective.

And even if these questions are answered, a police department may still have difficulty accommodating two very different working cultures: the patrol officers and detectives who handle major crimes (murders, rapes, and robberies) and the cops who work on community problems and the seemingly minor incidents they generate. In every department we visited, some of the incident-oriented officers spoke disparagingly of the problem-oriented officers as "social workers," and some of the latter responded by calling the former "ghetto blasters." If a community-service officer seems to get too close to the community, he or she may be accused of "going native." The tension between the two cultures is heightened by the fact that in many departments becoming a detective is regarded as a major promotion, and detectives are often selected from among those officers who have the best record in making major arrests—in other words, from the ranks of the incident-oriented. But this pattern need not be permanent. Promotion tracks can be changed so that a patrol officer, especially one working on community problems, is no longer regarded as somebody who "hasn't made detective." Moreover, some police executives now believe that splitting the patrol force into two units—one oriented to incidents, the other to problems—is unwise. They are searching for ways to give all patrol officers the time and resources for problem-solving activities.

Because of the gaps in our knowledge about both the results and the difficulties of community-oriented policing, no chief should be urged to accept, uncritically, the community-oriented model. But the traditional model of police professionalism—devoting resources to quick radio-car response to calls about specific crime incidents—makes little sense at a time when the principal threats to public order and safety come from *collective*, not individual, sources, and from *problems*, not incidents: from well-organized gangs and drug traffickers, from uncared-for legions of the homeless, from boisterous teenagers taking advantage of their newfound freedom and affluence in congested urban settings.

Even if community-oriented policing does not produce the dramatic gains that some of its more ardent advocates expect, it has indisputably produced one that the officers who have been involved in it immediately acknowledge: it has changed their perceptions of the community. Officer Robin Kirk, of the Houston Police Department, had to be talked into becoming part of a neighborhood fear-reduction project. Once in it, he was converted. In his words, "Traditionally, police officers after about three years get to thinking that everybody's a loser. That's the only people you're dealing with. In community policing you're dealing with the good citizens, helping them solve problems."

Confronting Police Corruption: Organizational Initiatives for Internal Control

Robert J. McCormack

Dr. Robert J. McCormack is an assistant professor in the Department of Criminal Justice at Trenton State College in Trenton, New Jersey. He received his PhD in sociology at Fordham University in New York City and a master's degree in criminology at the University of California, Berkeley, where he was a [member of the] Law Enforcement Assistance Administration (LEAA). Dr. McCormack was a member of the New York City Police Department for twenty years.

The emergence of corruption as a criminal justice problem of major proportions is highlighted by exposes and investigations which have appeared in the national press. Many recent books and articles in professional police journals have focused on such problems as they relate to the law enforcement field; however, it is clear that corruption affects almost all agencies of national, state, and municipal government and the private sector as well.

The problem for the police is particularly critical at this time, and if anything, it has become more serious since the middle of the 1970s, with the introduction of narcotics as an important variable in the corruption equation. At the time of this publication, major police corruption investigations have been reported in New York City, Philadelphia, and Boston and throughout many of the municipalities of Dade County, Florida. The Dade County and New York City investigations are directly related to narcotics; in Philadelphia and Boston, the issues are gambling and organized crime.

The *New York Times* reports that

> The beleaguered Miami Police Department, with more than a dozen officers facing charges ranging from drug dealing to murder, is the focus of an inquiry by the Federal Bureau of Investigation into drug-related corruption. Twenty-five other police officers, some of them of high rank, have been subpoenaed as witnesses or as targets of the investigation.

The article concludes that

> while the temptation is greater in Miami than in most American cities because of the great volume of cocaine smuggled into south Florida from Latin America, the epidemic of police corruption is not seen as a purely local problem. Experts expect increased corruption to unfold in other cities with the rise in consumption of crack, a cheap and powerful cocaine derivative. ("Miami" special supplement to the *New York Times,* 2 August.)

This prediction was shortly followed by a major drug scandal in New York. In September of 1986, twelve New York City police officers from the seventy-seventh Precinct in Brooklyn were suspended after being charged with some 250 counts, including sale and possession of crack and other drugs, burglary, thefts, attempted gun selling, trespass, and bribery. A thirteenth officer, one of the ringleaders, committed suicide several months later, shortly before he was scheduled to surrender to authorities. The police commissioner indicated that the drastic shake-up of this police district reflected "a deep

From *Managing Police Corruption: International Perspectives,* Richard H. Ward and Robert McCormack, editors. Chicago, IL: Office of International Criminal Justice, University of Illinois at Chicago, 1987, pp. 151-165.

concern that drugs and the money they generate pose an increasing threat to the integrity of the force" (*New York Times,* 9, November 1986).

In the city of Philadelphia, widespread corruption among police has been linked to gambling and organized crime. The revelations were made as part of a continuing federal investigation into extortion and racketeering by Philadelphia police officers. The mayor said shortly after the story broke that police corruption was not pervasive but that it did, however, reach into each and every police district. A *Philadelphia Inquirer* editorial indicated that there was a growing body of information, largely on purported graft, found by an intense FBI investigation. "The allegations include widespread shake downs, extortion and methodical exploitation of police power for private profit." (12, April 1984). Over the two-year period since the probe began, more than twenty-five officers of the department have been tried and convicted of charges stemming from this investigation.

In October of 1986, the Boston Police Department, often the target of investigations of corruption over the years, announced a joint corruption probe involving its own internal affairs unit and a federal organized crime strike force. Allegedly, members of the department and unidentified outsiders are involved in State Liquor License Board violations. The illegal activity includes reported bribery of members of the department at senior levels of command. The investigation, according to reliable sources, has been going on for the past two years without the knowledge of the previous commissioner but with the full cooperation of the present administration.

These recent revelations once again underscore the seriousness of the problem of corruption in policing. Apart from the obvious economic costs, there are other latent and perhaps more serious consequences. In corrupt departments there is waste and inefficiency. Vital services which should be available to the public are either not provided or provided on a conditional basis. Officers preoccupied with selling crack or making a "score" have little interest in public service.[1]

Probably the most important consequences of a major police corruption scandal are the almost immediate reduction in confidence in city government and a heightened sense of insecurity among the general public. Lack of trust in the police is often generalized to include all governmental operations as the most visible representatives of local government. Law and justice and the lofty sentiments these terms conjure up become the subject of derision upon the realization that many of the community's protectors may also be listed among its criminals.

SHORT- AND LONG-TERM SOLUTIONS

Most experts agree that police corruption cannot be entirely eliminated and that control is the only realistic approach to the problem. Formal control systems that are designed to shape the perceptions and expectations of officers and at the same time reduce discretionary action have the greatest potential for producing behavioral change (Simpson 1977:129). While formal organizational initiatives are essential, any program that is meant to elevate the ethical standards of police officers must consider the informal organization as the dominant force for effective internal control. The ultimate goal of corruption management should be the development of an agency that regulates itself through positive peer pressure (Ward and McCormack 1979:85).

In departments where corruption is a serious problem, corruption management programs must address both short- and long-term remedies. Short-term approaches are basically Hobbesian in nature. They involve (1) heightening the perceptions of agency personnel regarding the problem of corruption, (2) setting specific policy guidelines for police conduct, (3) enforcing the guidelines by means of a proactive system of internal supervision, and (4) having agency-wide dissemination of information concerning the nature of the disciplinary action connected with each transgression. The long-term objective is to develop a consistently shared outlook among officers supportive of the new ethical policies of the department. *The secret to the success of a corruption-control program, then, is bridging this gap between coercion and cooperation.*

DEVELOPING ETHICAL PERCEPTION PATTERNS

While initially one may view the beginning phase of a corruption control program as a rather primitive attempt at producing behavioral change, the long-range effects of such a beginning should not be underestimated. If one assumes that most police officers are basically honest, hardworking people who wish to do a good job, a pervasive organizational effort to root out serious corruption provides these officers with an opportunity to resist peer group pressure in that direction. *A strong proactive internal affairs initiative provides "an excuse for being honest" that may be acceptable to many of the rank and file.* After all, every police officer recognizes the consequences of being caught in a corrupt act. Under intense supervision, reluctance to engage in unethical behavior may be viewed not only as acceptable but also perhaps as prudent. As a result, many officers who are seeking ethical guidance may secretly welcome such efforts if policies are realistic and fair.

This approach to corruption management requires accountability at every level of the agency. Control requires clear guidelines for subordinates, as this minimizes the use of discretion. Staff monitoring and inspection are essential. It should also be pointed out that this orientation is not purely theoretical. The reduction of police corruption through the implementation of more effective managerial control is well documented. Police scandal followed by organizational change and reform have been reported by Sherman (1975a) in the police departments of New York City; Oakland, California; Newburg, New York; and "Central City." Williams (1973) cites similar examples in the cities of Seattle, Washington, and Louisville, Kentucky. The Knapp Commission Report includes many recommendations for tightening administrative controls.[2] In several of the above departments, the long-term result of strong managerial leadership was permanent change.

One of the long-term effects of proper managerial acountability is its tendency to alter the perceptions of members of the organization. What were once operational procedures largely ignored become the actual operating guidelines of the agency; what was ethically acceptable under a previous managerial system is no longer condoned. As standards are enforced, they tend to become internalized by agency personnel and eventually may be viewed as legitimate expectations of the administration. They come to represent the consensus of officers regarding appropriate behavior. This type of change requires time. One sage police administrator with a reputation as a corruption fighter has indicated that a complete change in officers' perceptions about corruption might take ten years or more, even with the benefit of continuity of leadership and a reasonable attrition of older officers (Gain 1976).

This time frame is not inconsistent with other managerial efforts to improve the quality of personnel and services delivered to the public by the police. Change in most bureaucracies comes slowly and involves shaping the perceptions of officers in the organization. In the final analysis, officers' perceptions are the factors that determine the outcome of most police incidents. Wilson concludes that policies within a police agency should reflect a general underlying principle that will guide the use of discretion in cases where no rules seem to apply. Controlling subordinates depends only partly on sanctions and inducements; it also requires instilling in them a shared outlook or ethos that provides for them a common definition of the situations they are likely to encounter. (1969:131)

A MULTI-DISCIPLINARY APPROACH

The short-term effect of strong internal controls will produce noticeable behavioral change as a result of the heightened risk of detection. Long-term change depends more upon internalizing new ethical standards. It is here that knowledge generated by social scientists may be applied. If, for example, corruption is viewed as a function of anomie, the administrator may opt for a program that would increase salaries and reduce opportunities for illegal gain. If subcultural differences are seen as the primary cause of corruption, activities designed to align subcultural values more closely with those of the larger society may be effective on a long-term basis. Sociopsychological theories would suggest improved screening of recruits and more selective assignment.

The only effective approach to corruption management, therefore, is a multi-disciplinary one. While one does not need to understand fully the root causes of the problem to initiate a program that addresses it, long-term success depends upon resolving specific problems related to causality. It is in this area that the failure of many anti-corruption efforts can be found.

IMPLEMENTING AN ANTI-CORRUPTION PROGRAM

As indicated above, the administrator of an agency with an obvious corruption problem should assume that most officers in the department are basically honest and are seeking guidance relative to the agency's position on ethical issues. The first step, then, in the development of anti-corruption plans is to establish a clear definition of corruption. A national survey of over five hundred police agencies in the country (Ward and McCormack 1979:11) revealed that of the most commonly cited definitions of police corruption, the following definition provided by the National Advisory Commission on Criminal Justice Standards and Goals: Police was most often selected as closest to their own:

> Police corruption consists of acts which involve the misuse of police authority for the police employee's personal gain; activity of the police employee which compromises, or has the potential to compromise, his ability to enforce the law or provide other service impartially; the protection of illicit activities from police enforcement, whether or not the police employee receives something of value in return; the police employee's involvement in promoting the business of one person while discouraging that of another person. (1973:473)

It is recommended that this definition be used as an overall policy guideline and that activities such as a accepting gratuities, shopping in uniform, affording preferential treatment for personal gain, etc., be expressly prohibited. (This list may easily be expanded.) There may be other questionable activities of a local nature that the administrator may also wish to proscribe at the outset. An ethics board should be instituted so that requests for guidance in various areas may be forthcoming. Over time, the board's rulings will firmly establish an objective set of standards which will not be predicated on political or community values but on established ethical principles.

DETERMINING THE NATURE OF CORRUPTION

A planning team for the implementation of the anti-corruption program should be created. The group selected should be representative of all levels of the agency. They should be briefed regarding the administrator's concern about corruption. The administrator should meet frequently with the group, and a task force director should be designated to coordinate the group's activities. The task force should begin to analyze the existing anti-corruption procedures within the agency, including current and past memos; general orders and policy statements; past disciplinary fines, suspensions, and terminations; and the current effectiveness of internal affairs as indicated by an internal affairs audit. The group should begin to outline corruption-specific procedures to address the various hazards. A complete picture of the nature and scope of police corruption in the agency should be developed.

In the early stages of the program, the following activities should have been accomplished:

1. A satisfactory operational definition of police corruption developed by the chief administrator.
2. The selection of an anti-corruption task force to plan and implement the program.
3. A preliminary review of current and past anti corruption tactics and procedures and analysis of agency corruption.
4. The development of an ethics board assigned to a committee by the task force coordinator.

Each of these steps is preliminary to program development and is designed primarily to acquaint the anti-corruption task force, including the chief, with the nature and scope of the corruption problem. These steps will also focus the attention of the task force on some of the difficulties to be faced in implementing the program.

OBTAINING COMMITMENTS FROM AUTHORITIES

Because the chief of police or commissioner has the prime responsibility for the external relations of the department, he should seek commitments from local officials regarding his anti-corruption efforts. He should meet with the mayor, the board of commissioners, the town council, and other municipal officials with information on the extent of the problem in the agency.

For the administrator of an agency in which serious corruption exists, there may be a hidden agenda at some of these meetings. To the extent that community corruption opportunity results from municipal government and community tolerance, the anti-corruption efforts of the police department may be viewed by some as threatening. Fortunately, others will be supportive of the planned changes, and their advice and perhaps participation should be sought during the planning and implementation stages. By carefully assessing the level of commitment of supporters and resistance by protagonists, an administrator can gauge the degree of external pressure his reforms will generate and will be able to determine realistically the pace at which the program may proceed.

DEVELOPMENT AND DISSEMINATION OF THE ANTI-CORRUPTION POLICY

An anti-corruption policy must be characterized by clarity, fairness, and consistency. The policy should have a general framework or definition and a range of prevalent corrupt activities which the administration is attempting to eliminate. Meetings to disseminate policy should be conducted at every level of the agency. Responsibility for the corrupt acts of subordinates must be forcefully fixed at each level of command, and it should be clearly stated that a commander's anti-corruption efforts will be evaluated periodically to determine continuity of assignment and promotion.

DESIGNING THE ANTI-CORRUPTION PROGRAM

The anti-corruption task force should meet and report on its preliminary anti-corruption assignments. It should prepare to design a system-wide program for implementation. The policy already announced by the administration will provide the task force with a framework to guide its efforts. This stage should begin with a restructuring, if necessary, of the internal affairs unit of the department. This unit must function properly because, in addition to providing proactive anti-corruption capability, it should be providing control information to the task force director and the chief regarding the effectiveness of the new procedures. As the program to address each of the corruption-specific areas is beginning to function, a decentralized internal affairs capability (assuming the agency itself is decentralized) should be established to assist subordinate commanders. Personnel should be provided within subordinate commands to act specifically as integrity control officers. Once the capability for monitoring corruption is established, accountability for conditions can be exacted.

A written copy of the anti-corruption policy should be made available to each member of the department. Officers should be encouraged to discuss the policy with their immediate supervisors and to confer with the ethics board on issues which are unclear. Decisions of the ethics board should be published periodically, as they may have application to questions from other members of the department.

In addition to the above, the program design should include

1. improved procedures for handling civilian complaints;
2. a media program to inform the public of the new initiatives (a press conference should be planned in which the purpose of the anti-corruption program is explained and the events that prompted implementation discussed);
3. new written orders for internal distribution outlining the purposes of the new policies, proposals for carrying out the policies, and proposed sanctions attached to violations;
4. specifics regarding decentralized responsibility and accountability for corrupt practices and the reorganization of internal affairs;
5. the role of retraining as a form of positive discipline in cases where violations are not criminal in nature and when the use of probation as an alternative to termination seems appropriate;
6. a proposed agency response to the external pressure from citizens and businessmen who may be adversely affected by the plan;
7. a program to encourage and support officers who report the corrupt acts of their peers.

ANTI-CORRUPTION TRAINING

The anti-corruption task force should meet with police academy personnel early in the program planning to determine the role of this unit. Traditional training methods in police ethics have not proven effective in changing officers' behavior responses to corruption. More contemporary ethical awareness workshop training has not met with any better responses.[3] Anti-corruption training should be used to inform officers that corruption is not acceptable in the department.

Straightforward discussions with small groups of officers should be scheduled. The department's awareness of specific types of prevalent violations should be the major topic of consideration. It should be pointed out that much of the information under discussion was gathered by the task force and that no officers are specifically being accused of committing violations. The department's new procedures regarding the enforcement of regulations and laws in the area of corruption should be discussed in detail, particularly the department's efforts to reorganize internal affairs and to hold subordinate commanders accountable for corruption in their commands. The department's policy statements concerning corruption should be discussed, and each of the specifically prohibited activities should be reviewed along with the possible penalties for violations. The entire session should be conducted in an adult, dispassionate atmosphere with no recriminations. The fact that, except in extraordinary cases, retroactive enforcement of the regulations will not apply should be made clear. Sessions should close on a realistic note by indicating that what is being done is absolutely necessary and in the best interests of the community, the department, and the officers themselves.

IMPLEMENTING THE PLAN

The plan should be implemented on a specific date, and retroactive enforcement of its provisions should be avoided. A sustained effort should be made by subordinate commanders to secure the support of the officers by explaining the positive aspects of the program, such as a new image for the department, greater respect from the public, and the possibility of salary increases.

Once the initial phase of the anti-corruption program has been implemented, initiatives to resolve problems related to causality must be developed. These problems may have their antecedents in a variety of internal and external factors. Internally, one might expect problems related to recruiting and general personnel policies, inadequate discretionary guidelines, inadequate pay and/or working conditions to name a few. Externally, factors such as a corrupt political environment, community cultural traditions, and the influence of organized crime may be affecting the department's ability to operate with a higher level of integrity. Corruption-specific programs designed to counteract these and other causal factors must be developed if long-range anti-corruption efforts are to be successful.

Periodic reports on the progress of the anti-corruption program should be issued. These reports should include (1) internal affairs unit activities for the time period covered by the report, (2) disciplinary decisions based on official charges, (3) changes or additions to existing department policies in the corruption area, and (4) board of ethics decisions regarding issues requiring clarification. These reports should be distributed departmentwide for the information of all agency personnel.

The chief should continually indicate his support for the anti-corruption program and take swift action against all commanders and supervisors who do not support it. It is imperative, particularly at the outset of the program, that decisive action be taken against violators because the creditability of the administration and the progress of the program will ultimately depend on this.

CONCLUSION

According to proponents of organizational theory, the key to effective managerial accountability is to have clear operational policy guidelines for subordinates, as this minimized the use of discretion. Standards must also be set for all supervisors, and authority commensurate with responsibility delegated to each. Staff monitoring and inspection of administrative and operational units to insure disciplinary effectiveness of lower level supervisors is essential. The impact of improved managerial accountability will not only tend to improve the effectiveness and efficiency of the agency but also will, if applied with the same vigor to corruption management, go a long way in reducing systemic corruption.

Organizational theories have perhaps the greatest pragmatic value in the initial stages of corruption control. There is a sufficient amount of literature in the field to indicate that control by means of positive and negative discipline will have a significant impact. It has been suggested, however, that tight managerial controls should be applied in combination with other techniques: "what maintains conformity to organizational policy is a good balance of pride and fear, deterrence and voluntary compliance" (Sherman, 1975B:9). Simpson sagely points out that "the question of what constitutes a good balance" seems, however, to be what constitutes the problem in this discussion (1977:1346).

FOOTNOTES

1. A score by a police officer involves being "paid off" by a person who has been caught in an illegal act in return for not arresting him.

2. The Knapp Commission was formed by Mayor John Lindsay. It was formally titled The New York Commission to Investigate Allegations of Police Corruption and the City's Anti-corruption Procedures.

3. During a period of several years after the Knapp Commission scandal in New York in the early 1970s, the New York Police Department mandated that each of its thirty thousand plus officers attend a three-day Ethical Awareness Training Program at a cost of approximately ninety thousand man-days or over $100,000. There never was an evaluation of this costly program. How much of the post-Knapp improvement can be attributed to quality leadership, administrative reform, tighter discipline, or training no one knows. We are inclined to believe that training had the least impact. Research connected with this report indicates that given an exceptionally high opportunity for corruption, lack of administrative controls, poor morale, and generally questionable leadership corruption, exists no matter how mature the individual morality of a department's experienced officers and recruits.

BIBLIOGRAPHY

Bahn, Charles. 1975. The psychology of police corruption: Socialization of the corrupt. *Police Journal* 48 (January): 30–36.

Burnham, David. 1970. Graft paid to police here said to run into millions. *New York Times,* 27 April: 1.

Gain, Charles. 1976. Patrolling corruption from the top. Interview by Robert McCormack. *Law Enforcement News,* September 7: 9.

Goldstein, Herman. 1977. *Police corruption: A perspective on its nature and control.* Washington, D.C.: Police Foundation: 52.

Maas, Peter. 1973. *Serpico: The cop who defied the system.* New York: Viking.

National Advisory Commission on Criminal Justice Standards and Goals: Police. 1973. Washington, D.C.: U.S. Government Printing Office: 473.

Sherman, Lawrence, 1975a. *Controlling police corruption: Final Report* Washington, D.C.: National Institute of Law Enforcement and Criminal Justice, Grant no. 75NI-99-00-24-G.

.1975b. Controlling police corruption: What works? Paper Presented at the American Society of Criminology, Toronto: 9.

Simpson, Antony. 1977. *The literature of Police corruption,* Volume 1, *A guide to bibliography and theory.* New York: John Jay Press.

Ward, Richard, and McCormack, Robert. 1979. *An anti-corruption manual for administrators in law enforcement 1st edition.* New York: John Jay Press.

Williams, Robert. 1973. *Vice squad.* New York: Thomas Y. Crowell.

Wilson, James Q. 1969. What makes a better policeman? *Atlantic* 223. no. 3, March: 131.

FROM PRIVATE SECURITY TO LOSS CONTROL:

What Does the Future Hold?

William Van Wilkinson, Ph.D.

Dr. Wilkinson is a professor with the Department of Arts and Sciences with Pam American University at Brownsville, Texas.

The private security/loss control industry is a multi-billion dollar industry and is currently one of the fastest growing industries in the United States (Cunningham & Taylor, 1985). However, this rapidly expanding industry is a resource that almost all aspects of society have failed to sufficiently recognize. Not the least of the reasons for this lack of recognition has been the reluctance of law enforcement agencies to combine efforts with the various segments of security/loss control industry to effect greater protection for society as a whole.

Along with the problem of perception by the community and the police, security/loss control has suffered from a distorted and often incongruous self-perception. We have seen an emphasis on name changing within the profession—from private security to loss control. Yet, there seems to still be within the profession those that view themselves as little more than "rent-a-cops." Perhaps both of these perceptions, outside and inside, hinge upon the pivotal role that the coming decade can bring.

The focus of this article is the major areas of concern for the security/loss control industry during the next ten years;

1. legal aspects of private security/loss control,
2. standards for private security/loss control personnel,
3. education for private security/loss control managers and administrators, and
4. the effects of technology on private security/loss control.

While these categories have been developed for clarity and heuristic organization, they can in no way be considered orthogonal categories. Each of these categories is interrelated to the other. Only when considered as a "gestalt" can these four areas become truly meaningful.

Legal Aspects of Private Security/Loss Control

When large amounts of money are involved in an industry, concern over the potential for abuse and corruption within that industry must be addressed by those directly responsible for management and administration. If the security/loss control industry becomes involved in any illegal activities then attorneys will tend to gather where the negligence appears and criminal and/or civil action may ensue. The result of this action can be devastating to both the industry and the individuals involved.

Confusing the legal issues is the legal status of those involved in the security/loss control industry. According to Bilek, et. al. (1982) there

"From Private Security To Loss Control: What Does the Future Hold?" by William Van Wilkinson, *C.J. the Americas*, June/July 1989, pp. 1, 4, 8, 10. Reprinted by permission.

are three major groups of legal status involving all security personnel, and they include those security personnel with citizen powers, those security personnel with special powers, and those who are also police officers. This tends to cloud the separation of criminal and civil activities that may involve arrest by security personnel. Clearly each type of security personnel must understand his/her particular status when interacting with the public. Commingling of the three major groups of legal status within an organization only serves to exacerbate the problem, and the problem then becomes one primarily of civil, not criminal liability. If the action can withstand tort liability and is statutorily sound, then the activity should be legal.

The issue of civil liability is indeed a pervasive and confusing problem within the security/loss control industry. A typical scenario would involve a security person attempting to protect a company's assets by stopping a person attempting to take, damage, or destroy those assets. In the ensuing struggle, the perpetrator is inured. While the security person is protected against criminal actions (given a lack of any criminal intent), the perpetrator may bring civil action, and by using the principle of "respondent superior" may once more attack the company's assets. By winning a civil action, the company may lose far more than the value of the assets originally protected.

Legal information and training is the only sure method of addressing the legal aspects issue. This lack of legal knowledge has been reported in the Rand Report (Kakalik & Wildhorn, 1971) and by Shearing and Stenning (1983), and Cunningham and Taylor (1985) suggest that "Some minimum level of legal training should be provided for all security employees" (p. 261). This "minimum level" concept was based upon the relatively infrequent "police-like" duties required of most security personnel. However, Federal and Fogleman (1986) have provided data supporting the idea that while incidents may be infrequent, they can be quite costly. Other authorities have also suggested that legal training should be thorough and updated frequently (Security Systems Digest, 1987; Ohlhausen, 1987).

Standards for Private Security/ Loss Control Personnel

Anthony Potter (1975) described the problems of the private security system as a "vicious circle." Within this vicious circle, factors such as low salaries, marginal personnel, lack of promotional opportunities, high turnovers, and little or no training lead back to one another and result in ineffective performance. To attract and keep highly qualified personnel, salaries must be commensurate with experience, training, education, and job responsibilities. However, competition by private security companies tends to keep wages low because of the bidding process (Task Force, 1976). Cunningham and Taylor (1985) report that "senior executives in the national and regional security companies indicate that 'low balling' or unrealistically low bidding practices can force contract prices to artificially low rates" (p. 77).

This bidding process, in effect, creates a vicious circle where high caliber personnel cannot be provided unless there are higher wages, but on the surface, it appears that the consumer has been reluctant to pay these wages. In fact, a 1975 study of consumers of security/loss control services in the Philadelphia areas revealed that 72 percent of the respondents were willing to spend additional funds for security if the qualification of personnel and/or quality of security/loss control services were improved. Cunningham and Taylor have found that where "training has been mandated, a delivery system for training has emerged . . . [and] . . . there has been a proliferation of training resources and materials since the RAND and PSTF reports (p. 263). There is more than ample evidence to suggest that the establishment of standards and goals is an important step toward improving quality and effectiveness in the security/loss control industry, thereby eliminating the vicious circle.

Education for Private Security/Loss Control Managers and Administrators

Managers and administrators do much more than supervise. They are the leaders within an organization and a major force in the professionalization of any field. Managers and administrators should be multidisciplinarians and research oriented. Higher education programs tailored toward the security/loss control industry can directly affect the efforts toward this goal.

Green (1987) and Bilek, et al. (1982) recognized the interest in developing the "broad based security professional" and the diligent efforts of the American Society of Industrial Security (ASIS) in this regard. ASIS has long been interested and involved in creating standards of competence and professionalism to identify those security practitioners who have shown a willingness to devote their attention to achieving higher goals of education and training in their chosen career. The ASIS program designed to upgrade career security personnel who are willing and able to qualify for certification as a Certified Protection Professional (CCP) is an excellent example of their involvement and concern. However, ASIS cannot be expected to carry the ball alone, and higher institutions of education have an obligation to become involved in the professional development of private security/loss control personnel.

There are less than 200 colleges

and universities in the United States offering certified or degree programs in private security, and only 35 offer Bachelor's degrees and 10 Master's degrees (Cunningham and Taylor, 1985). The interest and need for educational efforts exists, but the response has been slow. While we must emphasize the need for the institutions of higher learning to move into this area, it must be remembered that education is also an industry, and students must be shown to exist in quantifiable numbers if additional curriculum is to be developed.

Currently educational degree programming for security/loss control exists at three levels;

- associate degree programs,
- baccalaureate degree programs, and
- graduate degree programs (Hertig, 1988).

Private security/loss control education can also be integrated rather easily with institutions currently offering criminal justice degrees. Efforts to avoid duplication of course offerings can be addressed, and specifically related private security/loss control courses can be developed to ensure quality programming and curricula designed to advance the professionalization of the private security industry.

Technology and Private Security/Loss Control

Cunningham and Taylor (1985) list four ways that the security/loss control industry will be influenced by technological change;

1. upgraded and new technology will be used to enhance existing security systems,
2. new technology will provide totally new approaches to security designs,
3. technology will provide greater integration of multiple protection systems and devices, and
4. technology will require greater integration with personnel.

. . . history has indicated that rather than decreased employment, technology will increase the need for employees that are educated with respect to the intergration of technology . . .

Technology has had, and will continue to have, an impact on security/loss control. It would be beyond the scope of this paper to attempt to list the changes, and imminent changes, that technology is having on the security/loss control industry. However, two major trends can be briefly summarized.

First, microprocessor technology will permit the development of systems that will require less space, perform instructions more rapidly, cost less, and integrate more subsystems into central units (Cunningham & Taylor, 1985). This will allow smaller companies to utilize security/loss control technology while larger companies can expand their security/loss control services into areas previously not available, or available to only the more affluent organizations.

Second, the use of fiber optics has had, and will continue to have, a profound effect on security/loss control technology. Since fiber optics take electric signals and transform them into light waves, more information can be transmitted over longer distances, faster, and more competitively priced (Barry, 1987). Fiber optics are more secure than shielded cables and are more resistant to electrical interference, providing less susceptibility to false alarms or inaccurate data transmissions (Cunningham & Taylor, 1985). Increased use of fiber optics and expanded microprocessor technology will significantly improve the ability of the security/loss control industries to protect assets.

While this increased technology will have an inestimable impact on the hardware component of the security/loss control industry, we would be remiss if the impact on the human element were not addressed. Without doubt, increased technology will result in employee displacement. Operations such as access control will be increasingly left to security technology (Barry, 1987). CCTVs and increasingly sophisticated intrusion devices will continue to replace human surveillance. While this preliminary analysis leads to a conclusion that jobs will be lost due to increased technology, history has indicated that rather than decreased employment, technology will increase the need for employees that are educated with respect to the integration of technology and security/loss control. Rather than replacing secretaries in the business community, the increased use of computers has caused an increase in the need for computer literate workers (Buffa, 1983).

Conclusions

The preceding analysis has been an attempt to focus on the major issues facing the private security/loss control industry during the 1990s. This decade will play a pivotal role in determining where this rapidly expanding industry will be in the next century. The major issue facing the security/loss control industry is that of identity. Acceptance as a viable industry by the community, law enforcement, and the public at large can only succeed if the industry itself recognizes its potential and moves progressively toward self-identity. It is increased and improved education and training that can make that move possible.

The four sub-areas that have

been discussed are all tied to a common bond—education and training. Continuing high-cost law suits can only be diminished through a thorough knowledge of the legal aspects of private security/loss control. Acceptance of the security/loss control personnel as professionals can only come with increasing training and education. Private security/loss control managers and administrators will be expected on an equal basis with other mid- and high-level managers and administrators if they are equal with respect to education. And increasing reliance on technology in the security/loss control industry presupposes education and training in order to understand and operate this increasingly sophisticated equipment.

References

Barry, J. The world of indoor space: Part 2 Security Management, July, 1987, pp. 39–42.

Bilek, A., Klotter, J., and Federal, R. Legal Aspects of Private Security. Cincinnati, OH: Anderson Publishing Col, 1982.

Buffa, E. Modern Production/Operations Management. New York: John Wiley & Sons, 1983.

Cunningham, W. and Taylor, T. Private Security and Police in America: The Hallcrest Report. Portland, OR: Chancellor Press, 1985.

Federal, R. and Fogleman, J. (eds.) Avoiding Liability in Retail Security: A Casebook. Atlanta, GA: Strafford Publications, 1986.

Green, G. Introduction to Security (4th ed.) Boston: Butterworth Publishers, 1987.

Hertig, C. An inside view of security education. A paper presented at the Academy of Criminal Justice Sciences, San Francisco, CA, March, 1988.

Kakalik, J. and Wildhorn, S. The Rand Report. Santa Monica, CA: The Rand Corp., 1971.

Ohlhausen, P. Update on security liability insurance. Security Management, February, 1987, p. 88.

Potter, A. An address to the First Annual Conference on Private Security, University of Maryland, College Park, MD: December, 1985.

Private Security: Report of the Task Force on Private Security. Washington, DC: National Advisory Committee on Criminal Justice Standards and Goals, 1976.

Security Systems Digest. Who's guarding the guards? Some contracting employees are creating mayhem across the U.S., 1987, 18(18), 1.

Shearing, C. and Stenning, P. Private Security: Implications for social control. Social Problems, 1983, 30, 503–504.

Police Officers Tell of Strains of Living as a 'Black in Blue'

Lena Williams

James Hargrove remembers the time he saw a robbery in progress in Manhattan. As a police officer, he wanted to jump out of his patrol car. As a black man in civilian clothes, carrying a weapon, he knew better.

So Patrolman Hargrove did what most other off-duty black police officers have been trained by instinct and by the job to do in such situations: he stayed in the car and radioed for help.

The episode, recalled recently by Mr. Hargrove, who is now an Assistant Police Commissioner in New York City, reflects some of the special problems faced by black police officers as they try to reconcile their race with their work.

Conflicts and Ambiguities

It also underscores a more complex issue: how the pervasive stereotype of criminals as young black males may influence police officers' responses. That point was illustrated in December in Prince Georges County, Md., when a black Washington police officer was shot and killed in his home by a white county police officer who mistook him for an armed burglar.

In interviews around the country, black police offices said the conflicts and ambiguities that arise from being "black in blue" can be humiliating and demoralizing.

"When the white guys finish work, they go home to their white neighborhoods and the black guys go home to the black community," said Ronald Hampton, a black Washington police officer who lives in a predominantly black section of the capital.

Another black officer in Washington said: "You may be their partner on the job, but the minute you're off duty, it's a different story. It's like you'll find a bunch of white cops hovering in the locker room snickering at something, then when you walk in they stop. Now what are you supposed to think?"

A Belief in Opportunities

Despite such problems, most of those interviewed said that their jobs were satisfying and that they believed there were opportunities to advance. The number of black police officers nationwide has more than doubled since 1972, to 42,000 from 20,000. There are 12 black police chiefs in cities, including New York, Chicago, Washington and Houston.

The black officers also overwhelmingly expressed the belief that regardless of personal likes, dislikes or prejudice, white officers would come to their aid and that they would aid white officers. All shared the view that the relationship between black police officers and the black community, where the black officer is sometimes regarded as a traitor and is often shunned, has improved in recent years, in part because of attempts by black police officers to control crime in black neighborhoods.

"We're tied to the black community by this umbilical cord," said Mr. Hampton, who is also the information director for the National Black Police Association, which has 35,000 members. "We can't sever it because we have a commonality, and that is our color. We know that if we take off our uniforms, whites would treat us the same as they do other blacks in Anacostia," a predominantly, low-income black community in the District of Columbia.

"On the one hand, we're asked to think of ourselves as being blue, not black," Sgt. Donald Jackson of the Los Angeles Police Department said in a telephone interview. "I had one fellow officer, who was white, tell me that if he calls blacks niggers it shouldn't offend me because I'm blue, not black."

Sensitivity to race is now stressed in training.

But when Mr. Jackson began to speak out against such racial slurs, first to his superior officers and then to the local news media, he said he was ostracized by whites in the department.

Integration vs. Solidarity

Charles Bahn, professor of forensic psychology at the John Jay College of Criminal Justice in New York City, said the comments of these and other black officers illustrated the contradictory nature of the job.

"The police fraternity has not stretched to the point of fully embracing blacks or women," Mr. Bahn said. "It is true, in part, because black officers have segregated themselves to be a force for their own people. Self-integration interferes with the issue of solidarity, which says anyone in blue is your brother or sister."

In his book "Black in Blue: A Study of the Negro Policeman," Nicholas Alex wrote: "The black policeman can never escape his racial identity while serving in his official role. He attempts to escape his uniform as soon as possible after his tour of duty. He avoids the friends of his youth in order to avoid learning of their criminal behavior. He does not socialize with white cops after duty hours. In short, he is drawn into an enclave of black cops and becomes a member of a minority group within a minority group."

Most law-enforcement officials acknowledge that racial prejudice exists in their profession, but they say it is no more pervasive than in the rest of American society. "The police department is not much different than broader society to the extent that you have racism in the broader society," said Chief Lee P. Brown of the Houston police. He is black.

Shift in Training Emphasis

To combat this, nearly all the nation's 19,000 police departments are shifting some emphasis from training at the firing range to training in judgment and sensitivity. A few have brought in experts in an attempt to identify racially biased officers.

Referring to the shooting in Maryland, Sergeant Jackson of the Los Angeles police said rhetorically: "Had an armed white man been in that house, would he have been shot? I doubt it. He would have been given the benefit of the doubt by any officer, black or white."

That is vigorously disputed by other police organizations. "That's garbage," said Buzz Sawyer, president of the Prince Georges County's Fraternal Order of Police, a social and professional organization that is the bargaining unit for the 915-member force. "When someone turns at you with a gun, you don't sit there and determine what color he is. Color has nothing to do with the fact that a person is armed." Mr. Sawyer is white.

Statistics do not support the notion that race is a significant factor when police officers decide to shoot. A 1986 study by the Crime Control Institute, a nonprofit research organization in Washington, reported a sharp decline from 1971 to 1984 in killings by police officers in cities with populations over 250,000. The researchers concluded that the 39 percent reduction was "almost entirely" a result of fewer blacks being killed.

In 1971, the report said 353 people were killed by police officers. In 1984, 172 were killed. The number of blacks killed dropped by nearly 50 percent, from an average of 2.8 per 100,000 in 1971 to 1.4 per 100,000 in 1984.

Assignments and Promotions

Black offices frequently complain that they are treated differently from whites in assignments and promotions. In a 1981 study, Dr. James J. Fyfe, chairman of the Department of Justice, Law and Society at American University in Washington, a white former New York City police officer, concluded that black police officers were more likely to be assigned to high-crime areas in which minority groups live.

"Fewer than one in three white police officers or detectives is assigned to narcotics, street crime and A precincts," those where violent crime is likely, Dr. Fyfe said, "while nearly half the blacks and more than 4 of 10 Hispanics work in these units. On the other hand, whites are more than three times as likely to work in traffic or emergency as are blacks or Hispanics."

Some of the black officers interviewed said they preferred to work in minority communities, even with the greater potential for danger.

"We serve a dual purpose in the black community in that we are seen as protectors of the community and in some respects as role models," said Inspector Harold Washington of the Detroit police. He is the president of the National Organization of Black Law-Enforcement Executives.

Most black police officers say they have learned how to respond to the pressures they face on and off the job, but most also concede that constant stress may eventually begin to take its toll.

"It was destroying me as a black man," said Sergeant Jackson, who is 29 years old, a graduate of California Lutheran College and the son of a retired Los Angeles police officer. "When I joined the force eight years ago I went along with the racial slurs in order to be accepted by the police fraternity. It began to turn me against my own people. I began to see fellow blacks as untrustworthy, as thieves and criminals. I began to shut myself off from my family and friends."

Officer Jackson said he did not begin to feel better until he started to speak out against racists in the department. Three months ago he formed an organization of black police officers to address racism in the Los Angeles Police Department. Last month the department began a racial sensitivity program and established a panel to examine acts of racism and discrimination in the department.

Rock N Roll

Civilian Review Boards: A Means to Police Accountability

TERRY HENSLEY, Division Chief, Staff Inspections, St. Petersburg Police Department, Florida

Recently, there has been a resurgence of interest in the concept of civilian review of law enforcement officers' actions. Renewed interest has been sparked by a series of incidents involving the use of force and, in some cases, the unfortunate deaths of citizens at the hands of law enforcement officers. As a result, some communities are considering the implementation of a civilian review board.

During times of tension and crisis it is imperative that decisions are made on the basis of accurate information and consideration for the long-term implications. Prior to making a decision regarding the implementation of a civilian review board, everyone involved should have a clear understanding of the concept and its advantages and disadvantages.

The civilian review concept originated in the 1930s, and is defined as "an independent tribunal of carefully selected outstanding citizens from the community at large" (Bopp 1972, p. 146). Ideally, board members' backgrounds include judicial, legal, investigative and educational experience. Merit, not race, religion or membership in any group, would be the criterion for selection.

In some forms, the board has the power to hear complaints, investigate and make recommendations only. Its function is purely advisory. It has no disciplinary powers whatsoever. Recommendations are forwarded to the police chief or law enforcement authorities who choose whether or not to act. Clearance or punishment of an individual thus remains where it is presently—in the hands of the law enforcement officials who are legally responsible for the running of their own agencies. In all cases, the complainants and interested parties should be informed in detail and in a reasonable time as to the disposition of their complaints.

In other forms, the civilian review board is empowered to determine guilt and assess penalties. This is the form that is the most controversial and the one on which this discussion will focus.

Pros and Cons of Civilian Review

Both proponents and opponents of the civilian review board system present what they perceive as valid arguments to defend their stand on the issue. While it appears that law enforcement is generally opposed to the idea, community and civil liberty organizations are generally in support.

A review of the current literature regarding the civilian review process and civilian review boards reflects a consensus on the pros and cons of a civilian review board. Proponents of the system assume the following (Walker 1983, p. 240):

1. A lack of communication and trust exists between the law enforcement and minority group communities.
2. The lack of trust is accentuated by the belief that law enforcement agencies fail to discipline their own employees who are guilty of misconduct.
3. Civilian review would theoretically provide an independent evaluation of citizen complaints.
4. Civilian review would ensure that justice is done and actual misconduct is punished.
5. Civilian review would improve public trust in law enforcement.
6. Civilian review provides for better representation of the entire community.

Those opposed to civilian review boards submit the following point of view (Geller 1985, p. 157-198):

1. Civilian review boards ignore other legal resources that citizens have for registering complaints, i.e., state attorney's office, federal EOC, civil suits, FBI civil rights investigations, and so forth.
2. It is difficult for citizens to understand operations of law enforcement agencies and have a thorough understanding of laws, ordinances and procedures which law enforcement officers must uphold and operate within.
3. Civilian review boards have a destructive effect upon internal morale.
4. Civilian review boards invite abdication of authority by the line supervisors and lower-level management. These are the levels of supervision that should exercise maximum control.
5. Civilian review boards weaken the ability of upper-level management to achieve conformity through discipline.
6. The creation of a civilian review board is tantamount to admitting that the police cannot "police" themselves.

What Does Research Reveal?

Considerable discussion and rhetoric have surrounded the issue of civilian review boards, but there has been only a limited amount of research. In 1978, Douglas Perez completed a well-documented study of the civilian review process, which includes a comparison of citizen satisfaction rates, a review of exoneration rates, a comparison of penalties, and findings as to the reasons

Reprinted from *The Police Chief* magazine, Vol. LV, No. 9, September 1988, pp. 45-47.

for some of the problems with the system. The major findings in Perez's study include the following:

1. The experience with some form of civilian review in several major cities shows that civilian review is *less likely* than police internal review to find officers guilty of misconduct.

2. In those cities where the civilian review board has the authority to dictate penalties, they are *more lenient* in disciplinary recommendations than the internal review process.

3. Regardless of whether the complaint is investigated by a civilian review board or an internal affairs review, there is a direct correlation between the final decision and citizen satisfaction. There is a much higher level of dissatisfaction with the investigative process when the complaint is found *not* to be justified, regardless of what entity investigated the complaint.

One of Perez's conclusions illustrates the dilemma that is present in reviewing police conduct. The conclusion is that "policemen act legally and properly in the vast majority of their interactions with citizens and a majority of alleged cases of abuse." This conclusion appears to be borne out by the available data. Statistically, a very small number of police actions are found to be inappropriate, regardless of what procedure is used to review those actions.

Police Accountablity

Both the proponents and the opponents of a civilian review board process would appear to have essentially one goal in mind: police accountablity to the public. When it becomes clear that accountability is a real issue, it is also clear that the integrity and objectivity of the process of reviewing complaints are far more important than whether the process is staffed by civilians or by sworn law enforcement personnel. This is especially true when the chief reserves the final determination regarding disciplinary action (Fyfe 1985).

"Each community must decide what is best . . . "

There are four objectives that, when met, will ensure police accountablity to the public (Fyfte 1985, p. 82). These objectives are

1. To determine whether individual complaints against officers are founded and, where appropriate, to provide a basis for discipline or other corrective action.

2. To identify patterns of wrongful conduct by officers. Such patterns begin to emerge when an officer becomes the subject of repeated complaints by independent citizens, none of which can be individually sustained. Any complaint mechanism, therefore, should have the power to review individual complaints in the context of an officer's whole career history and to make recommendations that go beyond the findings in individual complaints.

3. To provide feedback on policies and practices. The system should have the ability to recommend to the chief that policies be brought into line with community expectations.

4. To demonstrate police credibility and responsiveness and to assure citizens that their grievances are welcomed and will be taken seriously.

Attaining these objectives does not require that civilians investigate or review complaints against police. Instead, it requires that citizens be strongly encouraged to make complaints; that complaints be investigated thoroughly and objectively; that departmental reporting requirements provide sufficient openness so that it becomes nearly impossible to cover up misconduct; and that the system be perceived as credible and fair by citizens and officers.

St. Petersburg's Community/Police Council

It appears that a system providing for civilian review of policies and procedures with meaningful input for change would best serve the needs of the community. Such a system is currently in place in the city of St. Petersburg, Florida. The core of the system is the Community/Police Council.

The Community/Police Council is a biracial group that meets periodically with the chief and police department staff to review topics of mutual concern. Members of the council are encouraged to suggest changes that they feel will improve the department's operations and relationship with the community.

Each community must decide what is the best vehicle to use to find solutions for its problems. An approach similar to St. Petersburg's Community/Police Council is an example of a program that is successful without incurring the long-term negative impacts of a civilian review board. ★

BIBLIOGRAPHY

1 Bopp, William J. and Donald O. Schultz. *A Short History of American Law Enforcement*. Springfield, IL: Charles C. Thomas, 1972.

2 Geller, William A. *Police Leadership in America* New York: Praeger Publishers, 1985.

3 Perez, Douglas. 1978. "Police Accountablity: A Question of Balance." Ph.D. dissertation, University of California, Berkeley.

4 Walker, Samuel. *The Police in America*. New York: McGraw-Hill, 1983.

5 Fyfe, James J. *Police Management Today*. Washington, D.C.: International City Management Association, 1985.

The Judicial System

The courts are an equal partner in the American justice system. Just as the police have the responsibility of guarding our liberties by enforcing the law, the courts play an important role in defending these liberties by applying the law. The courts are where civilized "wars" are fought, individual rights are protected, and disputes are peacefully settled.

The Supreme Court of the United States is the ultimate forum for interpreting the Constitution and guaranteeing our rights. In the 1988–1989 term, the Court handed down a few significant decisions on criminal law issues. Perhaps the most controversial case involved the right of a demonstrator to burn the American flag as a symbol of protest, a right which was protected by the First Amendment (*Texas v. Johnson*).

In the cases concerning the death penalty, the Court held that executing a criminal who was as young as 16 years of age when he committed the crime did not necessarily violate the Constitutional provision against cruel and unusual punishment (*Stanford v. Kentucky*). The Court also held that the Eighth Amendment was not violated by the imposition of the death penalty against a criminal who was mentally retarded, but not legally insane, and was competent to stand trial (*Penry v. Lynaugh*).

In the area of search and seizure, a divided Court held that the warrantless observation of the interior of a greenhouse from a helicopter hovering at a height of 400 feet was not an illegal search (*Florida v. Reilly*). On the other hand, the Court did hold that police roadblocks came within the scope of the Fourth Amendment (*Brower v. Inyo County*). The Court also upheld the constitutionality of drug testing of railroad employees in sensitive jobs, and of certain Custom Services employees (*Skinner v. Railway Labor Executives' Assoc.; National Treasury Employees Union v. Von Rash*).

The articles in this unit discuss several issues concerning the judicial process. Ours is an adversary system of justice and the protagonists, the State, and the defendant are usually represented by counsel. The articles "The Duty of the Defense Counsel" and "The Prosecutor as a 'Minister of Justice' " discuss the roles of these participants and raise certain ethical issues. The issue of plea bargaining is discussed in "A Prosecutor's View of Plea Bargaining." "White Justice, Black Defendants" raises the sensitive issue of racial discrimination in the judicial process.

A controversial program of allowing jurors to question witnesses is the subject of "After 200 Years, the Silent Juror Learns to Talk." Three articles raise questions about the fairness of the judicial system: "Convicting the Innocent," "A Criminal Lack of Common Sense," and "Liberals and Crime."

As technology develops, so must the justice system, and DNA printing is one of the most revolutionary developments in the law of evidence. "Genetics Meets Forensics" asks if the system can handle this issue.

Looking Ahead: Challenge Questions

Is the judicial system racially biased?

Should jurors be allowed to question witnesses?

Is plea bargaining a valid part of the judicial process?

Does our justice system make it too easy for innocent people to be convicted?

Unit 4

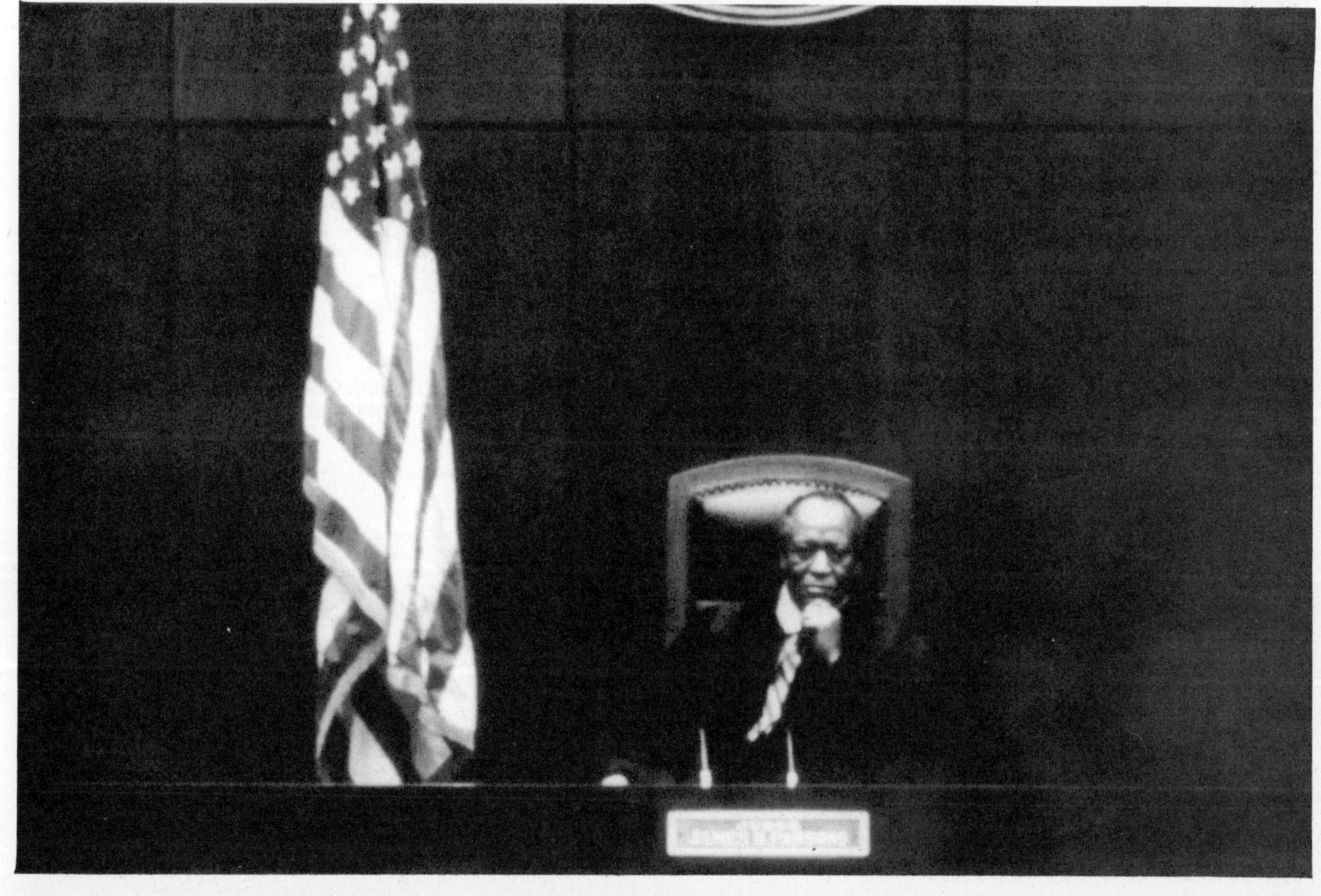

The Judicial Process: Prosecutors and Courts

The courts participate in and supervise the judicial process

The courts have several functions in addition to deciding whether laws have been violated

The courts—
• settle disputes between legal entities (persons, corporations, etc.)
• invoke sanctions against law violations
• decide whether acts of the legislative and executive branches are constitutional.

In deciding about violations of the law the courts must apply the law to the facts of each case. The courts affect policy in deciding individual cases by handing down decisions about how the laws should be interpreted and carried out. Decisions of the appellate courts are the ones most likely to have policy impact.

Using an arm of the State to settle disputes is a relatively new concept

Until the Middle Ages disputes between individuals, clans, and families, including those involving criminal acts, were handled privately. Over time, acts such as murder, rape, robbery, larceny, and fraud came to be regarded as crimes against the entire community, and the State intervened on its behalf. Today in the United States the courts handle both civil actions (disputes between individuals or organizations) and criminal actions.

An independent judiciary is a basic concept of the U.S. system of government

To establish its independence and impartiality, the judiciary was created as a separate branch of government coequal to the executive and the legislative branches. Insulation of the courts from political pressure is attempted through—
• the separation of powers doctrine
• established tenure for judges
• legislative safeguards
• the canons of legal ethics.

Courts are without the power of enforcement. The executive branch must enforce their decisions. Furthermore, the courts must request that the legislature provide them with the resources needed to conduct their business.

Each State has a system of trial and appeals courts

Generally, State court systems are organized according to three basic levels of jurisdiction:

• **Courts of limited and special jurisdiction** are authorized to hear only less serious cases (misdemeanors and/or civil suits that involve small amounts of money) or to hear special types of cases such as divorce or probate suits. Such courts include traffic courts, municipal courts, family courts, small claims courts, magistrate courts, and probate courts.

• **Courts of general jurisdiction**, also called major trial courts, are unlimited in the civil or criminal cases they are authorized to hear. Almost all cases originate in the courts of limited or special jurisdiction or in courts of general jurisdiction. Most serious criminal cases are handled by courts of general jurisdiction.

• **Appellate courts** are divided into two groups, intermediate appeals courts, which hear some or all appeals that are subject to review by the court of last resort, and courts of last resort, which have jurisdiction over final appeals from courts of original jurisdiction, intermediate appeals courts, or administrative agencies. As of 1985, 36 States had intermediate appellate courts, but all States had courts of last resort.

The U.S. Constitution created the U.S. Supreme Court and authorized the Congress to establish lower courts as needed

The Federal court system now consists of various special courts, U.S. district courts (general jurisdiction courts), U.S. courts of appeals (intermediate appellate courts that receive appeals from the district courts and Federal administrative agencies), and the U.S. Supreme Court (the court of last resort). Organized on a regional basis are U.S. courts of appeals for each of 11 circuits and the District of Columbia. In Federal trial courts (the 94 U.S. district courts) more than 300,000 cases were filed in 1985; there was one criminal case for every seven civil cases. In 1985 more than half the criminal cases in district courts were for embezzlement, fraud, forgery and counterfeiting, traffic, or drug offenses.

Court organization varies greatly among the States

State courts of general jurisdiction are organized by districts, counties, dual districts, or a combination of counties and districts. In some States the courts established by the State are funded and controlled locally. In others the court of last resort may have some budgetary or administrative oversight over the entire State court system. Even within States there is considerable lack of uniformity in the roles, organization, and procedures of the courts. This has led to significant momentum among States to form "unified" court systems to provide in varying degrees, for uniform administration of the courts, and, in many cases, for the consolidation of diverse courts of limited and special jurisdiction.

From *Report to the Nation on Crime and Justice,* Bureau of Justice Statistics, U.S. Department of Justice, March 1988, pp. 81-82, 71-72, 74-75.

Most felony cases are brought in State and local courts

The traditional criminal offenses under the English common law have been adopted, in one form or another, in the criminal laws of each of the States. Most cases involving "common law" crimes are brought to trial in State or local courts. Persons charged with misdemeanors are usually tried in courts of limited jurisdiction. Those charged with felonies (more serious crimes) are tried in courts of general jurisdiction.

In all States criminal defendants may appeal most decisions of criminal courts of limited jurisdiction; the avenue of appeal usually ends with the State supreme court. However, the U.S. Supreme Court may elect to hear the case if the appeal is based on an alleged violation of the Constitutional rights of the defendant.

State courts process a large volume of cases, many of them minor

In 1983, 46 States and the District of Columbia reported more than 80 million cases filed in State and local courts. About 70% were traffic-related cases, 16% were civil cases (torts, contracts, small claims, etc.), 13% were criminal cases, and 1% were juvenile cases. Civil and criminal cases both appear to be increasing. Of 39 States that reported civil filings for 1978 and 1983, 32 had increases. Of the 36 States that reported criminal filings for both years, 33 showed an increase in the volume of criminal filings.

In the 24 States that could report, felony filings comprised from 5% to 32% of total criminal filings with a median of 9%.

Victims and witnesses are taking a more significant part in the prosecution of felons

Recent attention to crime victims has spurred the development of legislation and services that are more responsive to victims.

- Some States have raised witness fees from $5–10 per day in trial to $20–30 per day, established procedures for victim and witness notification of court proceedings, and guaranteed the right to speedy disposition of cases
- 9 States and the Federal Government have comprehensive bills of rights for victims
- 39 States and the Federal Government have laws or guidelines requiring that victims and witnesses be notified of the scheduling and cancellation of criminal proceedings
- 33 States and the Federal Government allow victims to participate in criminal proceedings via oral or written testimony.

Courts at various levels of government interact in many ways

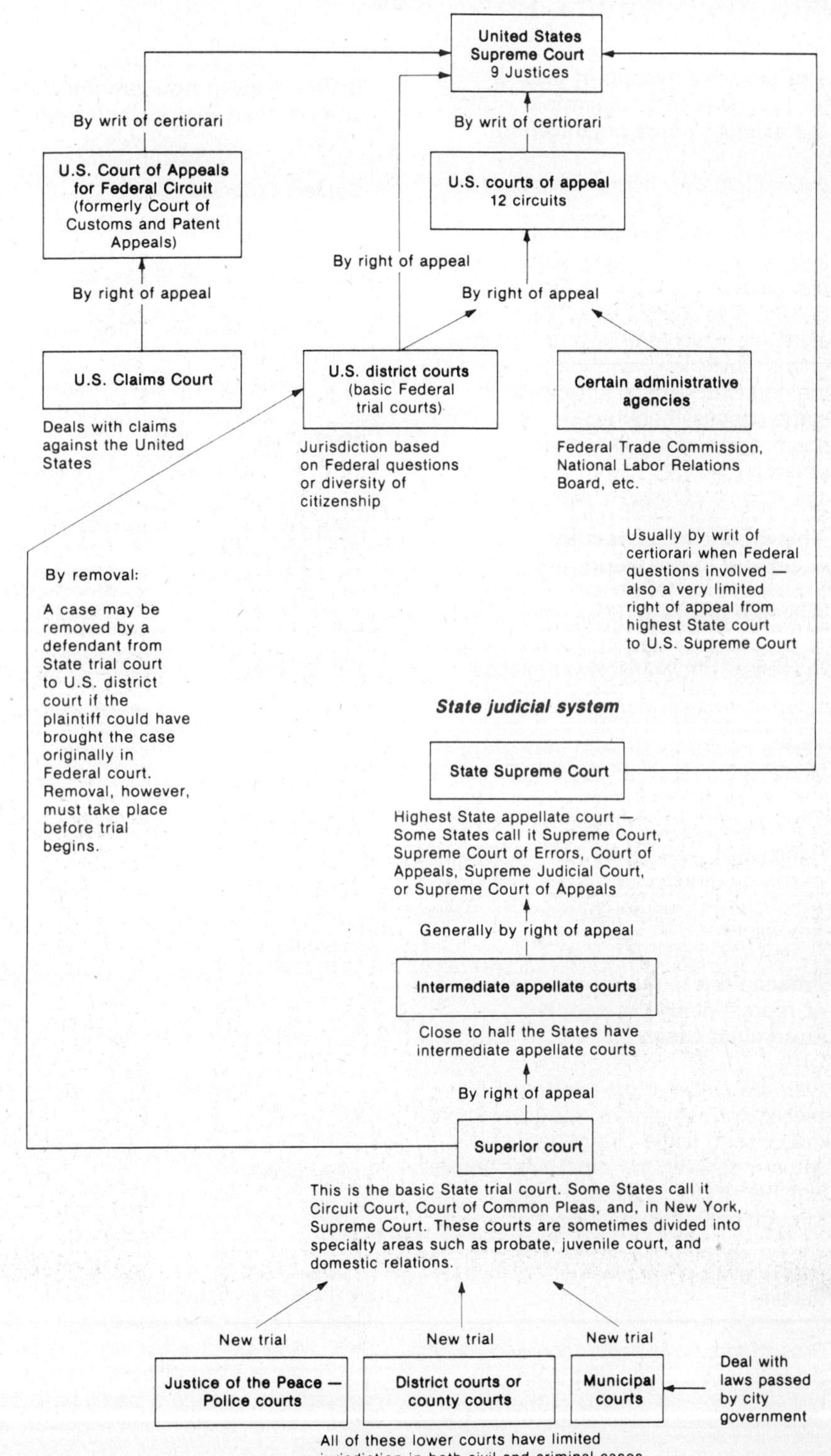

Updated and reprinted by permission from *The American Legal Environment* by William T. Schantz.

The prosecutor provides the link between the law enforcement and adjudicatory processes

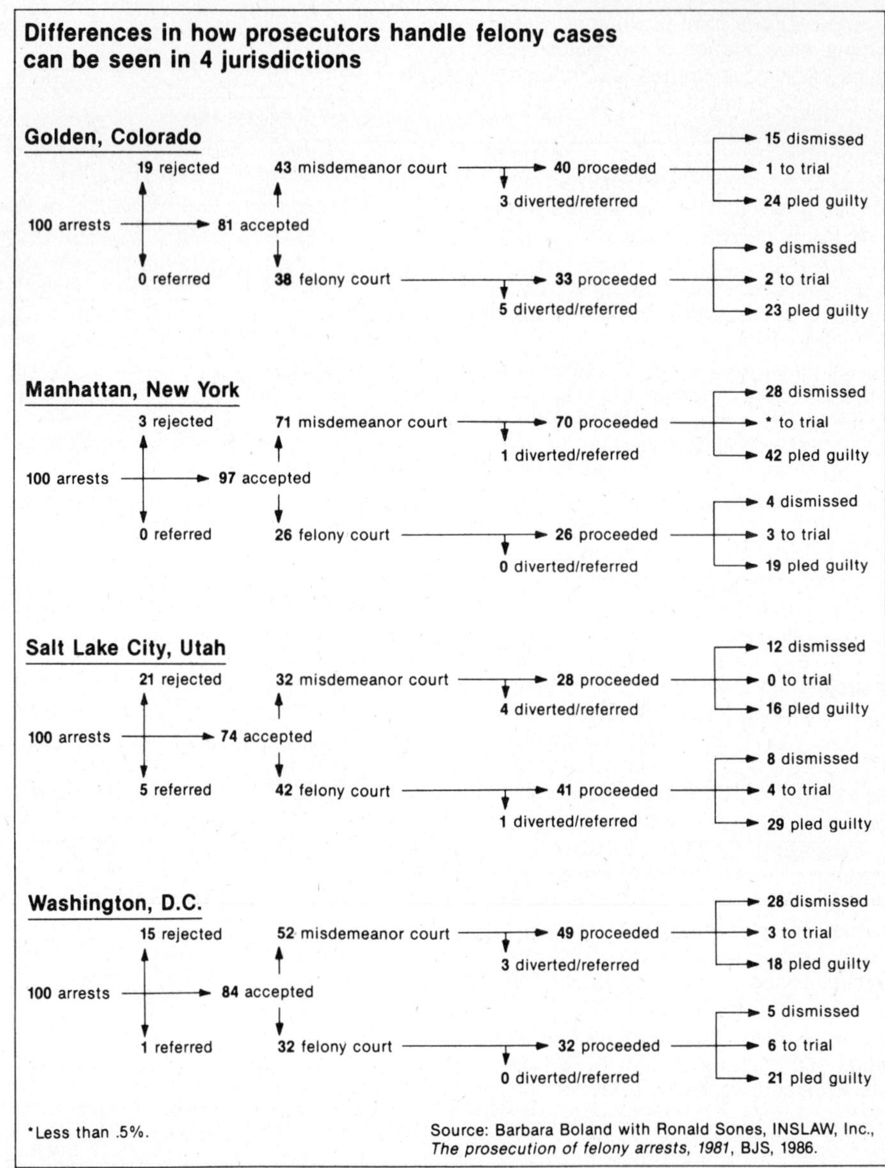

The separate system of justice for juveniles often operates within the existing court organization

Jurisdiction over juvenile delinquency, dependent or neglected children, and related matters is vested in various types of courts. In many States the juvenile court is a division of the court of general jurisdiction. A few States have statewide systems of juvenile or family courts. Juvenile jurisdiction is vested in the courts of general jurisdiction in some counties and in separate juvenile courts or courts of limited jurisdiction in others.

The American prosecutor is unique in the world

First, the American prosecutor is a public prosecutor representing the people in matters of criminal law. Historically, European societies viewed crimes as wrongs against an individual whose claims could be pressed through private prosecution. Second, the American prosecutor is usually a local official, reflecting the development of autonomous local governments in the colonies. Finally, as an elected official, the local American prosecutor is responsible to the voters.

Prosecution is the function of representing the people in criminal cases

After the police arrest a suspect, the prosecutor coordinates the government's response to crime—from the initial screening, when the prosecutor decides whether or not to press charges, through trial. In some instances, it continues through sentencing with the presentation of sentencing recommendations.

Prosecutors have been accorded much discretion in carrying out their responsibilities. They make many of the decisions that determine whether a case will proceed through the criminal justice process.

Prosecution is predominantly a State and local function

Prosecuting officials include State, district, county, prosecuting, and commonwealth attorneys; corporation counsels; circuit solicitors; attorneys general; and U.S. attorneys. Prosecution is carried out by more than 8,000 State, county, municipal, and township prosecution agencies.[1] In all but five States, local prosecutors are elected officials. Many small jurisdictions engage a part-time prosecutor who also maintains a private law practice. In some areas police share the charging responsibility of local prosecutors. Prosecutors in urban jurisdictions often have offices staffed by many full-time assistants. Each State has an office of the attorney general, which has jurisdiction over all matters involving State law but generally, unless specifically requested, is not involved in local prosecution. Federal prosecution is the responsibility of 93 U.S. attorneys who are appointed by the President subject to confirmation by the Senate.

The decision to charge is generally a function of the prosecutor

Results of a 1981 survey of police and prosecution agencies in localities of over 100,000 indicate that police file initial charges in half the jurisdictions surveyed. This arrangement, sometimes referred to as the police court, is not commonly found in the larger urban areas that account for most of the UCR Index crime. Usually, once an arrest is made and the case is referred to the prosecutor, most prosecutors screen cases to see if they merit prosecution. The prosecutor can refuse to prosecute, for example, because of insufficient evidence. The decision to charge is not usually reviewable by any other branch of government.

Some prosecutors accept almost all cases for prosecution; others screen out many cases

Some prosecutors have screening units designed to reject cases at the earliest possible point. Others tend to accept most arrests, more of which are dismissed by judges later in the adjudication process. Most prosecutor offices fall somewhere between these two extremes.

Arrest disposition patterns in 16 jurisdictions range from 0 to 47% of arrests rejected for prosecution. Jurisdictions with high rejection rates generally were found to have lower rates of dismissal at later stages of the criminal process. Conversely, jurisdictions that accepted most or all arrests usually had high dismissal rates.

Prosecutorial screening practices are of several distinct types

Several studies conclude that screening decisions consider—
- evidentiary factors
- the views of the prosecutor on key criminal justice issues
- the political and social environment in which the prosecutor functions
- the resource constraints and organization of prosecutorial operations.

Jacoby's study confirmed the presence of at least three policies that affect the screening decision:
- Legal sufficiency—an arrest is accepted for prosecution if, on routine review of the arrest, the minimum legal elements of a case are present.
- System efficiency—arrests are disposed as quickly as possible by the fastest means possible, which are rejections, dismissals, and pleas.
- Trial sufficiency—the prosecutor accepts only those arrests for which, in his or her view, there is sufficient evidence to convict in court.

The official accusation in felony cases is a grand jury indictment or a prosecutor's bill of information

According to Jacoby, the accusatory process usually follows one of four paths:
- arrest to preliminary hearing for bindover to grand jury for indictment
- arrest to grand jury for indictment
- arrest to preliminary hearing to a bill of information
- a combination of the above at the prosecutor's discretion.

Whatever the method of accusation, the State must demonstrate only that there is probable cause to support the charge.

The preliminary hearing is used in some jurisdictions to determine probable cause

The purpose of the hearing is to see if there is probable cause to believe a crime has been committed and that the defendant committed it. Evidence may be presented by both the prosecution and the defense. On a finding of probable cause the defendant is held to answer in the next stage of a felony proceeding.

The grand jury emerged from the American Revolution as the people's protection against oppressive prosecution by the State

Today, the grand jury is a group of ordinary citizens, usually no more than 23, which has both accusatory and investigative functions. The jury's proceedings are secret and not adversarial so that most rules of evidence for trials do not apply. Usually, evidence is presented by the prosecutor who brings a case to the grand jury's attention. However, in some States the grand jury is used primarily to investigate issues of public corruption and organized crime.

Some States do not require a grand jury indictment to initiate prosecutions

Grand jury indictment required	Grand jury indictment optional	Grand jury lacks authority to indict
All crimes	Arizona	Pennsylvania
New Jersey	Arkansas	
South Carolina	California	
Tennessee	Colorado	
Virginia	Idaho	
	Illinois	
All felonies	Indiana	
Alabama	Iowa	
Alaska	Kansas	
Delaware	Maryland	
District of Columbia	Michigan	
Georgia	Missouri	
Hawaii	Montana	
Kentucky	Nebraska	
Maine	Nevada	
Mississippi	New Mexico	
New Hampshire	North Dakota	
New York	Oklahoma	
North Carolina	Oregon	
Ohio	South Dakota	
Texas	Utah	
West Virginia	Vermont	
	Washington	
Capital crimes only	Wisconsin	
Connecticut	Wyoming	
Florida		
Louisiana		
Massachusetts		
Minnesota		
Rhode Island		

Note: With the exception of capital cases a defendant can always waive the right to an indictment. Thus, the requirement for an indictment to initiate prosecution exists only in the absence of a waiver.

Source: Deborah Day Emerson, *Grand jury reform: A review of key issues*, National Institute of Justice, U.S. Department of Justice, January 1983.

The secrecy of the grand jury is a matter of controversy

Critics of the grand jury process suggest it denies due process and equal protection under the law and exists only to serve the prosecutor. Recent criticisms have fostered a number of reforms requiring due process protections for persons under investigation and for witnesses; requiring improvements in the quality and quantity of evidence presented; and opening the proceeding to outside review. While there is much variation in the nature and implementation of reforms, 15 States have enacted laws affording the right to counsel, and 10 States require evidentiary standards approaching the requirements imposed at trial.

The defense attorney's function is to protect the defendant's legal rights and to be the defendant's advocate in the adversary process

Defendants have the right to defend themselves, but most prefer to be represented by a specialist in the law. Relatively few members of the legal profession specialize in criminal law, but lawyers who normally handle other types of legal matters may take criminal cases.

The right to the assistance of counsel is more than the right to hire a lawyer

Supreme Court decisions in *Gideon* v. *Wainwright* (1963) and *Argersinger* v. *Hamlin* (1972) established that the right to an attorney may not be frustrated by lack of means. For both felonies and misdemeanors for which jail or prison can be the penalty, the State must provide an attorney to any accused person who is indigent.

The institutional response to this Constitutional mandate is still evolving as States experiment with various ways to provide legal counsel for indigent defendants.

The Duty of the Defense Counsel

J. Radley Herold

Presently in private practice in White Plains and Katonah, New York; Town Justice and Acting Village Justice in Scarsdale, New York; Westchester County Assistant District Attorney, 1961 to 1968; and Chief Counsel of the Criminal Division of the Westchester County Legal Aid Society, 1968 to 1973. Chairman of the Criminal Justice Section of the Westchester County Bar Association.

The duty of the defense counsel is to represent the client zealously within the bounds of the law. The defense counsel is ordinarily[1] an advocate who, for the most part, deals with past conduct. As such he must take the facts as he finds them. While serving as advocate, the lawyer should resolve any doubts as to the bounds of the law in favor of the client.[2] Quite obviously this duty is different from that of the prosecutor, who is obliged to see that justice be done and *not* merely to convict.[3] That obligation—of seeing that justice is done—falls on defense counsel only to the extent that it is consistent with the interests of the accused and not otherwise.

The general public views these duties of the defense counsel with understandable suspicion and probable contempt. The public often asks a defense counsel how it feels to represent a person they know[4] to be guilty when that person is acquitted of the charge.[5] By doing so the questioner mistakenly believes that the attorney *alone* "engineered" the outcome, thereby ignoring the fact that the decision was by a jury of 12 citizens—who are no different than the questioner—or a judge who simply decided that the prosecutor did not have enough evidence to prove the charge beyond a reasonable doubt. In order to get this point across to the public they should be asked how they would feel as an attorney representing a client whom they believed[6] was innocent which client was found guilty. It really comes down to a person giving their opinion from the position that they occupy at the time they are posing the question. An illustration of that may be learned from the jocular definitions of a conservative and a liberal. A conservative is someone who has just been mugged. A liberal is the person charged with the mugging.[7] The public must be made to appreciate as well as understand that every accused, whether in fact innocent or guilty, is entitled to representation by counsel. That counsel, in order to give meaning to the term "effective assistance of counsel," must owe no duty other than to the client so long as that duty is carried out within the strictures of the law.

". . . it is a part of the counsel's obligation of fidelity to his client that in his role as advocate, his conduct of the case not be governed by his personal views of right or justice but by the task he has assumed of furthering his client's interest to the fullest extent that the law and the standards of professional conduct permit."[8]

It has been correctly stated that if the legal rights of those most detested in our society are not held inviolable then the rights of all others are in equal danger of vanishing.[8] It is not a question of whether a particular accused *deserves* the rights accorded to him. It is simply that he is *entitled* to these rights lest by diminishing his we diminish our own.

In 1770 Captain Thomas Preston and the British soldiers under his command were prosecuted for the killings in the Boston Massacre. An attorney successfully defended all but two of the soldiers and was called a traitor to the Patriot cause. In time the devotion of the attorney to the cause of representing the unpopular was vindicated. The attorney was John Adams who was to become the second President of the United States.[10]

"The first duty of an attorney is to keep the secrets of his clients."[11] The first stage at which such a duty becomes apparent is when the initial conferences with the client about the charge take place. "Both the fiduciary relationship existing between lawyer and client and the proper functioning of the legal system require the preservation by the lawyer of confidences and secrets [of the client]."[12] The privilege of confidentiality of communications between the attorney and client is provided for by statute in New York.[13] "It

The second in a series on the duties of three of the parties in the Criminal Justice System—the Prosecutor, the Defense Counsel and the Judge.

From *Westchester Bar Journal*, Vol. 12, No. 3, Summer 1985, pp. 217-221, 223-224.

exists to ensure that one seeking legal advice will be able to confide fully and freely in his attorney, secure in the knowledge that his confidences will not later be exposed to public view to his embarrassment or legal detriment."[14] This assurance of confidentiality is the basis upon which the free flow of information between attorney and client is encouraged and founded. This privilege must remain unpierced even if it entails the details of a heinous crime crying out for solution and punishment.[15]

It is essential that the attorney make it clear at the beginning of the initial conference, and again whenever necessary, that a privilege exists. This is done so as to avoid at least three misapprehensions by the defendant: (1) the client who believes that everything told the attorney *must* be reported to the court and the prosecutor; (2) the client who withholds information and lies to the lawyer, resulting in actions taken by the attorney in reliance thereon, which cannot be reversed and which ordinarily work to the detriment of the client and (3) client, who though in fact guilty, tells his attorney he is innocent in the belief that the attorney will otherwise report his "guilt" to the judge and prosecutor and further because he believes the attorney will thus work harder for him.[16]

The client should be told that certain matters will be revealed by the attorney such as the information necessary for a bail application, to file proper pre-trial motions, to negotiate a disposition without a trial and to adequately defend the charge. To this extent the privilege will be impliedly or explicitly waived for those purposes only.

There is a further duty on counsel not to intentionally misrepresent matters of fact and law to the Court.[17] There is also a corollary duty that counsel must not knowingly make false statements concerning the evidence in the course of plea negotiations with the prosecutor.[18] These duties can come into conflict with the privilege of confidentiality. For example, in a bail application the fingerprint record of the client may not be available but counsel is aware of a criminal conviction—of a nature which would possibly make bail prohibitive or non-existent. The attorney cannot assert that there is no criminal conviction and, *if asked* by the court about whether a criminal conviction exists, must either answer honestly or remain mute. The former alternative is the best since the latter leaves the Court totally "in the dark" and a remand without any bail likely. Furthermore, a misrepresentation would not only cause possible damage to the cause of the client, it would be a violation of the ethical standards imposed on the attorney. As for the future of the attorney—if he or she has not been disbarred—all future clients will be hampered by the reputation for untruthfulness created by but one incident.[19]

The author once experienced a situation where two brothers were waiting court action on two unrelated charges. The second offense chronologically took place at a time when one brother was in custody on the first offense. It became known that the brothers were switching places for the court appearances apparently in the hope that a mistaken identification would take place at a felony preliminary hearing. The associate in the author's office at the time was instructed to tell the clients not to "switch" and to inform the court, if inquiry were made, of the identity of the person standing before the court. The associate followed the instructions to the letter and did not misrepresent anything to the court and prosecutor. As it happened the prosecutor and the Court did not seem to grasp (or hear) the significance of what was being told[20] them and the witness identified the unaccused brother as his assailant. Suffice it to say that both honesty and confusion reigned supreme.[21]

On occasion the attorney will learn of future planned conduct of the client, or others, of a criminal nature. The former is least likely but the latter occurs often enough. There no privilege of confidentiality exists and the obligation is to inform the proper authorities.[22] This may result in withdrawal from any further representation of the client but it is nevertheless the right thing to do. The author in one instance was informed by a client that, among other things, a certain person was to be murdered by someone unknown. The client was informed that it must be reported and made no objection.[23] The information was then reported to the law enforcement authorities. The facts given were sufficient to protect the "victim" and not to be attributable to the client—although nothing would have been improper if the identity of the "informant" were to have become known.[24]

Where a number of defendants on the same charge seek to be represented by the same attorney, a potential for a conflict of interest becomes evident. The attorney should discuss any potential conflict openly with the clients and, regardless of the outcome, be prepared to advise the court that a conflict either exists or is non-existent.[25] Whether this is done by the attorney or not—and it should be—the trial court has a duty to protect the right of the defendant to the effective assistance of counsel and should recognize that a defendant may not perceive the existence of a conflict of interest in such joint representation. As a consequence, the Court must inquire on the record if the decision of the defendants to proceed with the same attorney is an informed one.[26]

The attorney has the duty to investigate the facts, to research the applicable law, to explain the options (to enter a plea of guilty or to stand trial) to the client, to show the weaknesses of the charge or the lack of evidence; to present every valid defense and to be familiar with and able to employ at trial the basic principles of criminal law and procedure.[27]

The attorney has the additional duty to control and direct the conduct of the case. As a consequence, there are a number of decisions in which the client, after hearing the advice and recommendation of the attorney has the absolute right to determine what course to take. They are: (1) whether to plead guilty or not guilty; (2) whether to waive a jury trial; and (3) whether to testify in his own behalf. All others decisions as to strategic and tactical matters are the exclusive province of the attorney after consultation with the client. As a practical matter, not all of them can be discussed with the client but as many as can be should be.[28] On most occasions the client will follow the advice of the attorney on those matters concerning which the former has the right to decide and will further make no complaint about the strategy and tactics of the attorney in presenting his case. But where a disagreement does arise, a record of its circumstances, the advice given, the reasons for the advice and the conclusion arrived at should be made.

When it comes to the testimony of defense witnesses it is up to the counsel to determine who, if anyone, is to be called. When it is believed or known that they will commit perjury, the attorney is obliged not to call them as witnesses. The situation is far more difficult with the client. If it becomes known that he will commit perjury every proper effort, including withdrawal from the case, must be used to prevent such testimony. But if time does not permit withdrawal and every other effort has failed, the client has the absolute right to testify. At that point, the impossible duty of the counsel is not to assist other than in conducting a circumscribed direct examination. Furthermore, the testimony may not be argued by the attorney as being worthy of belief. The obligation is understandably valid but nearly impossible of execution.[29]

These comments are just a broad overview of the duties of defense counsel in a criminal case. These duties, like those of a prosecutor, are complex, burdensome and not simple of implementation. It is hoped that the comments in this article will provide a common sense response to the misapprehensions of the public and their sometimes unjust criticisms of the defense bar.[30]

NOTES

1. The Code of Professional Responsibility of the New York State Bar Association provides for a lawyer serving as either or both an advocate or an adviser. An adviser primarily assists a client in determining the course of future conduct and relationships. In such capacity the lawyer should give a professional opinion as to what the ultimate decisions of the court would likely be as to the applicable law, Canon 7, EC-3. In the overwhelming number of cases, a defense counsel is dealing with past conduct and acts as an advocate. In the small number of instances in which he acts as an adviser he must be exceedingly cautious not to countenance future criminal conduct and become a criminal himself, Daily News, March 12, 1985, p. 19, New York Times, March 12, p. A24, 26th, p. A27 and April 8th, 1985.

2. The interests of the client are paramount over any considerations of personal or professional advantage to the attorney, Canon 7, EC 7-1 and American Bar Association Project on Standards for Criminal Justice Standards Relating to the Prosecution Function and the Defense Function, hereinafter referred to as Standards, section 1.6.

3. "The Duty of the Prosecutor," Herold, Westchester Bar Journal, Winter, 1985, Vol. 12, No. 1, p. 11. The best and most obvious example of the difference in duties is that the defense counsel has no duty to inform the authorities of inculpatory evidence while the prosecutor must inform him of exculpatory evidence.

4. As used in this context, the author refers to situations where the client tells the attorney he is guilty, as distinct from the attorney concluding guilt on his own instincts or judgment.

5. As an individual and not as an attorney advocate, the attorney may be "incensed" at the "guilty dirt bag getting away with it" but the attorney knows that the reason is simply that the State lacked the evidence to prove its case.

6. By "believes" in this context is meant the client tells the attorney that he is not guilty and the attorney believes him. There are, of course, instances where clients will tell the attorney they are not guilty and the attorney does not believe them for any number of reasons. In those circumstances the obligation of the attorney is to truthfully explain to the client why that "story" will not be credited. After that the attorney, if the client persists in the story, is obliged to defend the client with that claim as his basis. This is not, despite the misgivings of some, subornation of perjury. See *infra,* regarding perjury by the client and defense witnesses. Criticisms are also made of the courtroom histrionics of the defense counsel and the "technicalities" on which the "guilty" get "off" the charge. Histrionics is an occurrence divided between the prosecutor and the defense counsel and most juries, presumed to be composed of people with common sense, are able to separate the "wheat from the chaff." And there is always the obligation of the Court to curb such actions in certain situations provided it is done in a way which does not prejudice either party. As to "technicalities" it once again depends on the position one occupies at the time of such criticism and the nature of the "technicality." Lack of proof beyond a reasonable doubt is one thing. The failure to file a required number of copies of a document is another. Suffice it to say that when the critic or someone close to him is charged with a crime they rush to a lawyer "who gets them [defendants] off on technicalities."

7. Lawyers and non-lawyers alike involved in the Watergate Scandals, when accused of criminal violations, were quick to condemn what they thought were the unfairnesses of the criminal justice system as it affected them. Nothing had been heard from them before that and little has been heard since, "The Terrors of Justice," by Maurice H. Stans.

8. Standards, Part I, Sec. 1.1, Commentary, p. 173, *Johns v. Smyth,* 1959, E.D. Va., 176 F. Supp. 949 and The Ethics of the Advocate, 1961, Thode, 39 Tex L. Rev. 575, 583–584.

9. "How Can You Defend Those People," James S. Kunen, p. 27.

10. The American Heritage History of Law in America, pp. 32–33.

11. *Taylor v. Blacklow,* C.R. 1836, 3 Bing. N.C. 235, 249, 132 Eng. Rep. 401, 406.

12. Canon 4, EC 4-1.

13. Civil Practice Law and Rules, section 4503(a).

14. *Matter of Priest v. Henness,* 51 N.Y. 2d 62, 67–68 (1980), and *People v. Investigation,* 113 Misc. 2d 348, 350 (1982), Supreme Court, Kings County.

15. *People v. Belge,* 85 Misc. 2d 186, County Court, Onondaga County, 1975, affd. 50 A.D. 2d 1088 (4th Dept., 1975). "Privileged Information," by Tom Alibrandi and Frank H. Armani. This book and the *Belge* decision dealt with a murder trial in which the defense of insanity included the revelation of the whereabouts of the bodies of other victims of the defendant. These revelations had been made known earlier in confidential communications between the attorneys [Francis Belge and Frank H. Armani] and the client [Robert Garrow].

16. A takeoff on these cases can be where a client is represented by a former prosecutor just entering private practice. The client will claim innocence to "test" the sincerity of the attorney. When the attorney "passes the test" the client will "confess" guilt and authorize the best possible plea bargain.

17. Standards, Part I, section 1.1(d).

18. Standards, Part VI, section 6.2(b).

19. Standards, Commentary, p. 175.

20. That the person before the Court was not the accused in that case.

21. The Judge threatened to hold the associate in contempt of court until the author told the court he was acting under the instructions of the author. This case has remained in the memory of the author as an example of "How Not to Handle a Difficult Situation." After the transcript of the proceedings was sent to another Judge in the same Court, an apology was made to the author and his associate. The author then made the mistake in judgment of agreeing not to publicly comment on the controversy which had developed unless inquiry was made of the author about the proceedings. That is a mistake which would not be repeated now. The author should have issued a statement responding to the criticism of his office implicit in the media.

22. Standards, Part III, section 3.7(d). The Standard mandates the obligation where it is the client who intends to commit a crime. The author firmly believes that the obligation is the same where the future crime is to be committed by another.

23. Had the client made an objection it would have made no difference. The information would still have been reported and the author would have withdrawn from any further representation.

24. Anonymity was not requested by the client in any event. The means used to impart the information to the police and to protect the identity of the source were straight out of a cops and robber movie: an anonymous call from a payphone near a police headquarters by a person other than the author—the voice of the author was distinctive and familiar enough to be recognized by many police officers at the time. As an aside the author realized later that he had attended the same class in grade school with the daughter of the "victim" and a relation of the client. As another example during the time that the author was a prosecutor a defense counsel furnished information coming from a client as to a planned "jail break" from the holding facilities at the County Courthouse.

25. Standards, Part III, section 3.5.

26. *People v. Gomberg,* 38 N.Y. 2d 307, 313–314 (1975).

27. Standards, Part IV, section 4.1; *People v. Bennett,* 29 N.Y. 2d 462, 467 (1972); *People v. LaBree,* 34 N.Y. 2d 257, 261 (1974), and *People v. Jesus Rodriquez,* 94 A.D. 2d 805 (2d Dept., 1983). See also "Effective Assistance of Counsel: An Impossible Dream?", Herold, Westchester Bar Journal, Fall 1983, Vol. 10, No. 4, p. 281 at 286.

28. Standards, Part V, section 5.2. And see also "Critique of the ABA Standards for Criminal Justice," The Defense Function, Herold, Special 1976 Issue, pp. 86–87.

29. Standards, Part VII, sections 7.5(b) and 7.7. See also "Critique," *supra,* fn. 28, pp. 88–90.

The United States Supreme Court has just granted certiorari in the case of *Nix v. Whitestone.* In that case, the defense counsel told his client that he would testify against him at a state murder trial if the client committed perjury. The United States Court of Appeals for the 8th Circuit held that this violated the right of the client under the Sixth Amendment to the effective assistance of counsel, his right to testify and to due process. 37 Criminal Law Reporter 4008. See also *Whiteside v. Schurr,* 744 F. 2d 1323.

30. Unfortunately some of these misapprehensions and criticisms emanate from some members of the Bench and Bar—who should know better.

The Prosecutor as a "Minister of Justice"

BENNETT L. GERSHMAN

The author is an Adjunct Professor of Law at Pace University School of Law, and practices law in White Plains, New York. He was a prosecutor for ten years in the offices of Frank S. Hogan and Maurice H. Nadjari, and has written extensively about prosecutorial and police conduct.

These are heady times for prosecutors. Gone are the days when the Supreme Court every other week, it seemed, would invoke a new due process right for criminal defendants; when prosecutors would frantically prepare for strange new hearings labeled "Mapp", "Huntley", and "Wade"; would be embroiled in sensational, political trials—Harlem 6; Chicago 7; Harrisburg 8; Boston 5; Panther 21—only to be rebuked by defense counsel, the press, the public, and juries. Prosecutors were often on the defensive in those days.

Times have changed. Today, prosecutors are on top of the world. Their powers are enormous, and constantly reinforced by sympathetic legislatures and courts. The "awful instruments of the criminal law," as Justice Frankfurter described the system,[1] are today supplemented with broad new crimes,[2] easier proof requirements,[3] heavier sentencing laws,[4] and an extremely cooperative judiciary, from district and state judges, to the highest Court in the land.

Indeed, Supreme Court watchers, and I am one of them, carefully analyze the oracles from our Nation's legal equivalent of Mt. Olympus, and try to discern trends. Some trends are easy to decipher, such as the Death of the Fourth Amendment; the continuing drift from adjudicative fair play, symbolized by the Due Process Revolution of the Nineteen-Sixties, to crime control, epitomized by what I have termed the Counter-Revolution of Harmless Error;[5] and the increasing availability and use of draconian forms of punishment, whether labeled preventive detention,[6] consecutive jail sentences for overlapping criminal acts,[7] and more and more executions.[8]

Another trend, more subtle, perhaps, has been a change in the role of the prosecutor. Twenty-five years ago, in one of the great cases of this or any generation — *Brady* v. *Maryland*[9] — the Supreme Court could write this about the prosecutor's duty: "Society wins not only when the guilty are convicted but when criminal trials are fair; our system of the administration of justice suffers when any accused is treated unfairly."[10]

This statement was a kind of banner under which enthusiastic young men and women began legal careers in prosecutors offices, particularly in the office of New York County District Attorney Frank S. Hogan. Indeed, the cover story of one issue of the *New York Times Magazine* profiled that office, under the title: "Hogan's Office Is a Kind of Ministry of Justice."[11] For a long time it has been an accepted part of the conventional legal wisdom, translated into one of the principal Standards of Criminal Justice of the American Bar Association, that it is the duty of the prosecutor "to seek justice, not merely to convict."[12]

There are, however, serious practical and conceptual difficulties in squaring the prosecutor's function with that of a "Minister of Justice." The concept was seriously eroded in two important decisions of the Supreme Court —*Coolidge* v. *New Hampshire*[13] and *Gerstein* v. *Pugh*[14]—in which the Court recognized that it is realistically impossible for a prosecutor to play the dual roles of vigorous advocate and protector of public justice. In *Coolidge,* the Court said that the prosecutor is too heavily involved in the "competitive enterprise of ferreting out crime" to pass on the sufficiency of a search warrant in a case being investigated under his supervision. Only a judge is neutral and impartial enough to do so. And in *Gerstein,* the Court held that an information drafted by a prosecutor is not "judicial" enough to provide an objective guarantee of probable cause comparable to that furnished by a grand jury, because the prosecutor is inherently partisan, while the grand jury is an arm of the court.

From *New York State Bar Journal,* Vol. 60, No. 4, May 1988, pp. 8-12, 63-64.

Furthermore, anybody who has carefully followed recent developments in criminal justice, and particularly the Supreme Court's treatment of prosecutorial behavior, must view such references to the prosecutor's purported justice function with considerable skepticism. This is not to suggest that prosecutors by and large behave unfairly. They do not. However, the prosecutor's role is not that of a justice-giver, but of an advocate, a "Champion of the People," in the same way that defense counsel's role is not a defender of abstract justice, but, rather, a Champion of the Defendant. Frequent ceremonial language about the prosecutor's quasi-judicial function[15] is not only misleading, but may be detrimental. It places the prosecutor in an untenable conflict, forcing him constantly to walk a tightrope, and it invites the judiciary to display a kind of obeisance towards the prosecutor, suggesting that he or she stands above the fray, omnipotent and infallible.

To be sure, the prosecutor has a fundamental commitment to fair dealing, not foul play.[16] The respect, and success, of any prosecutor's office depends on a high degree of skill, good judgment, and fairness. If the prosecutor plays fairly and by the rules, justice probably will work itself out under our system of adversarial testing. However, to the extent that some courts, particularly the Supreme Court, continue to evince a consistent and unyielding philosophy of judicial permissiveness in the face of prosecutorial excesses, many prosecutors will get the wrong message, namely, that misconduct pays.[17] And to the extent that bar disciplinary committees wink at prosecutorial excesses, the message is reinforced.[18]

Clearly, prosecutors have legal and ethical obligations different from their defense counterparts. Prosecutors are guided by stricter rules, many of which are embodied in the constitution. Moreover, in contrast to defense counsel, prosecutors wield tremendous power and tremendous discretion. The juxtaposition of such power and discretion can be dangerous, especially if courts display restraint, passivity, and even withdrawal in the face of prosecutorial misbehavior. Indeed, such combination can be lethal. For example, in the recent capital case of *Darden* v. *Wainwright*,[19] the prosecutor, among other things, characterized the defendant as an "animal;" told the jury that the only guarantee against his future crimes would be to execute him; that he should have "a leash on him;" and that he should have "his face blown away by a shotgun." Darden's trial was "not perfect," said the Supreme Court in upholding his conviction and death sentence. "Few are." "But neither was it fundamentally unfair."[19a]

Obviously, we can never know to what extent the jury in finding guilt and imposing death, was influenced by the prosecutor's outrageous remarks. Was Darden treated unfairly? The answer depends, in part, on where one sits. One of the major problems with the Supreme Court's prosecutorial jurisprudence — and that of appellate courts generally — is that these courts look at trial proceedings retrospectively, and can only guess, quantitatively or qualitatively, at the prejudicial impact of such misconduct, or its influence on the fairness of the trial.[20]

To be sure, the Supreme Court has not tolerated every form of prosecutorial misconduct. In one case — *Batson* v. *Kentucky*[21] — the Court at long last outlawed the pernicious prosecutorial practice of peremptorily challenging minority jurors from jury service. *Batson*, as well as *Vasquez* v. *Hillery*,[22] which dealt with grand jury discrimination, are clearly long overdue and are to be applauded. However, they involve equal protection concerns to which the Court has displayed far greater sensitivity than to due process concerns. Indeed, virtually every important decision of the Supreme Court over the past several terms addressing the prosecutor's conduct involved a lower court judgment — state or federal — which had sustained the defendant's claim of improper prosecutorial behavior. In virtually every case, the Supreme Court reversed. It also should be noted that among the dozens of summary reversals by the Court — done without briefs or oral argument — well over 90% were decided in the prosecutor's favor.[23]

Any lingering notion that the prosecutor is obligated to dispense justice has been dispelled by recent decisions of the Supreme Court. For example, the increasingly expansive use of the harmless error doctrine is one of the principal themes in the Court's treatment of prosecutorial misconduct. Thus, in *United States* v. *Mechanik*,[24] the Court for the first time held that prosecutorial misconduct in the grand jury, reviewed on appeal following a conviction, could be harmless error. Similarly. in *United States* v. *Lane*,[25] the Court held for the first time that improper conduct in mischarging crimes, reviewed on appeal following a conviction, could be harmless error. Further, in *United States* v. *Hasting*,[26] the Court held that lower federal courts could not use their supervisory powers to discipline errant prosecutors who had consistently violated that circuit's rules. These courts were ordered to apply the harmless error test instead.

It is in the area of nondisclosure of exculpatory evidence, however, that the Supreme Court has rendered most meaningless notions of fundamental fairness and constitutional protections afforded criminal defendants. This is the one area above all else that depends on the integrity and good faith of the prosecutor. If the prosecutor hides evidence, it will probably never be known. Moreover, as an advocate, the prosecutor, if candid, will concede that his or her inclination is not to disclose. By way of rough analogy, we do not enjoy paying taxes. Since the government's auditing powers are severly limited, the tax system depends largely on the integrity of the individual taxpayer. Many evaders are not apprehended. But if a tax cheat is caught, the chances are good that the courts will impose severe sanctions, mostly for deterrent purposes.

So, it seems, should it be with prosecutorial suppression of evidence. But in this one area, where the prosecutor's fairness is so dramatically put to the test, the Supreme Court has continued to default. First, according to the Court, the prosecutor's good or bad faith in secreting evidence is irrelevant.[27] But surely if one seeks to deter prosecutors from hiding exculpatory evidence, willful violations should be severely punished. Not so, according to the Court. The hidden evidence has to be "material," that is, as the Court wrote recently in *United States* v. *Bagley*,[28] a case involving a prosecutor's false representations to defense counsel about monetary inducements to government witnesses, it has to be shown that *but for* the nondisclosure, the verdict *would* have been different.

Examples of this quagmire spawned by the Court are numerous. In *Smith* v. *Phillips*,[29] the prosecutor suppressed information that a juror in a murder trial had sought employment with the same prosecutor's office. The Supreme Court reversed the Second Circuit, which had granted the habeas corpus petition. The Court said first, that there was no showing of actual bias, nor, secondly, any showing that the defendant was prejudiced by the nondisclosure. Ethical standards may be overlooked, said Justice Rehnquist for the majority, because the "touchstone of due process analysis is the fairness of the trial, not the culpability of the prosecutor." But, *quaere*, how does one demonstrate prejudice if the juror swears: "I was not prejudiced"? Similarly, in *United States* v. *Valenzuela-Bernal*,[30] the prosecutor ordered the deportation of illegal-alien eyewitnesses to the defendant's crime before they could be interviewed by defense counsel. The Supreme Court reversed the Ninth Circuit, which had reversed the conviction. The prompt deportation of illegal-aliens is an overriding duty of the Executive Branch, the Court said, to which the Court will defer absent a plausible showing that the lost evidence would be material and favorable to the defense. Of course, as the dissent correctly pointed out, showing the importance of evidence without an opportunity to examine that evidence can be exceedingly difficult. And in *California* v. *Trombetta*,[31] the Court reversed the state court which had reversed the defendant's intoxicated driving conviction because the prosecutor had failed to preserve as evidence the contents of a breathilyzer test. The evidence was not sufficiently material, said the Court. To be material, a defendant is required to show that the evidence possessed an exculpatory quality that was apparent before the evidence was destroyed, and was of such nature that the defendant would be unable to obtain comparable evidence. Again, how does a defendant show the importance of evidence that is no longer available?

Moreover, the Supreme Court's undue deference to the prosecutor, as noted above, can result in wholesale abdication of traditional judicial functions. With due respect to the judiciary, the prosecutor is the most dominant and powerful official in the criminal justice system. The prosecutor runs the show. The prosecutor decides whether or not to bring criminal charges; who to charge; what charges to bring; whether a defendant will stand trial, plead guilty, or be conferred with immunity. The prosecutor even possesses broad sentencing powers, as the New York Court of Appeals' decision in *People* v. *Farrar* illustrates.[32] The prosecutor enjoys virtual independence. He has no superiors. He cannot be compelled to bring charges or to terminate them. Moreover, in using these vast powers, the prosecutor is presumed to act in good faith. The Supreme Court wrote a few months ago in a case involving the use of a private prosecutor: "Between the private life of the citizen and the public glare of criminal accusation stands the prosecutor, with the power to employ the full machinery of the state in scrutinizing any given individual."[33] And, one might add, to stigmatize that person for life. To be sure, the prosecutor's vast charging discretion is contrained by a few modest doctrines: the prosecutor must not be unfairly selective, vindictive, or demagogic in using his charging powers. These doctrines, however, are rarely invoked, and hardly ever successful.

No area of criminal justice is more complex and controversial than that of the prosecutor's discretion, particularly as it relates to charging, plea bargaining, dismissing, and granting immunity. It is here, in my judgment, that the courts should exercise more vigilance and control. Yet here, more than any other area, the courts have withdrawn more than ever.[34] Several recent cases illustrate the ineffectiveness of doctrine as it relates to the prosecutor's discretion. In *Wayte* v. *United States*,[35] for example, the defendant, a vocal opponent of the Selective Service system, was one of a handful of nonregistrants who was prosecuted, out of nearly a million non-vocal nonregistrants. Wayte made a colorable showing that he was impermissibly targeted for prosecution based on his exercise of First Amendment rights. He sought to discover information in the prosecutor's files. When the prosecutor resisted, the district court dismissed the indictment. The Supreme Court treated the case not as a discovery problem. The Court found that there was no showing that the defendant was selected "*because of* his protest activities," a showing of prosecutorial motivation that seems almost impossible to prove. Given the presumption of prosecutorial good faith, the prosecutor's expertise, and the prosecutor's law enforcement plans and priorities, matters which are ill-suited to judicial review, said the Court, there would be no interference with the prosecutor's discretion, even in this obvious instance of a prima facie case of selective prosecution.

Unfair selectivity is matched by prosecutorial retaliation in the form of increased charges after defendants raise statutory or constitutional claims. Prosecutors, however, may not be vindictive in response to a defendant's exercise of rights. Proving prosecutorial vindictiveness, however, is another matter. The courts have indulged the prosecutor in this area as well. Thus, prosecutorial retaliation by increasing charges after a plea offer is refused is not legally vindictive, said the Supreme Court in *United States* v. *Goodwin,*[36] reaffirming *Bordenkircher* v. *Hayes,*[37] even though such tactics may demonstrate actual vindictiveness. The concerns are purely pragmatic. Prosecutors need this leverage to run the system. If prosecutors could not threaten defendants by "upping the ante," they would obtain fewer pleas. Further, in virtually every pretrial context in which prosecutors have increased charges after defendants have exercised rights, courts uniformly have found no vindictiveness. This can result in some patently unfair decisions. In one recent New York case,[38] the prosecutor charged the defendant with perjury after his motion to suppress evidence was granted. The hearing court found that the defendant was a credible witness, and the police witnesses were not. This is a blatant instance of prosecutorial vindictiveness, or alternatively, of prosecutorial bad faith, particularly after a judge already had made a credibility determination in the defendant's favor.

Prosecutorial behavior in plea bargaining is standardless and often highly coercive. A plea bargain is a constitutional contract. The prosecutor must keep his promise. However, the prosecutor's decisions usually are deferred to by the Courts, and the prosecutor's interpretation of the bargain usually controls. A good example of this is *Ricketts* v. *Adamson,*[39] decided by the Supreme Court last June. The case arose out of the murder of Arizona newspaper reporter Don Bolles. The prosecutor and Adamson agreed that Adamson would testify fully and completely in return for a plea to a reduced murder charge and a reduced sentence. Adamson testified at the murder trial of two other co-defendants and was sentenced. All told, Adamson made 14 court appearances in 5 separate cases — 31 days of testimony and over 200 interview sessions with the prosecutor — but balked at testifying at a retrial after the above murder convictions were reversed. He claimed that his plea agreement, reasonably construed, did not require such additional testimony. The prosecutor disagreed, claimed that Adamson breached his agreement, and notwithstanding Adamson's willingness to accede to the prosecutor's interpretation, nonetheless indicted and convicted Adamson of first degree murder, and obtained a death sentence. A majority of the Court upheld the prosecutor's interpretation of the agreement, and found there was no double jeopardy bar to Adamson's conviction. The four dissenting Justices, on the other hand, said that Adamson had not breached, that there was a reasonable basis for his interpretation, and that the matter should have been submitted to the courts for resolution. Overzealousness may be an appropriate characterization of the prosecutor's conduct here. He behaved more like an "Avenging Angel" than a "Minister of Justice."

Although prosecutors may need "leverage" in plea bargaining, they do not need leverage when seeking a defendant's agreement to release the police or municipality from civil liability following an arrest, and using the dismissal of charges as a weapon to compel such agreement. In *Newton* v. *Rumery,*[40] the First Circuit, as had several other circuits, found such release-dismissal agreements invalid as contravening public policy. The Supreme Court reversed, finding that the agreement was voluntarily and knowingly entered into, as in the case of plea bargains. But as the dissent pointed out, the release-dismissal agreement is inherently coercive and unfair, there being no mutuality of advantage, as there is in plea bargaining. Moreover, there is a conflict of interest between the prosecutor's interest in furthering legitimate law enforcement objectives, and at the same time protecting the town, police, or other public officials, from civil liability.

Finally, as noted above, the standards applied by the courts to prosecutors often are unrealistic. Clearly, the search for a prosecutorial *mens rea,* or guilty mind, is hazardous at best. Prosecutors do not confess their misdeeds, and presumptions are rarely invoked. Thus, in *Oregon* v. *Kennedy,*[41] a case in which a prosecutor's misconduct provoked the defendant to ask for a mistrial, the Supreme Court was asked to decide whether retrial should be barred on double jeopardy grounds. Several courts, including some New York courts, looked to the seriousness of the misconduct in deciding whether to bar retrial.[42] The Supreme Court, however, adopted the most restrictive approach possible, requiring proof that the prosecutor's specific intention was to goad the defendant into seeking a mistrial, rather than prejudicing the defendant generally. Proving such specific intent, said the four dissenting justices, is "almost inconceivable."[43]

For some prosecutors, the temptation to cross over the allowable ethical line often must be irresistible, particularly because misconduct frequently creates distinct advantages to prosecutors in helping to win their case. It takes a steadfast effort on the part of prosecutors to maintain high moral and professional standards necessary to avoid such temptations. Regrettably, many courts, notably the Supreme Court, have provided few incentives to prosecutors to avoid misconduct. As with punishment generally, deterring misconduct requires the imposition of realistic sanctions. Such sanctions are either nonexistent or not used. Prosecutors are generally immune from civil liability.[44] Imposition of discipline by bar committees is virtually unheard of.[45] Contempt rulings by trial judges are rare.[46] Appellate reversals may punish society more than the prosecutor.[47] And although appellate courts occasionally issue stinging rebukes, the decisions rarely if ever identify the offending prosecutor by name. Perhaps if the prosecutor were forced to appear before the appellate tribunal to defend his or her conduct, the incidence of courtroom misconduct might diminish.

Although not a Minister of Justice, the prosecutor's role may well be the most exacting of any public official. But by the same token, the public has a right to require of that official the highest measure of responsibility, professionalism, and integrity. Prosecutors who use their prodigious powers gracefully and fairly are no less effective as Champions of the People, and will be far worthier of respect and admiration. Courts and bar associations have to send out better messages, and provide stronger incentives for prosecutors to behave fairly.

[1] *McNabb* v. *United States*, 318 U.S. 332, 343 (1943).

[2] *See, e.g.* 18 U.S.C. §§ 1961 *et. seq.* (Racketeer and Corrupt Organizations Act); 18 U.S.C. § 1952 (A) (murder for hire); 18 U.S.C. § 1952 (B) (commission of violent crimes in aid of racketeering activity).

[3] *See* 18 U.S.C. § 1623 (lessening proof requirements in perjury prosecutions); Fed.R.Evid. 801 (d)(2)(E) (lessening proof requirements in conspiracy prosecutions, as interpreted in *Bourjaily* v. *United States*, 107 S.Ct. 2775 (1987).

[4] *See* 21 U.S.C. § 841 (b)(1) (increasing penalties for drug trafficking); 18 U.S.C. § 924 (c) (imposing mandatory penalty for use of firearms during commission of violent crime).

[5] Gershman, "The Harmless Error Rule: Overlooking Violations of Constitutional Rights," 14 West.B.J. 3 (1987).

[6] *United States* v. *Salerno*, 107 S.Ct. 2095 (1987) (upholding 18 U.S.C. § 3142 (e) of Bail Reform Act of 1984).

[7] *Albernaz* v. *United States*, 450 U.S. 333 (1981); *United States* v. *Blocker*, 802 F.2d 1102 (9th Cir. 1986).

[8] *See* "Rise in Executions Widening Debate," *N.Y. Times*, Nov. 1, 1987, p. 30. In *McCleskey* v. *Kemp*, 107 S.Ct. 1756 (1987), the Supreme Court upheld the imposition of the death penalty over claims that the penalty was imposed disproportionately against racial minorities. This decision may have involved the last major challenge to the death penalty as violative of the Eighth Amendment's proscription against "cruel and unusual punishments."

[9] 373 U.S. 83 (1963).

[10] *Id.* at 87.

[11] Mayer, "Hogan's Office is a kind of Ministry of Justice," *N.Y. Times Magazine*, July 23, 1967, p. 7.

[12] ABA, Standards for Criminal Justice, 3-1.1(c) (1980).

[13] 403 U.S. 443 (1971).

[14] 420 U.S. 103 (1975).

[15] *United States* v. *Young*, 470 U.S. 1, 7 (1985), quoting *Berger* v. *United States*, 295 U.S. 78, 88 (1935).

[16] *Berger* v. *United States*, *supra*.

[17] *See Rose* v. *Clark*, 106 Sup.Ct. 3101, 3112 (1986) (Stevens, J., concurring). *See also* Gershman, "Why Prosecutors Misbehave," 22 *Crim. L. Bull.* 131 (1986).

[18] Bar Committees rarely impose discipline on offending prosecutors. *But see In re Rook*, 276 Ore. 695, 556 P.2d 1351 (1976) (misconduct in plea bargaining). It is virtually unheard of for disciplinary sanctions to be imposed for misconduct in the courtroom.

[19] 106 Sup.Ct. 2464, 2471-73 (1986).

[19a] On March 15, 1988, Willie Darden was executed in Florida's electric chair. *N.Y. Times*, March 16, 1988, p. A15.

[20] *See* R. Traynor, THE RIDDLE OF HARMLESS ERROR (1969); Note, "Prosecutor Indiscretion: A Result of Political Influence" 34 Ind. L. J. 477, 486 (1959).

[21] 106 S.Ct. 1712 (1986).

[22] 106 S.Ct. 617 (1986).

[23] *See United States* v. *Benchimol*, 471 U.S. 453, 458 (1985) (dissenting opinion).

[24] 475 U.S. 66 (1986).

[25] 474 U.S. 438 (1986).

[26] 461 U.S. 499 (1983).

[27] *United States* v. *Agurs*, 427 U.S. 97 (1976); *Giglio* v. *United States*, 405 U.S. 150 (1972).

[28] 473 U.S. 667, 682 (1985).

[29] 455 U.S. 209 (1982).

[30] 458 U.S. 858 (1982).

[31] 467 U.S. 479 (1984).

[32] 52 N.Y.2d 304, 419 N.E.2d 864, 437 N.Y.S.2d 961. (1981).

[33] *Young* v. *United States ex rel. Vuitton et Fils S.A.*, 107 S.Ct. 2124, 2141 (1987).

[34] *See* A. Goldstein, THE PASSIVE JUDICIARY: PROSECUTORIAL DISCRETION AND THE GUILTY PLEA (1981).

[35] 470 U.S. 598 (1985).

[36] 457 U.S. 368 (1982).

[37] 434 U.S. 357 (1978).

[38] *People* v. *Stephens*, 122 A.D.2d 608, 505 N.Y.S.2d 393 (4th Dept. 1986).

[39] 107 S.Ct. 2680 (1987).

[40] 107 S.Ct. 1187 (1987).

[41] 456 U.S. 667 (1982).

[42] *See People* v. *Cavallerio*, 104 Misc.2d 436, 428 N.Y.S.2d 585 (1980). *See also Petrucelli* v. *Smith*, 544 F.Supp. 627 (W.D.N.Y. 1982).

[43] 456 U.S. at 688.

[44] *Imbler* v. *Pachtman*. 424 U.S. 409 (1976).

[45] *See* B. Gershman, PROSECUTORIAL MISCONDUCT § 13.6 (1985).

[46] *See* B. Gershman, PROSECUTORIAL MISCONDUCT § *13.3 (1985).*

[47] *See United States* v. *Modica*, 663 F.2d 1173, 1182-86 (2d Cir. 1981), *cert. denied*, 456 U.S. 989 (1982).

White Justice, Black Defendants

Many believe the courts are still biased

The verdict confirmed the worst suspicions of many of the 200 blacks who live in the East Texas town of Hemphill. Last month a jury in that tiny village (pop. 1,350) found three white police officers not guilty of violating the civil rights of Loyal Garner, a black truck driver who had been arrested for drunken driving and died after an alleged jailhouse beating. Lamented Will Smith, a local black minister: "It seems as if there's justice for whites only in this society."

From the beginning many townspeople doubted that the Garner family could get a fair hearing in Hemphill. Their concern was validated when Dorie Lee Hudson Handy, a 45-year-old cleaning woman and the lone black on the jury, confessed to the Fort Worth *Star-Telegram* that she believed the lawmen were guilty but voted for their acquittal because "I was just one black against all those [white] people."

Cries of whites-only justice echo as well in New York City. "No justice! No peace!" bellows the Rev. Al Sharpton at innumerable demonstrations on behalf of Tawana Brawley, the black teenager from Wappingers Falls, N.Y., who says she was abducted and raped by six white men. For more than eight months, Sharpton and Activist Attorneys C. Vernon Mason and Alton Maddox Jr. have waged guerrilla warfare against the state officials looking into the case and effectively prevented any significant investigation of the charges. The trio's wild claims and controversial tactics have alienated many blacks as well as whites, but their allegation that the girl was treated unfairly—and verdicts like the one in Hemphill—have stirred up new concern about an old question: Is the criminal-justice system biased against blacks?

JAIL TIME IN BLACK AND WHITE

Average sentence in months

	Blacks	Whites
Murder	91.7	79.8
Rape	55	43.9
Kidnaping	41	37
Robbery	37.4	33.3
Arson	22.5	23.3
Drug trafficking	17.7	17.9
Drug possession	14.6	13.3
All offenses	25.2	22.1

Source: Bureau of Justice Statistics

TIME Chart by Cynthia Davis

Many blacks are apparently convinced that it is. When the *New York Times* and WCBS-TV News conducted a poll on attitudes toward the justice system last January, only 28% of the blacks questioned felt that the courts are evenhanded toward white and black defendants. Such sentiments may reflect, in part, black discontent with the handling of several recent racially charged events in New York City, including the Howard Beach and Bernhard Goetz cases. These impressions also point to a deep-rooted distrust of the system, engendered by years of legally sanctioned injustice against blacks and other minorities.

Significant gains have been made since the days when blacks in the South were allowed to sit on only one side of the courtroom. In 1986, for example, the Supreme Court made it more difficult for prosecutors to use peremptory challenges to keep blacks off juries. A few months later, an all-white jury in Alabama awarded $7 million to a black mother who sued the United Klans of America over the lynching death of her son, a far cry from the days when an all-white Mississippi panel freed two white men in the infamous 1955 murder of 14-year-old Emmett Till.

Nevertheless, the perception lingers that justice remains far from color-blind. "There is a view in this country that if you're poor and black or Hispanic or Native American, you won't get a fair deal," says James B. Eaglin, chairman of the National Association of Blacks in Criminal Justice. "And the basic contentions that there are biases at every level of the system are well founded."

Awards for black victims in civil suits are a third or

sometimes even half the amount of those given to white plaintiffs. A 1985 Rand Corp. study of 9,000 civil cases in Cook County, Ill., from 1959 to 1979 found that the median award to a white in a wrongful-death auto accident was $79,000; for a black it was $58,000. Other studies show that sentences for black criminals tend to be longer than those handed down to whites convicted of similar crimes. While blacks make up only 12% of the general population, they account for nearly half of all prison inmates and about 40% of those on death row.

Defenders of the existing system say sentencing decisions are based on objective measures such as prior arrests, employment history and stability of family background, factors that are commonly believed to predict whether a culprit will err again. But critics argue that these standards stack the deck against a member of a minority group; they are likened to the literacy tests once used to prevent Southern blacks from voting. "Some of the criteria that sound neutral and nonracially discriminatory are in effect proxies for race," says Criminologist Marvin Wolfgang.

In a landmark 1972 study that tracked 10,000 Philadelphia boys, Wolfgang discovered that 77% of white juveniles were let go after an arrest with just a warning, vs. 56% of nonwhites. In a follow-up study published in 1985, Wolfgang found that 49% of the white youngsters were let off, vs. 40% of the nonwhites, an improvement he attributes to the increasing number of black police officers.

More black faces on the bench, or even at the stenographer's table, might prove to be just as helpful. "When a black person walks into a court and sees a white judge, white prosecutors, white clerks white stenographers, do you think they're going to believe they're going to get justice?" asks Franklin Williams, chairman of the New York State Judicial Commission on Minorities. Black attorneys frequently complain that they are not accorded the same respect that their white colleagues receive. Archibald Murray, executive director of the Legal Aid Society in New York City, says black members of his staff have been stopped and searched because court offices assumed that a black entering the courtroom must be a defendant.

Only 500 or so blacks sit among the nearly 13,000 judges currently on the bench nationwide. Many are found in states where judges are elected rather than appointed. "I never would have been a judge if I sat around waiting for someone to appoint me. I went out and got myself elected," says Justice Kenneth N. Browne, who was first elected to the New York Supreme Court in 1973 and is an outspoken advocate of the need for more black judges. "No judge is infallible. They all bring to their jobs their predilections and their experiences," says Browne. "There can be no progress in the criminal-justice system without the contribution of men of color."

Several states, including Washington, Michigan and New York, have already convened special commissions to consider ways to balance inequities in their systems by, among other things, hiring more blacks at all levels and holding seminars and other training programs to help sensitize white court officers to minority cultures. Programs have also begun to encourage victim-assistance workers to reach out to blacks and Hispanics, assuring them that they too are entitled to their day in court. It is only through such measures that minorities may begin to believe in equal justice for all.

—By Janice C. Simpson/New York

A Prosecutor's View of Plea Bargaining

Nick Schweitzer

Nick Schweitzer is an Assistant District Attorney for the State of Wisconsin, now in Dane County, formerly in Rock County. The views expressed in this article do not necessarily reflect those of either office or of Mothers Against Drunk Driving.

More than nine out of ten cases are disposed of by plea bargain. Yet, despite the pervasiveness of the practice, plea bargaining is often criticized as improper at best, and at worst a conspiracy to emasculate the criminal justice system.

The view of one who uses it frequently is that plea bargaining is a useful, often vital, tool. It is a response to a court system which could never accord the luxury of a trial to every case brought before it. It is a practical way to dispose of matters which do not require full legal procedure. Plea bargaining in criminal cases is the equivalent of negotiation and mediation in civil cases, but while the latter are praised and encouraged, the former is frequently condemned. Why?

At one level, legal thinkers disapprove of prosecutors' unbridled right to discretion as not fitting into an orderly scheme, but criticism more often arises out of dissatisfaction with a particular case, and expands to the generalization that "plea bargaining is bad." I find two reasons for such criticism. The first is that a particular plea bargain may be genuinely bad: an offender is offered a charge reduction, a sentence concession, or both, unmerited by the offender and unjustified by any necessity. The second source of criticism is much more common: an interested party is dissatisfied with the outcome, finding it inadequate to salve his or her injured feelings. This is nearly as likely to occur with a "good" plea bargain, reasoned, conscientious, and practical, as it is with a "bad" one.

The reason for such disappointment, I believe, lies in the difference between the expectations held by experienced criminal attorneys and those of the general public. Experienced attorneys know the inherent constraints of our criminal justice system, which impose practical limits on the punishment of an offender even if he or she were convicted at trial, but if the case is disposed of by a negotiated plea, critics may ascribe their disappointments to the plea bargain.

Looking Ahead To Sentencing

An essential aspect of plea bargaining is the need to be fair. Plea negotiations reflect the need to individualize justice. For any given defendant, on any given charge, there is a wide range of penalties. Most criminal statutes carry a maximum penalty and some a minimum penalty. In addition, sentencing options may include community service and probation, as well as conditions on probation such as counseling, restitution, jail time, and alcohol and drug treatment. Except in cases for which sentencing guidelines have been set,[1] sentencing is a human decision. At some stage in the lengthy process from arrest to judgment, some person must decide what sentence, without being unduly harsh, will sufficiently deter future acts by this offender and by other potential offenders, and will at the same time sufficiently assuage the victim.

The function of a trial is to determine facts, but the essential facts are at issue in only a small fraction of criminal cases. The great majority of people charged with crimes are guilty and know it, but before they plead guilty or no contest, want to know what punishment they face. Often, the only argument is over mitigating factors which don't constitute legal defenses, so a trial would be a waste of time. Sentencing is the "bottom line" for most defendants, and if they can live with the sentence, most are happy to save the court system and themselves the trouble of a trial. When the advantage to the defendant of an acceptable, known sentence meets the advantage to the prosecutor of concluding the case for what it is realistically worth, a bargain can usually be struck.

The Prosecutor's Role

The responsibility for sentencing ultimately lies with a judge, but no judge has the time to check into the details of every felony, misdemeanor, and ordinance that comes before him or her. Most judges want a recommendation from someone who has already taken the time to investigate the offense, the situation of any victims, and the background of the defendant: skills, education, prior offenses, rehabilitation potential, and attitude. In serious cases, a judge can accom-

From *MADDvocate*, Vol. 1, No. 2, Fall 1988, pp. 18-19. Originally published in *Wisconsin Bar Bulletin*. Reprinted by permission of the author.

plish this by ordering the local probation office to conduct a pre-sentence investigation, but resources limit this option to the more serious cases.

The prosecution and defense attorneys are the ones to present alternative sentencing recommendations after a trial. The prosecuting attorney knows the details of the offense and the defendant's prior record, while the defense attorney knows the defendant and any mitigating factors. These two are in the best position early on to discuss the case, and are also best able to find the time to negotiate before trial. If these two sides can reach agreement, the judge's decision can be reduced to review and ratification.

Another reason for negotiations to take place at this level is the prosecutor's exclusive discretion to reduce or amend charges. A charge may be dismissed only with the court's approval,[2] but the judge has no mandate to amend or reduce a charge. The discretion to amend charges is vested in the prosecutor[3] to cover those relatively rare cases where the wrong charge was issued. This authority is even more useful in the frequent cases where a penalty is inappropriate. As an example, cooperative first offenders are usually offered some alternative, such as a county ordinance, which would allow them to avoid a criminal record. This discretion to amend adds a second dimension to plea negotiations: the parties can consider not only the range of penalties associated with the original charge, but also the ranges associated with all related charges.

There are other reasons for a prosecutor to make concessions in return for a guilty or no contest plea. The prosecutor will often dismiss or read in one or more offenses for a defendant facing multiple charges. The prosecutor will still usually insist on a sentence consistent with the total number of offenses, but there is a general belief that reducing the number of convictions on the defendant's record is necessary to induce him or her not to tie up the court system by trying all the cases. The prosecutor may also face some obstacle to conviction (other than the defendant's innocence), such as an unavailable witness or a witness who would be compromised or traumatized by having to testify; in such cases, any conviction, even on a reduced charge, is generally seen as better than a dismissal or an acquittal. Then, there are the infrequent cases in which a concession is necessary to secure the defendant's testimony against a co-defendant or in an unrelated case. Finally, plea bargaining can be used to expedite cases which would otherwise take months or years. A prosecutor may agree to a charge or sentence concession in return for a speedy disposition which benefits a victim or takes an offender out of circulation quickly.

Editor's Note: Some MADD chapters encourage victims to supply prosecutors with their Victim Impact Statement early in the case for this very purpose.

The Quality of the Bargain

The real issue is the quality of the decisions made. Plea bargaining is a tool; its mark depends largely on the skill and care of the craftsman. The quality of the plea bargain depends on the values, interests, and abilities of the attorneys. If both sides are interested in finding a "just" sentence, the result is as likely to be "good" as is that made by a conscientious judge. But if one or both sides are interested mainly in expedience, primarily want to "win," or have other priorities unrelated to the merits of the defendant and the case, then the bargain may well be "bad." It is unfortunately true that prosecutors and defense attorneys make some "bad" plea bargains. Judges, too, can make sentencing decisions which are injudicious, but since the majority of cases are disposed of by negotiated plea, the opportunity for a "bad" decision by a prosecutor is that much greater.

There are two weaknesses in the plea bargaining process. First, it can become routine, and thereby an end rather than a means. Very few cases crossing a prosecutor's desk deserve a trial; as a result, the overwhelming majority of cases do settle, and prosecutors develop a strong work habit of managing their caseloads that way. Consequently, a holdout case may be seen as a nuisance, causing plea-bargaining to deteriorate into coercion, concession, and compromise, without regard for the merits of the case. The indiscriminate use of plea bargaining to clear court calendars has been justly condemned, but under pressure, a prosecutor's definition of a "reasonable" plea-bargain has an unfortunate tendency to expand.

The second problem with plea bargaining is that it does not encourage participation by the victim. The criminal justice system historically has treated victims cavalierly, and only with the recent development of victim/witness programs is their involvement being encouraged. Most victims want to have a voice in the outcome of a case, but this seldom happens when cases are plea bargained. One reason is that the negotiations are often informal and unscheduled. More importantly, talking to victims can be time-consuming and painful, as a victim's viewpoint is naturally very different from that of an experienced criminal attorney. Victims are deeply hurt by the offenses, and have difficulty accepting the concept of "what a case is worth" in criminal justice terms and understanding the realistic limitations on punishment. The prosecutor risks becoming the focus of all the victim's anger, disappointment, and abuse, so the task of explaining even a reasonable plea bargain tends to be pushed far down on the list of priorities. Since there is no requirement to contact victims, a prosecutor will commit the time and effort only if he or she is deeply committed to the victims' inclusion in the process.

Suggestions

There are no standards or checks imposed on plea bargaining by statute or case law. Whether to subject plea bargaining to some degree of quality control is a policy decision balancing discretion and accountability, but I offer here a few suggestions to district attorneys and judges.

First, guidelines can be set. A well-understood set of policies for reductions and sentencing recommendations can effectively limit the possibilities for poor judgment. Guidelines can be developed on a statewide basis, similar to the sentencing guidelines for judges, which set standard dispositions, yet allow departure from the standards for good reason. Second, plea bargains could be put into writing and reviewed within the D.A.'s office before final agreement. Although this would add a step or two to the process, it would help to establish uniformity, avoid "bad" decisions, and, if part of the policy, assure that victims' views were considered. Third, any judge who is concerned about the quality of the plea bargains brought before him or her could develop a litany of questions for accepting a plea bargain, like those for the taking of a guilty plea. This would allow the judge to play a more active role, or at least to signal that certain aspects of plea bargaining are open to scrutiny, without taking part in the actual negotiations. One of the questions might be to ask the attorneys for a specific justification of any reduction or sentencing recommendation; another might be to ask whether a victim was involved, and if so, whether he or she was consulted.

Conclusion

Despite my reservations about the potential and the occasional weaknesses of plea bargaining, I wholeheartedly accept and strongly defend the practice, as a very practical solution to some of the needs and pressures of our criminal justice system. Plea bargaining is a vital part of the complex system of powers and responsibilities which has evolved in our efforts to make justice as equal, fair, and efficient as resources permit. Without plea bargaining, other parts of the system would have to absorb vastly increased stress. Specifically, if we wanted judges to make all the decisions, we would need more judges, more courtrooms, more jurors, and more trials. This is not because defendants want trials, but largely because most defendants will "plead in" only if they know ahead of time what sentence is likely to be imposed. Until and unless society decides to allocate sufficient resources to these ends, plea bargaining will be essential. When exercised with a due regard to the case, the victim, and the defendant, it can result in outcomes as "just" as any available in our current system.

NOTES

1. "Wisconsin Sentencing Guidelines Manual," July 1985, State of Wisconsin Sentencing Commission, Madison, WI.
2. *State v. Kenyon*, 85 Wis. 2d 36, 270 N.W. 2d 160 (1978).
3. Section 971.29, Wis. Stats.

Genetics meets forensics

Courts are now grappling with double-helix models and population databases

Ricki Lewis

Ricki Lewis of the State University of New York, Albany, writes about and teaches biology.

In recent months, headlines and televised news reports have heralded the arrival of a powerful new forensic technology—DNA printing, sometimes called DNA fingerprinting—the highlighting of DNA sequence differences between individuals to establish identity. The steps and interpretation of the procedures are part of the standard vocabulary of molecular biologists. But many judges and juries, who are increasingly being asked to evaluate the technology, and even some crime laboratory personnel who will actually implement it, lack the biological knowledge to understand DNA printing. For many people, the biotechnology on which DNA printing is based has evolved in the years since they have been inside a biology classroom. The knowledge gap also extends in another direction. Many biologists are unfamiliar with the legal labyrinth new evidence must pass through before it is admitted in a court of law. The coming merger between genetics and forensics will require cooperation from both sides.

A trio of techniques, companies, and uses

Courts in many states are now grappling with double-helix models, aligning Southern blots, and consulting population databases. At the California attorney general's office, a task force plans to store DNA prints of 5000 sex offenders already in custody. The National Institute of Justice has provided grants to several medical examiners' offices to develop forensic application of DNA printing.

DNA printing has led to convictions in more than a dozen US cases

The technology is under the most intense scrutiny at the FBI's Forensic Research and Training Laboratory in Quantico, Virginia, where three DNA printing methods are being compared to determine which combination of approaches best suits particular forensic situations. Says James J. Kearny, microbiologist and section chief for the project, "The FBI has a conservative approach. We are following the same protocol with this as any other method, not accepting it at face value. We are taking it into our research group to work it over, then transfer the technology to other crime labs."

The three methods under FBI investigation are multilocus probes (each of which binds to repeated sequences at several chromosomal sites), single-locus probes (each of which highlights known sites on a single chromosome pair), and the dot-blot method (which detects known HLA variants and can be used on smaller samples of DNA than the other techniques). Single-locus and multilocus probes detect restriction fragment length polymorphisms (RFLPs)—inherited variations in DNA sequence—an approach already in wide use in basic research and in diagnosing genetic disease.

Basically the three DNA printing approaches differ in the clarity and sensitivity of the final result, and in the minimal amount of material needed for processing. Prints made with single-locus or multilocus probes have been compared to a thumbprint and require at least a drop of blood or similar amounts of other tissue. The dot-blot method is analogous to a single swirl in a thumbprint; although it provides less information, its great promise is that it works on minute amounts of DNA.

Three companies currently provide DNA printing: Lifecodes in Valhalla, New York, specializes in combinations of single-locus probes; Cellmark Diagnostics in Germantown, Maryland, uses multilocus and single-locus probes; and Cetus Corp. in Emeryville, California, is pioneering dot-blots. So far DNA printing has found three major applications: comparisons between crime scene material and tissue (usually white blood cells) from the victim and the accused; between a child, a mother, and two or more possible biological fathers in paternity cases; and between purported relatives living in two nations in immigration disputes.

From scientific to legal acceptance

What exactly will it take for DNA printing to become as firmly entrenched in the justice system as conventional fingerprints? For a new type of evidence to be admissible, a judge must be convinced of the technology's reliability and scientific acceptance in a pretrial hearing called a Frye hearing. This convention stems from the 1923 case of *Frye v. United States,* in which the US Court of Appeals in the District of Columbia affirmed the trial court's refusal to accept polygraph test results. Since then, the evaluation of dozens of new procedures and tests has rested on the language of the Frye decision:

> Just when a scientific principle or discovery crosses the line between the experimental and demonstrable stages is difficult to define. Somewhere in this twilight zone the evidential force of the principle must be recognized, and while courts will go a long way in admitting expert testimony deduced from a well-recognized scientific principle or discovery, the thing from which the deduction is made must be sufficiently established to have gained general acceptance in the particular field in which it belongs.

If after a Frye acceptance the evidence leads to a conviction, the next step is for the appellate court to affirm the use of the technology. Daniel Dwyer, Chief District Attorney for Albany County, New York, who participated in the state's version of a Frye hearing, which cleared the use of DNA printing, explains, "If the appellate court rules on it and decides in a well-written and documented form that it satisfies the Frye requirement, then this will serve as a springboard for all the rest of the tests pending in other states. Another state will adopt it, and then another, and then another, until it is generally accepted. The doubters will all fall in line."

But many legal and scientific professionals feel that the Frye requirement carries inherent flaws. It seeks demonstration of general acceptance, rather than evaluation of the evidence or rationale behind such acceptance—a situation philosophically opposite to the scientific method. In the past, the courts have looked to the credentials of expert witnesses to validate the rather vague "general acceptance" requirement. Even if technical or scientific information is presented by the most qualified and eloquent expert, the Frye procedure assumes that a judge, and later a jury, has the scientific background to evaluate the basis of general acceptance.

The importance of the expert witness in evaluating the acceptability of new scientific evidence has grown since 1983, when a group at the National Conference of Lawyers and Scientists recommended replacing Frye with direct evaluation of scientific evidence. And James E. Starrs, a professor of Law and Forensic Sciences at George Washington University in Washington, DC, and his co-workers suggest a game plan to evaluate new technology that converts the scientific method into legal lingo.

Those who must be convinced by expert witnesses are understandably a little gun-shy about new technologies, because they have been burned before, says Robert Shaler, Chief of Forensic Sciences at Lifecodes. "Remember paraffin? It showed if someone had shot a gun by looking for nitrates on the hand. But you can get nitrates on your hand if you work with or sell fertilizer, or play cards! It's the pattern of nitrates on the hand that correlates with having fired a gun. Courts perceive those exceptions as false positives."

Attorneys and forensic scientists are likely to be especially on guard if the technology involves biochemicals that are not as easily seen as a nitrate stain or conventional fingerprints. Scientists on the stand must make complex molecular technology tangible and accessible. To complicate matters, DNA printing is going under the gun at a time when judges and juries are moving away from blind acceptance of expert testimony. They are adopting a "show me" approach—they want to see just what it is that makes the experts so sure of their powerful conclusions. DNA printing lends itself well to show-and-tell testimony, provided the story is unveiled in a logical step-by-step sequence.

Michael Baird of Lifecodes has testified at several hearings in which DNA printing itself essentially stood trial. Using DNA models, diagrams of restriction enzymes and DNA probes, electrophoresis gels, and Southern blots, he elegantly leads the audiences through the history of genetics, which in a sense parallels the steps of DNA printing—patterns of inheritance, chromosomes, the double helix, exons and introns—also including basics of population genetics.

This last step—the population statistics that determine the likelihood that two individuals could have the same DNA pattern—is crucial. At the first trial of accused serial rapist Tommie Lee Andrews in Orlando, Florida, last October, omission of the statistical backup provoked the strongest challenge to DNA printing so far. Says Baird, "There was a mistrial, and the reason was that I wasn't able to talk about variability. The judge allowed testimony about DNA, but he would not allow me to mention the numbers. I think the judge was being conservative. He didn't want his ruling overturned by the appellate courts because he was introducing too much new technology. He was already going out on a limb with this new technology."

The key statistic—the chance that the sperm collected at the scene of the crime came from someone other than Tommie Lee Andrews—was one in ten billion. A few weeks later, at Andrews' trial for the rape and assault of a different woman, statistics were permitted after the prosecution cited precedents of using statistics from populations to derive databases, such as in protein and blood typing. Andrews was convicted. Although a DNA print does not provide absolute certainty, in a statistical sense it is clearly an improvement over the numbers generated by conventional forensic tests, such as sharing a protein blood marker with 30% of the population.

Defense attorneys, in their quest for flaws in DNA printing, point to its perceived newness. But whether it is in fact novel or not depends upon whom you ask. RFLP analysis dates from the mid-1970s, with use in human gene mapping suggested in 1980 by Ray White, Arlene Wyman, and David Botstein at the Massachusetts Institute of Technology in Boston. The technique made its clinical debut in presymptomatic diagnosis of genetic disease in 1983.

A pivotal application came in

1985, when Alec Jeffreys and his colleagues at the University of Leicester demonstrated how the short repeated stretches of DNA that pepper everyone's chromosomes in different locations could be used to establish biological identity. It was Jeffreys who coined the appealing phrase "DNA fingerprint." So to molecular biologists, the steps and rationale behind DNA printing are 13 years old; to others, including many forensic scientists, judges, juries, attorneys, and the press, these techniques are but 3 years old. Albany County (New York) Assistant District Attorney Michael Katzer says, "The application to forensics is what is new."

The future

DNA printing has now led to convictions in more than a dozen US cases, with at least 100 more trials waiting. How long will it be until the technology becomes standard fare in the crime lab? Many experts, including Lifecodes' Robert Shaler and the FBI's James Kearny, feel it has already arrived. Even the chief public defender of Albany County, Douglas Rutnik, sees a bright future for the technology, although he is currently charged with questioning its acceptability.

"It will eventually be as good for the defense as for the prosecution. After all, all you'd have to show is a different DNA band pattern in the semen from an accused rapist," says Rutnik. Recently a Florida man accused of rape was found innocent when his blood DNA print did not match that in the semen taken from a vaginal swab of the victim. Daniel Dwyer adds that if he were defending an accused rapist who refused to be DNA printed, he would doubt the man's innocence.

Already criminals are being affected by the mere possibility of matching up DNA prints. In a recent case, John Haynes, a 35-year-old Tacoma, Washington, bus driver, was accused of raping a 57-year-old Alzheimer's disease patient whom he transported daily to a care facility. Because the victim could not testify due to her medical condition, deputy prosecutor Barbara Corey-Boulet sent semen samples from the woman's body to Lifecodes for DNA printing. But the case never got to court. Upon hearing of the impending DNA test, John Haynes admitted his guilt. Says Lifecodes' Robert Shaler, "Did he confess under threat of DNA fingerprinting? We'll never know."

Ultimately, though, the power of DNA printing lies in the genetic material itself, in the three billion bits of information that define who we are, and particularly in those regions that vary from person to person. Kearny says, "For the first time we have a situation with the potential to prove the identity of the donor of biological material at a crime scene. We can exclude everyone else in the United States, potentially in the world." And, with a homicide occurring every 28 minutes and a rape every 6 minutes, that is quite an important potential.

Table 1. Some cases in which DNA printing was used.

Case	City	Date of trial*	Type	Outcome
Oklahoma v. B. J. Hunt†	Norman	09/15/87	Murder	Acquitted‡
New York v. J. Zambrana	New City	10/30/87	Murder	Convicted
Florida v. T. L. Andrews†	Orlando	11/06/87	Rape	Convicted
Florida v. D. Hill	Melbourne	01/20/88	Rape	Convicted
Florida v. T. L. Andrews§	Orlando	02/03/88	Rape	Convicted
Washington v. J. Haynes	Tacoma		Rape	Confessed
Florida v. F. Martinez	Deland	04/18/88	Rape	Convicted
South Carolina v. S. Ford	Georgetown	04/26/88	Rape	Convicted
Georgia v. J. G. Smith	Gainesville		Rape	Cleared
Kansas v. V. R. Pioletti	Wichita	05/09/88	Murder	Convicted
Idaho v. T. Horsley	Sandpoint	05/11/88	Rape	Convicted
Oklahoma v. M. Reed	Oklahoma City	05/20/88	Rape	Convicted
Florida v. S. Jenkins	Orlando	06/03/88	Rape	Convicted
Virginia v. T. Spencer†	Arlington	07/12/88	Rape/Murder	Convicted
Florida v. K. Baier	Jacksonville		Rape	Confessed
New York v. Wesley‖	Albany	07/15/88	Rape	Evidence admissible
New York v. Bailey‖	Albany	07/15/88	Rape	Evidence admissible
Florida v. G. Forrest	West Palm Beach	07/20/88	Rape	Convicted
Ohio v. G. Dascenzo†	Dayton	08/05/88	Murder	Convicted
Texas v. S. Delce	Bryon	08/19/88	Rape	Convicted
Michigan v. J. Fagan	Flint	09/09/88	Rape	Convicted

*Scientists from Lifecodes Corporation testified in these trials.
†Includes testimony in evidentiary hearing.
‡Body of victim was not found until after trial.
§Retrial.
‖Testimony in Frye hearing.

Convicting the Innocent

JAMES MCCLOSKEY

James McCloskey is Director of Centurion Ministries, Inc, Princeton, N.J.

On most occasions when it has been discovered that the wrong person was convicted for another's crime, the local law enforcement community, if it has commented at all, has assured the public that such instances are indeed rare and isolated aberrations of a criminal justice system that bats nearly 1,000 percent in convicting the guilty and acquitting the innocent. And this view is shared, I think, not only by the vast majority of the public but also by almost all of the professionals (lawyers and judges) whose work comes together to produce the results.

I realize that I am a voice crying in the wilderness, but I believe that the innocent are convicted far more frequently than the public cares to believe, and far more frequently than those who operate the system dare to believe. An innocent person in prison, in my view, is about as rare as a pigeon in the park. The primary purpose of this article is to delineate why and how I have come to believe that this phenomenon of the "convicted innocent" is so alarmingly widespread in the United States. Although no one has any real idea of what proportion it has reached, it is my perception that at least 10 percent of those convicted of serious and violent crimes are completely innocent. Those whose business it is to convict or to defend would more than likely concede to such mistakes occurring in only 1 percent of cases, if that. Regardless of where the reader places his estimate, these percentages, when converted into absolute numbers, tell us that thousands and even tens of thousands of innocent people languish in prisons across the nation.

Allow me to outline briefly the ground of experience on which I stand and speak. For the past eight years I have been working full time on behalf of the innocent in prison. To date, the nonprofit organization I founded to do this work has freed and vindicated three innocent lifers in New Jersey. Another, on Texas's death row, has been declared "innocent" by a specially appointed evidentiary hearing judge, who has recommended a new trial to Texas's highest court. Currently we are working on ten cases across the country (New Jersey, Pennsylvania, Virginia, Louisiana, Texas, and California). We have received well over 1,000 requests for assistance and have developed extensive files on more than 500 of these requests, which come to us daily from every state of the nation from those who have been convicted, or from their advocates, proclaiming their innocence. We serve as active advisors on many of those cases.

Besides being innocent and serving life or death sentences, our beneficiaries have lost their legal appeals. Their freedom can be secured only by developing new evidence sufficient to earn a retrial. This new evidence must materially demonstrate either that the person is not guilty or that the key state witnesses lied in critical areas of their testimony. We are not lawyers. We are concerned only with whether the person is in fact completely not guilty in that he or she had nothing whatsoever to do with the crime. When we enter the case it is usually five to fifteen years after the conviction. Our sole focus is to reexamine the factual foundation of the conviction -- to conduct an exhaustive investigation of the cast of characters and the circumstances in the case, however long that might take.

We find and interview as often as necessary anyone who has knowledge about the case and/or the people who are related to the case. We search for documentation and employ whatever forensic scientific tests are available that in any way shed light on, point to, or establish the truth of the matter. While developing this new information, we retain and work with the most suitable attorney in seeking judicial relief for our clients. We raise and disburse whatever funds are required to meet the legal, investigative, and administrative costs of seeking justice for these otherwise forgotten and forsaken souls buried in our prisons all across the land.

Appellate Relief for the Convicted Innocent

As all lawyers and jurists know, but most lay people do not, innocence or guilt is irrelevant when seeking redress in the appellate courts. As the noted attorney F. Lee Bailey observed, "Appellate courts have only one function, and that is to correct legal mistakes of a serious nature made by a judge at a lower level. Should a jury have erred by believing a lying witness, or by drawing an attractive but misleading inference, there is nothing to appeal." So, if the imprisoned innocent person is unable to persuade the appellate judges of any legal errors at trial, and generally he cannot, even though he suffered the ultimate trial error, he has no recourse. Nothing can be done legally to free him unless new evidence somehow surfaces that impeaches the validity of the conviction. Commonly, the incarcerated innocent are rubber-stamped into oblivion throughout the appeals process, both at the state and at the federal level.

So where does that leave the innocent person once he is convicted? Dead in the water, that's where! He is screaming his head off that he is innocent, but no one believes him. One of our beneficiaries standing before his sentencing judge told him,"Your Honor . . . I will eat a stone, I will eat dust, I will eat anything worse in the world for me to prove my innocence. I am not the man. I am innocent. I am not the man." The jury didn't believe him. The judge didn't. Certainly the prosecutor didn't, and more important than all of these put together, neither did his trial attorney nor his appellate lawyer. And so it goes for the convicted innocent. Their cries of innocence will forever fall on deaf ears and cynical minds.

Once he is convicted, no one in whose hands his life is placed (his lawyer and the appellate judges) either believes him or is concerned about his innocence or guilt. It is no longer an issue of relevance. The only question remaining that is important or material is whether he "legally" received a fair trial, not whether the trial yielded a result that was factually accurate. Appellate attorneys are not expected to, nor do they have the time, inclination, and resources to, initiate an investigation designed to unearth new evidence that goes to the question of a false conviction. Such an effort is simply beyond the scope of their thinking and beyond the realm of their professional responsibility. It is a rare attorney indeed who would dare go before any American appellate court and attempt to win a retrial for his client based on his innocence. That's like asking an actor in a Shakespearian tragedy to go on stage and pretend it's a comedy. It is simply not done.

Causes of Wrongful Conviction

But enough of this post-conviction appellate talk. That's putting the cart before the horse. Let's return to the trial and discuss those elements that commonly combine to convict the innocent. Let me state at the outset that each of these ingredients is systemic and not peculiar to one part of the country or one type of case. We see these elements as constant themes or patterns informing the cases that cross our desks. They are the seeds that sow wrongful convictions. After one has reflected on them individually and as a whole, it becomes readily apparent, I think, how easy it is and how real the potential is in every courthouse in America for wrongful convictions to take place.

(a) *Presumption of Guilt* The first factor I would like to consider is the "presumption-of-innocence" principle. Although we would all like to believe that a defendant is truly considered innocent by those who represent and judge him, this is just not so. Once accusations have matured through the system to the point at which the accused is actually brought to trial, is it not the tendency of human nature to suspect deep down or even believe that the defendant probably did it? Most people are inclined to believe that where there is smoke, there is fire. This applies to professional and lay people alike albeit for different reasons perhaps.

The innate inclinations of the average American law-abiding citizen whose jury experience is that person's first exposure to the criminal justice system is to think that law enforcement people have earnestly investigated the case and surely would not bring someone to trial unless they had bona fide evidence against the person. That is a strong barrier and a heavy burden for the defense to overcome. And how about judges and defense lawyers? These professionals, like members of any profession, have a natural tendency to become somewhat cynical and callous with time. After all, isn't it true that the great majority of the defendants who have paraded before them in the past have been guilty? Why should this case be any different? As far as defense attorneys are concerned, if they really believe in their clients' innocence, why is it that in so many instances they are quick to urge them to take a plea for a lesser sentence than they would get with a trial conviction? So, by the time a person is in the trial docket, the system (including the media) has already tarnished him with its multitude of prejudices, which, of course, would all be denied by those who entertain such prejudices.

Most people are inclined to believe that where there is smoke, there is fire.

(b) *Perjury by Police* Another reason for widespread perversions of justice is the pervasiveness of perjury. The recent District Attorney of Philadelphia once said, "In almost any factual hearing or trial, someone is committing perjury; and if we investigate all of those things, literally we would be doing nothing but prosecuting perjury cases." If he is guilty, the defendant and his supporters would lie to save his skin and keep him from going to prison. That is assumed and even expected by the jury and the judge. But what would surprise and even shock most jury members is the extent to which police officers lie on the stand to reinforce the prosecution and not jeopardize their own standing within their own particular law enforcement community. The words of one twenty-five-year veteran senior officer of a northern New Jersey police force still ring in my ears: "They [the defense] lie, so we [police] lie. I don't know one of my fellow officers who hasn't lied under oath." Not too long ago a prominent New York judge, when asked if perjury by police was a problem, responded, "Oh, sure, cops often lie on the stand."

(c) *False Witnesses for the Prosecution* What is more, not only do law officers frequently lie, but the primary witnesses for the prosecution often commit perjury for the state, and do so under the subtle guidance of the prosecutor. Inveterately, common criminals who are in deep trouble themselves with the same prosecutor's office or local police authority are employed as star state witnesses. In exchange for their false testimony, their own charges are dismissed, or they are given non-custodial or greatly reduced prison sentences. In other words a secret deal is struck whereby the witness is paid for his fabricated testimony with that most precious of all commodities -- freedom!

Such witnesses are usually brought forward by the state to say either that the defendant confessed the crime to them

Jailhouse confessions are a total perversion of the truth-seeking process.

or that they saw the defendant near the crime scene shortly before it happened, or they saw him flee the scene of the crime as it was occurring. If I have seen one, I have seen a hundred "jailhouse confessions" spring open the prison doors for the witness who will tell a jury on behalf of the state that the defendant confessed the crime to him while they shared the same cell or tier. When the state needs important help, it goes to its bullpen, the local county jail, and brings in one of the many ace relievers housed there to put out the fire. As several of these "jailhouse priests" have told me, "It's a matter of survival: either I go away or he [the defendant] goes away, and I'm not goin'." Jailhouse confessions are a total perversion of the truth-seeking process. Amazingly enough, they are a highly effective prosecutorial means to a conviction. Part and parcel of a jailhouse confession is the witness lying to the jury when he assures them that he expects nothing in return for his testimony, that he is willing to swallow whatever pill he must for his own crimes.

(d) *Prosecutorial Misconduct* The right decision by a jury depends largely on prosecutorial integrity and proper use of prosecutorial power. If law enforcement officers, in their zeal to win and convict, manipulate or intimidate witnesses into false testimony, or suppress evidence that impeaches the prosecution's own witnesses or even goes to the defendant's innocence, then the chances of an accurate jury verdict are greatly diminished. Sadly, we see this far too often. It is frightening how easily people respond to pressure or threats of trouble by the authorities of the law. Our insecurities and fears as well as our desires to please those who can punish us allow all of us to be far more malleable than we like to think.

Few of us have the inner strength we think we have to resist such overreaching by the law. This applies to mainline citizenry as well as to those living on the margins. However, the underclasses are particularly vulnerable and susceptible to police pressure because they are powerless; and both they and the police know it. A few examples will illustrate.

In 1981 three white high school janitors were threatened by the Texas Rangers into testifying that they had seen Clarence Brandley, their black custodial supervisor, walking into the restroom area of the high school where the victim had entered only minutes before she had disappeared. Brandley was convicted and sentenced to death based on the inferential testimony that since he was the last person seen near her, then he must have killed her. Eight years later Brandley was exonerated by the judge who conducted his evidentiary hearing when one of these janitors came forward and told how they had lied in implicating Brandley because of coercion by the investigating law officer.

On the eve of the Rene Santana trial in Newark, New Jersey, which was a year and a half after the crime, the prosecutors produced a surprise "eyewitness" who said he saw Mr. Santana flee the scene of the crime. A decade later that same witness visited Mr. Santana at New Jersey's Rahway State Prison and asked for his forgiveness after admitting to him that he had concocted the "eyewitness" testimony in response to intense pressure from the prosecutor's investigator. Since this "eyewitness" was from Trujillo's Dominican Republic police state, his innate fear of the police made him vulnerable to such police coercion.

Or how about the Wingo case in white, rural northwestern Louisiana? Wingo's common-law wife came forward on the eve of his execution and admitted that she had lied at his trial five years earlier because the deputy sheriff had threatened to put her in jail and forever separate her from her children unless she regurgitated at trial what he wanted her to say.

And in the Terry McCracken case in the suburbs of Philadelphia, a fellow high school student of the caucasian McCracken testified that he saw McCracken flee the convenience store moments after a customer was shot to death during the course of a robbery. The teenager was induced to manufacture this false eyewitness account after three visits to the police station. Among the evidence that vindicates McCracken are the confessions by the real robber/killers. So, you see, it not only can happen anywhere, it does happen everywhere; and it does happen to all different people, regardless of race and background.

Another common trait of wrongful convictions is the prosecutor's habit of suppressing or withholding evidence which he is obliged to provide to the defendant in the interests of justice and fairness. Clarence Darrow was right when he said, "A courtroom is not a place where truth and innocence inevitably triumph; it is only an arena where contending lawyers fight not for justice but to win." And so many times this hidden information is not only "favorable" to the defendant but it clears him. In Philadelphia's Miguel Rivera case the district attorney withheld the fact that two shopkeepers had seen the defendant outside their shop when the art museum murder was actually in progress. And in the Gordon Marsh case near Baltimore, Maryland, the state failed to tell the defendant that its main witness against him was in jail when she said she saw him running from the murder scene. One has to wonder what the primary objective of prosecutors is. Is it to convict, regardless of the factual truth, or is it to pursue justice?

The prosecution is the "house" in the criminal justice system's game of poker. The cards are his, and he deals them. He decides whom and what to charge for

The prosecution is the "house" in the criminal justice system's game of poker.

crimes, and if there will be a trial or whether a plea is acceptable. He dominates. Unfortunately, his power is virtually unchecked because he is practically immune from punishment for offenses, no matter how flagrant or miscreant. According to many state and federal courts, prosecutorial misbehavior occurs with "disturbing frequency." When the "house" cheats, the innocent lose. Lamentably, we see prosecutors throughout the nation continually violating the standards set for them by the U.S. Supreme Court in 1935 when it said that the prosecutor's

> interest in a criminal prosecution is not that it shall win a case, but that justice shall be done. . . . He is in a peculiar and very definite sense the servant of the law, the twofold arm of which is that guilt shall not escape or innocence suffer. . . . While he may strike hard blows, he is not at liberty to strike foul ones. It is as much his duty to refrain from improper methods calculated to produce a wrongful conviction as it is to use every legitimate means to bring about a just one.

It is human nature to resist any information that indicates that we have made a grievous mistake. This is particularly true of prosecutors when presented with new evidence that impeaches a conviction and goes to the innocence of a person convicted by their office at a prior time, whether it occurred four months or forty years before. Not only are they coldly unresponsive to such indications but they quickly act to suppress or stamp them out. New evidence usually comes in the form of a state witness who, plagued with a guilty conscience, admits that he lied at the trial; or from a person completely new to the case who comes forward with his exculpatory knowledge. Without exception, in my experience, the prosecutor's office will treat that person with total contempt in its usually successful attempt to force the person to retreat into silence. If that doesn't work, it will dismiss such testimony as somehow undeserving of any credibility and blithely ignore it. This prosecutorial impishness reminds me of a little boy holding his hands to his ears on hearing an unpleasant sound.

The Joyce Ann Brown case is a poignant illustration of this kind of prosecutorial posturing. One year after Joyce's 1980 conviction for being one of two black women who had robbed a Dallas, Texas furrier and killed one of the proprietors, the admitted shooter was captured and pleaded guilty while accepting a life sentence. She also told her attorney that the district attorney had convicted the wrong woman (Joyce Brown) as her partner in the crime. She had never known or even heard of that Joyce Brown. With the district attorney fighting her with all of his might, Joyce sits in prison to this day trying to win a retrial as we try to develop new evidence on her behalf.

(e) *Shoddy Police Work* The police work of investigating crimes, when done correctly and thoroughly, is indeed a noble profession. Law and order are essential to a cohesive and just society. Because police work is fraught with so many different kinds of pressures, it is rather easy for an investigation to go awry. The high volume of violent crime plagues every urban police department. Skilled detectives are few, and their caseloads are overwhelming. The "burnout" syndrome is a well-documented reality within police ranks. Interdepartmental politics and the bureaucracy stifle initiative and energy. The pressure to "solve" a case is intensely felt by the line detective and comes both from his superiors and the community and from his own ambitious need for recognition and advancement. If today's climate of "burn or bury" them puts more pressure on the detective to resolve, it also gives him more license to do so by whatever means.

If today's climate of "burn or bury them " puts more pressure on the detective to resolve, it also gives him more license to do so by whatever means.

Too often, as a result of the above factors, police officers take the easy way out. Once they come to suspect someone as the culprit, and this often occurs early within the investigation and is based on rather flimsy circumstantial information, then the investigation blindly focuses in on that adopted "target." Crucial pieces of evidence are overlooked and disregarded. Some witnesses are not interviewed who should be, while others are seduced or coerced into telling the police what they want to hear. Evidence or information that does not fit the suspect or the prevailing theory of the crime is dismissed as not material or is changed to implicate the suspect. Good old-fashioned legwork is replaced by expediency and shortcuts. Coercive confessions are extracted and solid leads are ignored.

Before too long, momentum has gathered, and the "project" now is to put it on the suspect. Any information that points to the suspect, no matter how spuriously secured, is somehow obtained; and anything that points away from him is ridiculed and twisted into nothingness. The task is made much easier if the suspect has a police record because he should be "taken off the streets" anyhow. That kind of person is not only a prime suspect but also a prime scapegoat. An example of this is Clarence Brandley, who was mentioned earlier. He was arrested in late August four days after the crime and on the weekend before school was to begin. The high school where the rape and murder took place was flooded with telephone calls by scared parents who refused to send their children to school until the murderer was caught. The arrest of Brandley calmed the community, and school started as scheduled. It was after Brandley's arrest that the investigation then spent five hundred hours building the case against him.

(f) *Incompetent Defense Counsel* The wrongly convicted invariably find themselves between the rock of police/prosecutorial misconduct and the hard place of an incompetent and irresponsible defense attorney. While the correct decision by a jury hinges on a fair prosecution, it also depends on dedicated and skilled defendant lawyering. And there is such a paucity of the latter. Not only are there very few highly competent defense lawyers but there are very few criminal defense lawyers, period. They are rapidly becoming an extinct species.

The current Attorney General of New Jersey not too long ago told the New Jersey State Bar Association that finding quality private defense attorneys "may be the most crying need that we have." He also told this same assemblage that unless there is an adequate number of well-trained private defense lawyers, there will be little hope for justice. Of the 30,000 lawyers in New Jersey, the number of those doing primarily criminal defense work is only in the hundreds. At this same conference the First Assistant Attorney General pointed out that 85 percent of New Jersey's criminal cases are handled by the public defender system; and he wondered if there would be a private defense bar by the year 2000.

This means, of course, that 85 percent of those charged with a crime cannot afford an attorney, so they are forced to use the public defender system. As competent as New Jersey's full-time salaried public defenders generally are, their resources (budget and people) are vastly inadequate and are dwarfed by those of their adversaries (the local prosecutor's office). Moreover, they are so overwhelmed by the sheer volume of caseload that no defender can give quality attention to any one of his cases, let alone all of them. So, in response to this shortage, public defender cases are farmed out to "pooled" attorneys, who are paid a pittance relative to what they earn from other clients who retain them privately.

The experience of these pooled attorneys in criminal matters is often limited and scanty. In addition, they do not bring to their new-found indigent client the desired level of heart and enthusiasm for their cases. All of these conditions leave the defendant with an attorney somewhat lacking in will, effort, resources, and experience. Thus, the defendant goes to trial with two strikes against him.

What we have discovered as a common theme among those whose cases we have studied from all over the country is that their trial attorney, whether from the public domain or privately retained, undertakes his work with an appalling lack of assiduity. Communication with the defendant is almost nonexistent. When it does take place, it is carried on in a hurried, callous, and dismissive manner. Attempts at discovery are made perfunctorily. Prosecutors are not pressed for this material. Investigation is shallow and narrow, if conducted at all. Preparation meets minimal standards. And advocacy at trial is weak. Cross-examination is superficial and tentative.

Eighty-five percent of those charged with a crime cannot afford an attorney.

Physical evidence is left untested, and forensic experts are not called to rebut whatever scientific evidence the state introduces through its criminalists. I cannot help thinking of the Nate Walker case, where, at Nate's 1976 trial for rape and kidnapping, the doctor who examined the victim the night of her ordeal testified that he found semen in her vaginal cavity. Walker's privately retained attorney had no questions for the doctor when it came time for cross-examination, nor did he even ask anyone to test the vaginal semen for blood type. Twelve years later, that test was peformed at our request, and Walker was exonerated and immediately freed.

This is not to say, however, that we have not encountered some outstanding examples of vigorous and thorough defense lawyering that left no stones unturned. What a rare but inspiring sight! We could not do our work without the critically important services of the extremely able and dedicated attorneys with whom we team up. If only the preponderance of attorneys would heed the admonition of Herbert Stern, a former U.S. Attorney and U.S. District Court judge in Newark, New Jersey, when he addressed a new crop of attorneys who had just been sworn in. He told them that they were free to choose their own clients. "But," he continued, "once that choice is made, once a representation is undertaken, then that responsibility is as sacred to us as the one assumed by a surgeon in the operating room. You must be as committed and as selfless as any surgeon." He further challenged them to "be an advocate. Represent your clients -- all of them -- fearlessly, diligently, unflinchingly. . . . Withhold no proper legal assistance from any client. And when you do that, you thereby preserve, protect, and defend the Constitution of the United States, just as you have this day sworn to."

(g) *Nature of Convicting Evidence* The unschooled public largely and erroneously believes that convictions are mostly obtained through the use of one form of tangible evidence or another. This naive impression is shaped by watching too many TV shows like Perry Mason or Matlock. The reality is that in most criminal trials the verdict more often than not hinges on whose witnesses -- the state's or defendant's – the jury chooses to believe. It boils down to a matter of credibility. There is no "smoking gun" scientific evidence that clearly points to the defendant. This puts an extremely heavy burden on the jury. It must somehow ferret out and piece together the truth from substantially inconsistent and contradictory testimony between and within each side. The jury is forced to make one subjective call after another in deciding whom to believe and what inferences to draw from conflicting statements.

For example, how can a jury accept a victim's positive identification at trial of the defendant as her assailant when she had previously described her attacker in physical terms that were very different from the actual physical characteristics of the defendant, or when the defense has presented documented information that precludes the defendant from being the assaulter? Several cases come to mind. Boy was convicted of robbing a convenience store in Georgia. The clerk initially told the police that since she was 5 feet 3 inches, was standing on a 3-inch platform, and had direct eye contact with the robber, he must have been about 5 feet 6 inches tall. Boy is 6 feet 5 inches tall. Four teenage girls identified Russell Burton as their rapist on a particular day in Arkansas. Burton introduced evidence that on that day his penis was badly blistered from an operation two days before for removal of a wart. And a Virginia woman was certain that Edward Honaker was her rapist even though her rapist had left semen within her, and Honaker had had a vasectomy well in advance of the assault.

Criminal prosecutions that primarily or exclusively depend on the victim's identification of the defendant as the perpetrator must be viewed with some skepticism unless solid corroborating evidence is also introduced. Traumatized by a crime as it occurs, the victim frequently is looking but not seeing. Victims are extremely vulnerable and can easily be led by the police, through unduly suggestive techniques, into identifying a particular person. The victim in Nate Walker's case, for example, was with her abductor/rapist for two and a half hours with ample opportunity to clearly view him. She told the jury without hestitation eighteen months later that "he's the man." Nate had an ironclad alibi. The jury struggled for several days but in the end came in with a guilty verdict. As mentioned earlier, he was scientifically vindicated twelve years later.

When juries are confronted with a choice between a victim's ringing declaration that "that's the man" and solid evidence that "it couldn't be him," they usually cast their lot with the victim. I suggest that this can be a very dangerous tendency and practice. And this is particularly so when identification crosses racial lines, that is, when a white victim says it was that black person. Future jurors should be aware that identifications can be very unreliable forms of evidence.

Another type of evidence that can be misleading and even confusing to jurors is that offered by laboratory scientists. Results of laboratory tests that are presented by the forensic scientists are not always what they appear to be, although they strongly influence jury decisions. A recent New York Times article pointed out that there is a "growing concern about the professionalism and impartiality of the laboratory scientists whose testimony in court can often mean conviction or acquittal." This article went on to say that the work of forensic technicians in police crime laboratories is plagued by uneven training and questionable objectivity.

The reality is that in most criminal trials the verdict more often than not hinges on whose witnesses -- the state's or defendant's -- the jury chooses to believe.

We share this mounting concern because we see instance after instance where the prosecutor's crime laboratory experts cross the line from science to advocacy. They exaggerate the results of their analysis of hairs, fibers, blood, or semen in such a manner that it is absolutely devastating to the defendant. To put the defendants at a further disadvantage, the defense attorneys do not educate themselves in the forensic science in question, and therefore conduct a weak cross-examination. Also, in many cases,the defense does not call in its own forensic experts, whose testimony in numerous instances could severely damage the state's scientific analysis.

One case profoundly reflects this common cause of numerous unjust convictions. Roger Coleman sits on Virginia's death row today primarily because the Commonwealth's Bureau of Forensic Science expert testified that the two foreign pubic hairs found on the murdered victim were "consistent" with Mr. Coleman's, and that it was "unlikely" that these hairs came from someone other than Mr. Coleman. The defense offered nothing in rebuttal, so this testimony stood unchallenged. In a post-conviction hearing Mr. Coleman's new lawyer introduced the testimony of a forensic hair specialist who had twenty-five years of experience with the F.B.I. He testified that "it is improper to conclude that it is likely that hairs came from a particular person simply because they are consistent with that person's hair because hairs belonging to different people are often consistent with each other, especially pubic hairs."

Another problem that we continually observe within the realm of forensic evidence is the phenomenon of lost and untested physical evidence. Often, especially in cases up to the early 1980s, the specimens that have the potential to exclude the defendant have not been tested and eventually get misplaced. At best this is gross negligence on the part of both the police technician and the defense attorney in not ensuring that the tests be done.

Conclusion

We agree with a past president of the New Jersey Division of the Association of Trial Lawyers of America who said that "juries are strange creatures. Even after taking part in many, many trials, I still find them to be unpredictable. The jury system isn't perfect, but it does represent the best system to mete out justice. They're right in their decisions more often than not." Remember when I quoted a former District Attorney who said that "in almost any factual hearing or trial someone is committing perjury." So, a wide margin of error exists when earnest but all too fallible juries are only right "more often than not" and when trial testimony is so frequently and pervasively perjurious. My contention is that at least 10 percent of those convicted for serious, violent crimes are incorrectly convicted because some combination of the trial infirmities described in this article results in mistaken jury determinations.

Everyone will agree that the system is not perfect, but the real question is this: To what extent do its imperfections prevail? I contend that for all the reasons detailed above the system is a far leakier cistern than any among us has ever imagined. Untold numbers of innocents have tumbled into the dark pit of prison. Some of them have eventually gained their freedom, but a majority remain buried in prison, completely forsaken and forgotten by the outside world.

Other than my own wholly inadequate organization, no person or agency, private or public, exists anywhere that works full time and serves exclusively as an advocate and arm for the innocent in prison. The body of justice that has evolved over the centuries has many members. But not one part that functions within this whole has been created or is properly equipped specifically to secure the freedom of the incarcerated innocent.

Publications Received

Timo Airaksinen, *Ethics of Coercion and Authority: A Philosophical Study of Social Life* (Pittsburgh, PA: University of Pittsburgh Press, 1988), ix + 219 pp.

George F. Cole, *The American System of Criminal Justice* (5th ed) (Pacific Grove, CA: Brooks/Cole Publishing Co., 1989), xxiv + 706 pp.

Joshua Dressler, *Understanding Criminal Law* (New York: Mathew Bender & Co., 1987), xli + 540 pp.

Franco Ferracuti, ed. *Trattato Di Criminologia, Medicina Criminologia E Psichiatria Forense* (Milano: Dott. A. Guiffre Editore, 1988) *IX. Forme di Organizzazioni Criminali e terrorismo* xiii + 403 pp.

Mark S. Gaylord & John F. Galliher, *The Criminology of Edwin Sutherland* (New Brunswick: Transaction Inc., 1988) xiv + 183 pp.

Jean Harris, *"They Always Call Us LADIES": Stories from Prison* (New York: Charles Scribner's Sons, 1988), vii + 276 pp.

Geoffrey C. Hazard, Jr. & Deborah L. Rhode, *The Legal Profession: Responsibility and Regulation* (2nd ed) (Westbury, NY: The Foundation Press, Inc., 1988), viii + 505 pp.

Jack Katz, *Seductions of Crime: Moral and Sensual Attractions in Doing Evil* (New

York: Basic Books, Inc., 1988), viii + 367 pp.

Kelsey Kauffman, *Prison Officers and their World* (Cambridge: Harvard University Press, 1988), ix + 290 pp.

Robert Klitgaard, *Controlling Corruption* (Berkeley & Los Angeles: University of California Press, 1988), xiii + 220 pp.

Richard A. Myren & Carol Henderson Garcia, *Investigation for Determination of Fact: A Primer on Proof* (Pacific Grove, CA: Brooks/Cole Publishing Co., 1988), xv + 240 pp.

David W. Neubauer, *America's Courts and the Criminal Justice System* (3rd ed) (Pacific Grove, CA: Brooks/Cole Publishing Co., 1988), xvi + 464 pp.

Andrew Oldenquist, *The Non-Suicidal Society* (Bloomington & Indianapolis: Indiana University Press, 1986), viii + 263 pp.

Richard Polenberg, *Fighting Faiths: The Abrams Case, the SupremeCourt, and Free Speech* (New York: Viking Penguin Inc., 1987), xiv + 431 pp.

Joycelyn M. Pollock-Byrne, *Ethics in Crime & Justice: Dilemmas and Decisions* (Pacific Grove, CA: Brooks/Cole Publishing Co., 1989), xiii + 169 pp.

Curtis Prout & Robert N. Ross, *Care and Punishment: The Dilemmas of Prison Medicine* (Pittsburgh, PA: University of Pittsburgh Press, 1988), x + 276 pp.

Lionel Tiger, *The Manufacture of Evil -- Ethics, Evolution and the Industrial System* (New York: Harper & Row, 1987), 345 pp.

Michael Tonry & Norval Morris, eds. *Crime and Justice: A Review of Research* (Vol. 10) (Chicago: The University of Chicago Press, 1988), x + 343 pp.

UMI, ed. *Criminal Justice Periodical Index* (Vol. 13) (Ann Arbor: University Microfilms Inc., 1988), xi + 391 pp.

H. Richard Uviller, *Tempered Zeal -- A Columbia Law Professor's Year on the Streets with the New York City Police* (Chicago & New York: Contemporary Books, 1988, xvii + 234 pp.

Samuel Walker, *Sense and Nonsense about Crime: A Policy Guide* (2nd ed) (Pacific Grove, CA: Brooks/Cole Publishing Co., 1989), xvi + 276 pp.

Stanton Wheeler, Kenneth Mann, & Austin Sarat, *Sitting in Judgement: The Sentencing of White-Collar Criminals* (New York: Yale University Press, 1988), xii + 199 pp.

AFTER 200 YEARS, THE SILENT JUROR LEARNS TO TALK

Lis Wiehl

For more than 200 years, the American jury has been a passive audience in the courtroom, breaking its silence only to deliver a verdict. But now an experiment in more than 100 courts nationwide is giving the jury a voice.

Judges in a least 30 states, including New York, California and Connecticut, are allowing juries in criminal and civil trials to question witnesses and tell judges when they want more information.

The experiment is bringing juries into a courtroom dialogue that has until now been the exclusive province of lawyers, judges and witnesses. Although the rules for state court procedures rarely prohibit juror participation, few judges have flouted custom and used their discretion to allow jurors to ask questions, said Prof. Steven Penrod at the University of Minnesota law school.

Professor Penrod is a co-director of the experiment in juror participation, which was organized by two national organizations concerned with the administration of justice.

RESTLESSNESS OVER SYSTEM

Legal scholars say the experiment is the latest milestone in a decade-long liberalization of the roles of judge and jury, often at the expense of the lawyer's control over presenting evidence.

"There is growing restlessness with a system that gives trial lawyers so much power over the questions that are asked in court, sometimes at the price of the truth," said David Wilkins, an assistant professor at the Harvard Law School. "Increasingly, judges have been interrupting lawyers to interrogate witnesses from the bench, and in much the same way, jurors' questions chip away at the trial lawyer's domination of courtroom interrogation."

The aim of the experiment is to make jury verdicts more reliable, Professor Penrod said. "We depend on juries to find the truth, but jurors are often frustrated because they can't ask for clarifications or additional facts."

The experiment, which is expected to involve 500 trials from now until November, is supported by the American Judicature Society, a national organization of judges, and the State Justice Institute, a Congressionally financed organization for state court reform.

Professor Penrod and the other director of the experiment, Larry Heuer, a psychologist at Northwestern University, said they expected the experiment to improve jurors' attentiveness and give lawyers and judges an indication of jury concerns during a trial.

"It's valuable for a lawyer to know what the jurors are thinking as the trial unfolds, and for a judge to receive an early warning if the jury is hung up on an irrelevant tangent," Mr. Heuer said.

But the experiment is spawning concern rather than enthusiasm among many lawyers and judges. "American juries are supposed to hear the evidence rather than join the inquisition," said Lawrence M. Lapine, a plaintiff's lawyer in Connecticut who is appealing a case in which jurors were permitted to ask questions. "As soon as we let jurors ask questions, the juror is no longer a fact-finder, but a second prosecutor or defender."

Other lawyers say the experiment raises troubling issues of how far juries will be allowed to go: Will jurors one day have the power to bring witnesses back to the stand two and three times? Will jury questioning lengthen trials and worsen court caseloads?

Professor Penrod acknowledged those concerns but said there was room to increase juror participation without risking an inexorable march toward an inquisitorial system.

"This is still just an experiment," he cautioned. "Moreover, to insure that jurors' questions do not run roughshod over a fair trial, judges who participate in the experiment are making certain that the questions comply with the rules of evidence and other safeguards."

Professor Penrod said participating judges usually let jurors ask questions only when lawyers on both sides consented to take part in the experiment, and even then only after the lawyers finished interrogating a witness.

The guidelines sent to participating judges suggest that jurors submit written questions to lawyers on both sides and that a lawyer submit any evidentiary objections in a handwritten note to the judge.

"Otherwise, a juror might feel slighted by the objecting lawyer and hold it against him the rest of the trial," Mr. Heuer said. For the same reason, the merits of an objection are usually argued outside the jury's earshot, he said.

But some lawyers worry that such safeguards could be illusory. "A jury member can see which lawyer objected to his question by body language if nothing else," said Roy S. Wilcox, a defense lawyer in Eau Claire, Wis. "A juror might feel alienated if I objected to his question, but even worse, he might conclude that I have something to hide."

Some lawyers are wary because jurors' questions have been known to stop a lawyer's case dead in its tracks. "It's a well-known maxim that a trial lawyer never asks a question if he doesn't know how the witness is going to answer," Mr. Lapine said.

JUROR's TELLING QUESTION

In a recent Wisconsin case, the defendant, on trial on charges of shooting his former wife and her boyfriend, denied that he had ever intended to fire his weapon. Then a juror asked if he had unlocked the safety mechanism on the trigger before confronting the victims. The defendant said he had, a fact the prosecutor had failed to elicit. "That question finished the trial," said Judge Thomas H. Barland, who presided in the case.

But not all questions are so probing, and some lawyers fear that trials may be waylaid by irrelevant questions unless they are tightly controlled from the bench.

Judges are watching the experiment to see whether questions from the jury lead to premature deliberation between jurors.

"Jurors aren't supposed to begin deliberating until all the evidence is in," said Judge John D. Farrell of Superior Court in Los Angeles. "But by asking questions, jurors begin sending signals to each other about their thinking."

Professor Wilkins predicted that jury questioning would eventually find wider acceptance in the legal system, but he added that state supreme courts and legislatures would first have to clarify court rules and establish some guidelines. "Sooner or later, a juror's question will be the basis for a high court appeal," he said.

Jurors who have been part of the experiment thus far appear to welcome their newly found power.

"It's a great idea," said Lila S. Winter of Northfield, Minn., who served on a recent experimental jury. "Next time I'll be more confident and ask more questions," she said. "I just kept thinking that my questions were so obvious that the lawyers would ask them, but they never did."

But Mr. Wilcox reflected the ambivalence of fellow lawyers. "If this takes off, I'll live with it," he said "But I'll live in deathly fear of the devastating question that I didn't want asked."

A criminal lack of common sense

JOHN LEO

The life story of Warren Bland is one of those tales evenly divided between the viciousness of the criminal and the folly of the criminal-justice system. Consider this career:

In 1958, Bland stuck a knife in the stomach of a man in a Los Angeles bar and got off with probation. In 1960, he was arrested in a series of sexual assaults on women in Los Angeles County. Three women fought back and avoided rape. One had her jaw broken in the process. Originally charged with one rape, three attempted rapes, a kidnapping and a robbery, he plea-bargained down to one rape and one kidnapping and was sent to a state mental hospital under the state's "mentally disordered sex offender" program, which has since been abandoned. The hospital warned that Bland was a sexual psychopath who would be "assaultive and/or homicidal toward women" if released.

For seven years, Bland was studied, interviewed, counseled, psychoanalyzed and "treated." In the process, the hospital disregarded its own warning. Always expert at simulating rehabilitation, Bland was hailed in a probation report for his "complete change and attitude toward his problem," and the hospital set him free.

Within months, he was back at his chosen life's work, violent sexual attacks. He was convicted of two more rapes. At his sentencing, another dark report announced that Bland was "clearly a dangerous individual who warrants segregation from society for the longest time that is possible under existing laws."

Existing laws being what they are, Bland served just seven years. Shortly after his release, he kidnapped an 11-year-old girl and her mother. The mother was molested. The girl was sexually assaulted and tortured.

In yet another of those compassionate criminal-justice breaks that kept coming his way, Bland plea-bargained and served only three years for those crimes. The crimes were growing more violent; the jail terms were getting shorter.

Lethal habits. Eight months after his release, Bland was back in jail, this time for sodomizing and torturing a small boy. At this point, in any sensible society, Bland would have been tossed into a dungeon for the rest of his life, but in California he plea-bargained for 9 years and served only 4½ years.

Bland got out again in early 1986. In December, Phoebe Ho, age 7, disappeared while walking to school in South Pasadena. She was found dead in a ditch in Riverside County, mutilated with the kind of instruments Bland had used before. A 14-year-old girl in Orange County died the same way, and an 81-year-old San Diego woman was found bound, nude and choked to death, with Bland as the chief suspect.

Sought in the Ho murder, Bland fled and was found by police—working under an alias in a McDonald's in Pacific Beach. He was wounded in the buttocks while trying to escape. In his car, police found a gun and evidence linking him to Ho. He was charged with her murder.

Enter the Feds. Larry Burns, an assistant U.S. Attorney in San Diego, filed federal charges against Bland under the Armed Career Criminal Act, the brainchild of Senator Arlen Specter (R-Pa.). This fairly new, fairly obscure legislation was passed in 1984. As originally written, it provided that anyone caught with a gun after three burglaries or robbery felonies will go to jail for a minimum of 15 years to a maximum of life imprisonment, with no possibility of parole. The act was amended and enlarged in 1986 to apply to anyone who had committed three crimes of violence or serious drug offenses.

In his brief to the court, Burns noted dryly that "a public perception has arisen, in California in particular, that the stewards of our criminal-justice system have failed to come to grips in a realistic and common-sense manner with the mounting crime wave." This is lawyerly understatement. What he might have said is that the state of California botched the Bland case for three decades and is implicated by its incompetence in the savage murder of little Phoebe Ho. It has known for 29 years that Bland is a violent sexual psychopath, yet it let him go five times.

This casual approach did not end with Bland's latest arrest in Pacific Beach. Nearly three years after Ho's death, the Riverside County prosecutor still has not managed to hold even a preliminary hearing in the case. If it continues at its current pace, the case could easily drag on for another three to five years.

As Burns notes, if the criminal-justice system fails to protect the citizens, the public will lose confidence and turn to vigilantism. Yes. And if the nation is serious about crime, it will not release sexual monsters like Bland every few years and simply let victims pay the price for the next brief round of confinement.

The lack of seriousness about violence was the real source of the outrage over Willie Horton, just as it was in the outrage over the misguided policies at the Patuxent Institution in Maryland, where a triple-murderer serving a life sentence was allowed unsupervised furloughs. The Patuxent program is being revamped, a straw in the wind. Another such straw is the announcement by New York Governor Mario Cuomo that he now favors a lifetime sentence without parole for some hardened criminals, a position he adopted when opponents of his seventh annual veto of the death penalty appeared to have enough votes to override.

The Armed Career Criminal Act also fits this new realism. Under this act, it took only 30 minutes in court for Larry Burns to accomplish what the state of California failed to do for 30 years—take Bland off the streets permanently. With no fanfare at all, the sentencing came last week. Warren Bland will stay in federal prison for the rest of his life.

The reclaiming of an issue.

LIBERALS AND CRIME

GEORGE KANNAR

George Kannar is associate professor at the SUNY-Buffalo School of Law.

BY A QUARTER of an inch, I missed growing up as the son of an Irish cop in New York City. Because my father flunked the height exam, I ended up as the son of an international automobile executive instead. Only in America. I consequently came of age in a faraway country with stylish people and broad boulevards, a Spanish-speaking Paris; with gauchos, and pampas, and steak every day. A beautiful country where the judiciary was weak, where habeas corpus was usually ignored, and where official investigations were unhampered by cumbersome procedures. A society as cosmopolitan and sophisticated as our own, in which a few years later thousands of innocent men, women, and children were kidnapped, tortured, and made to "disappear." And all as part of a good-faith effort, performed by sincere officers, to re-establish "law and order."

In 1968 Richard Nixon was elected president by talking about crime and the liberals' supposed "softness" on it, as exemplified by the Warren Court. This year George Bush was elected by talking about crime again. But in 1988 there is an important difference. Having controlled the White House for 16 of the last 20 years, and having appointed every Supreme Court justice for the last 21, the Republicans ought rightfully to be explaining why their lengthy reign has apparently done so little to assuage Americans' fear of crime. Yet the Warren Court's legacy endures. Those rules that let criminals off on "technicalities"—*Miranda*, the exclusionary rule, and miscellaneous procedural contortions that delay final resolution of so many cases—have not been stricken from the law, even in the Burger/Rehnquist era. The reason is simple: despite 20 years of debate and study, no one has come up with any better devices for protecting individual rights in the criminal justice process.

In other respects, America has become much tougher on its criminals since Earl Warren left the Court. Because of stricter sentencing laws (particularly new "habitual offender" statutes), as well as changes in judicial sensibilities, according to David C. Anderson's *Crimes of Justice*, since 1968 the inmate population in this country has more than tripled. The United States now incarcerates a greater percentage of its population than any industrialized country except the Soviet Union and South Africa. As Elliot Curie pointed out in *Confronting Crime*, such massive "incapacitation" has indeed kept crime rates lower than they would otherwise have been—not because of any deterrent effect, but simply by keeping would-be criminals off the streets.

Still, this vast increase in punishment has not satisfied anyone, and has not come without substantial costs, both human and financial. At latest count, according to Anderson, 36 states were under expensive court orders to relieve prison overcrowding, whose truly hellish human consequences no reader of *Presumed Innocent* or *The Bonfire of the Vanities* can doubt. We require new prison beds at the rate of a thousand every week. This cannot go on forever, and communities throughout the country balk at the idea of paying for more prisons, or letting them be built nearby. Budget pressures and community resistance are far more responsible for the nation's many furlough programs and work-release alternatives than are woolly-headed liberals or weak-kneed judges.

But, aside from distorting our discussion of crime control for the last two decades, have there been any socially significant costs to those Warren Court "technicalities"? The evidence is overwhelming that the Warren Court—clumsily, and no doubt in part by accident—in fact managed to enhance protection of individual liberties (greater insurance than ever that "it can't happen here") without any real dilution of legitimate law enforcement efforts. If anything, the reality is just the opposite of what the public thinks. Sentimental liberalism has not been a major problem. The problem comes from the other side. Conservative sentimentalism, particularly on our highest court, has in complex ways probably impaired both constitutional rights *and* effective law enforcement.

CONSIDER THE exclusionary rule, the remedy the Warren Court imposed on the states to enforce the

Fourth Amendment's protections against unreasonable search and seizure. The premise of the rule is simple: if evidence is obtained unconstitutionally, it may not be introduced at trial. The reasons for it, originally, were two. First, it was thought to corrupt the system of justice for courts to use the products of illegal searches—a "judicial integrity" rationale. Second, it was hoped that police would conduct fewer illegal searches if they knew the result would not help gain convictions—a "deterrence" rationale.

Because the Burger Court discarded the "judicial integrity" idea, recent criticism of the exclusionary rule has focused on its deterrent purpose. Does it make sense, as Benjamin Cardozo once put it, to "let the criminal go free because the constable has blundered"? Taking the analysis at this level, the answer is easy: in the case of a well-intentioned officer, doing his or her level best to observe constitutional proprieties, it certainly does not make sense. If the officer was *already* trying to do what was right, what deterrent purpose could possibly be served by suppressing the evidence obtained?

But if we don't intend for the Constitution to become a dead letter, then *some* kind of enforcement mechanism is essential. And constructing a workable constitutional remedy means taking a *systemic* view of the criminal justice process, not one that focuses sentimentally on the "innocent," well-meaning cop. The Burger/Rehnquist Court consistently gave into just such sentimentalism. A prime culprit is the so-called "good faith" exception to the exclusionary rule. This sensible-sounding change allows the use of illegally gathered evidence when the officer who obtained it did not know that what he did was wrong. The Burger Court created this exception to "protect" the officer who relied upon what later turned out to be a defective search warrant, issued by a magistrate based on insufficient evidence. Many conservatives have urged the Court to create a "good faith" exception for mistakes committed by the officer himself, an exception deleted from the latest drug bill only at the very last minute.

But if such an exception becomes available, what smart officer, at a pretrial suppression hearing, will *not* say that he "meant well"—and believe it? Of course he "means well"; fighting crime is hard, boring, and highly dangerous work. People don't do it so that they can become millionaires. Moreover, even if the question is narrower—whether the police officer sincerely thought his actions were permitted by the Constitution—does society want the officer's opinion to be the only one that matters? Although individual cases of suppressing "good faith" evidence may seem stupid, the only real alternative is to delegate the entire matter to the individual cop. With all the considerable respect that's due our law enforcement officers, trusting solely in the individual officer's "good faith" would create a completely lawless system. The effective result of a broad "good faith" exception of the sort now widely proposed would be to eliminate entirely the opportunity for meaningful judicial review.

IN ITS OBSESSION with the predicament of the forgivably mistaken officer—its uncontrollable frustration at seeing undeniably guilty individuals go free—the Burger Court abdicated its prime institutional responsibility within the criminal justice system: to establish comprehensible and enforceable ground rules.

The Fourth Amendment's "warrant clause" could easily be read to establish an ironclad rule that searches and arrests may be conducted only with a formal written warrant, issued by a magistrate on the basis of sworn testimony establishing "probable cause." Even the Warren Court recognized that such an absolute rule was inadequate for the myriad unanticipated situations of modern life. Consequently, that Court, and the ones before it, allowed a few "jealously and carefully drawn" exceptions, for example allowing police to search suspects for weapons while making an arrest, and to inspect automobiles without detaining the driver while a warrant is obtained or allowing him to drive away.

The Burger Court consistently failed to recognize that exceptions of this sort can only be kept from swallowing the rule if they are *kept* narrowly—and clearly—limited. Out of a misplaced zeal to punish individual malefactors, it began behaving like a neighborhood police court, cluttering its docket with insignificant cases simply because it could not bear the sight of particular individuals going free. In the process, the Republican-dominated Court converted Fourth Amendment jurisprudence into the impossibly confused quagmire it is today—piling exception upon exception, creating exceptions *to* exceptions, until not even the legal treatise writers can figure out exactly what the law is, or conscientious officers figure out how to act. In short, it was the conservative Burger Court, not the liberal Warren Court, that made search and seizure law a labyrinth of muddled "technicalities." And then opponents of the exclusionary rule seized upon the mess conservatives had themselves created as an excuse for abolishing the rule completely.

Because releasing clearly guilty suspects to vindicate the Constitution is indeed unattractive, it is frequently proposed to replace the exclusionary rule with some kind of civil damage suit by the person whose rights are violated. In fact, such tort remedies *already* exist, and everyone knows from long experience that juries will hardly ever award any substantial damages against a cop, even to an innocent citizen. "Everyone" includes the police themselves, which means lawsuits will never have any serious deterrent value. Civil lawsuits also put the burden of enforcing the Constitution on the shoulders of private citizens who may not, individually, have the time, resources, or inclination to pursue every violation. For all its faults, the exclusionary rule is at least self-executing. Although there are various ideas floating around to address these questions, no one has really shown how to get around the basic problem that a civil action simply has no credible bite.

Criminal prosecution of errant police—another oft-suggested alternative to the exclusionary rule—wouldn't work either. According to Professor Stephen A. Saltzburg of the University of Virginia (now deputy head of the Justice Department's Criminal Division), both the federal government and his home state have long had perfectly fine criminal statutes on their books prohibiting illegal searches. No officer, however, has ever been convicted under the federal statute, and the Virginia one, in all its history, has never once been used. And vigorously prosecuting cops would just make it impossible for the district attorneys and the officers to work together anyway.

WHAT ABOUT the supposed costs of enforcing the exclusionary rule with rigor? Of course there are individual horror cases: the man who raped your wife—or you—but goes free because a well-intentioned officer accidentally goofed. Still, despite the terrible human pain such incidents inflict, any policy-maker or justice who worries obsessively about criminals going free because of "soft" criminal procedures faces a statistical uphill battle in a society where half the crimes go unreported, two-thirds of those reported go unsolved, and four out of every five crimes committed therefore never get to court at all.

Even among cases that get to court, the "cost" of the exclusionary rule is very small. Critics often cite a 1982 report by the National Institute of Justice reviewing the experience of California, which allegedly concluded that 4.8 percent of state court prosecutions fail because evidence has been thrown out on exclusionary rule grounds. In fact, 4.8 percent is the proportion of *rejected* cases in which the prosecution fails for search and seizure reasons. In other words, only one out of every 20 that are *dismissed* can be blamed on the exclusionary rule. The percentage of *all* criminal cases that founder on search and seizure issues is 0.8 percent, hardly a major public policy concern.

A comprehensive 1979 General Accounting Office study of the exclusionary rule's effect on federal prosecutions found similar results. According to the GAO, in only 1.3 percent of the federal cases was any evidence excluded on Fourth Amendment grounds. And in more than half of those cases—a factor that is usually overlooked—the defendant was convicted *anyway*. In other words, the effective cost of the exclusionary rule to federal prosecutors, *before* the Burger Court created the "good faith" standard, was—at worst—a negligible 0.65 percent. And since the vast majority of these cases involve drug possession, rather than violent offenses against person or property, the threat to public order represented by the rule diminishes to the vanishing point. A 1979 study of Washington, Salt Lake City, Los Angeles, and New Orleans found in all those cities exactly one homicide case that was aborted because of the exclusionary rule, and no rape arrests at all.

Although politicians still clamor for exclusionary rule reform, in light of these realities it is no surprise that growing numbers of law enforcement experts agree with Reagan-appointed FBI Director William Sessions, who told the Senate Judiciary Committee during his confirmation hearings in 1987, "As a former judge, . . . I know that the protections that are afforded by the exclusionary rule are extremely important to . . . fair play, and the proper carrying out of the law enforcement responsibility. . . . [B]y and large, I am happy with it the way it is."

NOW LET'S TAKE *Miranda*. This notorious decision required officers to warn those they arrest of their rights to be silent and to consult a lawyer. It also required the police to refrain from interrogation if a suspect refused to waive those rights. Liberals won't admit it, but as an example of judicial craftsmanship *Miranda* v. *Arizona* is a terrible piece of work, and a highly inflammatory one. Long, rambling, drawing on dubious authority, and full of smarmy '60s rhetoric, it undeniably represents a highly overt form of judicial activism. It is not surprising that it was greeted with a storm of protest when first issued back in 1966.

But what the Court actually did should not have been so controversial. Earl Warren didn't invent the *Miranda* warnings. J. Edgar Hoover did. *Miranda* merely extended to the states the FBI's internal regulations on interrogating suspects, which the agency had adopted at its own initiative more than 20 years before. Civil liberties advocates had urged the Court to go further than it did in *Miranda*: to require not only that suspects be informed of their rights, but that they be precluded from *waiving* them. They would have required not just notice of a "right" to a lawyer before a suspect could be questioned, as *Miranda* does, but the presence of an *actual* lawyer. And an actual lawyer would indeed have prevented all but the most demonstrably innocent suspects from talking.

This year, however, the big story about *Miranda* is that it isn't a big story. In large part, this is because of an emerging consensus among scholars and police officials that *Miranda* "works." One reason, as a series of studies has shown, is that the *Miranda* procedure, precisely because it is so intrusive, specific, and detailed—in short, so resolutely "activist"—is easily enforceable, and easy to train officers to obey. Whatever its jurisprudential deficiencies, it is at least not very hard to follow.

Moreover, *Miranda* also streamlines the criminal justice process. Even before *Miranda*, suspects' confessions were not just automatically admitted. Defendants frequently made motions to suppress them under the vague "voluntariness" standard that previously applied. Consequently, courts and police officers were required to conduct time-consuming, fact-intensive hearings concerning the details of a particular incident, to determine whether a suspect's statements had been improperly coerced. Since *Miranda*, courts need only inquire whether the more mechanical requirements of *Miranda* were observed: whether the prescribed warnings were delivered at the appropriate times. If they were, the confession almost always gets admitted.

Like the Fourth Amendment exclusionary rule, *Miranda* turns out to have virtually no effect on the system's ability to convict guilty suspects. At the time that the decision was issued, leading experts estimated that it would cut the conviction rate by something like four percent. However, despite an initial drop, after about a year conviction rates were higher than they'd been before it. Two factors were responsible.

First, despite the warnings, an amazing number of suspects continued to waive their rights, having more faith than was justified in their ability to "talk their way out of it," being so guilt-stricken (or such tough guys) that they couldn't keep their mouths shut, or—as with so many other consumer warnings—simply disregarding them. Second, it turned out that the necessity of getting confessions in order to secure convictions had been overestimated. Juries turned out to be just as willing to convict on solid evidence of other kinds, and this knowledge quickly filtered into plea bargaining calculations. The "worst case" study, performed in Pittsburgh shortly after *Miranda* came down, found a drop-off in the confession rate of 17 percent, but no reduction in the conviction rate. After Ernest Miranda's own confession was thrown out, he was retried. And reconvicted.

UNLIKE THE exclusionary rule, *Miranda* really was about protecting the innocent. Former prosecutors Earl Warren and Hugo Black both knew that the "third degree" wasn't something out of Hollywood, and that innocent people were regularly being subjected to it. Their concern was not just that formal proprieties were being violated, or that undue pressure was being applied.

But if large numbers of innocent people were previously being convicted, why didn't *Miranda* reduce the conviction rate? Either the Warren Court overestimated the innocence problem or it may be that *Miranda*'s protections have been so watered-down by Burger Court interpretations that they aren't effective. Because *Miranda* only applied to (1) "interrogation" of suspects who were (2) "in custody" and who (3) refused to "waive" their rights—not one of which terms was seriously defined—there was plenty of room for vitiating interpretation. Despite an almost total lack of evidence that the *Miranda* rules were broken, the Burger Court did an awful lot of fixing.

IN 1980 the Burger Court upheld a conviction obtained because officers in the front seat of their squad car carried on a conversation, ostensibly between themselves, in the presence of a murder suspect in the back who had asserted his right to silence, about how tragic it would be if the missing murder weapon were accidentally discovered by a handicapped child at a nearby school. The remorseful suspect, "overhearing" their conversation, took them to the weapon and thereby slipped the noose around his neck. The Court held this wasn't an "interrogation." According to Columbia Law Professor Richard Uviller's new book, *Tempered Zeal*, which recounts a year's experience working in a New York precinct house, since 1980 an astonishing number of officers now suddenly seem to get worried about many different things whenever they're driving suspects to the station house.

Some people will think it's good to try to trick presumptively innocent suspects out of their basic rights, even after they've asserted them. Others will think the practice makes a mockery of *Miranda*'s clear intent. But either way it certainly helps explain why nobody is still complaining about *Miranda*.

Although conservatives still undermine police morale by complaining about the "handcuffs" *Miranda* placed on them, no one is even really trying anymore to get it overturned. Even former Attorney General Edwin Meese, despite continually expressing outrage on the subject, never even attempted to use a considerable weapon at his disposal: Title II of the Omnibus Crime Control and Safe Streets Act of 1968, in which Congress tried to outlaw *Miranda*'s application in federal courts. Neither Meese, nor any of his predecessors, has directed federal agencies to observe this statute, or even shape a single test case in which to try the statute's constitutionality. Perhaps in the end Meese was forced to agree with the nation's best-known crime fighter, U.S. Attorney Rudolph Giuliani of New York, that "the *Miranda* warnings are simple and easy to give and are known by everyone. As a matter of reality and practicality, [*Miranda*] doesn't prevent anyone from confessing who wants to confess." And perhaps this is why the 1988 Republican Party platform, which complains about everything else in the criminal justice system, is conspicuously silent about *Miranda*.

A third conservative complaint about "liberal" technicalities, created by the Warren Court, that let criminals off the hook concerns the right to federal habeas corpus, which the Warren Court expanded. Habeas is one of the most basic principles of Anglo-American jurisprudence, going back to the Magna Charta, which guarantees that someone held in custody can have a court determine if that custody is legal. As the barons at Runnymede knew, a strong right to habeas review represents the ultimate protection against governmental tyranny, and the ultimate guarantee that a free society will stay that way. In our federal system, federal habeas review of state convictions ensures that our constitutional liberties are enforced in a nationally uniform way. We don't want one Constitution to be applied in Rhode Island and a different one in Georgia. And the mere threat of such review helps keep the state courts constitutionally honest.

Although the public's basic gripe with federal habeas concerns the delay it imposes on obtaining a final disposition of criminal cases, the politicians have chosen to articulate this concern in terms of the supposed clogging of the federal courts. Supporters of restricting habeas, led by Democratic Senator Bob Graham of Florida, point at the surge in federal habeas filings in recent years; since 1980 habeas petitions have risen more than 225 percent. But what else should you expect in a country where incarceration has more than tripled? Moreover, as figures recently compiled by the ACLU have shown, the 9,500 petitions attacking state convictions filed in 1987 represent just 3.9 percent of the more than 238,000 cases filed that year in federal district courts.

TO BE SURE, there is something illogical about a system that permits endless, repeated federal re-evaluations years after the original conviction. But the reasons for this system are ones its critics ought to like. Out of respect for state autonomy (to give them first crack at catching their own mistakes), and to control that worrisome federal docket, the law requires that a prisoner exhaust all opportunities for state review before a federal habeas suit can even be commenced. Here in Buffalo it can take four years just to get to the *first* level of *state* appeal.

Yet Congress might still struggle to draft a docket-clearing statute, designed to eliminate repetitive attacks on state convictions, provided just one thing: that prisoners be guaranteed a court-provided lawyer who knows the ins and outs of federal habeas procedure. Much of today's profusion of wasteful and repetitious habeas cases is due to the fact that 95 percent of all habeas cases are filed by the uneducated prisoners themselves (which also no doubt accounts for the remarkable fact that 98.8 percent of them never get to trial). Giving prisoners lawyers would not only help assure fairness, but would make the cases clearer, allowing them to be more efficiently, and finally, disposed of. In that situation, the law could give the ordinary prisoner just one more shot, to guarantee the abstract value of presenting all the claims *the prisoner* thinks important. Further petitions in non-capital cases could be limited to a few specified circumstances—like the discovery of constitutionally significant new evidence, or changes in the law. Where capital punishment is at stake—that statistically insignificant number of cases where *no* mistakes are tolerable—the limits would not apply.

ALTHOUGH NO ONE now remembers it, each of the Warren Court's big cases was preceded by others, in which the Court gave fair warning to criminal justice policy-makers that it saw deficiencies that needed to be corrected. In each instance, the Court invited the other players to act first, and waited a decent interval before creating remedies of its own. The Warren Court's "judicial activism" was quite real, and the politicians who complained about it were the ones who made it happen. For the contemporary American politician, from Richard Nixon on, the Supreme Court of Earl Warren has been a political godsend. Someone other than themselves could be blamed for crime.

But as drugs and their disorder spread, even the politicians are being forced to recognize that the crime problem in America is caused by something larger than constitutional procedures. Frustrated businessmen on New York's "restaurant row" don't call in the Guardian Angels because they dislike *Miranda*. Frightened residents of D.C. housing projects don't turn to the Nation of Islam because of the exclusionary rule. The reason isn't that there are "handcuffs on the police." The reason is not enough police with handcuffs. Effective law enforcement means more than merely making the criminal justice process more efficient. It means making it stronger. But more police—if that's part of what an effective war on crime requires—means stronger controls on their behavior too.

Efficiency is not the only goal. Justice is another one, and so is maintaining a free society. No one says that having trials is efficient either. It would be a lot easier just to let "law and order" forces shoot a suspect when they catch him. That's what they used to do in Argentina. So far, fortunately, no one is proposing that we do it here.

In the recent successful effort to achieve meaningful reform of welfare, it was the left that had to swallow hard and make some painful counterideological admissions—that dependence had indeed been fostered by well-intended programs. When it comes to crime, the situation is reversed. If our approach to crime is ever to get serious, it is the other side's turn to be the first to blink.

At the level of constitutional enforcement, clearer rules, even overbroad ones—the kind that will inevitably generate a distressing amount of pain to individuals—nonetheless have a more positive net effect on the criminal justice process than superficially tougher ones, overly fine-tuned, that subsequently break down in practice. There are, to be sure, plenty of "technicalities" that could go, but they're mostly at the state court level.

As a man President Reagan has called a "national hero" once told reporters with characteristic melodrama through the window of his jeep, thousands of good Americans have "died face down in the mud" to protect a defendant's rights in the criminal justice process. Supreme Court justices should protect them too.

Juvenile Justice

A century ago children found guilty of committing crimes were punished as if they were adults. Since there were few specialized juvenile detention institutions, children were thrown into jails and prisons with murderers, thieves, drunks, tramps, and prostitutes, with no protection and no programs for rehabilitation.

The establishment of a special criminal justice system for the handling of juvenile offenders was hailed in the 1920s by humanitarians, reformers, and social scientists, and accepted, somewhat reluctantly, by the legal profession and the police. Only recently has the cry of dissent been heard.

Judge Ben Lindsay and others who pioneered the juvenile court movement believed that juveniles sinned out of ignorance, because of the growing pains of adolescence, or because they were corrupted by adults. They believed that a juvenile court should concern itself with finding out why a juvenile was in trouble and what society could do to help him or her. They saw the juvenile judge as parental, concerned, and sympathetic, rather than judgmental. They viewed the juvenile justice process as diagnostic and therapeutic, rather than prosecutive and punitive.

The proponents of this system were, of course, thinking of the delinquents of their time—the runaway, the truant, the petty thief, the beggar, the sexual experimenter, and the insubordinate. Now, however, the juvenile in court is more likely to be on trial for murder, gang rape, arson, or mugging. The 1990s also differ from the 1920s in other ways. Juvenile courts are everywhere, as are juvenile police, juvenile probation officers, and juvenile prisons. Literally hundreds of thousands of American juveniles enter this system annually.

It is clear at this time that the winds of change are blowing across the nation's juvenile justice system. Traditional reforms are being replaced by a new and more conservative agenda. This new reform movement emphasizes the welfare of victims, a punitive approach toward serious juvenile offenders, and protection of children from physical and sexual exploitation. Policies which favor diversion and deinstitutionalization are less popular. After many years of attempting to remove status offenders from the juvenile justice system, there are increasing calls for returning truants, runaways, and other troubled youth to juvenile court jurisdiction. In spite of these developments, however, there are many juvenile justice reformers who remain dedicated to advancing due process rights for children and reducing reliance on incarceration.

Clearly, there is conflict and tension between the old and new juvenile justice reform agendas. The articles in this section evaluate problems with the current juvenile justice system and present some possible solutions.

The first essay, "Handling of Juvenile Cases," draws distinctions between juvenile cases and adult cases, explains the circumstances under which juveniles may be tried in criminal courts, and reveals that juveniles receive dispositions rather than sentences.

Shelden, Horvath, and Tracy, in "Do Status Offenders Get Worse?" maintain that "escalation" among status offenders is dependent upon gender and the specific type of status offense committed. According to "Our Violent Kids," juvenile crime is more widespread and vicious than ever before. Statistics are cited to document an upsurge in the most violent types of crimes by teens.

Are existing delinquency causation theories adequate to the task of explaining female delinquency and official reactions to girls' deviance? The answer is clearly "no," according to the author of the next essay, "Girls' Crime and Woman's Place." She maintains that the academic study of delinquent behavior usually focuses on male delinquency alone.

Confining children in adult jails continues to be a significant problem nationwide, according to "The Hard Facts About Children in Jails." The section closes by exploring information about drug abuse among teenagers, in "Teenage Addiction."

Looking Ahead: Challenge Questions

When the juvenile court was first conceived, what convictions did its pioneers hold about juvenile offenders?

Some argue that the failure of the juvenile court to fulfill its rehabilitative and preventive promise stems from a grossly oversimplistic view of the phenomenon of juvenile criminality. Do you agree? Why or why not?

What are "status offenders"? Do you believe family court jurisdiction over status offenders should be abolished? What substitute, if any, do you propose? Do you believe family court jurisdiction over status offenders should be redefined? How?

Unit 5

Handling of Juvenile Cases

Cases involving juveniles are handled much differently than adult cases

The juvenile court and a separate process for handling juveniles resulted from reform movements of the late 19th century

Until that time juveniles who committed crimes were processed through the criminal courts. In 1899 Illinois established the first juvenile court based on the concepts that a juvenile was a salvageable human being who needed treatment rather than punishment and that the juvenile court was to protect the child from the stigma of criminal proceedings. Delinquency and other situations such as neglect and adoption were deemed to warrant the court's intervention on the child's behalf. The juvenile court also handled "status offenses" (such as truancy, running away, and incorrigibility), which are not applicable to adults.

While the juvenile courts and the handling of juveniles remain separated from criminal processing, the concepts on which they are based have changed. Today, juvenile courts usually consider an element of personal responsibility when making decisions about juvenile offenders.

Juvenile courts may retain jurisdiction until a juvenile becomes legally an adult (at age 21 or less in most States). This limit sets a cap on the length of time juveniles may be institutionalized that is often much less than that for adults who commit similar offenses. Some jurisdictions transfer the cases of juveniles accused of serious offenses or with long criminal histories to criminal court so that the length of the sanction cannot be abridged.

Juvenile courts are very different from criminal courts

The language used in juvenile courts is less harsh. For example, juvenile courts—

- accept "petitions" of "delinquency" rather than criminal complaints
- conduct "hearings," not trials
- "adjudicate" juveniles to be "delinquent" rather than find them guilty of a crime
- order one of a number of available "dispositions" rather than sentences.

Despite the wide discretion and informality associated with juvenile court proceedings, juveniles are protected by most of the due process safeguards associated with adult criminal trials.

Most referrals to juvenile court are for property crimes, but 17% are for status offenses

Reasons for referrals to juvenile courts

11%	**Crimes against persons**	
	Criminal homicide	1%
	Forcible rape	2
	Robbery	17
	Aggravated assault	20
	Simple assault	59
		100%
46%	**Crimes against property**	
	Burglary	25%
	Larceny	47
	Motor vehicle theft	5
	Arson	1
	Vandalism and trespassing	19
	Stolen property offenses	3
		100%
5%	**Drug offenses**	100%
21%	**Offenses against public order**	
	Weapons offenses	6%
	Sex offenses	6
	Drunkenness and disorderly conduct	23
	Contempt, probation, and parole violations	21
	Other	44
		100%
17%	**Status offenses**	
	Running away	28%
	Truancy and curfew violations	21
	Ungovernability	28
	Liquor violations	23
		100%
100%	Total all offenses	

Note: Percents may not add to 100 because of rounding.
Source: *Delinquency in the United States 1983*, National Center for Juvenile Justice, July 1986.

Arrest is not the only means of referring juveniles to the courts

While adults may begin criminal justice processing only through arrest, summons, or citation, juveniles may be referred to court by law enforcement agencies, parents, schools, victims, probation officers, or other sources.

Law enforcement agencies refer three-quarters of the juvenile cases, and they are most likely to be the referral source in cases involving curfew violations, drug offenses, and property crimes. Other referral sources are most likely in cases involving status offenses (truancy, ungovernability, and running away).

"Intake" is the first step in the processing of juveniles

At intake, decisions are made about whether to begin formal proceedings. Intake is most frequently performed by the juvenile court or an executive branch intake unit, but increasingly prosecutors are becoming involved. In addition to beginning formal court proceedings, officials at intake may refer the juvenile for psychiatric evaluation, informal probation, or counseling, or, if appropriate, they may close the case altogether.

For a case involving a juvenile to proceed to a court adjudication, the intake unit must file a petition with the court

Intake units handle most cases informally without a petition. The National Center for Juvenile Justice estimates that more than half of all juvenile cases disposed of at intake are handled informally without a petition and are dismissed and/or referred to a social service agency.

From *Report to the Nation on Crime and Justice*, Bureau of Justice Statistics, U.S. Department of Justice, March 1988, pp. 78-79, 95.

Initial juvenile detention decisions are usually made by the intake staff

Prior to holding an adjudicatory hearing, juveniles may be released in the custody of their parents, put in protective custody (usually in foster homes or runaway shelters), or admitted to detention facilities. In most States juveniles are not eligible for bail, unlike adults.

Relatively few juveniles are detained prior to court appearance

One juvenile case in five involved secure detention prior to adjudication in 1983. Status offenders were least likely to be detained. The proportion of status offenders detained has declined from 40% in 1975 to 11% in 1983.

Under certain circumstances, juveniles may be tried in criminal courts

Age at which criminal courts gain jurisdiction of young offenders ranges from 16 to 19

Age of offender when under criminal court jurisdiction	States
16 years	Connecticut, New York, North Carolina
17	Georgia, Illinois, Louisiana, Massachusetts, Missouri, South Carolina, Texas
18	Alabama, Alaska, Arizona, Arkansas, California, Colorado, Delaware, District of Columbia, Florida, Hawaii, Idaho, Indiana, Iowa, Kansas, Kentucky, Maine, Maryland, Michigan, Minnesota, Mississippi, Montana, Nebraska, Nevada, New Hampshire, New Jersey, New Mexico, North Dakota, Ohio, Oklahoma, Oregon, Pennsylvania, Rhode Island, South Dakota, Tennessee, Utah, Vermont, Virginia, Washington, West Virginia, Wisconsin, Federal districts
19	Wyoming

Source: "Upper age of juvenile court jurisdiction statutes analysis," Linda A. Szymanski, National Center for Juvenile Justice, March 1987.

All States allow juveniles to be tried as adults in criminal courts

Juveniles are referred to criminal courts in one of three ways—

- **Concurrent jurisdiction**—the prosecutor has the discretion of filing charges for certain offenses in either juvenile or criminal courts
- **Excluded offenses**—the legislature excludes from juvenile court jurisdiction certain offenses usually either very minor, such as traffic or fishing violations, or very serious, such as murder or rape
- **Judicial waiver**—the juvenile court waives its jurisdiction and transfers the case to criminal court (the procedure is also known as "binding over" or "certifying" juvenile cases to criminal courts).

12 States authorize prosecutors to file cases in the juvenile or criminal courts at their discretion

This procedure, known as concurrent jurisdiction, may be limited to certain offenses or to juveniles of a certain age. Four States provide concurrent jurisdiction over juveniles charged with traffic violations. Georgia, Nebraska, and Wyoming have concurrent criminal jurisdiction statutes.

As of 1987, 36 States excluded certain offenses from juvenile court jurisdictions

Eighteen States excluded only traffic, watercraft, fish, or game violations. Another 13 States excluded serious offenses; the other 5 excluded serious offenses and some minor offenses. The serious offenses most often excluded are capital crimes such as murder, but several States exclude juveniles previously convicted in criminal courts.

48 States, the District of Columbia, and the Federal Government have judicial waiver provisions

Youngest age at which juvenile may be transferred to criminal court by judicial waiver	States
No specific age	Alaska, Arizona, Arkansas, Delaware, Florida, Indiana, Kentucky, Maine, Maryland, New Hampshire, New Jersey, Oklahoma, South Dakota, West Virginia, Wyoming, Federal districts
10 years	Vermont
12	Montana
13	Georgia, Illinois, Mississippi
14	Alabama, Colorado, Connecticut, Idaho, Iowa, Massachusetts, Minnesota, Missouri, North Carolina, North Dakota, Pennsylvania, South Carolina, Tennessee, Utah
15	District of Columbia, Louisiana, Michigan, New Mexico, Ohio, Oregon, Texas, Virginia
16	California, Hawaii, Kansas, Nevada, Rhode Island, Washington, Wisconsin

Note: Many judicial waiver statutes also specify offenses that are waivable. This chart lists the States by the youngest age for which judicial waiver may be sought without regard to offense.

Source: "Waiver/transfer/certification of juveniles to criminal court: Age restrictions: Crime restrictions," Linda A. Szymanski, National Center for Juvenile Justice, February 1987.

A small proportion of juvenile cases are referred to criminal court

Recent studies found that most juveniles referred to criminal court were age 17 and were charged with property offenses. However, juveniles charged with violent offenses or with serious prior offense histories were more likely to be adjudicated in criminal court. Waiver of juveniles to criminal court is less likely where court jurisdiction extends for several years beyond the juvenile's 18th birthday.

Juveniles tried as adults have a very high conviction rate, but most receive sentences of probation or fines

More than 90% of the judicial waiver or concurrent jurisdiction cases in Hamparian's study resulted in guilty verdicts, and more than half the convictions led to fines or probation. Sentences to probation often occur because the criminal courts view juveniles as first offenders regardless of their prior juvenile record. However, serious violent juvenile offenders are more likely to be institutionalized. In a study of 12 jurisdictions with Habitual Serious or Violent Juvenile Offender Programs, 63% of those convicted were sentenced to prison and 14% to jail. The average prison sentence was 6.8 years.

Correctional activities for juveniles tried as adults in most States occur within the criminal justice system

In 1978, in more than half the States, youths convicted as adults and given an incarcerative sentence could only be placed in adult corrections facilities. In 18 jurisdictions, youths convicted as adults could be placed in either adult or juvenile corrections facilities, but sometimes this discretion was limited by special circumstances. Only 6 jurisdictions restricted placements of juveniles convicted as adults to State juvenile corrections institutions. Generally, youths sentenced in this manner will be transferred to adult facilities to serve the remainder of their sentence on reaching majority.

Juveniles receive dispositions rather than sentences

Juvenile court dispositions tend to be indeterminate

The dispositions of juveniles adjudicated to be delinquent extend until the juvenile legally becomes an adult (21 years of age in most States) or until the offending behavior has been corrected, whichever is sooner.

Of the 45 States and the District of Columbia that authorize indeterminate periods of confinement—
- 32 grant releasing authority to the State juvenile corrections agency
- 6 delegate it to juvenile paroling agencies
- 5 place such authority with the committing judges
- 3 have dual or overlapping jurisdiction.

Most juvenile cases are disposed of informally

In 1982 about 54% of all cases referred to juvenile courts by the police and other agencies were handled informally without the filing of a petition. About 20% of all cases involved some detention prior to disposition.

Of about 600,000 cases in which petitions were filed, 64% resulted in formal adjudication. Of these, 61% resulted in some form of probation, and 29% resulted in an out-of-home placement.

The juvenile justice system is also undergoing changes in the degree of discretion permitted in confinement decisions

Determinate dispositions are now used in six States, but they do not apply to all offenses or offenders. In most cases they apply only to specified felony cases or to the juveniles with prior adjudications for serious delinquencies.

California imposes determinate periods of confinement for delinquents committed to State agencies based on the standards and guidelines of its paroling agency. Four States have similar procedures, administered by the State agencies responsible for operating their juvenile corrections facilities.

As of 1981 eight States had serious-delinquent statutes requiring that juveniles who are either serious, violent, repeat, or habitual offenders be adjudicated and committed in a manner that differs from the adjudication of other delinquents. Such laws require minimum lengths of commitment, prescribe a fixed range of time for commitment, or mandate a minimum length of stay in a type of placement, such as a secure institution.

Dispositions for serious juvenile offenders tend to look like those for adults

Aggregate statistics on juvenile court dispositions do not provide an accurate picture of what happens to the more serious offenders because many of the cases coming before juvenile courts involve minor criminal or status offenses. These minor cases are more likely to be handled informally by the juvenile court.

An analysis of California cases involving older juveniles and young adults charged by the police with robbery or burglary revealed more similarities in their disposition patterns than the aggregate juvenile court statistics would suggest. For both types of offenses, juvenile petitions were filed and settled formally in court about as often as were complaints filed and convictions obtained in the cases against adults. The juveniles charged with the more serious offenses and those with the more extensive prior records were the most likely to have their cases reach adjudication. At the upper limits of offense and prior record severity, juveniles were committed to secure institutions about as frequently as were young adults with comparable records.

The outcomes of juvenile and adult proceedings are similar, but some options are not available in juvenile court

For example, juvenile courts cannot order the death penalty, life terms, or terms that could exceed the maximum jurisdiction of the court itself. In Arizona the State Supreme Court held that, despite statutory jurisdiction of the juvenile courts to age 21, delinquents could not be held in State juvenile corrections facilities beyond age 18.[3]

Yet, juvenile courts may go further than criminal courts in regulating the lifestyles of juvenile offenders placed in the community under probation supervision. For example, the court may order them to—
- live in certain locations
- attend school
- participate in programs intended to improve their behavior.

The National Center for Juvenile Justice estimates that almost 70% of the juveniles whose cases are not waived or dismissed are put on probation; about 10% are committed to an institution.

Most juveniles committed to juvenile facilities are delinquents

	Percent of juveniles
Total	100%
Delinquents	74
Nondelinquents	
Status offenders	12
Nonoffenders (dependency, neglect, abuse, etc.)	14

Source: BJS Children in Custody, 1985, unpublished data.

Do Status Offenders Get Worse?

Some Clarifications on the Question of Escalation

Data from a longitudinal study of juvenile court referrals reveal that whether or not status offenders "escalate" is dependent upon gender and the specific type of status offense committed. Specifically, male status offenders were found to be more likely than females to escalate. Also, runaways and unmanageables were far less likely to escalate than those who were first referred for truancy, curfew, and liquor law violations. Status offenders are also compared with other offenders in terms of the total number of subsequent referrals and whether or not a youth had an arrest record as an adult. Some of the problems associated with the study of status offenders are discussed.

Randall G. Shelden, John A. Horvath, and Sharon Tracy

Randall G. Shelden: Associate Professor and Chair, Department of Criminal Justice, University of Nevada—Las Vegas. John A. Horvath: Assistant Professor, Department of Criminal Justice, University of Nevada—Las Vegas. Sharon Tracy: Instructor, Department of Criminal Justice, University of Nevada—Las Vegas.

It has always been part of the philosophy of the juvenile court that minor forms of misbehavior known as "status offenses" committed by children must be addressed at an early age if those children are to avoid a life of serious crime. Over the years a large number of youths who run away from home, who are "unmanageable" or "incorrigible," who are habitually truant from school, and who commit other status offenses are formally processed by the juvenile court. This practice has continued despite the fact that little data exist to demonstrate the success of such treatment.

Recently the vagueness of status offense laws has been attacked. Many children who violate these laws (but who commit no crime) are placed in secure detention (and sometimes in adult jails), and a significant number have been committed to training schools as a result of unclear or ambiguous statutes. In the early 1970s a "deinstitutionalization" movement focused on removing status offenders from institutions and secure detention facilities. This practice, while supported by the federal government (through the Office of Juvenile Justice and Delinquency Prevention), beginning with the Juvenile Justice and Delinquency Prevention Act of 1974 (Chesney-Lind, 1988a), has had varying impact. Some states have removed status offenders from their institutions, while in several states status offenders can still be found in adult jails (Krisberg et al, 1985; Logan and Rausch, 1985; Chesney-Lind, 1988b).

One reason for these mixed results is that the terms *status offense* and *status offender* are vague. Is the "status offender" a unique individual, completely different from the "delinquent"? Or is the status offender just like every other "delinquent"? More important, do status offenders "get worse" in terms of "progressing" or "escalating" to more serious offenses, as the juvenile court philosophy suggests?

PRIOR RESEARCH

Most of the previous research on this topic has found that status offenders also engage in various other delinquent acts; that is, most do not specialize in just status offenses. Further, most of them do not "escalate" (Weis, 1980; Clarke, 1975; Rojek and Erickson, 1982).

Thomas (1976) studied 2,092 youths who were brought into the juvenile court during a five-year period. His findings revealed that 38% of the status offenders returned to court a second time, compared to 21.5% of those whose first charge was a misdemeanor and 31% of those first charged with a felony. Of the status offense group returning a second time, 46% were charged with another status offense, while 17.5% were charged with a felony and 36% were charged with a misdemeanor. Almost one-half (49.8%) of these status offenders did not return for a third court appearance. Of those who did, one-third had committed a status offense. Among those who returned for a fourth court appearance (and 48.1% did not return for the fourth time), 34.6% were charged with another status offense. What is important to emphasize from this study is that 62% of the status offenders *never returned to court again.* Only 20.5% "escalated" toward more serious misbehavior and 108 (18.9%) of the original status offender group had three or more total referrals to court.

In a reanalysis of the Philadelphia cohort study (Wolfgang, Figlio, and Sellin, 1972), Clarke (1975) found little evidence to support the escalation hypothesis. Similarly, a study of 265 status offenders in Cook County, Illinois, found that 68% did not escalate to delinquent acts (cited in Rankin and Wells, 1985, pp. 13, 173). Rojek and Erickson (1982), in their study of 1,619 juvenile offenders in Arizona, found a very random distribution of offenses. The latter depicted juveniles as being quite versatile in the offenses they committed during their delinquent careers.

Studies using self-report data have had mixed results. Weis (1980) found that most of the offenders committed a variety of offenses, both status and delinquent, without escalating from status to delinquent acts. Finally, Rankin and Wells (1985) used data from a longitudinal study, following over 2,000 males from 1966 through 1970. They found little evidence of escalation; in fact, about two-thirds either remained status offenders or never committed another offense.

When the question of escalation is discussed, at least two issues often fail to be addressed in the literature. First, the distinction should be made between male and female status offenders (as well as male and female offenders generally). Second, *different types of status offenses* must be distinguished, rather than viewing status offenses as one unitary or global phenomenon.

It should first be noted that there are several types of status offenses and the categorized behaviors vary from state to state. Usually, status offenses include running away from home, unmanageable (also known as ungovernable, incorrigible, beyond control, and so on), truancy, curfew, and liquor law violations. In some states behavior such as "engaging in immoral activity," "growing up in idleness or crime," "knowingly associating with vicious or immoral persons," "in danger of becoming delinquent," and other vaguely worded statutes are also included under the status offense rubric.

It is wrong to categorize all of these offenses under one general heading, as the offenses reflect different problems in a young person's life. For instance, while running away and being unmanageable are similar offenses, they are very different from truancy, curfew, and liquor law violations. Parents are usually the source of the referral or complaint to the court for youth who run away and are unmanageable. These offenses may be reflective of some problems within the family, such as abuse and/or neglect (Teitelbaum and Gough, 1977; Chesney-Lind, 1988a). On the other hand, many cases of truancy probably stem from school-related problems, and violators are either referred by the school district or by the police. In contrast, curfew and liquor law violations are almost always referred by the police and are very different behaviors. Reactions to these behaviors differ among parents, friends, the police, and the juvenile court. An additional difference is that girls are more apt to be referred to court for running away and for being unmanageable; boys are more often referred for truancy, curfew, and liquor law violations (Shelden, 1987).

One might hypothesize that those committing curfew, truancy, and liquor law violations may also be committing delinquent offenses. Indeed, a large proportion of delinquent offenses are committed during the day when school is in session and late at night after curfew. These often occur in conjunction with drinking alcohol. Could it be that these offenses are more likely to result in "escalation" than are running away and being unmanageable?

Another hypothesis is that, given the higher rates of lawbreaking among males, male status offenders might be more likely to "escalate" than female status offenders.

It may also be hypothesized that during a typical delinquent "career" some youth will commit a wide variety of offenses. Rankin and Wells (1985) suggest the term "offense heterogeneity" to describe such a pattern. Some of these offenses will be status ones, while others will be delinquent violations. Also, some offenses will be violations of probation or parole rules, or violations of other court orders. It is important to be aware of such offenses (known as "administrative" offenses in Las Vegas) as some status offenses will be labeled as "delinquent" if the commission of one status offense is followed by another status offense and is therefore handled as any other "delinquent" offender (e.g., does not come under "deinstitutionalization" guidelines and is instead placed in detention and/or committed to a training school) (Chesney-Lind, 1988a).

From the above review, the following hypothesis is offered:

> Whether or not a status offender "escalates" to more serious offenses will vary according to the type of initial status offense and gender.

THE PRESENT STUDY: DATA AND METHODS

The present study used data collected from a much larger project involving a longitudinal study of a sample of youth who were first referred to the Clarke County Juvenile Court in Las Vegas during 1980 (Shelden, 1987, 1988). Court records contained referral histories (including abuse and neglect referrals) for each youth in the sample. From an original sample of 1,000, 863 youths were selected whose first referral was for either a status or delinquent offense (137 were first referred for abuse and neglect and are excluded from the present analysis).

For each subject, every charge, or "referral reason" (as some were subsequently referred for abuse/neglect, not a "charge" against the youth), was tabulated for each referral subsequent to the initial referral. (The total N of charges/referral reasons was greater that 863 because many had more than one charge/referral reason on a particular referral.) Offense categories for the initial referral were divided as follows: (1) status (runaway, unmanageable, curfew, truancy, and liquor law violations); (2) personal (rape, robbery, assault, and use/possession of weapons); (3) serious property (burglary, grand larceny, motor vehicle theft, stolen property); (4) minor property (petty larceny, trespassing, vandalism, and so on); and (5) other (mostly victimless and public order offenses). For subsequent referrals, two additional types were included with the "other" category: (1) administrative offenses (this category refers to violations of various court orders, mostly violation of probation and parole rules, and was included because a sufficiently large number of offenses that brought youth into court were of this variety); and (2) abuse and neglect.

In order to examine the extent to which status offenders "escalate," it was necessary to define this term operationally. Escalation was defined as offenses subsequent to the initial status offense that were *more serious than status offenses.* These included the following: personal crimes, property crimes, and drug offenses. Another method utilized was a comparison of the extent of one's "career," the number of times a youth was referred to court following his or her initial appearance. Therefore, first referral offense was matched with the number of subsequent referrals. An additional method of measuring escalation was to determine whether or not a youth had an arrest record as an adult. A limitation of this study was that only the arrest records in the Las Vegas area were available. However, the extent of one's adult arrest record was correlated with first referral offense wherever possible.

TABLE 1 First Referral Offense and Total Number of Referrals by Gender (in percentages)

	First Referral Offense				
Total Referrals	*Status*	*Personal*	*Serious Property*	*Minor Property*	*Other*
Male					
One	40.3	43.2	33.6	48.0	46.9
Two	16.7	24.3	20.2	13.5	24.0
Three or more	43.0	32.5	46.2	38.5	29.1
Total	100.0 (n = 72)	100.0 (n = 74)	100.0 (n = 119)	100.0 (n = 243)	100.0 (n = 96)
$\chi^2 = 15.8$ ($p < .05$)					
Female					
One	43.4	61.9	50.0	67.6	58.8
Two	26.4	19.0	14.3	11.8	17.6
Three or more	30.1	19.0	35.7	20.6	23.5
Total	100.0 (n = 53)	100.0 (n = 21)	100.0 (n = 14)	100.0 (n = 136)	100.0 (n = 34)
$\chi^2 = 10.5$ (ns)					
Total					
One	41.6	47.4	35.3	55.0	50.0
Two	20.8	23.1	19.5	12.9	22.3
Three or more	37.6	29.5	45.1	32.1	27.7
Total	100.0 (n = 125)	100.0 (n = 95)	100.0 (n = 133)	100.0 (n = 380)	100.0 (n = 130)
$\chi^2 = 25.0$ ($p < .01$)					

FINDINGS

In the sample of 863 youths, a total of 125 first came to court on a status offense; 95 for a personal offense; 133 for a "serious" property offense; 380 for a "minor" property offense; 130 were charged with other offenses (mostly victimless or public order offenses).

The data analysis begins with the relationship between first referral offense and the total number of referrals. Table 1 shows that those whose first referral was for a serious property offense were more likely than other offenders to have three or more referrals. However, the gap between these offenders and first time status offenders was negligible. In fact, status offenders ranked second in terms of the number of referrals (regardless of gender). A comparison of males and females showed that, regardless of original offense, males had the most subsequent referrals.

Table 2 shows a cross-tabulation between specific type of status offense and the total number of referrals that reveals significant differences. Those with the most referrals were those whose first referral was for truancy, followed closely by those first referred for being unmanageable or a runaway. When runaways and unmanageables were combined, 50% were referred three or more times, while only 25% did not return. In contrast, about 30% of those first charged with other status offenses returned three or more times, while just over half (51.9%) never returned again. Those first brought into court on liquor law violations were the least likely to return to court again (61%). About 44% of the curfew violators had no repeat appearances.

When comparing males and females, no significant differences were found (offenses were combined because the numbers of cases falling within each specific category were too small for analysis), although as indicated in Table 3, males charged with other status offenses were about twice as likely as females to have three or more referrals.

The total number of referrals is only one way of measuring escalation. When considering the nature of the subsequent referrals of those who were returned to court at least once, a slightly different picture emerged. In Table 4 all of the subsequent charges/referral reasons were cross-tabulated with the initial offense. For both males and females, and for the sample as a whole, there was a great deal of heterogeneity. When comparing males and females whose first referral was for a status offense, there were significant differences in their subsequent referral history. For female status offenders, *almost one-half (46.6%) of subsequent referrals were status offenses, twice the proportion for males.* Considering both males and females, it is clear that status offenses were not the exclusive preserve of those initially brought before the court on a status offense charge. For both serious and minor property offenders, a sizable proportion of subsequent referrals were status offenses; this was especially the case for females. Thus the conclusions to be drawn are that for those first referred for a personal or serious property offense, one-fifth of all subsequent charges were status offenses; for those originally brought in on a minor property offense, about one-fourth (24.5%) of subsequent referral charges were status offenses. For females who were first referred for a personal crime, almost one-half of the subsequent referrals were status offenses, compared to only 17% for their male counterparts first referred on a personal crime.

A somewhat different view is that there were a total of 594 status offense charges for the combined careers of the entire sample. Almost one-half (44.4%) were charged against those whose first referral was for a minor property offense (incidentally, the bulk of these were shoplifting charges). Only about one out of five (18.9%) were committed by those whose first referral was a status offense. In other words, status offenses were committed by more than merely those categorized as "status offenders." (These data are not shown within these tables.)

The most critical questions was, did these status offenders "escalate" or

TABLE 2 Type of Status Offense on First Referral and Total Number of Referrals (in percentages)

Type of Status Offense on First Referral	Total Referrals One	Two	Three +	Total
Runaway	23.1 (3)	30.8 (4)	46.1 (6)	100 (13)
Unmanageable	25.7 (9)	22.9 (8)	51.4 (18)	100 (35)
Curfew	43.8 (7)	25.0 (4)	31.2 (5)	100 (16)
Truancy	40.0 (8)	5.0 (1)	55.0 (11)	100 (20)
Liquor laws	61.0 (25)	21.9 (9)	17.1 (7)	100 (41)

$x^2 = 49.95$ ($p < .001$)

TABLE 3 Type of Status Offense on First Referral and Total Number of Referrals, by Gender (in percentages)

	Type of Status Offense					
Total Referrals	Runaway/ Unmanageable* Male	Female	Other** Male	Female	Total*** Male	Female
One	27.2	23.1	46.0	63.0	40.3	43.4
Two	13.6	34.6	18.0	18.5	16.7	26.4
Three +	59.2	42.3	36.0	18.5	43.0	30.2
Total	100.0 (n = 22)	100.0 (n = 26)	100.0 (n = 50)	100.0 (n = 27)	100.0 (n = 72)	100.0 (n = 53)

*$x^2 = 2.85$ (ns); **$x^2 = 2.71$ (ns); ***$x^2 = 2.80$ (ns).

"get worse"? Tables 5 through 8 provide the answer to this question in some detail. First, Table 5 reveals that a clear majority (two-thirds) of all of those first referred on a status offense charge did not escalate and commit more serious offenses. This was especially true for those whose first referral was for either running away or being unmanageable. While it is true that unmanageables were the most likely to return, they usually returned on either the same charge or something of nearly the same degree of seriousness ("other offenses," such as disturbances and other "public order" offenses), or for something clearly less serious (e.g., administrative offenses abuse/neglect). Those first referred for other status offenses were far more likely to escalate than were runaways and unmanageables. However, the majority of these offenders did not escalate either.

Table 6 compares males and females for offense escalation. First, it is clear that the great majority of female status offenders do not escalate; male status offenders were more than twice as likely as females to commit more serious offenses. These differences were even more pronounced when considering runaway and unmanageable charges, where males were about five times as likely as females to escalate. When considering other status offenses, males and females were about equally as likely to escalate.

The data presented in Table 7, which examine each individual status offense according to gender, revealed significant differences between males and females for those first referred for running away, being unmanageable, and curfew violation. Girls first referred for running away and being unmanageable were significantly less likely than males to escalate. However, girls first referred for curfew violation were about twice as likely as males to escalate, although the degree of significance is moderate. Males and females initially referred for truancy and liquor law violations were about equally likely to escalate. The large gaps between males and females for both runaway and unmanageable offenses suggest that these offenses have quite different implications for the subsequent "delinquent careers" of boys and girls.

Finally, in Table 8, the relationship between the nature of the first referral and the existence of an adult arrest record is considered. No significant relationship was found between first referral offense and the existence of an adult record. Indeed, the majority of subjects had no records as adults. For females, however, those first referred for a property or other offense were significantly more likely to have an adult record. It is clear that status offenders did not "escalate" into adult criminals. However, when males first referred as runaways or unmanageables were compared with females, about one-half of the males (45.5%), but only 11.5% of the females, had adult records. In addition, males were more than three times as likely to have a felony record (chi-square = 6.89, $p < .05$—not shown in Table 8).

SUMMARY AND CONCLUSIONS

The data reported here confirm what many other researchers have found; Young offenders commit a wide variety of offenses during their "careers" within the juvenile court system. It appears that the majority of those whose first referral was a status offense did not become serious delinquents. If anything, they became something considerably less than serious delinquents. The data clearly and unambiguously demonstrate that those first referred to court on a status offense are more likely to return for a second or third time than most other offenders. However, if they do return it will not be for a more serious offense.

It is also quite clear that there are significant differences between males and females who commit status offenses. Also, there are very significant differences between the status offenses of runaway and unmanageability and other types of status offenses (in this study, truancy, curfew, and liquor law violations). Those referred to the court for violations of liquor laws, truancy, and curfew were much more likely to escalate into more serious offenses than were runaways and unmanageables. It is also apparent that there were significant differences between males who were runaways and unmangeables and their female counterparts. One interpretation of this difference is that these two offenses are differentially applied to girls and boys on the part of their parents. Males and females may not be engaging in the same sorts of behavior, even though the charge is the same. Previous research has suggested that, while boys and girls are about equally as likely to "defy parental authority" and to run away from home (Cernkovich and Giordano, 1979), girls are far more likely to be referred to court on such charges. Also, when girls are charged with being runaways and/or unmanageables, they are often being sexually abused by someone in the home, usually the father or stepfather (Chesney-

TABLE 4 First Offense and Subsequent Referral History, by Gender (in percentages)

Subsequent Referrals	First Offense Status	Personal	Serious Property	Minor Property	Other
Male					
Status	24.5	17.0	19.7	22.6	17.6
Personal	4.1	17.4	11.1	9.4	5.6
Serious Property	17.3	14.2	16.5	16.4	7.9
Minor Property	14.1	13.7	18.9	15.4	9.3
Other	40.0	37.7	33.8	32.6	59.5
Total	100.0 (n = 220)	100.0 (n = 212)	100.0 (n = 461)	100.0 (n = 871)	100.0 (n = 301)
Female					
Status	46.4	45.4	31.6	32.7	16.4
Personal	5.6	9.1	5.3	2.9	1.5
Serious Property	3.2	0.0	15.8	8.8	6.0
Minor Property	8.8	9.1	13.2	14.1	23.9
Other	36.0	36.4	34.2	41.5	52.2
Total	100.0 (n = 125)	100.0 (n = 33)	100.0 (n = 38)	100.0 (n = 205)	100.0 (n = 67)
Total					
Status	32.5	20.8	20.6	24.5	17.4
Personal	4.6	16.3	10.6	8.2	4.9
Serious Property	12.2	12.2	16.4	15.0	7.6
Minor Property	12.2	13.1	18.4	15.1	12.0
Other	38.6	37.6	33.9	37.2	58.1
Total	100.0 (n = 345)	100.0 (n = 245)	100.0 (n = 499)	100.0 (n = 1076)	100.0 (n = 368)

NOTE: Totals represent the total number of referral reasons/charges and, since on a given referral there may be more than one charge, the number adds up to more than 863.

TABLE 5 First Referral Status Offense and Seriousness of Subsequent Referrals (in percentages)

First Referral Status Offense	More Serious	Same or Less Serious	Total
Runaway/Unmanageable	19.6 (31)	80.4 (127)	100 (158)
Other Status	43.3 (81)	56.7 (106)	100 (187)
Total	32.5 (112)	67.5 (233)	100 (345)

$\chi^2 = 21.2$ ($p < .01$)

Lind, 1973, 1978, 1988a). Thus such a referral for a female suggests victimization within the home but not an indication that such behavior will "escalate" into a serious delinquent career.

Juvenile courts should seriously question the inexact use of the concept "status offender." It should not be assumed that this group of youths represents a unique category that commits only one type of offense or that they, and they alone, commit status offenses. As the data here indicate, most of the status offenses are actually committed by those whose first referral was for something other than a status offense. Rather than offense specialization, these youths typify a sort of "jack of all trades and master of none" syndrome. If there is any limited degree of specialization, it is among females. Juvenile courts should pay special attention to girls that are brought before them, for it is rare indeed that any of them become serious delinquents. More often than not (especially if the charge is runaway or unmanageable), girls are being victimized at home and hence require a completely different response by the court. The male status offenders, overwhelmingly, are the ones who will escalate. Still, the courts should realize that even most of these males will not become hardened offenders.

REFERENCES

Cernkovich, Steven and Peggy C. Giordano. 1979. "A Comparative Analysis of Male and Female Delinquency." *Sociological Quarterly* 20:131–145.

Chesney-Lind, Meda. 1973. "Judicial Enforcement of the Female Sex Role." *Issues in Criminology* 8:51–70.

_____ 1978. "Young Women in the Arms of the Law." In *Women, Crime and Criminology,* edited by Lee Bowker. Lexington, MA: Lexington Books.

_____ 1988a. "Girls and Status Offenses: Is Juvenile Justice Still Sexist?" *Criminal Justice Abstracts* 20:144–165.

_____ 1988b. "Girls in Jail." *Crime & Delinquency* 34:150–168.

Clarke, Steven H. 1975. "Some Implications for North Carolina of Recent Research in Juvenile Delinquency." *Journal of Research in Crime and Delinquency* 12:57–60.

Krisberg, Barry, Ira Schwartz, Paul Litsky, and James Austin. 1985. *The Watershed of Juvenile Justice Reform.* Minnesota: Hubert Humphrey Institute of Public Affairs.

Logan, Charles H. and Sharla P. Rausch. 1985. "Why Deinstitutionalizing Status Offenders is Pointless." *Crime & Delinquency* 31:501–517.

Rankin, Joseph H. and L. Edward Wells. 1985. "From Status to Delinquent Offenses: Escalation?" *Journal of Criminal Justice* 31:171–180.

Rojek, Dean and Maynard L. Erickson. 1982. "Delinquent Careers: A Test of the Career Escalation Model." *Criminology* 20:5–28.

Shelden, Randall G. 1987. "The Chronic Delinquent: Gender and Racial Differences." Paper presented at the annual meeting of the American Society of Criminology, Montreal, November.

_____ 1988. "Delinquent Careers and the Chronic Delinquent." Paper presented at the annual meeting of the Academy of

TABLE 6: Seriousness of Subsequent Offenses of First Referral Status Offenders, by Type of Status Offense and Gender (in percentages)

First Referral Status Offense	*Seriousness*[a] *More Serious*	*Same or Less Serious*	*Total*
Runaway/Unmanageable			
Male	33.3 (26)	66.7 (52)	100 (78)
Female	6.3 (5)	93.7 (75)	100 (80)
$x^2 = 13.1$ ($p < .01$)			
Other Status			
Male	44.4 (63)	55.6 (79)	100 (142)
Female	40.0 (18)	60.0 (27)	100 (45)
$x^2 = 0.1$ (ns)			
All Status			
Male	40.5 (89)	59.5 (131)	100 (220)
Female	18.4 (23)	81.6 (102)	100 (125)
$x^2 = 18.5$ ($p < .01$)			

a. More serious: personal crimes, property crimes and drug offenses. About same or less serious: other status offenses, administrative offenses, abuse/neglect referrals, other.

TABLE 7 Percentage of Subsequent Charges that Were More Serious, by Gender (specific status offenses considered)

First Referral Status Offense	*Level of Seriousness* *More*	*Same or Less*	*Total*
Runaway			
Male	21.4 (3)	78.6 (11)	100 (14)
Female	3.2 (1)	96.8 (30)	100 (31)
$x^2 = 5.2$ ($p < .05$)			
Unmanageable			
Male	35.9 (23)	64.1 (41)	100 (64)
Female	8.2 (4)	91.8 (45)	100 (49)
$x^2 = 12.6$ ($p < .001$)			
Curfew			
Male	28.0 (7)	72.0 (18)	100 (25)
Female	56.3 (9)	43.7 (7)	100 (16)
$x^2 = 3.9$ ($p < .05$)			
Truancy			
Male	49.2 (33)	50.8 (34)	100 (67)
Female	36.8 (7)	63.2 (12)	100 (19)
$x^2 = 1.1$ (ns)			
Liquor laws			
Male	46.0 (23)	54.0 (27)	100 (50)
Female	20.0 (2)	80.0 (8)	100 (10)
$x^2 = 2.0$ (ns)			

TABLE 8 First Referral Reason and Adult Record, by Gender (in percentages)

Adult Record	*Run. & Unman.*	*Other Status*	*Personal*	*Serious Property*	*Minor Property*	*Other*
Males						
None	54.5	64.0	62.2	63.9	70.1	67.7
Misdemeanor	31.8	16.0	16.2	15.1	12.3	14.6
Felony	13.6	20.0	21.6	21.0	17.6	17.7
Total	100.0	100.0	100.0	100.0	100.0	100.0
$\chi^2 = 8.1$ (ns)						
Females						
None	88.5	66.7	71.4	100.0	86.0	73.5
Misdemeanor	7.7	25.9	14.3	0.0	7.4	8.8
Felony	3.8	7.4	14.3	0.0	6.6	17.6
Total	100.0	100.0	100.0	100.0	100.0	100.0
$\chi^2 = 19.2$ ($p < .05$)						
Both						
None	72.9	64.9	64.2	67.7	75.8	69.2
Misdemeanor	18.8	19.5	15.8	20.0	10.5	13.1
Felony	8.3	15.6	20.0	12.3	13.7	17.7
Total	100.0	100.0	100.0	100.0	100.0	100.0
$\chi^2 = 13.4$ (ns)						

Criminal Justice Sciences, San Francisco, April.

Teitelbaum, Lee E. and Aidan R. Gough, eds. 1977. *Beyond Control: Status Offenders in the Juvenile Court.* Cambridge, MA: Ballinger.

Thomas, Charles W. 1976. "Are Status Offenders Really So Different? A Comparative and Longitudinal Assessment." *Crime & Delinquency* 22:438–455.

Weis, Joseph. 1980. *Jurisdiction and the Elusive Status Offender: A Comparison of Involvement in Delinquent Behavior and Status Offenses.* Washington, DC: Report of the National Juvenile Justice Assessment Centers.

Wolfgang, Marvin E., Robert Figlio, and Thorsten Sellin. 1972. *Delinquency in a Birth Cohort.* Chicago: University of Chicago Press.

Our Violent Kids

A rise in brutal crimes by the young shakes the soul of society

ANASTASIA TOUFEXIS

Beating. Rape. Murder. Screams in the night. Bricks in the face. Sirens drowning out the crying. These are the images of violent crime—the crime generally associated with the most depraved individuals. No one is shocked any longer to hear of atrocities committed by mobsters, drug pushers or psychopaths. But the boy next door? That harmless-looking kid in biology class? The captain of the football team?

It is hard to believe, and harder still to comprehend, but it is true. Some atrocious crimes in America are being committed by those who should be the most innocent—the young. Recent weeks have brought news of two particularly brutal acts: the gang rape and near murder of a jogger in Manhattan's Central Park by a group of youths 14 to 16, and the alleged sexual assault on a mentally impaired girl by high school students in affluent Glen Ridge, N.J. These crimes have awakened the country to the beast that has broken loose in some of America's young people.

The Central Park and Glen Ridge attacks are only the most highly publicized of the cases occurring across the U.S. More and more teenagers, acting individually or in gangs, are running amuck. In the Central Park incident, young toughs said they were "wilding," which apparently means marauding with no purpose in mind but to create havoc and hurt people. In Philadelphia packs of youths chant "Beat, beat, beat" as they roam the streets looking for victims.

To be sure, teenagers have never been angels. Adolescence is often a troubled time of rebellion and rage. From *West Side Story* to *Rebel Without a Cause,* the violence of youth has been chronicled on stage and screen. But juvenile crime appears to be more widespread and vicious than ever before. "Burglars used to rob a house and then run away. Now they urinate or defecate in the home or burn it up before leaving," says Shawn Johnston, a forensic psychologist in Sacramento. "Thieves mugged a person and ran off. Now they beat their victims." Or rape or murder them.

Do you think teenage violence is a bigger problem today than it was in the past?

Yes: 88%

From a telephone poll of 506 adult Americans taken for TIME/CNN on June 1 by Yankelovich Clancy Shulman. Sampling error is plus or minus 4.5%.

Statistics show an upsurge in the most violent types of crimes by teens. In part, this trend may result from better reporting, but some experts believe it reflects a true increase in violence. According to the FBI, between 1983 and 1987 arrests of those under 18 for murder jumped 22.2%, for aggravated assault 18.6% and for rape 14.6%. Those figures may not seem dramatic, but they should be seen in the context of a 2% decline in the total number of teenagers in the U.S. since 1983.

Many of the tales behind the numbers are horrifying. In Springfield, Mass., last April, a 13-year-old girl was walking through a park with a girlfriend when she was allegedly attacked by five boys no older than 16. They fondled her breasts and appeared to be preparing to rape her when her screams brought help. Last September a 15-year-old Houston boy raped and murdered a 66-year-old woman, then burglarized her home. In May a 15-year-old Detroit boy was charged with killing another teenager with a sawed-off shotgun, apparently in a dispute over a stolen bicycle. Ten months ago, a 16-year-old boy drove 150 miles from his home in Princeton, Ky., and shot to death a woman he did not know. The boy, who came to be known as "Little Rambo" to his schoolmates, told police that he "just wanted to get away and kill somebody."

Adolescents have always been violence prone, but there are horrendous crimes being committed by even younger children. In Detroit last April, an eleven-year-old boy was charged with joining a 15-year-old in the rape of a two-year-old girl. The two allegedly left their victim in a garbage Dumpster. When he was only ten, a boy in San Antonio began sexually abusing three of his four younger sisters and continued until he was caught at 16.

The teen crime wave flows across all races, classes and life-styles. The youths who went on the Central Park rampage were blacks and Hispanics from Harlem, but they were not desperately poor. Three of the five suspects charged in the Glen Ridge sexual assault were idolized football stars, and two of them were co-captains of their high school team. Eight other Glen Ridge High School students, including the son of a local police lieutenant, allegedly stood by and watched the assault. In Denver a 16-year-old boy charged with first-degree murder in a stabbing death was a high school honors student.

The offenders are overwhelmingly male, but girls too are capable of vicious crimes. In Escondido, Calif., a 16-year-old girl and three teenage boys went on an arson spree last March. The group set four fires at three schools, causing damage that will cost more than $1 million to repair. A 16-year-old girl from Cape Cod, Mass., who had been drinking stabbed her male cousin, severely injuring him.

What is chilling about many of the young criminals is that they show no remorse or conscience, at least initially. Youths brag about their exploits and shrug off victims' pain. A Chicago case in which four teenagers raped and killed a medical student was solved because of good police work and what Pat O'Brien, Cook County deputy state's attorney, describes as "the defendants' inability to keep their mouths shut" about the crime. "It was a badge," he explains. "It was something they talked about as if it gave them status within that group of guys." Youngsters offhandedly refer to innocent passersby caught in the line of gunfire between two gangs as "mushrooms." "That is callous," observes Edward Loughran, commissioner of the Massachusetts department of youth services. "Alienated is too weak a word to describe these kids."

How could this be happening? The experts offer a raft of reasons, everything from physiological and psychological abnormalities to family and cultural decay. By themselves, none of the explanations are wholly satisfactory. But each of these factors may contribute to at least some of the violence. Generalizations are difficult because every case is unique. Each young criminal has his own genes, his own family background and his own response to the many forces in modern culture that encourage indiscriminate sex and violence.

A frequently advanced—and hotly disputed—theory is that aggression is a biologically rooted impulse of young males. Some experts suggest that there may be a genetic component to hostile behavior; others attempt to tie it to levels of different chemicals that circulate through the body and brain. One of them is testosterone. Production of this male sex hormone rises dramatically during puberty, a period usually marked by intense sexual desire and strong aggressive tendencies. Some studies indicate that particularly rough athletes or violent prisoners have higher than normal testosterone levels.

Violent youths frequently have neurological problems and learning disorders, many of which result from brain injuries inflicted in beatings by parents and others. Some suffer from paranoia and hallucinations, and others experience seizures. Some of the most violent children tend to have grossly abnormal electroencephalograms.

But it is too easy to say that biology is destiny and that all violent youths are simply captives of their physiology or "raging hormones." Society has generally been able to control and channel aggressive impulses through its basic institutions—home, schools and church. But these moral pillars are crumbling.

Too many children are growing up in families headed by one overburdened parent, usually the mother. Even when two parents are present, both often have demanding jobs and are absorbed in their own concerns. Sometimes the parents are strung out on alcohol or drugs. The result is that children do not get the nurturing, guidance or supervision necessary to instill a set of values and a proper code of behavior.

Children normally learn to trust and develop attachments to people within the first two years of life. By then they have also acquired a sense of compassion and empathy for others. And they have begun to be taught the difference between right and wrong and that hurtful actions have consequences. Many youngsters, though, fail to acquire those early curbs on conduct. Later on, when children misbehave, indulgent parents make excuses and forgo punishments. Young boys who grow up with absent or uninvolved fathers suffer doubly in that they often fail to develop a healthy sense of masculinity.

The neglect is frequently compounded by outright abuse. Says Dorothy Otnow Lewis, professor of psychiatry at New York University: "Kids are being raised by more and more disturbed parents. And what this lack of parenting breeds is misshapen personalities." Parents punch each other verbally and physically—and frequently do the same with their children. In fact, the large majority of violent kids have been physically, and often sexually, abused by parents, relatives or others. One mother, reports Lewis, broke her son's legs with a broom; a father threw his child down a set of stairs.

As a consequence of indifference and abuse, children are left emotional cripples, self-centered, angry and alienated. And fated to repeat the chilling lessons they have learned. "These children are dead inside," says psychologist Johnston. "For them to feel alive and important, they engage in terrible types of sadistic activity."

Their innocent victims are usually surrogate targets; the parents may be the ones they really hate. A 17-year-old boy who is now in a treatment program in San Bernardino, Calif., began sexually molesting younger members of his family when he was about twelve. He himself had been molested at the age of six, first by his father and then by a twelve-year-old friend. Says the boy: "My father used to beat my mom all the time. That makes me kind of angry. He was always out partying, getting high. My fantasy is making him suffer. First I'd shoot him in the kneecaps and let him suffer for about an hour, screaming. Then I'd shoot him in the nuts and let him suffer some more, and then I'd put a bullet through his head."

TEENS UNDER PRESSURE
Family Violence
The number of children reported abused and neglected almost doubled between 1980 and 1987, from 1.2 million to 2.2 million.
Educational Failures
The percentage of teens who drop out of high school is consistently above 25%.
Absentee Parents
Many youngsters lack attention and supervision in part because their parents are too busy making a living. Of women with children under 18, the percentage who work rose from 54% in 1980 to 65% in 1988.
Today 24% of families with children are headed by a single parent.
Poverty
One of every five children in the U.S. lives in a household with an income below the poverty level ($11,611 in 1987 for a family of four).
Drugs
Between 1983 and 1987, arrests of juveniles under 18 for drug-abuse violations rose 5% even though the total size of the teenage population shrank 2%.
Peer Influence
Teenagers often adopt the values of their peer group rather than those of parents and teachers.

Signals of violence surface early but frequently go ignored or denied. Serial killer Ted Bundy's family insisted for years that he had a normal childhood, points out psychiatrist Lewis. It was only recently revealed that "by the time he was

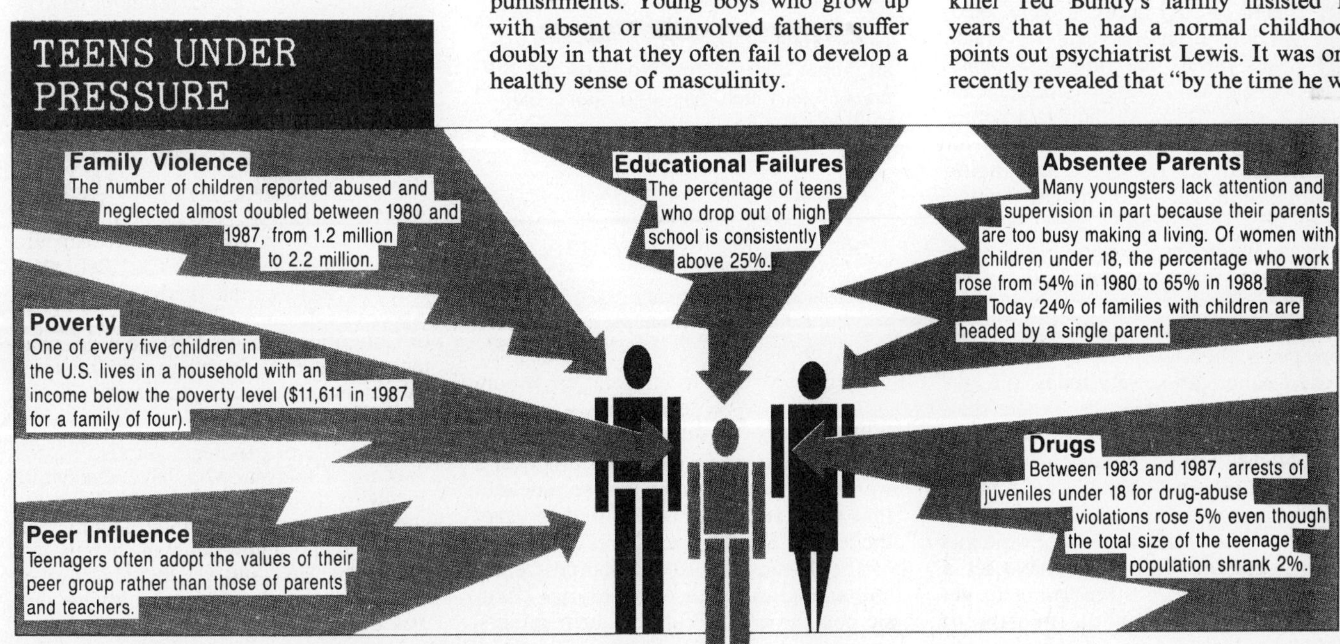

three, he was putting knives in his aunt's bed." The youngster who taunts siblings, bullies schoolmates, tortures pets or peeks in windows is sending up warning flares.

Children abandoned physically or emotionally by their parents look elsewhere for companionship, acceptance and values. Odell Edwards, a 20-year-old serving time in a Ventura, Calif., juvenile facility for attempted murder and other offenses, recalls that by the age of 14 he was spending most of his time away from home and hanging out with a group of friends that he called his "homeboys." Says Edwards: "I never really had anyone to talk to. My father was gone. I had no one to turn to when I was in trouble, except my homeboys. They became my family."

Members of a group learn about sex from one another, experiment with drugs together and look to their friends for a sense of belonging and approval. Notes Alan Morris, chief of the adolescent unit of the Illinois State Psychiatric Institute in Chicago: "Some kids, especially younger adolescents, have an exquisite sensitivity to what their peers think. They won't go to school if their shoelaces are the wrong color."

But the group's influence is often treacherous. Explains young Edwards: "It's peer pressure and wanting to be accepted by your friends and trying to prove yourself in the best way you know how, which is being violent." Gangs allow even the most cowardly and impotent to feel brave and powerful. And they override inhibitions and diminish any feelings of guilt. Violence becomes contagious. Some youngsters revel in the mayhem; others, too weak to break away, become trapped and are swept along.

In many instances, the violence is fueled by easy access to guns, alcohol and drugs, particularly crack. Users often "fall into a sadomasochistic ritual after smoking together," says Terry Williams, a senior research scholar at the New School for Social Research. "They are angry, hallucinating, and get into violent fights." Crack can also leave users sexually aroused. When they do not find a willing partner, Williams asserts, they may be tempted to rape.

If teenagers often get their values from peers, then just what are those values? In American society today, the emphasis is less on caring for others than on getting money and instant gratification. Notes Arnold Goldstein, director of the Center for Research on Aggression at Syracuse University: "We are a nation whose role models, Presidents and leaders on Wall Street have set a tone in the country—'I'm going to get mine.' " If the big-shot investment banker can take what he wants, often by illegal means, then a teenager may think he should be able to grab the spoils in the only way he knows how. Declares Harvard psychiatrist Robert Coles: "Our culture accentuates instinct instead of inhibiting it."

The entertainment media play a powerful role in the formation of values. Today's children, unlike those of earlier generations, are fed a steady diet of glorified violence. Television cartoons feature dehumanized, machinelike characters, such as the Transformers and Gobots, engaged in destructive acts. But viewers see no consequences. Victims never bleed and never suffer. Youngsters mimic the behavior with toys based on the shows. Later they graduate to TV programs and movies that depict people killing or degrading other people. By the age of 16, the typical child has witnessed an estimated 200,000 acts of violence, including 33,000 murders. Inevitably, contend many experts, some youngsters will imitate the brutality in real life. In a 22-year study, researchers tracked the development of 875 third-graders from a rural community in New York. Among the discoveries: those who watched the greatest amount of violent television at the age of eight were the most likely to show aggressive behavior at 19 and later. About one-quarter of the students were considered violent at 30—they had been convicted of a crime, had multiple traffic violations or were abusive to spouses.

Rock music has become a dominant—and potentially destructive—part of teenage culture. Lyrics, album covers and music videos, particularly in the rock genre called heavy metal, romanticize bondage, sexual assaults and murder. The song *Girls L.G.B.N.A.F.* by Ice-T contains the words "Girls, let's get butt naked and f______." Or consider these lyrics from Mötley Crüe's *Girls, Girls, Girls,*, an album that reached No. 2 on the *Billboard* chart and has sold more than 2 million copies:

The blade of my knife
Faced away from your heart
Those last few nights
It turned and sliced you apart . . .
Laid out cold
Now we're both alone
But killing you helped me keep you home.

Guns N' Roses put out an album called *Appetite for Destruction,* which has sold more than 6 million copies. The jacket cover, featuring a robot looming over a woman in torn clothing, was so repellent that some record stores refused to carry the album. Says Tipper Gore, co-founder of the Parents' Music Resource Center and a longtime critic of rock lyrics: "Music companies are cultural strip miners, profiting from the sex and violence and ignoring the scars."

Even today's comic books are not immune from the violent trend. While parents may fondly remember the dating shenanigans of Archie and Veronica or the wholesome exploits of superheroes, their children are now being offered a titillating blend of sadism and sex. A stripper was crucified in one issue of *Green Arrow.* Superman, in a story called *Bloodsport,* battled a deranged Viet Nam veteran who was shooting people at random on the streets of Metropolis with a gun in each hand.

Among the most offensive purveyors of brutality to women are slasher films. The movies that inaugurated the trend, including *Friday the 13th, Halloween* and *Nightmare on Elm Street,* are now tame compared with such opuses as *I Spit on Your Grave* or *Splatter University.* The main features: graphic and erotic scenes of female mutilation, rape or murder. Slasher films are widely shown on cable TV, and video shops do a booming business in rentals, especially among eleven-to-15-year-olds. Youngsters watch three or four at a clip at all-night "gross-out" parties. In some fraternity houses on college campuses, slasher movies play continually in lounges, along with pornographic films.

Sexually explicit movies may lead some young men to reaffirm the all-too-common male attitude that when a woman says no she really means yes. Many experts believe that such films may be a contributing factor in date rape, one of the most common adolescent sexual crimes. "Teenagers are only doing what they are told to do," says sociologist Gail Dines-Levy of Boston's Wheelock College. "They are being conformists, not deviants."

In some cases, poverty can help spur violent crime. Many ghetto residents have little sense of hope or opportunity, and feel they have little stake in preserving society. Boys often have trouble forging a masculine identity without one of the primary accompaniments—a job. Teen unemployment is endemic among poor youth, running more than 40% in many communities. Meanwhile, welfare and social programs suffered drastic cutbacks during the Reagan era. Says Chicago psychiatrist Carl Bell: "Violence is the weapon of the powerless." Agrees Professor Leah Blumberg Lapidus of Columbia Teachers College in Manhattan: "It relieves boredom and makes a statement, like graffiti, that says, 'Notice me.' "

But a life of privilege can also be corrupting. Children who have everything given to them may come to believe that they are entitled to anything, that they are above their fellow human beings and above the law. And yet their busy, overachieving parents may not be giving pampered teens what they need most:

attention and supervision. "Neglect is abuse," says Randa Dembroff, an official of the Los Angeles County Bar Association. "A workaholic parent is just as abusive as one who physically abuses his children."

Can anything be done about violent youngsters? Many Americans are calling for stronger laws and punishments. They argue that juveniles should be prosecuted as adults and that prison sentences should be longer. "These kids are getting away with murder," declares Robert Contreras, a police detective in Los Angeles. "They are not afraid, have no respect for anything and joke that in jail they'll at least get three square meals a day." Syracuse's Goldstein surveyed 250 juvenile delinquents for their solutions to violence and found that they too favored harsher sentences. Many thought that jail was too "cushy."

Others have offered an even more radical idea: locking up parents. California is trying to do just that. Under an eight-month-old statute, parents can be held responsible for the criminal activity of their offspring. In April, Los Angeles police arrested a woman whose 15-year-old son has been charged with participating in the rape of a twelve-year-old girl by a dozen members of a street gang. If she is convicted of violating the parental-responsibility law, she faces a maximum penalty of a year in jail and a $2,500 fine.

Such solutions offer only illusory security. Parents contend that they cannot control their children. And most youngsters are eventually released from jail. Many return more hardened than before. "You need to break delinquents from the group where antisocial behavior is reinforced," explains psychologist Michael Nelson of Xavier University in Cincinnati. "But we're caught in a catch-22 dilemma. We place delinquents in reform schools, where they have more access to individuals who are poor role models."

An unpopular but more sensible approach, say experts, is to offer rehabilitative treatment. Various communities across the U.S. are trying such programs—with considerable success. The programs call for individual and group therapy for the offender and sometimes for his family as well. The strategy is to get violent youngsters to recognize the inappropriateness of their actions and to accept responsibility for them. That is a difficult task, particularly with sexual offenders, who are often imitating what was done to them.

In some programs, youngsters discuss or write up their own cases in an effort to identify the behavior patterns or situations that are liable to trigger hostile actions. For example, sexual offenders are advised to avoid baby-sitting. In the program operated by the Justice Resource Institute in Massachusetts, members concentrate on overcoming aggressive thinking patterns—for instance, assuming that they are the butt of the joke whenever people are laughing.

The treatment centers also try to elicit a sense of empathy. At Giddings, a maximum-security facility for juveniles in Texas, murderers keep a daily journal of their feelings and act out their crime, taking the roles of both their victim and surviving family members. Sexual offenders meet with groups of victims every few months. At its prisons and work camps, the California Youth Authority runs voluntary classes in which inmates study property crimes, domestic violence, sexual assault, child abuse, homicide and victims' rights. Some offenders do eventually express remorse. Says one Giddings boy, a middle-class 15-year-old from Austin who raped his eight-year-old neighbor: "I realize how society really looks at rape. Sometimes at night I sit up crying. I look back and say that could never have been me."

Such programs are clearly valuable, but the treatment is costly. Therapists say the optimum time needed for counseling sex offenders ranges from twelve to 18 months. (It can take about six months just to break through the denial phase.) Follow-up and outpatient therapy are also necessary. As a result, not enough youths get treatment.

No matter how effective the programs are, they are indisputably too late. Violence-prone youths need to be identified and helped before they explode in rage. Reporting of physical and sexual abuse in particular should be encouraged. The earlier the intervention, the greater the chance of success. All youngsters could also benefit from improved sex-education programs that explore the emotional as well as the mechanical aspects of sex.

Some schools have begun offering special courses in preventing violence. A ten-session curriculum, designed by Dr. Deborah Prothrow-Stith, the Massachusetts commissioner of public health, is being used in several high schools in Boston, Detroit and Denver. "We tell them anger is potentially constructive but they need to learn how to handle it," explains Prothrow-Stith. Students examine how fights begin and analyze videotapes of arguments.

Yet the lessons learned at school can easily be undermined by today's popular culture. The messages that blare from stereos, TVs and movie screens amount to a second education for the young. And much more money goes into the development of this after-school curriculum than goes into education. Rock stars earn millions, but a high-school teacher is lucky to get $30,000 a year.

A growing band of activists is lobbying TV, movie and record producers to reduce the level of sex and violence in entertainment. Terry Rakolta of Bloomfield Hills, Mich., the mother of four children, has started a group called Americans for Responsible Television. She has suggested that networks devote the first two hours of evening programming to family shows and has also asked major advertisers to avoid sponsoring programs that the group finds objectionable. One of Rakolta's first targets was *Married . . . With Children*, a racy prime-time sitcom. Parents' Music Resource Center, meanwhile, has successfully pressured the Recording Industry Association of America to create a rating system that alerts parents to sexually explicit lyrics. Warning labels are now printed on record jackets. The group also provides printed lyric sheets and encourages parents to complain to radio and TV stations about raunchy and violent programming.

Even the activists admit, however, that removing all sex and gore from the media would make no more than a small dent in the teen crime problem. Much more fundamental changes in society are needed. Government at all levels should step up the battles against drugs, poverty and racism. Far more money should be poured into education, day-care and recreational opportunities for the young. Youngsters need more of their parents' time, and they need to know that society cares about them.

Above all, parents should take a long, hard look in the mirror. The values of today's youth are merely magnified reflections of the values of their elders. Parents should remember the words of the father in Harry Chapin's song *Cat's in the Cradle*, when he comes to a sudden realization about his insensitive, uncaring son:

He'd grown up just like me
My boy was just like me.

—Reported by Mary Cronin/New York, Melissa Ludtke/Boston and Sylvester Monroe/Los Angeles, with other bureaus

Girls' Crime and Woman's Place: Toward a Feminist Model of Female Delinquency

This article argues that existing delinquency theories are fundamentally inadequate to the task of explaining female delinquency and official reactions to girls' deviance. To establish this, the article first reviews the degree of the androcentric bias in the major theories of delinquent behavior. Then the need for a feminist model of female delinquency is explored by reviewing the available evidence on girls' offending. This review shows that the extensive focus on disadvantaged males in public settings has meant that girls' victimization and the relationship between that experience and girls' crime has been systematically ignored. Also missed has been the central role played by the juvenile justice system in the sexualization of female delinquency and the criminalization of girls' survival strategies. Finally, it will be suggested that the official actions of the juvenile justice system should be understood as major forces in women's oppression as they have historically served to reinforce the obedience of all young women to the demands of patriarchal authority no matter how abusive and arbitrary.

Meda Chesney-Lind

Meda Chesney-Lind: Associate Professor of Women's Studies and an Associate Researcher with the Center for Youth Research at the University of Hawaii, Manoa.

I ran away so many times. I tried anything man, and they wouldn't believe me. . . . As far as they are concerned they think I'm the problem. You know, runaway, bad label. (Statement of a 16-year-old girl who, after having been physically and sexually assaulted, started running away from home and was arrested as a "runaway" in Hawaii.)

You know, one of these days I'm going to have to kill myself before you guys are gonna listen to me. I can't stay at home. (Statement of a 16-year-old Tucson runaway with a long history of physical abuse [Davidson, 1982, p. 26].)

Who is the typical female delinquent? What causes her to get into trouble? What happens to her if she is caught? These are questions that few members of the general public could answer quickly. By contrast, almost every citizen can talk about "delinquency," by which they generally mean male delinquency, and can even generate some fairly specific complaints about, for example, the failure of the juvenile justice system to deal with such problems as "the alarming increase in the rate of serious juvenile crime" and the fact that the juvenile courts are too lenient on juveniles found guilty of these offenses (Opinion Research Corporation, 1982).

This situation should come as no surprise since even the academic study of delinquent behavior has, for all intents and purposes, been the study of male delinquency. "The delinquent is a rogue male" declared Albert Cohen (1955, p. 140) in his influential book on gang delinquency. More than a decade later, Travis Hirschi, in his equally important book entitled *The Causes of Delinquency,* relegated women to a footnote that suggested, somewhat apologetically, that "in the analysis that follows, the 'non-Negro' becomes 'white,' and the girls disappear."

This pattern of neglect is not all that unusual. All areas of social inquiry have been notoriously gender blind. What is perhaps less well understood is that theories developed to describe the misbehavior of working- or lower-class male youth fail to capture the full nature of delinquency in America; and, more to the point, are woefully inadequate when it comes to explaining female misbehavior and official reactions to girls' deviance.

To be specific, delinquent behavior involves a range of activities far broader than those committed by the stereotypical street gang. Moreover, many more young people than the small visible group of "troublemakers" that exist on every intermediate and high school campus commit some sort of juvenile offense and many of these youth have brushes with the law. One study revealed, for example, that 33% of all the boys and 14% of the girls born in 1958 had at least one contact with the police before reaching their eighteenth birthday (Tracy, Wolfgang, and Figlio, 1985, p. 5). Indeed, some forms of serious

Reprinted from *Crime & Delinquency,* Vol. 35, No. 1, January 1989, pp. 5-29.

delinquent behavior, such as drug and alcohol abuse, are far more frequent than the stereotypical delinquent behavior of gang fighting and vandalism and appear to cut across class and gender lines.

Studies that solicit from youth themselves the volume of their delinquent behavior consistently confirm that large numbers of adolescents engage in at least some form of misbehavior that could result in their arrest. As a consequence, it is largely trivial misconduct, rather than the commission of serious crime, that shapes the actual nature of juvenile delinquency. One national study of youth aged 15-21, for example, noted that only 5% reported involvement in a serious assault, and only 6% reported having participated in a gang fight. In contrast, 81% admitted to having used alcohol, 44% admitted to having used marijuana, 37% admitted to having been publicly drunk, 42% admitted to having skipped classes (truancy), 44% admitted having had sexual intercourse, and 15% admitted to having stolen from the family (McGarrell and Flanagan, 1985, p. 363). Clearly, not all of these activities are as serious as the others. It is important to remember that young people can be arrested for all of these behaviors.

Indeed, one of the most important points to understand about the nature of delinquency, and particularly female delinquency, is that youth can be taken into custody for both criminal acts and a wide variety of what are often called "status offenses." These offenses, in contrast to criminal violations, permit the arrest of youth for a wide range of behaviors that are violations of parental authority: "running away from home," "being a person in need of supervision," "minor in need of supervision," being "incorrigible," "beyond control," truant, in need of "care and protection," and so on. Juvenile delinquents, then, are youths arrested for either criminal or noncriminal status offenses; and, as this discussion will establish, the role played by uniquely juvenile offenses is by no means insignificant, particularly when considering the character of female delinquency.

Examining the types of offenses for which youth are actually arrested, it is clear that again most are arrested for the less serious criminal acts and status offenses. Of the one and a half million youth arrested in 1983, for example, only 4.5% of these arrests were for such serious violent offenses as murder, rape, robbery, or aggravated assault (McGarrell and Flanagan, 1985, p. 479). In contrast, 21% were arrested for a single offense (larceny, theft) much of which, particularly for girls, is shoplifting (Sheldon and Horvath, 1986).

Table 1 presents the five most frequent offenses for which male and female youth are arrested and from this it can be seen that while trivial offenses dominate both male and female delinquency, trivial offenses, particularly status offenses, are more significant in the case of girls' arrests; for example the five offenses listed in Table 1 account for nearly three-quarters of female offenses and only slightly more than half of male offenses.

More to the point, it is clear that, though routinely neglected in most delinquency research, status offenses play a significant role in girls' official delinquency. Status offenses accounted for about 25.2% of all girls' arrests in 1986 (as compared to 26.9% in 1977) and only about 8.3% of boys' arrests (compared to 8.8% in 1977). These figures are somewhat surprising since dramatic declines in arrests of youth for these offenses might have been expected as a result of the passage of the Juvenile Justice and Delinquency Prevention Act in 1974, which, among other things, encouraged jurisdictions to divert and deinstitutionalize youth charged with noncriminal offenses. While the figures in Table 1 do show a decline in these arrests, virtually all of this decline occurred in the 1970s. Between 1982 and 1986 girls' curfew arrests increased by 5.1% and runaway arrests increased by a striking 24.5%. And the upward trend continues; arrests of girls for running away increased by 3% between 1985 and 1986 and arrests of girls for curfew violations increased by 12.4% (Federal Bureau of Investigation, 1987, p. 171).

Looking at girls who find their way into juvenile court populations, it is apparent that status offenses continue to play an important role in the character of girls' official delinquency. In total, 34% of the girls, but only 12% of the boys, were referred to court in 1983 for these offenses (Snyder and Finnegan, 1987, pp. 6–20). Stating these figures differently, they mean that while males constituted about 81% of all delinquency referrals, females constituted 46% of all status offenders in courts (Snyder and Finnegan, 1987, p. 20). Similar figures were reported for 1977 by Black and Smith (1981). Fifteen years earlier, about half of the girls and about 20% of the boys were referred to court for these offenses (Children's Bureau, 1965). These data do seem to signal a drop in female status offense referrals, though not as dramatic a decline as might have been expected.

For many years statistics showing large numbers of girls arrested and referred for status offenses were taken to be representative of the different types of male and female delinquency. However, self-report studies of male and female delinquency do not reflect the dramatic differences in misbehavior found in official statistics. Specifically, it appears that girls charged with these noncriminal status offenses have been and continue to be significantly overrepresented in court populations.

Teilmann and Landry (1981) compared girls' contribution to arrests for runaway and incorrigibility with girls' self-reports of these two activities, and found a 10.4% overrepresentation of females among those arrested for runaway and a 30.9% overrepresentation in arrests for incorrigibility. From these data they concluded that girls are "arrested for status offenses at a higher rate than boys, when contrasted to their self-reported delinquency rates" (Teilmann and Landry, 1981, pp. 74–75). These findings were confirmed in another recent self-report study. Figueira-McDonough (1985, p. 277) analyzed the delinquent conduct of 2,000 youths and found "no evidence of greater involvement of females in status offenses." Similarly, Canter (1982) found in the National Youth Survey that there was no evidence of greater female involvement, compared to males, in any category of delinquent behavior. Indeed, in this sample, males were significantly more likely than females to report status offenses.

Utilizing Canter's national data on the extensiveness of girls self-reported delinquency and comparing these figures to official arrests of girls (see Table 2) reveals that girls are underrepresented in every arrest category with the exception of status offenses and larceny theft. These figures strongly suggest that official practices tend to exaggerate the role played by status offenses in girls' delinquency.

Delinquency theory, because it has virtually ignored female delinquency, failed to pursue anomalies such as these found in the few early studies examining gender differences in delinquent behavior. Indeed, most delinquency theories have ignored status offenses. As a consequence, there is considerable question as to whether existing theories that were admittedly developed to explain male delinquency can adequately explain female delinquency. Clearly, these theories were much influenced by the notion that class and protest masculinity were at the core of delinquency. Will the "add women and stir approach" be sufficient? Are these really theories of delin-

TABLE 1: Rank Order of Adolescent Male and Female Arrests for Specific Offenses, 1977 and 1986

Male				*Female*			
1977	*% of Total Arrests*	*1986*	*% of Total Arrests*	*1977*	*% of Total Arrests*	*1986*	*% of Total Arrests*
(1) Larceny-Theft	18.4	(1) Larceny-Theft	20.4	(1) Larceny-Theft	27.0	(1) Larceny-Theft	25.7
(2) Other Offenses	14.5	(2) Other Offenses	16.5	(2) Runaway	22.9	(2) Runaway	20.5
(3) Burglary	13.0	(3) Burglary	9.1	(3) Other Offenses	14.2	(3) Other Offenses	14.8
(4) Drug Abuse Violations	6.5	(4) Vandalism	7.0	(4) Liquor Laws	5.5	(4) Liquor Laws	8.4
(5) Vandalism	6.4	(5) Vandalism	6.3	(5) Curfew & Loitering Violations	4.0	(5) Curfew & Loitering Violations	4.7

Male	*1977*	*1986*	*% N Change*	Female	*1977*	*1986*	*% N Change*
Arrests for Serious Violent Offenses[a]	4.2%	4.7%	2.3	Arrests for Serious Violent Offenses	1.8%	2.0%	+1.7
Arrests of All Violent Offenses[b]	7.6%	9.6%	+10.3	Arrests of All Violent Offenses	5.1%	7.1%	+26.0
Arrests for Status Offenses[c]	8.8%	8.3%	−17.8	Arrests for Status Offenses	26.9%	25.2%	−14.7

SOURCE: Compiled from Federal Bureau of Investigation (1987, p. 169).
a. Arrests for murder and nonnegligent manslaughter, robbery, forcible rape, and aggravated assault.
b. Also includes arrests for other assaults.
c. Arrests for curfew and loitering law violation and runaway.

quent behavior as some (Simons, Miller, and Aigner, 1980) have argued?

This article will suggest that they are not. The extensive focus on male delinquency and the inattention the role played by patriarchal arrangements in the generation of adolescent delinquency and conformity has rendered the major delinquency theories fundamentally inadequate to the task of explaining female behavior. There is, in short, an urgent need to rethink current models in light of girls' situation in patriarchal society.

To understand why such work must occur, it is first necessary to explore briefly the dimensions of the androcentric bias found in the dominant and influential delinquency theories. Then the need for a feminist model of female delinquency will be explored by reviewing the available evidence on girls' offending. This discussion will also establish that the proposed overhaul of delinquency theory is not, as some might think, solely an academic exercise. Specifically, it is incorrect to assume that because girls are charged with less serious offenses, they actually have few problems and are treated gently when they are drawn into the juvenile justice system. Indeed, the extensive focus on disadvantaged males in public settings has meant that girls' victimization and the relationship between that experience and girls' crime has been systematically ignored. Also missed has been the central role played by the juvenile justice system in the sexualization of girls' delinquency and the criminalization of girls' survival strategies. Finally, it will be suggested that the official actions of the juvenile justice system should be understood as major forces in girls' oppression as they have historically served to reinforce the obedience of all young women to demands of patriarchal authority no matter how abusive and arbitrary.

THE ROMANCE OF THE GANG OR THE *WEST SIDE STORY* SYNDROME

From the start, the field of delinquency research focused on visible lower-class male delinquency, often justifying the neglect of girls in the most cavalier of terms. Take, for example, the extremely important and influential work of Clifford R. Shaw and Henry D. McKay who beginning in 1929, utilized an ecological approach to the study of juvenile delinquency. Their impressive work, particularly *Juvenile Delinquency in Urban Areas* (1942) and intensive biographical case studies such as Shaw's *Brothers in Crime* (1938) and *The Jackroller* (1930), set the stage for much of the subcultural research on gang delinquency. In their ecological work, however, Shaw and McKay analyzed only the official arrest data on male delinquents in Chicago and repeatedly referred to these rates as "delinquency rates" (though they occasionally made parenthetical reference to data on female delinquency) (see Shaw and McKay, 1942, p. 356). Similarly, their biographical work traced only male experiences with the law; in *Brothers in Crime,* for example, the delinquent and criminal careers of five brothers were followed for fifteen years. In none of these works was any justification given for the equation of male delinquency with delinquency.

Early fieldwork on delinquent gangs in Chicago set the stage for another style of delinquency research. Yet here too researchers were interested only in talking to and following the boys. Thrasher studied over a thousand juvenile gangs in Chicago during roughly the same period as Shaw and McKay's more quantitative work was being done. He spent approximately one page out of 600 on the five of six female gangs he encountered in his field observation of juvenile gangs. Thrasher (1927, p. 228) did mention, in passing, two factors he felt accounted for the lower number of girl gangs: "First, the social patterns for the behavior of girls, powerfully backed by the great weight of tradition and custom, are contrary to the gang and its activities; and secondly, girls, even in urban disorganized areas, are much more closely supervised and guarded than boys and usually well incorporated into the family groups or some other social structure."

Another major theoretical approach to delinquency focuses on the subculture of lower-class communities as a generating milieu for delinquent behavior. Here again, noted delinquency researchers concentrated either exclusively or nearly exclusively on male lower-class culture. For example, Cohen's work on the subculture of delinquent gangs, which was written nearly twenty years after Thrasher's, deliberately considers only boys' delinquency. His justification for the exclusion of the girls is quite illuminating:

> My skin has nothing of the quality of down or silk, there is nothing limpid or flute-like about my voice, I am a total

TABLE 2: Comparison of Sex Differences in Self-Reported and Official Delinquency for Selected Offenses

	Self-Report[a] *M/F Ratios (1976)*	*Official Statistics*[b] *M/F Arrest Ratio* *1976*	*1986*
Theft	3.5:1 (Felony Theft) 3.4:1 (Minor Theft)	2.5:1	2.7:1
Drug Violation	1:1 (Hard Drug Use)	5.1:1	6.0:1 (Drug Abuse Violations)
Vandalism	5.1:1	12.3:1	10.0:1
Disorderly Conduct	2.8:1	4.5:1	4.4:1
Serious Assault	3.5:1 (Felony Assault)	5.6:1	5.5:1 (Aggravated Assault)
Minor Assault	3.4:1	3.8:1	3.4:1
Status Offenses	1.6:1	1.3:1	1.1:1 (Runaway, Curfew)

a. Extracted from Rachelle Canter (1982, p. 383).
b. Compiled from Federal Bureau of Investigation (1986, p. 173).

loss with needle and thread, my posture and carriage are wholly lacking in grace. These imperfections cause me no distress—if anything, they are gratifying—because I conceive myself to be a man and want people to recognize me as a full-fledged, unequivocal representative of my sex. My wife, on the other hand, is not greatly embarrassed by her inability to tinker with or talk about the internal organs of a car, by her modest attainments in arithmetic or by her inability to lift heavy objects. Indeed, I am reliably informed that many women—I do not suggest that my wife is among them—often affect ignorance, frailty and emotional instability because to do otherwise would be out of keeping with a reputation for indubitable femininity. In short, people do not simply want to excel; they want to excel as a man or as a woman [Cohen, 1955, p. 138.]

From this Cohen (1955, p. 140) concludes that the delinquent response "however it may be condemned by others on moral grounds has least one virtue; it incontestably confirms, in the eyes of all concerned, his essential masculinity." Much the same line of argument appears in Miller's influential paper on the "focal concerns" of lower-class life with its emphasis on importance of trouble, toughness, excitement, and so on. These, the author concludes, predispose poor youth (particularly male youth) to criminal misconduct. However, Cohen's comments are notable in their candor and probably capture both the allure that male delinquency has had for at least some male theorists as well as the fact that sexism has rendered the female delinquent as irrelevant to their work.

Emphasis on blocked opportunities (sometimes the "strain" theories) emerged out of the work of Robert K. Merton (1938) who stressed the need to consider how some social structures exert a definite pressure upon certain persons in the society to engage in nonconformist rather than conformist conduct. His work influenced research largely through the efforts of Cloward and Ohlin who discussed access to "legitimate" and "illegitimate" opportunities for male youth. No mention of female delinquency can be found in their *Delinquency and Opportunity* except that women are blamed for male delinquency. Here, the familiar notion is that boys, "engulfed by a feminine world and uncertain of their own identification . . . tend to 'protest' against femininity" (Cloward and Ohlin, 1960, p. 49). Early efforts by Ruth Morris to test this hypothesis utilizing different definitions of success based on the gender of respondents met with mixed success. Attempting to assess boys' perceptions about access to economic power status while for girls the variable concerned itself with the ability or inability of girls to maintain effective relationships, Morris was unable to find a clear relationship between "female" goals and delinquency (Morris, 1964).

The work of Edwin Sutherland emphasized the fact that criminal behavior was learned in intimate personal groups. His work, particularly the notion of differential association, which also influenced Cloward and Ohlin's work, was similarly male oriented as much of his work was affected by case studies he conducted of male criminals. Indeed, in describing his notion of how differential association works, he utilized male examples (e.g., "In an area where the delinquency rate is high a boy who is sociable, gregarious, active, and athletic is very likely to come in contact with the other boys, in the neighborhood, learn delinquent behavior from them, and become a gangster" [Sutherland, 1978, p. 131]). Finally, the work of Travis Hirschi on the social bonds that control delinquency ("social control theiry") was, as was stated earlier, derived out of research on male delinquents (though he, at least, studied delinquent behavior as reported by youth themselves rather than studying only those who were arrested).

Such a persistent focus on social class and such an absence of interest in gender in delinquency is ironic for two reasons. As even the work of Hirschi demonstrated, and as later studies would validate, a clear relationship between social class position and delinquency is problematic, while it is clear that gender has a dramatic and consistent effect on delinquency causation (Hagan, Gillis, and Simpson, 1985). The second irony, and one that consistently eludes even contemporary delinquency theorists, is the fact that while the academics had little interest in female delinquents, the same could not be said for the juvenile justice system. Indeed, work on the early history of the separate system for youth, reveals that concerns about girls' immoral conduct were really at the center of what some have called the "childsaving movement" (Platt, 1969) that set up the juvenile justice system.

"THE BEST PLACE TO CONQUER GIRLS"

The movement to establish separate institutions for youthful offenders was part of the larger Progressive movement, which among other things was keenly concerned about prostitution and other "social evils" (white slavery and the like) (Schlossman and Wallach, 1978; Rafter, 1985, p. 54). Childsaving was also a celebration of women's domesticity, though ironically women were influential in the movement (Platt, 1969; Rafter, 1985). In a sense, privileged women found, in the moral purity crusades and the establishment of family courts, a safe outlet for their energies. As the legitimate guardians of the moral sphere, women were seen as uniquely suited to patrol the normative boundaries of the social order. Embracing rather than challenging these stereotypes, women carved out for themselves a role in the policing of women and girls (Feinman, 1980; Freedman, 1981; Messerschmidt, 1987). Ultimately, many of the early childsavers' activities revolved around the monitoring of young girls', particularly immigrant girls', behavior to prevent their straying from the path.

This state of affairs was the direct consequence of a disturbing coalition between some feminists and the more conservative social purity movement. Concerned about female victimization and distrustful of male (and to some degree female) sexuality, notable women leaders, including Susan B. Anthony, found common cause with the social purists around such issues as opposing the regulation of prostitution and raising the age of consent (see Messerschmidt, 1987). The consequences of such a partnership are an important lesson for contemporary feminist movements that are, to some extent, faced with the same possible coalitions.

Girls were the clear losers in this reform effort. Studies of early family court activity reveal that virtually all the girls who appeared in these courts were charged for immorality or waywardness (Chesney-Lind, 1971; Schlossman and Wallach, 1978; Shelden, 1981). More to the point, the sanctions for such misbehavior were extremely severe. For example, in Chicago (where the first family court was founded), one-half of the girl delinquents, but only one-fifth of the boy delinquents, were sent to reformatories between 1899–1909. In Milwaukee, twice as many girls as boys were committed to training schools (Schlossman and Wallach, 1978, p. 72); and in Memphis females were twice as likely as males to be committed to training schools (Shelden, 1981, p. 70).

In Honolulu, during the period 1929–1930, over half of the girls referred to court were charged with "immorality," which meant evidence of sexual intercourse. In addition, another 30% were charged with "waywardness." Evidence of immorality was vigorously pursued by both arresting officers and social workers through lengthy questioning of the girl and, if possible, males with whom she was suspected of having sex. Other evidence of "exposure" was provided by gynecological examinations that were routinely ordered in virtually all girls' cases. Doctors, who understood the purpose of such examinations, would routinely note the condition of the hymen: "admits intercourse hymen rupture," "no laceration," "hymen ruptured" are typical of the notations on the forms. Girls during this period were also twice as likely as males to be detained where they spent five times as long on the average as their male counterparts. They were also nearly three times more likely to be sentenced to the training school (Chesney-Lind, 1971). Indeed, girls were half of those committed to training schools in Honolulu well into the 1950s (Chesney-Lind, 1973).

Not surprisingly, large numbers of girls'reformatories and training schools were established during this period as well as places of "rescue and reform." For example, Schlossman and Wallach note that 23 facilities for girls were opened during the 1910–1920 decade (in contrast to the 1850–1910 period where the average was 5 reformatories per decade [Schlossman and Wallach, 1985, p. 70]), and these institutions did much to set the tone of official response to female delinquency. Obsessed with precocious female sexuality, the institutions set about to isolate the females from all contact with males while housing them in bucolic settings. The intention was to hold the girls until marriageable age and to occupy them in domestic pursuits during their sometimes lengthy incarceration.

The links between these attitudes and those of juvenile courts some decades later are, of course, arguable; but an examination of the record of the court does not inspire confidence. A few examples of the persistence of what might be called a double standard of juvenile justice will suffice here.

A study conducted in the early 1970s in a Connecticut training school revealed large numbers of girls incarcerated "for their own protection." Explaining this pattern, one judge explained, "Why most of the girls I commit are for status offenses, I figure if a girl is about to get pregnant, we'll keep her until she's sixteen and then ADC (Aid to Dependent Children) will pick her up" (Rogers, 1972). For more evidence of official concern with adolescent sexual misconduct, consider Linda Hancock's (1981) content analysis of police referrals in Australia. She noted that 40% of the referrals of girls to court made specific mention of sexual and moral conduct compared to only 5% of the referrals of boys. These sorts of results suggest that all youthful female misbehavior has traditionally been subject to surveillance for evidence of sexual misconduct.

Gelsthorpe's (1986) field research on an English police station also revealed how everyday police decision making resulted in disregard of complaints about male problem behavior in contrast to active concern about the "problem behavior" of girls. Notable, here, was the concern about the girls' sexual behavior. In one case, she describes police persistence in pursuing a "moral danger" order for a 14-year-old picked up in a truancy run. Over the objections of both the girl's parents and the Social Services Department and in the face of a written confirmation from a surgeon that the girl was still premenstrual, the officers pursued the application because, in one officer's words, "I know her sort . . . free and easy. I'm still suspicious that she might be pregnant. Anyway, if the doctor can't provide evidence we'll do her for being beyond the care and control of her parents, no one can dispute that. Running away is proof" (Gelsthorpe, 1986, p. 136). This sexualization of female deviance is highly significant and explains why criminal activities by girls (particularly in past years) were overlooked so long as they did not appear to signal defiance of parental control (see Smith, 1978).

In their historic obsession about precocious female sexuality, juvenile justice workers rarely reflected on the broader nature of female misbehavior or on the sources of this misbehavior. It was enough for them that girls' parents reported them out of control. Indeed, court personnel tended to "sexualize" virtually all female defiance that lent itself to that construction and ignore other misbehavior (Chesney-Lind, 1973, 1977; Smith, 1978). For their part, academic students of delinquency were so entranced with the notion of the delinquent as a romantic rogue male challenging a rigid and unequal class structure, that they spent little time on middle-class delinquency, trivial offenders, or status offenders. Yet it is clear that the vast bulk of delinquent behavior is of this type.

Some have argued that such an imbalance in theoretical work is appropriate as minor misconduct, while troublesome, is not a threat to the safety and well-being of the community. This argument might be persuasive if two additional points could be established. One, that some small number of youth "specialize" in serious criminal behavior while the rest commit only minor acts, and, two, that the juvenile court rapidly releases those youth that come into its purview for these minor offenses, thus reserving resources for the most serious youthful offenders.

The evidence is mixed on both of these points. Determined efforts to locate the "serious juvenile offender" have failed to locate a group of offenders who specialize only in serious violent offenses. For example, in a recent analysis of a national self-report data set, Elliott and his associates noted "there is little evidence for specialization in serious violent offending; to the contrary, serious violent offending appears to be embedded in a more general involvement in a wide range of serious and non-serious offenses" (Elliott, Huizinga, and Morse, 1987). Indeed, they went so far as to speculate that arrest histories that tend to highlight particular types of offenders reflect variations in police policy, practices, and processes of uncovering crime as well as underlying offending patterns.

More to the point, police and court personnel are, it turns out, far more interested in youth they charge with trivial or status offenses than anyone imagined. Efforts to deinstitutionalize "status offenders," for example, ran afoul of juvenile justice personnel who had little interest in releasing youth guilty of noncriminal offenses (Chesney-Lind, 1988). As has been established, much of this is a product of the system's history that encouraged court officers to involve themselves in the noncriminal behavior of youth in order to "save" them from a variety of social ills.

Indeed, parallels can be found between the earlier Progressive period and current national efforts to challenge the deinstitutionalization components of the Juvenile Justice and Delinquency Prevention Act of 1974. These come complete with their celebration of family values and concerns about youthful independence. One of the arguments against the act has been that it allegedly gave children the "freedom to run away" (Office of Juvenile Justice and Delinquency Prevention, 1985) and that it has hampered "reunions" of "missing" children with their parents (Office of Juvenile Justice, 1986). Suspicions about teen sexuality are reflected in excessive concern about the control of teen prostitution and child pornography.

Opponents have also attempted to justify continued intervention into the lives of status offenders by suggesting that without such intervention, the youth would "escalate" to criminal behavior. Yet there is little evidence that status offenders escalate to criminal offenses, and the evidence is particularly weak when considering female delinquents (particularly white female delinquents) (Datesman and Aickin, 1984). Finally, if escalation is occurring, it is likely the product of the justice system's insistence on enforcing status offense laws, thereby forcing youth in crisis to live lives of escaped criminals.

The most influential delinquency theories, however, have largely ducked the issue of status and trivial offenses and, as a consequence, neglected the role played by the agencies of official control (police, probation officers, juvenile court judges, detention home workers, and training school personnel) in the shaping of the "delinquency problem." When confronting the less than distinct picture that emerges from the actual distribution of delinquent behavior, however, the conclusion that agents of social control have considerable discretion in labeling or choosing not to label particular behavior as "delinquent" is inescapable. This symbiotic relationship between delinquent behavior and the official response to that behavior is particularly critical when the question of female delinquency is considered.

TOWARD A FEMINIST THEORY OF DELINQUENCY

To sketch out completely a feminist theory of delinquency is a task beyond the scope of this article. It may be sufficient, at this point, simply to identify a few of the most obvious problems with attempts to adapt male-oriented theory to explain female conformity and deviance. Most significant of these is the fact that all existing theories were developed with no concern about gender stratification.

Note that this is not simply an observation about the power of gender roles (though this power is undeniable). It is increasingly clear that gender stratification in patriarchal society is as powerful a system as is class. A feminist approach to delinquency means construction of explanations of female behavior that are sensitive to its patriarchal context. Feminist analysis of delinquency would also examine ways in which agencies of social control—the police, the courts, and the prisons—act in ways to reinforce woman's place in male society (Harris, 1977; Chesney-Lind, 1986). Efforts to construct a feminist model of delinquency must first and foremost be sensitive to the situations of girls. Failure to consider the existing empirical evidence on girls' lives and behavior can quickly lead to stereotypical thinking and theoretical dead ends.

An example of this sort of flawed theory building was the early fascination with the notion that the women's movement was causing an increase in women's crime; a notion that is now more or less discredited (Steffensmeier, 1980; Gora, 1982). A more recent example of the same sort of thinking can be found in recent work on the "power-control" model of delinquency (Hagan, Simpson, and Gillis, 1987). Here, the authors speculate that girls commit less delinquency in part because their behavior is more closely controlled by the patriarchal family. The authors' promising beginning quickly gets bogged down in a very limited definition of patriarchal control (focusing on parental supervision and variations in power within the family). Ultimately, the authors' narrow formulation of patriarchal control results in their arguing that mother's work force participation (particularly in high status occupations) leads to increases in daughters' delinquency since these girls find themselves in more "egalitarian families."

This is essentially a not-too-subtle variation on the earlier "liberation" hypothesis. Now, mother's liberation causes daughter's crime. Aside from the methodological problems with the study (e.g., the authors argue that female-headed households are equivalent to upper-status "egalitarian" families where both parents work, and they measure delinquency using a six-item scale that contains no status offense items), there is a more fundamental problem with the hypothesis. There is no evidence to suggest that as women's labor force participation accelerated and the number of female-headed households soared, aggregate female delinquency measured both by self-report and official statistics either declined or remained stable (Ageton, 1983; Chilton and Datesman, 1987; Federal Bureau of Investigation, 1987).

By contrast, a feminist model of delinquency would focus more extensively on the few pieces of information about girls' actual lives and the role played by girls' problems, including those caused by racism and poverty, in their delinquency behavior. Fortunately, a considerable literature is now developing on girls' lives and much of it bears directly on girls' crime.

CRIMINALIZING GIRLS' SURVIVAL

It has long been understood that a major reason for girls' presence in juvenile courts was the fact that their parents insisted on their arrest. In the early years, conflicts with parents were by far the most significant referral source; in Honolulu 44% of the girls who appeared in court in 1929 through 1930 were referred by parents.

Recent national data, while slightly less explicit, also show that girls are more likely to be referred to court by "sources other than law enforcement agencies" (which would include parents). In 1983, nearly a quarter (23%) of all girls but only 16% of boys charged with delinquent offenses were referred to court by non-law enforcement agencies. The pattern among youth referred for status offenses (for which girls are overrepresented) was even more pronounced. Well over half (56%) of the girls charged with these offenses and 45% of the boys were referred by sources other than law enforcement (Snyder and Finnegan, 1987, p. 21; see also Pope and Feyerherm, 1982).

The fact that parents are often committed to two standards of adolescent behavior is one explanation for such a disparity—and one that should not be discounted as a major source of tension even in modern families. Despite expectations to the contrary, gender-specific socialization patterns have not changed very much and this is especially true for parents' relationships with their daughters (Katz, 1979). It appears that even parents who oppose sexism in general feel"uncomfortable tampering with existing traditions" and "do not want to risk their children becoming misfits" (Katz, 1979, p. 24). Clearly, parental attempts to adhere to and enforce these traditional notions will continue to be a source of conflict between girls and their elders. Another important explanation for girls' problems with their parents, which has received attention only in more recent years, is the problem of physical and sexual abuse. Looking specifically at the problem of childhood sexual abuse, it is increasingly clear that this form of abuse is a particular problem for girls.

Girls are, for example, much more likely to be the victims of child sexual abuse than are boys. Finkelhor and Baron estimate from a review of community studies that roughly 70% of the victims of sexual abuse are female (Finkelhor and Baron, 1986, p. 45). Girls' sexual abuse also tends to start earlier than boys (Finkelhor and Baron, 1986, p. 48); they are more likely than boys to be assaulted by a family member (often a stepfather)(DeJong, Hervada, and Emmett, 1983; Russell, 1986), and as a consequence, their abuse tends to last longer than male sexual abuse (DeJong,Hervada, and Emmett, 1983). All of these factors are associated with more severe trauma—causing dramatic short- and long-term effects in victims (Adams-Tucker, 1982). The effects noted by researchers in this area move from the more well known "fear, anxiety, depression, anger and hostility, and inappropriate sexual behavior" (Browne and Finkelhor, 1986, p. 69) to behaviors of greater familiarity to criminologists, including running away from home, difficulties in school, truancy, and early marriage (Browne and Finkelhor, 1986).

Herman's study of incest survivors in therapy found that they were more likely to have run away from home than a matched sample of women whose fathers were "seductive" (33% compared to 5%). Another study of women patients found that 50% of the victims of child sexual abuse, but only 20% of the nonvictim group, had left home before the age of 19 (Meiselman, 1978).

Not surprisingly, then, studies of girls on the streets or in court populations are showing high rates of both physical and sexual abuse. Silbert and Pines (1981, p. 409) found, for example, that 60% of the street prostitutes they interviewed had been sexually abused as juveniles. Girls at an Arkansas diagnostic unit and school who had been adjudicated for either status or delinquent offenses reported similarly high levels of sexual abuse as well as high levels of physical abuse; 53% indicated they had been sexually abused, 25% recalled scars, 38% recalled bleeding from abuse, and 51% recalled bruises (Mouzakitas, 1981).

A sample survey of girls in the juvenile justice system in Wisconsin (Phelps et al., 1982) revealed that 79% had been subjected to physical abuse that resulted in some form of injury, and 32% had been sexually abused by parents or other persons who were closely connected to their families. Moreover, 50% had been sexually assaulted ("raped" or forced to participate in sexual acts)(Phelps et al., 1982, p. 66). Even higher figures were reported by McCormack and her associates (McCormack, Janus, and Burgess, 1986) in their study of youth in a runaway shelter in Toronto. They found that 73% of the females and 38% of the males had been sexually abused. Finally, a study of youth charged with running away, truancy, or listed as missing persons in Arizona found that 55% were incest victims (Reich and Gutierres, 1979).

Many young women, then, are running away from profound sexual victimization at home, and once on the streets they are forced further into crime in order to survive. Interviews with girls who have run away from home show, very clearly, that they do not have a lot of attachment to their delinquent activities. In fact, they are angry about being labeled as delinquent, yet all engaged in illegal acts (Koroki and Chesney-Lind, 1985). The Wisconsin study found that 54% of the girls who ran away found it necessary to steal money, food, and clothing in order to survive. A few exchanged sexual contact for money, food, and/or shelter (Phelps et al., 1982, p. 67). In their study of runaway youth, McCormack, Janus, and Burgess (1986, pp. 392–393) found that sexually abused female runaways were significantly more likely than their nonabused counterparts to engage in delinquent or criminal activities such as substance abuse, petty theft, and prostitution. No such pattern was found among male runaways.

Research (Chesney-Lind and Rodriguez, 1983) on the backgrounds of adult women in prison underscores the important links between women's childhood victimizations and their later criminal careers. The interviews revealed that virtually all of this sample were the victims of physical and/or sexual abuse as youngsters; over 60% had been sexually abused and about half had been raped as young women. This situation prompted these women to run away from home (three-quarters had been arrested for status offenses) where once on the streets they began engaging in prostitution and other forms of petty property crime. They also begin what becomes a lifetime problem with drugs. As adults, the women continue in these activities since they possess truncated educational backgrounds and virtually no marketable occupational skills (see also Miller, 1986).

Confirmation of the consequences of childhood sexual and physical abuse on adult female criminal behavior has also recently come from a large quantitative study of 908 individuals with substantiated and validated histories of these victimizations. Widom (1988) found that abused or neglected females were twice as likely as a matched group of controls to have an adult record (16% compared to 7.5). The difference was also found among men, but it was not as dramatic (42% compared to 33%). Men with abuse backgrounds were also more likely to contribute to the "cycle of violence" with more arrests for violent offenses as adult offenders than the control group. In contrast, when women with abuse backgrounds did become involved with the criminal justice system, their arrests tended to involve property and order offenses (such as disorderly conduct, curfew, and loitering violations) (Widon, 1988, p. 17).

Given this information, a brief example of how a feminist perspective on the causes of female delinquency might look seems appropriate. First, like young men, girls are frequently the recipients of violence and sexual abuse. But unlike boys, girls' victimization and their response to that victimization is specifically shaped by their status as young women. Perhaps because of the gender and sexual scripts found in patriarchal families, girls are much more likely than boys to be victim of family-related sexual abuse. Men, particularly men with traditional attitudes toward women, are likely to define their daughters or stepdaughters as their sexual property (Finkelhor, 1982). In a society that idealizes inequality in male/female relationships and venerates youth in women, girls are easily defined as sexually attractive by older men (Bell, 1984). In addition, girls' vulnerability to both physical and sexual abuse is heightened by norms that require that they stay at home where their victimizers have access to them.

Moreover, their victimizers (usually males) have the ability to invoke official agencies of social control in their efforts to keep young women at home and vulnerable. That is to say, abusers have traditionally been able to utilize the uncritical commitment of the juvenile justice system toward parental authority to force girls to obey them. Girls' complaints about abuse were, until recently, routinely ignored. For this reason, statutes that were originally placed in law to "protect" young people have, in the case of girls' delinquency, criminalized their survival strategies. As they run away from abusive homes, parents have been able to employ agencies to enforce their return. If they persisted in their refusal to stay in that home, however intolerable, they were incarcerated.

Young women, a large number of whom are on the run from homes characterized by sexual abuse and parental neglect, are forced by the very statutes designed to protect them into the lives of escaped convicts. Unable to enroll in school or take a job to support themselves because they fear detection, young female runaways are forced into the streets. Here they engage in panhandling, petty theft, and occasional prostitution in order to survive. Young women in conflict with their parents (often for very legitimate reasons) may actually be forced by present laws into petty criminal activity, prostitution, and drug use.

In addition, the fact that young girls (but not necessarily young boys) are defined as sexually desirable and, in fact, more desirable than their older sisters due to the double standard of aging means that their lives on the streets (and their survival strategies) take on unique shape—one again shaped by patriarchal values. It is no accident that girls on the run from abusive homes, or on the streets because of profound poverty, get involved in criminal activities that exploit their sexual object status. American society has defined as desirable youthful, physically perfect women. This means that girls on the streets, who have little else of value to trade, are encouraged to utilize this "resource" (Campagna and Poffenberger, 1988). It also means that the criminal subculture views them from this perspective (Miller, 1986).

FEMALE DELINQUENCY, PATRIARCHAL AUTHORITY, AND FAMILY COURTS

The early insights into male delinquency were largely gleaned by intensive field observation of delinquent boys. Very little of this sort of work has been done in the case of girls' delinquency, though it is vital to an understanding of girls' definitions of their own situations, choices, and behavior (for exceptions to this see Campbell, 1984; Peacock, 1981; Miller, 1986; Rosenberg and Zimmerman, 1977). Time must be spent listening to girls. Fuller research on the settings, such as families and schools, that girls find themselves in and the impact of variations in those settings should also be undertaken (see Figueira-McDonough, 1986). A more complete understanding of how poverty and racism shape girls' lives is also vital (see Messerschmidt, 1986; Campbell, 1984). Finally, current qualitative research on the reaction of official agencies to girls' delinquency must be conducted. This latter task, admittedly more difficult, is particularly critical to the development of delinquency theory that is as sensitive to gender as it is to race and class.

It is clear that throughout most of the court's history, virtually all female delinquency has been placed within the larger context of girls' sexual behavior. One explanation for this pattern is that familial control over girls' sexual capital has historically been central to the maintenance of patriarchy (Lerner, 1986). The fact that young women have relatively more of this capital has been one reason for the excessive concern that both families and official agencies of social control have expressed about youthful female defiance (otherwise much of the behavior of criminal justice personnel makes virtually no sense). Only if one considers the role of women's control over their sexuality at the point in their lives that their value to patriarchal society is so pronounced, does the historic pattern of jailing of huge numbers of girls guilty of minor misconduct make sense.

This framework also explains the enormous resistance that the movement to curb the juvenile justice system's authority over status offenders encountered. Supporters of the change were not really prepared for the political significance of giving youth the freedom to run. Horror stories told by the opponents of deinstitutionalization about victimized youth, youthful prostitution, and youthful involvement in pornography (Office of Juvenile Justice and Delinquency Prevention, 1985) all neglect the unpleasant reality that most of these behaviors were often in direct response to earlier victimization, frequently by parents, that officials had, for years, routinely ignored. What may be at stake in efforts to roll back deinstitutionalization efforts is not so much "protection" of youth as it is curbing the right of young women to defy patriarchy.

In sum, research in both the dynamics of girls' delinquency and official reactions to that behavior is essential to the development of theories of delinquency that are sensitive to its patriarchal as well as class and racial context.

REFERENCES

Adams-Tucker, Christine. 1982. "Proximate Effects of Sexual Abuse in Childhood." *American Journal of Psychiatry* 193: 1252–1256.

Ageton, Suzanne S. 1983. "The Dynamics of Female Delinquency, 1976–1980.," *Criminology* 21:555–584.

Bell, Inge Powell. 1984. "The Double Standard: Age." in *Women: A Feminist Perspective,* edited by Jo Freeman. Palo Alto, CA: Mayfield.

Black, T. Edwin and Charles P. Smith, 1981. *A Preliminary National Assessment of the Number and Characteristics of Juveniles Processed in the Juvenile Justice System.* Washington, DC: Government Printing Office.

Browne, Angela and David Finkelhor, 1986. "Impact of Child Sexual Abuse: A Review of Research," *Psychological Bulletin* 99:66–77.

Campagna, Daniel S. and Donald I. Poffenberger, 1988. *The Sexual Trafficking in Children,* Dover, DE; Auburn House.

Campbell, Ann. 1984. *The Girls in the Gang.* Oxford: Basil Blackwell.

Canter, Rachelle J. 1982. "Sex Differences in Self-Report Delinquency," *Criminology* 20:373–393.

Chesney-Lind, Meda. 1971, *Female Juvenile Delinquency in Hawaii,* Master's thesis, University of Hawaii.

_____1973. "Judicial Enforcement of the Female Sex Role," *Issues in Criminology* 3:51–71.

_____1978. "Young Women in the Arms of the Law," In *Women, Crime and the Criminal Justice System,* edited by Lee H. Bowker, Boston: Lexington.

_____1986. "Women and Crime: The Female Offender," *Signs* 12:78–96.

_____1988. "Girls and Deinstitutionalization: Is Juvenile Justice Still Sexist?" *Journal of Criminal Justice Abstracts* 20:144–165.

_____and Noelie Rodriguez 1983. "Women Under Lock and Key," *Prison Journal* 63:47–65.

Children's Bureau, Department of Health, Education and Welfare, 1965. *1964 Statistics on Public Institutions for Delinquent Children.* Washington, DC; Government Printing Office.

Chilton, Roland and Susan K. Datesman, 1987, "Gender, Race and Crime: An Analysis of Urban Arrest Trends, 1960–1980," *Gender and Society* 1:152–171.

Cloward, Richard A. and Lloyd E. Ohlin, 1960. *Delinquency and Opportunity,* New York: Free Press.

Cohen, Albert K., 1955. *Delinquent Boys: The Culture of the Gang,* New York: Free Press.

5. JUVENILE JUSTICE

Datesman, Susan and Mikel Aickin, 1984, "Offense Specialization and Escalation Among Status Offenders," *Journal of Criminal Law and Criminology*, 75:1246–1275.

Davidson, Sue, ed. 1982. *Justice for Young Women*. Tucson, AZ; New Directions for Young Women.

DeJong, Allan R., Arturo R. Hervada, and Gary A. Emmett, 1983. "Epidemiologic Variations in Childhood Sexual Abuse," *Child Abuse and Neglect* 7:155–162.

Elliott, Delbert, David Huizinga, and Barbara Morse, 1987, "A Career Analysis of Serious Violent Offenders," In *Violent Juvenile Crime: What Can We Do About It?* edited by Ira Schwartz, Minneapolis, MN: Hubert Humphrey Institute.

Federal Bureau of Investigation, 1987. *Crime in the United States 1986*, Washington, DC; Government Printing Office.

Feinman, Clarice, 1980. *Women in the Criminal Justice System*, New York; Praeger.

Figueira-McDonough, Josefina, 1985. "Are Girls Different? Gender Discrepancies Between Delinquent Behavior and Control," *Child Welfare* 64:273–289.

_____1986, "School Context, Gender, and Delinquency," *Journal of Youth and Adolescence* 15:79–98.

Finkelhor, David, 1982. "Sexual Abuse: A Sociological Perspective," *Child Abuse and Neglect* 6:95–102.

_____and Larry Baron. 1986. "Risk Factors for Child Sexual Abuse," *Journal of Interpersonal Violence* 1:43–71.

Freedman, Estelle, 1981. *Their Sisters' Keepers*, Ann Arbor; University of Michigan Press.

Geltshorpe, Loraine, 1986. "Towards a Sceptical Look at Sexism," *International Journal of the Sociology of Law* 14:125–152.

Gora, JoAnn, 1982. *The New Female Criminal: Empirical Reality or Social Myth*, New York: Praeger.

Hagan, John, A. R. Gillis, and John Simpson, 1985. "The Class Structure of Gender and Delinquency: Toward a Power-Control Theory of Common Delinquent Behavior," *American Journal of Sociology* 90:1151–1178.

Hagan, John, John Simpson, and A. R. Gillis, 1987. "Class in the Household: A Power-Control Theory of Gender and Delinquency," *American Journal of Sociology* 92:788–816.

Hancock, Linda. 1981. "The Myth that Females are Treated More Leniently than Males in the Juvenile Justice System." *Australian and New Zealand Journal of Criminology* 16:4–14.

Harris, Anthony, 1977. "Sex and Theories of Deviance," *American Sociological Review* 42:3–16.

Herman, Jullia L. 1981. *Father-Daughter Incest*. Cambridge, MA; Harvard University Press.

Katz, Phyllis A. 1979. "The Development of Female Identity," In *Becoming Female: Perspectives on Development*, edited by Claire B. Kopp, New York; Plenum.

Koroki, Jan and Meda Chesney-Lind. 1985, *Everything Just Going Down the Drain*. Hawaii; Youth Development and Research Center.

Lerner, Gerda. 1986. *The Creation of Patriarchy*. New York: Oxford.

McCormack, Arlene, Mark-David Janus, and Ann Wolbert Burgess, 1986. "Runaway Youths and Sexual Victimization: Gender Differences In an Adolescent Runaway Population," *Child Abuse and Neglect* 10:387–395.

McGarrell, Edmund F. and Timothy J. Flanagan, eds. 1985. *Sourcebook of Criminal Justice Statistics—1984*. Washington, DC; Government Printing Office.

Meiselman, Karen. 1978. *Incest*. San Francisco: Jossey-Bass.

Merton, Robert K. 1938. "Social Structure and Anomie." *American Sociological Review* 3(October):672–782.

Messerschmidt, James, 1986. *Capitalism, Patriarchy, and Crime: Toward a Socialist Feminist Criminology*, Totowa, NJ: Rowman & Littlefield.

_____1987. "Feminism, Criminology, and the Rise of the Female Sex Delinquent, 1880–1930," *Contemporary Crises* 11: 243–263.

Miller, Eleanor, 1986. *Street Woman*, Philadelphia: Temple University Press.

Miller, Walter B. 1958, "Lower Class Culture as the Generating Milieu of Gang Delinquency," *Journal of Social Issues* 14:5–19.

Morris, Ruth, 1964, "Female Delinquency and Relational Problems," *Social Forces* 43:82–89.

Mouzakitas, C. M. 1981, "An Inquiry into the Problem of Child Abuse and Juvenile Delinquency," In *Exploring the Relationship Between Child Abuse and Delinquency*, edited by R. J. Hunner and Y. E. Walkers, Montclair, NJ: Allanheld, Osmun.

National Female Advocacy Project, 1981. *Young Women and the Justice System: Basic Facts and Issues*. Tucson, AZ; New Directions for Young Women.

Office of Juvenile Justice and Delinquency Prevention, 1985. *Runaway Children and the Juvenile Justice and Delinquency Prevention Act: What is the Impact?* Washington, DC; Government Printing Office.

Opinion Research Corporation, 1982, "Public Attitudes Toward Youth Crime: National Public Opinion Poll." Mimeographed. Minnesota; Hubert Humphrey Institute of Public Affairs, University of Minnesota.

Peacock, Carol, 1981. *Hand Me Down Dreams*. New York: Shocken.

Phelps, R. J. et al. 1982. *Wisconsin Female Juvenile Offender Study Project Summary Report*, Wisconsin: Youth Policy and Law Center, Wisconsin Council of Juvenile Justice.

Platt, Anthony M. 1969. *The Childsavers*, Chicago: University of Chicago Press.

Pope, Carl and William H. Feyerherm. 1982. "Gender Bias in Juvenile Court Dispositions," *Social Service Review* 6:1–17.

Rafter, Nicole Hahn, 1985. *Partial Justice*. Boston: Northeastern University Press.

Reich, J. W. And S. E. Gutierres, 1979, "Escape/Aggression Incidence in Sexually Abused Juvenile Delinquents," *Criminal Justice and Behavior* 6:239–243.

Rogers, Kristine, 1972. "For Her Own Protection. . . . Conditions of Incarceration for Female Juvenile Offenders in the State of Connecticut," *Law and Society Review* (Winter):223–246.

Rosenberg, Debby and Carol Zimmerman, 1977. *Are My Dreams Too Much To Ask For?* Tucson, A. Z: New Directions for Young Women.

Russell, Diana E. 1986. *The Secret Trauma: Incest in the Lives of Girls and Women*, New York: Basic Books.

Schlossman, Steven and Stephanie Wallach, 1978. "The Crime of Precocious Sexuality: Female Juvenile Delinquency in the Progressive Era," *Harvard Educational Review* 48:65–94.

Shaw, Clifford R. 1930. *The Jack-Roller*, Chicago: University of Chicago Press.

_____1938. *Brothers in Crime*, Chicago: University of Chicago Press.

_____and Henry D. McKay, 1942. *Juvenile Delinquency in Urban Areas*, Chicago: University of Chicago Press.

Shelden, Randall, 1981. "Sex Discrimination in the Juvenile Justice System: Memphis, Tennessee, 1900–1917." In *Comparing Female and Male Offenders*, edited by Marguerite Q. Warren. Beverly Hills, CA: Sage.

_____and John Horvath, 1986. "Processing Offenders in a Juvenile Court: A Comparison of Males and Females." Paper presented at the annual meeting of the Western Society of Criminology, Newport Beach, CA, February 27-March 2.

Silbert, Mimi and Ayala M. Pines, 1981. "Sexual Child Abuse as an Antecedent to Prostitution," *Child Abuse and Neglect* 5:407–411.

Simons, Ronald L., Martin G. Miller, and Stephen M. Aigner, 1980. "Contemporary Theories of Deviance and Female Delinquency: An Empirical Test," *Journal of Research in Crime and Delinquency* 17:42–57.

Smith, Lesley Shacklady, 1978. "Sexist Assumptions and Female Delinquency," In *Women, Sexuality and Social Control*, edited by Carol Smart and Barry Smart, London: Routledge & Kegan Paul.

Snyder, Howard N. and Terrence A. Finnegan, 1987. *Delinquency in the United States*. Washington, DC: Department of Justice.

Steffensmeier, Darrell J. 1980 "Sex Differences in Patterns of Adult Crime, 1965–1977," *Social Forces* 58:1080–1109.

Sutherland, Edwin, 1978. "Differential Association." in *Children of Ishmael: Critical Perspectives on Juvenile Justice*, edited by Barry Krisberg and James Austin. Palo Alto, CA: Mayfield.

Teilmann, Katherine S. and Pierre H. Landry, Jr. 1981. "Gender Bias in Juvenile Justice." *Journal of Research in Crime and Delinquency* 18:47–80.

Thrasher, Frederic M. 1927. *The Gang*. Chicago: University of Chicago Press.

Tracy, Paul E., Marvin E. Wolfgang, and Robert M. Figlio. 1985. *Delinquency in Two Birth Cohorts: Executive Summary*. Washington, DC: Department of Justice.

Widom, Cathy Spatz. 1988. "Child Abuse, Neglect, and Violent Criminal Behavior." Unpublished manuscript.

THE HARD FACTS ABOUT CHILDREN IN JAILS

Mark I. Soler
Executive Director, Youth Law Center
San Francisco, California

The incarceration of children in adult jails and police lockups is a problem of crisis proportions nationwide.

THE NUMBERS

According to the U.S. Department of Justice, approximately 479,000 children are held in adult jails and police lockups in this country each year. Over nine percent of these children (more than 43,000) are under the age of 14, and over 19,000 are abused and neglected juveniles who have not committed any sort of offense. Twenty percent (95,800) are detained for status offenses such as underage drinking, disobeying parents, or running away from home.

THE DANGERS

Children in adult jails commit suicide **eight times** as often as children in juvenile detention centers. Children in jails are routinely — and illegally — exposed to frequent contact with adult inmates. Jail staff are not trained to handle the emotional and family problems of children in crisis. These children rarely receive schooling, exercise, or recreation.

Children have been beaten, raped, and murdered in county jails. In Boise, Idaho, 17-year-old Christopher Peterman was locked up in the Ada County Jail for failing to pay $73 in traffic fines. Over a 14-hour period, he was tortured and eventually murdered by other prisoners in his cell. In Ohio, a 15-year-old girl ran away from home and later returned to her parents. She was put in the Lawrence County Jail by the local juvenile court judge "to teach her a lesson." On the fourth night of her confinement, she was sexually assaulted by a deputy jailer. In Washington, D.C., an 11-year-old boy was sexually assaulted by two inmates while incarcerated in the Superior Court cell block.

THE REASONS

Children are often incarcerated in adult jails because the jails are closer and more easily accessible to law enforcement officers who make arrests than are county juvenile detention centers. This is particularly the case in rural counties. In some instances, children are held in jails because local juvenile detention centers are seriously overcrowded. In other communities, local officials are unaware that children can be safely placed in alternative community-based programs.

The large majority of children incarcerated in jails are **not** guilty of violent crimes: most are charged with minor property crimes, drug-related offenses, or "status offenses" that would not be considered crimes if they were committed by adults.

THE COSTS

Incarcerating children in adult jails is more expensive than placing them in community-based alternatives. In May, 1982, the Office of Juvenile Justice and Delinquency Prevention of the U.S. Department of Justice published a **Jail Removal Cost Study.** According to the Justice Department, some communities spend over **three times** as much to incarcerate children in jails as they do to place children in supervised programs in the community.

In a 1983 study by the U.S. Department of Justice, **Juveniles in Adult Jails and Lockups,** researchers found that jailing a juvenile costs $24 a day, while small group homes averaged only $17 a day, and home detention $14. In addition, the State of Maryland, according to the Justice Department report, found that "the cost of placing a youngster in a state correctional institution is between a reported $12,000 and $14,000 (per year), but a greater number of juveniles are being sent to group homes, which cost $8,200 or placed in foster care at a cost of $2,400."

THE ALTERNATIVES

Jailing of children is unnecessary. Communities across the nation offer a variety of alternatives to incarceration. These include:

* GROUP HOMES. These residential programs offer 24-hour adult supervision, counseling, and educational and recreational opportunities.
* FOSTER HOMES. Foster parents provide supervision and support for children who can benefit from a stable, home-like environment.
* WILDERNESS PROGRAMS. These programs are based on the premise that young people develop self-confidence and the ability to work constructively with others by participating in group outdoor survival programs.
* COMMUNITY SUPERVISION. A probation officer may determine that a child should return to the community. The child may then be required either to report regularly to the probation officer or to work with trained paraprofessional staff while placed at the child's own home.
* FAMILY COURT COMMUNITY AIDE PROGRAMS. A community aide works on a daily basis with the young person to provide counseling, link the young person with community resources, and accompany him or her to court.
* FAMILY CRISIS COUNSELING. Counselors visit the family at home soon after the young person's problems come to the attention of the authorities. Regular sessions are held, and counselors are available 24 hours a day in case of emergencies.
* PROCTOR PROGRAMS. Youths live with a proctor in the proctor's home. The proctor must demonstrate to authorities that the young person has made constructive use of his or her time and is working on those problems that led to involvement in the juvenile justice system.
* SERVICE-ORIENTED PROGRAMS. For those children who do not require constant supervision, some communities have provided an array of after-school or evening programs. These include recreational programs, counseling, alternative schools, employment training programs,

From *Perspectives*, American Probation and Parole Association, Vol. 11, No. 1, Winter 1986/87, pp. 14-15. Reprinted by permission.

and homemaking and financial planning classes.

THE LAW

Detention of children in adult jails, without adequate separation from adult inmates, violates the federal Juvenile Justice Delinquency Prevention Act and state law in most states. In addition, a number of states, including Pennsylvania, North Carolina, Tennessee and Virginia, have passed laws prohibiting the incarceration of children in adult jails.

Children in institutions are also entitled to adequate health and mental health care, exercise and recreation, education, and a homelike environment, none of which is available in jails and lock-ups. Moreover, the United States District Court in Oregon has ruled that **any** detention of children in adult jails violates the children's constitutional rights (**D.B. Tewksbury,** 545 F. Supp. 896 (D. Or. 1982).

The Youth Law Center, a public interest law office located in San Francisco, is working to end the incarceration of children in jails and police lock-ups nationwide. In Idaho, Ohio, Maine, California, New Mexico, Kentucky, and Colorado, Youth Law Center attorneys successfully brought litigation to stop the jailing of children. Center staff have also worked with public officials, parents, children's advocates, and community groups throughout the country to end this dangerous practice. The center works to stop the jailing of children throughout the country by providing training and technical assistance to juvenile court judges, probation officers, sheriffs, citizen groups, attorneys, and others concerned with juvenile justice and the welfare of children. Where dangerous conditions and practices threaten the lives and safety of confined children, they also bring litigation to protect children's civil and constitutional rights. The center can provide posters, bumperstickers and T-shirts (from children's small to adult's extra-large.)

For more information, please call or write Mark I. Soler, Executive Director, Youth Law Center, 1663 Mission Street, Fifth Floor, San Francisco, California 94103 (415) 543-3379.

TEENAGE ADDICTION

Chemical dependency is a problem that discriminates against no one, old, young, rich or poor, black or white. Yet, the tragedy of addiction seems more acute when it afflicts our adolescents, those whose bright futures seem threatened by drugs alcohol. In this section, we present three reports: one on the differences in treating teenage and adult chemical dependents; another on a successful school-based program on helping adolescent addicts; and finally, summaries of recent research on adolescent drug and alcohol abuse.

DON'T TREAT CHEMICALLY DEPENDENT TEENAGERS AS ADULTS

Martin N. Buxton, M.D., F.A.A.C.P.

Martin Buxton is director of the Chemical Dependency Program at Carter Westbrook Hospital, Richmond, Virginia and a member of the Editorial Advisory Board of The Addiction Letter.

Despite what they think, teenagers are not adults. Unfortunately, many of us treating chemically dependent adolescents forget that truism and use expertise we developed with adults on teenaged clients. It's not our fault; most training programs use adults as prototype patients, and while there has been an increasing reflection on the child-oriented family as part of the alcoholic system, there is still a dearth of literature on the chemically dependent adolescent patient.

In my experience in treating both adults and teenagers, I have found there are both subtle and not-so-subtle differences between the two groups. Dealing with adolescents requires the use of certain techniques that would be unsuccessful, if not extremely provocative, if tried on adults. Here are five techniques that I have found successful:

1. Don't treat the adolescent as an adult. This may be obvious, but it is vitally important. I would guess that 98% of the adolescents entering our treatment program are co-dependent, having at least one parent who is either chemically dependent and/or co-dependent themselves. Most come from at least a three-generational chemically dependent family system. Their age-expected developmental denial lulls them into taking risks in using chemicals, thinking "damage can't happen to me." The denial is exacerbated by the fact that as co-dependent, pseudo-adult, pseudo-precocious, omnipotent-thinking adolescents, they and

From *When Children Need Help*, Manisses Communications Group, 1987, pp. 15-27. Published with permission of The Brown University Child Behavior and Development Letter, Manisses Communications Group, Inc., Three Governor Street, P.O. Box 3357, Wayland Square, Providence, RI 02906-0357.

the world often see themselves as being older than they really are. If you aren't careful, you'll be lulled into the same attitude that enables their addiction. You must subtly recognize co-dependent adolescents' need to be friendly in an adult-to-adult fashion and deal with them in a way that does not reject them. At the same time, however, you must softly but realistically identify the fact that there is an age difference and that they are not adults.

2. Encourage them to develop relationships. Alcoholics Anonymous wisely teaches adults not to have a relationship within the first year of recovery, or else they risk an impulsive and ill-timed marriage or commitment. And adolescents, too, during their active co-dependency, may be prone to making serious but unhealthy commitments at a young age. Once this issue is worked out sufficiently, however, adolescents, as part of their healthy identity formation as heterosexual beings, should be encouraged to have involvement in relationships. Your need to see adolescence as a developmental entity distinct from adults requires you to encourage them to have healthy relationships that are not compulsively rife with sexuality or co-dependent caretaking.

3. Intervene more to keep adolescents in therapy. As caregivers, we are very aware of the concept of "parens patriae" which implies that we, who work in an institution or other treatment facility, often function as surrogate parents. But we also recognize the importance of the "Serenity Prayer," accepting the things we cannot change. These notions lead to a "laissez-faire" approach to treating adults, who may need to face more consequences of their addiction before they can be treated successfully.

The nature of chemically dependent adolescents, however, requires a different approach, at least at the beginning of treatment. More often than with adults, chemically dependent adolescents enter treatment not of their own volition but because they either attempted suicide, showed other self-destructive tendencies, or because of trouble with the law. As a result, more heroics and activism must be used by the therapist in order to keep a teenager in treatment, at least until the adolescent becomes enlisted in the therapeutic process.

You cannot go overboard, however, and seduce the adolescent into oppositional resistance. Evoking opposition is one of the dangers of working with adolescents, who often are contrary in order to establish their identity and autonomy. So you must be careful not to let the issues of staying sober and sticking with recovery become involved in the adolescent autonomy struggle, while trying to intervene assertively and clarify identity confusions.

4. Hold marathon sessions. We use this technique in our inpatient unit where we try to undo the alcoholic family types of communication and replace it with healthy family communication. Often, we'll find that a number of the youngsters have know that another has been using drugs or is planning on going AWOL. Yet they did not speak up despite the fact that they themselves are doing well in recovery. As we track this down, we come to understand that the youngsters are recapitulating the unrecovered alcoholic system's communications in that there are coalitions and alliances that do not address the truth of what is happening. We'll "close" the unit and keep the youngsters in a marathon intervention session, perhaps for hours at a time. The enabling denial of the process is addressed and resistance wears down, setting the stage for the reunification of healthy family lines of communication.

5. Use paradoxical intervention. Pioneered by the family systems people in Philadelphia, this technique is invaluable if used delicately. I have found it most helpful, given my personality style, when a youngster is entrenched in a co-dependent position and cannot see it objectively. In such cases, I'll have the co-dependent youngster be in charge of all ashtrays or being responsible for seeing that another youngster is on time for group therapy. It helps show the co-dependent adolescent their tendency to try to take care of people and control things as a way of avoiding their own issues. You must be careful that the patient has enough insight to be able to understand the abstract nature of what is being said and does not take it literally. If a tone of humor, without sarcasm is used, paradox can be a very successful intervention technique.

These aren't the only techniques that are helpful with adolescents. But they should stimulate more ideas in your own practice in dealing with the unique characteristics of adolescents. Certainly, both in a transferential and counter-transferential sense, you may find yourself more of a parent than a friend or counselor. But, as long as you are aware of the complications, you can use it in helping your teenaged patient attain recovery.

SCHOOL: AN AVENUE FOR CHANGE FOR DRUG-USING TEENAGERS

Matthew C. Green, M. Ed., C.A.C.

Matthew C. Green is co-director of the Newton Youth Drug/Alcohol Program, 100 Walnut Street, Newtonville, MA 02160 (617-552-7679).

Alcohol, drugs, and teenagers have been a troublesome problem for high schools since the 1960's. Whether they used pot, LSD, or cocaine—not to mention the ever-present alcohol—adolescents using chemicals have been a problem for two decades and most communities are frustrated in their inability to stem the tide of drug use on a broad scale.

Since teenagers, by law in most states, are required to participate in some kind of formal education process through the age of 16, schools have a large stake in the drug issue. In most cases, teens bring their drug problems to the schoolhouse door, forcing the school as well as communities and parents to have equal responsibility in dealing with the problem.

In recent years, there has also been an increase in the number of teenagers appearing in courts throughout the country for drug and alcohol-related violations. Most courts send the teenagers to correctional facilities or put them on probation, completely ignoring what created the problem: drugs and alcohol. In addition, physicians, social workers and teachers have seen increasing numbers of adolescents with drug problems. These professionals rarely have adequate training or experience in substance abuse to enable them to feel comfortable and competent in helping teens who abuse drugs.

In Newton, Massachusetts, we have formed an unusual alliance between schools and the courts, the two institutions most important in the life of the drug-abusing teenager. Now in its eighth year, the Newton Youth Drug/Alcohol Program has worked together with court probation departments and public school staff to meet the needs of about 40 adolescents in trouble with drugs each year.

I should note that, in Massachusetts anyway, school administrators are cool towards the concept of alcohol and drug treatment operated through public school. Schools are for education, they believe, not for medical or mental health treatment. School does not own the responsibility for the students' emotional and physical problems, they say.

The Newton community, however, believes that when school is the only constant in an adolescent's life and when children bring their drug and alcohol problems into the school environment, then the educational system is obligated to implement change.

At Least a Year

Students enter the Newton Youth Drug/Alcohol Program either as a condition of probation or as a school requirement. Court-referred teens remain in the program for the duration of their probation, usually one to three years or until they fail to comply with the program's requirements. School-referred students commit themselves for a least one year.

Satisfactory completion of the program means earned high school credit for all participants. Unsatisfactory performance means denial of credit for those referred from school and surrender and final disposition for those on probation.

Participants must attend either Alcoholics Anonymous and/or Narcotics Anonymous as well as group therapy and individual counseling. Vocational assistance, court liaison and interpretation of events are available to each student. Students are required to attend all meetings on time. Absence and tardiness are not tolerated and result in termination from the program. Furthermore, students must attend meetings sober and free of any mind-altering chemical.

Lack of Limits

The program's philosophy is based on the premise that the lack of limits in an adolescent's life promotes the drug abusing life-style. Adolescents are frightened of the decisions they are forced to make in their teenage years—on values, and life goals—so they respond to firm guidance and strict limits. Program workers are available to students 24 hours per day, seven days per week, and 52 weeks a year in case of crisis.

The program has grown during the past five years. In the 1980–81 school year, the courts referred eight youngsters, seven of whom completed the program and remained in school. None was referred by school officials. During 1984–85, 53 were enrolled in the program, 46 referred by the courts and 7 by the schools. Completing the program last year were 30 of the 46 on probation (40 are still in school) and 5 of the 7 school-referred youths. (All 7 are still in school). Of the 46, 24 were new enrollees while the remainder had continued from the previous year.

The program is designed to provide:

- A framework to help students understand their drug-using behavior.
- Skills for self-awareness.
- A non-threatening environment for discussion.
- Experiences which encapsulate various life situations (through AA, NA, and discussion).
- High school credits as an added incentive for success and a road back for those who dropped out of school.
- A mechanism for the schools and courts to monitor the student/offenders' behavior.

Successful Completion

A student will have successfully completed the program if he or she is able to state thoughts and feelings which lead to abusive drinking and/or drug use; identify moments when the student is beginning to feel out of control concerning alcohol or drugs; list alternatives to use at such moments; and practice skills or alternatives (ways of handling arguments, conflict, tension and boredom) which take control of his or her future, by describing specific actions in his or her personal plan for future development.

Individuals with drug and alcohol problems continually suffer from unrealistic aspirations. Our students learn through discussion the type of risks they usually take. The effect of consistently taking high risks is discussed in our groups, in the context of resolving family disputes, work, recreational activities, driving and abusive drinking and drug use. Our students are encouraged to seek help from other professionals, and to view it as a way of using resources rather than as a weakness or character defect. We emphasize seeking personal change that is realistic and have benchmarks for testing the program periodically. For many students, plans for maintaining sobriety and continued treatment become an essential part of their future plans. The program has had extensive contact with inpatient detoxification and treatment/rehabilitation facilities throughout the Northeast, making referrals as well as being used as an aftercare placement for students coming back from these facilities.

Treatment and prevention are closely allied, and the Newton program combines the two effectively. Once a student is "straight," he or she becomes a staunch advocate of abstinence and an evangelist in approaching their drug-using friends. We have young people—ages 17 to 22—who are teachers by example to their peers. One such group of young people started an NA and AA group of their own in Newton and are speaking to other young adults about alcohol and drug dependency.

The program is broader than the cooperation between schools and courts implies. Students are not only referred by school officials and probation departments but by police and city human services departments. It provides support services to adolescents returning to school from residential chemical dependency programs and to parents and staff who are being trained in the identification of potential problems in adolescence.

All referrals coming from the various community agencies are the same adolescents who are also having difficulties in school. Therefore the Newton program is able to coordinate these groups to provide appropriate services for the adolescent with difficulties, avoiding outside placement and providing early identification of special needs.

Attitudes of disbelief and denial are often found in communities. We are finding kids coming to school either hungover, stoned or tripping; some are even coming to school drunk. For the most part, our students are ingesting their drugs outside of the school building, but are playing out their trip either in the classrooms, the corridors, the washrooms, or the cafeteria. Most often when questioned about their drug problem, these kids don't see it as a problem at all.

One 17-year-old we interviewed provides a stark example. He said he began using drugs and alcohol at the age of 10 and identified his use of illegal substances as "moderate" by the time he reached the age of 12. At that time, he smoked an ounce of marijuana and drank a six-pack of beer daily. He used LSD weekly. He was identified in school and in the community as delinquent because of his occasional criminal behavior and was remanded to the State Department of Youth Services for a two-year period. It was upon incarceration, that he stated, "My drug use then began to get bad."

This case simply exemplifies the attitude of individuals as well as the community surrounding a teenager's use of drugs and alcohol. The outward behavior, criminal activity, is punished, and the root of the problem continues to grow. In addition, teens are often unaware that their drug use or their friends' drug use is dangerous, life-threatening, and producing negative consequences.

The Newton program is set up on the premise that education is the primary tool to break through this denial. Legal controls have proved largely ineffective in controlling alcohol and drug use by youth. Preaching and scare tactics generally have also met with failure.

If the problem of alcoholism and drug abuse is to be managed in the future, it will be because young people have adopted a responsible attitude. They gain this through adult examples of responsible behavior as well as learning all the facts, positive and negative. Programs like the Newton Youth Drug/Alcohol Program, which link education, adjudication and rehabilitation, accomplish this task.

INDIRECT INDICATORS OF CHEMICAL ABUSE

How can we tell whether children are abusing chemicals?

Abusive use itself (being drunk at school, using drugs to get high, etc.) is, of course, a direct indicator of a problem with chemicals. But the Johnson Institute, a Minneapolis training center for addiction professionals, found in a 1984 survey of Minnesota teenagers several other indicators—some related to chemical use, some lacking any apparent connection—that correlated with chemical abuse by teenagers.

The presence of one or two of the following indicators hardly suggests chemical abuse, but the presence of several, perhaps five or more, should at least raise the question of chemical abuse:

- Low grades—a consistent pattern of below average grades or a recent drop in grades. Low grades are three times as likely among heavy users (11%) as among abstainers (4%).
- Absenteeism from school. Heavy users are four times more likely than abstainers to miss school (37% vs. 10%).
- A negative opinion of school. Heavy users are much more likely than abstainers to complain that they don't like school (37% vs. 16%) or to complain that they don't get along with their teachers (18% vs. 6%).

- Cigarette smoking. Two-thirds of heavy users smoke tobacco vs. 6% of infrequent users vs. 3% of abstainers.
- Drinking hard liquor (as opposed to beer or wine).
- Using marijuana.
- Avoiding parties where no chemicals are available or attending parties where drugs other than alcohol are available.
- Drinking in cars (86% of heavy users vs. 13% of infrequent users vs.—of course—0% abstainers).
- Lack of involvement in community activities, organized sports or other school activities. (Heavy users are less likely to have a part-time job or be involved in organized sports. They are much less likely than infrequent users or abstainers to be involved in other school activities (21% vs. 72% vs. 63%).
- The student is a male in grades 10–12.

***

RECENT STUDIES PROVIDE INSIGHT INTO DRUG USE AMONG TEENS

Reflecting the general public's increasing concern about teenagers' use of drugs and alcohol, numerous recent studies attempt to shed light on why adolescents experiment with alcohol and drugs, how use and experiment progress to dependency, and which teenagers are more at risk of developing chemical dependency. Here are several of the more significant recent studies:

The Role of Personality

Does a teenager's personality predict whether he or she will use drugs or alcohol? A recent study by Erich W. Labouvie and Connel R. McGee at Rutgers' Center of Alcohol studies says yes, strongly suggesting that personality may cause later use of alcohol and drugs. The study was published in Journal of Consulting and Clinical Psychology (1986, 54:289–293).

The researchers randomly selected 882 adolescents in three waves in 1979, 1980 and 1981. Initially tested at the ages of 12, 15 and 18, participants in the first two waves were retested after three years at the ages of 15, 18 and 21 years. The researchers asked the teenagers how often and how much they used alcohol, cigarettes, marijuana and cocaine. They also measured whether they used alcohol, cigarettes and illicit drugs as a coping device; their personality attributes; and, finally, their self-esteem.

After testing, researchers divided the sample into three groups, light, moderate and heavy users of substances. They found that male adolescents used marijuana and alcohol more than females, but that females smoke cigarettes more.

Light users in early adolescence tend to use only alcohol by age 21 and to maintain limited usage. Moderate users, by age 15, exhibit fairly regular use of alcohol and cigarettes, and by age 18, regular use of marijuana. Heavy users indulge in marijuana, cigarettes and alcohol by age 15 and use cocaine occasionally by age 21. The heavy users are involved with multiple drugs.

Heavy users scored high on the personality test on autonomy, exhibitionism, impulsivity, and play. They scored low on achievement, cognitive structure and harm avoidance. Light users scored the opposite. The authors suggest strongly that personality causes later alcohol and drug use. Personality changes were not significant over time, they said, indicating that use did not cause the personality characteristics. They found, however, that self-esteem did not correlate with use levels, suggesting that use among today's adolescents may no longer represent deviance or self-rejection. They note that adolescents who scored lower in achievement, cognitive structure and harm avoidance are not only more likely to use substances, but also to underdevelop those characteristics over time.

They caution, however, against concluding that heavy adolescent use predicts adult alcoholism. They hypothesize that the heavy using teenager find the substances as instant gratification for needs of play and impulsivity with little effort or skill expended. Second, the researchers suggest that alcohol and drug use may help the teens express needs for affiliation, autonomy, and exhibitionism. Finally, adolescents with risk-taking attributes are likely to be at odds with their environment and alcohol and drug use would relieve that stress via rebellion and expression of individuality.

Drug Use Begins in Sixth Grade

A longitudinal study of more than 1,100 children in two New England towns, published in the Journal of Drug Education (1986, 16: 203–220), shows that drug use begins as early as sixth grade and that there are critical periods for onset of use that may be helpful in designing effective prevention strategies.

The researchers, Katherine Grady, David L. Snow, and Marion Kessen of Yale University, and Kelin E. Gersick of the California School of Professional Psychology at Los Angeles, first studied the youngsters during their sixth grade and re-evaluated them in their seventh and eighth grades.

They had noted that other studies showed patterns of use that include significant experimentation and use in increasingly early grades. Youths typically move from initial experimentation to increasing experimentation and that they move from beer and wine, then tobacco and hard liquor, then to marijuana and other illicit drugs.

For their study, the authors divided use into four stages: none-use, experimental use (less than once monthly), regular use (one to two times monthly) and heavy use (once a week or more).

The study used a two-part questionnaire: the first asked them how often they had been offered any of ten listed drugs: tobacco, LSD, marijuana, alcohol, amphetamines, barbiturates, heroin, inhalants, cocaine, and other drugs. The second asked them if and how often they had used the drugs.

The study confirmed that alcohol, tobacco, and marijuana are gateway drugs. Sixty-five percent of the sixth graders had at least experimented with alcohol. That increased to 68% in seventh grade, and 74% in eighth grade. Experimentation or use of tobacco increased from 36% in sixth grade to 59% in the eighth. Experimentation and use of marijuana increased from 11% in sixth grade to 38% in the eighth. For other drugs, the study indicated sizable increases in experimentation but not in regular or heavy use over the three years.

Males used more alcohol, marijuana and other substances in the sixth grade, but by the eighth grade, there were no gender differences. Females used tobacco more in seventh and eighth grades. Whites used more than blacks in all grades. Rates of use were higher in the town having a middle school structure than in the town having a K-6, 7-8, and 9-12 system.

Family situations also affected use rates. Students from broken homes used tobacco and marijuana more in all three grades and higher use of alcohol in sixth grade. Students with remarried parents had slightly lower use rates than students reporting separated or divorced parents. Religious background showed little correlation, except for seventh grade tobacco use. Protestants used more than Catholics.

Offer rates were higher than use rates by the eighth grades. By then, 78% had been offered alcohol, 77% tobacco, 58% marijuana, 18% inhalants, 20% amphetamines, 19% barbiturates, and 16% cocaine.

Few students rejected alcohol in all three years, while rejection rates were moderate for tobacco and high for marijuana. Over the three years, the percentage of students rejecting decreases.

The authors concluded that prevention programs in the younger grades may need to focus on boys' use of alcohol and drugs and girls' use of tobacco. Students from broken homes need programs to meet their special needs.

The critical period for initiation into alcohol use occurs prior to the middle school years, they conclude, requiring earlier prevention programs and intensive parent and school involvement. Prevention programs should aim at preventing experimentation and increasing rejection of alcohol when offered.

The critical period for tobacco use seems to be the sixth grade. Prevention programs should include earlier grades with the middle school focus being on increasing the capacity to reject offers of tobacco.

For marijuana the researchers suggest sixth grade as the best time for prevention programs since use is most evident in seventh and eighth grades. Prevention programs for non-gateway drugs need to build on these programs when experimentation with such drugs as amphetamines and cocaine are just beginning.

Polydrug Abusers Seek Pleasure or Escape Pain

A study of 433 high school students, published in Adolescence (1985, 20: 853–861) found that 12% were polydrug users or abusers and that the reason they used drugs was to seek pleasure or escape pain.

Polydrug use, in this case, means that the users used more than one drug at the same time or in close sequence to produce different effects. They researcher, Loyd S. Wright, a psychologist at Southwest Texas State University, noted the dangers of the synergistic effects that polydrug use pose to users and abusers. In his study, seniors at two Texas high schools filled out confidential questionnaires on their drug using habits as well as how they perceived their parents and themselves.

Polydrug users and abusers more likely:

- Were physically abused or in conflict with their parents;
- Rated themselves as lazy, bored, rejected and unhealthy;
- Have serious suicidal thoughts, delinquent behavior, early use of marijuana and alcohol and the tendency to drink more than six alcoholic drinks at a sitting; and
- Agreed with the statements "If something feels good, I usually do it and don't worry about the consequences" and "I try to play as much as possible and work as little as possible."

Wright concluded that the results confirmed the notion that polydrug users seek either relief or pleasure and, therefore, do not see their drug use as a problem. He writes, "a variety of treatment and prevention strategies are necessary. Any drug abuse treatment program that hopes to have an impact on the pleasure seekers must get them to reexamine their basic philosophy, remove their peer support, and provide alternatives that will meet their needs for excitement and adventure."

Model College Drug and Alcohol Treatment Program

A model program to treat drug and alcohol abusers in college was proposed by three researchers after a national study of currently available university-based programs.

James Dean, DMIN, Hannah Dean, RN, Ph.D., and Donna Kleiner, MA, writing in the Journal of Substance Abuse Treatment (1986, 3 95–101), maintain that current use levels and accompanying problems require greater involvement than currently exists.

They propose that each institution form a planning committee to set attainable goals for the institution. Variables would include the extent of alcohol and drug problems, campus and community political climate, available resources and the financial capacity of the school. These factors will dictate the degree of involvement possible on a continuum ranging from no response to crisis intervention, identification and assessment only, or identification, assessment, and treatment. Most universities have counseling services for career, academic and personal needs. Only half have alcohol and drug services, they said.

The structural style of a program will reflect campus size, location, affiliation, student age, financial resources, state and local laws. Off-campus referral might be most applicable for some, while others might better utilize on-campus treatment. On-campus treatment would need to be offered through the counseling center. Friction with traditional psychological counseling service providers can be minimized by considering the chemical problem as central with psychological services potentially available, the authors suggest.

Physical services need to be available in support of alcohol and drug abuse crisis situations. Campus police, residence hall and dean of students' staffs, and crisis response team members need special training.

Treatment philosophy in the national survey was found by the authors to reflect a variety of models including AA/NA, psychoanalytical, behavioral, cognitive, family systems, Gestalt, religious, disease and eclectic approaches. The authors urge avoid use of labels in any model such as "alcoholic" or "drug addict," but rather to focus on the specific problems behavior associated with chemical use.

They note the need for trained staff with alcohol and drug treatment approach as most useful with attention focused on chemical use, on environmental and intrapsychic factors that influence use. They cite the University of North Dakota assessment as most helpful. They collect family and personal history, history of previous treatment, arrests, and psychological disorders. This data is supplemented with tests such as the MMPI and Beck Depression Inventory.

Referral to counseling comes via word of mouth, radio and TV publicity campaigns, and linkage to housing and resident hall disciplinary systems. They note the North Dakota system as most effective. It involves observing the problem behavior, encountering the problem by presenting facts to the student and referral. The student has the choice of accepting assistance or facing disciplinary action. A similar model is used by the Greek system and is run as a peer intervention system.

The authors stress the need for high-level administrative support and financial budgeting. Primary and secondary prevention are both the legitimate concerns of academic institutions to prevent problems before they occur, and to arrest them before they become serious and disabling, they conclude.

Youth 'Heavy Involvements' in Drugs and Alcohol

More than one-quarter of all senior high school students use marijuana, and one in ten 12th graders used cocaine during the 1985–86 school year, according to the results of a survey conducted for the Parents' Resource Institute for Drug Education (PRIDE) of Atlanta, Georgia.

The survey also reported that, based on interviews with 40,000 students in 17 states in grades 6 through 12, few students use drugs or alcohol during school hours. Only 1% of all students used alcohol, and 2% marijuana, during school hours.

"However, this does not suggest that drug and alcohol abuse is not a school problem. Students who have smoked marijuana while waiting for the bus or who have a hangover from too much alcohol the night before will be less receptive to instruction during the school day," PRIDE said.

PRIDE also reported that alcohol abuse among students was high, with more than one quarter of students in grades 6–8 reporting some use of liquor during the past year, a figure that jumps to 60% for ninth through 12th graders.

Students reported an even higher incidence of beer or wine use, with just under half of all junior high school students, and nearly three quarters of all senior high students admitting to some experience with those products.

Although the incidence of alcohol abuse far outpaced that of drug abuse, PRIDE officials reserved their direst warnings for parents of students using drugs, particularly cocaine.

"Only 1.6% of the junior high students reported any cocaine use while 6.4% of the senior high school students reported cocaine use," the survey's summary reported. Cocaine use increased with age, with 10.4% of 12th grade students admitting to some experience with the drug," the report stated.

Worse, PRIDE reported, cocaine users admitted that, when they used alcohol or marijuana, they did so expressly to get "bombed" or "very high."

Almost half of all students who have used cocaine report that they become intoxicated when using any drug or alcohol products. By comparison, only 4.5% of students who use only beer or wine reported intoxication.

Finally, the report concluded that students—particularly older high school students—abuse drugs and alcohol outside of parents' purview, and, alarmingly, continue to do so while driving. Nine percent of beer and wine drinkers, and 6% of marijuana abusers, are combining substance use with driving.

"This use of alcohol and marijuana outside the home and the reported direct use of these substances in a car suggest a serious problem with teenagers driving under the influence," PRIDE concluded.

(Parents Resource Institute for Drug Education, 100 Edgewood Ave., #1002, Atlanta, GA 30303, 800-241-7946.)

Teens Concerned About Health Consequences of Drinking

A new study sponsored by the Alcoholism Council of Greater New York, suggests that teenagers are as concerned about the personal health problems associated with heavy drinking as about the social consequences.

The study, by an Albert Einstein College of Medicine researcher, involved 108 adolescents, ages 12 through 18, in three New York City community centers of the Children's Aid Society.

In a questionnaire which never mentions alcohol, the youths were asked to indicate their level of concern about specific health problems (such as acne, cancer, diabetes, and obesity) and behavior problems (peer acceptance, relationship with parents, and so on).

On 34 health issues, 19 represented problems that can be associated with heavy drinking, and 15 were not alcohol-related. All of the 19 behavioral items could be alcohol-related.

In an analysis of the responses, Thomas Ashby Wills, an assistant professor of psychology and epidemiology in Albert Einstein's Department of Epidemiology and Social Medicine, found the youths' concern about health problems "comparable to, and possibly greater than, their level of concern about behavioral problems."

"Concern about health consequences of alcohol may be an effective component of educational programs to reduce rates of alcohol abuse, in addition to the social consequences approach used in current alcohol education," he said.

The study was part of the Alcoholism Council's current Health Awareness Campaign designed to inform the public of alcohol's hidden effects on health, fitness and appearance.

(Alcoholism Council of Greater New York, 133 East 62nd St., New York, NY 10021; 212-935-7075)

Reasons for Drug Use

For teenagers, drugs: serve as rationalization vehicles for otherwise unacceptable behavior, enhance identity states, enable users to find companionship, and fulfill expectations of effects, as a hostility releaser, as a deepening of consciousness, or as an expression of civil disobedience.

These are the conclusions of Craig R. Thorne and Richard R. DeBlassie, who surveyed numerous recent studies and published their findings in Adolescence (1985, 78: 335-347).

According to the researchers, onset of use involves opportunity. At first, the teenager does not use at the first opportunity, but if his or her peer group uses drugs or alcohol, he or she, gradually, will follow suit. Young adults 18-25 years of age are most likely to use illicit drugs—especially if living away from family, alone or with peers. Perceived availability of drugs also influences use, with marijuana being seen as the universally most available, followed, in order, by psychotherapeutic drugs, barbiturates, cocaine, hallucinogens, opiates and heroin.

Marijuana is the most widely used illicit drug among high school seniors with 60% having used it, but alcohol and tobacco are the most widespread with 93% having tried alcohol and 71% having tried tobacco.

Use of illicit drugs occurs in the last three years of high school. Marijuana, alcohol, and tobacco are tried prior to high school. Inhalant use occurs typically prior to 10th grade while illicit drugs excluding inhalant and marijuana use begin after 10th grade. Marijuana use is increasing in all grade levels down to 8th grade, but on a declining curve.

Males and females exhibited difference in frequency of use with males using more of all substances except tobacco. Early aggressiveness and shyness correlate to later substance abuse in males only. Males rank peer and school bonds as primary. Females ranked family and school bonds as most important for them. Strong peer bonds correlates with use. College aspirations correlate with lower rates of illicit drug use. Northeastern American residents have highest rates of use, the Southern, the lowest. Urban areas outscore rural areas on use, except for tranquilizers, sedatives, stimulants, and tobacco which show no association to setting.

Family influence in this report involves older siblings' examples, mothers who smoke and drink moderately. Fathers' use does not appear, according to the authors, to be a significant factor.

Virtually all students perceived parental attitudes to be disapproving of drug use. Peer attitude is closest to the student's attitude toward use.

Prevention programs surveyed have largely focused on the individual, take place in an institutional setting rather than in the community, are directed at the middle-class, white population, aim at prevention of all drug use, and are presented to rather large audiences.

Four models of treatment are prevalent—legal, medical, traditional (AA, abstinence), and emergent (learned behavior/controlled use outcome). Increased opportunity for use relates with gradual increase in use. There is much cause of continuing concern and continued prevention efforts, work in the legal, research, and treatment areas.

The authors cite recognition of our individual and collective attitudes and beliefs as primary elements in overcoming substance abuse worldwide.

Self-image and Alcohol Use

Teenagers' self-images and social images were found to be factors as to whether they drank alcohol, according to researchers Laurie Chassin, Christine Tetzloff, and Miriam Hershey, who published the results of their study in the Journal of Studies on Alcohol (1985, 46: 39–47). They hypothesized that adolescents would drink if their self-concepts were consistent with a drinking image (consistency theory), or if their peers admired a drinking image (impression management theory).

They studied 266 students in a southwestern suburban high school, 51% male, 49% female and 92.5% white, 4.7% Hispanic, 2.4% Indian. The average age was 15 years old.

They were shown slides of youths holding beverage cans—beer or soft drinks—in pairs. Questions were asked on the desirability of the model as a friend, and how much like the model the student was. The Adolescent Alcohol Involvement Scale was given, testing frequency and quantity of use, and social and psychological problems resulting. Finally, adolescents gave intentions for future use.

The social image associated with alcohol use was ambivalent. They saw the adolescent drinker as projecting an image of toughness and precocity—a perceived social asset. It also conveys the association of rebellion against authority. On the negative side, they associated users with being less happy and honest, and more socially rejected regardless of sex of model. Drinking alcohol was noted by the authors as having significantly more social acceptability to adolescents than smoking. The authors suggest that the distress associated with use may be seen as teens viewing drinkers as more likely to bear dysphoric symptoms. They may see use as increasing positive mood states.

Adolescent boys tend to aspire to the drinking image and to believe that the drinker attributes are valued by their peers (toughness and precocity).

Girls who did not misuse alcohol followed this pattern. Significantly, girls who did misuse alcohol had ideal self-images that were less like the drinker image than their actual self-descriptions. The authors infer that these girls may be using alcohol to control mood or reduce stress.

Adolescents of both sexes who saw themselves as similar to a drinking image were more involved with alcohol (consistency hypothesis). Seeing peers as admiring the drinking image correlates with intent to use in the future (impression management hypothesis). Males who saw their ideal self-image as similar to the drinking image used more (self enhancement hypothesis).

The precise mechanics of causes of use by adolescents is unclear. Peer influence, modeling, opportunities, and social reinforcement are all cited as being involved by the authors. More work is needed to provide adequate programs for prevention. Finding ways to work around the social image associated with drug use—finding alternatives—is the course they suggest.

Punishment and Corrections

In the American system of criminal justice, the term "corrections" has a special meaning. It designates programs and agencies that have legal authority over the custody or supervision of persons who have been convicted of a criminal act by the courts.

The correctional process begins with the sentencing of the convicted offender. The predominant sentencing pattern in the United States encourages maximum judicial discretion and offers a range of alternatives from probation (supervised conditional freedom within the community), through imprisonment, to the death penalty. Selections in this unit focus on the current condition of the penal system in the United States, and the effects sentencing, probation, imprisonment, and parole have on the rehabilitation of criminals.

"Sentencing and Corrections" illustrates how society, through sentencing, expresses its objectives for the correctional process. The objectives are deterrence, incapacitation, rehabilitation, retribution, and restitution.

Some 60 percent of inmates released from state and federal lockups return to prison. Recidivism contributes greatly to the overcrowding that plagues prisons throughout the United States. Crowded, tense conditions make survival the principal goal. Rehabilitation is pushed into the background in the effort to manage incipient chaos.

The survival ethic continues after release. A parolee is released to the street with 40 dollars in his pocket, no home, and no job. The result: more crime. The three-part *Christian Science Monitor* series on prisons, "State Prisons: Crucibles for Justice," emphasizes that inmate populations are growing at a rate that is overwhelming prisons in spite of the huge expansion of prison space in recent years. "Prison Crowding in the United States" also addresses this serious issue.

Other issues and aspects of the correctional system—house arrest, whipping, AIDS, alternatives to incarceration, and privatization of prisons and the death penalty—are topics addressed in this unit. Fred Scaglione discusses a new high-tech, yet age-old approach to confinement in "You're Under Arrest—at Home." William Slicker's essay "Whipping" advocates the restoration of whipping as a statutory punishment. "Learning to Live With AIDS in Prison" examines more enlightened attitudes and policies toward convicts with AIDS. The authors of "Alternatives to Incarceration" contend that punishing non-violent offenders behind bars is counterproductive. Instead, they maintain that program options which deal with offenders in the community should be used.

"Prison Overcrowding and Privatization" gives a progress report on the "prisons for profit" movement. The most controversial punishment of all is under discussion in the concluding article, " 'This Man Has Expired.' "

Looking Ahead: Challenge Questions

If you were to argue the pathology of imprisonment, what points would you make? On the other hand, if you were to justify continued imprisonment of offenders, what would you stress?

Some authorities would have us believe that probation and parole are ineffective correctional strategies, and should be abandoned. Others maintain that they have yet to really be tried. What is your view?

Do you support work release or community service for any offenders? Which ones?

If you were a high-level correctional administrator and had the luxury of designing a "humane" prison, what would it be like? What aspects of a traditional prison would you keep? What would you eliminate? What new strategies or programs would you introduce?

What are your feelings about the death penalty? Do you think it is an effective deterrent to murder?

Unit 6

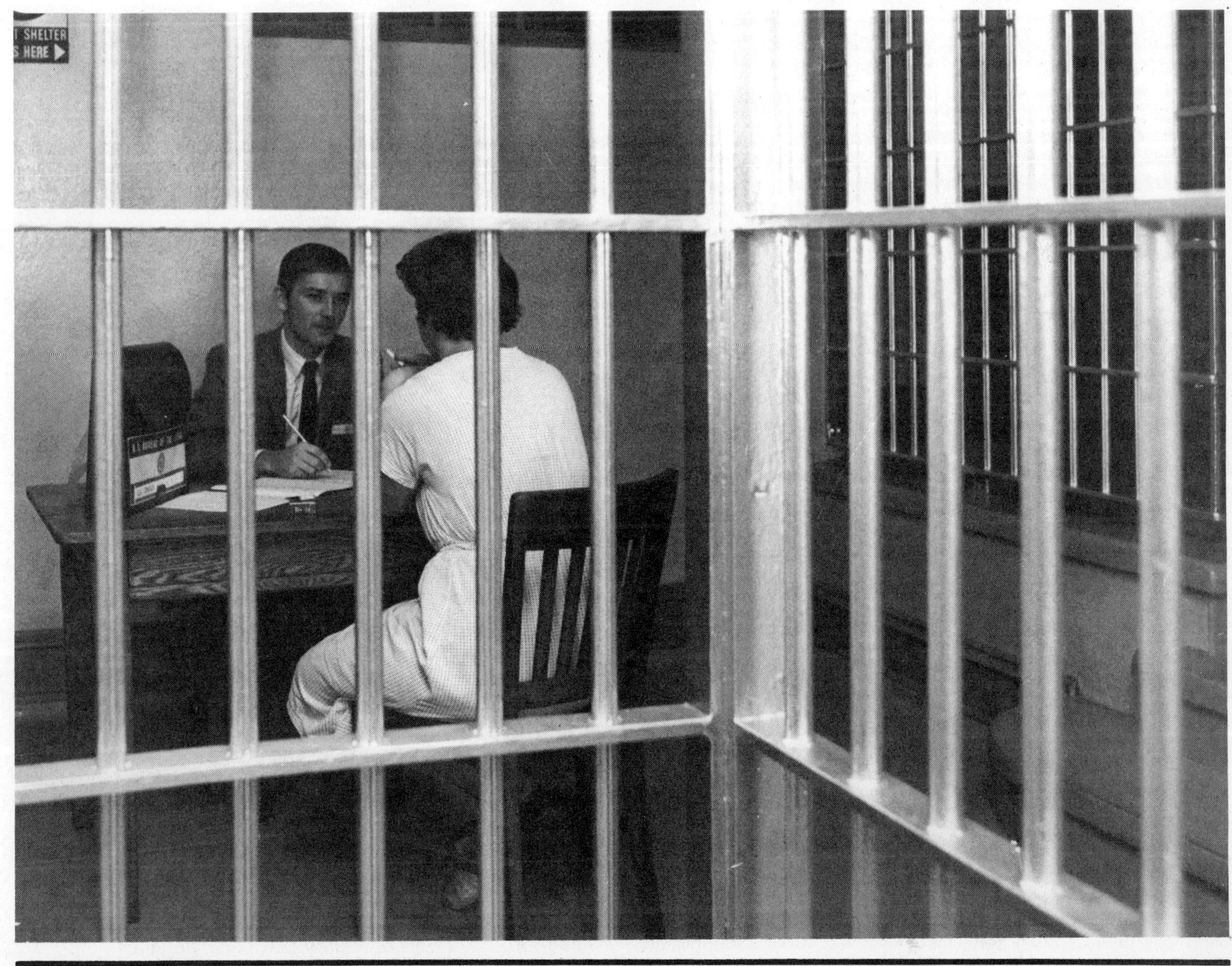

Sentencing and Corrections

Through sentencing, society attempts to express its goals for the correctional process

The sentencing of criminals often reflects conflicting social goals

These objectives are—
• **Retribution**—giving offenders their "just deserts" and expressing society's disapproval of criminal behavior
• **Incapacitation**—separating offenders from the community to reduce the opportunity for further crime while they are incarcerated
• **Deterrence**—demonstrating the certainty and severity of punishment to discourage future crime by the offender (specific deterrence) and by others (general deterrence)
• **Rehabilitation**—providing psychological or educational assistance or job training to offenders to make them less likely to engage in future criminality
• **Restitution**—having the offender repay the victim or the community in money or services.

Attitudes about sentencing reflect multiple goals and other factors

Research on judicial attitudes and practices in sentencing revealed that judges vary greatly in their commitment to various goals when imposing sentences. Public opinion also has shown much diversity about the goals of sentencing, and public attitudes have changed over the years. In fashioning criminal penalties, legislators have tended to reflect this lack of public consensus.

Sentencing laws are further complicated by concerns for—
• **Proportionality**—severity of punishment should be commensurate with the seriousness of the crime
• **Equity**—similar crimes and similar criminals should be treated alike
• **Social debt**—the severity of punishment should take into account the offender's prior criminal behavior.

Judges usually have a great deal of discretion in sentencing offenders

The different sentencing laws give various amounts of discretion to the judge in setting the length of a prison or jail term. In a more fundamental respect, however, the judge often has a high degree of discretion in deciding whether or not to incarcerate the offender at all. Alternatives to imprisonment include—
• probation
• fines
• forfeiture of the proceeds of criminal activity
• restitution to victims
• community service
• split sentences, consisting of a short period of incarceration followed by probation in the community.

Often, before a sentence is imposed a presentence investigation is conducted to provide the judge with information about the offender's characteristics and prior criminal record.

Disparity and uncertainty arose from a lack of consensus over sentencing goals

By the early 1970s researchers and critics of the justice system had begun to note that trying to achieve the mixed goals of the justice system without new limits on the discretionary options given to judges had—
• reduced the *certainty* of sanctions, presumably eroding the deterrent effect of corrections
• resulted in *disparity* in the severity of punishment, with differences in the sentences imposed for similar cases and offenders
• failed to validate the effectiveness of various rehabilitation programs in changing offender behavior or predicting future criminality.

Recent sentencing reforms reflect more severe attitudes and seek to reduce disparity and uncertainty

Reforms in recent years have used statutory and administrative changes to—
• clarify the aims of sentencing
• reduce disparity by limiting judicial and parole discretion
• provide a system of penalties that is more consistent and predictable
• provide sanctions consistent with the concept of "just deserts."

The changes have included—
• making prison mandatory for certain crimes and for recidivists
• specifying presumptive sentence lengths
• requiring sentence enhancements for offenders with prior felony convictions
• introducing sentencing guidelines
• limiting parole discretion through the use of parole guidelines
• total elimination of discretionary parole release (determinate sentencing).

States use a variety of strategies for sentencing

Sentencing is perhaps the most diversified part of the Nation's criminal justice process. Each State has a unique set of sentencing laws, and frequent and substantial changes have been made in recent years. This diversity complicates the classification of sentencing systems. For nearly any criterion that may be considered, there will be some States with hybrid systems that straddle the boundary between categories.

From *Report to the Nation on Crime and Justice,* Bureau of Justice Statistics, U.S. Department of Justice, March 1988, pp. 90-93.

The basic difference in sentencing systems is the apportioning of discretion between the judge and parole authorities

Indeterminate sentencing—the judge specifies minimum and maximum sentence lengths. These set upper and lower bounds on the time to be served. The actual release date (and therefore the time actually served) is determined later by parole authorities within those limits.

Partially indeterminate sentencing—a variation of indeterminate sentencing in which the judge specifies only the maximum sentence length. An associated minimum automatically is implied, but is not within the judge's discretion. The implied minimum may be a fixed time (such as 1 year) for all sentences or a fixed proportion of the maximum. In some States the implied minimum is zero; thus the parole board is empowered to release the prisoner at any time.

Determinate sentencing—the judge specifies a fixed term of incarceration, which must be served in full (less any "goodtime" earned in prison). There is no discretionary parole release.

Since 1975 many States have adopted determinate sentencing, but most still use indeterminate sentencing

In 1976 Maine was the first State to adopt determinate sentencing. The sentencing system is entirely or predominantly determinate in these 10 States:

California	Maine
Connecticut	Minnesota
Florida	New Mexico
Illinois	North Carolina
Indiana	Washington

The other States and the District of Columbia use indeterminate sentencing in its various forms. One State, Colorado, after changing to determinate sentencing in 1979, went back to indeterminate sentencing in 1985. The Federal justice system has adopted determinate sentencing through a system of sentencing guidelines.

States employ other sentencing features in conjunction with their basic strategies

Mandatory sentencing—Law requires the judge to impose a sentence of incarceration, often of specified length, for certain crimes or certain categories of offenders. There is no option of probation or a suspended sentence.	Mandatory sentencing laws are in force in 46 States (all except Maine, Minnesota, Nebraska, and Rhode Island) and the District of Columbia. In 25 States imprisonment is mandatory for certain repeat felony offenders. In 30 States imprisonment is mandatory if a firearm was involved in the commission of a crime. In 45 States conviction for certain offenses or classes of offenses leads to mandatory imprisonment; most such offenses are serious, violent crimes, and drug trafficking is included in 18 of the States. Many States have recently made drunk driving an offense for which incarceration is mandated (usually for relatively short periods in a local jail rather than a State prison).
Presumptive sentencing—The discretion of a judge who imposes a prison sentence is constrained by a specific sentence length set by law for each offense or class of offense. That sentence must be imposed in all unexceptional cases. In response to mitigating or aggravating circumstances, the judge may shorten or lengthen the sentence within specified boundaries, usually with written justification being required.	Presumptive sentencing is used, at least to some degree, in about 12 States.
Sentencing guidelines—Explicit policies and procedures are specified for deciding on individual sentences. The decision is usually based on the nature of the offense and the offender's criminal record. For example, the prescribed sentence for a certain offense might be probation if the offender has no previous felony convictions, a short term of incarceration if the offender has one prior conviction, and progressively longer prison terms if the offender's criminal history is more extensive.	Sentencing guidelines came into use in the late 1970s. They are— • used in 13 States and the Federal criminal justice system • written into statute in the Federal system and in Florida, Louisiana, Maryland, Minnesota, New Jersey, Ohio, Pennsylvania, and Tennessee • used systemwide, but not mandated by law, in Utah • applied selectively in Massachusetts, Michigan, Rhode Island, and Wisconsin • being considered for adoption in other States and the District of Columbia.
Sentence enhancements—In nearly all States, the judge may lengthen the prison term for an offender with prior felony convictions. The lengths of such enhancements and the criteria for imposing them vary among the States.	In some States that group felonies according to their seriousness, the repeat offender may be given a sentence ordinarily imposed for a higher seriousness category. Some States prescribe lengthening the sentences of habitual offenders by specified amounts or imposing a mandatory minimum term that must be served before parole can be considered. In other States the guidelines provide for sentences that reflect the offender's criminal history as well as the seriousness of the offense. Many States prescribe conditions under which parole eligibility is limited or eliminated. For example, a person with three or more prior felony convictions, if convicted of a serious violent offense, might be sentenced to life imprisonment without parole.

Sources: Surveys conducted for the Bureau of Justice Statistics by the U.S. Bureau of the Census in 1985 and by the Pennsylvania Commission on Crime and Delinquency in 1986.

Sentencing guidelines usually are developed by a separate sentencing commission

Such a commission may be appointed by the legislative, executive, or judicial branch of State government. This is a departure from traditional practice in that sentences are prescribed through an administrative procedure rather than by explicit legislation.

In some States the guidelines are prescriptive in that they specify whether or not the judge must impose a prison sentence and the presumptive sentence length. In other States the guidelines are advisory in that they provide information to the judge but do not mandate sentencing decisions.

To determine whether a prison sentence should be imposed, the guidelines usually consider offense severity and the offender's prior criminal record. A matrix that relates these two factors may be used.

Sentencing matrix

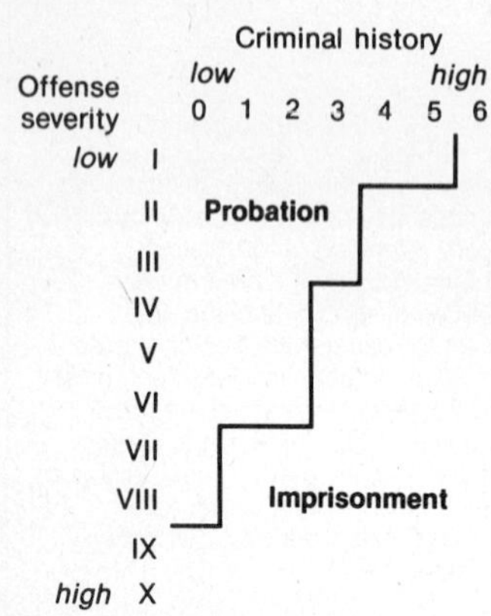

Adapted from *Preliminary report on the development and impact of the Minnesota sentencing guidelines*, Minnesota Sentencing Guidelines Commission, July 1982.

Sentencing guidelines used in the Federal justice system were developed by the United States Sentencing Commission. The guidelines provide for determinate sentencing and the abolition of parole. Ranges of sentence length are specified for various offense classifications and offender characteristics. The judge must provide written justification for any sentence that deviates from the guideline range; sentences that are less severe can be appealed by the prosecution, and sentences that are more severe can be appealed by the defense.

Changes in sentencing have brought changes in correctional practices

Many sentencing reforms have led to changes in the way correctional systems operate:

The proliferation of determinate and mandatory sentences during the past decade, together with dissatisfaction about the uncertainties of indeterminate sentencing (especially the linking of release decisions to rehabilitative progress or predictions of future behavior), have led to modifications in parole decisionmaking. Many States now use parole guidelines, and many have modified their use of "goodtime" and other incentives for controlling inmate behavior and determining release dates.

New administrative requirements, such as collection of victim restitution funds, operation of community service programs, and levying fees for probation supervision, room and board, and other services, have been added to traditional correctional practices.

Changes in sentencing laws and practices may be affecting the size of the correctional clientele. Such changes include—

- using determinate and mandatory sentencing
- limiting or abolishing parole discretion
- lowering the age at which youthful offenders become subject to the adult criminal justice system
- enacting in a few jurisdictions laws providing for life imprisonment without the possibility of parole.

Forfeiture is a relatively new sanction

What is forfeiture?

Forfeiture is government seizure of property derived from or used in criminal activity. Its use as a sanction aims to strip racketeers and drug traffickers of their economic power because the traditional sanctions of imprisonment and fines have been found inadequate to deter or punish enormously profitable crimes. Seizure of assets aims not only to reduce the profitability of illegal activity but to curtail the financial ability of criminal organizations to continue illegal operations.

There are two types of forfeiture: civil and criminal

- **Civil forfeiture**—a proceeding against property used in criminal activity. Property subject to civil forfeiture often includes vehicles used to transport contraband, equipment used to manufacture illegal drugs, cash used in illegal transactions, and property purchased with the proceeds of the crime. No finding of criminal guilt is required in such proceedings. The government is required to post notice of the proceedings so that any party who has an interest in the property may contest the forfeiture.

- **Criminal forfeiture**—a part of the criminal action taken against a defendant accused of racketeering or drug trafficking. The forfeiture is a sanction imposed on conviction that requires the defendant to forfeit various property rights and interests related to the violation. In 1970 Congress revived this sanction that had been dormant in American law since the Revolution.

The use of forfeiture varies greatly among jurisdictions

The Federal Government originally provided for criminal forfeiture in the Racketeer Influenced and Corrupt Organization (RICO) statute and the Comprehensive Drug Prevention and Control Act, both enacted in 1970. Before that time civil forfeiture had been provided in Federal laws on some narcotics, customs, and revenue infractions. More recently, language on forfeiture has been included in the Comprehensive Crime Control Act of 1984, the Money Laundering Act of 1986, and the Anti-drug Abuse Act of 1986.

Most State forfeiture procedures appear in controlled substances or RICO laws. A few States provide for forfeiture of property connected with the commission of any felony. Most State forfeiture provisions allow for civil rather than criminal forfeiture. A recent survey responded to by 44 States and territories found that under the controlled substances laws most States provide only for civil forfeiture. Eight States (Arizona, Kentucky, Nevada, New Mexico, North Carolina, Utah, Vermont, and West Virginia), however, have criminal forfeiture provisions.[1] Of the 19 States with RICO statutes, all but 8 include the criminal forfeiture sanction.[2]

What is forfeitable?

Originally most forfeiture provisions aimed to cover the seizure of contraband or modes of transporting or facilitating distribution of such materials. The types of property that may be forfeited have been expanded since the 1970s to include assets, cash, securities, negotiable instruments, real property including houses or other real estate, and proceeds traceable directly or indirectly to violations of certain laws. Common provisions permit seizure of conveyances such as airplanes, boats, or cars; raw materials, products, and equipment used in manufacturing, trafficking, or cultivation of illegal drugs; and drug paraphernalia.

How long does it take to determine if property can be forfeited?

In most cases some time is provided before the actual forfeiture to allow persons with an interest in seized property to make a claim. Seized property is normally kept for 6 months to 1 year before being declared forfeit and disposed of. Contraband or materials that are illegal *per se*, such as drugs, are disposed of relatively quickly. Cars, airplanes, boats, and other forms of transportation are usually kept for about 6 months before disposal. Real property is often kept for longer periods. Administrative forfeitures usually take less time than ones that require judicial determination.

Because of the depreciation in value of many assets over time and the cost of storing or caring for such assets, forfeiture may result in a cost rather than revenue to the prosecuting jurisdiction.

What happens to forfeited property?

The disposition of forfeited property is controlled by statute or in some States by their constitutions. In many cases, the seizing agency is permitted to place an asset in official use once it has been declared forfeit by a court. Such assets are usually cars, trucks, boats, or planes used during the crime or proceeds of the crime.

For assets that are sold, the proceeds are usually used first to pay any outstanding liens. The costs of storing, maintaining, and selling the property are reimbursed next. Some States require that, after administrative costs are reimbursed, the costs of law enforcement and prosecution must be paid. More than half the States provide that any outstanding balance go to the State or local treasury, or a part to both.

In eight States law enforcement agencies can keep all property, cash, or sales proceeds. If the State constitution governs distribution, the receiving agency is usually the State or local school system. Some States have specified the recipients to be special programs for drug abuse prevention and rehabilitation.

In 1984 the Federal Government established the Department of Justice Assets Forfeiture Fund to collect proceeds from forfeitures and defray the costs of forfeitures under the Comprehensive Drug Abuse Prevention and Control Act and the Customs Forfeiture Fund for forfeitures under customs laws. These acts also require that the property and proceeds of forfeiture be shared equitably with State and local law enforcement commensurate with their participation in the investigations leading to forfeiture.

STATE PRISONS

Crucibles for Justice

American prisons tend to dehumanize most prisoners. Rehabilitation, as a systemwide policy, is hit-or-miss. The latest crisis facing our prisons is an explosive growth in the number of prisoners, which is overwhelming an unprecedented boom in prison construction. The result, more often than not, is a prison experience that may mollify society, but damages people. Below, the first of a three-part series looks at troubled prisons and their effects on several inmates.

INSIDE LOOKING OUT

Jim Bencivenga
Staff writer of The Christian Science Monitor

Smyrna, Del.

"I love you."

The words are at the same time defiant and sustaining, even a little courageous. In the din of the early morning hour, Leamond Pierce Jr. rises from a narrow bed in a cell smaller than a pickup truck. He looks into the stainless-steel mirror screwed to the wall of his cell and tells his out-of-focus face, "I love you."

He steadies himself, trying to balance the terrible odds against himself by reaffirming what he knows he must know. First things first. Survival next. He is in the Delaware State Penitentiary for life, convicted of murder.

After putting on his clothes, he lifts a pair of cherry-red, wraparound sunglasses to his eyes as if the glasses are a piece of armor or a veil. Coolly he moves out of the cell, a lanky, muscular man in his late 20s, heading for the prison mess hall, trying hard for a cherry-red day.

"I struggle daily not to be bitter," he says.

After 7½ years, the daily routine is ingrained, but not the fact that he is here for life. Despite the wary hope he has for a cherry-red day, he never forgets he is here for life.

The public rationale is that justice has been done in the case of Mr. Pierce. He committed murder and his penalty is life imprisonment. The man is out of sight behind bars and doing hard time. Justice operating to a tee.

But the difficult question, one that still befuddles the experts and pokes a stick in the ribs of justice, is what on earth should be done with Pierce and tens of thousands of other felons while they are in prison.

For almost 200 years penologists and policymakers in the United States have never really found anything but the most inconsistent answers in deciding what our prisons should do and be, and at what cost.

Because of a lack of policy consensus, US prisons are historically prone to stagger from one palliative to another, from one crisis to another. The latest crisis, the most formidable ever, is the explosive growth in prison populations that is even overwhelming an unprecedented boom in prison construction.

Currently, there are 582,000 inmates in state and federal prisons, an increase of more than

120,000 in the last five years, the highest level in the nation's history. At the same time, during the last eight years, a whopping $15 billion has been spent on new prisons around the country.

A chain reaction has set in: While national crime rates have risen slightly, recidivism is up, hovering at an alarming rate of about 60 percent. Thus more often than not, prisons are like crude, bubbling pots, seldom able to cook the crime out of criminals or alter behavior. Most inmates are released after a median incarceration of nearly 17 months. Many hit the streets, unable to cope with conventional life.

Yet a fearful and sometimes vindictive public wants tougher mandatory-sentencing laws and more and more prisons. Educational or rehabilitation programs get short shift, because overcrowding busts state budgets.

"How can the public know they are getting value for their money?" asks Jim Austin, one of the nation's premier corrections researchers at the National Council on Crime and Delinquency in San Francisco. "They can't," he answers. "The public looks at prisons as solving crime problems. They aren't."

What the public gets for its money is a mean, ugly place that controls, limits, and dehumanizes.

"There are so many men who hurt and hate in here," says Pierce. "It's tough to deal with. You have to fight daily not to let it get your spirit." By 7:30 in the morning he is in the prison print shop working on the same old machine, an A. B. Dick duplicator. For three years, up to seven hours a day, he has fed paper in and watched paper spit out. It fills his time. It creates purpose, even a little control over his life.

"I make 38 cents an hour," he says. "That's up from 16 cents. I won't ask my mother for money. She works two jobs to make ends meet." She has also seen two of her other sons do time in this same prison.

"People in here get crazy over a couple of bags of potato chips, a bar of soap," says Pierce. By earning money, he never has to borrow, thus avoiding a dangerous position in prison. "No one can come up to me and say, you owe. Once a week I'm allowed to make purchases at the commissary. Candy, ice cream. Sardines, if I feel real hungry."

Control. Limit. Dehumanize.

Several years ago a federal court, in deciding an overcrowding suit, declared that "prisoners cannot be free of discomfort." The ruling agreed with the assertion that it was permissible to place two prisoners in a cell designed for one.

"We're stuck with the wrong visions," says Anthony Travisono, executive director of the American Correctional Association.

"The public has no idea what it means to work and live in one of these facilities for any length of time. People just don't visualize what it means to operate a prison with 800 to 1,000 men in it when it was built to accommodate 500. In the desire to put somebody someplace, they just don't visualize what that is on a daily basis."

Nor is there much public awareness of the costs involved. To incarcerate Pierce for a year, the State of Delaware spends $15,890, about the same as a year at an Ivy League college.

In California and some Northern urban states, the figure is nearly $30,000 a year to house, feed, and guard an inmate. Between now and 1990, California alone will spend a minimum of $2 billion on new prison construction. The cost per cell can go as high as $75,000. Over the 30-year life of the prison, this will be but 1/16th of the cost of keeping a man locked in it.

But despite new prison construction, the somber, monolithic state prisons found in each of the 50 states, many over 100 years old, are coming under attack by the courts. Currently, 38 state corrections departments, either entirely or at least at one major facility, are under court order for unconstitutional living conditions: overcrowding, lack of exercise areas, limited visiting rights, or unsanitary food preparation.

"After work," says Pierce, "I need a letter waiting for me, especially on Friday." It is the proverbial letter from home, carrying with it a double impact in the cage that is a prison. Not only the contents of the letter are important, but the fact that it is there, in his hands, as evidence of Pierce's link to the outside.

On Sundays he sings in the prison choir. "It's like flying," he says. "A chance to stand up and give." He pauses. "The absolute best is a visit," he says. "Fifteen minutes with somebody is a vacation, an absolute vacation for me. I can do another month after a visit." He is allowed visitors for 90 minutes a week.

The penitentiary here in Smyrna is banal. Manila brick bunkers squat in an open field, the entire compound intricately laced with steel fences and miles of razor-sharp wire. Relatively new (built in 1971), it is clean, efficient, not overly crowded, housing about 50 inmates more than its 1,266-bed capacity. It is miles from any town or city of size.

A new segregation unit looms a stone's throw away. It has beds for 64 inmates. Such units are safety valves. They allow prison officials to isolate inmates who break prison rules. For Pierce, the "seg unit" means that predators, gangs, and rapists will not roam at will; that criminals will not run the joint. It means his hard time will be less hard.

Food is ample but bland. "Like spaghetti, only they always forget the sauce," Pierce says with a sad laugh. He must contend with the pervasive smell of industrial cleansers and disinfectants. Smyrna's one redeeming architectural feature is the recreation yard. It creates a campus effect and affords a horizon inmates in more notorious lockups only dream about.

Less than 5 percent of the cost of Pierce's incarceration goes for work or education programs. Two counselors are here, should he want to arrange for education or religious instruction. Such individuals' worth is immeasurable to Pierce. He cannot petition the state pardon board for clemency until he completes his 10th year. He's doing "natural life."

"You ain't right."

The statement pops up often in prison, says Pierce. It is a charge intentionally cruel and part of the prison lingo that digs into you and transforms you until you start to believe, "You ain't right." You are dead "wrong," because you're here, looking at yourself in the mirror, doing hard time, wearing cherry-red glasses. "You ain't right" because you were convicted of what you know is a stupid, violent act.

The snap of the handcuffs told you this when you were caught; you suffocated on it in court when the sentence was read. When you saw "You ain't right" in the eyes of a family member. "You ain't right" because, once, you tried to take your life here. "You ain't right," chants the daily prison count, six counts a day to make sure you're still here. "You ain't right," says Pierce of himself when he thinks of the young girl whose father he murdered.

"You ain't right."

GETTING 'RIGHT,' STAYING OUT

Bronx, N.Y.

DANNY SANDERS doesn't remember what he ate for his first meal in a restaurant after eight years in prison. What he does remember is that he stole the silverware.

The slight, quiet, youthful-looking black man, spooning down a pint of chocolate Häagen-Dazs ice cream and sipping a root beer, smiles and shakes his head as he leans back in his chair. "It wasn't funny then," he says. "I was a block-and-a-half from the restaurant when I froze on the street. I realized I had a knife and fork in my hands."

One of the rules at the Elmira prison in New York where he did a major stint was that each inmate carry his fork and spoon to the back of the mess hall and then, in the presence of a correction officer, toss both into a garbage can. Since prison officials viewed the plastic utensils as potential weapons, this was the "ticket" out of the dining area.

Leaving meals with silverware in hand was a habit he picked up while in prison, a jailhouse lesson, one that, though not serious, took a while to unlearn. It wasn't the only lesson he had to unlearn. And Danny Sanders, out for more than 10 years now and a successful counselor of ex-offenders in New York City, is not the only inmate to leave prison with lessons to unlearn.

Yet tragically, in state after state, the most important lesson we expect a prison to teach an inmate – how to leave and not return – is not being taught. Graded on this basis, prisons are failing, miserably.

The share of inmates who commit another crime and do another stretch in a state prison approaches 60 percent. These thousands of repeat offenders are the greatest reason for overcrowded prisons and the prison crisis in America today, says James Q. Wilson, a professor of political science at the University of California at Los Angeles. Whatever went wrong in their lives to get them locked up in the first place is still going wrong when they get out.

Putting it simply, the typical inmate's stay in prison serves as punishment. It does little to help him learn to behave in a way that society deems right.

The overwhelming number of inmates are left to their own initiative to change so that they become law abiding upon release. And they are to do this while confined in overcrowded prisons, experiencing a life radically different from anything that they are going to face when they return to the streets.

INDEED, for many poorly educated, unskilled, drug-using, often minority inmates, it is as if prison life were designed to thwart successful adjustment back into lawful society. Prison offers little else than a severely diminished chance to get their lives right again.

It is critical that you make the decision to reform while you are still inside, the earlier the better, says Willy Oxendine, out seven months now after four years in New York prisons. Otherwise, "you can become much worse," he says. Not claiming to be anybody's angel, he says it hit him like a ton of bricks once he settled into the routine at the Wyoming penitentiary in upstate New York that "half the guys I was in with I would never associate with on the street."

When did Mr. Oxendine make his decision to reform? "I started cleaning house about six months after I was in," he says, referring to mental "ripples" all inmates have when they finally come to terms with the hostility and isolation of prison, whether it's being alone in your cell, playing basketball in the yard, or trying to put your head under a pillow and sleep in the bedlam of crowded dormitory bunking.

"Ripples happen to your mind in prison," says Oxendine. "I thought about how my wife drove herself to deliver my baby; my sister was raped and I wasn't there to console her; my parents needed to have a house built and my two hands were behind bars," he says, looking down at his big hands that go with his hulking 6-foot, 3-inch frame.

And especially the ripple of his wife's face at his sentencing. "I never seen that much hurt on a person's face," he says.

"Ripples are what start you to change," he says. "Before I went to prison, if I didn't have enough clothes, or whatever, I'd grab a gun, I'd go to scheming. If you see it, you want it, you grab it," he recalls. "I had bad values, I knew this. You have to change your values in prison if you want to change them when you're out."

Enrolled at Bronx Community College in New York City in a unique paralegal studies program, one that he began while behind bars, he knows he landed in a safety net. He is given a good chance of succeeding, of extricating himself from the criminal-justice system and leading a fulfilling, productive, and free life.

About 40 percent of state inmates enter some form of pre-release program at the end of their sentence. The rest get a one-way bus ticket, a new suit, and anywhere from $40 to $200, depending on the state.

Reform and preparation for a successful transition back to straight society must start the second week after you're in, says Jo Ann Page, a New York lawyer who works with ex-offenders. "People come out angry – and part of the transition is working with that anger," she says.

One of the biggest criticisms you can level at pre-release programs in many state prison systems, she says, is that they are so artificial, so incapable of dealing with the experience the inmate has just had emotionally, as well as the experience he is going to have when he goes back out on the street.

"We know how to leave people alone, and we know how to throw them into Attica, . . . we don't know how to do anything [much] in between," says Ms. Page. "A job and a place to live after you're out are the two most important 'transition' programs you can have," she says. "Just what most inmates don't have."

'A FEW of the states have got a handle on it, but not many,'' says Warren Burger, former chief justice of the United States. "If we don't train [inmates], they are going to be worse when they come out. Who's going to hire them," he asks, "and if they don't work, what will they do?"

"The first three to six months out are the most critical for a man," says Dr. Allan Wolk, director of paralegal studies at Bronx Community College. "This is when the risk of falling back into old habits is greatest."

But one of the big myths of prison reform is that rehabilitation programs abound behind bars, says John DiIulio, a professor at the Wilson School of Government at Princeton University. "They don't," he says.

"And when they do, you are only talking about 3 to 5 hours of a 24-hour day," says Lacey Williams an ex-offender in New York City. For the majority of inmates, most of their prison time is decidedly unproductive, he says.

"The struggle is to redefine yourself from what the institution says you are," says Jim Proctor, an inmate at the Maryland Penitentiary in Baltimore. Once you decide you want to reform, and you alone must make this decision, he says, then you can look for programs.

"Inmates adapt to the environment," says James N. Rollins, warden at the Maryland Penitentiary in Baltimore. "If the environment says you must arm yourself, join a gang, they do that. If the environment says work on schooling, work on job training, they do that." Mr. Rollins runs a prison that works hard to provide the latter environment.

Because of overcrowding in many states, combined with a threat of violence, thoughts of reform, which do not predominate in the first place, come even harder for many young first offenders, corrections officials say. They run up against one of the harder facts of prison life, the need to form alliances with other inmates, relationships that often run counter to any desire to improve themselves.

"You must form alliances when you are in prison," says Harold Walker, recently out after a 5-year, 4-month stint. He has spent 21 of his 54 years doing hard time and has been in and out of most major prisons in New York. He was wounded in the Attica riot of 1971. "That's just the way it is or your chances of being killed are very high," he says. Because "at some point in time you have to attach yourself to someone or some group," says Mr. Walker. "Otherwise, if there is a throwdown [a brawl, a riot], you're alone."

But no one should kid himself, the challenge of making the transition from prison life to mainstream society will always be great, Walker says. Laughing, he recalls a funny, yet painful, experience that points out the challenge of making a successful transition.

He and two other inmates were due for release. "Everything was so highly coordinated, from the door of my cell right through the sign-out," he says. "A guard escorted us each step of the way. But as soon as we got outside the door, and it was snowing heavily, all supervision ended. Momentarily, I didn't know what to do or where to go. Neither did the other two inmates who were with me, even though all we were going to do was cross the street and catch a bus."

WHAT CAN BE DONE NOW

San Quentin, Calif.

'COME to San Quentin to learn how not to build a prison," says Daniel Vasquez, the latest of the "blood-and-guts" wardens at the notorious prison "on the bay."

"They spilled our guts and we spilled theirs," he says, in referring to the bloody history of San Quentin, where he has charge of 1,750 inmates – more on death row (224) than any other prison in the United States. In his 20 years in the line of duty, he has seen six inmates shot and killed by guards from the towers that sit atop the prison walls.

After 135 years, this maximum-security prison is scheduled for downgrading to a medium-security facility. The more incorrigible inmates will be farmed out to other lockups around the state, principally a massive new complex, a prison city called Del Norte, soon to open in northern California.

"I'm the first to cheer San Quentin's downgrading," says Mr. Vasquez. "When I took over, I couldn't feed, shower, or exercise the number of inmates I had in a normal [work] shift." He just barely can today.

In about 38 states around the country, courts have had to step in to demand better conditions for inmates. But can anything corrections officials do really improve conditions and help reduce a 60-percent recidivism rate? Or will the extra beds resulting from the most explosive growth in prison construction in US history continue to be outdistanced by an even more rapid rate of incarceration?

Conventional wisdom has it that "no one ever got elected by calling for better-run prisons." And yet in some of the more-populous states, such as California, the high numbers of inmates and the high costs of locking them up will force just such a campaign, says the California state superintendent of public instruction, Bill Honig. He has already seen his plans for building more elementary schools, "just to stay even with our rising younger population," collide, then lose, to funding commitments for more prisons.

"You want to know where prison reform starts?" asks Mr. Honig. "I'll tell you. It's the third grade. We know the high risk groups who will drop out of school. We know individuals from these groups make up a disproportionate share of prison inmates. Give me part of the $20,000 a year we now spend [in California] on these kids as adults, give it to me now, and we can make sure they won't wind up in prison, costing the sta. money not only to lock them up, but for the crimes they've committed, and for the welfare payments if they have a family."

For this spending shift to happen, it would take a major sea change in the way we sentence people, says Ken Schoen, director of the criminal-justice program at the Edna McConnell Clark Foundation. Mr. Schoen was a co-author of a Minnesota sentencing bill in the 1970s that has given that state one of the lowest per-capita incarceration rates in the country.

MINNESOTA'S plan is not on many states' agenda, though, says Anthony Travisono, executive director of the American Correctional Association. The big industrial states have so far been able to absorb the increased costs of expansion and provide more beds. He does not expect a fiscal crunch to hit hard enough to make changes in the status quo for at least five years. If and when it does, it will still take eight to 10 more years to straighten things out, he says.

What can be done in the interim? Three steps could be taken by state corrections departments to help create better prisons in both the short and long term, says John DiIulio, an authority on prison management at the Woodrow Wilson School of Government at Princeton University:

1. Provide continuity in the commissioner's office. For the last 15 years, less than one-third of all state adult corrections departments have had a commissioner with a tenure of more than five years. In more than one-third of the states, the commissioner has held office for less than three years. This high turnover fosters a lack of continuity and a power vacuum at many levels of management. Each state must find a way for its commissioner to be independent of the four-year political cycle of the governor, yet still be accountable to elected officials.

2. Adopt the practice of unit management. The concept has been employed since 1970 by the Federal Bureau of Prisons. Under this system, senior corrections officers are given broad authority to run a cellblock or dormitory as a separate unit. In this way early signs of trouble are more easily read (troublemakers, such as drug dealers and rapists, can be identified, separated, or sent to different quarters), and potential suicides are more easily spotted.

Unit management also results in fewer staff rotations, allowing management to measure performance better. Officers, given more responsibility, act more as professionals. Morale is boosted both for staff and inmates.

Under unit management, more opportunities are provided for visits from family and friends. Prison officials concede that the risk of contraband entering a prison grows as more visits are allowed. But a staff

The incarceration rate continues to climb

Year	US population (in millions)	Numbers of Prisoners	Prisoners per 100,000 population
1988	246	582,000	237
1987	244	546,000	224
1983	235	420,000	180
1980	227	321,000	142
1970	203	196,000	97
1960	179	213,000	119
1950	151	166,000	110
1940	132	174,000	132
1930	123	148,000	121
1925	106	93,000	88
1918	92	75,000	82
1900	76	57,000	75
1890	63	45,000	71
1870	40	33,000	83
1860	31	19,000	60
1850	23	7,000	30
1840	17	4,000	24

Source: American Correctional Association

familiar with the conduct and habits of its inmates is also able to deal better with the potential increase in contraband. Meanwhile, one study indicates that inmates who receive six or more visits while in prison have less than half the recidivism rate of inmates who have no visits.

3. Allow products manufactured by inmates in state prisons to be sold to the federal government, subject to minimum wage laws and regular competitive bidding regulations.

Currently, prison industries in the federal system have a large ready market, the federal bureaucracy. State prison industries, where they exist, are severely limited in what they can produce and to whom they can sell. The result is endless hours of unproductive idleness for inmates. Even when there is a prison industries program in place, too often it is nothing more than a make-work project, with equipment used and job skills learned having little bearing to a real-world labor market.

MEANWHILE, says Mr. Travisono, a new-old way to ease overcrowding is being looked at nationwide: "shock incarceration." First used in the 1930s, it is a kind of "boot camp" targeted at young felons doing their first hard time. It is an effort to impose an intense dose of order on young, often chaotic and directionless, lives.

In return for serving fewer years, young inmates agree to a six-month regimen of military drills, drug treatment, physical exercise, back-breaking work, and academic study. A 16-hour day includes such activities as a two-mile run, calisthenics, chopping trees, and carrying logs.

"I have been very surprised to see how fast this idea has taken off with politicians," says Travisono. Its main appeal is that it has a quid pro quo, enough punishment (which the public demands), before a sentence is reduced, he says. Five states now run variations of shock incarceration. "There will be 30 states with similar programs by 1990," he says.

The only pitfall, says Mr. Schoen, is the danger that judges who normally wouldn't sentence a young offender to two or three years of hard time will now see shock incarceration as a workable option. "Teaching him a lesson for six months" might be the thinking, says Schoen, in effect widening the net of individuals who come under the control of a state's criminal-justice system. Schoen favors New York's plan whereby an individual must first be sentenced before he can apply for shock incarceration.

Privatization of prisons is another development that has the potential to provide better, more humane, and more economically run prisons, say corrections officials. In privatization, for-profit companies take over from the state some, or all, of the functions of running a prison.

But the verdict is out as to the effects privatization of prisons may have, says Allen F. Breed of the National Council on Crime and Delinquency. Only a few states are experimenting with the concept. Nevertheless, "It will provide a fresh stimulus to make the government sector, as a result of competition, work more efficiently," he says.

A study by Joan Petersilia, published by the RAND Corporation, cites counties in more than 40 states as adopting "intensive supervision" probation programs, most of which include paying into a victims' fund or providing mandated community service. These programs, between probation and imprisonment, provide for daily, if not hourly, checks on the status of the offender. They have received widespread attention in many states as the costs of incarceration have climbed.

A novel idea recommended by former Chief Justice of the United States Warren Burger – one that he says would increase public awareness about what goes on behind prison walls – would be to return to the practice of assigning "official visitors" to each prison. This was a common practice before World War II, he says.

These visitors would report to the governor (and the news media) on conditions. Mr. Burger recommends that leading community figures, such as corporation heads, educators, or church officials, be appointed to these positions.

Prison Crowding In The United States: The Data

STEVEN R. SCHLESINGER, Ph.D.
Director
Bureau of Justice Statistics
U.S. Department of Justice

This paper was presented as part of the Beto Chair, Visiting Distinguished Professor series (1985-86) at the College of Criminal Justice, Sam Houston State University, Huntsville, Texas.

The problem of prison crowding, as you know, is severe and pervasive. As the constant demand for more prison beds collides with limited correctional resources, we are forced to confront one of the most serious issues in criminal justice today.

Four out of five states have been found to be operating prison facilities under conditions that violate the Eighth Amendment. The courts have placed entire state correctional systems in receivership, appointed masters to operate state systems, and ordered the early release of thousands of offenders. The courts have even threatened some state officials with fines and jail terms for noncompliance with orders to relieve prison conditions.

But crowding creates other problems for correctional officials as well. Overcrowded prisons mean major management problems: staff morale declines; staff turnover increases; population control becomes formidable; and the outbreak of violence constantly threatens. And as prison facilities reach their saturation point, state prisoners back up in city and county jails reproducing all the problems of crowding at the local level.

This was the state of affairs at the end of 1985: Prison systems were operating at 106 percent to 121 percent of capacity. (Incidentally, the American Correctional Association recommends that a facility never operate at more than 90 percent of capacity. Prison officials always need some room for maneuvering). More than two percent of the prison population was backed up in local jails. (In Louisiana, Kentucky, New Jersey, and Mississippi the backup was running at more than 10 percent.) And 19 states reported releasing a total of more than 18,600 inmates ahead of schedule specifically for the purpose of relieving crowded conditions. This meant that more than one out of every three inmates leaving prison in these 14 states received an early release.

Between 1979 and 1984, the states added 126 new prisons, increasing the total available housing space by more than 3.7 million square feet. Expansion in existing prison facilities over the same years increased available housing space by nearly 1.6 million square feet. Together, these additions represented a 29 percent increase in total space available to house the nation's prisoners over the five years, a period in which the prison population grew by 45 percent.

In 1984, 9.6 persons were committed to prison by the courts for every ten thousand adults in the general population. Between 1978 and 1983 court commitment rates for the nation increased from 7.2 per ten thousand adults to 10.1. This dramatic change is probably the result of heightened public concern about crime as it is expressed in such sentencing reforms as mandatory prison terms and determinate sentencing. At these rates of commitment to prison, three to five percent of the males born today could expect to be imprisoned at least once in their lifetime.

Both the number of prison admissions per 100 of the most serious crimes reported to the police and the number of admissions per 100 arrests have also increased considerably. Between 1978 and 1984 admissions per 100 of these serious crimes rose from 2.7 per 100 to 3.9; while the number of admissions relative to adult arrests rose from 18.5 per 100 arrests to 24.6 per 100.

Now, look at prison crowding from a different perspective. In the 27 years between 1957 and 1984, serious crime — that is murder, rape, robbery and burglary — increased by 414 percent. You will be heartened to learn that arrests for serious crime also grew considerably, increasing by 385 percent over the 27 year period. The state prison popula-

"Prison Crowding In The United States: The Data," by Steven R. Schlesinger, from *Criminal Justice Research Bulletin*, Vol. 3, No. 1, 1987, pp. 1-3. Reprinted by permission.

tion, on the other hand, grew by only 165 percent, and prison capacity grew at the slowest rate of all, an estimated 79 percent. In other words, the prison population grew less than half as fast as serious crime, and prison capacity grew less than half as fast as the prison population.

Who Enters Prison?

Who are the people flooding through the prison gates and breaking population records year after year? Four out of five come directly from trial courts or from probation with a median sentence of three years. Most of the rest are parole and mandatory release violators, though a few hundred each year are returned escapees.

Bureau of Justice Statistics data indicate that persons entering prison are mostly male, mostly young, and disproportionately black: 93 percent are men; 48 percent are under 25; 54 percent are white, 45 percent, black; and one percent, Asians, Pacific Islanders or Native Americans.

What offenses brought them to prison? Murder and manslaughter accounts for six percent; rape and other sexual assaults for five percent; robbery, 14 percent; aggravated assault, seven percent; burglary, 26 percent; larceny, 11 percent; auto theft, two percent; forgery, fraud, and embezzlement, six percent; drugs, eight percent; and public order and miscellaneous crimes, nine percent.

In other words, one in every three persons entering prison has been convicted of a violent offense. If you add to this group persons who are not currently sentenced for a violent crime, but who have served time for a violent crime in the past, you find that more than half the persons committed to prison by the courts are convicted violent offenders. More than four-fifths of the offenders entering prison have a record of prior convictions. More than three-fifths have served time and more than two-fifths were on probation or parole at the time of admission.

Property offenders entering prison are especially likely to be recidivists. More than two-thirds of the burglars, auto thieves, forgers, defrauders, and embezzlers going to prison have been there before. Violent offenders, on the other hand, are more likely to be entering prison for the first time. The explanation, when you think about it, is fairly simple.

The likelihood of going to prison for a given offense is related both to the seriousness of the offense and to the criminal record of the offender. In the absence of a criminal record, it usually takes a rather serious offense to receive a term of confinement. However, combined with a record, a less serious crime can earn a prison term. This is, in effect, a sensible system of allocating a scarce resource: prison space.

A final point about persons entering prison: Half the recidivists have been out of prison less than 23 months and recidivists returning to prison for robbery, burglary or auto theft have not been out that long. About half the recidivists — more than one-fourth of all persons entering prison — would not have been out on the street at the time they committed their current offense if they had served the full amount of their previous sentence. Theoretically, at least, their present crime could have been averted if they served their maximum prison sentence.

Who Leaves Prison?

Now, let's look at the people getting out. They have, as you would expect, about the same overall race and sex composition as those entering prison. They are, as you would also expect, a little bit older. While 48 percent of prison admittees are under 25, about 35 percent of the releases are in this age range. The median age of persons leaving prison is 27, a year older than that for those arriving.

One of the most interesting things about persons leaving prison is how they are getting out. In 1978, more than 70 percent of all those leaving prison were released by a parole board decision. That number declined steadily in each of the next six years, and in 1984, 43 percent of the departing prisoners had received a parole board release. Concurrently, mandatory releases rose from six percent of those released to 27 percent. Prisoners who "maxed out," that is, who left only after the expiration of their full sentence, remained a stable 14 to 17 percent of all releasees during this six year period.

These numbers dramatically illustrate the sharp shift away from the parole board as the principal way out of prison. This shift has led a number of states to abolish or limit parole board decisionmaking in the last nine years. The shift away from parole release has been brought about by rising public concern about the effectiveness of parole decisions — as they affect public safety and as they undermine the certainty of sentences imposed. The ability of parole boards to reshape and remodel judicially imposed sentences has been sharply curtailed in most states through the enactment of mandatory minimum and determinate sentencing laws.

Actual Time Served in Prisons

In 1983, the average prisoner released had served 26 months, including credit for jail time. By offense, average time served for those released was: murder, seven and a half years; manslaughter, three years; rape, four and a half years; robbery, three years; aggravated assault, two years and five months; burglary, 21 months; larceny, 16 months; auto theft, 17 months; forgery, fraud, or embezzlement, 19 months; drugs, 19 months; public order, 13 months. Other than for murder, the time to be served for those admitted during 1983 was approximately equal to that actually served by those released in 1983.

The median time served of 19 months for all offenses is just about what prisoners have been serving since 1926. Excluding World War II, when potential soldiers were not put in prison except for serious crimes carrying lengthy sentences, median time served has ranged between 16 and 21 months. Some caution has to be used when comparing 1983 to earlier years. A different set of reporting states, new reporting criteria, and different computational procedures for the calculation of median time served were all introduced and may affect some of the comparisons.

Nevertheless, stability in median time served for those released over time is quite remarkable, especially since today's prison population is considerably more violent than those in the past. In 1982 one-third of all exiting prisoners had been convicted of a violent crime. In 1933 it was only one-fifth. Yet median time served in 1982 was a month less than it was in 1933. For this to be the case, crime for crime, offenders must be serving less time now than they did before.

Let's compare: Robbery — in 1933, 32 months; in 1982, seven months less. Rape — in 1933, also 32 months; in 1982, 4 months more. (Of course, in 1933 the rape of an adult woman was still a capital crime.) Aggravated assault — 17 months in 1933 and 15 in 1982. Burglary — also 17 months in 1933; in 1982, three months less. Larceny — in 1933, 16 months; in 1982, six months less.

It is not accurate, then, to say that prisoners are serving as much time today as they did in time past. For some crimes like aggravated assault, time served is about the same, but for crimes like burglary and robbery — the two most common offenses among the prison population, median time served for those released is actually less than it has been in the past.

Alternatives to Prison

It has been suggested that one answer to the problem of prison crowding lies in alternatives to prison, that these can and should be used to a greater degree than they are now. Popular alternatives are community supervision, community service, restitution, and sentences served only on weekends.

At the end of 1985 nearly three million convicted offenders were under some form of correctional supervision. Nearly three out of every four of these were already being supervised in the community as probationers or parolees. In recent years, probation populations have been growing at a faster rate than prison populations. If we are going to add to their number, we must decide on the criteria to be used. What combination of offense severity and criminal history suggests that an offender can be left in the community and what combination of these factors suggests that he belongs behind prison bars?

Suppose we decided that we would eliminate imprisonment for anyone who had never been convicted of a violent crime. Based on our sample survey of prison inmates in 1979, we estimate that we could reduce our prison population by a third! But suppose, on reflection, we decided that offenders who had a history of prior incarceration should serve time in prison for their current offense. Then the candidates for release drop to 11 percent of the prison population. If, on further reflection, we decided not to release anyone who had received probation on a previous conviction, we would find ourselves down to less than five percent.

In other words, about 95 percent of those in prison in 1979 were convicted violent offenders, or were convicted recidivists. Most of the remaining five percent were convicted of arson, weapons violations, drug trafficking, burglary, or of multiple offenses. Thus, less than two percent of the males in prison in 1979 were first-time offenders, convicted of a single non-violent crime other than those I listed before, remaining for possible placement in the community.

Conclusion

My overall perception is that states are willing to build to accommodate the growth in prisoner populations and will need to continue these construction efforts to avert the problems of having to resort to early releases or increased crowding in local jails. Based upon our findings from self-report inmate studies, it is clear that imprisonment is rarely used as a first resort; rather, most inmates are either chronic or violent offenders.

Our studies of inmates also indicate that about half of those released from prisons will return. One way of looking at this finding is to become pessimistic and contend that prisons do little to effect behavioral change. Alternatively, however, we could focus greater energy and resources on understanding why half of those released **do not** return and attempt to understand the reasons for disengagement from a criminal career. It could very well be true that the harsh realities of prison deter many from continued criminal activity. My sense is that such a course of research may be just as important for public policy as learning why people commit crime in the first place.

You're Under Arrest—AT HOME

With a jail's daily operating costs of $35-$125 per prisoner, home detention represents big savings for hard-pressed correction officials.

Fred Scaglione

Mr. Scaglione is a New York free-lance writer.

NOBODY wants a prison in his or her neighborhood, but don't be surprised if that split level next door is already a jail cell. As the nation's penal system staggers under the weight of an ever-rising inmate population, corrections officials are taking a new, high-tech look at an age-old technique—house arrest. Jurisdictions in 32 states now are sending almost 2,000 offend ers to their homes, rather than to traditional lock-ups, and outfitting them with an array of electronic equipment to ensure they stay there. "We believe this is an important enhancement to a criminal justice system that is already overburdened," says James K. Stewart, director of the National Institute of Justice (NIJ).

Offenders accepted into these programs are given a daily schedule, allowing them to leave the house for work, approved counseling sessions, and religious services. Some are fitted with continuously signaling anklets or wristlets which broadcast to a second unit attached to their home telephone lines. If the offender leaves the house and takes the transmitter out of the broadcast range, the telephone-based receiver automatically calls the program's central monitoring station. There, a computer programmed with the offender's daily schedule determines if the absence is authorized or if a violation report is warranted.

Other jurisdictions use a computer-generated random calling system, requiring the offender to verify his presence in a variety of ways each time the phone rings. The central schedule monitoring station works the same in both cases. Neither system eavesdrops on the offender's conversations or activities, nor can they track him if he leaves the house. "The monitor is the baby sitter and I'm your mom," explains In-House Arrest Officer Trish Dosset to new program participants in Palm Beach County, Fla. "For the next 30 days, you don't go anywhere without asking me first."

The programs also require regular face-to-face meetings, verification of employment and hours worked, telephone checks, and occasional site visits at the offender's home and workplace. Clients with drug and alcohol problems may be required to attend counseling sessions and undergo randomly scheduled urine tests.

Inmates may be the nation's fastest growing community group. By June, 1986, there were over 750,000 residents of Federal, state, and local penal institutions, twice the number of 10 years earlier. The American Correctional Association expects the population to double again by soon after the year 2000, as legislators continue to demand longer sentences generally and mandatory imprisonment for specific offenses.

Law enforcement officials have been unable to accommodate their burgeoning clientele. Prisons in Connecticut, California, and Ohio, for example, were 83%, 76%, and 69%, respectively, above their designed capacities in 1986. Almost one-quarter of all city and county jails now have court orders limiting their populations.

Efforts to expand the prison system have been devastatingly expensive. The average construction cost of a new jail cell is estimated at $75,000. Jurisdictions then go on to pay operating costs ranging from $35 to $125 per night. It's not surprising that correctional expenses are now the fastest growing segment of state government spending.

Electronic monitors, on the other hand, cost anywhere from $2 to $10 per day for each offender, depending on the type of equipment and the size of the program. Staff costs will vary according to the level of personal supervision a program specifies. Clackamas County, Ore., estimates

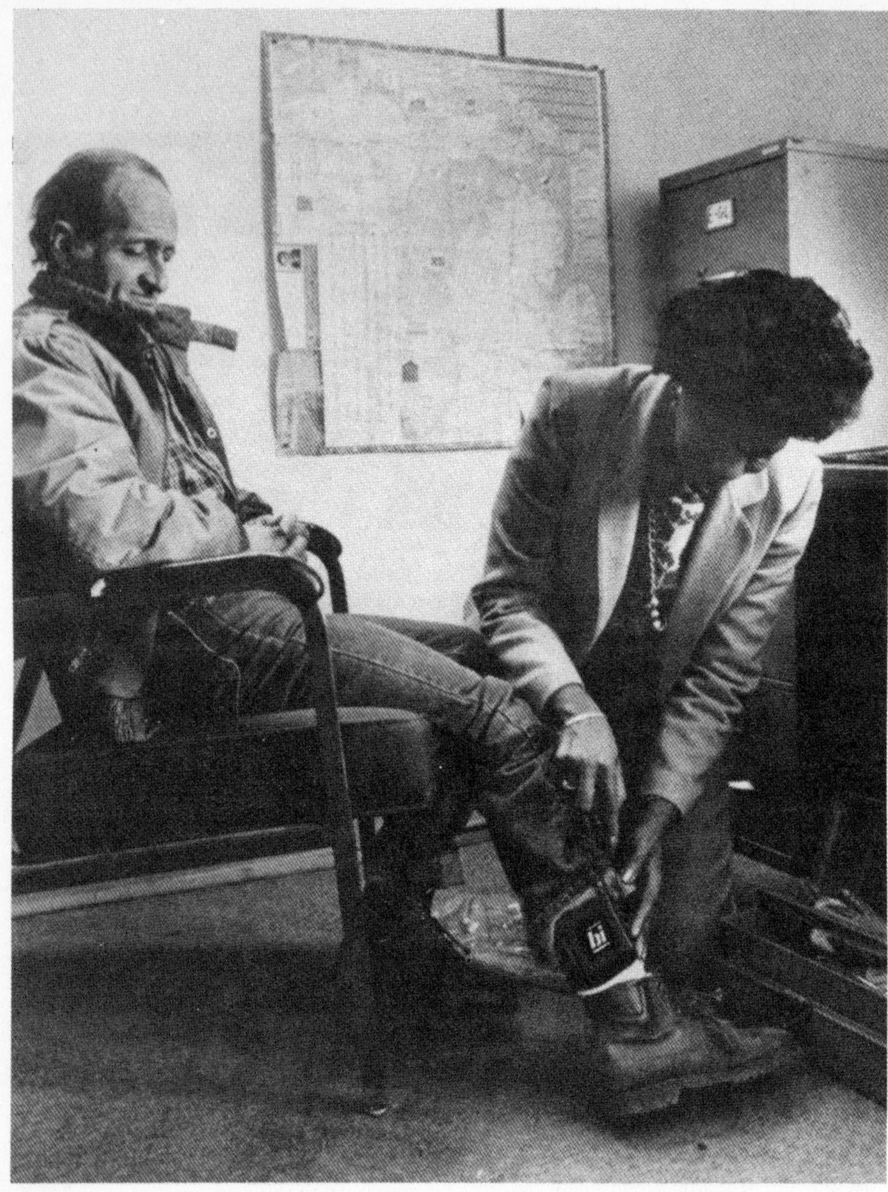

A continuously signaling device is installed on the ankle of a man under house arrest. A telephone-based receiver will call authorities if his body transmitter is taken out of broadcast range.

total costs at $12 per day; Utah officials quote $17.

No matter how you add it up, home detention represents big savings for hard-pressed corrections officials. "We're buying additional jail beds for $10," says Marie Whittington as Orange County, Calif., prepares to expand its house arrest program from 25 to 75 slots.

New Jersey, with 400 felons on pre-release from its overcrowded prison system, estimates that its Intensive Supervision Probation (ISP) program is saving approximately $6,700,000 in direct expenditures annually. In addition, working program participants usually make a wide range of payments that further offset the costs of supervision; most programs collect a fee from participants to cover the cost of monitoring equipment. Palm Beach County's PRIDE, Inc., for example, charges the fairly typical amount of $7 per day. Offenders also pay taxes, fines, and restitution as required. They often are obligated to work on community service projects as well. New Jersey estimates that these payments and activities add up to an additional $1,400,000.

Life-saving programs

Yet, these programs may be saving more than money. They may be saving lives. Success stories are depressingly rare in the world of correction, but many administrators of home detention programs like to tell one—the same one. It's about the offender who comes to their program near the end of his personal rope. He's sick—busted in more ways than one. He gets a monitor and a curfew, and goes to work every morning and comes home every night. He stops seeing his friends on the corner or at the bar and they don't bother to visit him. He gets to know his wife and kids, stops drinking or doing drugs, saves his money, and works around the house. Nine months later, they take off the monitor and he still comes home at night. He's got a job, a bank account, and a whole new relationship with his family. The monitor and house arrest have made him healthy, wealthy, and wise.

If it sounds like a law-enforcement fairy tale, it is. However, for certain offenders it's also true. "I now own my own deli," says a 25-year-old man after five years on cocaine, six months in prison, and 10 months on the New Jersey ISP program. "I do not do drugs and I will not go back to doing drugs. This program was a lifesaver for me."

An auto mechanic, also in his mid-20's and convicted on drug charges, stands in the service station where he works, talking about his wife, baby, and the five-year sentence he started serving in state prison. "I'm going to make it," he asserts, explaining how he's regained much of the weight he lost to drugs. "That cost me $2,800," he adds, pointing to a large metal tool cabinet. "I never could save up to buy decent tools before."

"We've had people who, for the first time in their lives, are working. They're going home and they're providing some kind of support for their family," says Ingrid Lewis, administrator of the house arrest program in Clackamas County. "They're at home and they have to take care of responsibilities at home," explains Capt. Ken Lane of the Fairfax County, Va., Sheriff's Office. However, corrections officials, perhaps out of experience, are quick to burst their own bubble. They are cautious about predicting success or prescribing monitoring programs for too many offenders.

Many of the plans which have sprung up in recent years mirror the two original Palm Beach County models established in 1984. Approximately one-third of all participants throughout the county are traffic offenders, predominately drunk-drivers. Some jurisdictions extend participation to work-release inmates and to those convicted of low-level property crimes. A history of violence, drug abuse, or sexual misconduct often will disqualify an applicant. White-collar criminals also make appearances in many of the local programs. In July, 1987, for example, a Los Angeles court sentenced a local slumlord to house arrest in one of his rat-infested buildings.

Growth also has come through monitoring a wide range of offenders with varying, and more serious, backgrounds. Clackamas County, for example, assigns offenders convicted of violent felonies like armed robbery and manslaughter. They are also one of the few programs to accept sex offenders. "We look at the individual, not just the crime," says Ingrid Lewis.

As the technology has grown more reliable, a number of states have incorporated monitoring into pre-release programs aimed at freeing up bed space in crowded prisons. Inmates agree to a variety of conditions, including monitoring and curfews, in exchange for the chance to get out of prison early. Michigan, for example, began providing monitors to convicted felons in its Extended Furlough Program in April, 1987. It now monitors nearly 1,000 offenders.

About 90% of all participants successfully complete home-monitoring programs. "I'm continuously amazed with the level of compliance that prisoners give us," states Jim Putnam of the Michigan Department of Correction. However, there still is relatively little hard data to support the gut feelings of administrators that these successful graduates go on to live crime-free lives. A recent survey of 327 offenders who completed the New Jersey ISP program since 1984 did find that only four percent had been rearrested in the state, an excellent result compared with typical studies of recidivism. The National Institute of Justice is funding a series of tests to follow offenders randomly assigned to electronic monitoring as opposed to other programs.

Of the 10% who fail to complete the programs, the majority are sent back to jail for violating in-house rules—missed curfews, refusal to attend counseling sessions, or failed urine tests. A small fraction are sent back because of new arrests. In county-run programs, these tend to be relatively infrequent and for minor offenses.

State-run pre-release programs generally have a greater return rate with more serious rearrests despite screening out 70-80% of all potential candidates. The New Jersey ISP program, for example, has returned approximately seven percent of its participants to prison because of new charges, with approximately two-thirds of those for felonies. Michigan's program recently suffered a murder/suicide by one of its participants, the most serious crime committed by a monitored offender to date. Incidents such as these appear inevitable when offenders are sent back into the community. Yet, so far, electronically monitored home detention seems to have drawn high marks in protecting the public safety.

If anything, administrators, particularly on the local level, have been criticized for being too cautious in their selection of offenders. "Judges are gun shy," says Joan Petersilia of the Rand Corporation, a research/consulting firm in Santa Monica, Calif. "They're picking people who they are fairly sure won't embarrass the program." If this means that monitoring is used for offenders who wouldn't normally draw jail time and pose little risk to the public safety, she argues that the program is self-defeating. "It's costly. It's intrusive. I don't think we can afford to do those symbolic punishments anymore."

Monitoring probation

However, there is a group now walking the streets of society for which electronic monitoring is appropriate, Petersilia believes. The nation's overflowing prisons have swelled the probation caseload to over 1,800,000, more than twice the number incarcerated. At the same time, dwindling resources have reduced routine probation supervision to an exercise in paper-shuffling. "Half of all people now on probation are convicted felons," she states, "and a quarter of them are convicted of violent crimes." A recent Rand study found that 65% of California probationers are rearrested within 40 months, 75% for serious crimes. This population, she feels, is much too dangerous to be receiving nominal probation supervision. "The system must develop intermediate forms of punishment more restrictive than routine probation, but not as severe or expensive as prison."

Electronic monitoring may be at least part of the answer. Some officials worry, however, that monitoring will become a popular and counterproductive crutch. "I'm concerned about programs that put too much emphasis on the equipment and not enough emphasis on a balanced program of equipment and personal supervision," says Marie Whittington, director of Orange County's Work Furlough Program. "The monitors are only a back-up," agrees New Jersey ISP officer Mike McCree. "What makes this program work is close personal contact."

In fact, New Jersey puts electronic monitors on only 20 problem cases out of its total of 400 participants. Another 200 receive computer-generated nightly telephone calls, but are not required to wear a bracelet to verify their identities. Unlike many jurisdictions which require only one office visit per week, New Jersey's program averages 27 contacts per month, many of them face to face in the offender's home. Participants attend weekly rap sessions, special ISP-sponsored drug counseling sessions, and 16 hours per month of community service. They also must maintain an up-to-date diary and personal budget.

"We get involved in every aspect of their lives," McCree says, adding with a smile, "I've been to two or three weddings and we've got a wall full of baby pictures."

Although offenders with monitors may certainly feel that Big Brother is watching, the American Civil Liberties Union (ACLU) has yet to take issue with any of the house arrest programs. "The overarching problem in correction is overcrowding," says Ed Koren, an attorney with the ACLU's National Prison Project. "We'd like to see this happen if it can get people out of prison." Therefore, while it remains sensitive to the threat of abuse through overutilization and to possibilities of discrimination in selection and offender contribution requirements, the ACLU basically is watching as the strategy continues to develop.

While programs similar to those already in existence are likely to continue to grow rapidly, new technological developments are offering the possibility of even more comprehensive electronic surveillance. One manufacturer has added a blood alcohol-level monitoring system to its house arrest equipment. At least two others are developing methods to track an offender's position geographically as he travels throughout a metropolitan area and report it back to a computerized central control station for comparison with his approved daily schedule.

Some corrections officials respond favorably to this prospect of expanded surveillance. Others, however, are skeptical. "I think the technology is a long way off," says Joan Petersilia, "but I think the public acceptance of that is an even longer way off." Nevertheless, electronic monitoring and house arrest clearly are here to stay as correctional strategies. "The future of this is very bright," concludes the NIJ's Stewart.

Whipping

William D. Slicker

William D. Slicker practices law in St. Petersburg, Florida. He received his B.A. and J.D. degrees from Florida State University.

During January, 1989, a Delaware senator introduced in bill in the Delaware legislature that would mandate five to forty lashes "well laid on" in public as punishment for drug trafficking in hard drugs.[1] Since whipping as legal punishment has not been in use in most of the states for many years, such a bill piqued my curiosity.

The Delaware bill was not the first attempt to restore whipping as a statutory punishment. In 1905, President Teddy Roosevelt recommended the whipping post for wife beaters, and a bill was introduced in the Massachusetts legislature that would have so provided.[2] In 1931, there was an effort to restore whipping in Georgia.[3] In 1937, a bill was introduced in Massachusetts that would have allowed whipping as punishment for driving while intoxicated.[4]

Some History

Until it fell into disuse, whipping as legal punishment had a long history. The Mosaic law provided for forty lashes.[5] Whipping was included in England's early statutory penalties for, inter alia, begging without a license.[6] After the 1689 English Bill of Rights prohibition against "illegal and cruel punishments,"[7] whipping was still a legal punishment reported by Blackstone.[8]

The English brought whipping with them when they came to America. The official records of New Castle, Delaware show that on June 3, 1679, Robberd Hutchinson was given 39 lashes for stealing.[9] The Colonies punished a variety of crimes with public whippings of up to forty lashes.[10] The territories[11] and the states[12] continued using whipping (commonly 39 lashes) well into the 1800's. After an outbreak of robberies in which the victims were garrotted, England enacted a statute in 1863 allowing up to 50 strokes as punishment for robbery with violence.[13]

However, curbs on whipping were also being enacted during the 1800's. In 1820, England abolished the whipping of women.[14] The United States abolished whipping in federal institutions in 1839 and on board sailing vessels in 1850.[15] By the end of the Civil War,[16] most states had dropped whipping as an authorized penalty. By the early 1900's, many states had prohibited whipping as a form of discipline of prisoners, although a number of states still allowed it.[17]

In 1923, Martin Tabert, a North Dakota youth aged 22, set out to travel and work his way as he went. He made it into north Florida where he ran out of money. He was arrested for riding a train without a ticket. When he could not pay the $25.00 fine, he was imprisoned and leased out to a lumber company. While working in swamp water up to his waist, he caught a fever and could not work fast enough to please the whipping boss who whipped Tabert when he would come in from work. One Saturday night, the whipping boss laid Tabert on the ground and beat him with a leather strap about 50 times. The whipping boss told Tabert to get up, but he could not, so the whipping boss beat him some more, and left him unconscious. The next morning Tabert died.[18] As a result, Florida and several other states outlawed corporal punishment of prisoners.[19]

In 1948, England abolished whipping of males.[20] In 1951, Colorado outlawed whipping prisoners after a warden whipped some escapees.[21] In 1967, a court stopped the practice of whipping prisoners in Arkansas.[22]

By that time, the only state that still provided for whipping as a statutory penalty was Delaware. In 1963, a sentence of 20 lashes for auto theft was upheld as punishment for Franklin Cannon.[23]

Arguments in Favor

In debating whether to allow whipping as a punishment, the arguments in favor of it seem to sift down into two. The first argument is that some crimes need to be punished by a humiliating form of punishment. As one judge wrote:

> The general rule of the Common Law was, that the punishment of all infamous crimes should be disgraceful—as the pillory for every species of crimen falsi; as forgery, perjury, and other offenses of the same kind. Whipping was more peculiarly appropriated to petit larceny, and to crimes which betray a meanness of disposition, and a deep taint of moral depravity.[24]

A warden who administered one of Delaware's public whippings stated, "The lash doesn't hurt them, and it's not the whipping that bothers them. It's the humiliation."[25]

The second argument in favor of whipping is that it is not unduly harsh and that just as an errant child sometimes needs to be spanked, so some criminals do not respond to anything else except corporal punishment. It is the "spare the rod and spoil the child" analogy used by U.S. Representative Franklin Brockson in 1913[26] and by Judge Stewart Lynch in 1963.[27]

Arguments Against

The arguments against allowing whipping as a punishment are also basically two. First whipping is humiliating and degrading.[28] Secondly, whipping is unduly harsh; nothing more than a form of torture.[29]

Both the pro-whipping and the anti-whipping groups agree that whipping is humiliating. The groups differ however in their conclusions as to whether humiliation is good as a deterrent or bad as degrading. With no easily assessable first-hand revelations or research studies on the humiliation argument, neither argument has much evidence to prove or disprove it. Perhaps both arguments are correct.

The "too harsh" argument gives us more to analyze. The pro-whipping analogy with the right of a parent to discipline his child only holds up so long as it is recognized that the right is a limited one. The right of a parent over his child does not mean that a father would be excused for inflicting a blow upon his child for every act displeasing to him.[30] While a parent has the right to discipline his child, a parent does not have the right to beat his child to the point where there are bruises and broken bones.[31] We have been left some eyewitness accounts of whippings which we can review to see if the whippings were limited or not.

Examples

In the 1600's, four Quaker women, Anna Coleman, Mary Tompkins, Alice Andrews, and Alice Ambrose, were sentenced to be tied to the back of a cart, drawn through twelve towns of Massachusetts and New Hampshire, and given ten lashes in each town. These women were whipped until blood ran down their shoulders and breasts, and then men in Salisbury rose up in disgust and tore the women away from the cart and the constables.[32]

Dr. Samuel Willard recounted a whipping he saw in Illinois in the 1800's:

> I saw a man brought from the jail by the sheriff and a constable, to be whipped thirty lashes for the theft of a horse. He was stripped naked to the hips, his hands were tied and the rope was carried to the cross-piece and drawn as tight as could be without taking his feet from the ground. Then Sheriff Fry took that terrible instrument of punishment and torture, a rawhide. Probably many of you have not seen one. To make it, a taper strip of soft wet cowskin was twisted until the edges met, and the thing was dried in that position. It was hard, ridgy, and rough, but flexible as a switch, three quarters of a yard long. The Sheriff began laying strokes on the culprit's back, beginning near his neck and going regularly down one side of his backbone, former Sheriff Young counting the strokes aloud. Each stroke made a red blood-blister. When fifteen blows had been counted, the officer paused, and someone ran to the

> poor wretch with a tumbler of whiskey, then the other side of the man received like treatment. Then the man's shirt was replaced and he was led away to the jail. One of the by standers said, 'O Lord! He isn't as bad cut up as G. H. was when L. M. flogged him three or four years ago.'[33]

From our own century, we have this account:

> The strap which is referred to throughout this opinion is made of leather and is between four and five feet long and four inches wide. This leather is braided to a wooden handle approximately six inches in length. The strap is about one-fourth inch thick at the end attached to the handle and is gradually tapered toward the end which comes in contact with the person being whipped. . . . On July 20, 1966 . . . Captain Mayes . . . gave (Ernst) ten lashes with the strap . . . Ernst was required to lower his pants and was whipped on his bare buttocks . . . Some forty-five minutes later Captain Bruton instructed Captain Mayes to give Ernst ten lashes. He was again required to lower his pants and lie face down on the contrete floor to receive the licks. Ernst testified that this whipping left large bruises and caused him to bleed.[34]

Conclusion

A proper "discipline that brutes will understand" or a "barbarous torture"?—I will let the reader decide. I will point out that before the colonists came to America, they left behind some of the earlier punishments such as boiling in water, burning at the stake, drawing and quartering, and the rack. The colonists brought with them whipping, the pillory, the stocks, the ducking stool, branding, pressing to death, breaking on the wheel, and cutting off of ears. In time all these methods of punishment were also left behind.[35] For people to want to bring any of these punishments back reminds me of what Rivarol said:

> The most civilized people are as near to barbarism as the most polished steel is to rust.

---

1 St. Petersburg Times, January 29, 1989

2 Current History 38:487, June, 1905

3 Literary Digest 108:22, February 7, 1931

4 11 Rocky Mt. (Univ. Colo.) L Rev 186 (1939)

5 Deuteronomy 25:3

6 22 Henry VIII cap. XII (1530), 4 Pickering's Statutes at Large 207 (1763)

7 1 William and Mary Second-Session cap. II (1688), 9 Pickering's Statutes at Large 68 (1764)

8 4 Blackstone Commentaries 369-72 (1st ed. 1769)

9 Newsweek 53:39, May 11, 1959

10 Powers, Crime and Punishment in Early Massachusetts, Beacon Press, Boston, 1966; New Haven's Settling In New-England and Some Lawes for Government, London, 1656 reprinted in Cushing, The Earliest Laws of the New Haven and Connecticut Colonies, Michael Glazier, Inc., Wilmington, Delaware, 1977

11 Garcia v Territory, 1 NM 415 (1869); Thompson, Early Corporal Punishments, 6 Ill Law Q 37 (1923)

12 State v Kearney, 8 NC (1 Hawks) 53 (1820) The Commonwealth v Wyatt, 27 Va (6 Rand) 694 (1828)

13 26 & 27 Victoria cap. 44 (1863); 104 Pickering's Statutes at Large 151 (1863)

14 1 George IV cap 57 (1820); 60 Pickering's Statutes at Large 204 (1820)

15 5 Stat. 322 (1839); 9 Stat 515, Rev. Stat. 4611 (1850)

16 Earle, Curious Punishments of Bygone Days, Herbert S. Stone & Company, Chicago, 1896

17 Cal. Penal Code Ann. Sec. 2652 enacted 1941 (predecessor statute enacted 1913) ND Cent. Code Sec. 12-47-26 enacted 1943 (predecessor statute enacted 1883)

18 Literary Digest 77:40, April 21, 1923

19 Florida Laws Chap. 9332 Sec. 1 (1923) now Fla. Stat. 951.17

20 11 & 12 George VI cap. 58 (1948), 28 Halsburg's Statutes of England 352 (1951)

21 Time 58:19, July 30, 1951

22 Jackson v Bishop, 268 F Supp 804 (ED Ark 1967)

23 State v Cannon, 55 Del 587, 190 A2d 514 (1963)

24 State v Kearney, 8 NC (1 Hawk) 53 at 54 (1820)

25 Saturday Evening Post 236:7, March 30, 1963

26 Literary Digest 47:1100, December 6, 1913

27 Saturday Evening Post 236:7, March 30, 1963

28 Literary Digest 47:1100, December 6, 1913

29 Literary Digest 47:1100, December 6, 1913

30 Sheridan v Furbur, 21 Fed. Cases 12,761 (1834)

31 Compare *In the Interest of W.P.*, 534 So2d 905 (Fla 2d DCA 1988) with Spankie v Department of H.R.S., 505 So.2d 1357 (Fla 5th DCA 1987), rev. den., 513 So.2d 1063 (Fla. 1987)

32 Thompson, Early Corporal Punishments, 6 Ill Law Q. 37 at 40 (1923)

33 Thompson, Early Corporal Punishments, 6 Ill Law Q. 37 at 49 (1923)

34 Jackson v Bishop, 268 F Supp 804 at 810 (ED Ark. 1967) see also Lewis v State, 176 So2d 718 (La App), appeal denied, 248 La 364, 178 So2d 655 (1965)

35 See James v Commonwealth, 12 Serg. & Rawle (Penn) 220 (1824) for an opinion on the decline of the ducking stool

Learning to Live With AIDS in Prison

Behind bars, there is a new death row, but its inmates are being dealt with in enlightened ways

Inside the walls of American prisons, convicts call it "the package." AIDS, an agonizing, protracted form of execution, has created a new death row, more dreaded than the old. Over the years, cellblock grapevines buzzed with tales of prisoners who were beaten and stabbed by other inmates, or thrown into solitary confinement by guards—just for having AIDS. But now prisons, sometimes prodded by lawsuits filed by prisoner-rights organizations, are beginning to adopt enlightened policies toward convicts with AIDS. In New York state, for example, inmates who are not currently hospitalized with an AIDS-related illness can return to the "mainstream" prison population. To reduce fear among staff and inmates, many prison systems have set up AIDS-education programs. Guards no longer automatically wear masks and gloves when escorting inmates with AIDS. Some states even allow inmates to go home to die.

When the AIDS epidemic hit in 1981, doomsayers predicted prison hospitals would overflow with junkies, homosexual rapists and cellblock "queens." "We're going to see a whopping epidemic," complained one Maryland prison official a few years ago. But to date, this grievous scenario has proved exaggerated. According to a study funded by the Justice Department, there have been only 3,136 confirmed cases of AIDS behind bars, less than 4 percent of the national total. The number of prison AIDS cases increased by 60 percent last year, but on the outside, the rate of increase was 76 percent. Of the 49,414 federal prisoners tested for AIDS antibodies since 1987, only 1,417 inmates tested positive. In 1988 less than 3 percent of new federal inmates coming in from the outside were found to be HIV positive. Says James Riley of the Texas Department of Corrections, "It's a myth that prisons are breeding grounds."

One reason that the AIDS rate in prison may be lower than expected is caution on the part of the prisoners. Some inmates say that high-risk behavior—unsafe sex in which body fluids are exchanged, sharing smuggled drugs and needles, even tattooing—has dropped off substantially. "It's gone down to a minimum," says AIDS patient Robert DeMaio, 36, who is serving time for second-degree murder in New York's Sing Sing prison.

While the stigma of AIDS has eased, reports of serious abuse continue. In a well-publicized case last year, guards in a federal prison in Richmond, Va., allegedly handcuffed Michael Henson, 33, and tossed him into "the hole" after he tested positive for AIDS antibodies. (The prison denies Henson's charges.) In Nocatee, Fla., Scott Brewer—who later tested negative—told a jailer that he might have been exposed to the virus. "They stuck me in an isolation cell with an AIDS patient," Brewer said. "The officer yelled, 'I've got one with AIDS here'." A bigger problem than abuse is unreliable medical treatment. At the U.S. Medical Center for Federal Prisoners in Springfield, Mo., Michael Lingard had to sue for the right to take regular doses of AZT, the drug that appears to prolong the lives of people with AIDS. Around the country, numerous inmates have died prematurely because prison doctors misdiagnosed their symptoms. A New York state study made last year found the mean survival of AIDS inmates was 128 days—about eight months less than on the outside.

Home to die: But even the most critical AIDS activists concede that some progress has been made. One of the most welcome reforms has been the "compassionate release" parole. California has had the policy for three years, but only two patients have gone home. New York's plan is little more than a year old, and 46 parolees have taken advantage. "Most families accept them," says Ann Quinlan, nurse administrator at Sing Sing. "They see how we deal with patients, and learn by osmosis." Some families still say no. "No one wants to die in jail," said "Lucky," 39, a Georgia convict, "but that's the way it is sometimes." (Last month Lucky died in a prison hospital.)

Allowing prisoners access to condoms for "safe sex" in prison has been the most controversial new policy. Prisons in Vermont and Mississippi, as well as New York City jails, make prophylactics available. But in Bible-belt Mississippi, where sodomy laws are still on the books, church groups protested loudly. Nationwide, prison officials are largely opposed on the ground that free condoms might encourage sexual activity, even rape, as well as create other problems. "Our security people are concerned about this," says Texas administrator Riley. "These things can be turned into slingshots. They can be filled up with a variety of items, and turned into bombs."

Several states, including California, cite the threat of homosexual rape and needle sharing to justify quarantine policies. At the California Medical Facility at Vacaville, healthy HIV-positive inmates are segregated alongside AIDS patients. Some officials fear the situation could erupt into violence. "Parole violators are living with lifers and murderers," says physician Jan Diamond who treats AIDS patients at Vacaville, "and that creates stress." David Wayne Smith, 33, a petty thief housed in the unit, agrees: "Something's not clicking and the tension is mounting all the time," he says. In a recent incident at an AIDS unit in the California Institution for Men in Chino, 15 HIV-positive inmates broke 220 windows to protest their segregation. Elsewhere, even in states that allow AIDS inmates to live in the general population, anyone with a potentially violent nature is isolated: in 1987 a Florida convict laced a

For Women: Education and Mutual Support

They tell a parable about "Blackie" at the Bedford Hills Correctional Facility, New York's maximum-security prison for women. Blackie, an inmate who died of AIDS last year, used to say she could always leave her things lying around because she knew no one would dare touch them for fear of being exposed to the virus. Then in 1985 the prison had its first AIDS Counseling and Education program (ACE), and attitudes started to change. "Eventually everyone started stealing [Blackie's things]," an ACE participant recalls. "That was a good sign."

Around the country, some of the most innovative AIDS-education programs have been developed for women behind bars. In San Francisco, Sean Reynolds, an AIDS counselor for the county public-health department, uses tough talk to teach women in the tanks. "Think of condoms as your American Express card, honey," she says. "Don't leave home without it." In Boston, an activist organization called Social Justice for Women developed "AIDS 101" that features "speak outs" where inmates can go to an open mike and say what's on their minds about the disease. "Before, if women tested positive, [inmates] would call them 'AIDS-carrying bitches'," says Francine Melanson, a former drug addict who runs AIDS 101 at the Massachusetts Correctional Institute at Framingham. "Now they're knocking down my door, asking how they can help."

The programs often inspire women to take the antibody test. "I'm going to get tested when I get out," said Michelle Thompson, 23, after one of Reynolds's seminars. "I've been on the streets since I was 11 . . . doing heroin." ACE has stayed in touch with a number of parolees and hopes to set up counseling groups on the outside. But the biggest benefit may be to prisoners who are dying of AIDS. Says Sonya, a frail Bedford Hills inmate who can remember what it was like to be harassed for having AIDS, "These people take care of you."

guard's coffee with his own AIDS-infected blood.

But at the federal medical center in Springfield, AIDS patients find a potentially positive advantage in being forced to live on a rigid schedule: they welcome being guinea pigs for experimental drugs such as CD-4, which impedes the virus's destruction of the immune system. "You've got inmates in a controlled environment," says Michael Miller, 43, who is HIV positive. "I, for one, would be standing in line for any test."

Prisons sometimes actually involve AIDS activists in policymaking, bringing them in to develop education programs. "We do role playing," says John Egan of the Mid-Hudson AIDS Task Force in White Plains, N.Y. "Inmates act out scenes like being tested or being told they're antibody positive." But some activists say prison officials, reluctant to concede that sex and drug use cannot be controlled, provide too little education. And even when programs exist, the critics say, institutions do not require attendance, rarely offer follow-up sessions and rely on printed material for people with a high illiteracy rate.

If ignorance is one obstacle, complacency is another. Many prison officials are encouraged by the low number of AIDS cases in federal prisons, but they know that most inmates are in state facilities. Only 13 states, largely in areas where AIDS is relatively rare, screen for antibodies. Moreover, the full force of the epidemic may not have hit prisons yet. "There's no hotbed now," says Dr. C. E. Alexander, medical director of Texas prisons. "But what's going to happen in 1995?" Indeed, on the outside, AIDS continues to spread rapidly among i.v.-drug addicts, and in New York state alone, the Department of Correctional Services estimates that between 60 and 70 percent of all inmates have a history of i.v.-drug abuse. Epidemiologists now believe the incubation period for the virus can be more than eight years, maybe as high as 20. Prison officials have to stay vigilant: if the numbers start to climb in the 1990s, the new death row may yet become as overcrowded as was originally feared.

JAMES N. BAKER *with* SUE HUTCHISON *in Boston,* NADINE JOSEPH *in Vacaville,* HOWARD MANLY *in Atlanta,* DANIEL PEDERSEN *in Houston,* KAREN SPRINGEN *in Springfield and* NED ZEMAN *in New York*

A Conservative Perspective
Alternatives to Incarceration

Charles Colson and Daniel W. Van Ness

Charles Colson serves as chairman of the Board of Prison Fellowship Ministries, a Christian outreach to prisoners, ex-prisoners and their families. Former special counsel to President Nixon, Colson spent seven months in prison for a Watergate-related offense.

Daniel W. Van Ness is president of Justice Fellowship, the criminal justice reform arm of Prison Fellowship Ministries. Justice Fellowship advocates alternatives to incarceration for non-violent offenders, a formal role for victims in criminal cases, victim-offender reconciliation and victim assistance.

In Michigan, conservative Republican legislators Jack Welborn and William Van Regenmorter worked with liberal Democrat Carolyn Cheeks Kilpatrick to pass a Community Corrections Act (CCA). The result: Non-violent offenders will be punished in their communities instead of prison, which will save money and ease the state's prison overcrowding crisis.

In Indiana, Republican State Sen. Ed Pease led a successful legislative effort to establish home detention as a means of easing the pressure of the state's expanding prison population. Russ Pulliam, editorial writer of the conservative Pulliam newspaper chain, voiced support for the legislation as "one step in the right direction for the future of the criminal justice system in Indiana" (*Indianapolis News* Jan. 20, 1988). (The bill was included in The Council of State Governments' *Suggested State Legislation*, 1989).

In Florida, conservative businessman Jack Eckerd and former Federal Bureau of Prisons Director Norm Carlson are leading a campaign for expanded use of house arrest, drug treatment and restitution centers as alternatives to imprisonment for non-violent offenders.

In Alabama, conservative Democratic Rep. Claud Walker is sponsoring a Community Corrections Act aimed at reducing the large percentage of non-violent inmates in state prisons. Alabama Commissioner of Corrections Morris Thigpen and the Alabama Sheriffs Association are backing the bill.

In Arizona, Republican State Sen. Tony West sponsored the Community Punishment Act. The legislation, which recently passed with the support of Arizona Chief Justice Frank Gordon and Maricopa County Chief Presiding Judge B. Michael Dann, will provide communities with state money to establish restitution, community service, victim-offender reconciliation and other non-prison programs for non-dangerous offenders.

Conservatives are often typecast as champions of the "lock 'em up and throw away the key" battle cry of this "get tough on crime" era. Yet, increasingly, all around the country, conservatives of both parties are advocating alternatives to incarceration for non-violent offenders. They may well be the single most potent force for practical, prudent criminal justice reform today.

What's Going On?

No one can deny the crying need for reform in our nation's criminal justice system. In December 1988 there were 627,402 state and federal prisoners in American institutions — twice as many as in 1978 (Department of Justice press release April 23, 1989). The prison population explosion has filled prisons to overflowing. Federal prisons are 73 percent over capacity, while state

From *The Journal of State Government*, March/April 1989, pp. 59-64, published by The Council of State Governments. Reprinted by permission.

prisons are on average 20 percent over capacity, according to the Bureau of Justice Statistics (BJS 1988a).

Prison systems in 45 states have been sued because of overcrowding. In 37 states, at least one major institution is under court order or consent decree. In nine of those 37 states, the entire prison system is under court order. Litigation is pending in eight states (National Prison Project 1988).

The future looks no brighter. The National Council of Crime and Delinquency (NCCD 1988a) estimates that U.S. prison populations will increase by an additional 50 percent in the next 10 years.

Although our country is incarcerating more people than ever, violent and property crimes continue to escalate (BJS 1988b). The indiscriminate "get tough" approach is a grand success in filling prisons. But it fails miserably at reducing crime.

Thankfully, many conservatives actively are pushing saner, wiser solutions to crime's stranglehold on our nation and the prison population explosion.

Why conservatives? Based on Justice Fellowship's work with politicians across the United States, it's clear that many see alternatives to incarceration for non-violent offenders as a natural extension of conservative political philosophy. Legislators cite the following principles: Punishment is appropriate; it should serve victims' needs; public safety is essential; local is better, and wise use of limited government resources is needed.

Let's look at each.

Punishment is appropriate. Since the first "penitentiary" was established in 1790, American criminal justice has been predicated on the belief that crime is the result of environmental or psychiatric factors. Criminals were seen as victims and were sent to prison to be rehabilitated.

This human engineering approach has proven a dismal failure. Studies over the last two decades consistently have concluded that three out of four ex-offenders are rearrested within four years of their release form prison (Federal Bureau of Investigation 1975; Petersilia, Turner and Peterson 1986). Far from rehabilitating offenders, prisons seem better suited to train them in the finer arts of crime.

Pursuing false dreams of rehabilitation undermines the principle of personal accountability. No matter how many environmental factors weigh upon the individual, committing a criminal act is a personal choice. By treating victimizers as victims, society robs them of the dignity belonging to moral agents. They are denied the opportunity to "pay the price" and move on with life. C. S. Lewis ([1949] 1983) put it this way, "To be punished, however severely, because we have deserved it, because we 'ought to have known better' is to be treated as a human person made in God's image."

Treatment programs should be available to offenders who would be helped by them — but justice requires that offenders also must be held accountable for their behavior.

The issue should not be *whether* to punish but *how*. The problem is that our society has increasingly equated "punishment" with "prison" and seems unable to conceive of the notion of punishments aside from prison. Prisons are, of course, necessary for violent offenders. But nearly 50 percent of the American prison population is behind bars for non-violent offenses. Many of them would pose little danger to their communities; they are imprisoned solely for punishment.

For the reasons that follow, many conservatives are concluding that society is not well served by punishing non-violent offenders behind bars. Sound alternatives to prison are available. Restitution, community service and intensive supervision probation are tough and effective punishments that limit freedom and place demands for compensation upon offenders.

Punishment should serve victims' needs. While victims suffer most from crime — physically, emotionally and financially (to the tune of $13 billion per year) (BJS 1988c) — victims' interests are represented least. From the moment a crime is committed, through the time the offender is convicted and sent to prison, the victim is virtually ignored by the criminal justice system. As Roberta Roper, whose daughter was murdered seven years ago, said, "Crime doesn't pay — but victims do."

This injustice has sparked the growth of victims' rights groups across the United States. In addition to supporting an increased role for victims in the system, many have promoted restitution and other alternatives to incarceration — not to make life easier for offenders but to benefit victims.

For example, the Alabama Victims Compensation Group and Victims of Crime Against Leniency are supporting the Alabama Community Corrections Act because it holds offenders accountable for their crimes and provides for victim assistance officers to help victims secure restitution and compensation. In Maryland, Justice Fellowship worked with the effective and well-respected Stephanie Roper Committee to promote recently passed mandatory restitution legislation.

Victim restitution must become an essential part of criminal punishments. This a matter of simple justice. In an article describing the Sentencing Improvement Act of 1983, U.S. Sens. William Armstrong, R-Colorado, and Sam Nunn, D-Georgia, (1986) recognized the importance of alternative punishments based on restitution: "Because of growing public concern for crime victims, the restitution concept holds great promise of gaining broad public support. . . . Recent surveys indicate that a great percentage of Americans would prefer to have the non-violent offender repay his victim rather than serve time at public expense."

Public safety is essential. Non-violent offenders who might be sentenced to alternative punishments are taking up precious prison space that should be reserved for violent criminals. (As noted, nearly half of all state prisoners were convicted of non-violent crimes. And 34 percent have *never* committed a violent crime (BJS 1988d).)

But, prisons are so overcrowded that many states rely on early release to reduce prison populations. This means that some dangerous offenders are let out well before they have served their full sentence. This is the irony of the "get tough" response to crime: By indiscriminately sending more people to prison, communities are less safe.

The case of Charlie Street is illustrative. Street was released from Florida's Martin Correctional Institution in the fall of 1988 after serving only half of his sentence for attempted murder. Ten days later, he gunned down two Dade County police officers — a tragedy that could have been avoided if Street had been kept off the streets and in prison where he belonged. As Jack Eckerd wrote in the *Orlando Sentinel* (Dec. 4, 1988), "We must restore sanity to the system, slamming the door and keeping it shut on violent and career criminals like Charlie Street, while expanding alternate punishments for non-violent offenders."

Any discussion of public safety eventually includes the issue of deterrence. The argument that prisons alone deter is defeated by the facts. Swift and certain punishment deters, not harsh punishment that is neither swift nor certain.

Consider the odds. The federal government reports that out of 100 crimes, 33 will be reported to the police and seven will result in an arrest. Four will end with a conviction, with one offender going to jail, one to prison and two to probation. In other words, for every 100 crimes committed in the United States, one person goes to prison (Colson and Van Ness 1989).

Can we reasonably believe that doubling or tripling the number of people in prison would significantly deter crime? Would a 2 or 3 percent chance of imprisonment actually deter more crime than a 1 percent chance of imprisonment?

Fortunately, experienced criminal justice practitioners know that tough alternative punishments are feared more by convicted offenders than prison. Trial judges in Florida, for example, say that defendants request prison sentences to avoid the state's tough Community Control Program.

Alternatives promote public safety in other ways as well. For example, they keep the non-violent offender out of prison, the ideal training ground for becoming a more accomplished and dangerous criminal. The Rand Corporation found in a 1986 study (Petersilia, Turner and Peterson) that a group of probationers committed fewer new crimes than an identical group of ex-prisoners. The researchers concluded that "imprisonment was associated with a higher probability of recidivism."

A federal study of Georgia's Intensive Probation Supervision program (National Institute of Justice 1987) found that probationers committed fewer new crimes than comparable prisoners and no violent new crimes.

Community safety depends on increased use of community sanctions.

Local is better. Many alternatives to incarceration significantly benefit local communities. Community corrections acts, for example, allow communities to tailor programs to meet their own needs, by dealing with non-violent offenders in their own ways. This also means that communities are involved with their own offenders, who will most likely continue to live in the community after serving their sentences.

Local punishments benefit the state as well. Every offender who stays in a local program is one less person taking up scarce prison space at state expense.

Community service performed by offenders can be another important local benefit. Instead of sending offenders to state prisons, some communities reap the benefits of free or low-pay labor for charitable or governmental agencies. Genesee County, New York, has honed this practice into an art form. Since the establishment of the county's widely acclaimed Genesee Justice program in 1981, offenders performed more than 97,000 hours of community service for 118 community agencies, a total value of $389,000 (Genesee County Sheriff's Department 1988).

Wise use of limited government resources. There is no question that states will have to increase their prison capacities. But state governments cannot afford to rely on prison construction as the sole means to solve the overcrowding crisis. It costs an average of $15,900 to keep an inmate in prison for one year (Camp and Camp 1988). In fiscal 1987 alone, state and federal governments spent almost $5 billion in new prison construction (American Correctional Association 1988).

This is placing an extraordinary strain on state budgets. Norman Carlson (1988), writing of the situation in Florida, summarizes the dilemma facing many states, "Constructing sufficient prison space is not a viable solution. The tremendous costs involved in building and operating the required number of new prisons would overwhelm the limited resources available in the state treasury and would compete with other high priority needs, such as education, medical care and transportation."

Explaining why he worked so hard for passage of the Michigan Community Corrections Act, Michigan State Rep. William Van Regenmorter (1988) said, "Michigan's prison system has been overcrowded since 1975. (In) . . . 1984, the system held about 300 prisoners more than its intended capacity. To combat this problem, the Department of Corrections constructed many new prisons, almost doubling the system's capacity in just three years. The result of this expensive building program? The system was still overcrowded, this time by some 3,000 prisoners!"

And because of the extraordinary increase (141 percent over the last five years), in the corrections budget — due to the massive prison construction program (*Grand Rapids Press* Jan. 2, 1989) — Michigan now faces cuts in social service programs.

New prison construction costs an average of $80,000 per maximum security cell. The total cost of all current or planned prison construction will be $25 billion (NCCD 1988b). States cannot afford to make such budget-busting investments in concrete and steel condominiums with bars.

To reduce overcrowding and avoid bankrupting other key state programs, conservatives argue in favor of investing in alternatives to prison, so that prisons can be reserved for the dangerous offenders who must be locked away from society. Some states are taking initiatives to do so.

Program Profiles

Community Corrections Acts (CCAs). These acts provide a statewide mechanism allowing local governments to design, develop and deliver — and state governments to fund — local correctional tools such as intensive supervision, restitution, community service, and drug and alcohol treatment. Thirteen states now have CCAs.

Tennessee diverted 504 offenders from prison in fiscal 1987-88 at a cost of $7,599 per offender, compared to the state average of $19,710 for incarceration. In addition, offenders sentenced to community corrections paid $59,145 in restitution to victims and performed 76,294 hours of community service. The estimated total savings to the state was $6.1 million (Mike Jones, Tennessee Department of Corrections, telephone interview, September 1988).

Virginia diverted 699 felons from its prisons and jails in fiscal 1987-88. As a result, it saved more than $8 million, which does not include savings realized by diverting more than 6,500 local felons and misdemeanants from jails. Diverted offenders performed 229,812 hours of community service and paid $76,870 in restitution (Gwen Cunningham, Virginia Department of Corrections, telephone interview, September 1988).

House arrest confines offenders to their own homes. They are not allowed out except for approved activities such as health care, special religious services, community service or employment, which in turn most often leads to restitution payments to victims (Petersilia 1987). Many jurisdictions are using electronic surveillance measures to ensure compliance.

Florida's Community Control Program is a nationally recognized house arrest program. Established in 1983, Community Control uses community service and restitution sanctions for some 8,000 offenders statewide. The cost to the state is $2,650 per year per offender, which is 80 percent less than the $13,140 cost for imprisonment (Carlson 1989). By reducing prison commitments by 180 people a month, Community Control has proven a valuable weapon in Florida's fight against overcrowding. Because only 9 percent of its offenders commit new crimes, it is also an effective weapon against crime.

Intensive Probation Supervision (IPS). The key to this program's success is low caseloads. Ideally, officers maintain caseloads of 15-25 people — as opposed to the supervision possible when harried officers in "normal" probation programs carry caseloads of between 120 and 300 offenders. In many IPS programs, offenders must make daily contact with their officers. Most intensive supervision programs require offenders to maintain employment or go to school and to abide by a strict curfew. Many also include restitution and community service as sanctions.

Illinois regularly supervises 570 offenders in its IPS program — a ratio of 25 offenders for every two officers. The annual cost per offender is $2,367. Since the program was established in 1984, Illinois has collected approximately $1 million in restitution, taxes, fines and court costs. Its Intensive Probation Supervision participants performed 145,349 hours of public service valued at $489,921. All told, the state saved $7.7 million in the last five years through IPS (Anderson 1988). And prospects look good for expanding the program to more offenders.

Restitution centers are residential facilities designed to house offenders requiring more supervision than regular or intensive supervision probation but less than total confinement in prison. These centers, which are a tightened-up version of "work release" with a focus on restitution, are used in six states as an alternative to imprisonment.

Georgia's restitution centers can house 2,600 offenders yearly. During fiscal 1987, the state collected from offenders $256,817 in restitution, $626,516 in family support, $1.4 million in room and board, $940,274 in fines and court fees and $1.4 million in taxes. The offenders also performed community service worth $266,516. The annual cost per offender was $8,249. Seventy-five percent of the residents successfully complete the program (Larry Anderson, Georgia Department of Corrections, telephone interview, 1988).

Florida's Probation and Restitution Centers can hold 382 offenders, far below the 900 offenders who would have qualified for the program in 1987, according to a 1988 report by the state Office of the Auditor General. The annual cost per offender is $10,909, which the state partially defrays by collecting average annual fees of $1,900 per offender. Jack Eckerd and Norm Carlson are among those calling for expanded use of these centers in Florida.

Conclusion

No one could deny the severity of America's criminal justice crisis. The time has come for real solutions rather than overheated rhetoric that fuels public passions, reinforces stereotypes about prisons and prisoners and, in the end, results in taxpayers being punished far more than offenders.

Historically, conservatives have been at the forefront of many great movements in the West: the battle for abolition of the slave trade and of slavery, the fight to end industrial abuses in the late 19th century and in efforts to establish public education. We believe the criminal justice arena is one in which conservatives are beginning to lead the way toward measures that will benefit offenders, victims, correctional officials and taxpayers.

Crime is not a partisan issue. Pursuing alternatives to prison for non-violent offenders will take the endurance, creativity and cooperation of men and women from every political perspective. And conservatives, working with moderates and liberals, can play a key role in forging that public consensus for effective criminal justice policy.

Sources

Administrative Office of the Illinois Courts. 1988. *Illinois Intensive Probation Supervision: Statewide Summary, Quarterly Statistical Report*. Prepared by Gregg Anderson. Springfield: Administrative Office of the Illinois Courts, July.

American Correctional Association. 1988. *1988 Directory: Juvenile and Adult Correctional Departments, Institutions, Agencies & Paroling Authorities*, ed. Anthony P. Travisono. College Park, MD: American Correctional Association.

Armstrong, William L., and Sam Nunn. 1986. "Alternatives to Incarceration: The Sentencing Improvement Act." *Crime and Punishment in Modern America*, ed. Patrick B. McGuigan and Jon S. Pascale, 337-348. Washington D.C.: Free Congress Research and Education Foundation.

Bureau of Justice Statistics (BJS), Department of Justice. 1988a. *Prisoners in 1987*. Washington D.C.: GPO, April.

____. 1988b. *Criminal Victimization 1987*. Washington D.C.: GPO, October.

____. 1988c. *Report to the Nation on Crime and Justice*. 2d. ed. Washington D.C.: GPO.

____. 1988d. *Profile of State Prison Inmates 1986*. Prepared by Christopher A. Innes. Washington, D.C.: GPO, January.

Camp, George M., and Camille Graham Camp. 1988. *The Corrections Yearbook 1988*. New York: Criminal Justice Institute.

Carlson, Norman A. 1988. *Findings and Recommendations on Florida's Prison Crisis*. Tallahassee: Florida Prison Crisis Project, March-April.

____. 1989. *Florida's Prison Crisis*. Tallahassee: Justice Task Force, January.

Colson, Charles, and Daniel W. Van Ness. 1989. *Convicted: New Hope for Ending America's Crime Crisis*. Westchester, IL: Crossway.

Council of State Governments. 1989. *Suggested State Legislation*, vol. 48. Lexington: Council of State Governments.

Federal Bureau of Investigation. 1975. *Crime in the United States 1975: Uniform Crime Reports for the United States*. Washington D.C.: GPO.

Genesee County (NY) Sheriff's Department. 1988. *Genesee Justice 1987-88 Annual Report: Community Service/Victim Assistance Program*. Batavia, NY: Genesee County Sheriff's Department.

Lewis, C.S. [1949] 1983. *The Humanitarian Theory of Punishment*. Reprint, in *God in the Dock: Essays on Theology and Ethics*, ed. Walter Hooper, 287-294. Grand Rapids: William B. Eerdmans.

National Council on Crime and Delinquency (NCCD). 1988a. *Crime and Punishment in the Year 2000: What Kind of Future?* San Francisco: NCCD.

____. 1988b. *Illusory Savings in the War Against Crime*. San Francisco: NCCD, July.

National Institute of Justice. 1987. *New Dimensions in Probation: Georgia's Experience with Intensive Probation Supervision*. Prepared by Billie S. Erwin and Lawrence A. Bennett. Washington D.C.: GPO, January.

National Prison Project. 1988. *Status Report: The Courts and Prisons*. Washington D.C.: National Prison Project.

Petersilia, Joan, Susan Turner and Joyce Peterson. 1986. *Prison versus Probation in California: Implications for Crime and Offender Recidivism*. Santa Monica: Rand.

Petersilia, Joan. 1987. *Expanding Options for Criminal Sentencing*. Santa Monica: Rand.

State of Florida Office of the Auditor General. 1988. *Performance Audit of the Department of Corrections Community-Based Facilities Program*. Tallahassee: Office of the Auditor General, March.

Van Regenmorter, William. 1988. "Helping Young Offenders in Michigan." *The Banner*, Nov. 14.

Prison Overcrowding and Privatization: *Models and Opportunities*

Keon S. Chi

Keon S. Chi, Ph.D., is a senior policy analyst at The Council of State Governments' Headquarters Office.

State and local governments have turned to the private sector — privatization — to expand their services and to manage their correctional facilities to reduce prison and jail overcrowding. Prison privatization should be further tested to provide more documented evidence of benefits as well as shortfalls.

In 1988, federal and state prisons held a record 627,402 offenders and operated from 7 percent to 72 percent over capacity. More than 14,000 prisoners were housed in local jails in 17 states because of crowded conditions in federal and state prisons. By early 1989, prisons and jails in 42 states and the District of Columbia were under court orders to relieve overcrowding.

State and local governments have taken measures to reduce prison and jail populations. These include construction, renovations, use of military facilities, pretrial diversion, probation and parole, intensive supervision, community treatment, emergency and work release, house arrest and sentencing guidelines. State and local governments also have turned to the private sector — privatization — to expand services and to manage correctional facilities for adult and juvenile offenders.

Policy-makers have debated extensively whether privatization is a sound public option for reducing prison and jail overcrowding. Proponents and opponents have disagreed on almost every issue relevant to prison privatization, especially on philosophical, ideological and legal grounds. Although the literature on the controversial topic is voluminous, more information is needed, including empirical studies based on pilot tests and experiments rather than much talked about claims for and against prison privatization.

The purposes of this article are to suggest that public and private sectors have begun working together to deal with the perpetual prison population crisis and that prison privatization be tested further to provide documented evidence of benefits and shortfalls. The first section describes prison privatization models, by citing examples; the second discusses opportunities for and circumstances conducive to prison privatization; and the conclusion calls for a comprehensive assessment of the effectiveness of prison privatization.

Privatization Models

The use of the private sector for correctional services is not new; however, new trends have emerged. First, some states have expanded the authority of corrections departments and local jurisdictions to make greater use of private organizations for correctional services. Second, there are now more than two dozen for-profit companies providing various types of correctional services including offender detention or incarceration services. And, third, state and local governments have contracts for larger and more secure correctional facilities.

Prison privatization activities can be grouped into five models: services, construction, management, take-over, and ownership and operation.

1. Private Services Model

Under the private services model, government

From *The Journal of State Government*, March/April 1989, pp. 70-76, published by The Council of State Governments. Reprinted by permission.

agencies contract selected correctional services, including work for inmates, to for-profit or non-profit organizations. The most frequently cited reasons for using the model include more effective and efficient provision of such services. This is the oldest and most familiar privatization model in use.

Over the last few years, however, several states have considered contracting for additional correctional services — administrative as well as institutional — once performed exclusively by public employees. For example, Arizona considered contracting for rehabilitation and conservation camps, while California studied the feasibility of contracting inmate classification, management of offender data systems and administrative work such as purchasing, payroll and accounting. New Jersey's Department of Corrections relies on private firms for data management and Illinois contracts parole services.

States also are relying on the private sector for correctional industries programs. A dozen state corrections departments have contracts with private firms. A unique example is Florida. The Prison Rehabilitation Industries and Diversified Enterprise Inc. (PRIDE) in 1981 assumed control of the management of all state correctional industries. In 1988, the company made a $4 million profit and paid 60 percent of inmates' wages to the state to defray correctional costs. Only a few states also had a profit from correctional industries programs. Several states are studying the feasibility of replicating the Florida model.

To most state and local governments, prison privatization activities fall under the private services model. Some correctional agencies, dissatisfied with privately provided services, have complained about their lack of control over services and increased costs for inferior services. While the cost-effectiveness of private correctional services should be assessed case by case, it appears that most jurisdictions will continue to contract selected correctional services.

2. Private Construction Model

Under the private construction model, private firms build correctional facilities, using short-term financing, lease-purchase or pooled financing. Private firms normally handle every aspect of prison construction, ranging from design to construction, free of government control. The model saves costs, speeds construction and avoids lengthy delays associated with general obligation bond issues. Of prison construction financing methods, lease-purchase is the most popular, having been used by more than a dozen states, including California and Missouri. California recently obtained $800 million for prison construction through a lease-purchasing arrangement without committing the state to any long-term debt. In 1986, Missouri selected the private firms of Corrections Development Corp. and Kidder Peabody to build a 500-bed maximum/minimum prison near Potosi. Under the lease-purchase agreement, private companies designed, financed, constructed and then leased the facility to Missouri for 30 years. Approximately $50 million of state appropriations would have been needed for the construction of a 500-bed facility. Other states that have built prisons on lease-purchase include Alaska, Louisiana, New York, Ohio and Rhode Island. A dozen other states have considered such agreements. In addition, many local jails were built through lease-purchase agreements.

In some states, governors' support for private construction failed to sway legislatures. In 1986, Tennessee's then-Gov. Lamar Alexander's proposal for private construction of two 512-bed, maximum security prisons was rejected by the Legislature. Despite Gov. Robert D. Orr's initial support, an amendment to House Bill 1072 before the 1988 Indiana Senate to build an 800-bed prison for medium-to-maximum security inmates was rejected by a 30-20 vote. In these states, the lack of capital budgets and projected lower costs were the primary reasons for considering private construction.

At issue is the constitutionality of lease-purchase for prison construction. A Michigan court ruled that attempts to have a private entity construct and lease back a prison facility with an option to purchase by any method other than through the state building authority is a long-term debt and, therefore, an unconstitutional transaction. In South Carolina, on the other hand, the attorney general said in 1984, "If the lease-purchase agreement contains a so-called 'non' appropriation clause, thereby binding the state only to the extent of currently appropriated revenues, such an agreement would not constitute a debt or indebtedness within the meaning of existing constitutional and statutory provisions and thus would not have the same effect as general obligation bonds."

3. Private Management Model

Under the private management model, state prisons and local jails built and owned by government would be run by private firms. Typically, a private company would provide corrections managers to operate a facility for a fee, which might be tied to performance. The managers might keep government corrections employees or replace them with private corrections workers.

No states have tried this model. But, in 1986, the Tennessee Senate Government Operations Committee first approved and then killed a bill that would have allowed a private company to run a maximum security state prison. The model, however, has been used for several county jails. The Corrections Corporation of America took over the management and operation of the 172-bed maximum security Santa Fe County, New Mexico jail in 1986. In September 1988, CCA, under a five-year contract, began managing the 532-bed county law enforcement center in Pecos, Texas. The contract provides that CCA receive reimbursement for its costs plus a guaranteed management fee of approximately $400,000 a year. The Pecos minimum-security facility, built in 1986 and owned by Reeves County, is used by the county, the Federal Bureau of Prisons and the U.S. Marshals Service. Since October 1988, CCA also has managed a new $7 million, 252-bed jail in Hernando, Florida, which the county designed, constructed and financed. The county is the primary user of the facility, but beds are available to the U.S. Marshals Service. The three-year contract may be renewed for successive two-year periods.

Variations of the private management model include allowing a company to manage one or more units within a correctional compound, to operate an entire facility for two to three years to relieve overcrowding or to provide specialized services for special needs inmates or inmates under protective custody.

4. Private Takeover Model

Under the private takeover model, private companies, under a lease and management contract, take over an entire state prison or county jail system. Private companies relieve a correctional department of most of its functions, including construction and management of correctional facilities. The corrections department, under this model, is responsible for planning, monitoring and evaluating the programs carried out by private firms.

CCA's 1985 proposal to take over Tennessee's state correctional system falls under the model. The Nashville-based company proposed to run for 99 years all existing institutions, adult and juvenile, including group homes. The only areas excluded in the proposal were probation and foster care. Describing Tennessee's prison system, which suffered riots in 1984, as one of the worst in the nation, a CCA official said, "In five years it will be the best in the country, period. We're betting the company that we can do it."

The CCA proposal called for building five new prisons: two maximum-security and three 612-bed, medium-security prisons. The company, offering to pump $150 million in capital into the system, proposed to have 8,564 beds — 4,304 of them new — in place by July 1989. With the new beds, CCA said the state could ask to be released from federal court control. Under the proposal, annual adjustments to the amount the state would pay CCA would have been tied to external factors, such as the Consumer Price Index, the overall state budget or another agreed-upon index. If the state had decided to terminate the agreement, it would have been able to buy prison buildings from CCA without paying interest.

Under the proposal, the company would have managed and employed the state's 4,500-employee corrections department. Crucial to implementation of the CCA proposal were: adequate financial resources, building or renovating facilities according to established standards, sufficient committed and trained personnel, effective inmate programs and efficient management of the overall system. The proposal was discussed in public forums arranged by the Department of Corrections. After a few months of heated debates, the Legislature rejected the takeover bid primarily for philosophical and political reasons.

5. Private Ownership and Operation Model

Under the private ownership and operation model, a private company owns, manages and operates a prison or jail. The model can speed efforts to open a facility to handle prison overcrowding. Other perceived advantages of this model include private capital, management quality control and construction and operational cost savings. The model also provides tax advantages and financial incentives for the private contractor and relieves government of construction and management of correctional facilities. This model appears to be more popular than others. More than 30 correctional facilities are or will be privately owned and operated.

The Federal Bureau of Prisons has used more than 220 private community-corrections facilities serving more than 3,000 prerelease or work-release inmates. The Immigration and Naturalization Service detains illegal immigrants in four large private detention facilities with 600 beds each and plans to use two more facilities for an additional 200 beds.

Juvenile corrections has the longest tradition of private facility contracting. But most private facilities are small. Examples are the Weaversville Intensive Treatment Unit, with 22 beds, in North Hamptonm, Pa., run by RCA since 1975 and a 30-bed juvenile facility in Phoenix run by Behavioral Systems Southwest. Since 1982, when the Eckerd Foundation took over the operation of the Okeechobee School for Boys in Florida (with 400 delinquents), private companies have built and managed several larger juvenile facilities. In 1985, CCA built the Shelby Training Center in Shelby County, Tenn., with 150 beds. In March 1989, CCA signed a contract to design, build, finance and manage a 144-bed secure juvenile facility in Jefferson County, Tenn., expected to open in 1990 for 120 male and 24 female offenders.

Privately owned and operated jails for juveniles and adults include Panama City in Bay County,

Fla., with 340 beds (CCA since 1985); Hamilton County jail in Tennessee, with 330 beds for pretrial detainees and convicted adults (CCA since 1984); a 96-bed medium-security jail in Butler County, Pa. (Buckingham Security Ltd.); a 768-bed private jail for low-risk inmates in Lubbock, Texas (Detention Services Inc.); Silverdale Detention Center in Hamilton County, Tenn., with 350 beds for coed adult-medium-security (CCA since 1984); and Fayetteville Community Treatment Center in North Carolina (CCA) for prerelease, alternative sentencing and drunk driver programs for the Federal Bureau of Prisons. In November 1988, CCA was chosen to negotiate contracts with Bernalillo County (Albuquerque), N.M., to design, finance, construct and manage a 425-bed county jail, with expected expansion to 850 beds. In January 1989, the company was awarded a contract from Tulsa County, Okla., to develop a plan to relieve jail overcrowding, including design, construction and management of a new 800-bed jail.

At the state level, three private minimum-security facilities are operating: an 80-bed facility in California for state parole violators (Eclectic Communications Inc. of Ventura, since 1986); a 158-bed work-release facility (Beckham House, since 1985) for state inmates in Florida; and the Marion Adjustment Center, a minimum-security facility for 450 inmates in Marion County, Ky. operated by U.S. Corrections Corporation since 1986.

In 1988, the Texas Board of Corrections contracted with private firms to locate, design and manage four 500-bed prerelease centers for state inmates. Two contractors were chosen by competitive bid from among 20 bidders nationwide. The new facilities in Kyle and Bridgeport were contracted by Florida-based Wackenhut Services and two facilities in Cleveland and Venus by CCA. Funding of approximately $24 million was provided through tax-exempt bonds secured by a lease-purchase agreement with the state. The facilities are expected to open July 1, 1989. Texas agreed to pay the contractors $34.79 per inmate a day, which could increase to $35.25 later. The agreement is for three years and can be renewed for a two-year period. In 1988, New Mexico awarded CCA a contract to design, build, finance and manage a mixed-security 200-bed female prison. The facility, expected to be completed in 1989, will accommodate all the state's female prisoners. The private company offers educational and vocational training programs along with a state-run correctional industry program. The non-profit Volunteers of America since 1984 has operated a 42-bed facility, the Roseville Regional Corrections Center in Roseville, Minn., for adult female inmates serving terms of less than one year.

In addition, a small Denver firm has joined large national and international corporations for a prison construction project on speculation in Ault, Colo. Participants in the $40 million joint venture are American Correctional Systems Inc. (designing and managing the facility), Bechtel Group Inc. (construction), Daewoo Corp. (financing) and Shearson Lehman (underwriting).

Opportunities for Prison Privatization

Many state and local officials are reviewing prison privatization in other states and localities. There are at least five reasons why they should consider prison privatization.

First, when a state or county wants to respond quickly to a court order to expand prison capacity, privatization is a practical option. Speedy mobilization of facilities and staff is the most valid and convincing reason for prison privatization. The much-publicized Kentucky case is illustrative. Like many states, Kentucky has been under court order to alleviate prison overcrowding. In 1985, a governor's corrections task force recommended the option of privatization and the Corrections Cabinet issued a request-for-proposal (RFP) for a 200-bed facility. When the initially successful bidder was unable to secure its designated facility, the state chose the second bidder, U.S. Corrections Corp., to manage a minimum-security prison, beginning January 1986. In 1988, satisfied with the corporation's management of the Marion Adjustment Center, the state renewed its contract and added 250 beds. Kentucky chose privatization primarily because a private contractor was able to open a facility more quickly than the state.

A second reason for privatization is the financial relief provided state and county governments, which might lack capital budgets for prison or jail construction. As inmate populations increase, additional prison space will be needed. In 1987-88, the states and federal government built nearly 80,000 new prison beds. New construction projects were funded by legislative appropriations in 26 states, bond issues in 20 states and both in 13. Some jurisdictions, however, were unable to obtain capital budgets or bond issues for prison construction. Voters have turned down more than half the proposed bond issues for jail construction. In addition, private financing for corrections can free government tax monies for other purposes.

Cost savings in prison privatization should be analyzed carefully, case by case. While privatization might not always save money, a major benefit of private construction, ownership and operation models is that government does not need to provide funding in advance to build prisons. Governments also can require private providers to meet cost ceilings. For example, the Texas Legislature, in authorizing the construction of four 500-bed facilities by private companies, required that contracts be at least 10 percent lower than correctional estimates of state costs to build and operate similar facilities. Government, however, should not propose cost restrictions that are unfeasible. In 1986, for example, Tennessee issued a request for proposal for private firms to manage and operate a 500-bed medium security prison (Carter County Work Camp) at least a 5 percent savings in operational costs. The RFP attracted only one bidder, who was rejected for not being responsive to the conditions set by the Department of Corrections.

Third, private prisons can be appropriate for some inmates. Many prisons and jails are occupied by inmates who could be supervised equally well by private providers. The prison overcrowding situation might be improved by handling certain types of inmates differently. For example, inmates near time of release, parole violators and inmates requiring minimum custody could be housed in private beds.

Other potential residents for private facilities are special-needs inmates, including the emotionally unstable, mentally ill and retarded. These inmates might require counseling services, specialized treatment programs or select housing in a supportive environment. Others are physically handicapped or chronically ill, requiring protective custody. By placing some of these inmates in private facilities for specialized services, space would be available for inmates requiring higher levels of custody. For example, there are approximately 3,000 (or 20 percent) special-needs inmates, out of a total inmate population of 15,000 in Pennsylvania's correctional system. Corrections agencies also might consider private facilities for drunk drivers, who usually receive relatively short sentences and require moderate supervision and specialized treatment services. Private corrections firms also might manage more effectively special prisons for inmates with AIDS.

Fourth, privatization should not threaten the job security of corrections employees. Privatization has not been used to force corrections workers out of jobs, even though some privatization opponents fear it might. To protect workers, government might require private providers to hire these employees. On the other hand, privatization might be used to contain or even reduce the size of the bureaucracy by requiring fewer new correctional employees.

The truth is that governments will have to hire new corrections workers as prison populations escalate. Employment has grown faster in corrections than any other area of government. There will be even a greater need for new corrections workers in the future. In New Jersey, for example, the prison population increases by 100 to 120 a month. The number of offenders behind bars nationwide is expected to reach the 1 million mark by 1990.

And fifth, privatization can be positive for government correctional management services and programs. While for the past 200 years, there has been a government monopoly in corrections, it is time to try different modes of operation, management philosophy and tools, new technology and program-oriented correctional services rather than punishment-oriented programs. In privatization, qualified providers compete to deliver better services. This is the key assumption on which the privatization option is based. More importantly, however, prison privatization encourages competition between private organizations and government for improved correctional services.

Competition between corrections agencies and private providers is a reality in Texas. Since 1987, the Texas Department of Corrections, as required by state sunset legislation, must estimate its costs for correctional management services, which are certified by the state auditor. The auditor sends the estimate to the State Purchasing and General Services Commission, which estimates the cost to purchase services from the private sector. The department is required to reduce its own cost to no more than 10 percent above the private sector estimate. Besides cost savings, healthy competition could lead to improved correctional programs.

Cost-effectiveness

Policy-makers and administrators need information on the effectiveness of prison privatization. They want documented evidence, based on performance evaluation rather than unproven claims. How is the cost-effectiveness of prison privatization assessed? Each privatization model should be assessed differently. For example, the private ownership and operation model would require policy analysts to review and study corrections performance, including the following:

- Confinement — crowding, housing conditions, institutional and recreational facilities, safety and sanitation measures, food services, health care programs and facilities.
- Security — number of escapes, inmate and room searches, freedom of movement in the facility, disciplinary problems, frequency of use of force, violence and victimization.
- Rehabilitation — inmate activities, counseling, grievances, substance abuse programs, academic programs, vocational training, job counseling and placement.
- Staff — recruitment and training, pay and fringe benefits, employee turnover rate, work environment, program goals, performance, grievances and inmate contacts.
- Outcome — inmate expectation and level of satisfaction, length of stay, prerelease, post-release, employment and recidivism.

• Costs — direct costs for personnel, meals, education, utilities, medical care, counseling, legal services, maintenance, transportation, insurance, liability, performance bond, capital construction and maintenance and property tax; indirect costs including administrative overhead and contract management; and other costs, such as inmate wages and gate fees.

Of the six areas, cost comparison might be the most difficult. State and county correctional agencies as well as private providers often use per-inmate per-day cost as the single most important criterion in contract award and program evaluation. The per-inmate per-day cost approach is a useful, but not necessarily the most accurate, method to compare costs between publicly and privately run corrections facilities. This is difficult unless the facilities are identical in location, size, building design, inmate characteristics and correctional programs. Adding to the difficulty of cost comparison, private providers tend to include every expense, while governments tend to underestimate costs. Finally, capital costs (assuming that government builds a facility) for a publicly run facility tends to increase government's per-inmate per-day cost considerably.

Conclusion

Most prison privatization activities began in the mid-1980s. In 1985, the policy of the American Correctional Association read, "Profit and non-profit organizations have resources for the delivery of services that often are unavailable from the public correctional agency. It is consistent with good correctional policy and practice to consider use of profit and non-profit organizations to develop, fund, build, operate and provide services, programs, and facilities when such an approach is cost-effective, safe and consistent with the public interest and sound correctional practice."

Although many state and local governments have studied privatization since 1985, few have yet to approve its use. Pennsylvania is an example. In 1986, the Pennsylvania Legislature imposed a moratorium on the operation of private prisons and created a legislative task force to study private correctional facilities. Earlier, Pennsylvania had considered a private maximum-security prison to house protective custody adult offenders from other states. On the national level, the American Bar Association in 1986 called for a moratorium on privatization of prisons and jails "until the complex constitutional, statutory and contractual issues are satisfactorily developed and resolved." A November 1988 ABA report on legal issues of privately owned and operated prisons and jails warned government officials to remain eternally vigilant when contracting these services. The report said, "If this critical government function is to be contracted out, it must be accomplished with total accountability."

Most states' constitutions and statutes do not specifically address privatization issues. New legislation should encompass a wide range of legal, administrative and technical issues. The issues that should be considered include delegation of government authority to private contractors, liability, contract mismanagement provisions, bankruptcy, contract monitoring, inmates' civil rights, corruption, quality of service, flexibility, security, accountability, dependency, equity and propriety. It is government's responsibility to require private providers to meet corrections standards.

Prison privatization is no panacea for prison overcrowding. It is, however, an option worth considering. Several models are available in prison privatization and state and local governments are experimenting with them. There are circumstances when governments should consider privatization. Finally, it is time to assess the cost-effectiveness of prison privatization.

James K. Stewart, director of the National Institute of Justice, said to the President's Commission on Privatization in December 1987, "Until private prison operators are given an opportunity to succeed or fail in meeting their promises, the debate over private prisons will continue to be clouded by the claims, counterclaims and vested interests that arise in response to any proposal which represents a dramatic departure from the status quo."

For states and localities there has never been a more opportune time for testing the benefits of private models for prisons.

Sources

Hackett, Judith, et al. October 1987. *Issues in Contracting for the Private Operation of Prisons and Jails*. Washington D.C.: The National Institute of Justice.

Logan, Charles H. December 1988. *Private Prisons: Cons and Pros*. A Report to The National Institute of Justice. Washington D.C.: The National Institute of Justice.

Mullen, Joan. et al. February 1985. *The Privatization of Corrections*. Washington D.C.: The National Institute of Justice.

Robinson, Ira P. 1988. "The Legal Dimensions of Private Incarceration." Chicago: The American Bar Association.

Stewart, James K. December 22, 1987. "Statement of the Honorable James K. Stewart, Director, National Institute of Justice before the President's Commission on Privatization." Washington D.C.: The National Institute of Justice.

The Commonwealth of Massachusetts. July 1986. "Prisons for Profit." Legislative Research Council.

'THIS MAN HAS EXPIRED'

WITNESS TO AN EXECUTION

9

ROBERT JOHNSON

ROBERT JOHNSON *is professor of justice, law, and society at The American University, Washington, D.C. This article is drawn from a Distinguished Faculty Lecture, given under the auspices of the university's senate last spring.*

The death penalty has made a comeback in recent years. In the late sixties and through most of the seventies, such a thing seemed impossible. There was a moratorium on executions in the U.S., backed by the authority of the Supreme Court. The hiatus lasted roughly a decade. Coming on the heels of a gradual but persistent decline in the use of the death penalty in the Western world, it appeared to some that executions would pass from the American scene [cf. *Commonweal*, January 15, 1988]. Nothing could have been further from the truth.

Beginning with the execution of Gary Gilmore in 1977, over 100 people have been put to death, most of them in the last few years. Some 2,200 prisoners are presently confined on death rows across the nation. The majority of these prisoners have lived under sentence of death for years, in some cases a decade or more, and are running out of legal appeals. It is fair to say that the death penalty is alive and well in America, and that executions will be with us for the foreseeable future.

Gilmore's execution marked the resurrection of the modern death penalty and was big news. It was commemorated in a best-selling tome by Norman Mailer, *The Executioner's Song*. The title was deceptive. Like others who have examined the death penalty, Mailer told us a great deal about the condemned but very little about the executioners. Indeed, if we dwell on Mailer's account, the executioner's story is not only unsung; it is distorted.

Gilmore's execution was quite atypical. His was an instance of state-assisted suicide accompanied by an element of romance and played out against a backdrop of media fanfare. Unrepentant and unafraid, Gilmore refused to appeal his conviction. He dared the state of Utah to take his life, and the media repeated the challenge until it became a taunt that may well have goaded officials to action. A failed suicide pact with his lover staged only days before the execution, using drugs she delivered to him in a visit marked by unusual intimacy, added a hint of melodrama to the proceedings. Gilmore's final words, "Let's do it," seemed to invite the lethal hail of bullets from the firing squad. The nonchalant phrase, at once fatalistic and brazenly rebellious, became Gilmore's epitaph. It clinched his outlaw-hero image, and found its way onto tee shirts that confirmed his celebrity status.

Befitting a celebrity, Gilmore was treated with unusual leniency by prison officials during his confinement on death row. He was, for example, allowed to hold a party the night before his execution, during which he was free to eat, drink, and make merry with his guests until the early morning hours. This is not entirely unprecedented. Notorious English convicts of centuries past would throw farewell balls in prison on the eve of their executions. News accounts of such affairs sometimes included a commentary on the richness of the table and the quality of the dancing. For the record, Gilmore served Tang, Kool-Aid, cookies, and coffee, later supplemented by contraband pizza and an unidentified liquor. Periodically, he gobbled drugs obligingly provided by the prison pharmacy. He played a modest arrangement of rock music albums but refrained from dancing.

Gilmore's execution generally, like his parting fete, was decidedly out of step with the tenor of the modern death penalty. Most condemned prisoners fight to save their lives, not to have them taken. They do not see their fate in romantic terms; there are no farewell parties. Nor are they given medication to ease their anxiety or win their compliance. The subjects of typical executions remain anonymous to the public and even to their keepers. They are very much alone at the end.

In contrast to Mailer's account, the focus of the research I have conducted is on the executioners themselves as they carry out typical executions. In my experience executioners—not unlike Mailer himself—can be quite voluble, and sometimes quite moving, in expressing themselves. I shall draw upon their words to describe the death work they carry out in our name.

DEATH WORK AND DEATH WORKERS

Executioners are not a popular subject of social research, let alone conversation at the dinner table or cocktail party. We simply don't give the subject much thought. When we think of executioners at all, the imagery runs to individual men of disreputable, or at least questionable, character who work stealthily behind the scenes to carry out their grim labors. We picture hooded men hiding in the shadow of the gallows, or anonymous figures lurking out of sight behind electric chairs, gas chambers, firing blinds, or, more recently, hospital gurneys. We wonder who would do such grisly work and how they sleep at night.

This image of the executioner as a sinister and often solitary character is today misleading. To be sure, a few states hire free-lance executioners and traffic in macabre theatrics. Executioners may be picked up under cover of darkness and some may still wear black hoods. But today, executions are generally the work of a highly disciplined and efficient team of correctional officers.

Broadly speaking, the execution process as it is now practiced starts with the prisoner's confinement on death row, an oppressive prison-within-a-prison where the condemned are housed, sometimes for years, awaiting execution. Death work gains momentum when an execution date draws near and the prisoner is moved to the death house, a short walk from the death chamber. Finally, the process culminates in the death watch, a twenty-four-hour period that ends when the prisoner has been executed.

This final period, the death watch, is generally undertaken by correctional officers who work as a team and report directly to the prison warden. The warden or his representative, in turn, must by law preside over the execution. In many states, it is a member of the death watch or execution team, acting under the warden's authority, who in fact plays the formal role of executioner. Though this officer may technically work alone, his teammates view the execution as a shared responsibility. As one officer on the death watch told me in no uncertain terms: "We all take part in it; we all play 100 percent in it, too. That takes the load off this one individual [who pulls the switch]." The formal executioner concurred. "Everyone on the team can do it, and nobody will tell you I did it. I know my team." I found nothing in my research to dispute these claims.

The officers of these death watch teams are our modern executioners. As part of a larger study of the death work process, I studied one such group. This team, comprised of nine seasoned officers of varying ranks, had carried out five electrocutions at the time I began my research. I interviewed each officer on the team after the fifth execution, then served as an official witness at a sixth electrocution. Later, I served as a behind-the-scenes observer during their seventh execution. The results of this phase of my research form the substance of this essay.

THE DEATH WATCH TEAM

The death watch or execution team members refer to themselves, with evident pride, as simply "the team." This pride is shared by other correctional officials. The warden at the institution I was observing praised members of the team as solid citizens—in his words, country boys. These country boys, he assured me, could be counted on to do the job and do it well. As a fellow administrator put it, "an execution is something [that] needs to be done and good people, dedicated people who believe in the American system, should do it. And there's a certain amount of feeling, probably one to another, that they're part of that—that when they have to hang tough, they can do it, and they can do it right. And that it's just the right thing to do."

The official view is that an execution is a job that has to be done, and done right. The death penalty is, after all, the law of the land. In this context, the phrase "done right" means that an execution should be a proper, professional, dignified undertaking. In the words of a prison administrator, "We had to be sure that we did it properly, professionally, and [that] we gave as much dignity to the person as we possibly could in the process....If you've gotta do it, it might just as well be done the way it's supposed to be done—without any sensation."

In the language of the prison officials, "proper" refers to procedures that go off smoothly; "professional" means without personal feelings that intrude on the procedures in any way. The desire for executions that take place "without any sensation" no doubt refers to the absence of media sensationalism, particularly if there should be an embarrassing and undignified hitch in the procedures, for example, a prisoner who breaks down or becomes violent and must be forcibly placed in the electric chair as witnesses, some from the media, look on in horror. Still, I can't help but note that this may be a revealing slip of the tongue. For executions are indeed meant to go off without any human feeling, without any sensation. A profound absence of feeling would seem to capture the bureaucratic ideal embodied in the modern execution.

The view of executions held by the execution team members parallels that of correctional administrators but is somewhat more restrained. The officers of the team are closer to the killing and dying, and are less apt to wax abstract or eloquent in describing the process. Listen to one man's observations:

> It's a job. I don't take it personally. You know, I don't take it like I'm having a grudge against this person and this person has done something to me. I'm just carrying out a job, doing what I was asked to do....This man has been sentenced to death in the courts. This is the law and he broke this law, and he has to suffer the consequences. And one of the consequences is to put him to death.

I found that few members of the execution team support the death penalty outright or without reservation. Having seen executions close up, many of them have lingering doubts about the justice or wisdom of this sanction. As one officer put it:

> I'm not sure the death penalty is the right way. I don't know if there is a right answer. So I look at it like this: if it's gotta be done, at least it can be done in a humane way, if there is such a word for it. . . . The only way it should be done, I feel, is the way we do it. It's done professionally; it's not no horseplaying. Everything is done by documentation. On time. By the book.

Arranging executions that occur "without any sensation" and that go "by the book" is no mean task, but it is a task that is undertaken in earnest by the execution team. The tone of the enterprise is set by the team leader, a man who takes a hard-boiled, no-nonsense approach to correctional work in general and death work in particular. "My style," he says, "is this: if it's a job to do, get it done. Do it and that's it." He seeks out kindred spirits, men who see killing condemned prisoners as a job—a dirty job one does reluctantly, perhaps, but above all a job one carries out dispassionately and in the line of duty.

To make sure that line of duty is a straight and accurate one, the death watch team has been carefully drilled by the team leader in the mechanics of execution. The process has been broken down into simple, discrete tasks and practiced repeatedly. The team leader describes the division of labor in the following exchange:

> the execution team is a nine-officer team and each one has certain things to do. When I would train you, maybe you'd buckle a belt, that might be all you'd have to do. . . . And you'd be expected to do one thing and that's all you'd be expected to do. And if everybody does what they were taught, or what they were trained to do, at the end the man would be put in the chair and everything would be complete. It's all come together now.
>
> So it's broken down into very small steps. . . .
>
> *Very small,* yes. Each person has *one* thing to do.
>
> I see. What's the purpose of breaking it down into such small steps?
>
> So people won't get confused. I've learned it's kind of a tense time. When you're executin' a person, killing a person—you call it killin', executin', whatever you want—the man dies anyway. I find the less you got on your mind, why, the better you'll carry it out. So it's just very simple things. And so far, you know, it's all come together, we haven't had any problems.

This division of labor allows each man on the execution team to become a specialist, a technician with a sense of pride in his work. Said one man,

> My assignment is the leg piece. Right leg. I roll his pants leg up, place a piece [electrode] on his leg, strap his leg in. . . . I've got all the moves down pat. We train from different posts; I can do any of them. But that's my main post.

The implication is not that the officers are incapable of performing multiple or complex tasks, but simply that it is more efficient to focus each officer's efforts on one easy task.

An essential part of the training is practice. Practice is meant to produce a confident group, capable of fast and accurate performance under pressure. The rewards of practice are reaped in improved performance. Executions take place with increasing efficiency, and eventually occur with precision. "The first one was grisly," a team member confided to me. He explained that there was a certain amount of fumbling, which made the execution seem interminable. There were technical problems as well: The generator was set too high so the body was badly burned. But that is the past, the officer assured me. "The ones now, we know what we're doing. It's just like clockwork."

THE DEATH WATCH

The death-watch team is deployed during the last twenty-four hours before an execution. In the state under study, the death watch starts at 11 o'clock the night before the execution and ends at 11 o'clock the next night when the execution takes place. At least two officers would be with the prisoner at any given time during that period. Their objective is to keep the prisoner alive and "on schedule." That is, to move him through a series of critical and cumulatively demoralizing junctures that begin with his last meal and end with his last walk. When the time comes, they must deliver the prisoner up for execution as quickly and unobtrusively as possible.

Broadly speaking, the job of the death watch officer, as one man put it, "is to sit and keep the inmate calm for the last twenty-four hours—and get the man ready to go." Keeping a condemned prisoner calm means, in part, serving his immediate needs. It seems paradoxical to think of the death watch officers as providing services to the condemned, but the logistics of the job make service a central obligation of the officers. Here's how one officer made this point:

> Well, you can't help but be involved with many of the things that he's involved with. Because if he wants to make a call to his family, well, you'll have to dial the number. And you keep records of whatever calls he makes. If he wants a cigarette, well he's not allowed to keep matches so you light it for him. You've got to pour his coffee, too. So you're aware what he's doing. It's not like you can just ignore him. You've gotta just be with him whether he wants it or not, and cater to his needs.

Officers cater to the condemned because contented inmates are easier to keep under control. To a man, the officers say this is so. But one can never trust even a contented, condemned prisoner.

The death-watch officers see condemned prisoners as men with explosive personalities. "You don't know what, what a man's gonna do," noted one officer. "He's liable to snap, he's liable to pass out. We watch him all the time to prevent him from committing suicide. You've got to be ready—he's liable to do anything." The prisoner is never out of at least one officer's sight. Thus surveillance is constant, and control, for all intents and purposes, is total.

Relations between the officers and their charges during the death watch can be quite intense. Watching and being watched are central to this enterprise, and these are always engaging activities, particularly when the stakes are life and death. These relations are, nevertheless, utterly impersonal; there are no grudges but neither is there compassion or fellow-feeling. Officers are civil but cool; they keep an emotional distance from the men they are about to kill. To do otherwise, they maintain, would make it harder to execute condemned prisoners. The attitude of the officers is that the prisoners arrive as strangers and are easier to kill if they stay that way.

During the last five or six hours, two specific team officers are assigned to guard the prisoner. Unlike their more taciturn and aloof colleagues on earlier shifts, these officers make a conscious effort to talk with the prisoner. In one officer's words, "We keep them right there and keep talking to them—about anything except the chair." The point of these conversations is not merely to pass time; it is to keep tabs on the prisoner's state of mind, and to steer him away from subjects that might depress, anger, or otherwise upset him. Sociability, in other words, quite explicitly serves as a source of social control. Relationships, such as they are, serve purely manipulative ends. This is impersonality at its worst, masquerading as concern for the strangers one hopes to execute with as little trouble as possible.

Generally speaking, as the execution moves closer, the mood becomes more somber and subdued. There is a last meal. Prisoners can order pretty much what they want, but most eat little or nothing at all. At this point, the prisoners may steadfastly maintain that their executions will be stayed. Such bravado is belied by their loss of appetite. "You can see them going down," said one officer. "Food is the last thing they got on their minds."

Next the prisoners must box their meager worldly goods. These are inventoried by the staff, recorded on a one-page checklist form, and marked for disposition to family or friends. Prisoners are visibly saddened, even moved to tears, by this procedure, which at once summarizes their lives and highlights the imminence of death. At this point, said one of the officers, "I really get into him; I watch him real close." The execution schedule, the officer pointed out, is "picking up momentum, and we don't want to lose control of the situation."

This momentum is not lost on the condemned prisoner. Critical milestones have been passed. The prisoner moves in a limbo existence devoid of food or possessions; he has seen the last of such things, unless he receives a stay of execution and rejoins the living. His identity is expropriated as well. The critical juncture in this regard is the shaving of the man's head (including facial hair) and right leg. Hair is shaved to facilitate the electrocution; it reduces physical resistance to electricity and minimizes singeing and burning. But the process has obvious psychological significance as well, adding greatly to the momentum of the execution.

The shaving procedure is quite public and intimidating. The condemned man is taken from his cell and seated in the middle of the tier. His hands and feet are cuffed, and he is dressed only in undershorts. The entire death watch team is assembled around him. They stay at a discrete distance, but it is obvious that they are there to maintain control should he resist in any way or make any untoward move. As a rule, the man is overwhelmed. As one officer told me in blunt terms, "Come eight o'clock, we've got a dead man. Eight o'clock is when we shave the man. We take his identity; it goes with the hair." This taking of identity is indeed a collective process—the team makes a forceful "we," the prisoner their helpless object. The staff is confident that the prisoner's capacity to resist is now compromised. What is left of the man erodes gradually and, according the officers, perceptibly over the remaining three hours before the execution.

After the prisoner has been shaved, he is then made to shower and don a fresh set of clothes for the execution. The clothes are unremarkable in appearance, except that velcro replaces buttons and zippers, to reduce the chance of burning the body. The main significance of the clothes is symbolic: they mark the prisoner as a man who is ready for execution. Now physically "prepped," to quote one team member, the prisoner is placed in an empty tomblike cell, the death cell. All that is left is the wait. During this fateful period, the prisoner is more like an object "without any sensation" than like a flesh-and-blood person on the threshold of death.

For condemned prisoners, like Gilmore, who come to accept and even to relish their impending deaths, a genuine calm seems to prevail. It is as if they can transcend the dehumanizing forces at work around them and go to their deaths in peace. For most condemned prisoners, however, numb resignation rather than peaceful acceptance is the norm. By the account of the death-watch officers, these more typical prisoners are beaten men. Listen to the officers' accounts:

> A lot of 'em die in their minds before they go to that chair. I've never known of one or heard of one putting up a fight. . . . By the time they walk to the chair, they've completely faced it. Such a reality most people can't understand. Cause they don't fight it. They don't seem to have anything to say. It's just something like "Get it over with." They may be numb, sort of in a trance.
>
> They go through stages. And, at this stage, they're real humble. Humblest bunch of people I ever seen. Most all of 'em is real, real weak. Most of the time you'd only need one or two people to carry out an execution, as weak and as humble as they are.

These men seem barely human and alive to their keepers. They wait meekly to be escorted to their deaths. The people who come for them are the warden and the remainder of the death watch team, flanked by high-ranking correctional officials. The warden reads the court order, known popularly as a death warrant. This is, as one officer said, "the real deal," and nobody misses its significance. The condemned prisoners then go to their deaths compliantly, captives of the inexorable, irresistible momentum of the situation. As one officer put it, "There's no struggle. . . . They just walk right on in there." So too, do the staff "just walk right on in there," following a routine they have come to know well. Both the condemned and the executioners, it would seem, find a relief of sorts in mindless mechanical conformity to the modern execution drill.

WITNESS TO AN EXECUTION

As the team and administrators prepare to commence the good fight, as they might say, another group, the official witnesses, are also preparing themselves for their role in the execution. Numbering between six and twelve for any given execution, the official witnesses are disinterested citizens in good standing drawn from a cross-section of the state's population. If you will, they are every good or decent person, called upon to represent the community and use their good offices to testify to the propriety of the execution. I served as an official witness at the execution of an inmate.

At eight in the evening, about the time the prisoner is shaved in preparation for the execution, the witnesses are assembled. Eleven in all, we included three newspaper and two television reporters, a state trooper, two police officers, a magistrate, a businessman, and myself. We were picked up in the parking lot behind the main office of the corrections department. There was nothing unusual or even memorable about any of this. Gothic touches were notable by their absence. It wasn't a dark and stormy night; no one emerged from the shadows to lead us to the prison gates.

Mundane considerations prevailed. The van sent for us was missing a few rows of seats so there wasn't enough room for all of us. Obliging prison officials volunteered their cars. Our rather ordinary cavalcade reached the prison but only after getting lost. Once within the prison's walls, we were sequestered for some two hours in a bare and almost shabby administrative conference room. A public information officer was assigned to accompany us and answer our questions. We grilled this official about the prisoner and the execution procedure he would undergo shortly, but little information was to be had. The man confessed ignorance on the most basic points. Disgruntled at this and increasingly anxious, we made small talk and drank coffee.

At 10:40 P.M., roughly two-and-a-half hours after we were assembled and only twenty minutes before the execution was scheduled to occur, the witnesses were taken to the basement of the prison's administrative building, frisked, then led down an alleyway that ran along the exterior of the building. We entered a neighboring cell block and were admitted to a vestibule adjoining the death chamber. Each of us signed a log, and was then led off to the witness area. To our left, around a corner some thirty feet away, the prisoner sat in the condemned cell. He couldn't see us, but I'm quite certain he could hear us. It occurred to me that our arrival was a fateful reminder for the prisoner. The next group would be led by the warden, and it would be coming for him.

We entered the witness area, a room within the death chamber, and took our seats. A picture window covering the front wall of the witness room offered a clear view of the electric chair, which was about twelve feet away from us and well illuminated. The chair, a large, high-back solid oak structure with imposing black straps, dominated the death chamber. Behind it, on the back wall, was an open panel full of coils and lights. Peeling paint hung from the ceiling and walls; water stains from persistent leaks were everywhere in evidence.

Two officers, one a hulking figure weighing some 400 pounds, stood alongside the electric chair. Each had his hands crossed at the lap and wore a forbidding, blank expression on his face. The witnesses gazed at them and the chair, most of us scribbling notes furiously. We did this, I suppose, as much to record the experience as to have a distraction from the growing tension. A correctional officer entered the witness room and announced that a trial run of the machinery would be undertaken. Seconds later, lights flashed on the control panel behind the chair indicating that the chair was in working order. A white curtain, opened for the test, separated the chair and the witness area. After the test, the curtain was drawn. More tests were performed behind the curtain. Afterwards, the curtain was reopened, and would be left open until the execution was over. Then it would be closed to allow the officers to remove the body.

A handful of high-level correctional officials were present in the death chamber, standing just outside the witness area. There were two regional administrators, the director of the Department of Corrections, and the prison warden. The prisoner's chaplain and lawyer were also present. Other than the chaplain's black religious garb, subdued grey pinstripes and bland correctional uniforms prevailed. All parties were quite solemn.

At 10:58 the prisoner entered the death chamber. He was, I knew from my research, a man with a checkered, tragic past. He had been grossly abused as a child, and went on to become grossly abusive of others. I was told he could not describe his life, from childhood on, without talking about confrontations in defense of a precarious sense of self—at home, in school, on the streets, in the prison yard. Belittled by life and choking with rage, he was hungry to be noticed. Paradoxically, he had found his moment in the spotlight, but it was a dim and unflattering light cast before a small and unappreciative audience. "He'd pose for cameras in the chair—for the attention," his counselor had told me earlier in the day. But the truth was that the prisoner wasn't smiling, and there were no cameras.

The prisoner walked quickly and silently toward the chair, an escort of officers in tow. His eyes were turned downward, his expression a bit glazed. Like many before him, the prisoner had threatened to stage a last stand. But that was lifetimes ago, on death row. In the death house, he joined the humble bunch and kept to the executioner's schedule. He appeared to have given up on life before he died in the chair.

En route to the chair, the prisoner stumbled slightly, as if the momentum of the event had overtaken him. Were he not held securely by two officers, one at each elbow, he might have fallen. Were the routine to be broken in this or indeed any other way, the officers believe, the prisoner might faint or panic or become violent, and have to be forcibly placed in the chair. Perhaps as a precaution, when the prisoner reached the chair he did not turn on his own but rather was turned, firmly but without malice, by the officers in his escort. These included the two men at his elbows, and four others who followed behind him. Once the prisoner was seated, again with help, the officers strapped him into the chair.

The execution team worked with machine precision. Like a disciplined swarm, they enveloped him. Arms, legs, stomach, chest, and head were secured in a matter of seconds. Electrodes were attached to the cap holding his head and to the strap holding his exposed right leg. A leather mask was placed over his face. The last officer mopped the prisoner's brow, then touched his hand in a gesture of farewell.

During the brief procession to the electric chair, the prisoner was attended by a chaplain. As the execution team worked feverishly to secure the condemned man's body, the chaplain, who appeared to be upset, leaned over him and placed his forehead in contact with the prisoner's, whispering urgently. The priest might have been praying, but I had the impression he was consoling the man, perhaps assuring him that a forgiving God awaited him in the next life. If he heard the chaplain, I doubt the man comprehended his message. He didn't seem comforted. Rather, he looked stricken and appeared to be in shock. Perhaps the priest's urgent ministrations betrayed his doubts that the prisoner could hold himself together. The chaplain then withdrew at the warden's request, allowing the officers to affix the death mask.

The strapped and masked figure sat before us, utterly alone, waiting to be killed. The cap and mask dominated his face. The cap was nothing more than a sponge encased in a leather shell with a metal piece at the top to accept an electrode. It looked decrepit and resembled a cheap, ill-fitting toupee. The mask, made entirely of leather, appeared soiled and worn. It had two parts. The bottom part covered the chin and mouth, the top the eyes and lower forehead. Only the nose was exposed. The effect of a rigidly restrained body, together with the bizarre cap and the protruding nose, was nothing short of grotesque. A faceless man breathed before us in a tragicomic trance, waiting for a blast of electricity that would extinguish his life. Endless seconds passed. His last act was to swallow, nervously, pathetically, with his Adam's apple bobbing. I was struck by that simple movement then, and can't forget it even now. It told me, as nothing else did, that in the prisoner's restrained body, behind that mask, lurked a fellow human being who, at some level, however primitive, knew or sensed himself to be moments from death.

The condemned man sat perfectly still for what seemed an eternity but was in fact no more than thirty seconds. Finally the electricity hit him. His body stiffened spasmodically, though only briefly. A thin swirl of smoke trailed away from his head and then dissipated quickly. The body remained taut, with the right foot raised slightly at the heel, seemingly frozen there. A brief pause, then another minute of shock. When it was over, the body was flaccid and inert.

Three minutes passed while the officials let the body cool. (Immediately after the execution, I'm told, the body would be too hot to touch and would blister anyone who did.) All eyes were riveted to the chair; I felt trapped in my witness seat, at once transfixed and yet eager for release. I can't recall any clear thoughts from that moment. One of the death watch officers later volunteered that he shared this experience of staring blankly at the execution scene. Had the prisoner's mind been mercifully blank before the end? I hoped so.

An officer walked up to the body, opened the shirt at chest level, then continued on to get the physician from an adjoining room. The physician listened for a heartbeat. Hearing none, he turned to the warden and said, "This man has expired." The warden, speaking to the director, solemnly intoned: "Mr. Director, the court order has been fulfilled." The curtain was then drawn and the witnesses filed out.

THE MORNING AFTER

As the team prepared the body for the morgue, the witnesses were led to the front door of the prison. On the way, we passed a number of cell blocks. We could hear the normal sounds of prison life, including the occasional catcall and lewd comment hurled at uninvited guests like ourselves. But no trouble came in the wake of the execution. Small protests were going on outside the walls, we were told, but we could not hear them. Soon the media would be gone; the protestors would disperse and head for their homes. The prisoners, already home, had been indifferent to the proceedings, as they always are unless the condemned prisoner had been a figure of some consequence in the convict community. Then there might be tension and maybe even a modest disturbance on a prison tier or two. But few convict luminaries are executed, and the dead man had not been one of them. Our escort officer offered a sad tribute to the prisoner: "The inmates, they didn't care about this guy."

I couldn't help but think they weren't alone in this. The executioners went home and set about their lives. Having taken life, they would savor a bit of life themselves. They showered, ate, made love, slept, then took a day or two off. For some, the prisoner's image would linger for that night. The men who strapped him in remembered what it was like to touch him; they showered as soon as they got home to wash off the feel and smell of death. One official sat up picturing how the prisoner looked at the end. (I had a few drinks myself that night with that same image for company.) There was some talk about delayed reactions to the stress of carrying out executions. Though such concerns seemed remote that evening, I learned later that problems would surface for some of the officers. But no one on the team, then or later, was haunted by the executed man's memory, nor would anyone grieve for him. "When I go home after one of these things," said one man, "I sleep like a rock." His may or may not be the sleep of the just, but one can only marvel at such a thing, and perhaps envy such a man.

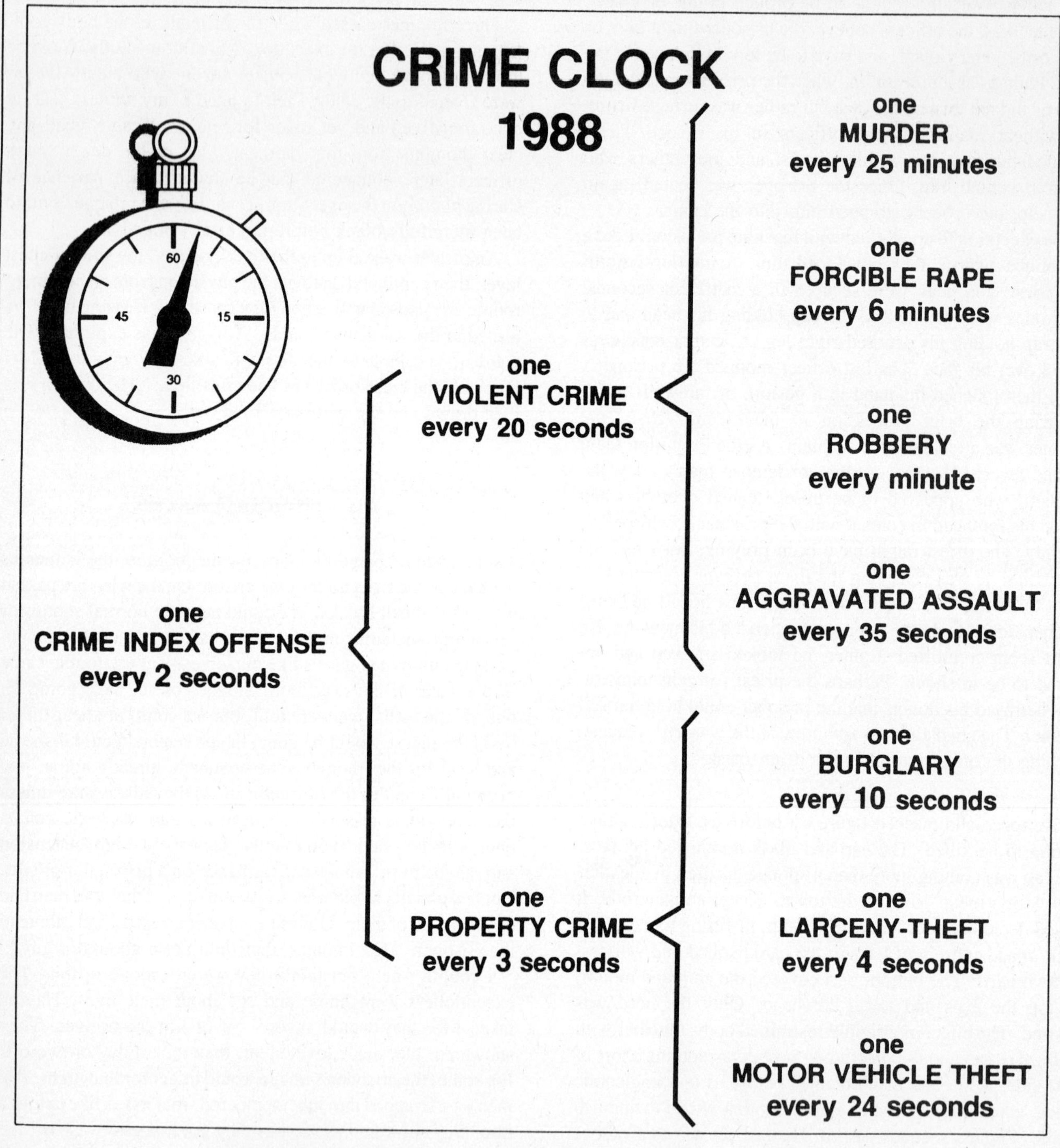

The crime clock should be viewed with care. Being the most aggregate representation of UCR data, it is designed to convey the annual reported crime experience by showing the relative frequency of occurrence of the Index Offenses. This mode of display should not be taken to imply a regularity in the commission of the Part I Offenses; rather, it represents the annual ratio of crime to fixed time intervals.

Crime in the United States 1988

The Crime Index total rose 3 percent to 13.9 million offenses in 1988. Five- and 10-year percent changes showed the 1988 total was 17 percent above the 1984 level and 14 percent higher than in 1979.

From 1987 to 1988, overall violent crime showed a 6-percent increase. Among the violent crimes, aggravated assault increased 6 percent; robbery, 5 percent; murder, 3 percent; and forcible rape, 2 percent.

The number of property crimes increased 3 percent for the 2-year period. Motor vehicle theft rose 11 percent, and larceny-theft was up 3 percent. Burglary showed a 1-percent decline.

Considering 5- and 10-year timeframes, the 1988 violent and property crime totals each showed increases. Violent crime was up 23 percent and property crime, 16 percent over 1984 figures. A comparison of 1979 and 1988 figures showed upswings of 30 percent for violent crime and 12 percent for property crime. National estimates of volume and rate per 100,000 inhabitants for all Crime Index offenses covering the past decade are set forth in Table 1, "Index of Crime, United States, 1979-1988." Crime rates relate the incidence of reported crime to population.

Table 1.—Index of Crime, United States, 1979-1988

Population[1]	Crime Index total[2]	Modified Crime Index total[3]	Violent crime[4]	Property crime[4]	Murder and non-negligent man-slaughter	Forcible rape	Robbery	Aggra-vated assault	Burglary	Larceny-theft	Motor vehicle theft	Arson[3]
Number of offenses:												
1979-220,099,000	12,249,500		1,208,030	11,041,500	21,460	76,390	480,700	629,480	3,327,700	6,601,000	1,112,800	
1980-225,349,264	13,408,300		1,344,520	12,063,700	23,040	82,990	565,840	672,650	3,795,200	7,136,900	1,131,700	
1981-229,146,000	13,423,800		1,361,820	12,061,900	22,520	82,500	592,910	663,900	3,779,700	7,194,400	1,087,800	
1982-231,534,000	12,974,400		1,322,390	11,652,000	21,010	78,770	553,130	669,480	3,447,100	7,142,500	1,062,400	
1983-233,981,000	12,108,600		1,258,090	10,850,500	19,310	78,920	506,570	653,290	3,129,900	6,712,800	1,007,900	
1984-236,158,000	11,881,800		1,273,280	10,608,500	18,690	84,230	485,010	685,350	2,984,400	6,591,900	1,032,200	
1985-238,740,000	12,431,400		1,328,800	11,102,600	18,980	88,670	497,870	723,250	3,073,300	6,926,400	1,102,900	
1986-241,077,000	13,211,900		1,489,170	11,722,700	20,610	91,460	542,780	834,320	3,241,400	7,257,200	1,224,100	
1987-243,400,000	13,508,700		1,484,000	12,024,700	20,100	91,110	517,700	855,090	3,236,200	7,499,900	1,288,700	
1988-245,807,000	13,923,100		1,566,220	12,356,900	20,680	92,490	542,970	910,090	3,218,100	7,705,900	1,432,900	
Percent change: number of offenses:												
1988/1987	+3.1		+5.5	+2.8	+2.9	+1.5	+4.9	+6.4	-.6	+2.7	+11.2	
1988/1984	+17.2		+23.0	+16.5	+10.6	+9.8	+12.0	+32.8	+7.8	+16.9	+38.8	
1988/1979	+13.7		+29.7	+11.9	-3.6	+21.1	+13.0	+44.6	-3.3	+16.7	+28.8	
Rate per 100,000 inhabitants:												
1979	5,565.5		548.9	5,016.6	9.7	34.7	218.4	286.0	1,511.9	2,999.1	505.6	
1980	5,950.0		596.6	5,353.3	10.2	36.8	251.1	298.5	1,684.1	3,167.0	502.2	
1981	5,858.2		594.3	5,263.9	9.8	36.0	258.7	289.7	1,649.5	3,139.7	474.7	
1982	5,603.6		571.1	5,032.5	9.1	34.0	238.9	289.2	1,488.8	3,084.8	458.8	
1983	5,175.0		537.7	4,637.4	8.3	33.7	216.5	279.2	1,337.7	2,868.9	430.8	
1984	5,031.3		539.2	4,492.1	7.9	35.7	205.4	290.2	1,263.7	2,791.3	437.1	
1985	5,207.1		556.6	4,650.5	7.9	37.1	208.5	302.9	1,287.3	2,901.2	462.0	
1986	5,480.4		617.7	4,862.6	8.6	37.9	225.1	346.1	1,344.6	3,010.3	507.8	
1987	5,550.0		609.7	4,940.3	8.3	37.4	212.7	351.3	1,329.6	3,081.3	529.4	
1988	5,664.2		637.2	5,027.1	8.4	37.6	220.9	370.2	1,309.2	3,134.9	582.9	
Percent change: rate per 100,000 inhabitants:												
1988/1987	+2.1		+4.5	+1.8	+1.2	+.5	+3.9	+5.4	-1.5	+1.7	+10.1	
1988/1984	+12.6		+18.2	+11.9	+6.3	+5.3	+7.5	+27.6	+3.6	+12.3	+33.3	
1988/1979	+1.8		+16.1	+.2	-13.4	+8.4	+1.1	+29.4	-13.4	+4.5	+15.3	

[1]Populations are Bureau of the Census provisional estimates as of July 1, except April 1, 1980, preliminary census counts, and are subject to change.
[2]Because of rounding, the offenses may not add to totals.
[3]Although arson data are included in the trend and clearance tables, sufficient data are not available to estimate totals for this offense.
[4]Violent crimes are offenses of murder, forcible rape, robbery, and aggravated assault. Property crimes are offenses of burglary, larceny-theft, and motor vehicle theft. Data are not included for the property crime of arson.

All rates were calculated on the offenses before rounding.

Data for 1988 were not available for the States of Florida and Kentucky; therefore, it was necessary that their crime counts be estimated.

CRIME INDEX OFFENSES REPORTED

MURDER AND NONNEGLIGENT MANSLAUGHTER

DEFINITION

Murder and nonnegligent manslaughter, as defined in the Uniform Crime Reporting Program, is the willful (nonnegligent) killing of one human being by another.

TREND

Year	*Number of offenses*	*Rate per 100,000 inhabitants*
1987	20,096	8.3
1988	20,675	8.4
Percent change	+2.9	+1.2

Volume

The total number of murders in th Jnited States during 1988 was estimated at 20,675 or 1 percent of the violent crimes reported. More persons were murdered in August than any other month, while the fewest were killed during February.

Geographically, the Southern States, the most populous region, accounted for 42 percent of the murders. The Western States reported 21 percent; the Midwestern States, 19 percent; and the Northeastern States, 18 percent.

Murder by Month, 1984-1988
[Percent of annual total]

Months	1984	1985	1986	1987	1988
January	8.3	8.1	7.7	7.7	8.2
February	7.5	7.9	7.0	7.9	7.2
March	8.1	8.1	8.3	8.2	7.7
April	7.9	7.6	8.0	7.6	7.7
May	8.0	7.6	8.2	8.6	7.8
June	7.8	8.2	8.3	7.8	7.7
July	8.6	9.3	9.4	8.6	8.9
August	8.8	9.1	9.4	8.9	9.5
September	8.7	8.1	9.1	8.3	8.9
October	8.8	8.4	8.3	8.8	8.9
November	8.6	8.2	8.0	8.3	8.2
December	9.0	9.4	8.4	9.1	9.2

Trend

The murder volume increased 3 percent nationwide in 1988 over 1987. The Nation's cities overall experienced an increase of 4 percent, while both the suburban and rural counties recorded 2-percent declines. Among city groupings, those of jurisdictions with populations over 25,000 registered increases ranging from 1 to 8 percent. The groupings of cities with smaller populations showed declines, 5 percent in those with 10,000 to 24,999 inhabitants and 3 percent in those with populations under 10,000.

Viewed regionally, the murder counts increased 10 percent in the Northeast, 4 percent in the South, and 1 percent in the West from 1987 to 1988. A 3-percent decline was experienced in the Midwestern States.

The accompanying chart reveals an 11-percent rise nationally in the murder counts from 1984 to 1988. The 10-year trend showed the 1988 total 4 percent below the 1979 level.

Rate

Up 1 percent from 1987, the 1988 United States murder rate was 8 per 100,000 inhabitants. On a regional basis, the Southern States averaged 10 murders per 100,000 people; the Western States, 9 per 100,000; the Northeastern States, 8 per 100,000; and the Midwestern States, 6 per 100,000. The murder rate in the Northeast was up 9 percent, 1988 versus 1987. In the South, it increased 3 percent, and in the West, it showed no change. A rate decrease of 4 percent was recorded in the Midwest.

The Nation's metropolitan areas reported a 1988 murder rate of 9 victims per 100,000 inhabitants. In the rural counties, the rate was 5 per 100,000, and in the cities outside metropolitan areas, it was 4 per 100,000.

Nature

Supplemental data provided by contributing agencies recorded information for 18,269 of the estimated 20,675 murders in 1988. Submitted monthly, the data consist of the age, sex, and race of both victims and offenders; the types of weapons used; the relationships of victims to the offenders; and the circumstances surrounding the murders.

Based on this information, 75 percent of the murder victims in 1988 were males. Ninety-one percent were persons 18 years of age or older, with 49 percent aged 20 through 34 years. Considering victims for whom race was known, an average of 50 of every 100 were white, 49 were black, and the remainder were persons of other races.

FORCIBLE RAPE

DEFINITION

Forcible rape, as defined in the Program, is the carnal knowledge of a female forcibly and against her will. Assaults or attempts to commit rape by force or threat of force are also included; however, statutory rape (without force) and other sex offenses are excluded.

TREND

Year	*Number of offenses*	*Rate per 100,000 inhabitants*
1987	91,111	37.4
1988	92,486	37.6
Percent change	+1.5	+.5

Volume

During 1988, there were an estimated 92,486 forcible rapes in the Nation. Rape offenses comprised 6 percent of the total violent crimes. Geographically, the Southern States, the region with the largest population, accounted for 37 percent of the forcible rapes reported to law enforcement. Following were the Midwest with 25 percent, the West with 23 percent, and the Northeast with the remainder.

Monthly totals showed the greatest number of forcible rapes was reported during the summer, with July recording the highest frequency. The lowest total was registered in December.

Forcible Rape by Month, 1984-1988
[Percent of annual total]

Months	1984	1985	1986	1987	1988
January	7.1	7.2	7.1	7.2	7.4
February	7.1	6.6	6.7	6.8	7.3
March	7.6	8.2	7.9	8.1	8.0
April	7.7	8.3	8.1	8.2	8.0
May	8.6	8.9	8.8	8.9	9.0
June	8.9	9.0	9.2	9.3	8.7
July	9.9	10.1	9.8	9.7	9.9
August	10.2	9.9	10.2	9.8	9.8
September	9.1	8.8	9.1	8.9	9.0
October	9.0	8.5	8.4	8.1	8.4
November	7.2	7.7	7.8	7.7	7.6
December	7.5	6.9	7.0	7.3	6.8

Trend

Compared to the previous year, the 1988 forcible rape volume increased 2 percent nationwide. In the suburban counties and cities collectively, the totals were up 1 percent. Rural counties recorded a 1-

percent decline. City trends ranged from a 12-percent increase in cities under 10,000 in population to a 4-percent decline in cities 500,000 to 999,999 in population.

National trends for 5 and 10 years show that the forcible rape total rose 10 percent over 1984 and 21 percent above 1979.

Rate

By Uniform Crime Reporting definition, the victims of forcible rape are always female. In 1988, an estimated 73 of every 100,000 females in the country were reported rape victims. The 1988 female forcible rape rate showed no change from 1987, but was 6 percent higher than in 1984.

Female forcible rape rates for 1988 showed there were 83 victims per 100,000 females in MSAs, 49 per 100,000 females in cities outside metropolitan areas, and 36 per 100,000 females in rural counties.

Regionally, the highest female rape rate was in the Western States, which recorded 81 victims per 100,000 females. Following were the Southern States with a rate of 78, the Midwestern States with 75, and the Northeastern States with 57.

Nature

Of all reported forcible rapes during 1988, 82 percent were rapes by force. The remainder were attempts or assaults to commit forcible rape. An increase of more than 2 percent was registered in the number of rapes by force, while attempts to commit rape decreased 5 percent from the 1987 figures.

Clearances

Nationwide and in the cities, 52 percent of the forcible rapes reported to law enforcement were cleared by arrest or exceptional means in 1988. Rural county law enforcement agencies cleared 55 percent of the offenses brought to their attention, while suburban county agencies cleared 53 percent.

Clearance rates for the regions ranged from 45 percent in the Midwestern States to 56 percent in the Southern States. In the Northeastern States, the clearance rate for forcible rape was 54 percent, and in the Western States, it was 51 percent.

In the country as a whole, the Nation's cities, and the rural counties, 9 percent of the forcible rape clearances involved only persons under the age of 18. Suburban counties recorded a 10-percent involvement of this age group.

Persons Arrested

From 1987 to 1988, the number of persons arrested for forcible rape showed virtually no change nationally. Arrests for this offense declined 1 percent in both suburban counties and the Nation's cities, while arrests in rural counties rose 5 percent. For the 5-year period, 1984 to 1988, increases of 3 percent were recorded for the total forcible rape arrests, and 4 percent for those of adults. A decrease of 2 percent was shown for arrests of persons under 18 years of age during this same period of time.

Of the forcible rape arrestees in 1988, 43 percent were persons under the age of 25, with 29 percent of the total being in the 18- to 24-year age group. Fifth-three percent of those arrested were white, 46 percent were black, and all other races comprised the remainder.

ROBBERY

DEFINITION

Robbery is the taking or attempting to take anything of value from the care, custody, or control of a person or persons by force or threat of force or violence and/or by putting the victim in fear.

TREND

Year	*Number of offenses*	*Rate per 100,000 inhabitants*
1987	517,704	212.7
1988	542,968	220.9
Percent change	+4.9	+3.9

Volume

Accounting for 4 percent of all Index crimes and 35 percent of the crimes of violence, the estimated robbery total in 1988 was 542,968. During the year, robberies occurred most frequently in December and least often in April.

Regionally, the most populous Southern States registered 33 percent of all reported robberies. Following were the Northeastern States with 28 percent, the Western States with 21 percent, and the Midwestern States with the remainder.

Robbery by Month, 1984-1988
[Percent of annual total]

Months	1984	1985	1986	1987	1988
January	8.9	8.6	8.7	8.9	8.6
February	8.2	7.4	7.7	8.1	7.9
March	8.1	7.9	8.2	8.2	8.0
April	7.6	7.3	7.6	7.5	7.3
May	7.6	7.5	7.7	7.5	7.6
June	7.5	7.7	8.0	7.6	7.6
July	7.9	8.6	8.4	8.3	8.4
August	8.5	8.9	9.3	8.7	8.7
September	8.2	8.4	8.6	8.5	8.7
October	9.0	9.1	8.7	8.8	9.1
November	8.6	8.8	8.3	8.5	9.0
December	9.9	9.7	9.0	9.2	9.2

Trend

Upward trends in robbery were evident nationwide and throughout all population groups in 1988. Nationally, the 1988 robbery volume was 5 percent higher than the 1987 level. The suburban counties experienced a 7-percent increase in robberies; the Nation's cities overall, a 4-percent rise; and the rural counties, a 3-percent increase. Of the cities, those with populations of 100,000 to 249,999 registered the greatest increase, 7 percent.

Two-year regional trends show the number of robberies were up in all but one region. The increases were 10 percent in the South; 6 percent in the Northeast; and 2 percent in the West. A 2-percent decrease was recorded in the Midwest.

Robbery, Percent Distribution, 1988
[By region]

	United States Total	North-eastern States	Mid-western States	Southern States	Western States
Total[1]	100.0	100.0	100.0	100.0	100.0
Street/highway	54.0	64.4	55.5	43.9	49.7
Commercial house	11.9	7.5	10.2	15.7	15.2
Gas or service station	2.9	2.2	3.7	3.3	2.7
Convenience store	6.4	2.1	4.3	13.4	6.3
Residence	10.5	11.4	10.5	11.0	8.8
Bank	1.4	.8	1.0	1.1	2.9
Miscellaneous	12.9	11.5	14.8	11.6	14.5

[1]Because of rounding, percentages may not add to totals.

Rate

The national robbery rate in 1988 was 221 per 100,000 people, 4 percent higher than in 1987. In metropolitan areas, the robbery rate was 278; in cities outside metropolitan areas, it was 55; and in the rural areas, it was 15. With 919 robberies per 100,000 inhabitants, the highest rate was recorded in cities with populations over 1 million.

A comparison of 1987 and 1988 regional rates showed the only decline—2 percent—was in the Midwest, which had a rate of 169 per 100,000 population. The South's rate of 209 was 9 percent higher; the Northeast's rate of 299 was up 5 percent; and the West's rate of 225 represented a 1-percent increase.

Nature

In 1988, a total estimated national loss of $343 million was due to robberies. The value of property stolen during robberies averaged $631 per incident. Average dollar losses ranged from $344 taken during robberies of convenience stores to $2,885 per bank robbery. The impact of this violent crime on its victims cannot be measured in terms of monetary loss alone. While the object of a robbery is to obtain money or property, the crime always involves force or threat of force, and many victims suffer serious personal injury.

As in previous years, robberies on streets or highways accounted for more than half (54 percent) of the offenses in this category. Robberies of commercial and financial establishments accounted for an additional 23 percent, and those occurring at residences, 10 percent. The remainder were miscellaneous types. Only gas or service station robberies declined from 1987 to 1988, down 1 percent. Among the other types, convenience store robberies showed the greatest increase, 16 percent.

AGGRAVATED ASSAULT

DEFINITION

Aggravated assault is an unlawful attack by one person upon another for the purpose of inflicting severe or aggravated bodily injury. This type of assault is usually accompanied by the use of a weapon or by means likely to produce death or great bodily harm.

TREND

Year	*Number of offenses*	*Rate per 100,000 inhabitants*
1987	855,088	351.3
1988	910,092	370.2
Percent change	+6.4	+5.4

Volume

Totaling an estimated 910,092 offenses nationally, aggravated assaults in 1988 occurred most frequently in the summer months. Geographic distribution figures show that 36 percent of the aggravated assault volume was accounted for by the Southern States, 25 percent by the Western States, 20 percent by the Midwestern States, and 19 percent by the Northeastern States.

The 1988 monthly figures show that the greatest number of aggravated assaults was recorded during July and August, while the lowest occurred in February.

Trend

In 1988, aggravated assault increased 6 percent nationwide in volume as compared to 1987. For the 2-year period, upward trends in the geographic regions ranged from an increase of 10 percent in the Northeastern States to 4 percent in the Midwestern States. Rises of 7 and 5 percent were recorded in the Southern and Western States, respectively.

By population grouping, cities with 250,000 to 499,999 inhabitants recorded the greatest rise in aggravated assaults from 1987, 11 percent. Upswings of 8 percent in the suburban counties, 6 percent in the cities collectively, and 1 percent in the rural counties were registered for this offense during the same time period.

Five- and 10-year trends show aggravated assaults up 33 percent above the 1984 level and 45 percent over the 1979 experience.

Aggravated Assault by Month, 1984-1988

[Percent of annual total]

Months	1984	1985	1986	1987	1988
January	7.0	7.0	6.8	7.3	7.2
February	7.0	6.8	6.3	7.0	7.0
March	7.8	8.2	8.0	7.8	7.9
April	7.9	8.2	8.1	8.1	8.1
May	8.7	8.8	9.1	8.9	8.9
June	9.1	9.0	9.7	8.9	9.0
July	9.6	9.5	10.0	9.5	9.8
August	9.5	9.5	10.0	9.5	9.8
September	8.8	8.9	8.8	8.7	9.0
October	8.9	8.8	8.3	8.5	8.4
November	7.6	7.9	7.6	7.9	7.5
December	8.1	7.4	7.4	7.8	7.5

Rate

Up 5 percent above the 1987 rate, there were 370 reported victims of aggravated assault for every 100,000 people nationwide in 1988. Higher than the national average, the rate in metropolitan areas was 422 per 100,000. Cities outside metropolitan areas experienced a rate of 286 and rural counties, a rate of 141.

Nationwide, the rate for aggravated assault showed increases of 28 percent over 1984 and 29 percent over 1979.

Aggravated Assault, Type of Weapons Used, 1988

[Percent distribution by region]

Region	Total all weapons[1]	Firearms	Knives or cutting instruments	Other weapons (clubs, blunt objects, etc.)	Personal weapons
Total	100.0	21.1	20.5	31.0	27.4
Northeastern States	100.0	15.9	23.5	34.3	26.4
Midwestern States	100.0	23.1	20.8	32.1	24.0
Southern States	100.0	26.3	23.1	29.7	20.9
Western States	100.0	18.4	15.6	29.3	36.7

[1]Because of rounding, percentages may not add to totals.

Nature

In 1988, 31 percent of the aggravated assaults were committed with blunt objects or other dangerous weapons. Of the remaining weapon categories, personal weapons such as hands, fists, and feet were used in 27 percent of the offenses; and knives or cutting instruments and firearms in 21 percent each.

From 1987 to 1988, aggravated assaults committed with knives or cutting instruments and personal weapons increased 4 percent while those assaults with blunt objects or other dangerous weapons increased 7 percent. Assaults where firearms were used showed the greatest increase during this 2-year period, 10 percent.

BURGLARY

DEFINITION

The Uniform Crime Reporting Program defines burglary as the unlawful entry of a structure to commit a felony or theft. The use of force to gain entry is not required to classify an offense as burglary.

TREND

Year	*Number of offenses*	*Rate per 100,000 inhabitants*
1987	3,236,184	1,329.6
1988	3,218,077	1,309.2
Percent change	−.6	−1.5

Volume

Estimated at over 3.2 million in 1988, burglaries accounted for 23 percent of all Crime Index offenses and 26 percent of the property crimes.

Distribution figures for the regions showed that the highest burglary volume occurred in the most populous Southern States, accounting for 42 percent of the total. The Western States followed with 23 percent, the Midwestern States with 19 percent, and the Northeastern States with 16 percent.

Like the previous year, more burglaries occurred in August than any other month. The lowest number was reported in April.

Burglary by Month, 1984-1988

[Percent of annual total]

Months	1984	1985	1986	1987	1988
January	8.3	8.2	8.4	8.4	8.4
February	7.9	7.2	7.5	7.8	7.8
March	8.0	8.2	8.3	8.3	8.1
April	7.8	7.8	7.9	7.6	7.5
May	8.0	8.0	8.1	8.0	8.1
June	7.8	7.9	8.1	8.0	8.0
July	8.7	9.0	8.9	8.8	8.8
August	8.9	9.1	9.0	9.1	9.3
September	8.3	8.5	8.5	8.4	8.6
October	8.8	9.0	8.4	8.4	8.5
November	8.4	8.5	8.1	8.4	8.4
December	9.0	8.8	8.8	8.8	8.5

Trend

Nationwide, the burglary volume decreased 1 percent in 1988 from the 1987 total. Cities with populations of 1 million or more registered the only increase, 2 percent. Both the rural and suburban counties showed no change in their burglary volumes.

Geographically, three of the four regions reported decreases in burglaries in 1988 compared to 1987. The declines were 4 percent in the Midwestern States, 3 percent in the Western States, and 1 percent in the Northeastern States. The Southern States recorded the only increase in burglaries, 2 percent.

Rate

A burglary rate of 1,309 per 100,000 inhabitants was registered nationwide in 1988. The rate decreased 2 percent from 1987 and was 13 percent below the 1979 rate. In 1988, for every 100,000 in population, the rate was 1,457 in the metropolitan areas, 1,042 in the cities outside metropolitan areas, and 672 in the rural counties.

Regionally, the burglary rate was 1,583 in the Southern States, 1,461 in the Western States, 1,039 in the Midwestern States, and 1,018 in the Northeastern States. A comparison of 1987 and 1988 rates showed declines of 4 percent in the Midwest and West and 1 percent in the Northeast. The South registered a burglary rate increase of 1 percent.

Nature

Two of every 3 burglaries in 1988 were residential in nature. Seventy percent of all burglaries involved forcible entry, 22 percent were unlawful entries (without force), and the remainder were forcible entry attempts. Offenses for which time of occurrence was reported were evenly divided between day and night.

Burglary victims suffered losses estimated at $3.3 billion in 1988, and the average dollar loss per burglary was $1,014. The average loss for residential offenses was $1,037, while for nonresidential property, it was $967.

Residential burglary showed a 2-percent decline from 1987 to 1988; nonresidential offenses showed no change during the same period.

Clearances

In 1988, 13 percent of the burglaries brought to the attention of law enforcement agencies across the country were cleared. Geographically, a 15-percent clearance rate was registered in the South. In the Northeast, the rate was 14 percent; in the West, 13 percent; and in the Midwest it was 11 percent.

Adults were involved in 82 percent of all burglary offenses cleared, and only young people under 18 years of age were offenders in the remaining 18 percent. Similar to the national experience, persons under age 18 accounted for 18 percent of the burglary clearances in cities and suburban counties. Rural county law enforcement agencies reported 19 percent of their burglary clearances involved only juveniles. The highest degree of juvenile involvement was recorded in the Nation's smallest cities (under 10,000 population) where young persons under 18 years of age comprised 26 percent of the clearances.

LARCENY-THEFT

DEFINITION

Larceny-theft is the unlawful taking, carrying, leading, or riding away of property from the possession or constructive possession of another. It includes crimes such as shoplifting, pocket-picking, purse-snatching, thefts from motor vehicles, thefts of motor vehicle parts and accessories, bicycle thefts, etc., in which no use of force, violence, or fraud occurs.

TREND

Year	*Number of offenses*	*Rate per 100,000 inhabitants*
1987	7,499,851	3,081.3
1988	7,705,872	3,134.9
Percent change	+2.7	+1.7

Volume

Larceny-theft offenses, estimated at 7,705,872 during 1988, comprised 55 percent of the Crime Index total and 62 percent of the property crimes. When viewed monthly, larceny-thefts were recorded most often during August and least frequently in February.

Regionally, the most populous Southern States recorded 37 percent of the total. The Western States registered 24 percent; the Midwestern States, 22 percent; and the Northeastern States, 17 percent.

Larceny-Theft by Month, 1984-1988

[Percent of annual total]

Months	1984	1985	1986	1987	1988
January	7.5	7.4	7.8	7.6	7.6
February	7.6	7.0	7.2	7.5	7.5
March	8.0	8.2	8.3	8.3	8.2
April	8.0	8.1	8.2	8.0	7.8
May	8.2	8.4	8.4	8.2	8.3
June	8.4	8.5	8.6	8.5	8.5
July	9.0	9.3	9.1	9.1	9.0
August	9.4	9.5	9.3	9.2	9.5
September	8.3	8.4	8.4	8.4	8.5
October	8.9	8.9	8.5	8.6	8.7
November	8.2	8.2	7.9	8.1	8.2
December	8.5	8.1	8.3	8.4	8.3

Trend

Compared to 1987, the 1988 volume of larceny-thefts increased 3 percent in the Nation and 2 percent in all cities collectively. Both the suburban and rural counties also showed 3-percent increases.

Volume increases were recorded in the Southern States, 4 percent; and in the Western and Northeastern States, 3 percent. The Midwestern States registered virtually no change.

The 5- and 10-year national larceny trends showed a 17-percent increase over the totals for both 1984 and 1979.

Rate

The 1988 larceny-theft rate was 3,135 per 100,000 United States inhabitants, 2 percent higher than in 1987. The 1988 rate was 12 percent above the 1984 level and 5 percent higher than in 1979. The 1988 rate was 3,506 per 100,000 inhabitants of metropolitan areas; 3,298 per 100,000 population in cities outside metropolitan areas; and 973 per 100,000 people in the rural counties.

Regionally, the Western States' larceny-theft rate increased 1 percent over the 1987 level to 3,642 per 100,000 inhabitants. The rates were 3,338 in the Southern States and 2,594 in the Northeastern States, up 3 and 2 percent, respectively. The Midwestern States' rate, 2,877, showed virtually no change in 1988 as compared to 1987.

Nature

The average value of property stolen due to larceny-theft during 1988 was $426, up from $404 in 1987. When the average value was applied to the estimated number of larceny-thefts, the loss to victims nationally was $3.3 billion for the year. This estimated dollar loss is considered conservative since many offenses in the larceny category, particularly if the value of the stolen goods is small, never come to law enforcement attention. Losses in 25 percent of the thefts reported to law enforcement in 1988 ranged from $50 to $200, while in 35 percent, they were over $200.

Losses of goods and property reported stolen as a result of pocket-picking averaged $384; purse-snatching, $228; and shoplifting, $104. Thefts from buildings resulted in an average loss of $673; from motor vehicles, $461; and from coin-operated machines, $144. The average value loss due to thefts of motor vehicle accessories was $297 and for thefts of bicycles, $188.

MOTOR VEHICLE THEFT

DEFINITION

Defined as the theft or attempted theft of a motor vehicle, this offense category includes the stealing of automobiles, trucks, buses, motorcycles, motorscooters, snowmobiles, etc.

TREND

Year	*Number of offenses*	*Rate per 100,000 inhabitants*
1987	1,288,674	529.4
1988	1,432,916	582.9
Percent change	+11.2	+10.1

Volume

An estimated total of 1,432,916 thefts of motor vehicles occurred in the United States during 1988. These offenses comprised 13 percent of all property crimes. The regional distribution of motor vehicle thefts showed 31 percent of the volume was in the Southern States, 25 percent each in the Northeastern and Western States, and 19 percent in the Midwestern States.

Motor vehicle theft figures by month showed that the greatest number occurred in August, while the lowest was in April.

Trend

The number of motor vehicle thefts increased 11 percent nationally from 1987 to 1988. This upward trend was evident in all population groups with cities having populations of 1 million and over showing the largest increase, 16 percent. Suburban and rural counties showed increases of 11 percent and 4 percent, respectively.

Geographically, all four regions experienced motor vehicle theft increases. The increases were 14 percent in both the Northeastern and Western Regions, 10 percent in the Southern Region, and 5 percent in the Midwestern Region.

Motor Vehicle Theft by Month, 1984-1988

[Percent of annual total]

Months	1984	1985	1986	1987	1988
January	8.0	7.8	7.9	7.9	8.0
February	7.7	7.1	7.1	7.5	7.6
March	8.0	8.1	8.1	8.4	7.9
April	7.8	7.8	7.8	7.9	7.4
May	8.0	8.0	8.0	8.0	7.8
June	8.0	8.2	8.2	8.1	8.0
July	8.8	8.9	8.9	8.8	8.8
August	9.1	9.1	9.5	9.0	9.4
September	8.7	8.7	8.7	8.4	8.7
October	8.9	9.1	9.0	8.8	9.0
November	8.5	8.6	8.5	8.5	8.7
December	8.6	8.7	8.3	8.7	8.7

Rate

The 1988 national motor vehicle theft rate—583 per 100,000 people—was 10 percent higher than the rate in 1987. The rate was 33 percent higher than in 1984 and 15 percent above the 1979 rate.

For every 100,000 inhabitants living in MSAs, there were 713 motor vehicle thefts reported in 1988. The rate in cities outside metropolitan areas (other cities) was 210 and in rural counties, 114. As in previous years, the highest rates were in the Nation's most heavily populated municipalities, indicating that this offense is primarily a large-city problem. For every 100,000 inhabitants in cities with populations over 250,000, the 1988 motor vehicle theft rate was 1,448. The Nation's smallest cities, those with fewer than 10,000 inhabitants, recorded a rate of 236 per 100,000.

Among the regions, the motor vehicle theft rates ranged from 713 per 100,000 people in the Northeastern States to 446 in the Midwestern States. The Western States' rate was 711 and the Southern States' rate, 526. From 1987 to 1988, rate increases were registered in all regions. In the Northeastern States, the increase was 13 percent; in the Western States, 12 percent; in the Southern States, 9 percent; and in the Midwestern States, 5 percent.

Motor Vehicle Theft, 1988

[Percent distribution by region]

Region	Total[1]	Autos	Trucks and buses	Other vehicles
Total	100.0	77.3	15.2	7.5
Northeastern States	100.0	92.4	4.5	3.0
Midwestern States	100.0	80.8	10.1	9.0
Southern States	100.0	72.7	18.8	8.6
Western States	100.0	65.7	24.6	9.7

[1]Because of rounding, percentages may not add to totals.

An estimated average of 1 of every 128 registered motor vehicles was stolen nationwide during 1988. Regionally, this rate was greatest in the Northeast where 1 of every 91 motor vehicles registered was stolen. The other three regions reported lesser rates—1 per 110 in the West, 1 per 147 in the South, and 1 per 172 in the Midwest.

Nature

During 1988, an estimated national loss of over $7 billion was due to motor vehicle theft. At the time of theft, the average value per vehicle stolen was $5,117.

Seventy-seven percent of all motor vehicles reported stolen during the year were automobiles, 15 percent were trucks or buses, and the remainder were other types.

Bibliography

Abraham, H., *The Judicial Process,* Oxford University Press, 1968.

Adler, F., *Sisters in Crime,* McGraw-Hill, 1975.

Allen, H. and C. Simonsen, *Corrections in America,* Glencoe Press, 1978.

Amos, W., *Delinquent Children in Juvenile Correctional Institutions,* C.C. Thomas, 1966.

Atkins, B. and M. Pogrebin, *The Invisible Justice System,* W.H. Anderson, 1978.

Balton, M., *European Policing,* John Jay Press, 1978.

Bartollas, C., S. Miller, and S. Dinitz, *Juvenile Victimization,* Sage Publications, Inc., 1976.

Bartollas, C. and S.J. Miller, *Correctional Administration: Theory and Practice,* McGraw-Hill, 1978.

Bartollas, C. and S.J. Miller, *The Juvenile Offender: Control, Correction and Treatment,* Allyn & Bacon, Inc., 1978.

Bayley, D., *Police and Society,* Sage Publications, Inc., 1978.

Beigel, H., *Beneath the Badge,* Harper and Row Publishers, Inc., 1977.

Bell, J.B., *Time of Terror: How Democratic Societies Respond to Revolutionary Violence,* Basic Books Inc., 1978.

Bequai, A., *Organized Crime,* Lexington Books, 1979.

Bequai, A., *White Collar Crime,* Lexington Books, 1979.

Berkeley, G., *The Democratic Policeman,* Beacon Press, 1969.

Berkley, G., *Introduction to Criminal Justice,* Holbrook, 1980.

Berns, W., *For Capital Punishment: Crime and the Morality of the Death Penalty,* Basic Books, Inc., 1979.

Best, A., *The Politics of Law Enforcement,* Lexington Books, 1974.

Bittner, E., *The Functions of Police in Modern Society,* U.S. Government Printing Office, 1970.

Bittner, E., and S. Krantz, *Standards Relating to Police Handling of Juvenile Problems,* Ballinger Publishing Co., 1978.

Blumberg, A.S., *Criminal Justice: Issues and Ironies,* New Viewpoints, 1979.

Bond, J., *Plea-Bargaining and Guilty Pleas,* Clark Boardman Co., 1975.

Bouza, A., *Police Administration,* Pergamon Press, Inc., 1979.

Bowker, L., *Women, Crime, and the Criminal Justice System,* Lexington Books, 1978.

Bowker, L., *Prison Victimization,* Elsevier, 1980.

Bracey, D.H., *"Baby-Pros"—Preliminary Profiles of Juvenile Prostitutes,* John Jay Press, 1978.

Butler, A., *The Law Enforcement Process,* Alfred Publishing Co., Inc., 1976.

Carlson, D.L., *Criminal Justice Procedure,* W.H. Anderson, 1979.

Carrington, F., *The Victims,* Arlington House, Inc., 1975.

Carte, G., *Police Reform in the United States,* University of California Press, 1975.

Carter, R. and L. Wilkins, *Probation, Parole and Community Corrections,* Wiley, 1976.

Challenge of Crime in a Free Society, The, Presidential Commission on Law Enforcement and Administration of Justice, 1967.

Chambliss, W., *Law, Order, and Power,* Addison-Wesley Publishing Co., 1971.

Chevigny, P., *Cops and Rebels: A Study of Provocation,* Random House, Inc., 1972.

Clinard, M.B., *Cities with Little Crime,* Cambridge University Press, 1978.

Cole, G., *The American System of Criminal Justice,* Duxbury, 1976.

Collins, M.C., *The Child-Abuser,* Publishing Sciences Group, 1978.

Conklin, J.,, *"Illegal But Not Criminal": Business Crime in America,* Prentice-Hall, Inc., 1977.

Conley, J.A., *Theory and Research in Criminal Justice,* W.H. Anderson, 1979.

Conrad, J., *Crime and Its Correction,* University of California Press, 1965.

Conrad, J., *The Dangerous and the Endangered,* Lexington Books, 1978.

Conrad, J. and S. Dinitz, *In Fear of Each Other: Studies of Dangerousness in America,* Lexington Books, 1977.

Cook, J.G., *Constitutional Rights of the Accused, The,* Lawyers Co-Operative Publishing Co., 1972.

Cotte, T.J., *Children in Jail,* Beacon Press, 1978.

Creamer, J., *The Law of Arrest, Search and Seizure,* W.B. Saunders Co., 1975.

Cressey, D., *Criminal Organization,* Harper & Row Publishers, Inc., 1972.

Davis, K., *Discretionary Justice,* University of Illinois Press, 1971.

Delin, B., *The Sex Offender,* Beacon Press, 1978.

Devine, P.E., *The Ethics of Homicide,* Cornell University Press, 1979.

Dowling, J., *Criminal Procedure,* West, 1976.

Drapkin, I. and E. Viano, *Victimology,* Lexington Books, 1974.

Empey, L.T., *American Delinquency: Its Meaning and Construction,* Dorsey, 1978.

Falkin, G.R., *Reducing Delinquency,* Lexington Books, 1978.

Felkenes, G., *Constitutional Law for Criminal Justice,* Prentice-Hall, Inc., 1977.

Felkenes, G., *The Criminal Justice System,* Prentice-Hall, Inc., 1973.

Felkenes, G., *Criminal Law and Procedure,* Prentice-Hall, Inc., 1976.

Felt, M., *The FBI Pyramid,* G.P. Putnam's Sons, 1979.

Field, H.S. and N.J. Barnett, *Jurors and Rape,* Lexington Books, 1978.

Folley, V.L., *American Law Enforcement,* Allyn & Bacon, Inc., 1980.

Fogel, D., *The Justice Model for Corrections,* W.H. Anderson, 1979.

Foucault, M., *Discipline and Punish,* Pantheon Books, Inc., 1978.

Fox, J.A., *Forecasting Crime Data,* Lexington Books, 1979.

Fox, J.G., *Women in Cages,* Ballinger Publishing Co., 1979.

Frankel, M., *Criminal Sentences,* Hill & Wang, 1972.

Freeman, J.C., *Prisons Past and Future,* Heinemann, 1979.

Gardiner, J. and M. Mulkey, *Crime and Criminal Justice,* Heath, 1975.

Gaylin, W., *Partial Justice,* Knopf, Inc., 1974.

Geis, G., *Not the Law's Business,* NIMH, 1972.

Geis, G. and R. Meier, *White Collar Crime,* Free Press, 1977.

Gerber, R., *Contemporary Punishment,* University of Notre Dame Press, 1972.

Germann, A., et al., *Introduction to Law Enforcement,* C.C. Thomas, 1973.

Gibbs, J., *Crime, Punishment, and Deterrence,* Elsevier North-Holland, Inc., 1975.

Gifis, S.H., *Law Dictionary,* Barron's, 1975.

Glaser, D., *Adult Crime and Social Policy,* Prentice-Hall, Inc., 1972.

Glaser, D., *Crime in Our Changing Society,* Holt, Rinehart & Winston, Inc., 1978.

Goldsmith, J. and S.S. Goldsmith, *Crime and the Elderly,* D.C. Heath, 1976.

Goldstein, A., et al., *Police Crisis Intervention,* Pergamon Press, Inc., 1979.

Goldstein, H., *Policing a Free Society,* Ballinger Publishing Co., 1977.

Gottfredson, M.R. and D.M. Gottfredson, *Decision-Making in Criminal Justice,* Ballinger Publishing Co., 1979.

Greenberg, D., *Corrections and Punishment,* Sage, 1977.

Greenwood, P., *The Criminal Investigation Process,* Rand McNally Co., 1975.

Grosman, B., *New Directions in Sentencing,* Butterworths, 1980.

Gross, Hyman, *A Theory of Criminal Justice,* Oxford University Press, 1978.

Guide to Criminal Justice Information Sources, National Council on Crime and Delinquency, 1977.

Hahn, P.H., *Crimes Against the Elderly,* Davis, 1976.

Hahn, P.H., *The Juvenile Offender and the Law,* W.H. Anderson, 1978.

Haskell, M.R. and L. Yablonsky, *Crime and Delinquency,* Rand-McNally Co., 1978.

Hemphill, C.F., *Criminal Procedure: The Administration of Justice,* Goodyear Publishing Co., Inc., 1978.

Heumann, M., *Plea-Bargaining,* University of Chicago Press, 1978.

Hills, S., *Crime, Power and Morality,* Chandler, 1971.

Jahnige, T., *The Federal Judicial System,* Holt, Rinehart and Winston, Inc., 1968.

James, H., *Crisis in the Courts,* McKay, 1971.

Johnson, N., *The Human Cage: A Brief History of Prison Architecture,* Walker, 1973.

Johnson, R.E., *Juvenile Delinquency and Its Origins,* Cambridge University Press, 1979.

Johnson, T.A., G. Mizner, and L.P. Brown, *The Police and Society,* Prentice-Hall, 1981.

Jones, D.A., *Crime and Criminal Responsibility,* Nelson-Hall Publishers, 1978.

Jones, D.A., *Crime Without Punishment,* Lexington Books, 1979.

Kalven, H. and H. Zeisel, *The American Jury,* Little, Brown and Co., 1966.

Kamisar, Y., *et al., Criminal Law and Procedure,* West, 1974.

Kassebaum, G., *Prison Treatment and Parole Survival,* Wiley, 1972.

Killinger, G. and P. Cromwell, *Penology,* West, 1973.

Killinger, G.G. and P.F. Cromwell, *Corrections in the Community,* West, 1978.

Klein, I., *Law of Evidence for Police,* West, 1973.

Klein, M., *The Juvenile Justice System,* Sage Publications, Inc., 1976.

Klotter, J. and J. Kanovitz, *Constitutional Law for Police,* Anderson, 1977.

Kratcoski, P. and D. Walker, *Criminal Justice in America,* Scott, Foresman and Co., 1978.

Kratcoski, P.C. and L.D. Kratcoski, *Juvenile Delinquency,* Prentice-Hall, Inc., 1979.

LaFave, W.R., *Principles of Criminal Law,* West, 1979.

LaPatra, J.W., *Analyzing the Criminal Justice System,* Lexington Books, 1978.

Levin, M., *Urban Politics and the Criminal Courts,* University of Chicago Press, 1977.

Lewis, P.W. and K.D. Peoples, *The Supreme Court and the Criminal Process,* W.B. Saunders Co., 1978.

Lipton, D., R. Martinson, and J. Wilks, *The Effectiveness of Correctional Treatment,* Praeger Publishers, Inc., 1975.

Loeb, R.H., *Crime and Capital Punishment,* Franklin-Watts, 1978.
MacNamara, D. and F. Montanino, *Incarceration,* Sage Publications, 1978.
MacNamara, D. and E. Sagarin, *Perspectives on Correction,* Thomas Y. Crowell Co., 1971.
MacNamara, D. and E. Sagarin, *Sex, Crime, and the Law,* Macmillan-Free Press, 1977.
MacNamara, D. and M. Riedel, *Police: Problems and Prospects,* Praeger Publishers, Inc., 1974.
MacNamara, D. and E. Sagarin, *Corrections, Punishment and Rehabilitation,* Praeger, 1972.
MacNamara, D.E.J. and L.W. McCorkle, *Crime, Criminals and Corrections,* John Jay Press, 1982.
Marmor, J., *Homosexual Behavior: A Modern Reappraisal,* Basic Books, 1979.
Mathias, W., *Foundations of Criminal Justice,* Prentice-Hall, 1980.
McDonald, W., *Criminal Justice and the Victim,* Sage Publications, 1976.
Menninger, K., *The Crime of Punishment,* Viking Press, 1968.
Miller, F., *The Correctional Process,* The Foundation Press, 1971.
Miller, F., *Prosecution,* Little, Brown and Co., 1970.
Mitford, J., *Kind and Usual Punishment,* Knopf, Inc., 1973.
More, H., *Effective Police Administration,* West, 1979.
Morris, N., *The Honest Politician's Guide to Crime Control,* The University of Chicago Press, 1970.
Morris, N., *The Future of Imprisonment,* The University of Chicago Press, 1974.
Munro, J., *Administrative Behavior and Police Organization,* W.H. Anderson, 1974.
Nagel, S., *Modeling the Criminal Justice System,* Sage Publications, 1977.
Nagel, S., *The Rights of the Accused,* Sage Publications, 1972.
Nagel, S. and H.G. Neef, *Decision Theory and the Legal Process,* Lexington Books, 1979.
Navasky, V. and D. Paster, *Law Enforcement: The Federal Role,* McGraw-Hill Book Co., 1976.
Neary, M., *Corruption and Its Management,* American Academy for Professional Law Enforcement, 1977.
Netter, G., *Explaining Crime,* McGraw-Hill Book Co., 1978.
Neubauer, D., *Criminal Justice in Middle America,* General Learning Press, 1974.
Newman, C., *Probation, Parole and Pardons,* C.C. Thomas, 1970.
Newman, G., *The Punishment Response,* J.P. Lippincott Co., 1978.
Niederhoffer, A., *The Ambivalent Force,* Ginn and Co., 1970.
Niederhoffer, A., *The Police Family,* Lexington Books, 1978.
O'Brien, J.T. and M. Marcus, *Crime and Justice in America,* Pergamon Press Inc., 1979.
Ohlin, L.E., *et al., Reforming Juvenile Corrections,* Ballinger Publishing Co., 1979.
Packer, H., *The Limits of the Criminal Sanction,* Stanford University Press, 1968.
Platt, A., *The Child Savers: The Invention of Delinquency,* The University of Chicago Press, 1977.
Platt, T. and P. Takagi, *Punishment and Penal Discipline,* Crime and Social Justice Press, 1979.
Price, B., *Police Professionalism,* Lexington Books, 1977.
Quinney, R., *Critique of the Legal Order,* Little, Brown and Co., 1974.
Rawls, J., *A Theory of Justice,* Harvard University Press, 1971.
Reid, S.T., *Crime and Criminology,* Holt, Rinehart, & Winston, Inc., 1979.
Reiss, A., *The Police and the Public,* Yale University Press, 1971.
Reppetto, T., *Residential Crime,* Ballinger Publishing Co., 1974.
Reppetto, T., *The Blue Parade,* The Free Press, 1978.
Rich, V., *Law and the Administration of Justice,* Wiley, 1979.
Rieber, R.W. and H.J. Vetter, *The Psychological Foundations of Criminal Justice,* John Jay Press, 1979.
Rifai, M.A., *Justice and Older Americans,* D.C. Heath and Co., 1977.
Ross, R. and P. Gendreau, *Effective Correctional Treatment,* Butterworths, 1980.
Rossett, A. and D. Cressey, *Justice by Consent,* J.P. Lippincott Co., 1976.
Rothman, D., *The Discovery of Asylum,* Little, Brown and Co., 1971.
Rubin, S., *Law of Criminal Correction,* West, 1973.
Rush, G.E., *Dictionary of Criminal Justice,* Holbrook Press Inc., 1977.
Sagarin, E., *Deviants and Deviance,* Praeger Publishers, Inc., 1976.
Sagarin, E., *Criminology: New Concerns,* Sage, 1979.
Saks, M.J., *Jury Verdicts,* D.C. Heath and Co., 1977.
Sanders, W., *Detective Work,* The Free Press, 1977.
Saunders, C., *Upgrading the American Police,* The Brookings Institution, 1970.
Schultz, D.D., *Modern Police Administration,* Gulf Publishing Co., 1979.
Schur, E., *Crimes Without Victims,* Prentice-Hall, Inc., 1965.
Senna, J. and L. Siegel, *Introduction to Criminal Justice,* West, 1978.
Shanahan, D.T. and Whisenand, P.M., *Dimensions of Criminal Justice Planning,* Allyn & Bacon, Inc., 1980.
Sheehan, S., *A Prison and a Prisoner,* Houghton Mifflin Co., 1978.
Sherman, L.W., *The Quality of Police Education,* Jossey-Bass, Inc., 1978.
Sherman, L.W., *Scandal and Reform: Controlling Police Corruption,* University of California Press, 1978.
Silberman, C., *Criminal Violence—Criminal Justice,* Random House, Inc., 1978.
Simon, R., *Women and Crime,* Lexington Books, 1975.
Simon, R., *The Jury System in America,* Lexington Books, 1979.
Simonsen, C.E. and M.S. Gordon, *Juvenile Justice in America,* Glencoe Press, 1979.
Skolnick, J. and T. Gray, *Police in America,* Little, Brown, 1975.
Snortum, J. and I. Hadar, *Criminal Justice,* Palisades Publishers, 1976.
Stanley, D., *Prisoners Among Us: The Problem of Parole,* The Brookings Institution, 1975.
Stead, P.J., *Pioneers in Policing,* Patterson Smith, 1977.
Strasburg, P., *Violent Delinquents,* Monarch Books, 1978.
Strickland, K.G., *Correctional Institutions for Women in the United States,* Lexington Books, 1978.
Stuckey, G.B., *Evidence for the Law Enforcement Officer,* McGraw-Hill Book Co., 1979.
Szasz, T., *Psychiatric Justice,* Macmillan, 1965.
Toch, H., *Living in Prison,* The Free Press, 1977.
Turk, A., *Legal Sanctions and Social Control,* NIMH, 1972.
Ungar, S., *F.B.I.,* Little-Brown and Co., 1976.
Ulviller, H., *Adjudication,* West, 1975.
Van Dyke, J.M., *Jury Selection,* Ballinger Publishing Co., 1977.
Vetter, H. and C. Simonsen, *Criminal Justice in America,* W.B. Saunders Co., 1976.
Viano, E.C., *Victims and Society,* Visage Press, 1976.
Von Grimme, T.L., *Your Career in Law Enforcement,* ARCO, 1979.
Von Hirsch, A., *Doing Justice: The Choice of Punishments,* Hill and Wang, 1976.
Walker, A., *A Critical History of Police Reform,* Lexington Books, 1977.
Warren, E., *The Memoirs of Chief Justice Warren,* Doubleday, 1977.
Weaver, S., *Decisions to Prosecute,* M.I.T. Press, 1977.
Weinreb, L., *Leading Constitutional Cases on Criminal Justice,* Foundation Press, 1978.
Wheeler, R. and H. Whitcomb, *Judicial Administration,* Prentice-Hall, 1977.
Whisenand, P., *Crime Prevention,* Holbrook Press, 1977.
Weiss, J.A., *Law of the Elderly,* Practicing Law Institute, 1977.
Wice, R., *Bail and Its Reform,* National Institute of Law Enforcement and Criminal Law, 1974.
Wilkins, L., *Evaluation of Penal Measures,* Random House, 1969.
Wilson, J., *Varieties of Police Behavior,* Harvard University Press, 1968.
Wilson, J., *Thinking About Crime,* Basic Books, 1975.
Wilson, J., *The Investigators: Managing the FBI and Narcotics Agents,* Basic Books, 1978.
Witt, J.W., *The Police, the Courts and the Minority Community,* Lexington Books, 1978.
Wolf, J.B., *The Police Intelligence System,* John Jay Press, 1978.
Wolfgang, M.E., *Prisons: Success and Failure,* Lexington Books, 1978.
Wolfgang, M.E. and F. Ferracuti, *Diagnosis in Criminal Justice Systems,* Lexington Books, 1978.
Wootton, B., *Crime and Penal Policy,* Allen & Unwin, 1978.
Wright, E., *The Politics of Punishment,* Harper & Row, 1973.
Zimring, F. and G. Hawkins, *Deterrence,* University of Chicago Press, 1973.

Glossary

Abet To encourage another to commit a crime. This encouragement may be by advice, inducement, command, etc. The abettor of a crime is equally guilty with the one who actually commits the crime.

Accessory after the Fact One who harbors, assists, or protects another person, although he knows that person has committed a crime.

Accessory before the Fact One who helps another to commit a crime, even though he is absent when the crime is committed.

Accomplice One who is involved in the commission of a crime with others, whether he actually commits the crime or abets others. The term *principal* means the same thing, except that one may be a principal if he commits a crime without the aid of others.

Acquit To free a person from an accusation of criminal guilt; to find "not guilty."

Affidavit A written declaration or statement sworn to and affirmed by an officer having authority to administer an oath.

Affirmation To swear on one's conscience that what he says is true. An *oath* means that one calls upon God to witness the truth of what he says.

Alias Any name by which one is known other than his true name. *Alias dictus* is the more technically correct term but it is rarely used.

Alibi A claim that one was in a place different from that charged. If the person proves his alibi, he proves that he could not have committed the crime charged.

Allegation The declaration of a party to a lawsuit made in a pleading, that states what he expects to prove.

Amnesty A class or group pardon (e.g., all political prisoners).

Appeal A case carried to a higher court to ask that the decision of the lower court, in which the case originated, be altered or overruled completely.

Appellate Court A court that has jurisdiction to hear cases on appeal; not a trial court.

Arraignment The appearance before the court of a person charged with a crime. He or she is advised of the charges, bail is set, and a plea of "guilty" or "not guilty" is entered.

Arrest To take a person into custody so that he may be held to answer for a crime.

Autopsy A post-mortem examination of a human body to determine the cause of death.

Bail Property (usually money) deposited with a court in exchange for the release of a person in custody to assure later appearance.

Bail Bond An obligation signed by the accused and his sureties, that insures his presence in court.

Bailiff A court attendant whose duties are to keep order in the courtroom and to have custody of the jury.

Bench Warrant An order by the court for the apprehension and arrest of a defendant or other person who has failed to appear when so ordered.

Bill of Rights The first ten amendments to the Constitution of the United States which define such rights as: due process of law, immunity from illegal search and seizure, the ban on cruel and unusual punishment, unreasonably high bail, indictment by a grand jury, and speedy trial.

Bind Over To hold for trial.

"Blue" Laws Laws in some jurisdictions prohibiting sales of merchandise, athletic contests, and the sale of alcoholic beverages on Sundays.

Booking The procedure at a police station of entering the name and identifying particulars relating to an arrested person, the charges filed against him, and the name of the arresting officer.

Burden of Proof The duty of affirmatively proving the guilt of the defendant "beyond a reasonable doubt."

Calendar A list of cases to be heard in a trial court, on a specific day, and containing the title of the case, the lawyers involved, and the index number.

Capital Crime Any crime that may be punishable by death or imprisonment for life.

Caseload The number of cases actively being investigated by a police detective or being supervised by a probation or parole officer.

Change of Venue The removal of a trial from one jurisdiction to another in order to avoid local prejudice.

Charge In criminal law, the accusation made against a person. It also refers to the judge's instruction to the jury on legal points.

Circumstantial Evidence Indirect evidence; evidence from which the principal fact can be proved or disproved by inference. Example: a finger-print found at the crime scene.

Citizen's Arrest A taking into custody of an alleged offender by a person not a law enforcement officer. Such an arrest is lawful if the crime was attempted or committed in his presence.

Code A compilation, compendium, or revision of laws, arranged into chapters, having a table of contents and index, and promulgated by legislative authority. Criminal code; penal code.

Coercion The compelling of a person to do that which he is not obliged to do, or to omit doing what he may legally do, by some illegal threat, force, or intimidation. For example: a forced confession.

Commit To place a person in custody in a prison or other institution by lawful order.

Common Law Law that derives its authority from usage and custom or court decisions.

Commutation To change the punishment meted out to a criminal to one less severe. Executive clemency.

Complainant The victim of a crime who brings the facts to the attention of the authorities.

Complaint A sworn written allegation stating that a specified person committed a crime. Sometimes called an *information.* When issued from a *Grand Jury,* it is called an *indictment.*

Compulsion An irresistible impulse to commit some act, such as stealing, setting a fire, or an illegal sexual act.

Confession An admission by the accused of his guilt; a partial admission (e.g., that he was at the crime scene; that he had a motive) is referred to as "an admission against interest."

Confinement Deprivation of liberty in a jail or prison either as punishment for a crime or as detention while guilt or innocence is being determined.

Consensual Crime A crime without a victim; one in which both parties voluntarily participate (e.g., adultery, sodomy, etc.).

Conspiracy A secret combination of two or more persons who plan for the purpose of committing a crime or any unlawful act or a lawful act by unlawful or criminal means.

Contempt of Court Behavior that impugns the authority of a court or obstructs the execution of court orders.

Continuance A delay in trial granted by the judge on request of either the prosecutor or defense counsel; an adjournment.

Conviction A finding by the jury (or by the trial judge in cases tried without a jury) that the accused is guilty of a crime.

Corporal Corporal punishment is pain inflicted on the body of another. Flogging.

Corpus Delicti The objective proof that a crime has been committed as distinguished from an accidental death, injury or loss.

Corrections Area of criminal justice dealing with convicted offenders in jails, prisons; on probation or parole.

Corroborating Evidence Supplementary evidence that tends to strengthen or confirm other evidence given previously.

Crime An act or omission prohibited and punishable by law. Crimes are divided into *felonies* and *misdemeanors;* and recorded as "crimes against the person" (murder, rape, assault, robbery) and "crimes against property" (burglary, larceny, auto theft). There are also crimes against public morality and against public order.

Criminal Insanity Lack of mental capacity to do or refrain from doing a criminal act; inability to distinguish right from wrong.

Criminalistics Crime laboratory procedures (e.g., ballistics, analysis of stains, etc.).

Criminology The scientific study of crime and criminals.

Cross-Examination The questioning of a witness by the party who did not produce the witness.

Culpability Guilt; *see also mens rea.*

Defendant The person who is being prosecuted.

Delinquency Criminality by a boy or girl who has not as yet reached the age set by the state for trial as an adult (the age varies from jurisdiction to jurisdiction and from crime to crime).

Demurrer In court procedure, a statement that the charge that a crime has been committed has no sufficient basis in law, despite the truth of the facts alleged.

Deposition The testimony of a witness not taken in open court but taken in pursuance of authority to take such testimony elsewhere.

Detention To hold a person in confinement while awaiting trial or sentence, or as a material witness.

Deterrence To prevent criminality by fear of the consequences; one of the rationalizations for punishing offenders.

Directed Verdict An instruction by the judge to the jury to return a specific verdict. A judge may not direct a guilty verdict.

Direct Evidence Proof of facts by witnesses who actually saw acts or heard words, as distinguished from *Circumstantial Evidence.*

Direct Examination The first questioning of a witness by the party who produced him.

Discretion The decision-making powers of officers of the criminal justice system (e.g., to arrest or not, to prosecute or not, to plea-bargain, to grant probation, or to sentence to a penal institution).

District Attorney Prosecutor; sometimes County Attorney, (U.S. Attorney in Federal practice).

Docket The formal record maintained by the court clerk, listing all cases heard. It contains the defendant's name, index number, date of arrest, and the outcome of the case.

Double Jeopardy To be prosecuted twice for the same offense.

Due Process Law in its regular course of administration through the courts of justice. Guaranteed by the 5th and 14th Amendments.

Embracery An attempt to influence a jury, or a member thereof, in their verdict by any improper means.

Entrapment The instigation of a crime by officers or agents of a government who induce a person to commit a crime that he did not originally contemplate in order to institute a criminal prosecution against him.

Evidence All the means used to prove or disprove the fact at issue.

Examination An investigation of a witness by counsel in the form of questions for the purpose of bringing before the court knowledge possessed by the witness.

Exception A formal objection to the action of the court during a trial. The indication is that the excepting party will seek to reverse the court's action at some future proceeding. *Objection.*

Exclusionary Rule Rule of evidence which makes illegally acquired evidence inadmissible; *see* Mapp vs. Ohio.

Expert Evidence Testimony by one qualified to speak authoritatively on technical matters because of his special training or skill.

Ex Post Facto After the fact. An ex post facto law is a criminal law that makes an act unlawful although it was committed prior to the passage of that law.

Extradition The surrender by one state to another of an individual accused of a crime.

False Arrest Any unlawful physical restraint of another's freedom of movement. Unlawful arrest.

Felonious Evil, malicious, or criminal. A felonious act is not necessarily a felony, but is criminal in some degree.

Felony Generally, an offense punishable by death or imprisonment in a penitentiary.

Forensic Relating to the court. Thus, forensic medicine would refer to medicine in relation to court proceedings and the law in general.

Grand Jury A group of 16 to 23 citizens of a county who examine evidence against the person suspected of a crime, and hand down an indictment if there is sufficient evidence to warrant one.

Habeas Corpus (Writ of) An order that requires a jailor, warden, police chief, or other public official to produce a person being held in custody before a court in order to show that they have a legal right to hold him in custody.

Hearsay Evidence not originating from the witness' personal knowledge.

Homicide The killing of a human being; may be murder, negligent or non-negligent manslaughter, or excusable or justifiable homicide.

Impeach To discredit. To question the truthfulness of a witness. Also: to charge a president or governor with criminal misconduct.

Imprisonment The act of confining a convicted felon in a federal or state prison.

In Camera In the judge's private chambers; in secrecy; the general public and press are excluded.

Indictment The document prepared by a prosecutor and approved by the grand jury which charges a certain person with a specific crime or crimes for which that person is later to be tried in court. Truebill.

Inference A conclusion one draws about something based on proof of certain other facts.

Injunction An order by a court prohibiting a defendant from committing an act.

Intent A design or determination of the mind to do or not do a certain thing. Intent may be determined from the nature of one's acts. Mens Rea.

Interpol International Criminal Police Commission.

Jail A short-term confinement institution for the detention of persons awaiting trial and the serving of sentences by those convicted of misdemeanors and offenses.

Jeopardy The danger of conviction and punishment that a defendant faces in a criminal trial. *Double Jeopardy.*

Judicial Notice The rule that a court will accept certain things as common knowledge without proof.

Jurisdiction The power of a court to hear and determine a criminal case.

Jury A certain number of persons who are sworn to examine the evidence and determine the truth on the basis of that evidence. Grand jury; trial jury.

Juvenile Delinquent A boy or girl who has not reached the age of criminal liability (varies from state to state) and who commits an act which would be a misdemeanor or felony if he were an adult. Delinquents are tried in *Juvenile Court* and confined to separate facilities.

L.E.A.A. Law Enforcement Assistance Administration, U.S. Dept. of Justice.

Leniency An unusually mild sentence imposed on a convicted offender; clemency granted by the President or a state governor; early release by a parole board.

Lie Detector An instrument which measures certain physiological reactions of the human body from which a trained operator may determine whether the subject is telling the truth or lies; polygraph; psychological stress evaluator.

Mala In Se Evil in itself. Acts that are made crimes because they are, by their nature, evil and morally wrong.

Mala Prohibita Evil because they are prohibited. Acts that are not wrong in themselves but which, to protect the general welfare, are made crimes by statute.

Malfeasance The act of a public officer in committing a crime relating to his official duties or powers. Accepting or demanding a bribe.

Malice An evil intent to vex, annoy, or injure another; intentional evil.

Malicious Prosecution An action instituted in bad faith with the intention of injuring the defendant.

Mandamus A writ that issues from a superior court, directed to any person, corporation, or inferior court, requiring it to do some particular thing.

Mens Rea A guilty intent.

Miranda Warning A police officer when taking a suspect into custody must warn him of his right to remain silent and of his right to an attorney.

Misdemeanor Any crime not a *Felony.* Usually, a crime punishable by a fine or imprisonment in the county or other local jail.

Misprision Failing to reveal a crime.

Mistrial A trial discontinued before reaching a verdict because of some procedural defect or impediment.

Modus Operandi Method of operation by criminals.

Motions Procedural moves made by either defense attorney or prosecutor and submitted to the court, helping to define and set the ground rules for the proceedings of a particular case. For example: to suppress illegally seized evidence or to seek a change of venue.

Motive The reason for committing a crime.

N.C.C.D. National Council on Crime and Delinquency.

No Bill A phrase used by a *Grand Jury* when they fail to indict.

Nolle Prosequi A declaration to a court, by the prosecutor that he does not wish to further prosecute the case.

Nolo Contendre A pleading, usually used by a defendant in a criminal case, that literally means "I will not contest."

Objection The act of taking exception to some statement or procedure in a trial. Used to call the court's attention to some improper evidence or procedure.

Opinion Evidence A witness' belief or opinion about a fact in dispute, as distinguished from personal knowledge of the fact. Expert testimony.

Ordinance A statute enacted by the city or municipal government.

Organized Crime The crime syndicate; cosa nostra; Mafia; an organized, continuing criminal conspiracy which engages in crime as a business (e.g., loan sharking, illegal gambling, prostitution, extortion, etc.).

Original Jurisdiction Trial jurisdiction.

Over Act An open or physical act, as opposed to a thought or mere intention.

Pardon Executive clemency setting aside a conviction and penalty.

Parole A conditional release from prison, under supervision.
Penal Code The criminal law of a jurisdiction, (sometimes the criminal procedure law is included but in other states it is codified separately).
Penology The study of punishment and corrections.
Peremptory Challenge The act of objecting to a certain number of jurors without assigning a cause for their dismissal. Used during the *voir dire* examination.
Perjury The legal offense of deliberately testifying falsely under oath about a material fact.
Petit Jury The ordinary jury composed of 12 persons who hear criminal cases. Determines guilt or innocence of the accused.
Plea-Bargaining A negotiation between the defense attorney and the prosecutor in which defendant receives a reduced penalty in return for a plea of "guilty."
Police Power The authority of the legislation to make laws in the interest of the general public, even at the risk of placing some hardship on individuals.
Post Mortem After death. Commonly applied to examination of a dead body. An autopsy is a post mortem examination to determine the cause of death.
Preliminary Hearing A proceeding in front of a lower court to determine if there is sufficient evidence for submitting a felony case to the grand jury.
Presumption of Fact An inference as to the truth or falsity of any proposition or fact, made in the absence of actual certainty of its truth or falsity or until such certainty can be attained.
Presumption of Law A rule of law that courts and judges must draw a particular inference from a particular fact or evidence, unless the inference can be disproved.
Prima Facie So far as can be judged from the first appearance or at first sight.
Prison Federal or state penal institution for the confinement of convicted felons. Penitentiary.
Probation A penalty placing a convicted person under the supervision of a probation officer for a stated time, instead of being confined.
Prosecutor One who initiates a criminal prosecution against an accused. One who acts as a trial attorney for the government as the representative of the people.
Provost Marshal Military police officer in charge of discipline, crime control and traffic law enforcement at a military post.
Public Defender An appointed or elected public official charged with providing legal representation for indigent persons accused of crimes.

Reasonable Doubt That state of mind of jurors when they do not feel a moral certainty about the truth of the charge and when the evidence does not exclude every other reasonable hypothesis except that the defendant is guilty as charged.
Rebuttal The introduction of contradicting testimony; the showing that statements made by a witness are not true; the point in the trial at which such evidence may be introduced.
Recidivist A repeater in crime; a habitual offender.
Recognizance When a person binds himself to do a certain act or else suffer a penalty, as, for example, with a recognizance bond. Release on recognizance is release without posting bail or bond.
Relevant Applying to the issue in question; related to the issue; useful in determining the truth or falsity of an alleged fact.
Remand To send back. To remand a case for new trial or sentencing.
Reprieve A stay of execution or sentence.

Search Warrant A written order, issued by judicial authority in the name of the state, directing a law enforcement officer to search for personal property and, if found, to bring it before the court.
Sentence The punishment (harsh or lenient) imposed by the trial judge on a convicted offender; major options include: fines, probation, indeterminate sentencing (e.g., three to ten years), indefinite sentencing (e.g., not more than three years), and capital punishment (death).
Stare Decisis To abide by decided cases. The doctrine that once a court has laid down a principle of law as applicable to certain facts, it will apply it to all future cases when the facts are substantially the same.
State's Evidence Testimony given by an accomplice or participant in a crime, tending to convict others.
Status Offense An act which is punishable only because the offender has not as yet reached a statutorily prescribed age (e.g., truancy, running away, drinking alcoholic beverages by a minor, etc.).
Statute A law.
Stay A stopping of a judicial proceeding by a court order.
Subpoena A court order requiring a witness to attend and testify in a court proceeding.
Subpoena Duces Tecum A court order requiring a witness to testify and to bring all books, documents, and papers that might affect the outcome of the proceedings.
Summons An order to appear in court on a particular date, which is issued by a police officer after or instead of arrest. It may also be a notification to a witness or a juror to appear in court.
Suspect One whom the police have determined as very likely to be the guilty perpetrator of an offense. Once the police identify a person as a suspect, they must warn him of his rights (Miranda warning) to remain silent and to have legal advice.

Testimony Evidence given by a competent witness, under oath, as distinguished from evidence from writings and other sources.
Tort A legal wrong committed against a person or property for which compensation may be obtained by a civil action.

Uniform Crime Reports (U.C.R.) Annual statistical tabulation of "crimes known to the police" and "crimes cleared by arrest" published by the Federal Bureau of Investigation.

Venue The geographical area in which a court with jurisdiction sits. The power of a court to compel the presence of the parties to a litigation. See also *Change of Venue.*
Verdict The decision of a court.
Victimology Sub-discipline of criminology which emphasizes the study of victims; includes *victim compensation.*
Voir Dire The examination or questioning of prospective jurors.

Waive To give up a personal right. For example: to testify before the grand jury.
Warrant A court order directing a police officer to arrest a named person or search a specific premise.
Witness One who has seen, heard, acquired knowledge about some element in a crime. An *expert witness* is one who, though he has no direct knowledge of the crime for which the defendant is being tried, may testify as to the defendant's sanity, the amount of alcohol in the deceased's blood, whether a signature is genuine, that a fingerprint is or is not that of the accused, etc.

Index

Credits/ Acknowledgments

Cover design by Charles Vitelli

1. Crime and Justice in America
Facing overview—Dushkin Publishing Group photo by Nick Zavalishin. 18—National Archives.

2. Victimology
Facing overview—United Nations photo by John Isaac.

3. Police
Facing overview—United Nations.

4. The Judicial System
Facing overview—EPA Documerica.

5. Juvenile Justice
Facing overview—United Nations photo by Jane Schreibman.

6. Punishment and Corrections
Facing overview—National Archives.

ANNUAL EDITIONS: CRIMINAL JUSTICE 90/91

Article Rating Form

Here is an opportunity for you to have direct input into the next revision of this volume. We would like you to rate each of the 48 articles listed below, using the following scale:

1. Excellent: should definitely be retained
2. Above average: should probably be retained
3. Below average: should probably be deleted
4. Poor: should definitely be deleted

Your ratings will play a vital part in the next revision. So please mail this prepaid form to us just as soon as you complete it.
Thanks for your help!

Rating	Article
	1. An Overview of the Criminal Justice System
	2. What Is Crime?
	3. Are Criminals Made or Born?
	4. A Law Enforcement Response to Legalizing Illicit Drugs
	5. Guns
	6. Hitting Kingpins in Their Assets
	7. Guardian Angels: A Unique Approach to Crime Prevention
	8. The Nation: As Racketeering Law Expands, So Does Pressure to Rein It In
	9. The Fear of Crime
	10. Crime Victims and the News Media: Questions of Fairness and Ethics
	11. Battered Families: Voices of the Abused; Voices of the Abusers
	12. Victims of Crime
	13. Death of a Bard
	14. Victim-Offender Mediation: A Survey of Program Characteristics and Perceptions of Effectiveness
	15. Police Response to Crime
	16. The Police in the United States
	17. The State of Police Education: Critical Findings
	18. Women on the Move? A Report on the Status of Women in Policing
	19. Making Neighborhoods Safe
	20. Confronting Police Corruption: Organizational Initiatives for Internal Control
	21. From Private Security to Loss Control: What Does the Future Hold?
	22. Police Officers Tell of Strains of Living as a "Black in Blue"

Rating	Article
	23. Civilian Review Boards: A Means to Police Accountability
	24. The Judicial Process: Prosecutors and Courts
	25. The Duty of the Defense Counsel
	26. The Prosecutor as a "Minister of Justice"
	27. White Justice, Black Defendants
	28. A Prosecutor's View of Plea Bargaining
	29. Genetics Meets Forensics
	30. Convicting the Innocent
	31. After 200 Years, the Silent Juror Learns to Talk
	32. A Criminal Lack of Common Sense
	33. Liberals and Crime
	34. Handling the Juvenile Cases
	35. Do Status Offenders Get Worse? Some Clarification on the Question of Escalation
	36. Our Violent Kids
	37. Girls' Crime and Woman's Place: Toward a Feminist Model of Female Delinquency
	38. The Hard Facts About Children in Jails
	39. Teenage Addiction
	40. Sentencing and Corrections
	41. State Prisons: Crucibles for Justice
	42. Prison Crowding in the United States: The Data
	43. You're Under Arrest—AT HOME
	44. Whipping
	45. Learning to Live with AIDS in Prison
	46. Alternatives to Incarceration
	47. Prison Overcrowding and Privatization: Models and Opportunities
	48. 'This Man Has Expired'

We Want Your Advice

Annual Editions revisions depend on two major opinion sources: one is our Advisory Board, listed in the front of this volume, which works with us in scanning the thousands of articles published in the public press each year; the other is you—the person actually using the book. Please help us and the users of the next edition by completing the prepaid article rating form on this page and returning it to us. Thank you.

(Continued on next page)

ABOUT YOU

Name ______________________ Date __________

Are you a teacher? ☐ Or student? ☐

Your School Name ______________________

Department ______________________

Address ______________________

City ______________ State ________ Zip ________

School Telephone # ______________________

YOUR COMMENTS ARE IMPORTANT TO US!

Please fill in the following information:

For which course did you use this book? ______________________

Did you use a text with this Annual Edition? ☐ yes ☐ no

The title of the text? ______________________

What are your general reactions to the Annual Editions concept?

Have you read any particular articles recently that you think should be included in the next edition?

Are there any articles you feel should be replaced in the next edition? Why?

Are there other areas that you feel would utilize an Annual Edition?

May we contact you for editorial input?

May we quote you from above?

No Postage Necessary if Mailed in the United States

ANNUAL EDITIONS: CRIMINAL JUSTICE 90/91

BUSINESS REPLY MAIL

First Class Permit No. 84 Guilford, CT

Postage will be paid by addressee

The Dushkin Publishing Group, Inc.
Sluice Dock
DPG **Guilford, Connecticut 06437**